The First Georgia
Cavalry in the Civil War

The First Georgia Cavalry in the Civil War

A History and Roster

MICHAEL BOWERS CAVENDER

McFarland & Company, Inc., Publishers

Jefferson, North Carolina

Photographs enhanced for publication by Wendell Tudor,
Tudor Photography, Stone Mountain, Georgia.

LIBRARY OF CONGRESS CATALOGUING-IN-PUBLICATION DATA [new form]

Names: Cavender, Michael Bowers, 1942– author.
Title: The First Georgia Cavalry in the Civil War : a history and roster /
Michael Bowers Cavender.
Description: Jefferson, North Carolina : McFarland & Company, Inc.,
Publishers, 2016. | Includes bibliographical references and index.
Identifiers: LCCN 2015045633 | ISBN 9780786499120 (softcover : acid free paper)
Subjects: LCSH: Confederate States of America. Army. Georgia
Cavalry Regiment, 1st. | United States—History—Civil War,
1861–1865—Regimental histories. | Georgia—History—
Civil War, 1861–1865—Regimental histories. | United States—
History—Civil War, 1861–1865—Campaigns.
Classification: LCC E559.6 1st .C38 2016 | DDC 973.7/458—dc23
LC record available at http://lccn.loc.gov/2015045633

BRITISH LIBRARY CATALOGUING DATA ARE AVAILABLE

ISBN (print) 978-0-7864-9912-0
ISBN (ebook) 978-1-4766-2112-8

Front cover: *Glorious Fighting*, painting by
Gilbert Gaul, 1885 (© 2016 PicturesNow)

Printed in the United States of America

*McFarland & Company, Inc., Publishers
Box 611, Jefferson, North Carolina 28640
www.mcfarlandpub.com*

To my dear wife of almost 50 years, Beverly Vaughn Cavender. I needed and generously received her prayer and support in writing the book. I also dedicate the book to my two sons, David and Matt Cavender; and my grandchildren, Bailey, Amber, Macie, Hayden and Liza Cavender. I'll never forget how Bailey wrote in an elementary school paper describing herself. She noted she would not be alive today had William Washington Cavender not recovered from his wound.

This book is especially dedicated to the men who served in the First Georgia Cavalry Regiment. I pray it brings them to life for this generation and those to come. We need to understand the extent of their devotion to the states rights of Georgia and the Confederacy. Though they suffered much, some proclaimed later that these were the best years of their lives.

Table of Contents

Preface

This effort began in 1976 after my parents, Lucy and Leon Cavender, died. I had not been interested in the tales my father related about our family enough to ask questions. As an orphan at the age of thirty-four, I had a need to know about my family history.

I began my quest by visiting grave sites. I remembered how to find them in Coweta County, Georgia, because my father had made me go with him when I was young. We went several times to pay respect, and he would tell stories about their lives. This time, however, I paid attention to what I read on those stones. The footstone of my grandfather, Guy Leon Cavender, Sr., stated he was in the 3rd Georgia Infantry during the Spanish American War. I reminisced about how he was sick with malaria all the years I had known him.

I found the grave of my great-grandfather, William Washington "Bill" Cavender. The footstone indicated that he had been in the Seventh Georgia Infantry, CSA. I recalled something my dad had said about Bill Cavender's being wounded at First Manassas. A silver plate had been placed in his head to cover the hole a cannon shell fragment had made. As a kid I thought that was neat, but now I couldn't recollect the details. The thought did cross my mind that had he not survived, I would not be here! I wanted to know more.

While working in downtown Atlanta on a slow day, I decided to visit the Georgia Archives. At that time the archives were located near the state capitol. I had never been there in my life. Someone at the front desk directed me to the Civil War Room. A nice lady, Charlotte Ray, pointed me to books, files, micro-film, and tons of information. As I read about events concerning my great-grandfather, I began to take notes.

Ms. Ray handed me a *Confederate Veterans* magazine with William Washington Cavender's obituary in it. He was known in Wheeler's Cavalry as Bill Cavender, the famous secret service man and scout. This was exciting news to me as my father never mentioned anything about his being in the secret service of Wheeler's Cavalry. A later issue had his picture and more information. I made copies. Both had been sent to the magazine by Major John Tench who had served with him in the First Georgia Cavalry. They were about the same age and served in the same company. Bill Cavender was likely a member of Captain Alexander M. Shannon's Special Scouts of General Joseph Wheeler's Cavalry Corps.

On another day, Ms. Ray showed me a newspaper article about a monument dedication to Sergeant Bill Moore who had been killed at the Battle of Peachtree Creek. The main speaker at the dedication was General Clement A. Evans. During the speech Evans gave, he referred to the notes given to him by Bill Cavender. General Evans then proceeded to read to the crowd what my great-grandfather had written. I was extremely proud and wanted to learn more about Bill Cavender and his regiment. (The monument dedicated that day is still on Howell Mill Road at I-75 in Atlanta, Georgia.)

I found information about William W. Cavender's being wounded on July 21, 1861, and his stay in a hospital in Lynchburg, Virginia. He was released in March 1862. Incredibly, by May 1862, he had joined Company K, First Georgia Cavalry Regiment. A few months later when I was visiting the archives, Ms. Ray handed me a letter from a man in Virginia. Ironically, he wanted information about William Washington Cavender. He possessed a photo of my great-grandfather made prior to July 21, 1861, while William was in the Seventh Georgia Infantry.

I could not write Dale Snair fast enough and provide the information he sought. In return, he sent me a glossy 8 × 10 picture of my great-grandfather's portrait. A photo portrait was the thing to do as a soldier back then, as it is today. I've seen a lot of those photos and they all seem pretty stiff, but twenty-year-old Bill Cavender was pointing his pistol at the camera! What a guy! I was hooked. The more I learned about Bill Cavender, I discovered he belonged to an extraordinary cavalry regiment. I wanted to learn where the First Georgia Cavalry went, who they fought, and what happened to the men involved.

It was impossible to find Georgia Cavalry information in one place and at one time. Hours turned into days, days into weeks, and weeks into years. After exhausting all the information I could find, I tried to put everything in order with an electric typewriter. All of a sudden, I didn't want to do this anymore. My hobby had gotten out of control. It had become work so I put it away. This was in the days before computer searches and word processors.

As time passed and moods changed, I'd work and dabble in this First Georgia Cavalry his-

Pvt. William Washington Cavender. Discharge description, March 1, 1862, 7th Ga. Inf., born Coweta Co., Georgia, age 20, 6'0", fair complexion, grey eyes, black hair. Enlisted May 1862. Col. J.J. Morrison's orderly and scout. Served in Wheeler's Secret Service and was a spy (courtesy Dale S. Snair).

tory. Then one day, I got "old" (68) and knew I had to finish it. I've included information about the journey of the First Georgia Cavalry and events that happened to the men individually, as a regiment, and as members of the Georgia Brigade as they fought, died, or deserted. So here it is. I hope you enjoy the adventures of these gallant and heroic men as much as I have. Their combat was up close and personal like none before or since.

1

Organizing the First
Georgia Cavalry Regiment

This Means War!

How could this happen? Abraham Lincoln won only 39.7 percent of the popular vote in 1860, but he received 180 (59.4 percent) of the 303 electoral votes.[1] The South could not stand for this and talk of division began with South Carolina's secession on December 20, 1860. Georgia, deeply divided on the issue, was progressing in all areas of commerce, agriculture, and population. It was the second largest state east of the Mississippi, had the best rail system in the Deep South, and was centrally located.[2] She had nothing to gain, because secession would mean war.

Alexander Stephens, a pro-unionist, was credited with a warning to Georgia's legislators about their vote and he spoke so true when he said, and later denied:

> The step once taken can never be recalled; and all the baleful and withering consequences that must follow will rest on the Convention for all coming time. When we and our prosperity shall see our lovely South desolated by the demon of war which this act will inevitably invite and call forth, when our green fields of waving harvest shall be trodden down by the murderous soldiery and fiery car of war sweeping over our land, our temples of Justice laid in ashes, all the horrors and desolation of war upon us, who but this convention will be held responsible?[3]

The vote was taken at the capitol in Milledgeville and no matter how you counted the vote, Georgia seceded on January 18, 1861, and joined the Confederacy in February. Still there was hope for reconciliation until the "Hot Heads" in Charleston, South Carolina, fired on Fort Sumter on April 12. Now there was no backing down or away from war!

Thirty-three-year-old Captain James Jefferson Morrison resigned his commission in the United States Cavalry and came home to Cedartown, Georgia. James Morrison knew the value of the cavalry and wanted to raise a regiment himself for Georgia. During these early days of getting a new country on a war footing, Captain Morrison left his home in Cedartown for a long trip to Montgomery, Alabama. Morrison knew Georgia needed cavalry as well as infantry to fight the pending war. He was on his way to see the Confederate president, Jefferson Davis, his old friend from the Mexican War. Morrison needed and sought President Davis' permission to raise a regiment of cavalry.[4]

As he rode the train to Montgomery, he may have thought about his leaving Franklin College in Nashville, Tennessee, during his freshman year, and how his parents, Major James

J. Morrison, Sr., and Agnes Cates, were surprised when they found out he had joined Captain Ed B. Gaithers's Co. B, U.S. Army Dragoons, for the Mexican War.[5]

Morrison might have reflected on the battles he saw at Vera Cruz, Bridge de Nacional, Alpa, Pass le Vega, Molina del Rey, and the cavalry charge at the Gates of San Augustine and been reminded of the importance of his mission. They had stormed Chapultepec and par-

Clockwise, starting top left: Major John Walter Tench. Promoted to captain by General William Martin, August 15, 1864, for gallantry and efficient conduct. Promoted to major by General Joseph Wheeler, December 21, 1864 (courtesy Alachua County Library District Heritage Collection).

The 2nd Lt. Washington Lafayette Ballew. Captured: Powell Valley, Tennessee. June 27, 1862. Exchanged November 22, 1862. Description: Age 23, 5'10", 170 lbs., blue eyes. Resigned March 13, 1863 (courtesy Mary Tom Donnelly Smith collection).

Pvt. Daniel Boone Curtis. Enlisted March 1862 at Fair Mount, Georgia. Brother of John Merrill, Thomas Newton, and William Naaman Curtis (courtesy Nathan Bryant).

Pvt. William T. Tinney. Enlisted March 1862. Wounded in action August 17, 1862, London, Kentucky. Present December 1863 and December 1864 (courtesy Mary Elizabeth Tinney Hill, Richard Finch, and Tammy Tinney Caine).

ticipated in the final capture of Mexico City. During all of this he was only slightly wounded. Whatever his reflections had been as the train pulled into Montgomery, he had to get to the business at hand, his meeting with the president. Morrison was more determined than ever to lead a regiment of cavalry.

During this meeting Davis discouraged Morrison from his idea because a more immediate need had to be met. The South had to supply the state of Virginia with men to defend her borders against Yankee invasion. Alexander Stephens, the vice president, had promised men to Virginia in order to bring her into the Confederacy. President Davis would not let Morrison have a cavalry regiment because Davis reasoned that the cavalry needed Virginia men in their ranks. They would know the state, and Davis felt most of the fighting would take place in Virginia.

Jefferson Davis convinced Morrison of a greater need and persuaded him instead to raise a regiment of infantry. James Morrison did extract from the president a promise that at the first opportunity for a cavalry regiment he would be notified. Meanwhile, in the state of Georgia, prominent men had been organizing companies of men for the services. Because of a disagreement, however, between Governor Joseph E. Brown and President Davis, these organizations were rejected.[6] When Morrison got back to Cedartown, he began organizing the Fourth Battalion of Georgia Infantry. The same prominent men organizing companies learned of Morrison's authorization from President Davis to raise a regiment of infantry and began to correspond with him. They met in the latter part of April 1861 to meld their companies with his battalion and formed the Twenty-first Georgia Infantry Regiment. Morrison was elected colonel. Daniel S. Printup, a lawyer in Rome, Georgia, was elected lieutenant colonel. Alexander M. Wallace, a captain in the Atlanta Greys, was elected major.

On July 17, the regiment as organized was submitted to President Davis, and he accepted the services of the regiment. However, he declined to accept the officers and claimed he had the right to appoint regimental officers. Col. Morrison suggested his cousin, John T. Mercer, who had just resigned as first lieutenant in the First Dragoons, to be the colonel. President Davis made the appointment and appointed Morrison lieutenant colonel. The Twenty-first Georgia Infantry was soon on its way to northwest Virginia to serve the cause.[7]

The War Department did remember Lt. Col. Morrison's request and sent a message to him in January 1862. He was authorized to raise a regiment of cavalry. Lt. Col. Morrison packed his bags on January 24, 1862, and returned home to Georgia on the pretense of a thirty-day sick leave. From Georgia, Lt. Col. Morrison wrote to the secretary of war on February 1 requesting "that my leave may be extended thirty days as I desire to complete the organization of a battalion or regiment of cavalry which I have underway by authority granted 25 January."[8] Morrison thought he could complete the regiment in sixty days.

On February 4, the *Rome Tri-Weekly Courier* recorded the arrival of Col. Mercer, Lt. Col. J.J. Morrison, and Captain D.M. Hood, all of the 21st Georgia Infantry, on Sunday morning, February 1. They were cordially greeted at the train station. News began to spread that Lt. Col. Morrison had been authorized to raise a regiment of cavalry. Posters began appearing on the streets of Rome, Georgia, proclaiming a regiment of cavalry was to be raised by Morrison. News spread as far as Meriwether County to the south and Walker County to the north and all counties in between.

On February 6, a letter to the editor of the *Rome Tri-Weekly Courier* appeared stating: "Notwithstanding Floyd County has done nobly in sending eleven companies, I believe, into service. There are still materials enough to furnish one or two more companies. I would suggest the name John L. Kerr as a suitable and competent person to raise and take command of one—he having some experience in military tactics and withal a brave and chivalrous young man." A week later John L. Kerr answered the challenge and offered to raise a company and asked all those interested to contact him.

Lt. Col. Morrison began his recruiting by contacting prominent men in the nearby counties. He had these men place advertisements in the local newspapers about the regiment's being raised, such as the one which appeared in the *Rome Courier* of Rome, Georgia, on February 20, 1862:

Cavalry

To the citizens of Floyd and adjacent counties:

The subscribers are now engaged in making up a cavalry company and already have a good list of names but many more are wanted. The entire Cherokee country has turned out nobly in the infantry service, and up to this time there has been but one Cavalry Company accepted. There is now a call upon Georgia for one Regiment of Cavalry and the Government has made arrangements to arm it with Sabers, Colts and Rifles.

From the late call of our government for troops, it must be evident to every intelligent mind that before this struggle is over every able bodied man will have to take part, and there is no doubt that this will be the last opportunity offered to the people of Georgia to enter the service as cavalry. The only advantage claimed for this arm of the service over the others is its healthfulness, which is very important. Each man will receive the bounty of $50.00, also $25.00 for clothing every six months. They will also receive $12.00 per month for their own services, and 40 cents per day for their horse, and in case the horse is killed it will be paid for by the government.

We have already been tendered several horses for those who are unable to furnish themselves. A few more of the same sort, are solicited. All who wish to go with this company are earnestly requested to report themselves immediately.

With the present arrangement, and the united and patriotic exertions of the citizens, this company can be placed on a war footing in the next ten or fifteen days.

All speak at once. J.L. Kerr

D.B. Hamilton

P.S. The regiment will be formed about the first of April next.[9]

The response as a result of John L. Kerr's article was tremendous. Within two days, he had one hundred volunteers to form his company. The men elected him as their captain; J.M. Pepper was first lieutenant; S.M. May, second

Pvt. Joseph Alavia Bohannon. Enlisted March 1862. Absent December 27, 1864, in General Hospital. Paroled May 3, 1865 (courtesy Susan Robinson Whatley and Mary Padget).

lieutenant; R.S. Zuber, third lieutenant; and C.W. Hooper, orderly sergeant. The company formed called themselves the "Highland Rangers" and later formed Company G of the regiment. Though this company was filling fast, other companies remained to be formed. Captain Kerr's advertisement appeared again in the Rome newspaper on February 27.

When Lt. Col. Morrison's thirty-day sick leave expired on February 24, the Twenty-first Georgia Infantry adjutant listed him as absent without leave. Morrison, however, was now near Cartersville. He had established Camp Morrison as the headquarters of the First Georgia Regiment of Cavalry. He teamed up with the very able twenty-seven-year-old Armstead R. Harper in organizing the regiment. More advertisements seeking volunteers for cavalry were placed in area newspapers. The counties of Floyd, Polk, Paulding, Carroll, Haralson, Coweta, Meriwether and others nearby supplied the lifeblood of the First Georgia Cavalry Regiment. On March 6, the *Rome Courier* printed a letter to the editor that gave insight into the genesis of the First Georgia Cavalry:

> Sir: I am glad to see that Lt. Col. Morrison of the 21st Georgia Regiment has been authorized by the President to raise a regiment of cavalry. I feel it my duty to say a word in his praise, and of recommendation to those whom he is to command. I have been in his regiment for six months and during this time, I have not seen anything in his deportment other that of a gentleman and soldier. He is brave and generous having the high regard for those who are subordinate to him and endeavoring at all times to advance the interest and welfare of his men.
>
> The service, in which he is entering, is greatly preferable to the Infantry and especially to those of a bold daring nature and who love the excitement of scouting and hunting the enemy in his den. Col. Morrison for such spirits will prove a gallant and brave leader. He combines all the elements of a commander of cavalry and will make his mark where ever an opportunity presents.
>
> One more and the greatest recommendation to Col. Morrison is that this honor was conferred upon him by the President, without the usual political log-rolling incident to such appointments. I can vouch for his honor, and am satisfied that those entering his regiment will never regret their choice.
>
> M.[10]

On March 6, Captain Milton H. Haynie submitted the names of his company from the Cave Spring area of Floyd County. They called themselves the "Cave Spring Rangers." They were accepted into Lt. Col. Morrison's regiment and became Company C. Advertisements were placed in papers requesting all persons with horses to sell, bring them to Rome for inspection and purchase. As the days passed, the fever to complete the enlistment for the First Georgia Regiment increased. Pressure was placed by advertisement upon those yet undecided about how they should serve with friends and friendly officers. An example of this pressure appeared on March 13, in the *Rome Courier*:

> More Cavalry
> The undersigned have authority to raise a company of cavalry to complete the regiment now being formed by Col. J.J. Morrison.
> It is well understood that our government will in a very short time call for more troops, which will in all probability take every able bodied man in the state. Would it not be better to volunteer at once and organize a company with such officers as you may prefer than to wait for a call, and run the risk of being attached to such companies as the authorities may

dictate? As soon as sufficient number of names is obtained, they will meet and select officers from among the number composing the list.

Daniel F. Booton

John Harkins

P.S. Those wishing to join this company will address Mr. Booton at Coosa, Ga., or Mr. Harkins, Rome, Ga.[11]

This advertisement appeared several times in the Rome newspapers, and on March 25 the list of people to contact included Judge William Truslow Newman. Judge Newman was a prominent businessman in Rome. During this time Captain Kerr and Captain Haynie began making preparations to move their companies to Camp McDonald for training.

Saturday, March 22, a flag presentation was made to Captain Milton H. Haynie and the Cave Spring Rangers as they prepared to depart for Camp McDonald. Three young ladies, Misses Gill, Haynie, and Simmons, had handmade the banner. It was presented to Captain Haynie by his daughter. The occasion was more somber due to the fact Miss Haynie was dressed in mourning clothes. Her brother, the son of Captain Haynie, had been killed in battle. The banner drooped over Miss Haynie's shoulder as she made a speech sending them off. Smiles appeared when the banner was accepted by her father. His speech was brief but to the point.

The regiment contained men who had served in other units and had completed their enlistments. Now they wished to continue to fight for their state in the cavalry. Others were just raw recruits itching for the glory of battle. The wealthy and the poor alike came to fight. Some recruits did not stay long in service due to illness or injury. On March 26, Pvt. William H.H. Barnett, Co. G, was discharged as disabled.

Captain Kerr's Company appeared on horseback for the first time in Rome in the early morning of March 28. Those men impressed the citizens as being first rate, but some of the horses appeared as not fit to go into service. Appeals again appeared for the citizens to provide horses that would be worthy of Rome, Georgia.

Soon those companies from the various counties began to report to Lt. Col. Morrison near Cartersville, Georgia. Rome's newspapers carried a notice Thursday morning, April 1, 1862. The notice was for the Highland Rangers. Captain Kerr had received orders to report to Camp McDonald in order to organize. Camp McDonald was located near Big Shanty, Georgia, and there the men would begin their training in cavalry tactics. Captain Kerr informed members of the command to meet on Broad Street, Rome, Georgia, on Friday, April 4, to "take up the line of march on the 5th at seven and a half o'clock A.M. Each man will prepare two days cooked rations."[12]

The First Georgia Regiment of Cavalry formally held its election for lieutenant colonel and major on April 1, 1862. James J. Morrison was elected the lieutenant colonel and Adjutant Armstead R. Harper, of the Eighth Georgia Infantry, was elected major. When Major Harper returned to Georgia from the 8th Georgia Infantry, he brought back with him a large sum of money given him by various men to take to loved ones in Georgia. Notice was published that they could receive the money at Harper and Pepper Hardware Store, Rome, Georgia.[13]

Though the government was supposed to supply the needs of the regiment, the men still needed various articles; such as guns, sabers, and uniforms. Lt. Col. Morrison had to use his own money to help outfit his new regiment. On April 25, the *Rome Weekly Courier* featured an advertisement:

GUNS

All persons who have double barreled shotguns to dispose of will please call at my store. I want them for Col. J.J. Morrison's Regiment of Cavalry, and will pay the best cash price for them

W.T. Newman[14]

Early excitement was provided to the regiment on April 12, 1862. A bugle call alerted Captain John L. Kerr and his Highland Rangers that the steam engine *General* was about to pass near them. The *General* had been stolen by Andrew's Raiders and was heading north. The Rangers gave chase through the mountains, but soon gave up. Privates David Wimpee, George Wimpee, and Matthew Wimpee took part in the chase.

On May 1, 1862, six companies under Lt. Col. Morrison's command mounted up and moved out of Camp Morrison headed for Chattanooga, Tennessee.

Sgt. Mansell D. Tidwell. Enlisted March 1862. Wounded in action July 13, 1862, Murfreesboro, Tennessee. Present December 1863 (courtesy Alice Huitt Preston).

Morrison's command passed through Rome and camped there a few days. On Monday, May 5, a beautiful flag was presented to the Polk County Rangers, later Company A, by Miss Lizzie Lyons of Polk County. The flag was received on behalf of the company by F.C. Shropshire, Esq., of Rome. Speeches were made and poetry read, as both had family members in the company.[15] The *Rome Courier* of May 8 issued a note that the regiment left town "Tuesday morning for a scene of active duty."[16] The paper also commented on their behavior and the makeup of the regiment: "The deportment of the men while here was very commendable. The Companies were composed of the bone and sinew of the land; hardy, healthy men, and well mounted and equipped."[17] At Chattanooga, Lt. Col. Morrison hoped to fully equip his men and receive their duty assignment. The governor of Georgia, Joseph E. Brown, had sent Morrison there at General Robert E. Lee's request. The six companies with Morrison were led by:

- Captain John C. Crabb, Company A—Polk County.
- Captain James H. Strickland, Company B—Coweta and Meriwether Counties;
- Captain Milton H. Haynie, Company C—Floyd County;
- Captain William R. Seawright, Company D—Paulding County;
- Captain James Blalock, Company E—Carroll County;
- Captain Nap Reynolds, Company F—Gordon County.

Major A.R. Harper remained at Camp Morrison to continue recruiting. Captain John L. Kerr's Highland Rangers from Floyd County (later known as Company G) remained with Harper. Major Harper would soon recruit three more companies to complete the regiment. They were led by Captain William Tumlin, Company H—Haralson County; Captain John F. Leake, Company I—Bartow County; and Captain Henry A. North, Company K—Coweta County.

Lt. Gen. Edmund Kirby Smith commanded the Department of East Tennessee headquartered in Chattanooga. On May 2, 1862, General Robert E. Lee wrote General Kirby Smith informing him that a regiment of infantry and a regiment of cavalry from Georgia were coming to him as the First Georgia Cavalry had been ordered to Chattanooga for his support: "These men will bring such arms as they have and 1,000 improved arms have been ordered to the same place. All arms that could be provided sent to you."[18]

At this time, Chattanooga and northern Alabama were being threatened by a portion of General Buell's army and part of General Ormsby Mitchell's army headquartered in Huntsville, Alabama. The governor of Alabama, J. Gill Shorter, was concerned for his state's northern border and wrote the secretary of war about this matter. On May 13, General R.E. Lee, in Richmond, Virginia, wrote the governor a letter. Lee let him know his plea was being heard. Lee's letter to Shorter stated: "The importance of defending the northern parts of Georgia and Alabama, particular[ly] the town of Rome and like places of importance is fully appreciated and steps with the view to that end have been taken. Col. Morrison's regiment of cavalry has already been ordered to Chattanooga to operate with the forces at that point in the protection of the northern frontier of Georgia and Alabama and the cavalry regiment referred to by you in your letter to the Secretary of War will be sent to that point as soon as it is equipped and armed."[19] Buell's movements proved not to be a direct threat to Chattanooga and as a result Lt. Col. Morrison's outfit was ordered to move to Kingston, Tennessee. From there, they moved to Big Creek Gap near Jacksboro, Tennessee, in the Cumberland Mountains.

Upon arrival, Lt. Col. Morrison was placed in command of a brigade of cavalry, which consisted of his own six companies of the First Georgia Cavalry and Col. Henry M. Ashby's Tennessee Regiment of Cavalry. From Big Creek Gap, Morrison's Brigade crossed the mountains going toward Archer's Place, where the Federals had a considerable force. The Federals learned that the Rebs were coming and departed rapidly. They left about fifty men to tend the commissary stores and other supplies just in case the Confederates did not attack as expected.

Morrison's Cavalry Brigade took four days to cross the mountains. The roads had been blocked by trees cut to fall across the narrow mountain road. The mounted cavalry dismounted and walked their horses over the rugged paths. The brigade was not well prepared for this trip, as some of the men were barefoot and not enough rations or forage had been brought with them. A perplexing lesson was learned as the discomfort grew.

Upon reaching the Federal outpost at Archer's, Morrison formed part of the brigade into lines of battle and quickly charged into the camp. They captured most of the remaining fifty Yankee troops with ease. Morrison's men fed their horses with the 500 bushels of corn they had just captured. The horses had been without food for the past four days. The men filled their bellies with the food found in the camp. Lt. Col. Morrison questioned the prisoners and paroled them. The parolees were not to fight again until they were exchanged. Morrison mounted his cavalry and took them back to Big Creek Gap to await further orders.

Before long, Lt. Col. Morrison received orders to return to Kingston with his six companies and assume command of the post. Col. John McLin and Col. Henry Ashby were also at this post. After arriving, Lt. Col. Morrison received word that a heavy attack could be expected by the Federals very shortly. He immediately sent out a strong picket and a large number of scouts to discover the enemy's intention.

Major A.R. Harper remained behind in Cartersville, Georgia, with four companies about a week after Morrison had departed with his six companies. At the conclusion of recruiting, Harper moved these men to Chattanooga to outfit them as Morrison had likewise done for his men. While in Chattanooga, Harper drilled his men in cavalry movement and tactics. The men were happy to receive their shotguns and sabers, but they were not happy measles had broken out among them. Harper's Brigade remained in Chattanooga almost two weeks. At this time, General Mitchell's presence in Huntsville threatened Chattanooga. Harper's men had to stay around Chattanooga to help guard against an imminent attack. Major Harper had to follow the command of Brigadier General Danville Leadbetter.

General Kirby Smith, concerned about his situation in Chattanooga, wrote to General Robert E. Lee again asking for reinforcements.

Lt. Col. James H. Strickland. Elected captain, Company B, March 1862. Promoted to lieutenant colonel by General William Martin April, 15, 1864. Wounded in action at Battle for Bald Hill, Atlanta, Georgia, July 22, 1864. Died of wounds August 3, 1864 (courtesy Susan Robinson Whatley).

Left: **Pvt. William P. Barnett. Enlisted March 1862. Absent sick August 1862 in Kingston, Tennessee. Discharged April 26, 1865 (courtesy Mary Brunette).**
    Right: **Sgt. Hiram Warner Camp. Discharge description from 7th Georgia Infantry. Born Coweta Co. Georgia, age 20, 6'4", fair complexion, blue eyes, and dark hair. Enlisted August 3, 1862. Present through December 31, 1864 (courtesy Judge Jack T. Camp).**

Lee's answer came back on May 27, stating that he had on April 29 requested Governor Brown of Georgia to "send the regiment of cavalry at Dalton, commanded by Col. [Jesse A.] Glenn and that at Cartersville under Col. Morrison to Chattanooga to report to the commanding officer at that point."[20]

Before General Smith had received General Lee's letter, he wrote to Lee again about his need for troops and cannon. General Lee then personally wrote to General Smith. He first congratulated him on his success; he then informed him of his efforts to get cannon, and discussed Colonels Glenn and Morrison. Lee became concerned that General Smith had no facts of the whereabouts of Glenn, Morrison, or the two regiments of infantry sent to him from Alabama. Lee asked Smith to inform him as to the status of these troops as soon as possible. General Smith soon learned of the First Georgia Cavalry's presence and sent Major Armstead R. Harper with his four companies to join Col. Morrison at Camp Allston near Kingston, Tennessee.

While in the Chattanooga, Tennessee, area, the day before the first bombardment of Chattanooga, Pvt. Jesse B. Hall and others of the First Georgia Cavalry were detailed on June 6 to scout up the Tennessee River. They were to destroy anything that would aid the enemy in crossing the river. Up around Harrison they heard a boat going downstream and chased it for about seven miles. They caught the boat, captured two prisoners and horses, and burned the boat. Afterwards, they returned to Chattanooga with the prisoners.[21] That Monday night, the same group was put in railcars and taken to Athens, Tennessee. From Athens, they went to Decatur and Bridgeport. They were going all the way up to Loudon to make sure the First Georgia Cavalry scouts were well placed to report enemy movements. Before they had traveled very far, they received a dispatch to meet Major Harper at Post Oak Springs, Tennessee.[22]

Major Armstead R. Harper's detachment, First Georgia Cavalry, had arrived at Kingston, Tennessee, and immediately received orders to move to Jacksboro.[23] They positioned themselves at Big Creek Gap. Colonel Benjamin Allston, commander of the First Cavalry Brigade, was to find Maj. Harper and send him with his command to Knoxville. Almost as quickly, General Kirby Smith sent orders to Lt. Col. Morrison to send Maj. Harper with four companies to Maynardville. Harper was to scout north to Powell's River and Tazewell and report the number and movement of the enemy. Major Harper took Captain Henry North's Co. K, Captain Napoleon Reynolds's Co. F, and two other companies.

Upon reaching Powell's River Valley, Maj. Harper came across an enemy encampment. He quickly formed his men up for a charge upon the unseen enemy. The mounted command of eighty men came crashing through the trees into the camp yelling and waving their sabers and captured the entire command of tents. The Yankees had so quickly abandoned their camp that they left behind all their tents and equipment. Major Harper had his men set up their camp and send out scouting parties. Harper was to locate Captain William P. Owen's Company D, Second Tennessee Cavalry, who was in the area, and have him join the command during this mission.

Meanwhile, on June 12, 1862, Lt. Col. Morrison wrote the secretary of war from Camp Allston in East Tennessee. He requested that he be promoted to colonel. Morrison based his case on the fact that he had organized a full regiment of cavalry under the authority of the War Department and was authorized to have the rank. Morrison complained that the regiment had been organized for two months and the absence of this rank had placed him in an awkward position. Morrison did not forget his friend, A.R. Harper, and stated that Harper had acted in the capacity of a lieutenant colonel with the rank of major. He added that the men of the regiment approved of them by a unanimous vote.

Morrison felt sure some captain working in the secretary's office must have misplaced all the previous information concerning the regiment. He forwarded to the secretary of war all the necessary records. Morrison requested permission not to appoint a major at this time as he wanted to select a man who would satisfy both himself and the War Department. Morrison asked for his appointment to be effective April 28, 1862. The War Department forwarded only Morrison's promotion with an effective date of May 21, 1862.

From Kingston, Tennessee, Colonel Morrison's mission was to scout the enemy's position, discover his intentions, and report immediately to Gen. Kirby Smith. Col. Morrison commanded the post at Kingston. One report concerned a large amount of bacon that had been captured from the Yankees. On June 17, General Smith's command staff sent the following message to Col. Morrison:

> Your communication of yesterday received. The commanding general directs that you will continue sending out scouting parties and watch the movements of the enemy toward Crab Orchard. If any advance is made, you will hold him in check as long as possible, reporting promptly to the headquarters all that transpires. The bacon mentioned by you had better be removed to this side of the river, except what is required for immediate consumption by your command. If you need other subsistence stores draw them from Loudon. If you require forage, notify the quartermaster here that it may be sent to you by boat. Col. Starnes' command will remain with you. Col. Reynolds at Loudon within supporting distance of you when needed. Keep the commanding general constantly advised of all movements.[24]

Col. Alexander W. Reynolds was the commanding officer of the Third Infantry Brigade. At that time, Captain James H. Strickland and Company B were detached to Col. Reynolds.

On June 22, Major Harper, near Maynardville, received orders to scout every inch toward Tazewell. He was to communicate with the Confederate forces at Blain's Crossroads by courier and to keep the commanding general informed of all movements of the enemy.[25] Kirby Smith also wanted to know if Major Harper had his courier lines posted and ready to report. Harper's lines of communication were ready. He sent General Smith by return courier a message that about eighty Union infantry had fired on one of his scouting parties near Hurst Ford on the Clinch River. He also reported that one of his lieutenants and four other men had been cut off by the enemy from the rest of his command, but he did not think they had been captured.[26] These men were of Company F: First Lt. Washington L. Ballew, Pvt. Robert C. Duckett, Pvt. Bailus M. Nally and Pvt. Nathan L. Stokes. First Lt. Washington L. Ballew had been ordered to take a platoon of Company F, First Georgia Cavalry, and scout for the enemy. Pvt. Jesse B. Hall stated: "We crossed the Clinch River in four miles of Maynardville and went across the valley towards Powell River and about 2 o'clock that evening we fell in with about 80 Yankees. They fired on us and we returned it in full on them and they commenced the charge and we the retreat. Some 10 of them had got in our rear in the road. We charged their line and myself and three or four others got through and made our escape back to camp and the lieutenant and four of the boys was taken prisoner."[27]

The next day, Harper gathered his whole force and chased after the enemy, but they were nowhere to be found. After that initial action report, other reports soon arrived at command headquarters. General Kirby Smith informed Major Harper that the enemy had been reported in a force at Tazewell. Harper kept his command vigilant and sent out scouts and pickets in that direction. Kirby Smith was preparing for a general movement against the enemy. As part of Smith's plan to meet the enemy, the detachment of the First Georgia Cavalry under Major Harper was attached to Col. Henry M. Ashby. Col. Ashby's First Tennessee Cavalry and Harper's First Georgia Cavalry were to cover all approaches from Tazewell and Powell's Valley. They were to report any movement of the enemy to General Kirby Smith.

Pvt. William T. Tinney, Co. B, reported in a letter to his parents on June 22, 1862: "I am in Louden, Tenn … and the regiment is in Kingston."[28] He bragged to his mother: "Our horses is as fast as you ever seen."[29] About coming home, he reported, "Captain [Strickland] says that we get 20 days [leave] every 6 months and we intend to have it."[30] Tinney was encouraging his father to come visit: "We are coming in 50 yards of the railroad now and we expect to be here some time."[31] Tinney reported Company B had been on a scout for the past five days looking for Yankees but found none.

Pvt. William Tinney, in a letter on June 27, 1862, to his brother Richard, told of life in camp: "I am living a unpleasant life for it is a raining today. When it's raining we have to stay about in the ground under the trees for shelter and pack up our bed close to a tree and when it comes night we make down on the ground and sleep. I have got so I can sleep on a rock or in mud."[32] Tinney goes on to tell about the war: "[T]he war is not the thing it is cracked up to be for men are sick and many die. There's about 250 men in the hospital since I've begun to write. I hear that three men died last night in the hospital."[33]

On June 28, Major Harper's scouts around Capp's Ford found a regiment of the enemy's infantry. They were camped within five miles of the ford on the main road from Tazewell to Knoxville, seven miles outside Tazewell. They discovered a company of the enemy infantry advancing toward Maynardville on the Owsely Ferry Road, seven miles from Maynardville. Harper's scouts found a party of enemy out foraging in his area. He reported all sightings to General Smith as instructed.[34]

General Kirby Smith instructed Col. Thomas H. Taylor to watch for the enemy and to meet them if they came up. Taylor was instructed to fall back to Blain's Crossroads if the force they met was too great. At that point, he was to form a junction with Col. Alexander W. Reynolds's Infantry. Major Harper was to continue his scout and communicate with both Colonel Taylor and Colonel Reynolds about any enemy movement he found and cooperate with them if an attack took place. That was all Major Harper needed to hear. He wanted to go after the foraging party and keep them from crossing the river, but, more importantly, he wanted to stop them from eating the valuable supplies that his horses needed. Harper gathered his four companies and one of the First Tennessee, about 125 men, and started in hot pursuit. The little command found the rear guard of the enemy force resting on the opposite side of Powell's River at Leach's Ford.

Harper and his men were so anxious for the attack that a proper scout of the enemy's position did not take place. Harper formed his men and crashed across the river with sabers drawn, attacking what they thought to be a small foraging party. The surprised Yankee rear guard rapidly fell back to their main body. As the First Georgia happily pursued them through the forest, a bigger surprise awaited the Georgians.

The enemy rear guard fell back to Col. Robert K. Byrd's command of eight companies of the First East Tennessee Infantry and two companies of the Third Kentucky Infantry, about 900 strong. Lt. John Tench, Co. K, First Georgia Cavalry, described the scene to the editor of the *Rome Courier*:

The charge was made and gallantly was it lead [*sic*], but the Major soon found that 900 infantry stood before him. Their bayonets glistening in the morning sun like a skein of silver. Had even 900 grim visage [*sic*] warriors been in battle line in open country, our gallant little Major, with his devoted men would have shaved the beard of the last face clean with their sabers, but he saw that it was impossible to charge them successfully on account of the precipitous hills on one side and the river on the other, nevertheless he ordered his men to charge them and fire both barrels of their guns which they did and always promptly will do right into the enemy's face.[35]

Col. Byrd's men, in the rear lines, held the charge of Harper's men and forced Harper to look for a way out before disaster struck. The retreat bugle called and the gallant cavalry retreated almost as rapidly as they had begun. The loss to the Union in the attack was eleven killed and five captured. Major Harper had none killed but three wounded and one man, Pvt. Maliachi Reeves, Co. K, was wounded and taken prisoner. In the fray some of the regiment lost their shotguns and sabers, but they performed well considering their position and the number of opposition troops.

Pvt. Jesse B. Hall wrote of the attack: "We succeeded in breaking their front line and my Captain [Napoleon Reynolds] and one more Captain [Henry A. North] and their companies was to charge their second line which they did with spirit, but was forced by superior numbers to retire and leave them. They fell back to the command and [Major] Harper saw that they was gaining his rear. He then recrossed the river and as we crossed the river they poured the ball at us from three sides and of all the singing ever hear of balls, it was there that I heard it."[36]

Lt. Tench reported that General Smith highly complimented Major Harper for the action and retreat. Tench did not report that Smith also chided Harper in the same letter of July 2, saying that it would "be better to send out scouts to find position and strength of the enemy." Gen. Smith closed his letter, however, with these words: "Congratulations on skill in withdrawing men from a difficult position."[37]

Pvt. Jesse B. Hall. Enlisted March 1862. Captured, December 24, 1863, near Dandridge, Tennessee. His widow was reading the *Atlanta Constitution* list of Confederate soldiers buried in Nicholasville, Kentucky. This was her only notice of his death January 28, 1864 (courtesy Steve Hall).

2

Murfreesboro

The organization of the Department of East Tennessee was in a state of constant change. On June 30, 1862, the department was commanded by Gen. E. Kirby Smith. Smith divided the department into one cavalry brigade and four infantry brigades. The Cavalry Brigade, Col. Benjamin Allston, contained three regiments: First Georgia Cavalry, Col. James J. Morrison; First Tennessee Cavalry, Col. Henry M. Ashby; and Second Tennessee Cavalry, Col. John B. McLin.

On July 3 changes were made again as the department grew larger. Kirby Smith still commanded the department, but it now contained two divisions: those of Gen. Carter L. Stevenson, First Division, and Gen. Henry Heth, Second Division. The Second Division contained two infantry and two cavalry brigades: First Infantry Brigade, Gen. Danville Leadbetter; Second Infantry Brigade, Col. William George Mackey Davis; First Cavalry Brigade, Col. Benjamin Allston; and Second Cavalry Brigade, Col. Nathan Bedford Forrest.

The First Cavalry Brigade contained the following regiments: First Georgia Cavalry, Col. Morrison; First Tennessee Cavalry, Col. Ashby; Second Tennessee Cavalry, Col. McLin; Third Tennessee Cavalry, Col. James W. Starnes; and Howitzer Artillery Battery, 1st Lt. Gustave A. Huwald. The Second Cavalry Brigade consisted of First Kentucky Cavalry, Lt. Col. Thomas Woodward; First Louisiana Cavalry, Col. John S. Scott; Eighth Texas Cavalry, Col. John A. Wharton; and Second Georgia Cavalry, Col. Winburn Joseph Lawton.

Col. Allston's first move after the reorganization was to consolidate the First Georgia Cavalry. Allston had Major Harper's detachment move from Maynardville to Kingston, Tennessee. Col. Morrison had his entire command together for combined work for the first time since he left Cartersville. Morrison's orders were to keep a sharp eye out for the enemy, who had been reported moving an infantry force down the Clinch Valley threatening Loudon, Tennessee.

The fear of Gen. Don Carlos Buell forced Gen. Kirby Smith to make some bold plans. The Confederate commanders wanted Col. Forrest to plan an expedition into middle Tennessee. Col. Forrest was still recovering from wounds received during the Confederate withdrawal from Shiloh. Wounded aside, he received orders June 11, to report to Chattanooga for further instructions. Urgency demanded Col. Forrest not take his brigade with him on this mission to Chattanooga. The brigade would follow in good order. Forrest did take some handpicked officers and an escort of twenty men commanded by Captain William Forrest, his brother.

Murfreesboro was chosen to be the target of Forrest's expedition. Forrest was to create a diversion to distract the Federals and take the pressure off Chattanooga. Murfreesboro was a major railroad center on the Nashville and Chattanooga line. Eleven major roads, some paved with tar and gravel, intersected near the town. Forrest's mission was to destroy the Federal force located there and also destroy lines of communication, both telegraph and railroad. Secondarily, he was to rescue a number of citizens who had been arrested and were expected to be executed.

Col. Morrison knew nothing of these plans being made in Chattanooga. On July 6, the following orders were handed Col. Morrison from Kirby Smith:

> You will put your regiment in marching order without delay, complete your preparations and on arrival of Major Harper, who left here [Knoxville] for Kingston this morning, push on with the effective part of your regiment by the most expeditious route to McMinnville. In arriving at that point you will await orders from Col. Forrest who, with a brigade from Chattanooga, will command the whole expedition. You will subsist your command on the country until your junction with Col. Forrest. He has funds for the subsistence of the whole command. You will attach to your command two companies of Col. Spiller's battery, provided two companies fit for service in the field can be found. You should at all events have with you some portion of Spiller's command, as the men are acquainted with the country and render you valuable service.[1]

Morrison's First Georgia Cavalry replaced Col. Scott's First Louisiana Cavalry in Forrest's Brigade. Scott was then sent to Kingston and took up Morrison's mission.

On July 9, Col. Forrest and his command of the Eighth Texas Rangers, Col. John Wharton, and the Second Georgia Cavalry, Col. Winburn Lawton, pulled out of Chattanooga. They began a forced march that reached Altamont the night of July 10.[2] Almost fifty miles were covered before the men got a chance to rest. The next morning Forrest moved his brigade another twenty miles to McMinnville. That night Col. Morrison and his command of the First Georgia Cavalry and two companies of Col. C.C. Spiller's battery under Major Baxter Smith, plus two companies of Kentucky Cavalry under Captains Taylor and Waltham, proceeded from their mountain camp to join Forrest's column.

The force now totaled around 1,400 effective men, all of whom were very tired after their long ride.[3] The horses were weary as well. Pvt. Jesse B. Hall's little mare was lame and both remained in McMinnville. Not much rest would come their way for awhile because at 1 P.M. on July 12 Col. Forrest moved his command toward Murfreesboro, over fifty miles away. There was no stopping except for a short period to feed both horses and men at Woodbury at midnight.[4]

The whole town seemed to be out on the street that night to see what all the turmoil was about. Everyone was trying to tell Forrest and his men that the Yankees had been there the night before. They told Forrest the Yankees had swooped down on the town and carried away almost every man there except the very young and very old. The Federals took the men to Murfreesboro to prison, as they were suspected of not being loyal to the Union. Forrest pledged to all who could hear that he would restore their loved ones to them before sunset the next day.[5]

One little girl ran up to Captain Haynie, the old patriot of the First Georgia Cavalry, wringing her hands and crying and begging him to bring her father back to her again. "The old man turned to her with his whole soul beaming in his face, and exclaimed, while manly tears started to his eyes and said, 'I will my daughter, I will.'"[6] Captain Milton H. Haynie was nearing sixty years of age. His company was made of men from Floyd and Polk counties, and his men loved him as a father figure. His temperament with his men and his paternal fondness for the boys caused those to greet him with affection throughout the regiment.

Forrest gathered the force together and gave the command to move out toward Murfrees-boro. Heretofore no one knew their destination except Forrest himself. As the march continued, the speed was constantly accelerated as Murfreesboro was approached. Lt. John W. Tench, in a letter to the editor of the *Rome Tri-Weekly Courier*, gave this description: "The excitement of the expected fight drove sleep from the eyes of the boys and the claims of Morpheus upon them were not honored that night. It was truly gratifying to witness the manifestations of approval of the people all along the route, who were up shouting and waving their handkerchiefs. The ladies were conspicuous in the demonstration made particularly in Murfreesboro and its vicinity. They were rejoiced that many of them stood in the street clapping their hands and shouting with joy at the prospect of being delivered from the terrible thralldom of Lincoln's minions who had been ruling over the people as they have everywhere in Tennessee, when they have had the power with an iron rod. Like the Roman Emperor Caligula, they liked to write their laws so high that the people cannot read them."[7]

At about 4:30 A.M., Sunday morning, July 13, Forrest and his cavalry began to approach Murfreesboro along the Woodbury Pike. Col. Forrest informed his command that this day was his birthday and asked as a present the town of Murfreesboro. The men cheered and swore to deliver the place to him. As the column moved closer to Murfreesboro, the Texas Rangers were posted in front. Their scouts reported pickets a short distance ahead. A small detachment was sent forward by Col. Wharton to deal with them without firing a shot. From those prisoners, Forrest learned that there were two regiments in and around Murfreesboro. The regiments were the Ninth Michigan and the Third Minnesota.

The Ninth Michigan Infantry was under the command of Colonel William Ward Duffield. Col. Duffield had been ordered to Nashville to take command of the Department of Kentucky. With Duffield in Nashville, this placed Lt. Col. John Gibson Parkhurst in command of the Ninth Michigan. Duffield's absence also caused Colonel Henry C. Lester, Third Minnesota Infantry, to be the commander of the Twenty-third Brigade, which occupied Murfreesboro.

Also, about Murfreesboro were around 200 of the Pennsylvania Cavalry, 100 of the Eighth Kentucky Cavalry, and Captain Hewett's battery of four guns. There were between 1,500 and 1,700 men under the command of General Thomas T. Crittenden.[8] General Crittenden arrived in Murfreesboro by train from Nashville on July 11 by order of General Buell. On the same train was Col. Duffield; he was to take back command of the Twenty-third Brigade.[9] Col. Lester had made changes in postings around Murfreesboro that would prove disastrous for the Union. He had them spread out because he claimed lack of adequate water. Gen. Crittenden had set up his temporary headquarters in the hotel in town about 75 yards from the courthouse.[10]

Soon other scouts returned with word that all was quiet in the camps and no notice of danger had been given to them. They also reported the enemy's location and number. Forrest then formulated his plan of attack. He decided to immediately attack the camp in town and the town's buildings. He would at the same time hold the enemy's artillery in check until the former was accomplished. It was important to the attack to hit all points simultaneously.

In columns of four the little army dashed into Murfreesboro. Echoes of the rattling of 4,800 hoofs on the stony streets awakened the townspeople. They rushed to their windows, balconies, and verandahs to see what was taking place. The sight of the Confederate cavalry by many of the people gave cause for them to kneel in prayer and give thanks to God for their deliverance.

The first force to be encountered was the Ninth Michigan Infantry and a squadron of cavalry on the Liberty Pike. Lt. Col. Parkhurst was awakened by a sentinel at his tent and informed of the rapidly approaching enemy. Parkhurst immediately gave the alarm and his troops began to form to take on the attacking rebels. He formed them up behind a cedar fence and had wagons overturned and bales of hay for the only barrier available.

Col. Wharton was leading his Texas Rangers in gallant style. They dashed at the Ninth Michigan encampment with horrific yells and armed with double barrel shotguns and navy Colt's revolvers. Col. Forrest didn't like sabers. He felt they made too much noise. Lt. John Tench, in the *Rome Weekly Courier*, stated: "This they did in gallant style, as the Rangers always do, killing and wounding over 100, taking a large number of prisoners, and driving them from their camps. Many of the Yankees were in bed and taken completely by surprise, and killed in their tents."[11] However, Col. Wharton did not realize several of his companies had peeled off to go with Col. Forrest to the courthouse.

Although surprised, Parkhurst's men put up quite a fight and repelled the first charge. Col. Wharton was severely wounded in the arm in this action and had to be replaced by Lt. Col. John G. Walker.[12] It was reported that Col. Wharton was the one who wounded Col. Duffield. Col. Walker backed the Rangers off some 200 yards and contained Parkhurst until help arrived.

Lt. Col. Parkhurst reported he was being attacked by Wharton's Texas Rangers and a battalion of Col. Morrison's First Georgia Cavalry. Parkhurst was surprised at the number of Rutherford County citizens who joined in the attack against him. Many of them had recently taken the oath of allegiance to the United States government. He had not considered that his men were really hated by the populace. Parkhurst was amazed as well by the number of Negroes attached to the Texas and Georgia troops. They were armed and took part in several of the engagements during the day.[13] Parkhurst sent out couriers to nearby units asking for help, but no reply or help was received. He was in this by himself. Col. Lester received the pleas for help, but just could not respond. He did alert the Third Minnesota troops and began a slow march toward the sounds of battle.[14]

Meanwhile, the main body of the command, the First and Second Georgia regiments with the Tennessee and Kentucky squadrons charged down the main street of town. They turned left on a street leading them to another street which ran parallel with the main street. They then went around to the Nashville Pike. On this pike, the command received a galling fire from the enemy who had collected in the courthouse.

The courthouse was occupied by Company B, Ninth Michigan, which was led by Captain Oliver C. Rounds. Lt. Tench described him as "the notorious Provost Marshall of the city, who had rendered himself conspicuous on account of his petty tyranny while clothed with his little brief authority."[15] The sixty or eighty men who had occupied the courthouse produced such a fire that it became of utmost importance to drive them out. Col. Forrest ordered Col. Morrison to take the building.

Col. Morrison took his First and Second Georgia Cavalry charging down the street to the public square of the city where the courthouse stood. Morrison was followed by four companies of the Texas Rangers who were supposed to be with Col. Wharton dealing with the Michigan camp. The Texans were promptly sent back to Col. Wharton.

Upon arrival at the square, Col. Forrest had Morrison dismount the command. Captain Rounds' men began to pick off the Georgians at will. In the exchange of fire, ten Confederates were killed and fifteen wounded to the enemy's one killed. It became evident to Col. Morrison that it would be impossible to dislodge the Yankees in the exchange of gunfire that was taking place. Morrison divided the First Georgia into two squadrons and placed one under the command of Captain John C. Crabb. Captain Crabb and Lt. William M. Hutchings, Company A, moved out to one of the three points Morrison had ordered for the assault. The other squadron was under Captain Milton H. Haynie and Captain William R. Seawright. The third point of attack was made up of men from the Second Georgia Cavalry. Most of their officers had already been severely wounded; therefore, Col. Morrison took command of them and led the assault.

The attacks upon the courthouse were made simultaneously from all three points. This attack was most hazardous duty, as they were being fired upon not only from the courthouse but also from behind fences and other buildings about town. At the signal, Captain Crabb, who had already been wounded, led his men in a charge to the door of the courthouse that faced east. During this charge, the gallant and daring Captain John Crabb was shot and killed. Lt. Hutchings ably continued to lead the men of Company A and was himself wounded. Privates Jasper York and Sam Brown broke down the door with axes procured from a nearby building, and they were the first to enter the courthouse.

Sgt. Alexander Hamilton Bohannon. Enlisted March 1862. Orderly for Major A.R. Harper December 1862. Surrendered April 26, 1865 (courtesy Susan Robinson Whatley and Mary Padget).

When Captain Milton H. Haynie, the old grey-haired chieftain, entered the courthouse, he realized that more lives would be lost in the attempt to go up the stairway to where the Yankees had their stronghold. Captain Haynie immediately set fire to the building, threatening to burn the place to the ground. At the moment the enemy smelled smoke, they sent up a yell to surrender. The First Georgia extinguished the flames and received the surrendered company.

Col. Morrison led the Second Georgia Cavalry in the assault on the front doors. Almost at the same time of the surrender, the noble and daring Captain William R. Seawright was mortally wounded as he reached the courthouse door. The courthouse was secured after two and a half hours of heavy battle. Privates A.H. York and Jesse Crabb were the first to go upstairs to release the prisoners. One of the captured Yankees exclaimed to them, "You fellers would charge Hell with a cornstalk."

In describing the results of the attack on the courthouse, Lt. Tench said, "Here fell the brave and chivalric Captains Crabb and Seawright. Here also was severely wounded Adj. Perkins, Lt. Hutchings and Lt. Trammel and Captain Kerr. Of the sixty men that made the charge nine fell dead, 21 wounded and of officers only escaped unscathed viz. our brave, noble, kind haired and generous Colonel and the white haired hero Captain Haynie."[16]

Captain Haynie reported to the *Rome Courier* the bravery and kindness the ladies of Murfreesboro had shown the First Georgia Cavalry: "The same fair ones were in the streets, in spite of the whistling of balls and the rain of lead, administering to the wants of our soldiers, filling their canteens with water and their haversacks with an abundance of provisions. Unheeding the shots from the enemy's guns, they thought only of the comfort of their gallant champions. One lady received a ball through her dress, whilst another had a parasol shot from her hand, the ball passing within two inches of her jeweled fingers. Such heroism has never before been known in the annals of war and it will illuminate to the remotest generation of the history of our glorious land."[17]

Meanwhile, Col. Forrest ordered Major Harper, with the balance of the First Georgia, and the Tennessee Cavalry commanded by Major Baxter Smith, and Kentucky Cavalry under Captains Taylor and Waltham to file around to the rear of the Third Minnesota and attack their camp. The Third had four pieces of artillery located on the Nashville Pike, which crossed Stones River one-and-a-half miles northwest of town. Harper was to occupy them while the town was being secured. This artillery had continued to hamper Forrest's troops in their attacks, and he wanted it silenced.

Forrest led this group himself through a wooded area and then a cornfield. Beyond the Whites' house, they came across the camp of the Third Minnesota, which was guarded by only one enemy company. The other companies were near the battery giving it support. Col. Lester had moved the bulk of the Third Minnesota down the road toward Murfreesboro but was not involved in any fighting.

The battalion of First Georgia, under Major Harper, soon arrived and with Captain Dunlop made a gallant charge almost to the mouths of the cannons firing at them. Then Col. Forrest took personal command of Col. Lawton's Second Georgia Cavalry and charged the rear of the artillery camp. It was still occupied by about 100 men posted behind a strong barricade of wagons and large limestone ledges that offered excellent protection. Forrest ordered a charge to be led by Majors Smith and Harper. Twice they charged and were repulsed. Forrest drew the men up for a third charge and appealed to their manhood. He then put himself at the head of the column and this time they had success. The camp was penetrated and the greater part of the Federals were either killed or captured.

Lt. Tench again described the scene: "In the camp, we found a number of contrabands, having gone there doubtless seeking the protection of their Yankee brethren. One of them, at least, had arms in his hands and had the boldness to shoot at the General [Col. Forrest] for which he forfeited his life very soon."[18] Besides the prisoners and slaves captured, there was a large number of army store wagons, mules and horses, plus the regimental colors. Forrest ordered the camp destroyed and all 150 tents burned.

He sent the First Georgia Cavalry and the Tennessee Squadron, under Major Harper's command, to the depot to burn it. Soon the depot was in flames along with a large number of commissary stores and quartermaster supplies destroyed. The postmaster was captured with all the Union mail. The telegraph office was captured and lines cut. The office equipment was carried away.

The other companies of the First Georgia Cavalry, under Col. Morrison, had been left to confront the main body of the Ninth Michigan. Upon hearing the battle going on in the rear, Morrison thought the other companies in the rear were being attacked by the Federals. He quickly charged them in front and broke their lines and swept through to the rear. The

Federals just as quickly reformed their divided lines and held their ground. The Yankees occupied an elevated ridge from which it had become very difficult to dislodge them.

Forrest formulated a new plan of attack. He sent Major Harper with three of his companies around to the rear to cut off the enemy's retreat toward Nashville. He sent Morrison with four companies as skirmishers into the front to prevent Federal movement on Murfreesboro. Forrest was afraid the enemy brigade would rally together and spoil his victory. With that in mind, he sent the prisoners, captured ammunition, and sundry supplies on their way to McMinnville. Forrest regrouped the rest of the command and surrounded the enemy.

As the battle progressed during the morning, Lt. Col. Parkhurst sent more couriers to Col. Lester asking for reinforcements. None returned until finally a courier from Col. Lester arrived telling Parkhurst that all his couriers had been arrested as spies.[19] Col. Lester was later court-martialed for cowardice. During the battle, Lt. Col. Arthur Hood, Second Georgia Cavalry, released about 150 political prisoners. They had been arrested in nearby counties, including those men from Woodbury. There was great rejoicing when these men were set free.

Around 11:30 A.M., Col. Forrest, wanting to save lives and end this battle, sent the following message to Lt. Col. Parkhurst:

> Murfreesboro
> July 13, 1862
> Col.:
>   I must demand an unconditional surrender of your force as prisoners of war or I will have every man put to the sword. You are aware of the overpowering force I have at my command, and this demand is made to prevent the infusion of blood.
>   I am Col. very respectfully
>   Your obedient servant,
>   N.B. Forrest[20]

After discussion with his officers and realizing the hopelessness of the situation, Parkhurst surrendered at twelve o'clock noon. In Parkhurst's defense, both he and Duffield were seriously wounded. General Thomas Crittenden and his staff were in a private house Captain Haynie had surrounded. Captain White, of Forrest's staff, received Crittenden's sword. After Haynie had Crittenden captured, he went to find Col. Morrison. Haynie came galloping up to Morrison frantic with joy and excitement. Captain Haynie exclaimed, "Col. I'll be damned if I haven't taken General Crittenden and all his staff."[21] Morrison, well pleased with Haynie, said, "You don't say so Captain."[22] The old man then replied: "If I haven't there's no Hell!"[23]

Meanwhile, Col. Lester had done little since the courthouse was attacked. As the fighting subsided, he wanted to talk with Col. Duffield. Under a flag of truce, he went to the Michigan encampment, where he saw the results of the battle.[24]

Col. Forrest had Col. Lester led into town to meet with the captured Union officers. Forrest had his brigade lined up in town to give the impression he was bigger than Col. Lester and was greatly outnumbered. Lester was so impressed with Forrest's defeat of the Ninth Michigan Infantry he was determined to surrender the Third Minnesota.

There were about 1,350 privates and noncommissioned officers captured and brought to McMinnville by the Georgia regiments. The noncommissioned prisoners were paroled July 15 on the condition they not serve until exchanged. The loss in Federal property and ammunition was estimated at one million dollars. Col. Duffield was so badly wounded he was paroled in Murfreesboro. He was permanently disabled and resigned from the Union army.[25] The 40 to 50 officers captured were taken to Knoxville by Col. Wharton. From there they went to Atlanta, Georgia, Madison, Georgia, and various other prisons in the South and were eventually paroled. Lt. Col. Parkhurst spent three months in prison and was exchanged in December 1862. The six captured companies of the Ninth Michigan were paroled and went to Nashville and from there to Camp Chase, Ohio. They were sent home to await word of their exchange. The Third Minnesota Infantry never took part in the War of Rebellion after Murfreesboro. They were sent west to fight the Indian Wars.

Major General J.P. McCown filed this after battle report: "Forrest attacked Murfreesboro at five o'clock Sunday morning July 13, and captured two Brigadier Generals, staff and field officers and 1,200 men, burned $200,000 worth of stores, captured sufficient stores with those burned to amount to $500,000, sixty wagons, 300 mules, 150 or 200 horses, and a field battery of four pieces, destroyed the railroad and depot at Murfreesboro. Forrest had to retreat to McMinnville owing to the large number of prisoners to be guarded. Loss 16 or 18 killed, 25 or 30 wounded."[26]

Col. John F. Miller, of the Twenty-ninth Indiana, investigated the Union disaster at Murfreesboro. He filed in his report that Col. Lester had become "stupid with fear and some complained of his cowardly action." The report indicated "jealousy between the officers caused a separation of the troops beyond supporting distance in sudden emergencies."[27] Other problems were "bad picketing, lack of skill, vigilance and personal courage of officers."[28]

Late in the afternoon of July 13, Col. Forrest sent a detachment of fifty men under Major Baxter Smith. It was composed of Captain John L. Kerr's Company G, First Georgia Cavalry, and Captain Francis Cunningham's Fourth Tennessee Cavalry, Company C. They were sent to burn the railroad bridge over Stones River, three miles below Murfreesboro. The bridge was well guarded by about 100 enemy troops. On arrival at the bridge, Major Smith formed up his command and charged the enemy, killing one and capturing three; all the others skedaddled. Major Smith then burned the bridge and returned to Murfreesboro.

After the victory at Murfreesboro, Nathan B. Forrest was promoted to the rank of Brigadier General. The First Georgia Cavalry remained with him a while longer and made camp on Mountain Creek, about ten miles north of McMinnville.

Lt. John W. Tench stated, "While I have seen many glowing accounts of the part taken by different troops in the action at Murfreesboro, I have never seen any praise awarded to the 1st Regiment. It may be, perhaps, it had no champion of the quill; if that is so, henceforth I will assume a pugilistic attitude and battle with it against the enemy and afterwards scribble for our share of the honors."[29]

On July 24, the *Rome Tri-Weekly Courier* reported Captains Seawright and Crabb and Surgeon Witcher were killed. Captain John L. Kerr, Adj. John Perkins, Lt. William M. Hutchings, and several privates had returned to Rome, Georgia, after recently being wounded in the Battle at Murfreesboro.[30]

On Friday, July 18, 1862, Brig. Gen. Nathan B. Forrest took 700 of his brigade on a reconnaissance mission from their encampment at Mountain Creek toward Nashville. When they arrived at Alexandria, Forrest was informed that some 700 Federal cavalry had been sent from Nashville to Lebanon. Upon hearing this, Gen. Forrest ordered up the entire brigade, including the First and Second Georgia Cavalry and the Tennessee and Kentucky squadrons. As soon as the Forrest Brigade was together, they began a forced march to

Lebanon.[31] They arrived there at sunrise on July 19. Forrest formed his command for a charge into Lebanon, which they did in fine style. The charging cavalry gave the Rebel yell as they galloped into town. The Confederates were surprised that they met with no resistance. It was because the enemy had pulled out at midnight. The fear of Forrest and his command was beginning to spread.

While in Lebanon, Lt. John Tench wrote a letter to the editor of the *Tri-Weekly Courier* in Rome, Georgia. In the letter, Tench described to the actions of the First Georgia Cavalry during the Battle of Murfreesboro. He prefaced his description with this statement: "No war since the beginning of time has been marked by as strange and important events as the present. So great is the extent of territory over which the war is spread, that we cannot determine today, when a blow will fall tomorrow. Little did the Federal invaders dream over a week ago, that they were in the slightest danger in the occupancy of the old capitol of Tennessee, Murfreesboro, but a bold and gallant spirit determined that they should be and it was done."[32]

The command stayed in Lebanon until Monday morning, July 21. The men were in need of a rest after their march from Alexandria. The people in Lebanon had welcomed them well enough and seemed loyal to the Confederacy with few exceptions; and it was a good place to rest. That morning, the Forrest Brigade headed toward Nashville.[33]

As the brigade moved to within five or six miles of Nashville, Forrest's men captured three enemy pickets.[34] They moved on around the city in a semicircular march. At the pike, Col. James J. Morrison was ordered to take the First Georgia Cavalry Regiment and the Kentucky squadron and hold the pike. Meanwhile, Forrest took the Eighth Texas Rangers and the Second Georgia Cavalry on around Nashville burning bridges. Morrison's mission was to prevent General Forrest from being cut off from behind.

Sgt. Augustus Silas McGregor. Enlisted May 1862. Wounded in action March 30, 1863, Somerset, Kentucky. Present through December 31, 1864. Sheriff of Polk Co., Georgia (courtesy Thomas F. Finley III).

Col. Morrison sent out a strong picket as Forrest departed. The First Georgia's wait had not been long when suddenly they were attacked. The pickets were being driven in by the advance of a strong enemy force. Col. Morrison, seeing the pickets fall back, ordered his men to mount up and charge into the attacking force. Morrison led the charge with the Kentucky Squadron in the lead.

As they galloped to attack, a misunderstanding of commands resulted in the Kentucky Squadron's halting. Col. Morrison, Sergeant Ben Pickett, and Pvt. Dick Lyons were unaware of the mix-up and continued the charge into the whole Yankee force. The three-man charge killed two and captured two Yankees. The remainder of the enemy ran back to Nashville. After a good laugh, as the troops returned to their post, there was a strong discussion of commands and how to follow them. At the assigned position, they waited for Forrest to return without further incident.

Forrest had taken the Eighth Texas and Second Georgia down the Nashville and Chattanooga railroad line to within three miles of the city. They captured some pickets along the way. As they went along the line, they removed railroad track and did as much damage as they could. The bridges were heavily picketed, and Forrest had to skirmish considerably to get them cleared. Forrest's men burned three bridges over Mill Creek. When they came upon Antioch, Tennessee; they took the place and burned all the supplies.

General Forrest's skill as an aggressive commander was again displayed during this raid toward Nashville. His men killed ten men, wounded between fifteen and twenty, and captured ninety-seven, including three commissioned officers. Forrest's command did not suffer any loss. Not only did they succeed in destroying railroad track, bridges, depots, and telegraph lines, but also they once again threw fear and terror into the hearts of the Yankee troops in Nashville. Forrest regretted not having a few thousand men to deal with Nashville as he did Murfreesboro. He felt if he had the men he could have dealt a blow to put Nashville "in possession of the South again."[35]

After the Forrest Brigade made their demonstration, they moved back to McMinnville. On July 24, Forrest filed his report to Kirby Smith of the actions of the previous day. On July 26, General Forrest ordered Major Armstead Harper and his detachment from the First Georgia Cavalry back to McMinnville. They had been on duty a Crossville.[36] Previously, Captain James Blalock, Co. E, had his pickets fired upon while on duty at the ferry near Clinton, Tennessee. Captain Blalock thought he was about to be surrounded and retreated. He reported the engagement to his headquarters.[37] Kirby Smith issued orders to Col. Thomas H. Taylor and Col. Alexander W. Reynolds, in light of Blalock's report, that if the enemy crossed the river to push them back across.

Almost at the same time that Major Harper and his command returned from their duty near Clinton and Crossville, Col. Morrison received orders to return again to Kirby Smith. Morrison was told "to select 300 good men, well mounted, with efficient officers, four days rations, and a full supply of ammunition and to send them back to Clinton without delay."[38] Morrison was to report to Kirby Smith by return courier when Major Harper departed. Major Harper was told that when he reached Clinton, he would find further orders there for him. Once again the First Georgia Cavalry took up their position to watch and report the actions of the enemy to Kirby Smith. The men thought this very light duty considering what they had accomplished in the last few weeks.

3

First Kentucky Campaign

In August 1862, the headquarters of the First Georgia Cavalry placed advertisements in local Georgia newspapers. It stated that all officers and privates who were absent from the regiment, either on furlough or otherwise, were ordered to report to Loudon, Tennessee, without delay and await further orders. It also stressed that the order would be rigidly enforced. Captain Milton H. Haynie placed the ads.[1] The First Georgia Cavalry was preparing for new action.

Colonel John S. Scott, First Louisiana Cavalry, was named commander of the Second Cavalry Brigade. He was replacing General Nathan B. Forrest. Col. Scott wanted to make an expedition through Kentucky to gather recruits and try to get the state to join the Confederacy. He also thought it a good idea to just permanently occupy the state if she refused to join.

Approval of the movement came to Col. Scott on August 9, 1862. He was to take the First Louisiana Cavalry, Lt. Col. James O. Nixon, and the First Georgia Cavalry Regiment, Col. James J. Morrison, on his proposed expedition. Col. James W. Starnes' Third Tennessee Regiment would join them later on the other side of the mountains. Immediately preparations were begun to make the long journey into Kentucky.

Col. Scott's plan was in concert with General Kirby Smith's plan as well. Scott's Brigade was to be the vanguard for Kirby Smith's Army. General Henry Heth moved his Second Division through Big Creek Gap on August 11. He was moving to Barboursville, Kentucky, in order to get to the rear of General George Morgan. General Carter L. Stevenson's First Division was to advance on Morgan's front.

With preparations complete, Col. Scott's Brigade left Kingston, Tennessee, in the late afternoon of August 13. The brigade's complement was made up of the First Georgia Cavalry, the First Louisiana Cavalry, and Captain Garnett's Buckner Guards. The brigade totaled 896 men.[2] Scott's Brigade made its way through Montgomery and Jamestown, Tennessee, to Monticello and Somerset, Kentucky, and moved on to London, Kentucky. The trip was about 170 miles long and was made in sixty hours. Thirty-six of those miles took five hours to traverse because it was over very primitive and rough mountain roads. The men did not give but one ration per day to their horses and very little water was to be found. The men themselves were on short rations. All these conditions made the trip very difficult.

As the First Georgia Cavalry was going through Jamestown, Colonel Morrison sent small parties of men to arrest some distrustful people who were thought to be Federal spies. While waiting out a driving rainstorm, the main body of the First Georgia Cavalry rested. At about two o'clock in the morning of August 14, the rain stopped, and the First Georgia took up the line of march to Monticello. The Georgians were met by Monticello's Home Guards, who put up a lively skirmish before they were driven away. After quiet was established, the First Georgia made camp for the night.[3]

By 2:00 A.M., Friday, August 15, the First Georgia was in the saddle and let the townspeople know of their departure by giving a fine rendition of "Dixie." The regiment had sung almost every song the Georgia boys knew while on the march to London. After leaving Monticello, they were headed for Somerset, Kentucky. Along the way, they crossed Fishing Creek and climbed the hills before them.[4]

Col. Scott's Cavalry Brigade failed to surprise the Yankees at Somerset. The Federals were already in position to receive Scott and his men. Col. Scott also failed to capture the telegraph office before the alert was given up the line. But after a heavy skirmish, the superior Confederate force soon cleared the town. They took 75 prisoners, wounded or killed at least 50 of the enemy, captured 40 or 50 wagons, 175 mules, the camp garrison equipment, about 50 stacks of guns with ammunition and a small amount of commissary stores. However, a considerable amount of clothing, commissary stores and arms were burned by the Yankees before they left town. Col. Scott's loss in the battle was one lieutenant and one private killed. Three or four others were wounded. Pvt. William W. Shaw, Co. E's blacksmith, was captured.

Scott's Brigade was still 25 miles from London on the night of August 15. Col Scott learned that five companies of the Third Tennessee Volunteers, U.S. Army, were stationed in London under Col. Leonidas C. Houk. Scott immediately made plans to attack them. He selected 500 men from the command which included the First Georgia Cavalry. They made a forced march toward London and reached the town about nine o'clock Sunday morning, August 17.[5]

Col. Scott's Louisiana Regiment attacked on the left. Col. Morrison led the First Georgia Cavalry in a charging attack on the right flank of town. The enemy, however, had deserted town, leaving only 150 men to defend London. After a brief skirmish and little resistance, the Federals were soon captured. In the action that morning, 13 men were killed, 17 wounded, and 111 captured. There were also 170 loaded wagons, 290 mules, and a large amount of arms and stores captured.[6] Scott's loss was one officer and one private killed and none wounded. The prisoners were immediately paroled, and they seemed anxious to get their papers and not have to fight. In taking London, the cavalry had cut off the supplies to the Federal forces in the Cumberland Gap. Forty-two of the wagons were burned and the remainder was sent to General Kirby Smith in Barboursville.

After the town was secured, at about eleven o'clock that morning, Col. Morrison sent out a scouting party of 55 men under Captain James H. Strickland to find the enemy and

Pvt. Seaborn J. Cavender. Enlisted May 1862. Sharpshooter who killed most Yankees for the regiment. Surrendered April 26, 1865 (by Michael B. Cavender).

determine his strength. Captain Strickland took his men eight miles toward Barboursville searching the countryside. His company was attacked by an infantry force and a skirmish ensued. Three of Strickland's men were wounded before they withdrew to London. Captain Strickland's men killed two of the enemy during this engagement.[7]

When Captain James H. Strickland's Company B returned to London, the First Georgia Cavalry cleared the town of any suspected enemy and cut telegraph wires. They all mounted up and took up the march again. Before long, the men almost fell asleep in their saddles from lack of sleep. Three miles out of London, the First Georgia made camp and rested for two days.[8] The Georgians feasted on what they had captured and were pleased over their victories.

After the Georgians had rested, Col. Morrison took six companies of the First Georgia Cavalry and three companies of the First Louisiana Cavalry, about 300 men, with one piece of artillery and began to make their way toward Richmond through Mount Vernon, Kentucky.[9] As Morrison and his men advanced, the enemy fell back rapidly, leaving equipment, wagons and mules behind. Col. Morrison drove them without firing a shot except for bushwhackers up on top of the nearby hills. Morrison's cavalry soon passed the place where the Wild Cat Fight had taken place and General Felix Kirk Zollicoffer had lost his life on January 19, 1862.[10] As the column moved toward Richmond, they gathered in the mules, horses, and wagons left by the Federals along the road. Morrison's command moved a few miles further and camped for the night.

Col. Morrison's orders were for him to occupy both Mount Vernon and Crab Orchard. On the morning of August 19, Morrison's command of six companies of the First Georgia and three companies of the First Louisiana Cavalry made a charge into the town of Mount Vernon. They took possession of the place, capturing some fifty or sixty prisoners, mostly Home Guards and some Federals, 76 wagons, 235 mules, and a large quantity of commissary stores. Morrison did not suffer the loss of a single man.[11] The Federals were so overwhelmed that they were able to fire only three or four times before capture.

In Col. Morrison's report to Col. Scott, he stated that they had taken about 137 wagons, mostly loaded with commissary stores and corn. He also took 335 mules and horses with harness and other equipment. Morrison continued his report: "I cannot conclude without remarking that notwithstanding the great inclemency of the weather much praise is due the officers and men for their soldier conduct—without food for two days, enduring hardships incident to a continuous march, they exhibited that fortitude and chivalry which only visits noble hearts in a just cause."[12]

After the town was secure and it was still early in the day, Col. Morrison sent a small detachment to Crab Orchard. He was able to take and hold Mount Vernon but could not hold Crab Orchard. It was heavily occupied by General Green Clay Smith's First Brigade. Gen. Smith had arrived several hours prior to the First Georgia's approach and secured their position and made a stiff resistance to the First Georgia's attack. The First Georgia Cavalry fell back to near Mount Vernon and stayed all day and night. On August 20, they fell back fifteen miles, where they were joined by Col. Scott and 250 men with two artillery pieces.[13] When Scott arrived, he decided to cross swords with General Clay Smith the next day. Scott moved his brigade back to Mount Vernon for the night.

Early the next morning, Scott's Brigade began their attack. The scouts skirmished with Clay Smith's pickets and drove them back. Scott's men were able to remove all the Federal wagons along the road intended for the Cumberland Gap. Soon the entire brigade was in line of battle north of Mount Vernon on the Crab Orchard Road. Scott's men were able to push the Yankees for two miles.[14]

Col. Scott was hoping to buy enough time for Col. James Starnes' Third Tennessee Cavalry to join them. Scott's advance came upon the pickets of General Clay Smith at Big Hill, seventeen miles from Richmond. At this point, Col. Leonidas K. Metcalf's Seventh Kentucky Cavalry came up to Rock Castle Creek on the Richmond Road. This newly formed regiment attacked Col. Scott's Brigade on August 23.

Scott's Brigade gave Col. Metcalf such a shower of shot and shell that Metcalf could not bring his men forward to attack. Instead, they broke and ran, some all the way to Richmond. Col. Metcalf had led a gallant charge under such conditions and was humiliated to find that not more than 100 of his regiment had followed him. General William "Bull" Nelson ordered the immediate arrest of those who ran. Lt. Col. John C. Childs, with his Union Third Tennessee Battalion, braved the bullets of Scott's men to rescue Col. Metcalf, who had been abandoned on the field by his regiment. Cpl. W.D. Hambrick, Co. H died of wounds.

During the chase, Col. Scott captured Metcalf's horse and coat. The coat contained Metcalf's private papers. Among the papers was a letter from General Lewis "Lew" Wallace commanding at Lexington (he would later write the novel *Ben Hur*). The letter stated that he would move a brigade of infantry and four pieces of artillery to Richmond that same day.

With information from General Wallace, Col. Scott sent the First Georgia Cavalry to Richmond hoping that they would get there before him. Col. Scott would bring the main body of the brigade the next day. The First Georgia Cavalry had moved toward Richmond only a few miles when the advance guard was fired on by the advance of the enemy infantry. The First Georgia's guard soon made the enemy take cover behind the long-range guns of their infantry and cavalry. The Yankees had formed a line of battle at a strong salient known as Big Hill. Their line was on the side of the hill under the cover of large trees and thick undergrowth. The engagement soon warmed and the firing between the First Georgia Cavalry and the enemy became consistent and very severe. Col. Scott, with the rest of the brigade, soon arrived to join the battle. Scott placed his artillery into position and quickly exhausted the brigade's small supply of ammunition. Col. Scott ordered a general assault upon the enemy position.

Col. Morrison saw the best way to attack was to turn the enemy's left flank. Col. Morrison dismounted every company of the regiment except for Captain Strickland's Company B. Morrison sent the dismounted men to attack the enemy's left flank. Morrison felt the dismounted cavalry could do a better job on foot than on horseback in the thick undergrowth. Major Armstead R. Harper led the attack. The dismounted Georgia cavalrymen had almost gained the enemy's left flank when the enemy began to retreat. Seeing the retreat, Col. Scott charged his First Louisiana, Ector's Dragoons, and Captain Strickland's Company B into the enemy. Captain Strickland's Company led the charge.[15]

After the charge, nothing but confusion filled the Yankee ranks. Guns, sabers, blankets, knapsacks, and even horses were left in the line of battle. The Federals fled wildly on foot. The First Georgia, which was on foot, mounted their horses and followed the retreating Federals in hot pursuit. Later some of the Federals returned to the Confederates to surrender.

About a mile down the mountain at the foot of Big Hill, the First Georgia Cavalry again met a portion of Col. Metcalf's cavalry and 500 infantry. They had blockaded the road with some overturned wagons at a bridge spanning the creek. The creek flowed through a three-foot deep embankment. In front of the creek was a rail fence and from there it was sixty yards to the foot of the mountain the Georgians were coming down.

Col. Morrison, seeing the position of the enemy, decided a charge was the best offensive to dislodge them. Morrison sent Major Harper with Captain Strickland's Company B and Lt. Jesse Crabb's Company A to charge their front. Meanwhile, Col. Morrison with the other companies led by Captain Milton H. Haynie charged them from the left. The enemy poured a galling fire into Major Harper and his men as they charged in the attack. The fence was quickly torn down and the creek crossed. Harper's men returned the fire rapidly and repeatedly and caused the Yankees again to see how fast they could retreat. Their retreat prevented Col. Morrison from taking them all prisoner. Morrison's men were able to catch about 300 prisoners, and later that evening they were paroled.

When the fight was over, Captain Strickland dismounted to attend to his wounded troops. He had one man killed, another mortally wounded, and seven others with various kinds of wounds. While Captain Strickland tended his wounded, he turned the company over to Lt. James Taylor to gallop off in pursuit of the scattered enemy.

The remaining First Georgia Cavalry followed Lt. Taylor in pursuing the enemy all the way to Richmond. The First Georgia Cavalry reached a point two miles beyond Richmond that same evening and took a position on the Lexington Road. Morrison found the next morning that those he had been chasing were now reinforced and were thus a much larger force than he could handle. Col. Morrison decided it would be best to fall back to Big Hill, where Col. Scott had established his camp. The First Georgia Cavalry had ridden over very broken country for twenty-five miles even before the fight started, and then they had chased the Yankees another ten miles to Richmond. It was time to give the regiment the rest they richly deserved. Lt. Jesse Crabb, Company A, was singled out for praise for his gallantry in the charge to the enemy's front and credit for the success of the attack.[16]

When Col. Morrison arrived back at Big Hill, he reported to Col. Scott about General Clay Smith's Cavalry Brigade at Crab Orchard. Col. Scott's men were busy collecting all the supplies, mules, wagons and arms left by the routed Federals. It took three days to gather all the material left. Scott also wanted to rest the men and horses and get them fed. The First Georgia Cavalry rested one day. They feasted on what they had captured and swapped stories of events and success in the battle. What they did not consume they sent down to General Kirby Smith.

Lt. John W. Tench in his letter to the *Rome Weekly Courier*, about the Battle at Big Hill, Kentucky, wrote of the bravery of Col. Morrison and Major Harper: "They are always in the thickest of the fight. Where the bullets whiz the thickest and the clash of arms and the yell of battle sounds the loudest, there they may be found."[17]

At the crossroad near Big Hill, Kentucky, Col. John S. Scott waited for Col. James W. Starnes' Third Tennessee Cavalry. Scott's Brigade was also waiting for General Patrick Ronayne Cleburne, who was the advance of Kirby Smith's Infantry. Finally, on August 27, Starnes arrived and Col. Scott moved the brigade toward Richmond.[18] Two days later, Col. Starnes made a reconnaissance ride around Richmond to locate the enemy's position and their number. He found the Federals were secure in their battle line about three miles from town. They occupied a high ridge commanding the turnpike. Brig. Gen. Mahlon D. Manson's First Brigade had formed his line with artillery on the flanks about two miles from town.

Captain Milton H. Haynie, Company C, First Georgia Cavalry was leading his squadron in advance of Scott's Brigade when his pickets came across the enemy and firing commenced. The Yankees began to retreat. Haynie followed them beyond the foot of Big Hill and on back toward Richmond. There the Yanks made another stand and opened up their artillery.

At about five o'clock in the afternoon, the Federals began a cannonade on Scott's Brigade that subsequently drove Scott away.[19] After the engagement, Col. Scott noted all the desired information and then fell back four miles to General Patrick Cleburne's advance infantry division. Col. Scott reported his findings to General Cleburne.[20] Scott did not notice the enemy had followed him. He told Cleburne that his brigade was camped in the road to his front and had posted pickets for the night. Scott also advised Cleburne the enemy would not advance upon them that night. General Cleburne listened to Scott but felt more secure with his own guards posted. Cleburne put his men in a battle front in the direction Col. Scott said the enemy was located.[21]

It was after dark before the guards were secured in the positions assigned by Cleburne. The general had summoned the regimental commanders to give them orders as to which locations they were to go in case of attack. The meeting was barely over when firing and yelling was heard from the front. Almost at the same time, Scott's Brigade came flying into the infantry's position. General Manson had sent his cavalry out to find the Rebels.[22]

The Federal Cavalry advanced in the dark to within twenty-five steps of the Confederate line. Two companies of the Forty-eighth Tennessee Infantry fired into the Yanks and checked their advance. The Federals dismounted and began to move again into the line of battle set up and were waiting for them. It was just as dark for the enemy as for the Confederates that night. However, the Federals could see the Rebel campfires but not the Confederates in their barricades. As the Union cavalry proceeded in the dark, they cursed and made threats to the Rebs, giving their locations away. When the order to fire was given, the firing from the Confederate line was so strong that the Yankees broke and ran back to their horses. They cut the reins from the trees to which they had been tied in order to make a faster retreat. Cleburne's men captured thirty prisoners and wounded several. Cleburne's men had only one man wounded.[23]

On August 30, Kirby Smith moved up four brigades of his infantry with artillery. They made a hammer-like attack on General Manson's untried troops near Richmond. Col. James J. Morrison and the First Georgia Cavalry were ordered in the advance of Kirby Smith and to move to the rear of Richmond.[24] Their mission was to cut off the retreat of the enemy, who were already beginning to fall back very fast from the heavy blows of Kirby Smith's forces.

There were three roads from Richmond to Lexington. Col. Scott's Louisiana Cavalry controlled one pike, and Col. Starnes' Tennessee Cavalry had one pike. Scott repulsed the enemy with blistering howitzer fire that sent the bewildered Yankees in another direction toward Morrison's Georgia boys.

Col. Morrison, in his initial movement, sent Captain James H. Strickland's Co. B and Captain Milton H. Haynie's Co. C to his right and left as flankers to prevent the column from being ambushed from the sides. Morrison was moving the First Georgia Cavalry to the Lexington Pike. About two miles from the pike, the column came across a wagon train with Union supplies moving in retreat. Lt. John Tench, Co. K, was leading the column. Tench took about sixty men and made a headlong charge into the train, stampeding the guards and teamsters away. Tench captured a large portion of the wagons and 300 prisoners. The First Georgia

Cavalry moved forward at full speed with the remaining six companies. Captains Haynie and Strickland were still on the flanks. Lt. Tench and Company K stayed with the wagon train until it was secured.

Kirby Smith, in attacking Manson's left wing, broke it with relentless fighting and sent that part of Manson's force in retreat. As Manson began to fall back, he had hopes of regrouping his lines. However, Kirby Smith's Confederates pressed even harder. Soon Manson's right, which had fought stubbornly, was crushed and the Union army was engaged in a full-scale rout.

Major General William "Bull" Nelson came upon the field at about two o'clock and replaced Manson. Nelson began directing the battle, but his efforts were fruitless. Each new position Nelson tried to establish was quickly overrun by Confederates who would not be denied victory. Full retreat from the field seemed the only option to General "Bull" Nelson to save his army of 7,000.[25] Nelson began moving them out to the Lexington Pike. Neither Union commander knew that the First Georgia Cavalry had been pressing hard to reach the Pike.[26]

The First Georgia Cavalry arrived just ahead of the Union infantry moving down that road. Col. Morrison had quickly placed his men in position to fire into the unsuspecting enemy. The fire was convulsive and threw the already defeated Union troops into confusion. They were so bewildered and astonished by this new attack they threw down their arms and prepared to surrender. They were especially demoralized since they believed they had at last escaped Kirby Smith's Infantry. Those who did not surrender immediately fled from the pike in every direction.

Confronted with the much larger number of enemy running away in uncontrolled confusion, Col. Morrison divided his force. He gave Lt. John W. Tench fifty men and the remainder to Lt. Col. Armstead R. Harper. Lt. Tench made a charge into a full regiment of Federal infantry on the right of the pike and took them all prisoner. Lt. Col. Harper led the remainder of the First Georgia in a brazen charge up the pike toward Lexington. They captured everyone and everything on the road. Morrison had thought that most of the Federals had already passed him, but Harper's charge proved him wrong, for which he was glad. Lt. Col. Harper ordered all the wagons captured to be overturned to prevent them from being driven away by the enemy.

Soon General Nelson was informed that the Rebel cavalry was destroying his advance in retreat. Nelson, in his usual rage, ordered his cavalry to locate the First Georgia Cavalry, charge into them and destroy them. He had previously tried retreating up the Frankfort Road, but Col. Scott's First Louisiana Cavalry and Col. Starnes' Third Tennessee Cavalry had foiled his efforts. Nelson was confident his cavalry could attack and defeat the single regiment that stood between him and freedom.

Col. Morrison was warned to watch for Nelson's attack. Morrison re-formed the regiment into an ambuscade. Strickland, Tench and Harper were now with Morrison and only Captain Haynie and Company C remained away. Col. Morrison hurriedly moved the regiment into a cornfield on the left of the pike. He concealed his men in a single line among the stalks of rustling corn. There was a stone wall at the edge of the field beside the road.

Almost at the moment the First Georgia Cavalry got into position, Nelson's Cavalry came charging down the road at full speed. The men of the First Georgia Cavalry sat quietly in their saddles watching the two Yankee cavalry regiments moving toward them followed by their artillery rumbling down the road. The artillery consisted of two Parrott guns and four brass eight pounders. The Yankees thundered down the road toward Lexington looking for Rebels.

Col. Morrison watched and as soon as the Yankees had almost reached the full length of his concealed cavalry, he ordered them to charge up to the stone fence while firing on the enemy. The First Georgia Cavalry responded promptly, moving forward and squaring up to the enemy, and commenced an awful slaughter. "The men stood firm and square to the fence, leading and firing very rapidly, each man loading and firing his gun three or four times besides firing their pistols."[27]

"The First Georgia poured a continuous galling fire into the enemy cavalry. They stood undaunted and volley after volley poured into the ranks of the terrified enemy. Horses and riders both rolled together in the dust.[28] The groans of the wounded and dying mingled in horrid discord with the clash of arms, the roar of coming artillery, and the wild neigh of wounded and frightened horses."[29] Thus did Lt. Tench describe the scene. Col. Morrison said, "The slaughter was awful, killing and wounding some 300, killing dead on the field some 70 or 80. Among them, Col. Wolfe of the Thirteenth Indiana Regiment and several captains and lieutenants, and taking a great many prisoners, amounting in all to nearly 3,000, together with six pieces of artillery."[30] This fatal blow to the Federal army lay open the heart of the retreating enemy and allowed most of it to be captured. Morrison said, "The road was literally strewn with the dead and dying horses and men, artillery, wagons, caissons, etc. The road was so completely blockaded that I had to have it cleared before any passing could be done."[31]

While Col. Morrison and the First Georgia Cavalry began rounding up the prisoners and clearing the road, Captain Milton H. Haynie and Company C were busy on another field. Captain Haynie had allowed himself and his company to fall into the hands of a regiment of enemy infantry. But Haynie did not allow himself to remain prisoner for long. In talking with the Union Officers of the regiment, Haynie persuaded them it was best they surrender to him before they, too, were destroyed. Col. Morrison said in his report in amazement, "They actually surrendered to him. His entire company numbering only 35 men."[32] Col. Morrison ended his report of the action with the following: "Both officers and men deserve the greatest credit for their coolness and bravery. Never in my life have I seen more determination exhibited by either men or officers to whip the fight, and nobly did they do it. They all deserve lasting honor."[33] Lt. John W. Tench, in his letter to the editor of the *Rome Courier*, wrote as follows,

> Col. Morrison deserves the greatest credit, for General Smith as General Claiborne remarked to me, would have secured none of the results scarcely of the victory had it not been for the cavalry, the enemy would have saved his artillery, his wagons, and 5,000 prisoners. Col Harper displayed a large share of his usual gallant conduct and no officer of his grade is more highly appreciated by General Smith than he is. Lt. [Jesse] Crabb deserves again to be mentioned. After the first gun had been captured he sprang to it, intending to load it. He called me to his assistance and we succeeded in loading the piece and brought it to bear on the enemy. But upon examination found that the Yankee gunners had thrown away their friction tubes and the piece could not be used.[34]

It became almost impossible for the First Georgia Cavalry to reap the harvest. They were so few and the enemy so great. A large number of the enemy just wandered away in bewilderment. No one was there to tell a man he was captured and where to go. Morrison's men searched the fields and woods for the enemy, rounding them up like scattered sheep. When it became so dark it was impossible to tell who was friend or foe, the search stopped for the night. All those that were captured were turned over to General Preston Smith.

The combined Confederate effort that day at Richmond against Generals Manson and Nelson yielded 206 killed, 844 wounded and 4,303 captured. There were nine artillery pieces captured with 8,000 to 10,000 arms, plus large quantities of stores and wagons. General Nelson was wounded and Illinois statesman William P. Morrison was captured. General Manson was captured when his horse was killed and fell on him, severely injuring him. The Confederates suffered only 450 killed or wounded.

A postscript to the battle at Richmond was that Union general Jefferson C. Davis, who had been insulted by General Nelson because of Davis' mismanagement of the battle, shot and killed General Nelson in a heated argument. General Davis had requested an apology from General Nelson for the treatment and Nelson slapped Davis twice and called him a coward. Davis procured a gun and returned to shoot General Nelson.

On the morning of September 1, 1862, the day after the victory at Richmond, Kentucky, Col. John Scott's Cavalry began to pursue the Federals who escaped capture during the night. Col. Scott pushed his brigade to the Kentucky River south of Lexington. At the bridge, the brigade met the rear guard of the enemy, who were across the river. Scott sent his men to drive them from the bank and continue the pursuit of the defeated army. The First Georgia Cavalry, with the brigade, captured another 1,200 prisoners. Along the way going to Lexington, the First Georgia Cavalry helped gather in Union stragglers.[35] As night approached, Col. Scott called off the pursuit and made camp near the city. The rest was welcomed by the men, as most had been awake for the past two days fighting a desperate enemy.

The morning of September 2, Col. Scott had his brigade mount up and move out toward Lexington. The city had been abandoned and surrendered without a fight. The brigade captured three tons of gunpowder in one house alone and a vast amount of supplies were also captured.[36] After the gunpowder and other supplies were secured, the brigade moved toward Georgetown, about fifteen miles north of Lexington. After the brigade arrived, they made camp for the night.

On September 3, Col. Scott led the cavalry brigade to Frankfort, the capital of Kentucky. Frankfort was surrendered to them by the citizens of the town. It was an odd feeling for the Rebel cavalry to be in the town with only 850 men while out on the hills from town 8,000 Federal troops watched them. Col. Scott took his cavalry right up to the capitol building and called for a Confederate flag. Unfortunately, none could be found among the men. Col. Scott called for the Battle Flag of the First Louisiana Cavalry and hoisted it up the flag pole. The men gave a yell like never before as that worn banner fluttered in the breeze.[37] The Yankees on the hillsides remained quiet and unwilling to challenge.

On September 4, while the Honorable Richard Hawes was being inaugurated as provisional governor of Kentucky, the boom of cannon startled the crowd. The sound came from the direction of Hardinsville, a town about 10 miles to the west. Scott's Brigade was engaging the enemy in a heavy skirmish, with several regiments of Yankees involved. This became a sharp fight and Col. Morrison's First Georgia Cavalry, which was in reserve at the time, came up to the rescue. Lt. Col. A.R. Harper led the center column and was able to hold the enemy in check until the brigade was able to disengage and move back behind the Kentucky River.[38]

That evening, Col. Scott called his commanders together for reports about their respective regiments. Scott found that he had only about 450 effective fighters. He ordered that in the morning they be prepared to move out, to be ready to pursue and harass the enemy. On September 5, before the sun was up, the 450 troops trotted out of camp toward Shelbyville. At about sunrise, they came upon the enemy in front of Shelbyville. Col. Scott had his brigade charge into them, through the town and out the other side. As they left Shelbyville, they crossed a large bridge and destroyed it. When the destruction was complete, Scott circled his men back around to Frankfort. The brigade remained there to rest, recover, and recruit for the next three days.

On September 8, Col. Scott prepared his command to move back south. That evening, the brigade fell back toward Lebanon. They arrived there at about nine on the morning of September 11. The First Georgia Cavalry was on point of the column and found the town deserted. The enemy had made great preparations for a fight, with streets barricaded, but decided to leave Lebanon two days before Scott's Brigade arrived.

From Lebanon, Col. Scott filed his report of the Kentucky campaign. He reported the loss of one officer killed, six privates killed, 21 men wounded and nine captured. He included that his brigade had captured 4,000 prisoners, 375 wagons with stores, 1,500 mules and a large number of horses. Col. Scott said of the campaign, "I cannot close this report without bearing testimony to the soldierly conduct of my command. They have endured unusual privations and fatigue without murmur. I cannot compliment the commanders of the regiments composing this brigade too highly for their assistance rendered me."[39]

General Kirby Smith in his report to General Samuel Cooper paid this tribute to the men in the ranks during the campaign: "As regards the intrepid behavior of the true patriots, I can only say that as long as the destinies of the South remain in such hands we need never fear Northern subjugation ... inspired only with the desire of being led against the invaders of their homes and oppressors of their liberties."[40]

Almost as soon as the First Georgia Cavalry and Scott's Brigade arrived in Lebanon, they were back in their saddles on their way to do battle again. This time they headed south to Greensburg, Kentucky and traveled along the Green River to Munfordville.

Col. John T. Wilder, commanding the garrison of the Seventeenth Indiana, occupied the "works" near Munfordville. The stronghold consisted of three distinct parts. On the right was a range of rifle pits that could hold 3,000 men in a semicircle formation. The right end ran into a strong stockade which stood upon the edge of the bluff overlooking the Green River. About 100 yards to the left of the stockade was another range of rifle pits capable of sheltering at least one regi-

Pvt. John Armistead Jones. Enlisted in 7th Georgia infantry May 31, 1861. Enlisted First Georgia Cavalry May 1, 1862, in Cartersville, Georgia. Present on all rolls. Absent 1863 and 1864 as teamster for the brigade. Paroled at Charlotte, North Carolina, May 3, 1865 (courtesy Lipscomb Collection in the Heritage Room at the Rome-Floyd County Library, Rome, Georgia, and Ricky Smith).

ment of infantry. The main works stood further to the left. It was a regular bastion earthwork. Inside were stationed about 300 men. There were passages to each segment and each was protected from enemy fire.[41]

Saturday night, September 13, Col. Scott arrived at Munfordville with his brigade. The brigade had five mountain howitzers in its command. Col. Scott knew his brigade and the support nearby outnumbered the enemy and thought it best for all concerned for the enemy to surrender. This would prevent loss of life and limb for both sides. At eight o'clock that night, Col. Scott summoned Col. Wilder to surrender unconditionally. Col. Wilder knew at that moment he was opposed only by Col. Scott's Brigade. He felt that with his strong defensive position he could resist them. Wilder also knew General Buell was close by and could either come to his aid or attack those who would aid Scott.

After receiving Wilder's refusal to surrender, Col. Scott made plans to attack the garrison. Scott was a little peeved with Wilder's excuse for not surrendering. Scott felt it should not matter that his strength was only a brigade of cavalry. Wilder's reasoning made Scott find a nearby infantry unit to aid him. Col. Scott sent one of his officers to find Gen. James R. Chalmers and to convince him to come join the attack for an easy victory. Scott was convinced that the enemy's strength and will to fight was low because they were raw troops. The officer sent to Chalmers was to say that Scott would attack at daylight.

Before hearing a reply from Chalmers, Scott began his attack before daylight. He had sent out his skirmishers to find and fire on Wilder's pickets. The Federals put up a stubborn resistance to Scott's attack. Scott was shocked that the pickets killed one of his officers and a guide. Col. Scott was still looking for an easy victory and decided to bring up his artillery to drive in the enemy pickets, which it did very rapidly.

By 5:30 A.M. on September 14, the fighting became general along the whole line of the works occupied by Wilder. Scott's men had also advanced to within 200 yards of the line. As the day wore on, the lack of coordination between Scott and Chalmers became more evident. Gen. Chalmers had organized his infantry for an assault upon the fortress and had advanced to within 25 yards. Suddenly artillery shells started falling on his troops. Chalmers was amazed that the artillery was coming from his rear. He immediately ordered the Seventh and Ninth infantry regiments to about-face and charge the artillery. These regiments promptly obeyed and charged the cannon. As they drove the artillery, they learned the battery belonged to Col. Scott. No one bothered to tell General Chalmers that they would be there.[42]

Once he discovered the battery was Confederate and had been stopped from firing on his men, Chalmers about-faced the Seventh and Ninth and led them back into the assault on the fort. Unfortunately, as Chalmers led them back to the battle, the other regiments thought he was leaving the field and they also began to withdraw. The field was in mass confusion. Chalmers realized all gains were now lost and decided to withdraw to a position in the woods to get everyone reorganized.

Later that afternoon, Col. Scott sent Col. Morrison with the First Georgia Cavalry and Col. John W. Starnes' Third Tennessee Cavalry Regiment to destroy the Louisville and Nashville railroad bridge across Bacon Creek a few miles north of Munfordville. Col. Morrison's men moved out, arriving near the bridge at sunset. Col. Morrison had purposefully moved carefully to the bridge, as he felt it would be heavily fortified.

After the First Georgia Cavalry arrived, Col. Morrison wisely sent out scouts to reconnoiter the bridge. After their reports, Morrison was satisfied that the bridge could not be taken with a regular cavalry charge. He ordered the two regiments to dismount and prepare for a fight on foot. Morrison had wished his scouts could have given him the troop strength of the enemy he was about to meet. He supposed that they must be at least equal a force to his. As the cavalry prepared to attack, Morrison had the artillery placed into position to do the most damage to the enemy. He finalized his plan with Lt. Col. Harper.

Everything was ready, the men were eager to fight, the artillery was ready to fire and the plans of attack were set. Col. Morrison sent Lt. Col. Harper under a flag of truce to demand the unconditional surrender of the garrison. Lt. Col. Harper was surprised that after he presented the situation to the commander of the garrison, he surrendered without a fight.

After the surrender and paroling of the prisoners, Col. Morrison proceeded to burn everything of use. He had the twelve nearby railcars pushed onto the bridge and all set on fire, both bridge and cars. The First Georgia Cavalry also destroyed arms and ammunition they couldn't use because they had no way to carry them. After Morrison was satisfied his mission was accomplished completely, he returned to Munfordville and rejoined Col. Scott. Scott sent the Georgians on to Lebanon and they arrived there September 15.

While the First Georgia Cavalry was demolishing the Bacon Creek Bridge, General Chalmers had been looking for Col. Scott to dress him down about the day's foul-ups. Col. Scott tried to convince Gen. Chalmers that he had repeatedly tried to inform him that his artillery was going to occupy the hill in question and support his infantry attack. He did not mention that the shells might be falling on Chalmers' men.

During that same evening, Col. Cyrus Livingston Dunham's 50th Indiana Infantry brought 400 of his men into the garrison at Munfordville to support Col. Wilder. Dunham was able to escape with these troops from Bacon Creek before Col. Morrison captured the place.[43]

As time went by, Col. Scott's Brigade played a lesser role at Munfordville. Braxton Bragg came up the morning of September 16, and General Leonidas Polk was not far behind. Bragg was waiting for Polk to be in place that evening before summoning Col. Wilder again to surrender. Wilder refused again because he did not believe that he could possibly be opposed by such a force as claimed. Wilder felt sure General Buell would have occupied at least part of the attacking Confederates. Col. Wilder consulted with General Simon Bolivar Buckner and demanded to inspect Bragg's force and check the batteries. After the inspection, Wilder realized the hopelessness of his position. He asked General Buckner what he would do. Wilder surrendered the whole force Wednesday morning, September 17, 1862,[44] with 4,600 prisoners taken and 600 stacks of arms. A prodigious amount of stores were captured, including a large quantity of clothing.[45] The First Georgia Cavalry with Scott's Brigade moved on.

4

From Kentucky to Stones River

The First Georgia Cavalry enjoyed a few days rest in Lebanon, Kentucky. Col. John S. Scott's Brigade mounted up and headed east, back to Richmond, Kentucky, to be the eyes and ears for General Kirby Smith. After arriving in Richmond, Scott's command was ordered to go to Irvine and Boonville. Kirby Smith was nervous that General John Fitzroy DeCourcey's Brigade was near Manchester. Smith did not want Union general George W. Morgan's Seventh Division to embarrass him because he was unprepared. Scott's Cavalry was to keep him alerted to their movements.[1] By the time Scott's Battalion arrived in Richmond, their assignment had changed. They were still to be the eyes and ears for Kirby Smith, but now at a different place. They were to go to Frankfort.[2]

The First Georgia Cavalry did not go with Col. Scott. They had orders to go north from Lebanon to Bardstown and drive the Yankees from that area. When the Georgians arrived at Bardstown, the Federals had already withdrawn. Col. Morrison kept his cavalry regiment in town until General Bragg brought up his infantry. When Bragg arrived, Col. Morrison moved the regiment to Frankfort to rejoin Col. Scott.

From Frankfort, Captain Milton H. Haynie was sent to procure clothing for the tattered First Georgia Cavalry. Haynie had to go to Lexington to get the uniforms. Upon completing that mission, he was sent down to Kingston, Tennessee, to retrieve all those of the First Georgia Cavalry who had been sick, on furlough, or otherwise absent from the regiment.[3]

Later the First Georgia Cavalry was sent as the advance picket for Kirby Smith's army almost to Middleton, Kentucky. After Col. Morrison arrived at the selected position near Middleton, he set out strong pickets as was his custom. Almost as soon as the men were in place, two regiments of Union cavalry, the Third Indiana and Seventh Pennsylvania, came crashing into the town driving the First Georgia Cavalry's pickets before them.

Col. Morrison heard the firing of guns in the distance and quickly mounted the standby company to reinforce the men on picket duty. When Morrison arrived, he found the Seventh Pennsylvania occupying the position where he had previously posted his pickets. Col. Morrison formed the two companies across the road and charged back into the Pennsylvania Cavalry. This drove them beyond the First Georgia Cavalry's original position.[4]

The Seventh Pennsylvania regrouped and reinforced their ranks and came charging back at the two companies of the First Georgia Cavalry, forcing them back again. In this seesaw battle, the First Georgia Cavalry in turn reinforced themselves to drive the Union cavalry back again, wounding several. The Union's next move was a show of full strength. They sent two regiments of infantry as flankers to the right and left of their cavalry. The Union moved in their long-range artillery and brought it to bear on the First Georgia Cavalry.[5]

Col. Morrison saw this overwhelming number of cavalry and infantry coming toward him, and he hurriedly withdrew across the bridge behind Middleton and one mile beyond. He felt sure the enemy would press him in his new position. With this in mind, he had the men build a strong defensive position rapidly. As night fell, Morrison had his men build large campfires to decoy the enemy to think they were in camp and not in the trenches, as they were. Col. Morrison's Brigade waited for the attack all night. The Yankees never came and Morrison sent his scouts out the next morning to find them.[6]

The scouts came in with news the enemy had fallen back to Middleton during the night. Morrison could not understand why they did not attack because they certainly outnumbered him and could have done the First Georgia Cavalry a lot of damage. He was relieved that they did not and felt it might be safe to return to the post assigned to him. As the First Georgia Cavalry arrived at the post, the firing started between the pickets. The light shooting continued until October 2. On that day, the Union commander wanted to smash the tenacious little Georgia Regiment.

Col. Morrison and his men watched as the Federals brought up their whole force. In all there were two cavalry regiments and eight regiments of infantry with six pieces of artillery. The Georgia boys watched as the enemy moved into line of battle and prepared to attack. Morrison had a little surprise for the Yankees this time.

Col. Morrison's men sat upon their saddles awaiting his orders. Their weapons were loaded and sabers extra sharp. When the Federals reached the place Morrison felt he could best deliver a blow, he charged his cavalry out at a full gallop. The Georgia Rebels were giving their yells at the top of their lungs as they came crashing into the Federal lines. The First Georgia Cavalry slammed into the Yankees with such great speed and force the Federals reeled backward. As the Georgians fought, they broke their lines and had the invaders on the run. The Union commander called for the artillery to do its work. This forced the First Georgia Cavalry to back off out of range.[7]

As all of this was going on, Col. John Scott's Louisiana Cavalry arrived to reinforce the First Georgia Cavalry. The Louisiana boys brought three pieces of artillery with them. The artillery was quickly placed into position in the road and loaded with grapeshot. Col. Morrison placed the two regiments on opposite sides of the road and waited for the Union's next move.

The wait was over as the Federals came charging down the road. As soon as the Yankees got in range, Morrison let them have it with grapeshot from all three pieces. The first round slowed their advance. The artillery was quickly reloaded and the second round stopped them. Morrison charged the Georgia and Louisiana cavalry into the shocked Federal cavalry, and the Yankees were forced from the field. Col. Morrison thought this a good time to withdraw before the enemy regrouped and brought their infantry back with them. He formed the regiments in columns of four and fell back toward Frankfort to Col. Scott's previous position. When Col. Morrison arrived at Col. Scott's headquarters, he reported the events that had taken place. The First Georgia Regiment meanwhile got in a day's rest.

On October 4, Col. Scott sent the First Georgia Cavalry out on the Louisville Pike toward Clay Village. They were to be the advance pickets for the infantry. Upon arrival at Clay Village, the First Georgia Cavalry encountered the enemy in heavy force. The enemy cavalry consisted of Col. Richard Taylor Jacob's Ninth Kentucky Cavalry and the Seventh Pennsylvania Cavalry. Both units were supported by a battery with six pieces. The Federals also had two brigades of infantry.

Col. Morrison knew his regiment could whip any two Yankee cavalry regiments and tried several times that day to engage them. Each time Morrison drew near for an attack, the enemy cavalry would run away. Col. Morrison decided to draw them out with a trap. He sent Captain Napoleon Reynolds and Company F out, with instructions to form a line of battle across the road. They were to keep concealed as much as possible and not fire until the enemy came to within a very short range. They were to fire and act as if in retreat before the enemy, hoping to draw them into Morrison's awaiting trap.[8]

The trap consisted of two platoons of the First Louisiana Cavalry on the right side of the road. They were commanded by Lt. E. Green Davis. Three companies of the First Georgia Cavalry were on the left side of the road commanded by Major James H. Strickland. These men were to wait for the enemy while they chased Captain Reynolds. When the Yankees passed their position, Major Strickland was to form in the road, blocking it and preventing the enemy from falling back. The doors of the trap would then be closed. Lt. Col. Armstead R. Harper was to charge into the Federals from the front with the remainder of the First Georgia Cavalry and crush the reluctant enemy.

Col. Morrison felt somewhat like a fisherman with Captain Reynolds and his men as bait. Morrison became hopeful as he saw the plan unfold. He watched the enemy cavalry coming down the road to Reynolds' position and wondered how long Company F could hold their fire. Company F bravely did hold its fire until the Yankees were right on top of them. Captain Reynolds had followed the plan perfectly. After Company F delivered its stunning blow, they rapidly moved down the road with the enemy after them in a hot chase.

Unfortunately, Col. Morrison had not planned on engaging the enemy infantry at the same time. The Federal Infantry was moving in a flanking movement on Major Strickland's position on the right. This unplanned-for infantry forced Strickland to abandon his position and the assignment of closing the doors of the trap. Strickland had his men move back to Lt. Col. Harper's position in the rear.

Disappointed, Col. Morrison saw his trap fall apart, but he also realized he had hooked a bigger fish than planned. He took two companies of the First Louisiana Cavalry, Lt. E. Green Davis, and cut off the advance guard of the enemy and demolished it. At the same time, Lt. Col. Harper took the First Georgia Cavalry in a charge on the flanking enemy infantry. On impact, the First Georgia Cavalry killed or wounded fifty or sixty of the enemy. This heavy blow broke the infantry's spirit to fight and the Georgians drove them in wild confusion. The First Georgia Cavalry continued to hack them with their sabers and blast them with shotguns in the continued slaughter. When the battle ended, a total of 202 Union men had been killed or wounded.[9]

Col. Morrison said in his report to Col. Scott that if it had not been for the enemy's long-range guns, he would have captured all of them. Only their artillery was able to force him back. Morrison ended his report as follows: "I am proud to say that although exposed to a heavy fire from the enemy artillery, my officers and men were never more cool, falling back slowly and in good order."[10] He continued: "My loss in killed and wounded was 26. I think it due the whole command to say they acted most gallantly showing additional proof of their valor and heroism."[11]

Col. Morrison withdrew his regiment back toward Hardinsville, where he again joined Col. John Scott. By sunrise on October 5, Col. Scott had moved his brigade to the west side of the Kentucky River near Frankfort. He maintained that position for the next few days.

On October 6, Col. John Pegram, chief of staff for General Kirby Smith, sent orders to Col. Scott that until otherwise ordered he would be under the command of Gen. Carter L. Stevenson.[12] Gen. Stevenson was located at McCown's Ferry near Versailles, Kentucky. Col. Pegram also informed General Stevenson and said that General Kirby Smith had directed him to say if "Scott did not obey orders to arrest him."[13]

When Col. Scott received these orders, he immediately began to comply. He sent General Stevenson a report that the enemy had crossed the river at Frankfort on October 7. The enemy had 20,000 men and had driven in his pickets on the Georgetown and Frankfort roads. Scott also gave Stevenson a present of two prisoners which belonged to the Ninety-third Ohio. At this time, the First Georgia Cavalry was located in Boston, Kentucky.

Gen. Stephen Bunbridge, First Division, Army of Kentucky, reported that Major Foley had made a reconnaissance ride through northern-most Kentucky and to within twelve miles of Georgetown and found no sign of the Rebels. The only unit Foley had heard of was Col. Scott's Cavalry near Frankfort on October 13.[14] On that same day, Col. Scott received orders from Kirby Smith to report to Col. Joseph Wheeler, chief of cavalry, who was near Crab Orchard. On October 14, Col. Scott sent Col. Wheeler a message that he was near him. Scott's position was on the Stanford Road two miles from Crab Orchard.

Scott's command was now a thousand strong. However, according to Scott they were tired and hungry. The horses were very much jaded, as they had been in front of Kirby Smith's Army since coming to Kentucky. Col. Scott told Col. Wheeler that he was going to Somerset for forage. Scott said that he had already consulted with General Bragg and got permission. Col. Scott added in his message that he would not go for forage if Wheeler needed him.[15]

Colonel Wheeler had earlier been ordered to protect the large wagon train which was now in the rear of the retreating Army of Mississippi and Kentucky. Wheeler was to collect all stragglers, disabled, and sick and get them mounted to leave Kentucky. Wheeler already had Morgan's and Allston's cavalries protecting the rear of Kirby Smith, but he also needed Col. Scott's men to help.

Wheeler began looking for Scott's Cavalry and sent out tracers to find him. Upon receiving Wheeler's request, Col. John A. Wharton sent him a message that Scott had gone to Somerset. Wharton had previously tried to get Scott to help protect the right flank of the infantry or to remain in position with him. Col. Scott refused Wharton and went on to Somerset. That evening Col. Wheeler reported all of these events to General Kirby Smith. Smith replied to Wheeler that Col. Scott had been ordered to report to him immediately.

The Confederate army was moving toward London, Kentucky, and would be there the night of October 14. That night Col. Wheeler was informed that Col. Scott had been arrested for disobedience of orders and his command turned over to the next man in rank.[16] The command was then ordered to report to Col. Wharton for duty. When Col. Scott reported to General Smith, he told him that he was following orders from General Bragg. He stated that he had been covering Bragg's lines. Kirby Smith was mad at Bragg anyway because he had abandoned Wild Cat Pass and exposed Smith's right flank. General Smith knew his army needed to be reorganized, but presently he needed to get them safely across the Cumberland River.

A communication was sent to the Rome, Georgia, newspapers giving a list of casualties of the two Floyd County companies in the First Georgia Cavalry during the raid into Kentucky. Those reported wounded were Captain Milton H. Haynie, Captain John L. Kerr, Lt.

George T. Watts, and Private Lewis R. Reynolds. Those left sick in Kentucky were Sergeant Stephen K. Hogue, Sergeant Martin Bobo, Cpl. John V. Bobo, and Privates James W. Wilkins, John Reeves, William H. Watson, J.W. Webb, Loverick Morris, and Dr. E.P. Dean. Those reported captured and paroled were George W. Witzell, Willis Morris, Z.F. McGuffee, J.S. Griswald, Robert Philips, John M. Cox, and Henry P. Waters.[17]

During this time, the Yankee press and rumor-mongers were spreading reports that Col. James J. Morrison had been killed in battle. Nothing was further from the truth. Though almost daily exposed to the dangers of war, he enjoyed excellent health. For that matter, the whole regiment, with a few exceptions, was in excellent condition.

Once the Confederate army got back across the Cumberland River to safety, a reorganization of the entire department ensued. The Department of East Tennessee commanded by General Kirby Smith was divided into three divisions: First Division, Gen. Carter Stevenson; Second Division, Gen. John McCown; and Third Division, Gen. Henry Heth.

Pvt. Littleton L. Brown. Enlisted March 1862. Company blacksmith. Absent December 1863 on furlough in Paulding County, Georgia. Last record December 1864 absent with leave (permission of the family of Arthur D. Brown, Jr.).

The organization of the Third Division included four infantry and three cavalry brigades: First Infantry Brigade, Gen. William Mackey Davis; Second Infantry Brigade, Gen. Archibald Gracie, Jr.; Third Infantry Brigade, Col. Sumner Smith; Fourth Infantry Brigade, Col. Alexander Reynolds; First Cavalry Brigade, Col. John H. Morgan; Second Cavalry Brigade, Gen. John Pegram; and Third Cavalry Brigade, Col. John Scott.

Pvt. John Henry Coleman. Enlisted May 1862. Captured and paroled December 1863 (courtesy Charmaine Malone).

The Third Cavalry Brigade contained the following regiments: First Georgia Cavalry, Col. James Morrison; First Louisiana Cavalry, Lt. Col. James Nixon; Second Tennessee Cavalry, Col. George McKenzie; Third Kentucky Cavalry, Col. Russell Butler; Twelfth Tennessee Cavalry Battalion, Major Thomas Adrian; Seventh North Carolina Cavalry Battalion, Lt. Col. George Folk; Sixteenth Battalion Georgia Partisans, Lt. Col. Francis M. Nix; Sixteenth Tennessee Cavalry Battalion, Major Edmund Rucker; Howitzer Artillery Battery, Captain W.H. Holmes; and Horse Artillery Battery, Captain W.R. Marshall.

The First Georgia Cavalry was sent to Sparta, Tennessee, on a mission to scout north toward the Cumberland River. They were to seek, find and report the enemy's position, movements and number. While in that region of Tennessee, Col. Morrison ran an advertisement in the local Georgia newspaper for members of the regiment who were on leave to report to Loudon, Tennessee, before October 22, 1862.

Lt. Col. Armstead Harper came home to Rome, Georgia, on a furlough to rest, but also to accomplish two other missions. Evidently the command was in need of clothing, as winter was coming and the worn summer clothing was not enough. He placed advertisements in the *Rome Tri-Weekly Courier* informing relatives with family in the First Georgia Cavalry of the needed clothing. He informed them to deposit all articles with Mr. E.V. Johnson, Kingston, Georgia, and he would see to it that they reached the intended destination.[18]

Harper's other mission was to issue Special Order 91. This order required all officers and soldiers of the First Georgia Cavalry to report immediately to Col. Morrison at Murfreesboro, Tennessee. All persons on parole were ordered to report for exchange. He warned that those who failed to comply would be treated as deserters.[19]

Pvt. William Eccles Wigley. Enlisted March 1862. Captured December 1, 1863, Loudon, Tennessee. Escaped and rejoined regiment (courtesy Rob Wigley).

A problem kept reappearing even in November 1862: The question of who was going to command the cavalry for the department. Though Kirby Smith commanded the department, General John Hood liked to interfere. General Nathan Forrest assumed great responsibility with the cavalry, but then newly promoted Brig. Gen. Joseph Wheeler arrived in the department headquarters with orders dated November 3, 1862. These orders were for him to relieve General Forrest. Wheeler was also to remove troops and stores from Sparta, Tennessee, where the First Georgia Cavalry was located.

During these days of confusion, Lt. John Tench wrote a letter to the editor of the *Rome (GA) Courier*. Tench was writing from Camp Haynie, Tennessee, November 11, 1862. His letter opened with: "Thinking it would be gratifying to the friends of the First Regiment Georgia Cavalry as well as members of the Regiment, I have concluded to give in detail the achievements, the hardships and the exposure of that gallant band, achievements for the time, the grandest of the struggle for Southern Independence, hardships unappreciated, exposure unknown to and unfelt by all save the gallant men I write of."[20]

Lt. Tench wanted all Georgians to hear their story and to be proud of their sons, brothers, and fathers in the First Georgia Cavalry. He wanted the people to write letters of encouragement to the men so they would feel the people at home appreciated their sacrifice for them. Tench said, "Beckon them on to newer and brighter deeds of chivalry and their bright blades will lay open the quivering flesh of the vandals and leave exposed the ghastly blackness of the heart within."[21]

Tench knew that the battles yet to come would be more difficult than those already experienced in Kentucky. If peace was ever to come, he felt the men had to rise to higher resolution to defeat the much larger Union army. With that preface, Tench wrote about some of the experiences of the First Georgia from Cartersville, Georgia, to Clay Village, Kentucky.

He did not tell all of the adventures and heroism of the First Georgia Cavalry, as that would be too much for the newspaper to print. He thought the war would be short and the men, when they came home, would "set by the cheerful winter fires, when the war battle is hushed and 'Peace on earth and goodwill to man' be choral hymns of nations."[22] Lt. Tench believed the South would win the war and longed to be home for Christmas in a peaceful Confederate States of America.

Before he closed, he mentioned Captain Samuel Davitte, quartermaster, as being "gentlemanly, cautious, and efficient."[23] Tench had been impressed with his gallantry at Murfreesboro and his cautious bearing. In closing this letter, Tench stated, "I must also mention our Surgeon, Dr. J.L. Branch, who is thoroughly efficient, and a gentleman in every respect, attention alike to sufferers, whether friends or foes."[24] Tench sent his letter to Rome, Georgia, with Captain Napoleon J. Reynolds and Captain Milton H. Haynie, who were on their way home for a few days' leave.

The First Georgia Cavalry did not stay at Camp Haynie long, because on November 15 General Kirby Smith sent orders for the First Georgia Cavalry, First Louisiana Cavalry, and Major Thomas W. Adrian's Twelfth Battalion of Tennessee Cavalry to proceed to Kentucky. They were to go through Monticello and Somerset, Kentucky, and cross the mountains to London and Mount Vernon, Kentucky. Their mission was to observe the enemy and his movements and ascertain if any force was going toward Knoxville.[25]

Almost as soon as the brigade started, General John Bell Hood ordered them back. Kirby Smith had Col. John Scott arrested. Col. Morrison, the next in rank, was placed in command. Morrison did not comply either with Kirby Smith but followed Hood's orders. General Smith requested General Bragg to enforce his orders, adding that the noncompliance of Col. Morrison may have endangered the department.

Meanwhile, Scott's Brigade busied itself between Gainesboro and Celina, Tennessee, along the Cumberland River. They were guarding the stock brought in from Kentucky and were also busy enforcing the conscript law.[26] Later, Scott's Brigade, now back under his command, crossed the Cumberland River and made their way to Tompkinsville, Kentucky. They went there looking for the enemy just across the Tennessee line. During this search, there was a brief skirmish with the pickets of the Nineteenth Illinois Infantry. They were commanded by Union Colonel Joseph R. Scott, who made a report of the incident. The Confederates had one man captured during this encounter. Afterwards, Col. Scott took his brigade back to Tennessee and resumed the watch at Celina.

Eventually, General Bragg stepped into the cavalry issue as Kirby Smith had requested. Smith wanted Col. Scott to be under his direct command. On November 29, Bragg issued Special Orders Number 9; Part 6 concerned the First Georgia Cavalry, as it stated: "The officer commanding the Third Cavalry Brigade of Smith's Corps composed of Morrison's Regiment and Scott's Louisiana Cavalry will report with his command to Brig. Gen. Wheeler without delay."[27]

On December 5, the First Georgia Cavalry reported to General Wheeler at Murfreesboro. At this time, the proposed orders for them was to go to Kentucky and relieve General John H. Morgan's command. However, while camped near Murfreesboro, the First Georgia Cavalry shivered under a heavy snow. Four inches of snow fell during that very cold and disagreeable time.[28]

The Department of East Tennessee was reorganized as the Army of Tennessee. It consisted of Lt. Gen. Leonidas Polk's Corps, Lt. Gen. William J. Hardee's Corps and Brig. Gen. Joseph Wheeler's Cavalry Corps. The cavalry corps was divided into four brigades: Gen. Joseph Wheeler's Brigade, Colonel Abraham Buford's Brigade, Gen. John Pegram's Brigade, and Gen. John Wharton's Brigade. Col. James Carter's First Tennessee Cavalry, Col. James Morrison's First Georgia Cavalry, and Col. John Scott's First Louisiana Cavalry made up the base for Gen. Pegram's Brigade.

Captain Milton H. Haynie, Co. C, had been home on a Christmas furlough during this time. As he was preparing for his return to the regiment, he was sitting at home with his family by the fire and cleaning his weapons. As he was in the process of working with his pistols, one of them accidently fired. The contents of the chamber entered his left leg above the knee. The wound became insufferable with inflammation. Captain Haynie did not return to the First Georgia Cavalry. First Lt. George T. Watts was commanding Company C in his absence.

John Pegram had been chief of staff for General Kirby Smith and begged the general for a line command while on his staff. In November, Pegram was promoted to brigadier general.[29] With the realignment in the cavalry corps, a small brigade was handed to him. Gen. Pegram's introduction to battle with his new brigade presented itself by a sudden Federal move. General Bragg was settling into his winter quarters and he hoped the Federals would do the same. On the day after Christmas, during a driving rainstorm, 60,000 effective Federals moved out of Nashville toward Murfreesboro. Their mission was to push the Rebels south.[30]

Gen. Pegram's Brigade, along with the other cavalry brigades, had been posted in front of the infantry between the enemy and Murfreesboro.[31] Gen. Pegram's Brigade patrolled an area northwest of Murfreesboro along the roads from Lebanon.[32] Though General William Starke Rosecrans' advance was unexpected at this time, his progress was impeded by the constant skirmishing with the cavalry corps who made sudden and unexpected attacks upon him. General Bragg commented in his report about the skillful manner in which the officers and men performed and about their gallantry. He concluded that their gallantry "must be attributed the four days' time consumed by the enemy in reaching the battlefield a distance only twenty miles from his encampment over fine macadamized roads."[33]

Wheeler led his brigade across Stones River and up the Lebanon Pike to a mile in front of General John C. Breckenridge. Wheeler's Brigade joined General Pegram's Brigade, which was east of the Lebanon Pike. On Tuesday morning, December 30, Gen. Wheeler, with his cavalry brigade and the First Tennessee Cavalry Regiment of General Pegram's Brigade, was ordered to attack the enemy's rear. By Tuesday morning, Wheeler was moving the command on the Jefferson Pike around the enemy's left flank. Wheeler gained the rear of the whole Union army and attacked their trains, guards, and the numerous stragglers. Wheeler succeeded in capturing several hundred prisoners and destroying hundreds of wagons loaded with supplies and baggage. After clearing the road, he made his way entirely around the enemy.

About ten o'clock, Wednesday, December 31, a report reached Gen. Bragg from Gen. Pegram that a heavy force of the enemy infantry (Brig. Gen. Horatio Van Cleve's Division) was advancing on the Lebanon Road. The enemy was about five miles in front of General Breckenridge. At this time, General Pegram's Brigade, except for the two regiments detached to Wheeler and Wharton, had been sent to that road to cover the flank of the infantry. Pegram's Brigade was ordered forward to meet any movement by the enemy. It was soon discovered by Pegram that a major assault was not forthcoming. Only a few sharpshooters had been placed to cause the Confederates concern.

Gen. Pegram was later criticized for not providing timely reports about the enemy's movements. General Breckenridge used this report to cover his refusal to send his brigades to aid General Bragg during a critical time in the battle. Pegram struggled as a cavalry commander and needed Wheeler's directions, but he did not receive instruction, as Wheeler was very active in the field.[34]

General Pegram was still probing with his cavalry when he discovered an enemy hospital and a large number of stragglers in the rear of the enemy lines across Stones River. Pegram charged his cavalry into them and captured about 170 prisoners.[35] Both armies were exhausted by the conflict, which had lasted a full ten hours. Battles like this were rarely surpassed for continued intensity and the heavy loss on both sides. As the sun sank and night came, perfect quiet prevailed.

On Thursday morning, January 1, 1863, the cavalry was ordered to the rear of the enemy again. They were to cut off the trains and attack any force they encountered. The cavalry soon discovered that the Federals were still in heavy force all along their front. The enemy occupied positions made strong by terrain and by their own work. The Confederate cavalry brigades busied themselves attacking wagon trains in the rear. They captured and paroled hundreds of prisoners on the spot.[36] General Wheeler and General Wharton returned Thursday night with their brigades exhausted from fighting and riding all day and part of the night. They had no rest or food for either horses or men. Later the men were quickly fed and they grabbed a few hours of sleep.

At daylight, Friday, January 2, Wheeler sent the two regiments that had been detached to him back to Pegram. Wharton was ordered to the right flank across Stones River to assume command in that quarter and keep watch for General Bragg.[37] Wheeler with his brigade was ordered to the enemy's rear again. Wheeler remained there in order to determine if the enemy was planning to retreat. The First Georgia Cavalry, with Lt. Col. Armstead Harper commanding, was engaged that evening with the enemy. None were killed but several of them were slightly wounded.[38]

General Bragg had special orders for the First Georgia Cavalry and Adrian's Battalion. General Joseph E. Johnston had ordered them to Knoxville to aid Kirby Smith in repelling the Union raid into that part of East Tennessee. William Truedail, chief of police in Nashville, Tennessee, reported to Rosecrans that the Georgians had departed Murfreesboro and were headed to reinforce Knoxville.

At Stones River the Federals were making their move against the whole of Breckenridge's Division. Breckenridge was ordered to drive them away. Wharton and Pegram's remaining brigades were attached to Breckenridge but were not used during the battle. Breckenridge was able to push the Yankees back, but the Confederates soon lost the ground gained and then some.

Saturday, January 3, the Army of Tennessee, commanded by General Bragg, had been in line of battle for five days and nights. They had gotten little rest and had no reserves for relief. Their baggage and tents had been loaded and sent with the wagons four miles away. Their provisions, if cooked at all, were not cooked very well. The weather had become very severe from cold and constant rain. The men had no change of clothing and could not dry them by a fire because the enemy would shoot them. The rain continued to fall all day and Stones River, which was usually fordable everywhere, was fast becoming unfordable anywhere.[39]

The Army of Tennessee was exhausted, and at eleven o'clock that night began to retire in order behind Duck River without incident. The cavalry acted as a screen for the infantry until Monday, January 5. The cavalry retired from that position in front of Murfreesboro and joined the infantry to cover its front.

The First Georgia Cavalry arrived in a cold rain on January 14, 1863, at Kingston, Tennessee. It rained the next day and snowed January 16. Private William H. Hood, Co. I, First Georgia Cavalry, took this time to write his parents a letter. He asked them "not [to] think hard"[40] of him because this was the first opportunity he had to write since December 26. That was the day Rosecrans moved against them at Murfreesboro. Pvt. Hood stated that he "had not slept in a tent since that night and had been in a fight at Murfreesboro."[41] He continued:

> We never had the saddle off our horses for eight days and nights. Nothing but the hand of Providence spared my life. The bullets and grape shot fell around me as thick as hail. I was standing behind a little cedar and a ball struck it and pieces of bark flew into my face. There was none of our company killed. There was one wounded and three missing. We don't know what became of them. We fought them eight days, but they kept reinforcing so we had to retreat. We had taken 6,000 prisoners but our loss was great. They came very near getting me. I was on piquet on the advance pail and they came very near cutting me off, if I staid ten minutes longer they wud have got me. I captured me a fine overcoat and canteen in the rounds. I wud not take $40.00 for my coat.[42]

William Hood closed his letter by asking his parents to excuse his mistakes and said; "I am so cold I can scarcely hold my pen."[43]

Later that month, a letter arrived for Col. Morrison from Lt. Gen. E. Kirby Smith to let Morrison know that he had not been forgotten and that people were trying to give him the rank he so richly deserved.

> Lynchburg, Virginia
> January 27, 1863
> Col. J.J. Morrison:
>   With pleasure I refer to your service while under my command. Your regiment was one of, if not the best disciplined and most efficient cavalry regiments in my Corps. I need only call attention to your official reports to show how important have been your services and how much they merit reward. I shall be gratified to know that they have been appreciated by the department.
>   E. Kirby Smith
>   Lt. Gen.[44]

The next few days a flurry of letters flew about Richmond, Virginia, to gain Col. Morrison's promotion. Pleas from Lucus Gartrell and Kirby Smith with endorsements from many contemporaries and members of the Legislature were sent to the War Department to this end.

5

Somerset, Kentucky

The First Georgia Cavalry, Pegram's Brigade, was facing a cold and hard winter in East Tennessee. Col. James J. Morrison was continually trying to keep his men clothed and fed. Forage for the animals was hard to find. Col. Morrison took his problems to Gen. Pegram and Pegram took his to General Henry Heth. Gen. Heth suggested Pegram take his brigade back into Kentucky to find the necessary forage.[1] The request for the brigade's movement was finally ordered February 2, 1863, by General Joseph E. Johnston.[2]

Col. Morrison's orders came to him February 11 while he was on furlough in Rome, Georgia. He had been there only a few days when he received a telegraphic message to report immediately to Rogersville, Tennessee. Morrison moved the entire First Georgia Cavalry to Rogersville.

Immediately, the regiments of the brigade readied themselves to move out toward Kentucky. Col. Morrison and the First Georgia Cavalry were to cross into Kentucky but were not to engage the enemy. Meanwhile, a detachment of the First Georgia Cavalry was sent to Kingston, Tennessee. They were to join with Col. Sumner J. Smith to be a part of a cavalry brigade containing the Tenth Confederate Cavalry and the First Tennessee Cavalry.

It was not only the cavalry having problems subsisting, but also the infantry. General Bragg's chief of commissary was of the opinion that by February 10, Middle Tennessee could not furnish meat for the army more than thirty days. General John H. Morgan, who was already in Kentucky, was ordered to bring cattle back to Tennessee to feed the army. General Pegram, located at the Kentucky and Tennessee border, was also ordered to help Morgan bring cattle back to Middle Tennessee.[3]

As the days went by gathering and herding cattle, the men of the cavalry felt like farmers again. Soon, most of the cattle were gone and Pegram took his cavalry deeper into Kentucky, but they never crossed the Cumberland River. Gen. Pegram wanted to put together an expedition of cavalry deeper into Kentucky and was making preparations to go. However, the heavy rains of the previous few weeks made the Cumberland River impossible to cross.

On February 14, the First Georgia Cavalry was located at Camp Woodlawn near Rogersville. The weather continued to be very cold, with snow 8 to 10 inches deep. The horses could hardly walk because their hooves got clogged with snow. Rogersville was a small town near the Kentucky border with Tennessee, but it did have something the men of the First Georgia Cavalry enjoyed. Women! There was a woman's college there with 300 beautiful Southern girls.

During these days several men and officers went home on furlough. Col. Morrison was just returning to the regiment as Lt. Col. A.R. Harper departed for home. When Lt. Col.

Harper arrived in Floyd County, Georgia, he discovered that Captain Milton H. Haynie was seriously ill. Haynie was suffering from the self-inflicted gunshot wound. Captain Haynie was not doing well at all, but still he could joke about going through the heat of battle and not getting a scratch. Captain Haynie was mad at himself for being careless while cleaning his pistols and shooting himself in his left thigh. Unfortunately, typhoid fever had taken over and everyone doubted he would ever be in his saddle again.[4] On March 14, Captain Milton H. Haynie, Co. C, died of typhoid fever. First Lt. George T. Watts, Co. C, was appointed captain to replace Haynie.

The expectation of the coming invasion by Rebel forces had the governor of Kentucky writing letters to General Haratio Wright. Governor James Robinson had been informed by his brother-in-law, Dr. Gano from Georgetown, of a clandestine meeting of Confederate officers of which Gen. Pegram was a member. The purpose of the meeting was to inform Confederate sympathizers of the coming movements and to help by burning bridges and destroying railroad lines from Cincinnati to Lexington. Governor Robinson said the date of the invasion was to be "March 20, 1863."[5] The governor also gave an insight concerning the conditions in Kentucky relating to the Union Army and the citizens themselves. In his letter of March 1, 1863, he stated:

> The present and prospective condition of Kentucky greatly troubles and annoys me.... I have information from various sources, rebel and union, all concurring that a heavy invasion of Kentucky has been determined on, and is being rapidly prepared....
>
> If Kentucky is permitted at this time to fall into the hands of the rebels, even so far as she was under Smith and Bragg, the consequences will be very different from those which then resulted. The wilting and withering effect of the proclamation upon the Union sentiment of Kentucky has been such that now they would receive, I fear, an aid and countenance far beyond any thus given.[6]

Governor Robinson's letter prompted General Wright to send General Rosecrans, in Murfreesboro, a message on March 6. Wright said: "Reports from Governor Robinson and some of our most intelligent and reliable citizens indicate a probable invasion of Kentucky within the next twenty days by the forces of Morgan, Pegram, and Marshall. I don't credit them, but must be prepared."[7]

General Wright expected the invasion to come through the Cumberland and Big Creek gaps into Kentucky.[8] Union spies and scouts were busy making trips to Middle Tennessee to find out what they could about the coming invasion. Union Lieutenant J.R. Edwards reported to General Wright that Pegram was at Beaver Creek, ten miles northwest of Knoxville, on March 3, with 10,000 to 12,000 men.[9] His report included the information that Pegram would have left for Kentucky two weeks earlier except that the Clinch River was too high to cross. Sergeant William S. Reynolds, a Union spy, reported about the same information as Edwards except for the troop strength, which he estimated as being near 6,000 men.

Meanwhile, back in Rome, notice was given that all persons holding promissory notes from the Confederate army signed by Col. James J. Morrison and Captain Napoleon J. Reynolds for the horses bought by Company F, First Georgia Cavalry, could now be paid. Mr. W.T. Newman was authorized to liquidate the notes. Instructions were for those holding them to report to him. Newman could be located at the Etowah House, Rome, Georgia.[10]

On March 10, General Rosecrans was beginning to grasp the real reason for Pegram's invasion into Kentucky. In his report to General Henry Halleck, Rosecrans stated: "We think they must intend to hold Middle Tennessee."[11] In order for the Confederate army to hold Middle Tennessee food for both men and horses must be supplied.

The Confederate Army was looking to the success of General Pegram's Cavalry Brigade and General John Stuart Williams' Brigade for them to be able to hold onto Middle Tennessee and from there pursue the war. General Joseph E. Johnston was told to expect 6,000 to 7,000 head of cattle to be herded into Tennessee by Pegram and Williams. The Union began to discount Pegram as a real threat to Kentucky. Their scouts were reporting that his brigade had been reduced by a number of widespread detachments.

March 19 brought changes to the Department of East Tennessee, which was now commanded by Gen. Daniel S. Donelson. Pegram's Brigade now contained the following regiments: First Florida Cavalry (3 companies), Captain William M. Footman; First Georgia Cavalry, Col. Morrison; First Louisiana Cavalry, Col. John Scott; First Tennessee Cavalry, Col. James Carter; Second Tennessee Cavalry, Col. Henry Ashby; Sixteenth Tennessee Battalion, Lt. Col. John R. Neal; and Huwald Tennessee Battery, Captain Gustave Huwald.

Decimated or not, Pegram was charged with bringing back food for the army. He watched the Clinch River and crossed it at the first opportunity. Saturday, March 21, the brigade was at Stegall's Ferry on the Cumberland River. By Monday morning, the whole force of 1,550 cavalry and Captain Huwald's battery of three pieces of artillery had crossed. They began a forced march north, along muddy roads, toward Danville, Kentucky.[12]

Pegram's force approached Danville at noon Tuesday, March 24, and by two o'clock they attacked the town. The enemy occupying Danville had five regiments of infantry, one cavalry regiment with seven pieces of artillery, and a number of armed citizens. The Union forces had formed themselves on the side of Danville facing the direction Pegram was making his approach. As Pegram's Brigade made its advance, the skirmishers were out in front of the main column. Pegram steadily brought his column forward and the enemy fell back with only light skirmishing. The Federals made their retreat down the road toward Camp Dick Robinson.[13]

As soon as Pegram saw the retreat, he ordered a charge into their rear and chased them into the streets of Danville. Lt. Col. James Nixon, First Louisiana Cavalry, led the column in the charge. While in hot pursuit and entering the suburbs of the town, the First Louisiana met an ambuscade set up for them in a thicket. The enemy infantry opened fire on the Louisiana cavalry when the cavalry got to within fifty yards.

The regiment stood the fire for several minutes with unyielding composure. Recovering, the Louisiana cavalry attacked the enemy infantry and forced them to flee from their position. The Yankees ran back into town and were followed by the Louisiana cavalrymen. Right behind them were two companies of the Second Tennessee Cavalry led by Col. Ashby and the First Georgia Regiment of cavalry led by Col. Morrison.[14]

The fighting downtown was very brisk for twenty minutes or more. This was mainly because Union sympathizers were firing at the Rebels from windows above the battle. Finally, the enemy was driven out of town and the citizens disarmed. As quiet came to Danville, Pegram was handed an intercepted dispatch from Col. Benjamin Runkle, 45th Ohio Regiment of Infantry, to General Samuel Perry "Powhatan" Carter telling him that he would arrive soon in Lancaster and to meet him at the Lexington Road by way of Camp Dick Robinson.

Pegram's mind was working fast and he had the idea to place the brigade between the two unsuspecting Union forces and wipe them both out. Lt. Col. Nixon was issued orders to follow up the rear of the enemy just defeated. The rest of the brigade was recalled to begin the march for one of the fords over the Dick's River.

As the command assembled, horses were breathing heavily and the men's faces were worn with fatigue. The brigade had been in battle and forced marching for the last 28 hours. General Pegram finally realized his command could not make another 61 miles of forced marching and then be expected to defeat an enemy twice its size. He congratulated his men on their victory and had them assemble the sixty prisoners, including Lt. Col. Silas Adams of Frank Wolford's Cavalry. Pegram had his officers talk with the prisoners and townspeople to gather what information they could about the enemy and their movements.[15]

Pegram discovered that the Yankees considered his force to be the advance of a heavy infantry column coming to occupy Kentucky. He was pleased to hear this and did not want to disappoint the Yankees with his efforts. Pegram decided to spend the next few days clearing the enemy out of the three nearby counties. All the command was involved with the clean-up except the First Louisiana Cavalry. They remained in Danville to hold the town as a support base for the brigade and to hold the prisoners.

Clearing the counties of Yankees also disguised Pegram's mission. This diversion took the brigade to within two miles of a place called Gibralter, which was on the Kentucky River near a bridge. This fortification was occupied with a force supported by infantry, artillery, and cavalry. The Union also greatly outnumbered Pegram. Pegram realized the situation of being faced with a superior enemy. He decided that it was time to accomplish the real mission for which he had been sent to Kentucky.[16]

On March 26, 1863, General Ambrose Burnside had directed General Quincy Adams Gilmore and General Jeremiah Tilford Boyle to concentrate all their available forces at Hickman's Bridge and Lebanon, Kentucky. They were to make simultaneous attacks upon General John Pegram's Brigade located near Danville.

Pegram was beginning to fall back to Danville with the cattle they had collected. His brigade burned two of the three bridges over the Dick's River; the river was too high to ford because of all the rain. Pegram was sure these conditions would slow any Union advances while he fell back slowly by the Stanford and Somerset Road.

The First Georgia Cavalry was reported, by Union spies, to be in Danville on March 26. While there, Gen. Boyle threw eighty of the Ninth Kentucky Cavalry at the First Georgia in a quick dash. The Federals drove in the Georgia pickets and captured some arms, but they were soon repulsed by the First Georgia Cavalry's counter charge.[17]

On March 27, the Union troops were ready to move. Gen. Gilmore purposed to move Gen. Samuel Carter's force against the Rebels that night and leave Gen. Charles Champion Gilbert in command. He wanted Gen. Carter to go to the front himself. Gilmore stated: "Pegram should not be

Pvt. Obediah Morgan Cavender. Enlisted June 1864. Surrendered April 26, 1865 (by Michael Bowers Cavender).

allowed to join Cluke or Marshall. This can be prevented better now than two days hence."[18] Burnside told Gilmore they ought to capture or disperse the whole of Pegram's force.

General Gilmore crossed the Kentucky River at Hickman's Bridge on March 28. When they reached the bridges over the Dick's River, they found them burned. General Boyle had occupied Danville that day because the First Georgia Cavalry and Pegram's Brigade had already withdrawn.

The morning of March 29, Col. Ashby, 2nd Tennessee Cavalry, sent General Pegram a message at Crab Orchard that he was being heavily pressed by the enemy. General Pegram hurried his force on to Somerset. By March 30, they were two miles outside of the town. Pegram selected the strongest position he could find to defend against the pressing army. He was forced into making a stand at this time because only half of the cattle had crossed the Cumberland River. He had to prevent the Federals from interfering with the crossing, which was taking place just six miles to the rear. The safety of the entire mission and the command depended upon Pegram's ability to check and hold the advance of the enemy.[19]

Pegram placed the Sixteenth Battalion of Tennessee Cavalry, Lt. Col. John Neal, on the road toward Stanford to watch for the advancing enemy. Neal was to hold long enough to give Pegram time to place the rest of the brigade into defensive position. At the junction of the Stanford and Crab Orchard Road, Pegram placed Col. Scott's First Louisiana Cavalry and Col. Carter's First Tennessee Cavalry. Both regiments were under the command of Col. Scott.[20]

The First Georgia Cavalry was dismounted and placed on the right of the selected position. Major Theopholus Steel's Battalion of General John H. Morgan's command was placed in the center. The Second Tennessee Cavalry was on the left. Captain Huwald, now with six pieces of artillery, was placed on a commanding point which enabled him to sweep the entire field of battle.[21]

The five-hour battle began with an artillery duel. Even though Pegram's artillery had the best position for a battle, it was bested because of inferior ammunition and lack of experience of his cannoneers. This was their first action under heavy combat conditions. The brigade stood the fire very well, with unflinching courage.

Pegram soon realized by the intensity of the attack that the enemy was pouring all his force against that one position. He sent for Col. Scott to reinforce him. When Col. Scott arrived at Pegram's position, Scott suggested that he should be allowed to move around the First Kentucky Cavalry's right flank and charge into his rear. Pegram thought this was a good idea and told Scott to do it quickly as everything depended upon his being prompt.[22]

Pegram's command held the position for more than an hour after Scott had left. Pegram became furious at Scott because the movement should have required only ten minutes to execute. Unknown to Pegram, almost as soon as Scott left on his circling mission to the enemy's rear the Louisiana regiment became separated in the confusion over poorly given orders. In that confusion, Gen. Gilmore's Union cavalry divided them by bisecting the column. Col. Scott later claimed that Pegram's aide Lieutenant J.F. Ranson caused half his command to halt.

General Pegram watched the Federals from his stronghold, anxiously waiting to see Scott charge into the rear of the enemy and scatter them. Instead, he watched three mounted infantry regiments dismount, fix bayonets, and form into lines of battle. Pegram realized that his men had not cleared the field of fire as well as they should. This allowed the enemy to advance up the hill under the protection of some undergrowth.

The First Georgia Cavalry had only 81 men in the battle line on the right. The others of the First Georgia were out on picket fully engaged or driving cattle across a swollen Cumberland River. The First Florida Squadron, commanded by Captain William Footman, was to their left and rear. The enemy was about to flank the brigade, and some broke and ran through the First Florida lines. All efforts of Pegram and other officers could not rally the men back into position.[23]

The First Georgia Cavalry and First Florida still held firm until the Federals got to within thirty yards of their line. To prevent imminent capture, Col. Morrison gave the command for his men to fall back to their horses. Once in their saddles, they retreated to a stronger position.

General Pegram stated in his report that the number of killed and wounded was small, but the loss in prisoners was heavy. This loss was due to the fact Pegram had sent three companies of the Second Tennessee Cavalry to occupy a thicket on the extreme left of their position in which the enemy was advancing, and they became trapped and were captured.[24]

Gen. Pegram and his officers put the brigade back in order before they had retreated a mile. They marched them in good order through the streets of Somerset with the exception of a few stragglers. As they marched through the town, Pegram knew more time had to be bought by his command for the sake of getting the cattle across the river.

Two and a half miles outside of Somerset, Pegram selected another strong position for his defensive effort. There the brigade waited for three long hours before the first advance of the enemy came into view. During this wait, General Pegram angrily censured the First Georgia Cavalry. He thought they were the first to break and run away from the enemy. The men of the First Georgia Cavalry were quite angry with Pegram and his censure and wanted the record set straight.

Meanwhile, the brigade watched as the enemy cautiously advanced into position and prepared for another fight. The Yankees blasted a few cannon shells at the Confederates and skirmished only slightly before night fell. They did not have the same zest for battle they had displayed before Somerset. As night came, the Federals retired from the field. Pegram made sure they were gone before he withdrew the brigade to the river near Stigall's Ferry.

Because there was only one ferryboat at Stigall's Ferry, Pegram, still peeved with the First Georgia Cavalry, sent them three miles down the river to Newell's Ferry.[25] The entire brigade worked all night in the crossing which was hazardous at best. By sunrise March 31, all were across except for about forty horses which drowned or otherwise died during the crossing. At about eight o'clock, the Yanks appeared on the other side of the river, but they did not make any attempt to molest the brigade.

General Pegram placed at 200 the number of men killed, wounded or missing from his command on the entire trip. He reported a rumor that eighty of the enemy had been killed, but the Union allowed only thirty as the number of their killed or wounded. Pegram said he captured and paroled 178 of the enemy during the expedition. As for the cattle to be collected in great numbers, Pegram was disappointed and reported: "The United States Government had gotten there first and stripped the land."[26] However, he did collect 750 head of cattle and brought 537 to the Confederate army.

The men of the First Georgia Cavalry had built a reputation for bravery which was unexcelled by any in the Confederate army. Fortunately for them, other officers respected them and went to General Pegram to set the record straight. Captain William Footman, First Florida Cavalry, was on the field beside the First Georgia. Captain Footman told Pegram that there was a body of men to the left and rear of the First Georgia. They were the ones that ran, not the Georgians. The First Georgia was on his right of his line and "stood manfully to their post."[27] Footman continued: "They stood firm and in an unswerving line until the enemy charged with fixed bayonets to within thirty paces of their front, at the same time flanking them right and left. The position now being untenable (for to remain would be capture) Col. Morrison ordered them to fall back to their horses. There were but 81 men of the regiment in the fight, the rest being on picket, and they stood the fire of three regiments of infantry until ordered back."[28]

General Pegram saw that he was in error in his judgment of the First Georgia Cavalry. He then wrote the following Special Order:

> April 4, 1863
>   The Brigade Commander being convinced on investigation of the case that his remarks on the 30th ult. To the 1st Ga. Regiment was under a misapprehension, hereby publically express regret for having unwittingly done injustice to a regiment which he believes to be composed of as gallant men as any other in the army.[29]

This apology appeared in the April 18 issue of the *Rome Tri-Weekly Courier.*

General Pegram included in his report of the action at Somerset the names of the officers that were "conspicuous in gallantry."[30] He named Col. J.J. Morrison, First Georgia Cavalry; Col. H.M. Ashby, Second Tennessee Cavalry; Lt. Col. A.R. Harper, First Georgia Cavalry and Captain William Footman, First Florida Cavalry. Pegram blamed the defeat at Somerset on Col. Scott. Pegram felt Col. Scott disobeyed his orders no matter what excuse Scott offered. Pegram stated in his closing remarks about the expedition "for Col. Scott's operations, I refer you to the accompanying report. Touching this curious document, I have only to say I cannot but admire the ingenuity with which Colonel Scott has attempted to account for his disobedience of orders and dilatoriness of action, which, it is my sincere belief, lost us the fight."[31]

General Pegram and his command should have been thankful to Union lieutenant Smyser, the officer in charge, for the issue of sabers at the place where Col. McCook was trying to arm his cavalry. McCook failed to get the proper requisition papers for the sabers and tried to force Smyser to issue them to Captain Semple. Lt. Smyser told

Pvt. George Washington Wright. Enlisted July 1863. Died July 14, 1864, Catoosa Hospital, Griffin, Georgia (courtesy Mary Jane Hobbs Pattillo).

Captain Semple to tell Col. McCook: "he had better send some more communications to Captain Semple about the sabers. I don't care a damn for him or any other McCook. They can all go to Hell. I don't care a damn for Captain Semple or any of the Brig. Generals or Major Generals and they all can go to Hell. I am a regular Officer and know how to attend to my business."[32] By Smyser attending to his business, he prevented Col. McCook's Cavalry from joining General Gilmore in attacking Pegram's Brigade at Somerset, Kentucky.

6

Monticello, Kentucky

On April 10, 1863, the First Georgia Cavalry was camped in the woods near Kingston, Tennessee. They were busy getting ready for another Kentucky campaign. They drew five days rations and spent all day cooking it. The next morning at eight o'clock, they would be in the saddle headed for Kentucky.

The area of operations was to be in Monticello, Wayne County, Kentucky. After the Battle at Somerset, they drove the few cattle they had collected south. Col. James Morrison's mission was to continue to gather food and forage for the Army of East Tennessee and provide information to Generals Joseph E. Johnston and Braxton Bragg about movements and strength of the Federals in the area.

General Pegram, in analyzing information provided by Col. Morrison's scouts, recognized that a strong force of enemy troops was moving slowly south. Pegram thought that another thrust into Kentucky by Generals Sam Jones and Humphrey Marshall would be enough to occupy the Federals and prevent them from concentrating on a Federal invasion.

General Ambrose Burnside knew that Pegram and Morrison were in Wayne County and proceeded April 11 to make plans to move against them. Burnside told General Halleck that he would soon attack them unless there was something else for him to do for General William Rosecrans' benefit. A week went by before much attention was paid to the Rebels.

On April 19, Col. Morrison assumed the command of Pegram's Brigade while Pegram visited Knoxville.[1] Lt. Col. Harper commanded the First Georgia Cavalry. Col. Morrison reported to the Army of East Tennessee that Burnside had concentrated a force of between 4,000 and 6,000 men at Columbia, Kentucky. Morrison also informed them of an even larger but unknown number of enemy troops at Lebanon, Kentucky. Morrison estimated the total of the Union Force to be 30,000 under Burnside.

Col. Morrison concluded that Burnside's mission was either to reinforce Rosecrans or to move against Morrison and East Tennessee through Jamestown, Tennessee. Morrison thought that the reinforcement of Rosecrans would be his best estimate of what Burnside was doing. Col. Morrison said that he was going to move his brigade to Albany, Kentucky. This would place him in Burnside's path. Morrison thought to delay Burnside as much as possible. He also indicated that he would keep the general advised of Burnside's movements.

Later that day, Col. Morrison moved the brigade to Albany, Kentucky. Col. David Waller Chenault created a controversy between himself and Col. Morrison. From Monticello, Col. Chenault complained to General John H. Morgan that since Col. Morrison had moved to Albany, he himself now had a long and heavy picket duty to perform. Chenault reported that he sent out his pickets that day and they discovered indications that the enemy had already crossed the Cumberland River. The scouts estimated that the enemy had to go back across because the river was too high to cross their artillery.

On April 22, Col. Morrison told Col. Chenault there were three regiments of Federals at Burkesville and that they were scattered all along the Cumberland River. Chenault in turn told General Morgan he had sent scouts out that night, and they had crossed the Cumberland River, traveled eight miles on the other side, and never saw the enemy. On April 25, the Department of East Tennessee's First Brigade of Cavalry was commanded by Col. James Morrison. It was official now. Morrison established his headquarters in Albany. This brigade was formally Pegram's old brigade. Morrison's Brigade contained the following units: First Georgia Cavalry, Lt. Col. Armstead Harper; First Tennessee Cavalry, Col. James Carter; Second Tennessee Cavalry, Lt. Col. Henry C. Gillespie; Twelfth Tennessee Battalion, Major Francis Leeper Phipps; Sixteenth Tennessee Battalion, Lt. Col. John Neal; and Huwald Tennessee Battery, Captain Gustave Huwald.

On April 26, the First Georgia Cavalry from Albany was watching the movements of Burnside and resting quietly. Burnside watched Morrison also. That same day, Burnside's scouts reported that the Rebels had moved out of Wayne County to Clinton County, Kentucky. They placed Morrison's First Georgia Cavalry six miles northwest of Albany on the Ellis farm on the road from Monticello to Burkesville. Col. Chenault was spotted on Cook's farm near the mouth of Beaver Creek. Thomas Bramlette, a Yankee spy, reported: "They were devouring everything," and felt they could be cut off easily from the Confederate army.[2]

General Pegram returned to his brigade on April 29 and resumed command. He reported to General Wheeler that since General Dabney Maury had ordered him to picket the Cumberland River around Clinton and Wayne counties, he would assume command of the regiments of Col. Leroy Cluke's Eighth Kentucky Cavalry and Col. Chenault's Eleventh Kentucky Cavalry. These regiments belonged to Gen. John H. Morgan. Pegram asked Wheeler to issue orders to the effect to prevent any misunderstanding. Pegram also told Wheeler that he would be in Albany, Kentucky.

Because of impending danger from Burnside, Pegram had more ammunition brought to him, and he was sending provisions to the rear as instructed. Pegram's men were stripping the country of all food and forage to prevent the Union from having it. Burnside continued to press southward toward Monticello.

Col. Chenault sent Col. Morrison a dispatch the morning of May 1. He stated he was being heavily pressed by superior forces of about 5,000 infantry and cavalry. Chenault wanted Morrison to reinforce him. He told Morrison he would hold at the crossroads three miles south of Monticello until relief came. Col. Chenault had been picketing the Cumberland from Greasy Creek to Stigall's Ferry. He reported the enemy crossed the river at the mouth of Greasy Creek.[3]

When Col. Morrison received Chenault's dispatch, he immediately ordered the First Georgia Cavalry, Major Samuel W. Davitte; First Tennessee Cavalry, Col. James Carter; Second Tennessee Cavalry, Major Pharaoh A. Cobb and Captain George W. Day's Twelfth Tennessee Battalion to take up the march on the Monticello Road. Col. Morrison ordered all his men who were sick, the disabled horses, and his wagon train to be moved to Travisville, Tennessee. Travisville was the last point on the Monticello and Jamestown Road where a junction was made with any other road. By moving them there, Morrison prevented the enemy from using other roads to flank him or get into his rear.[4]

This move by Col. Morrison was very smart because he disencumbered himself of his sick and the wagons, which would normally have slowed him down. Morrison knew he would probably be forced to fall back. Now he could move quickly to Travisville, which offered many places that could provide natural defensive positions.[5]

Simultaneously, at noon as the wagon trains with the sick departed, Col. Morrison double-quicked the brigade to Col. Chenault's last position some 25 miles away. Morrison was with Captain Day's Twelfth Tennessee Battalion in the advance. In two hours the brigade covered twenty miles. Abruptly, Day's Battalion was fired into. The enemy had hidden in an ambush to attack any Confederates on the road. This was the first sign Morrison had of the enemy on this march.[6]

Col. Morrison was a mile in front of the First Georgia Cavalry and Second Tennessee Cavalry. Chenault was nowhere to be found. Morrison only had Day's Battalion with him with which to fight. The brave battalion, after receiving fire, quickly returned it and fell back at Morrison's order. The Yankees came charging out of the woods after the retreating Rebels. Col. Morrison ordered an about-face and turned Day's battalion back on the Yankees and ordered a charge. "The gallant Day repeated the order and a wild Rebel Yell burst forth, a cloud of dust rolled up and the Battalion went thundering towards the Yankee Squadron."[7] The Yankees were in shock to see the Rebels coming at them and fell back rapidly to their infantry and artillery.

Shortly, the First Georgia Cavalry and Col. Ashby's Second Tennessee Cavalry came up, and Morrison began to lay out his plans. Col. Morrison knew he would not find Chenault as he had already fallen back from the position he had promised to hold. Morrison learned that the enemy had divided his forces. One arm was after Col. Chenault, who continued to retreat back beyond Travisville to Livingston, Tennessee. The other arm, which contained two regiments of cavalry, two regiments of mounted infantry, and eight pieces of artillery, were about to attack Morrison at Albany if he had not taken action. They had intended on trapping him as he fell back to Travisville. Just before leaving Albany, Morrison sent his scouts out toward Creelsboro, and now they returned with news the enemy was crossing the Cumberland River at Creelsboro and they were 4,000 strong. This force included cavalry and mounted infantry. The scouting report concluded that the Yankees intended to get to Morrison's rear and cut him off before he could reach Livingston, Tennessee.[8]

Pvt. William Allen Coleman. Enlisted March 1862. Present through December 1864 as company blacksmith. In skirmish line at Sunshine Church when General Stoneman surrendered (courtesy Charmaine Malone).

Col. Morrison thought it would be necessary to intercept the enemy who were after Col. Chenault. He knew this would have to be done before they reached Travisville because that was where he had sent his wagons and sick. Col. Morrison sent Major Pharaoh Cobb, commanding Ashby's Second Tennessee Cavalry, with orders to intercept and engage the enemy who were in route to Travisville. Major Cobb saluted and departed.[9]

Col. Morrison knew he was about to be attacked and selected a strong defensive position. He found a place that had a hill on each side of the Albany Road making a little valley in between. On the level ground between the hills, Col. Morrison ordered the First Georgia Cavalry to form across the road and said, "Every man die before the path should be given up."[10] Col. Morrison placed Captain George W. Day's Twelfth Tennessee Battalion on the left side of the First Georgia Cavalry. He put Col. James E. Carter's First Tennessee Cavalry as a reserve four miles to the rear.[11]

The wait was not long before the enemy attacked. The Union moved their artillery up to within 400 yards of the First Georgia's position, opened up their batteries upon them, and poured it to the Georgians. This account was given by a correspondent of the First Georgia Cavalry to the Editors of the *Atlanta Confederacy*:

> Round shot whistled overhead, while shells hissed like vipers at our feet. Now and then a shell would burst in the air above us sending fragments buzzing and shrieking through the files, tearing our clothes and cuffing our horses considerably. One man and horse were knocked by a round shot clear out of ranks, killing both instantly. The men gave one quick painful glance at their dead comrade, and closed in to the left as if nothing happened.[12]
>
> For thirty minutes the First Georgia stood under this hail storm of shot and shell, neither man nor horse moving a muscle. Major Sam Davitte riding slowly in front of the line calmly and quietly reminding the men and officers of their great responsibility and duty to their country. I do not think there is an instance parallel in the history of war, where a regiment of cavalry has stood the concentrated fire of a battery, well manned, at the distance of 400 yards.[13]

The Federals, not believing what was taking place before their eyes, sent out a regiment of cavalry supported by infantry. The Yankees came charging toward Day's Battalion intending to turn his left flank. As they got within range, the Confederates poured a galling fire into them. Finally, Captain Huwald's Parrott guns were able to speak. They opened up, sending shell after shell bursting in the ranks of bluecoats and turning them red. "Their lines wavier, they turn and now they scatter all over the valley, each vying the other to gain the front of the confused and flying mass."[14]

Huwald kept firing his artillery until he ran out of ammunition except for one gun which was slow opening up and it had only five rounds left. Captain Huwald had three guns available and did more damage that the enemy's eight.

As the enemy flew from the field, Col. Morrison knew his command had done more than anyone could have ever hoped. Now was the time to withdraw while the enemy was still disorganized. Morrison placed his sharpshooters on the crest of the hills with orders to keep up a continuous fire until he had the command well on its way on the Albany Road, then they were to form the rear guard.[15] Private Seaborn J. Cavender,

Pvt. William D. Jones, Jr. Enlisted August 1864 near Covington, Georgia. Surrendered near Raleigh, North Carolina (courtesy Lipscomb Collection in the Heritage Room at the Rome-Floyd County Library, Rome, Georgia, and Ricky Smith).

Co. K, First Georgia Cavalry, was among these men and it was said of him that he killed more Yankees than anyone in the regiment. As the brigade was moving, Col. Carter's Regiment fast approached to help with the fight, but it was over.

Col. Morrison's command consisted of two skeleton regiments and one battalion, which he used to protect his artillery. The command was low on ammunition, and the artillery had five rounds for three guns. Worse yet, they had twenty-five miles to travel on already jaded horses over the worst of mountain roads. The same writer described the situation: "Eighteen miles of this route we had to make straight toward the enemy in our rear for the Yankees had repulsed Major Cobb and compelled him to fall back on the Jamestown Road, the same on which Colonels Chenault, Clarke, and the First Louisiana had fallen back. Col. Morrison taking advantage of the darkness (knowing the Yankees were afraid to travel after night) marched within a few miles of the force that crossed the Creelsboro, and came to Travisville by daylight the next morning, in front of the force that was pursuing Col. Chenault. We now felt safe and rested our wearied bodies during the cool of the morning."[16] The same writer described Major Samuel Davitte and how he led the First Georgia Cavalry: "He acted with the coolness of an experienced commander—speaking to the men in that quiet, unimpassioned tone that tells so quickly that the man is determined to do what is undertaken."[17]

Again the writer described others involved: "Captain Huwald deserves great credit for the efficient and prompt management of his guns. Every shot sent a bundle of sad news to the Yankee states. Too much cannot be said for the gallant Captain Day. Tennessee may well be proud of such a son. Our countries [sic] honor will not suffer in his hands. The whole seems to be an impossibility, and if we had not been actors in and spectators of the scenes, we never could have believed that any man could have brought the brigade in safely away, and what seems marvelous still, is that from noon till daybreak, we marched fifty odd miles, and lost two hours of our time while engaging the enemy."[18]

While on the road to Travisville, Col. Chenault's courier again found Col. Morrison. He delivered a message that Chenault was still on the Jamestown Road and needed help. Chenault promised that he would hold until help arrived. Col. Morrison, anxious to help, dispatched Col. James Carter's First Tennessee Regiment to aid Chenault. When Col. Carter arrived at the designated place, he could find neither Chenault nor the enemy. Carter returned to Col. Morrison at Travisville and reported what had happened.

The men now felt safe in Travisville and rested. They talked with amazement of their escape from such an overwhelming force. They were proud to be commanded by a man like Col. Morrison. His decision making not only brought them out, but also the wagon train, the sick, the wounded, the disabled horses, and all of their equipment to the point not even a horseshoe was lost. The men also began the grim task of burying their dead.

Col. Morrison set up his headquarters at Travisville, Tennessee, with General Pegram. In his report, Morrison complimented the performance of his officers and men for their acts of courage under fire. During that day, Morrison lost three killed, twelve wounded, and one captured.

On May 2, 1863, General John Pegram received a message from General Dabney H. Maury, the new commander of the Army of East Tennessee. Maury emphasized to Pegram that he keep his command constantly vigilant and watch the enemy movements and report to him. Maury did not want them to be surprised by the enemy as others had been in previous days.[19] He let it be known that there was to be an inquiry into the incident at Monticello. He had to do this because of the conflicting reports by the parties involved.

General Maury was determined to retake Monticello because of the Confederate need to hold the line at the Cumberland River. He felt that Pegram should be able to retake the lost ground with his brigade. Maury also gave him the commands of Col. Leroy Cluke, Eighth Kentucky Cavalry, and Col. David Chenault, Eleventh Kentucky Cavalry. General Maury ordered General Archibald Gracie to send Col. John R. Hart's Sixth Georgia Cavalry to join Pegram on May 3.

The countryside around Travisville, Tennessee, was so barren that it could not support Pegram's Cavalry Brigade. Under these conditions, Pegram was forced to begin preparations to fall back to Clinton, Tennessee, on May 4. Maury urged Pegram to move into Wayne and Clinton counties of Kentucky and try to subsist there.

General Maury was irritated with Pegram and indicated these feelings to Joe Wheeler on May 4. Maury told Wheeler to have Gen. John H. Morgan move into Wayne County, Kentucky, regardless of what Pegram did. He told Wheeler to have Morgan communicate with Pegram and cooperate with him if possible.[20] General Morgan did not respect General Pegram, as he felt he had made too many mistakes in command, and because of his prima donna insistence that he outranked Gen. Morgan.[21] General Maury was concerned with the problem at hand. He knew that if Pegram's Cavalry left Kentucky, it would be very difficult for them to return unless they went back immediately. With that thought in mind, General Maury wrote Pegram a letter May 5, 1863 (Maury's salutation: "My Dear Pegram.")[22] Maury stated the importance of the position along the Cumberland River. He updated Pegram about the status of certain reinforcements that were expected. It turned out that General Gracie had a greater need for the Sixth Georgia Cavalry and would not let them go. Maury informed him that the arms and ammunition Pegram had requested was now on its way to him. Pegram could expect corn for the horses, but he would have to go to Clinton County, Kentucky, to get it. Maury assured him that his commanders, such as Col. James J. Morrison, were not afraid to engage the enemy. They could expect victory in pushing the enemy out of Monticello, and Col. Morrison saw no need to fall back.[23]

After Pegram received the letter from Maury, he began to receive the supplies as promised. Pegram felt assured that his men could be supplied long enough to drive the enemy out of Kentucky. He ordered up the cavalry from Kingston and some infantry from Wartburg. The First Georgia Cavalry was in camp near Robertsville on May 8. They were worn out from the hard times they had in Kentucky. They had to keep their horses saddled at all times ready to move at any moment, but they answered the call.

While Pegram was making plans to move back to Monticello, the Department of East Tennessee was changing commanders. Major General Simon Bolivar Buckner took over the department and was in place by May 14, 1863. General Buckner was trying to locate General Pegram to learn of his movements. Once Buckner found Pegram, he told him that the Federals had a force located at Barboursville, Kentucky. Pegram was ordered to operate against their flanks and rear. They were to retard the enemy progression south and destroy their supplies.[24]

On May 15, General Buckner was trying to soothe Gen. John H. Morgan. Buckner bragged about Morgan's success in the past and was glad they were now working together, if only for a short time. The crux of the matter, as Buckner reminded Morgan, was that General Pegram was his senior and as such Morgan would have to follow Pegram's orders. Buckner continued to assure Morgan that as soon as possible he would get him a permanent transfer to any other department.

Lt. Col. A.R. Harper became involved in the reorganization while Col. Morrison was away from the First Georgia Cavalry. Lt. Col. Harper reported as the commander of the First Georgia Cavalry on May 20 from Monticello. His report concerned the internal affairs of the regiment. A problem arose out of who was to be the major for the regiment. Harper stated that for some "private reason"[25] Col. Morrison postponed the nomination of a major. In the meantime, Captain James H. Strickland, the senior captain, acted as major. Strickland was not Col. Morrison's choice, but Captain Sam Davitte, the regiment quartermaster, was. Harper reported that Col. Morrison had instructed him to make that statement if it ever became necessary while he might be absent from the regiment.[26]

On May 26, Col. Morrison placed an advertisement in the local northwest Georgia newspapers such as the *Rome Courier.* The notice was to members of the First Georgia Cavalry who were either mounted or dismounted and absent from the regiment. Morrison was informing them to report to him in person or by surgeon's certificate by June 18, 1863. Those who failed to comply would thereafter be considered deserters.[27]

During the May 28 action at Mill Springs, Kentucky the following were captured: 2nd Lt. Francis M. Coulter, Co. G; Pvt. Asa Holcomb, Co. G; Pvt. William J. Holmes, Co. G; Pvt. Loverick Morris, Co. G; Pvt. James J. Tomlinson, Co. G: and Sgt. Simpson G. Tomlinson, Co. G.

During this time, Buckner had been looking for information about the enemy and Pegram had failed to provide what was required. His regular scouts had not provided the information Buckner wanted. Lt. John Tench, First Georgia Cavalry, was looking for the reason so many men of Company G had been captured by the enemy. On May 29, he took twenty men from Company G with him on scout near Mill Springs, Kentucky. Tench found the enemy in force on the south side of the Cumberland River. The Federals, seeing Tench and his party, prepared to attack them. As they came across the river, the Georgians charged into them driving the Yankees back. This allowed Tench enough time to lead the command back to safety.

During the charge, Lt. Tench was painfully wounded, but he made good their escape to bring the information to General Pegram. Pegram was very pleased with Tench and highly complimented him and his men for their bravery and for accomplishing a mission that others had failed.[28] From Lt. Tench's report, Pegram was able to inform General Buckner of the movements and strength of the enemy. There were no major engagements for the rest of May. The enemy continued to press forward and moved men and supplies into Kentucky. Pegram's Cavalry, including the First Georgia Cavalry, did enter Monticello but only because the Union forces withdrew.

June 1, 1863, brought rumors that the Federals would withdraw from Kentucky and go to Nashville. Another rumor was that the enemy was building a large force at Somerset. To counter the enemy buildup, Pegram wanted more supplies and men. He received word on June 5 that 15,000 rations were being sent to him at Wartburg, Tennessee. He was also to receive his reinforcements there. From Monticello, the First Georgia Cavalry observed that all was unusually quiet on June 6. Everyone was hoping that the enemy's movements were just a feint toward them to test their strength.

On the morning of June 9, the expected began to happen. Col. August V. Kautz, Second

Ohio Cavalry Brigade, began a drive through Monticello. At daylight, Kautz was joined by Lt. Col. Silas Adams' Second Tennessee and the Forty-fifth Ohio, Col. Benjamin Runkle. Lt. Col. Adams had previously driven in Pegram's pickets and captured six of them near Mill Springs.[29] Adams' advance did give a warning to Pegram of events yet to come.

General Pegram had time to set up his lines of battle four or five miles from West's Mill toward Mill Springs. The cavalry was now in position to meet the Federal advance. A heavy skirmish commenced for about twenty minutes as the enemy came forward. The Federals soon realized that they could not dislodge Pegram with a frontal assault. They brought in a section of howitzers to bear down on the stubborn Rebels. Pegram was soon forced to retreat from the position and lost two men killed and one officer wounded. The Federals suffered three wounded.

Once Pegram's Cavalry was dislodged, they could not find another strong position like the first to make another stand. Pegram decided the best thing to do was lead the enemy in a circle and attack his rear. The chase for the dog's tail was on. Pegram's Cavalry completed the circle by late afternoon.

As Pegram came upon the enemy, they attacked Col. Kautz's rear guard. The Yankees, surprised by the attack, were sent in a fast retreat. The retreating rear guard came upon Col. Kautz returning to camp for the night. Kautz had spent a hard day chasing Pegram and now here he was in his rear. Kautz had a company of Union Second Tennessee Cavalry with him. These men were unable to hold Pegram's advance, but Kautz was able to rally the retreating rear guard and began to push Pegram's advance back through the dense woods. Pegram's main body found a rock wall, from which they made their stand.

As Col. Kautz began to press forward, Pegram's Brigade gave him a good reply of fire that forced the Yankees to fall back out of range. Once Pegram saw the enemy retreating, he charged the brigade into them driving them further. The stampede did not last long because enough time had elapsed for Kautz to

Pvt. Patrick Asbury Carmical. Enlisted May 1862. Present through December 1864. Teamster for the Brigade. Cut off and captured at Oxford, Alabama. Paroled April 1865 (courtesy Pat Curry and dcarmichael).

Pvt. Joseph Thomas Tinney. Enlisted July 1863. Absent at General Hospital October 28, 1864 (courtesy Mary Elizabeth Tinney Hill, Richard Finch, and Tammy Tinney Caine).

be reinforced by the Seventh Ohio Cavalry and the remainder of the Second Tennessee, plus the battery of howitzers. This larger force stopped Pegram's advance as darkness began to fall. After dark, both sides ceased fire to remove their dead and wounded.

Col. Kautz reported that the Rebels under Pegram were driven off four miles beyond Monticello; two were killed, ten were wounded, and twenty prisoners were taken. Pvt. Osborn R. Witcher, Co. C, died, and Pvt. Thomas C. Ballin, Co. F, was captured.

On June 10, General Pegram resumed the initiative and attacked Col. Kautz at Mill Springs. Pegram's Cavalry forced Kautz to retreat toward Somerset by June 11. Pegram's Brigade still held Monticello, but the heat from the Union was beginning to become uncomfortably warm.

On June 12, a portion of the First Georgia Cavalry was located near Athens, Tennessee. The regiment assembled there to get ready to start back to Kentucky. When Col. Morrison arrived, he did not like what he saw. The men who were sick were being moved to Athens. The men who had been on furlough were returning, and talk among the men was that anybody who could afford a substitute was getting one. This kind of talk was not good for the morale of the regiment. This may have been in response to notices in the papers for members of the First Georgia Cavalry to report, in person or with a surgeon certificate, back to the regiment at Mouse Creek Station, Tennessee, by June 18 or be treated as a deserter.

On June 17, Col. Morrison rode into camp as Adj. John Tench was leaving. John Tench had been wounded again June 15 at Stubenville, Kentucky. Smallpox had broken out in camp and the sick were quarantined. There was talk again among the men that Col. Morrison was upset by the number of ineffective cavalrymen. The men were saying Col. Morrison was going to send all dismounted men to the infantry and swap for infantrymen who had a horse.

The Army of East Tennessee had approved of Pegram's valor and disposition of his command in Kentucky, but now they wished him to set up his headquarters at Wartburg, Tennessee. They urged him to operate as best he could against the Union flanks and rear. Pegram stayed in Monticello until June 18. At that time, he was forced to fall back to Wartburg because General Bragg had withdrawn his cavalry support from Pegram. This was a stressful time for Col. Morrison. In his personal life, for reasons unknown, he was selling some of his properties in Floyd and Polk counties, Georgia. While he was in Floyd County on furlough, he placed his 320 acre farm in Cedartown for sale. The brick building in Rome housing Morrison and Logan Livery Company with its surrounding buildings was also advertised.[30]

General Pegram was weakened by the lack of a strong cavalry force in Kentucky. The Union was putting heavy pressure on him, and on June 20 the Federals pushed Pegram to Jamestown, Tennessee, with 3,000 cavalrymen. Pegram informed East Tennessee headquarters that he expected the enemy to burn the Loudon Bridge or even go to Chattanooga. He said he would attack the enemy as soon as possible.[31]

Instead of attacking, Pegram fell back to Kingston, Tennessee.[32] They had their position fortified by June 25, and Pegram awaited the oncoming Union force. The Yankees were bringing up siege guns to attack him. Pegram's Cavalry was dismounted during this time. He sent the First Georgia Cavalry to Sweetwater,[33] which they were to fortify and hold. While at Sweetwater, Col. Morrison was informed that the enemy could be expected to come toward him if the other commands did not hold.

General Buckner left the Army of Tennessee June 26 to reinforce General Bragg at Tullahoma. General Pegram was placed in command of all forces of the army in the area. He was worried about his men and the ever pressing Union army. Pegram was in Knoxville as acting commander of the Army of East Tennessee and Col. Morrison was again acting commander of Pegram's Brigade.

The Sixth Georgia Cavalry was being moved to Pegram's Brigade and was assembling together with the First Georgia Cavalry around Lenoir's Station. This was going to be a good fit, as a lot of the men were relatives or knew each other from before the war. This was a good area for the brigade, as there was fine pasture and corn for the horses. Food was available for the men as they began getting themselves and equipment in order for the next campaign.[34]

On July 7, 1863, General Rosecrans wrote from Tullahoma to General Burnside in Cincinnati "that a brigade of Morgan's and all of Johnny Pegram's force have gone over to raid you. I hope you will kill or capture them all, and that Morgan will be no longer the terror of Kentucky."[35]

The Federals were reporting July 15 that Pegram and his force had left Kentucky to go down to the Sweetwater Valley. At Sweetwater, Pegram established his headquarters about 16 miles south of Loudon and commanded the cavalry corps of East Tennessee of about 3,000 men.

General Pegram sent a message to General Sam Jones about his concern that his men were ill equipped, and he was having to send them to Chattanooga. He wanted General Jones to send troops to hold his position. As July ended, Col. Morrison and the First Georgia Cavalry were still located in Sweetwater.

Those close to Col. Morrison realized how valuable he and the First Georgia Cavalry were to the cause of the Confederacy. General Pegram wrote the following letter to General Samuel Cooper:

> Headquarters
> Second Cavalry Brigade
> Sweet Water, Tennessee
> July 15, 1863
> General:
>   There being a vacancy in the Department of a Cavalry Brigadier, I write to urgently request that Col. J.J. Morrison, 1st Georgia Cavalry may be appointed to that position. Having served with Col. Morrison for nearly a year, I can testify to his being a gallant, sober, zealous and skillful officer and as being the best disciplinarian I have met among the Colonels of cavalry. His regiment is decidedly the best disciplined men in the cavalry service. Col. Morrison was strongly recommended for promotion last winter by Lt. Gen. E. Kirby Smith—the letter of recommendation is I think in the War Office in Richmond.
>   I am General very respectfully
>   Your Obedient Servant,
>   John Pegram
>   Brig. Gen.[36]

At the same time, General Buckner requested that Col. Morrison receive the appointment. However, for some reason, Col. Morrison would remain a colonel.

On July 30, General Cooper sent a note to President Davis with this cover: "Case of Col. Morrison recommendation by General Buckner for Brig. Gen. of Cavalry."[37] The note inside the cover read as follows:

"Respectfully submitted to the President:

The following Brigadiers who are fit for duty are unassigned viz. Lawton of Georgia, Blanchano of Louisiana, Drayton of South Carolina, Colson of Louisiana, and Rior of Georgia.

I doubt if either of these officers are equal to the commanding of a cavalry brigade. General Bragg's dispatch of July 16, states that he is in want of three Brigadiers of Cavalry—since then two Brigadiers (Deshler and Roddy) have been appointed and ordered to report to General Bragg, who doubtless assign them to cavalry brigades in his immediate command. These appear having jobs as Brigade of Cavalry in General Buckner's command wanting a Brigadier and Col. Morrison has been recommended by General Buckner for that appointment, Col. Morrison belongs to the First Georgia Regiment of Cavalry.[38]

The Army of East Tennessee was reorganized again on July 31, 1863. General Simon Buckner was commanding. It contained five infantry brigades and two cavalry: First Cavalry Brigade, Gen. John Pegram; and Second Cavalry Brigade, Col. John Scott.

The First Cavalry Brigade contained First Georgia Cavalry, Col. Morrison; Sixth Georgia Cavalry, Col. John R. Hart; Seventh North Carolina Cavalry, being reorganized; First Tennessee Cavalry, Col. James Carter; Rucker's Legion, Col. Edmund Winchester Rucker, and Huwald's Battery, Captain Gustave Huwald.

7

Chickamauga

During August 1863, the First Georgia Cavalry Regiment acted as a screen for General Simon Buckner's army in Knoxville, Tennessee. General John Pegram's Brigade was still being commanded in the field by Col. Morrison. Lt. Col. Armstead Harper commanded the First Georgia Cavalry Regiment.

On August 9, notices of a new company being formed for the First Georgia Cavalry began appearing in newspapers in Georgia. Captain John L. Kerr, Company G, stated he was authorized to raise as many men as he could to form a squadron. This new company would join his present company. He gave his location as Knoxville, Tennessee.[1]

On August 18, 1st Lt. S.W. Allman placed a notice in Georgia newspapers for recruits wanted for the First Georgia Cavalry. Allman stated he could receive them and place them in any company of the First Georgia Cavalry. The recruits with a suitable horse were to report to Rome, Georgia, by September 5 and be ready to proceed to the camp at Concord, Tennessee.[2]

The First Georgia Cavalry's last position had been around Sweetwater. On August 20 they moved to Winters Gap. A few days later General Buckner ordered Pegram's Brigade to report to Gen. Nathan B. Forrest at Kingston. General Buckner was moving his infantry to Kingston and was there by August 22. Buckner warned Forrest not to uncover his front in using Pegram's Brigade, but he could use them in any other action against the enemy that he desired. Buckner also warned Forrest to remove from Kingston all stores not needed by his troops. This was a precaution because General Burnside was still advancing.[3]

President Jefferson Davis proclaimed a day of fasting for the Confederacy to be observed on August 22. Col. Morrison was not so sure about his men going without food. To comply with the president, he ordered the brigade not to drill that day and had the chaplains observe a day of prayer. The men enjoyed the day off.

Every day the Army of East Tennessee fell back further south. Pegram's Brigade had formed a junction with Col. Scott's Brigade at Lenoir's Station on August 30. During that evening, the cavalry was ordered to go on to Loudon.[4]

General Buckner wrote to General Bragg on September 2 that Loudon had been shelled that afternoon. He also reported that Knoxville was now occupied by the enemy, and that his cavalry had been forced back to the Tennessee River. General Pegram was to move the remainder of his brigade at daylight September 3. Col. Scott was already in Athens, Tennessee, with the wagon trains.[5]

On September 3 Pegram's Brigade was picketing beyond Georgetown, and Gen. Forrest had not yet assumed command of Pegram's troops. At the same time, General Burnside believed that Forrest was going to move the cavalry to Dalton, Georgia. The First Georgia Cavalry continued to retreat and by the evening of September 3, they had moved to Diamond Gap, Tennessee.

Col. Morrison had the brigade prepare positions for the night. They had been pressured all day and forced to retreat, but that night Morrison had his cavalry ready to stand firm. The Federals moved in and made repeated efforts to dislodge them, but the Georgians were able to repel each Federal attack. During that night, the Georgians suffered two men wounded.[6]

During this time Chattanooga was being threatened by General Rosecrans' Army of the Cumberland, and Morrison fell back to help defend the city. General Pegram was able to place his command effectually under General Forrest on September 5. By September 8, Pegram's Brigade had crossed Lock's Ferry near Washington, Tennessee. However, his rear was spread all the way back to Charleston.[7]

On September 9 Col. Morrison was at Friars Island and engaged by Col. John Wilder's Cavalry. By one o'clock the First Georgia Cavalry was driven away with just a slight skirmish. Col. Wilder reported that the First Georgia Cavalry was headed toward Ringgold, Georgia. Wilder said that some deserters came to him and said Pegram's Brigade would be in Ringgold that night. These deserters may have been part of Gen. Bragg's plan to convince the enemy that the army was in full retreat.[8]

On September 10 General Pegram, with his brigade, went out on a reconnaissance ride from Ringgold north toward Graysville.[9] Early that morning, Pegram found part of General Thomas Crittenden's XXI Corps Infantry marching down the railroad track from Chattanooga. Pegram knew they were too far south to be reinforced by Gen. Rosecrans. Pegram quickly attacked them, capturing 45 prisoners. After the attack Pegram's command continued to fall back toward Rock Springs. His wagons arrived there at about 4:30 that afternoon.[10]

Later, General Pegram, with the First Georgia Cavalry, headed toward Ringgold. Pegram placed his brigade between General Armstrong's Cavalry and the enemy, and spent that afternoon skirmishing with Gen. Charles Cruft's First Brigade around Pea Vine Creek. General Rosecrans was anxious to defeat Bragg and had visions of taking Atlanta. In thinking like this, he spread his ranks very thin.[11]

General Forrest joined in the fight around Pea Vine Creek late in the afternoon. He saw the enemy could be soundly defeated with a little more help, so he sent a report about his plan to Generals Polk and Bragg asking for help. Both Generals had placed their headquarters with the infantry. General Forrest was certain that a deadly blow could be struck against Crittenden's XXI Corps, and he made preparations for the attack early the next morning. Unfortunately, neither Bragg nor Polk would come to the fight, and another opportunity passed for Southern victory.[12]

Col. Wilder was ordered by General Crittenden on September 10 to report that night to General Joseph Reynolds, Fourth Division, at La Fayette. Wilder was to go there by way of Leet's Tanyard. Unknown to the Federal generals, Pegram's Calvary and Armstrong's Cavalry lay in their path. The Federals thought the Rebels had gone further south.[13]

General Pegram had placed his pickets about four miles from Ringgold. Captain James H. Strickland, First Georgia Cavalry, selected twenty men to go with him to scout the enemy's position. As they traveled down the road, Strickland thought it would be best if the others in the command dismounted and rested their horses. Strickland sent Private R.T. Logan back to the lieutenant in charge of the company. Once Logan delivered the message, he wheeled his horse around and galloped off to rejoin the scouts.[14]

Strickland had moved down the road leaving only a cloud of dust for Logan to follow. Pvt. Logan was galloping down the road expecting any minute he would catch up with the party. As he spurred his little grey mare on in a rapid gait, he happened to notice that the party now in front of him were dressed in blue and aiming their carbines at him.

The Yankee sergeant yelled, "Halt!"[15] The yell was in such a tone that it brought Logan to an abrupt stop. He realized his plight of almost being shot and said, "Hold on, boys."[16] He hoped they would not shoot and acted as if he were about to surrender as he threw up his hands. The Union troopers thought they had captured another Reb and dropped their bead on Logan. At that instant, he wheeled his horse around, drove his spurs into its sides and galloped off.

The Yankees were dumbfounded for a moment, then took off after Logan in a hot chase. Logan was leaning low in his saddle and could hear the crack of the carbines and the whiz of the bullets passing by his ears. He knew that his little horse would soon be exhausted because she was already taxed from her previous gallop. He also knew if he did not stay ahead of the bluecoats, he would be dead in a minute.

As the race continued, Logan could feel the Union chargers gaining on him. He knew they had their sabers drawn ready to hack into him the moment they caught him. Feeling his horse begin to slow down, he knew all was about over. All of a sudden, the little horse stumbled and fell to the ground, throwing Logan some distance away.

As Logan fell, he caught a glimpse of Captain Strickland's First Georgia Cavalrymen coming his way. Strickland had heard the shooting and was coming to see what it was all about. The Union troops were now on Logan ready to kill him. Then a crack was heard and a shot hit the leading Federal trooper knocking him off his horse. Logan said that he could see his face "turn deadly white."[17] The Georgians came roaring in with a yell. They chased the rest of the enemy squad and all were soon captured.

Captain Strickland stopped near Logan and asked, "Are you hurt, Tom?"[18] "No, only a little bruised," was the reply.[19] Strickland smiled and said, "That was a narrow escape. You led them in a hot chase, but never mind, so long as you can't kill them yourself, go out and bring them to us and we will settle with them."[20]

Meanwhile, Col. Wilder brought his column south toward La Fayette on September 11. As the Yankee column approached Pegram's pickets, they stopped to sweep the Rebels away. But while Wilder was halted preparing to attack the pickets, General Pegram's Cavalry came out and immediately attacked Wilder's rear. Wilder decided to advance in a line of battle. As they went forward, Wilder found the rest of Pegram's Brigade had occupied the high wooded hill in his front just south of Leet's Tanyard. The woods were thick, making Wilder unable to utilize his artillery, but neither could Pegram.

Col. Wilder was fast becoming very concerned about his situation. Not only was Pegram in his front, but also General Armstrong's Cavalry was attacking his left flank. Armstrong was pressing in very close to him. At this point, Col. Wilder knew that he had to fight hard to save his command or surely be killed or captured. He sent his skirmishers out to both the front and rear. He ordered his command to make an oblique movement to the left across an open field and gain a ridge in the woods. From there, they drove for an opening to the road through Napier's Gap in the Pea Vine Ridge. With this move, they were finally able to escape both Pegram and Armstrong. The Confederates pursued them until dark, at which time they halted. Word came that night to the First Georgia Cavalry that General Forrest had been wounded at Dalton.[21]

In the fight Pegram got the better of Col. Wilder though allowing him to escape. Wilder had seven killed, twenty-three wounded, and one captured. Pegram had ten captured. On Saturday Sept.12, Pegram's Cavalry, with the First Georgia Cavalry, assumed a position on the right of General Polk's Corps. Armstrong was on the left.[22] Pegram was located twelve miles from La Fayette on the Alabama Road. During the day, Lt. Col. Harper had a telegraphic message sent to his wife in Rome, Georgia. He was telling her to remain in Rome. Mrs. Harper had planned to go further south away from the advancing Federal army. Harper told her that "the enemy is falling back."[23] Later that night, Pegram sent his scouts out toward Ringgold to discover the enemy's whereabouts.

Pvt. Cicero Columbus Ellis. Enlisted March 1862. Absent December 1963 on special duty for Col. J.J. Morrison (courtesy the Ellis and Kane family).

Early Sunday morning, Sept 13, the scouts came in with the news that Ringgold had been abandoned, and they had not seen anyone since leaving the brigade. Pegram notified General Cheatham that the enemy was gone. Pegram stated that he was going to move toward Ringgold with his effective force to the same position near Leet's Tanyard where he had engaged Wilder.[24] Senior captain James H. Strickland was appointed major for the First Georgia Cavalry Regiment.

Early that same morning, Braxton Bragg came up to the front and found no advance had been made against the enemy. He also found the Federals had come back across the Chickamauga. Bragg ordered Wheeler, with his two divisions of cavalry, to occupy the extreme left at the position which General Daniel Harvey Hill had vacated. Wheeler was then ordered to press the enemy and divert him from Bragg's real intentions. General Forrest's Corps, including Pegram and the First Georgia Cavalry, was to cover the front and right flank of the Confederate army in the advance.[25]

On September 15, Forrest was at Ringgold, Pegram was at Leet's Tanyard, and General Buckner was at Rock Springs. Pegram's Brigade remained at Leet's Tanyard through September 17.[26] Pegram sent his pickets up the Pea Vine Valley, and they set up an outpost at Pea Vine Church.

Pvt. Thomas Edward Shell. Enlisted December 1864 (courtesy Blake Adcock).

On September 18, Gen. Bragg sent Pegram orders to move out from Leet's to the front of his infantry. Pegram's Division consisted of two brigades: Gen. Davidson's Brigade and Col. John S. Scott's Brigade. Scott's Brigade was on the Ringgold Bridge Road at the Red House.

Gen. Henry Brevard Davidson had been promoted to Col. James J. Morrison's desired position with Pegram's Brigade on August 18, 1863. Davidson took his new command to near Alexander's Bridge.[27] General Polk was commanding the right wing of Bragg's Army. When Davidson's Brigade arrived, he placed them behind a pine thicket which was parallel to the river road.

One of General Polk's divisions, under General St. John Liddell, was in the process of crossing Alexander's Bridge. Col. Daniel Govan and Gen. Cary Walthall were busily engaging Col. Wilder's Union cavalry on the other side of the bridge. Though the First Georgia Cavalry was not actually engaged in the crossing, they came under fire from wild shots of those who were engaged. General Davidson decided that since the crossing at Alexander's Bridge was blocked, he would take the brigade to Fowler's Ford. The brigade crossed the Chickamauga in the late afternoon. Later General Liddell followed Davidson and crossed the stream at Lambert's Ford a short distance away.

After crossing, the First Georgia Cavalry led the brigade and filed to the right. They passed Cattlett's and arrived back on Alexander's Bridge Road, but beyond the bridge where they could not cross. The brigade turned right and then left and passed Jay's Saw Mill at about sunset. As dusk approached, the brigade rode on into the deep shadows of the woods. Private John W. Minnich, Sixth Georgia Cavalry, described the ride:

> Didn't know where to or how far [we rode]. Dark night soon settled about us, and we knew the enemy was not far off or at least supposed to be. We went along in the gloom making as little noise as possible, stopping every hundred yards or less often to look and listen. Even our horses seemed to feel the tension; not a chomping of the bits; not a snort, sniffle, or whinny; not a stamping of hoofs; not a word above a whisper. A ghostly procession in the deep gloom of the forest, 1,200 men and horses. We crossed a limestone ridge and sometimes a hoof would strike a loose "shingle" and it emits a sharp metallic ring. Then we'd clinch our teeth and cuss, under our breath.[28]

The brigade went down a little slope to softer ground where the hoofs would be quieter. They still stopped to listen every few yards. Nerves were tense in the darkness and one could easily hear his own heart pounding in his ears. Suddenly, after a quick halt, Col. Morrison whispered, "Left about, forward."[29] The order was

Pvt. Robert Haywood Jones. Enlisted March 1864. Lost one short Enfield rifle December 21, 1864 (courtesy Ricky Smith).

passed to the rear where the back of the column was still on the limestone ridge. The brigade slowly retraced its steps, went to camp in an open field below Alexander's Bridge, and slept there all night.

The Army of Tennessee on September 19, 1863, was commanded by General Braxton Bragg. It comprised the right wing, Lt. Gen. Leonidas Polk; the left wing, Lt. Gen. James Longstreet; and two cavalry corps.

General Joseph Wheeler's Corps contained Wharton's Division and Martin's Division. General Nathan B. Forrest's Corps contained Frank C. Armstrong's Division and John Pegram's Division. Pegram's Division contained: Henry B. Davidson's Brigade with First Georgia Cavalry, Col. Morrison; Sixth Georgia Cavalry, Col. John Hart; Sixth North Carolina Cavalry, Col. George N. Folk; Rucker's Tennessee Legion, Col. Edmund Rucker; 10th Confederate Cavalry, Col. Charles T. Goode; Huwald's Battery, Captain Gustave Huwald, and John Scott's Brigade.

Early in the morning, September 19, Davidson's Brigade was abruptly awakened by the sounds of guns being fired at them from close range. The First Georgia Cavalry was the first to pursue those firing. They chased the Federal cavalry and drove them up Reed's Bridge Road to near McDonald's place. At McDonald's a few Yankees were captured, but the others outran the Confederates. During the charge, Pvt. Walter T. Willis, Co. K, was knocked off his horse and trampled by those charging from behind him.

The First Georgia Cavalry disengaged and moved back by a logging road to point near Jay's Mill. The brigade rested, readjusted their saddles and equipment, and had a breakfast. The Sixth Georgia Cavalry was in the rear during the chase and was the first to return. This placed them on the left and the First Georgia Cavalry on the right, with Rucker in the middle.

During this rest, they were joined by Col. Folk's Battalion, Sixth North Carolina, and five companies of the Tenth Confederate Cavalry commanded by Col. Goode. This added force numbered less than 400 men. At about 7:15 A.M., a few minutes after they arrived, they were sent back over the route where the First Georgia Cavalry had chased the Federals. Meanwhile, Col. John Croxton's Brigade of Brannon's Division, Thomas's Corps, had maneuvered into a position to attack the unsuspecting Georgians. Croxton thought he was on Reed's Bridge Road but was south of that road. When he saw Folk's Battalion and Goode's Battalion coming up the road, he fired on both the First Georgia Cavalry and the two battalions in the road. The Sixth Georgia, far to the left, only heard the volleys of concentrated fire. Thus began the great Battle at Chickamauga near Jay's Mill.

Upon hearing the firing in the near distance, the Sixth Georgia Cavalry mounted and came galloping to the battle with Col. John Hart leading the charge. They were the first reinforcements to arrive during the battle. Before it would be over, thousands more would come to join it. Croxton's men poured a heavy fire into the two battalions, killing scores of horses and men and wounding many more. They turned and raced back toward the Sixth Georgia in a wild panic yelling, "The woods are full of Yankees!"[30] Private John Minnich described the scene: "Men hatless, without guns, a foot [afoot], and sometimes two men on one horse, rider less horses and at last some of the men limping painfully, and some unwounded, but a foot [afoot]."[31] All came crashing into the regiment.

Fortunately, the First Georgia Cavalry was partly in a line of battle, as Col. Morrison was always concerned to have a secure position. Those in line returned fire and those of the

First Georgia Cavalry not in line quickly fell into it. Their position was out in the open and not much natural protection was to be found. The enemy was firing from behind a fringe of small pines and blackjack oaks. Croxton's men were so well concealed the Georgians could see only puffs of smoke, not those who pulled the triggers. Minnich said, "We returned the fire, blind as we could not see anything to fire at except smoke and brush, nor did I see one man until Wilson came in more than three hours later."[32]

At about 8:00 A.M., Col. Ferdinand Van Deveer's Brigade came in on the Reed's Bridge Road and attacked the First Georgia Cavalry on their right rear. The attackers could also fire into the rear of the entire brigade. Although almost outflanked and greatly outnumbered, Davidson's Brigade held. Fortunately, neither of the enemy brigades tried to charge or the Confederates would have been forced to withdraw.

Both Pegram and Forrest had been in the front examining the roads. They hurried back to the brigade because they heard the fierce battle raging. Once on the scene of the battle, General Pegram and his staff officers worked feverishly trying to get the command in the proper line of battle to repel their attackers.[33]

General Forrest realized that his cavalrymen were in deep trouble being attacked by such a large number of enemy infantry. He saw that General Bragg was about to be outflanked unless something was done quickly. Forrest sent a messenger to Bragg with that information. The bearer of the report was to request that General Bragg send the infantry fast to help the cavalry. Forrest knew it would take Bragg a while to readjust his infantry divisions to the new situation. Forrest did not think the little cavalry brigade could hold out much longer against the two Federal infantry brigades. General Forrest sent Captain Anderson to General Armstrong, who was six or seven miles away, for help. Captain Anderson soon returned with Colonel Dibrell's Brigade. General Polk felt that he could not spare more than that. General Forrest quickly dismounted Dibrell's men and put them in line with Davidson's Brigade. Even with the added strength from Dibrell, the Confederates were still outnumbered.

Soon word was passed among the men that Forrest was there. The men somehow became more than themselves knowing he was near. General Forrest was furious when his fourth messenger to Bragg had not brought a response. The heat of battle was almost overwhelming. General Forrest told the Georgians, "You men are doing nobly. This is not a cavalry fight you are putting up, it is an infantry fight. Hold the line till the infantry comes. I am going for them myself and they'll soon be here."[34]

Before Forrest left, he ordered General Pegram to hold that position until he returned. Forrest spurred his horse and galloped off to the rear. Pegram's men held dearly to that piece of land in obeying Forrest. The price paid was the loss of about one fourth of the brigade either killed or wounded. Several officers and nearly every colonel had his horse shot from under him. Col. Morrison was also among the wounded during this battle.

Providence was with the Georgians, for soon after Forrest departed to fetch the infantry, the enemy ceased firing. The morning air hung heavy and was breathlessly still. The dense smoke from all the cannon and small arms fire hovered close to the ground. It became so thick the Yankees could not see the Rebels to shell them. The lulls in firing saved three quarters of the brigade.

General Pegram included in his report of the battle that the highest praise was due all the gallant men who fought that day. Pegram called it "a remarkable fight for cavalry."[35] Another observer of the battle was General D.H. Hill, who did not like cavalry and stated so while with the army in Virginia. General Hill came upon the scene and asked, "What infantry is that?" The reply: "Forrest Cavalry, Sir."[36]

To Pegram's delight, General Forrest returned about 10:30 A.M. with Col. Claudus C. Wilson's Brigade of Major Gen. William H.T. Walker's Corps. Walker's Corps was in reserve. Private Minnich described seeing their arrival: "Later one of the boys called out loud enough for the enemy to hear, 'Look there, Coming across the field!' We looked and could see between the tree tops, marching up the field a long line of infantry in grey, moving forward with colors waving gently with the slight breeze, as if on parade. The long prayed for infantry relief. We shouted our relief and threw our dusty hats into the air. Never was there a more welcome sight to tired dust filled eyes."[37]

At once Col. Wilson's Infantry Brigade moved into line and charged the Yankee position. The enemy poured a murderous fire into them, but they were not to be denied. Wilson's men poured back an equal fire into the Yankees and pushed them rapidly back. Wilson pushed them so far to the rear the dismounted cavalry could not keep up. However, the enemy was also reinforced and the battle began to swing the other way. As the Federals reinforced, the Confederates found themselves being pushed back again.

General Forrest again mounted his horse and with his linen duster flapping, he galloped off for more help. He soon returned with Brig. Gen. Matthew D. Ector's Brigade of Infantry, which had been in reserve, and they were quickly placed in line with Wilson's men. This pushed Pegram and Dibrell out to the right flank of the battle line. The battle raged on as Chickamauga lived up to its Indian name, River of Blood.

During the battle, General Forrest's horse, a gift from the people of Rome, Georgia, was killed. He had to find another horse fast, as he continued to look for more help. As the help came on line, Forrest moved his cavalry more and more to the right. He was hoping to get them into a flanking position on the enemy to be able to make a crushing attack. However, because of all the charges and countercharges, the cavalry was more in the rear of the enemy than on their flank.

As the day ended, the Confederates made one last bloody charge to within forty yards of the mouths of the enemy cannon. The Yankees poured a murderous fire of canister and grapeshot into the dying Confederates. Soon it was over. Smoke hung over the field like a vale of death and all seemed deadly quiet since the roar of the cannon had stopped. As both armies withdrew, the dead and dying were left in their own blood. The ghastly toll of a day's work at war lay strewn about the fields. General Forrest withdrew his cavalry to Jay's Saw Mill.

Sunday, September 20, as the Battle of Chickamauga raged on, General Forrest ordered Pegram's Division to be held in reserve on his right. They lay in Decherd's field about midway between the Dyer's Bridge Road and the Ringgold Road. Forrest took General Armstrong's division with him. He dis-

Pvt. Napoleon Bonaparte Terry. Enlisted March 1862. Present through December 31, 1864 (courtesy Sonja Garrett Fox).

mounted them and kept them in line with General Breckenridge's Infantry. Davidson's Brigade and the First Georgia Cavalry lay in Decherd's meadow listening to the roar of guns and the rattle of the small arms. They wondered about their brothers who were fighting in the distance.

General William S. Rosecrans' worries began early in the morning of September 21, 1863. Rumors were flying about that General Pegram's Division was crossing the Tennessee River to attack Chattanooga. Rosecrans wired Col. John T. Wilder to watch for Pegram. He warned that if the reports were true, he must find a way to protect his wagon trains on the north side of the river. General Rosecrans suggested leaving a regiment to watch the wagons and use the rest of his command to pursue Pegram.[38] Col. Wilder sent a message back to Rosecrans confirming his fears that Pegram had indeed crossed the Tennessee that morning at Thayer's Ford.

Whatever the Federals thought, until late Monday morning of September 21, Pegram's Division was located at Dechard's farm. General Pegram's Division was composed of General Henry B. Davidson's Brigade and Col. John S. Scott's Brigade. The division was recovering from the pounding they had taken at Jay's Mill the day before. Before noon Davidson's Brigade, along with the First Georgia Cavalry, was mounted and marching. They were going toward Ringgold on the road near McAfee's Church.

Col. Robert Minty's Federal cavalry had been fighting with Col. Scott's Brigade of Pegram's Division that morning. Col. Minty had fallen back to the McAfee Church as Davidson's Brigade appeared on his right. Col. Scott was moving his brigade up to continue chasing Minty.

Davidson's Brigade crossed the Ringgold Road, and Col. Minty continued his retreat. Minty had a section of the 125th Ohio Battery firing at Davidson's men, but they could not hit anyone. Davidson's Brigade continued skirmishing with the Seventh Pennsylvania Cavalry after the Ohio Battery withdrew. The two cavalries had a running battle through the open fields north of the Ringgold Bridge Road. Each side would exchange volleys, but no one was hurt. All during this time, Col. Minty was falling back fast toward Missionary Ridge.

Minty's Cavalry eventually disappeared over a ridge into a thinly wooded area. General Pegram saw the possible danger of an ambush and had his division dismount and continue their advance on foot. Col. Minty had placed two of his cannon in the road waiting for the charging rebels. Instead of crashing over the crest of the ridge, Pegram's division came slowly on foot. The enemy promptly fired their guns but again without effect. The Federals realizing that the Rebs were not falling for their trick, quickly disappeared around a bend in the road.

As the Georgians moved up on line at the crest of the ridge, they were ordered to lie down on the ground. From there they could see across the valley to Missionary Ridge. The ridge was heavily wooded and rose 500 feet above the valley floor. At the foot of Missionary Ridge, Pegram spotted a section of Minty's artillery ready for action.

The men of the First Georgia Cavalry watched the Union cannoneers and were somewhat amused to see smoke coming from the silent cannon mouths. Abruptly, a loud boom would rumble across the valley floor. Their amusement ended as the tops of pine trees began to fall on them from the passing enemy cannon balls. The Federals found the range and delivered lower shots that seemed to plow the ground all around Davidson's Brigade. Leaves and dirt was scattered all over the cavalry. Fortunately, the men were spaced far enough apart that no one was hurt. After about fifteen minutes of concentrated fire, the Federals limbered up their artillery and disappeared up the road deeper into the woods.

General Pegram ordered his men on their feet and marched them across the valley in open order. With each step, the men fully expected it would be their last. They knew that anything from artillery to small arms awaited them in those woods to their front. Davidson brought his men across in good order and not a shot was fired at them until they reached the foot of Missionary Ridge.

When they reached the foot of the ridge, the battle began. With each step up, the firing became more intense. Minty's men became more difficult to dislodge the further up the hill they were driven. The battle was difficult for the Confederates because the enemy was concealed behind the thick undergrowth. The Rebs could not shoot what they could not see. As Davidson's Brigade advanced to the ridge road, they were forced to halt because the Yankees poured a heavy artillery and small-arms fire into them at close range. The Confederates hugged the ground and tried to make themselves into very small targets.

Both sides kept up the firing until dusk arrived. Pegram withdrew his men back across the valley to their horses. Later that night, Col. Minty withdrew his men from the summit of Missionary Ridge. The top of Missionary Ridge was the only place Minty had been able to hold against the pressing Confederate cavalry that day.[39]

General Pegram stated in his report that his command had been subjected to a heavy fire of canister from 300 yards while holding the ground gained. Both General Davidson and Col. Scott lost several men during the battle. Pegram said that the gallant Lt. Col. Joel Cicero Fain, Sixth Georgia, was badly wounded. Pegram remarked on his command's bravery: "The steadfastness with which both brigades bore this artillery fire was admirable in extreme, especially as evidencing the discipline of the men."[40]

On September 22, General Benjamin Cheatham ordered Col. Scott and Gen. Davidson to cross the ridge on his right and sweep down the valley toward Chattanooga. They were to extend his lines from the ridge to the river. During this movement, Gen. Davidson's Brigade, with the First Georgia Cavalry, met the enemy on the Chattanooga and Hiwassee Road. Davidson took part of the brigade and attacked the Fifty-ninth Ohio Infantry. This attack sent the enemy back in a rout. The cavalry took a number of prisoners and arms but was prevented from capturing the entire regiment because of a mistake by one of the regiments. The errant regiment fired on Davidson thinking he was the enemy.

Col. Scott drove across the valley and swept the enemy back to within a mile of Chattanooga. They captured the enemy's first line of rifle pits and continued the push. General Pegram arrived about this time and ordered Col. Scott to fall back. Pegram did not know that Gen. Davidson was coming to support Scott.[41] After that bit of confusion, Col. Scott relocated his command at the foot of Missionary Ridge. After Scott was in position, Gen. Davidson's command came up as scheduled. They positioned themselves on Col. Scott's right. Col. Scott's report of the day stated, "What is most singular to say, all of the Yankees killed or taken prisoner had canteens of mean whisky that was issued to them to get up a little Dutch courage."[42]

That evening all was quiet around Chattanooga. General Pegram moved his headquarters to Chickamauga Station. At this time, the Confederate army began its siege of Chattanooga. Change was coming for the First Georgia Cavalry. General John Pegram was sent back to Virginia to take an infantry command. General Nathan B. Forrest was ordered by General Braxton Bragg to send his brigades, except for George Dibrell, to General Joseph Wheeler. General Forrest ordered General Davidson's Brigade and General Frank C. Armstrong's Division to report to General Wheeler. He then resigned his commission and rode away feeling betrayed by Bragg. Forrest went to Mobile, Alabama, to sulk. Later, he was granted an independent command by President Jefferson Davis to operate in Mississippi and Tennessee.

The First Georgia was without rations because they did not expect to be gone so long from their wagon trains. The Georgians had to be fed and their horses needed their shoes replaced. The horses had not been looked at by a blacksmith since the battle at Chickamauga.

During this time of changing cavalry division commanders from Forrest to Wheeler, the First Georgia Cavalry remained with General Henry B. Davidson's Brigade. After reporting to Gen. Wheeler, Davidson received orders to cross the Tennessee River with a portion of his command, and proceed to the enemy's rear. Davidson was to destroy their supplies and supply lines hoping to starve the Union Army that remained in Chattanooga.

After Gen. Wheeler's inspection of the three brigades Gen. Forrest gave him, he described them as "mere skeletons, scarcely averaging 500 effective men each."[43] Wheeler continued: "[They were] poorly armed, very little ammunition and their horses were in horrible condition having marched for the last eight weeks averaging thirty miles a day and some days never removing their saddles. The men were worn out and without rations."[44] The Brigade commanders made the most urgent protest against their commands for being called upon to move the men in these conditions. General Wheeler realized the state of this command and allowed the worst horses to be returned to the rear.[45]

On September 30, General Wheeler, with General Davidson's effective command, crossed the Tennessee River at Cotton Port in the face of the enemy. The Federal force was larger than Wheeler's, but he still attacked them. Even though the Federals poured a heavy fire into them, the Confederates were able to drive the enemy about three miles from the river. They moved next into the Sequatchie Valley. The march to the enemy's rear began with hardships which would continue throughout the entire trip.[46]

General Davidson took a route through Washington, Tennessee, at the foot of the Walden Hills. Rain began to fall on the cavalry column that cold October night. The horses and wagons made the road a quagmire. The column trudged along slowly and made only nine miles all night. To make matters worse, as dawn was barely breaking, the enemy cavalry sent a regiment to harass the rear of the column. This required measures to drive the enemy away, which was done shortly.[47]

Wheeler's force came across a 1,000-wagon train and captured everything, including several hundred prisoners. The entire day and night of October 1 occupied Wheeler's Cavalry in destroying the stores, locomotives, and train cars they found. They also destroyed the bridge over Hickory Creek. Whatever the members of the command needed or wanted from among the Yankee supplies was distributed to them. Everything else was destroyed.[48]

While on the march, Wheeler and his men came upon a garrison at Stones River. They captured it with the 52 men inside. Part of the day was spent cutting down a bridge nearby and thoroughly burning the timbers. Wheeler and his men ripped up three miles of railroad track and burned the cross ties below the bridge.[49]

On October 2, Wheeler's men destroyed stores at Christiana and Fosterville and supplies from Murfreesboro to Wartrace.[50] The next morning, Davidson's command attacked McMinnville. Major Michael Patterson, commander of the town and 4th East Tennessee Volunteers, surrendered both the town and garrison of 600 men after a battle of two hours.[51] The Confederates also liberated several million dollars' worth of stores, provisions, and munitions.

This included 31 days' rations for Rosecrans' army. Wheeler's command spent October 4, destroying all the supplies that could not be utilized by the Confederates.

Pvt. John W. Bunch, Co. F was being court-martialed as a bushwhacker. A guilty sentence was pronounced October 2, 1863, and the penalty was death. However, even though he associated with known bushwhackers, not enough strong evidence was given for a hanging. He was sent to prison instead.

The Federals reported that Wheeler paroled the men and robbed them of their money, clothing, shoes, and watches and turned them loose hatless, shoeless and almost naked. The 4th East Tennessee Volunteer Regiment ceased to exist when they were paroled, as all returned home. Wheeler also exchanged their old broken-down horses for the fresh horses the Yankees had.

As the Federal cavalry began to press Wheeler, he realized that the numbers were tilting out of his favor and decided to go back to the Confederate lines. On October 6, Wheeler's Cavalry was along the Duck River. That night, he ordered Davidson's Division to camp along the Duck River near Warner's Bridge. Two miles further down, he ordered Martin's Division to camp and two miles further down was General Wharton's Division.[52]

During the evening Wheeler learned that the enemy, who had been in hot pursuit of his forces, was camped for the night at Frazier's farm. Wheeler sent word to Gen. Davidson about the enemy's position and directed him to keep an eye out for the Yankees. Davidson was to fall back toward Wheeler if the enemy should advance. Wheeler sent Davidson another message later that night to clarify his position was at Crowley's Mill. Unfortunately, General Davidson failed to have his men watch for the enemy's movements. This usually has a bad result.

The Federal Cavalry who was in pursuit of the Confederates consisted of George Crook's Second Cavalry Division and General Robert Mitchell's First Cavalry Division. Crook was originally pursuing Wheeler and was joined by Mitchell during the night of October 6.[53]

On October 7, Mitchell ordered Crook to march on the road to Farmington south of the Duck River. As his column moved to within three miles of Shelbyville, he came across Davidson's Division. They were camped on the river two miles north of the road.

As Crook marched down the road, General Davidson's Division began to break camp at their leisure. Some units were moving down the river toward Farmington as ordered. Col. George Hodge's Brigade was in the road by nine in the morning. Col. Scott's Brigade was standing by the road in marching order waiting for Hodge's column to pass.

Crook's command of mounted infantry saw the Confederates breaking camp and the confusion involved in getting lined up to march. He charged his mounted infantry into the confusion on horseback. As they came charging in, the Confederates scattered. Some of them ran headlong away from their attackers. However, some of the division made a stand, forcing Crook to dismount his infantry. General Crook brought up Col. Eli Long's Brigade of cavalry to continue the charge. Long's Cavalry drove the Rebels three miles, killing and wounding a great number.[54]

General Davidson was able to rally a portion of the stampeded cavalry and make a stand in a cedar thicket. After placing them in a defensive position, he left to find the rest of his command. He found Col. Hodge's Brigade mixed up with Col. Scott's Brigade, thus creating the confusion. Davidson ordered Col. Hodge to send a regiment to the rear to stop the Federal advance. Hodge sent Lt. Col. Ezekiel Clay's Kentucky Battalion to stall the enemy. Lt. Col.

Clay soon asked to be reinforced as his command was being overwhelmed by the enemy cavalry. Col. Hodge galloped his brigade to the rear to meet the enemy.

Col. Hodge wrote in his report that on his way to meet the enemy, he encountered "Scott's whole brigade crowded in frightful and horrible confusion, wild and frantic with panic, choking the entire road and bearing down upon me at racing speed. It was too late to clear the way; they rode over my command like madmen. I was ridden over and my horse knocked down."[55]

Col. Hodge gallantly placed his command in the breach to buy Davidson enough time to rally Scott's Brigade and form a fresh line for Hodge to fall back behind. General Davidson could do nothing with Scott's men. They were still running in wild fright.

Meanwhile, General Wheeler was trying to ascertain Davidson's position. Couriers were telling Wheeler that Davidson was following along Duck River. General Wheeler questioned the courier further and found Davidson was really going down the road to Farmington.

With that information, Wheeler started a thrust toward Farmington with Gen. Martin's Division. Wheeler told General John Wharton and the wagon trains to follow General Martin. Wheeler's command reached Farmington just in time to place five regiments of Martin's Division in a defensive position before the enemy appeared. Wheeler ordered Gen. Davidson, with his effective men, to stand by on the pike in columns of four. They were to charge the Federals while Martin's Division repulsed their attack. Again Davidson failed to obey General Wheeler. Davidson did not form the columns and, therefore, was unable to charge the enemy. In turn, The Federals were able to recover from Martin's initial blow and come back with their full furry against Martin and Wheeler. Fortunately, General Wheeler was able to charge the enemy and drive them back for some distance.

This allowed time for General Wharton and the wagon trains to pass, and Wheeler withdrew the entire cavalry command behind them. They were able to withdraw without being followed by the enemy. General Wheeler estimated the enemy suffered 29 killed, 159 wounded. He placed his loss at one-fourth of the enemy's. He led his cavalry back to the Confederate line, and they crossed the Tennessee River at Muscle Shoals near Rogersville, Alabama.

An officer with Wheeler's command estimated they had captured 1,065 wagons and 4,500 mules. The command brought in 100 loaded wagons and 1,000 mules. They had to burn all the other wagons and stores captured. They also had to slaughter 3,500 mules. This was necessary to prevent the enemy from using them. They also destroyed 75 miles of railroad and burned numerous bridges. They left the country without supplies or transportation.

8

Philadelphia, Tennessee

Col. James J. Morrison had established his headquarters near the Wolf's River Bridge, Tennessee. From there the First Georgia Cavalry was ordered to proceed to Cleveland, Tennessee. Colonel Morrison mounted his command, and they made their way across Alabama, Georgia, and Tennessee. The First Georgia Cavalry was resupplied, horses and men fed. They were all rested from their experience along the Duck River and the long ride afterward.

By mid–October, Col. Morrison received orders from General Braxton Bragg to make a demonstration toward Philadelphia, Tennessee. He was to threaten the enemy's rear and drive them back as far as he could. Col. Morrison's Brigade and the First Georgia Cavalry were to be employed in this venture. More precisely, they were to be the advance of General Carter Stevenson's Army to capture or drive the enemy across the Tennessee River at Loudon back into Burnside's Army.[1]

The department ordered General Stevenson to provide infantry support. Col. George Gibbs Dibrell's Tennessee Cavalry Brigade (formally Forrest Brigade) was to cooperate with Col. Morrison. Col. Morrison's Brigade included the First Georgia Cavalry, Lt. Col. Armstead Harper; Sixth Georgia Cavalry, Col. John Hart; Third Confederate Cavalry, Col. Patrick Henry Rice; Tenth Confederate Cavalry, Col. C.T. Goode; Rucker's Legion, Col. Edmund Rucker; Sixty-fifth North Carolina, Lt. Col. George N. Folk; and Walker's Battalion, Lt. Col. James A. McKamy.

General Stevenson was delayed getting into position because the railroad failed to transport his troops as ordered. When Stevenson finally reached Charleston, he issued orders to Col. Morrison to move his brigade to be able to reach Philadelphia by daylight on October 20. Col. Dibrell was ordered to attack the enemy's front at daylight in conjunction with Morrison's thrust. The purpose of Dibrell's attack was to conceal Morrison's maneuver.[2]

No matter what, Morrison and Dibrell were to seek, capture, or drive the enemy across the Tennessee River even if the enemy moved out of Philadelphia. After either mission was accomplished, they were to attack Loudon and force the enemy from that place. Next on Col. Morrison's list was to send a select company to Kingston to destroy the ferry. Lastly, he was to set up pickets along the river on the left flank of the army.[3]

All day and night of October 19 was spent by the First Georgia Cavalry and the brigade in getting across the Hiwassee River. The crossing was a slow process. Most of the 1,800 men in the command were crossing at Kincannon's Ferry, and some forded the river where possible. As soon as they were across, they began the march to Decatur and to Philadelphia. Col. Morrison estimated that the distance to be traveled before morning was fifty miles. The conditions for the march were very bad, as it had been raining almost constantly. The roads were sloppy and getting worse as time went by.[4]

From Kincannon's Ferry, Col. Morrison sent General Stevenson a dispatch telling him that he could not get the command across the river before ten o'clock that night. It would be impossible for him to reach Philadelphia by morning. Morrison said he would be there by noon and when he reached Sweetwater, he would advise him of the locality and estimated strength of the enemy. From Sweetwater, Col. Morrison was going to update the precise time that he would reach the rear of Philadelphia.

Once across the Hiwassee River, the column was on line for Philadelphia. They reached their destination in fifteen hours on the muddy roads and through the cold rain. Morrison's report reflected "that the men and officers bore up astonishingly under the circumstances, having crossed the river and making the march, had lost two nights of sleep in succession."[5]

Upon reaching his desired position, Col. Morrison sent out his scouts to locate the enemy. The scouts returned with reports that Col. Frank Lane Wolford's Cavalry Brigade was set in line of battle. Col. Morrison sent word to Col. Dibrell suggesting that he should move up the railroad line and make his demonstration in front of Col. Wolford. Morrison informed Dibrell that he would be in place by 12 noon, and Dibrell was to begin a cannonade five minutes later. This would enable Morrison's Cavalry to move without interruption or discovery to the enemy's rear.

Col. Morrison moved his cavalry around to their target. At Pond Creek, a point to the left of the railroad line near Philadelphia, the command struck a wagon train and some stragglers who were passing from Col. Wolford's to General Burnside's camp. During the brief skirmish the First Georgia captured forty prisoners.[6] Col. Wolford learned of the attack on the trains six miles from him at 10 A.M. Wolford sent out the Union's 1st Kentucky and 11th Kentucky Cavalry regiments. He held back the 12th Kentucky Cavalry and the 54th Ohio (mounted) Infantry.[7]

After the prisoners were secure, Col. Morrison sent a detachment of his cavalry out on each road leading to Philadelphia. They were to drive in the Federal pickets and hold their position. The main objective was to prevent the Federals from learning the true direction the main body of the brigade was taking. While this order was being followed, Col. Morrison moved the First Georgia Cavalry to the rear of Philadelphia. At this time, the First Georgia Cavalry had marched fifty miles in fifteen hours without being discovered. When the two Yankee cavalry regiments arrived, they were dealt with by being either captured or scattered.

Morrison ordered Lt. Col. George Folk's Sixty-fifth North Carolina Regiment to make a feint toward Loudon, which was only four miles away. This was to prevent General Julius White's Brigade of four infantry regiments from reinforcing Col. Wolford. When Col. Morrison's Brigade reached the objective nearly two miles north of Philadelphia, they cut the telegraph wires.

After the North Carolina Regiment moved toward Loudon, Col. Morrison held a council of war with Lt. Col. Armstead Harper and Col. John Hart, Sixth Georgia Cavalry. Lt. Col. Harper wanted the First Georgia and the Sixth Georgia to be dismounted and make a combined attack against the enemy artillery. Col. Morrison had other plans for the attack and overruled Harper's suggestion.

At the appointed hour of 12 noon, Col. Dibrell began an artillery duel with the enemy from their front. The cannons roared from both sides as Col. Morrison's Brigade moved from the rear and maneuvered into position for the attack. Col. Morrison ordered Col. Hart's Sixth Georgia Cavalry and Col. Rice's Third Confederate Cavalry to dismount and charge the enemy's left flank and silence those cannon.

The left flank had a battery of six guns supported by five times their number in Federal Infantry. After Col. Hart and Lt. Col. Harper received their orders, they shook hands and said a prayer together asking God that they would meet again. This was the last time Col. Hart saw his good friend Arm Harper in good health. The First Georgia Cavalry was still mounted along with Col. George McKenzie's Fifth Tennessee Cavalry and a portion of Major Jessie's command.[8] They were combined to make a frontal assault at the center of the Federals.

The dismounted Sixth Georgia Cavalry led by Col. Hart and the Third Confederate led by Col. Rice moved out on foot toward the enemy's left. As they made their advance, the Federals discovered their presence and turned their attention to them. When the two regiments came into range, the Federals opened fire with their cannon. Col. Hart's Sixth Georgia made a gallant charge across a field of death. Col. Hart said, "Never had men fought better that those [I] had the honor to command that day."[9] It was apparent to each and every man that they had to carry those six cannon rapidly or be killed or captured trying.

The Federals fought hard to drive back their attackers and did succeed briefly. Col. Morrison rallied the faltering men to continue their charge. The battle ran hot again and for a second time the forces of Morrison were thrown back. A third time, Morrison rallied his men for a charge. The Federals knew they could not withstand the onslaught of another charge and began to look for a way out. Col. Wolford devised a plan to send a flag of truce with three captured citizens to Col. Dibrell. As they parleyed, this stopped Dibrell's attack, and Wolford could concentrate his force elsewhere.

Col. Wolford saw the weakest point in the attack was the place on his right where the fewest attackers and the First Georgia Cavalry stood. Col. Dibrell's Brigade was in front of the enemy but not attacking. Col. Hart's Sixth Georgia Cavalry and Col. Rice's Third Confederate were on the left, fully engaged, but had not silenced the cannon. Col. Wolford swelled his force together as a swarm of angry hornets and charged out against Lt. Col. Harper and the First Georgia Cavalry.

Col. Hart was helpless as the whole force of the remaining 1,800 men shocked the First Georgia Cavalry. Hart's men had carried the cannon and held prisoners. Hart watched the cavalry battle as it ebbed back and forth. Harper led his gallant men again and again against ever increasing odds. The heroic command unbelievably held Wolford in the trap, but Wolford, becoming desperate himself, knew that he must break out with this last charge. Like a great tidal wave, Wolford swelled his command to wash over the Georgians. The toll for escape was heavy for the Federals and Georgians alike. A great number of brave souls fell from their saddles never to rise to them again. Lt. Col. Armstead R. Harper was among that number. Harper received a mortal wound which broke his right thigh bone. A shell exploded near him sending fragments that hit him while he was riding in front of his line ordering his men to charge the enemy.[10]

Col. Morrison was enraged that Col. Dibrell held back and did not join in the attack with his troops. Col. Dibrell offered that he did not come because the enemy was already routed, and he thought they were just fleeing in confusion toward Loudon. In truth, Col. Dibrell did see a flag of truce presented by the enemy, and at that point he decided not to advance. This was exactly what the Federals wanted him to do. They bought enough time to make their escape.[11]

General Vaughn saw they were heavily outnumbered and feared the Georgians would be cut to pieces; therefore, he took over Dibrell's command. He arrested the Yankee officer who was under the flag of truce and placed him under guard until the fight was over. General Vaughn charged into the enemy in hope of saving Lt. Col. Harper's First Georgia Cavalry from slaughter, but his attack was too late as most of the damage was already done.[12]

Col. Wolford complained that Gen. Vaughn did not respect the flag of truce. Actually his ruse worked. The Yankee officer made the mistake of inquiring about the presence of General Stevenson, as he was higher rank. After he asked more questions, he was arrested and held. Later the Yankee officer laughed and admitted he would have done the same thing.

Col. Morrison's report stated that the men and officers of the brigade had conducted themselves "handsomely"[13] from the commencement of the march to the rout of the enemy at Philadelphia. Col. Morrison gave special credit for the victory to "Col. Hart, Col. Rice, and Lt. Col. Harper."[14] He also paid tribute to his staff for their gallant efforts during the battle, especially pointing out "Lt. George Yoe, Captain Davidson Lamar, and his Adjunct John W. Tench."[15] Morrison placed his loss at fourteen killed and 82 wounded. The enemy's loss in killed and wounded was much larger and the captured placed between 500 and 700 men. They also captured all six pieces of the artillery, with ammunition, stores, wagons and mules.[16] General Bragg said, "Too much praise cannot be given Colonels Dibrell and Morrison and the brave command under them for the dash and daring displayed in the Expedition so completely successful."[17]

Col. Morrison's command soon rallied itself along with Col. Dibrell's and pursued the fleeing enemy toward Loudon, Tennessee. As night began to fall, Morrison decided not to attack during the night as the enemy had its infantry waiting in a line of battle.[18]

The wounded and dead from the battle at Philadelphia were cared for by those left in camp. Lt. Col. Harper was carried to the surgeon's tent to be cared for by Dr. John L. Branch and Dr. Mulky. John Tench described the moment:

> Col. Harper, poor fellow, has had his right leg amputated far above the knee. I hope he will recover, as there is no Colonel in the army that we could not spare as well. Tears gushed from the eyes of men when he fell and when his leg was amputated there was not a dry eye in the room.
>
> Drs. Branch and Mulky, assisted by Surgeon Boyd, performed the operation. They did it handsomely. Mulky is a ripe scholar, a good man, and not excelled in surgery by any man in the army. Branch has proven himself here, as he always does, self-sacrificing for his friends. He remained with Col. Harper with, not the risk, but the certainty of being taken to a Yankee prison.
>
> Col. Harper's little orderly, Tommy Sparks of Newnan, also remained there with him. A better boy than Tom is not in our army, and all boys and even men should emulate his attachment for his Colonel.[19]

Tench also gave a view of what East Tennessee was like through his eyes after Philadelphia: "We will attack the enemy at Loudon tomorrow morning. East Tennesseans are following Burnside's Army by hundreds, and East Tennessee is fast becoming purified. The country is filled with Vicksburg prisoners. You can find from one to three at almost every farm house. They seem to rely upon their 'paroles' and are quite unconcerned. Won't we make them hustle, though? General Vaughn is here after them."[20]

The arrested Yankee officer was now under the care of Adj. John Tench. They shared a room. After the Yankee finished writing his reports at the little table, he turned the table and pen over to Tench. From this place, Tench wrote his reports and letters to newspapers.[21]

On the morning after the battle at Philadelphia, Tennessee, October 21, 1863, brigade commander Col. James Morrison appointed Major Samuel W. Davitte to the temporary rank of lieutenant colonel. Lt. Col. Armstead R. Harper was gravely injured, and Morrison needed a new commander for the First Georgia Cavalry. Meanwhile, the First Georgia Cavalry was skirmishing with the Federal infantry's advance about 3,000 strong and located outside Loudon, Tennessee.[22]

Col. Morrison thought the Yankee cavalry might try a flanking sortie against him. He had learned from a local citizen that General Burnside had just reinforced Loudon with Gen. Robert Potter's Ninth Army Corps.[23] Morrison knew that the Confederate cavalry defense near Loudon was weak. During the day, the colonel had a war council with General John Vaughn and Col. George Dibrell. They agreed they needed more room and more men to be able to attack with any success against the Yankees, who were waiting in place. Caution was the watchword for the moment.

Col. Morrison needed information and sent his scouts to watch the enemy and discover any venture they might make. Since the brigade was not ready to attack, Morrison began preparations to fall back toward Sweetwater. By six o'clock in the evening, Morrison's Brigade was camped on the left of the railroad near Col. Dibrell at Sweetwater. The First Georgia Cavalry occupied the left side of the railroad that ran between Philadelphia and Sweetwater, and Col. Dibrell's Brigade was on the right side of the line.[24]

On October 22, Col. Morrison's pickets were still being fired upon, as they had been all night. Col. Frank Wolford's Cavalry Brigade was gathering strength to make an attack upon Morrison's Brigade.

General Carter Stevenson, in light of what Col. Dibrell failed to do at Philadelphia, placed Col. Morrison in command of both brigades. After being given that authority, Col. Morrison moved his headquarters to the Owen's house near Sweetwater and stayed there several days. During this time, plans were being made to drive the Federals from Loudon with a cavalry assault supported by infantry. Col. Morrison appointed Col. John Hart, 6th Georgia Cavalry, as commander of his old cavalry brigade.

Col. Morrison was looking for a report from Col. Dibrell about the property captured by his brigade after the battle at Philadelphia. Col. Dibrell refused to comply with this order. This forced Morrison to have Col. Dibrell arrested and charges filed against him. Dibrell on several occasions did not do his duty.

Once Col. Morrison felt they were ready to attack Loudon, he moved his division toward Loudon before dawn October 28, and arrived near Loudon by late morning. Morrison's scouts came in and told him that the enemy had moved across the river the day before. The scouts reported that General Burnside himself had been in Loudon and that the enemy was set in a line of battle on the opposite side of the river from Loudon. With all of this information, Col. Morrison sent out the pickets and put his command in a defensive posture in case of a counterattack. However, the Federals saw the large Confederate force coming and withdrew from town.[25]

The town of Loudon was astir with the arrival of the Confederates. The Federals had just evacuated, and now the Confederates occupied it. The citizens had a difficult decision, with the shift of occupation, as to whom to be loyal. Col. Morrison asked the citizens questions about the Yankees and any plans they might have. He learned that the Federals had Gen. Mahlon Manson's Twenty-third Army Corps and Gen. Robert Potter's Ninth Army Corps, together totaling about 10,000 infantry and 2,500 cavalry. Some of the citizens believed that the Ninth Army Corps had gone to Kingston. They also reported that the Yankees sent their wagon trains to Knoxville.

Col. Morrison reported all information he had learned from the citizens to General Joseph Wheeler. Morrison reported the enemy had twelve batteries including six 24-pounder guns. He wanted to know if Wheeler thought he should place his guns into position that night.[26]

Wheeler replied to Col. Morrison to put the guns in place and take any necessary action to hold the town. He told Morrison the infantry was on its way to support him. Wheeler advised Morrison to keep his main force out of range of the enemy guns, but that he should put his sharpshooters near the river and in the town. General Wheeler had another order for Morrison's scouts and pickets. He wanted the river picketed from Loudon to Kingston, and the scouts sent to Kingston and Morgantown. Wheeler had a question for Morrison about the status of the mills in and around Loudon.[27]

During the night of October 28, the Confederate infantry arrived. Their commanding officer, General Alfred Cumming, reported to Col. Morrison. Morrison advised Gen. Cumming not to move his infantry too close to town as his campfires would inform the enemy of his position. General Cumming informed Gen. Carter Stevenson of the situation in Loudon regarding Col. Morrison's displacement of his troops and scouts.

On October 29, Col. Morrison's scouts confirmed that Gen. Julius White's Infantry Division had gone to Kingston. A report from Col. John Hart, who was near Kingston, verified the scouts report. Other scouts reported that except for two regiments of Col. Wolford's Brigade, all the enemy had gone to Knoxville. Col. Morrison sent these reports to General Wheeler along with a prisoner. The prisoner, Melvin Porter, had two sons in Byrd's Federal Regiment. Porter had recently taken the oath to both the Confederacy and the Union. Col. Morrison suspected him of being a spy and wanted Wheeler to deal with him accordingly.[28]

The sad news of Lt. Col. Arm Harper's death reached Col. Morrison October 31. The news inflamed thoughts of how Colonel George Dibrell's inactivity at Philadelphia possibly resulted in Lt. Col. Harper's death. Sadly, Col. Morrison issued the following notice:

> To the First Georgia Cavalry:
>   It is my painful duty to announce to you the death of Lt. Col. Harper, of the First Georgia Cavalry, who died on the 28th instant, from the effects of a wound received in the late battle at Philadelphia. In losing him you have lost a high toned, bold and gallant officer. He possessed all the requisites necessary to make a leader. His place cannot be supplied either to you or to me. He has paid the greatest price of liberty; you and I have the consolation to know that he died as heroes only die, leading his men to victory or a glorious grave. Soldiers: let us avenge his death and emulate his example.
>   J.J. Morrison[29]

Privates Tommy Sparks and R.T. Logan were placed in charge of Lt. Col. Harper's remains and were sent with the body to meet Mrs. Harper and their two little boys. Lt. Col. Harper was loved by all in the First Georgia and every man would have died for him. Their hearts went out to the brave Mrs. Harper, who held back the tears to receive her deceased husband. His body was carried on to Cave Spring for burial. The First Georgia Cavalry would not be the same without Arm Harper.

On October 31, the Army of Tennessee was commanded by General Braxton Bragg. The army was made up of four corps led by General James Longstreet, General Benjamin F. Cheatham, General John Cabell Breckenridge, and General Joseph Wheeler. Gen. Wheeler's Corps was divided into four divisions: General John A. Wharton's; General William T. Martin's; General Frank C. Armstrong's; and General John Herbert Kelly's.

General Martin's Division was divided into two brigades: John T. Morgan's and James J. Morrison's. Col. Morrison's Georgia Brigade contained the following regiments: First Georgia Cavalry, Lt. Col. Samuel W. Davitte; Second Georgia Cavalry, Col. Charles C. Crews; Third Georgia Cavalry, Lt. Col. Robert Thompson; Fourth Georgia Cavalry, Col. Isaac W. Avery; and Sixth Georgia Cavalry, Col. John R. Hart.

During the time of mourning for Lt. Col. Harper, both Union and Confederate troops watched each other across the Holston River near Loudon and without much action. Col. Morrison sent Col. Dibrell with 700 men to Morgantown to watch the enemy from there. They were all that were fit for service in his command. Dibrell requested more men from Morrison, but Col. Morrison had to refuse the request. Morrison's command was also spread too thin to aid Dibrell. Pvt. James J. Buchannan, Co. G, was detailed to Robertson's Artillery. Morrison reported that his scouts were on the opposite side of the river from Lenoir's Station, Tennessee, and his pickets were in place there as well. Fortunately, all remained quiet through November 2. The scouts were to discover what property was in Loudon, Tennessee.

On November 3, Morrison overheard General Alfred Cumming's men report about the enemy infantry moving. Morrison realized that none of his scouts had reported any like maneuver to him. He told Gen. Wheeler he doubted if these reports were true, and that Col. Dibrell had been attacked below Morgantown by some of Wolford's Cavalry. The attack had come while Dibrell was crossing the river and was driven back across. Morrison reported that Dibrell had not notified him of any infantry aggression.

That night two of Col. Morrison's most valuable scouts did not return to him, and Morrison feared that they might have been captured.[30] The scouts, Sergeant Bill Moore and Pvt. Bill Cavender, indeed had been captured by the Yankees. That night as they lay by the river bank, Sergeant Moore kicked a chunk of driftwood into the river while acting as if he were restlessly sleeping. The chunk made noise rolling down the riverbank and the guard came to see what the noise was all about. The Yankee guard was suspicious at first, counted the prisoners, and watched closely. However, as the night passed and there was repeated shuffling by Sergeant Moore, the guard became less vigilant. When Sgt. Moore was convinced his men were not being watched, he kicked another stump into the river and at the same time the other Rebel scout slipped into the river along with it. This act continued until Bill Moore made his own escape.[31]

Col. Morrison sent out other scouts near the mouth of the Little Tennessee River. He wanted to know if the Yankees were building a pontoon bridge anywhere along the Holston River. Morrison's pickets had reported a constant noise of carpenter-like sounds from saws and hammers coming from that direction. Morrison was concerned for all his scouts who were out because the Federals had placed their pickets as "thick as hops."[32]

On November 4, all was quiet for Morrison in Loudon, but Col. Dibrell had been busy skirmishing with the enemy. Dibrell reported to Wheeler that he still had not received any orders from him or Col. Morrison.[33]

By November 5, Col. Morrison's Cavalry Brigade had spread itself from the mouth of the Hiwassee River all the way along the Tennessee River to Knoxville.[34] General Frank Armstrong advised General Wheeler that Morrison's command was not in any shape to picket any further. He added that if Wheeler wanted more ground picketed then he would have to send more cavalry.

As time passed, the need for the First Georgia Cavalry to be more active, no matter its condition, came to the forefront. As a result, more misfortune struck the First Georgia Cavalry. During an engagement near Sweetwater, an enemy artillery shell exploded just in front of Col. Morrison's horse while at a gallop. The horse stopped suddenly, throwing Col. Morrison ungracefully to the ground. The crash severely battered him and the resulting injuries would hamper his ability to command cavalry for the remainder of the war.

After the accident Col. James J. Morrison was sent home to Cedartown, Georgia. Col. Charles Cotilda Crews, who had commanded cavalry for some time, now replaced Morrison as commander of the brigade.[35] Col. Charles Crews was at one time a captain of a company in the Second Georgia Cavalry Regiment. Crews had been captured by the Yankees during the raid into Kentucky and exchanged. He was promoted to colonel of the Second Georgia Cavalry on November 1, 1862. Later, he was shot in the hip and severely wounded but soon recovered. Now he was the commander of Morrison's Brigade and the First Georgia Cavalry.

9

Sevierville, Tennessee

Colonel Charles C. Crews was now in command of Col. James J. Morrison's Georgia Brigade. The Georgia Brigade and commanders as of November 20, 1863, were as follows: First Georgia Cavalry, Lt. Col. Samuel W. Davitte; Second Georgia Cavalry, Lt. Col. Francis M. Ison; Third Georgia Cavalry, Lt. Col. Robert Thompson; Fourth Georgia Cavalry, Col. Isaac W. Avery; and Sixth Georgia Cavalry, Col. John Hart.

The Georgia Brigade, with the First Georgia Cavalry, was still a part of General William T. Martin's Division of Wheeler's Cavalry Corps of Braxton Bragg's Army of Tennessee. In a matter of one month, the First Georgia Cavalry lost the two men who had formed and guided the regiment. New leaders like Sam Davitte, James H. Strickland, and George T. Watts would step forward to lead the regiment.

General Martin had wanted a more active role in the war effort, and General Wheeler gave him a campaign to lead. General Martin's headquarters was located near Kingston, Tennessee. The Georgia Brigade was with Martin at Kingston except for the Sixth Georgia Regiment. The Sixth Georgia had been on a mission into Georgia but were now on their way to report back to General Martin at Kingston. They arrived November 19.[1]

Special Order No. 101, November 22, put General Martin's Division on the move. Generals Martin and Frank C. Armstrong were to move their divisions to Kingston. Col. Charles Crews' Georgia Brigade was around Kingston on picket duty and had been for the past few weeks.[2]

General Wheeler despised the idea that cavalry should have to herd livestock. However, the job had to be done. He ordered Col. Crews to detail some men to drive hogs that had been captured by Captain Kincade and deliver them to a suitable area for forage. After Col. Crews' men got the hogs to pasture in a remote location, they proceeded with the Georgia Brigade to join General Martin.[3] Martin's Division had been engaged in heavy fighting around Knoxville helping General Longstreet.

On November 23, Gen. Martin's Division attacked Kingston. A forced march was made from Knoxville to Kingston, and when they attacked the Federals, they failed to dent their fortified stronghold. The Federals poured a steady fire into the Confederates which forced them to withdraw.[4] On November 23, Pvt. Isaac Smith, Co. K, was discharged.

After that failed attack, General Wheeler was ordered to report to General Braxton Bragg. Wheeler placed the cavalry command in the hands of General Martin and departed on November 24 for Bragg's headquarters. After Wheeler left, Martin moved the entire command back to Knoxville and came under attack in another skirmish.[5]

The Confederate cavalry lacked sufficient forage and suffered as a result. The weather was bitterly cold, and the Georgia Brigade suffered right along with the rest of the cavalry. On the cold and rainy day of November 26, General Martin sent Col. Thomas Harrison's Brigade of Armstrong's Division and Col. Alfred Russell's Alabama Brigade of Morgan's Division across the Holston River just below Knoxville. Gen. Morgan was to lead them in an attack against the Federal cavalry brigades of Col. Edward McCook's First Division. The Union commanders in the field were Col. Archibald Campbell, First Cavalry Brigade, and Col. Oscar LaGrange, Second Brigade. Morgan dismounted his command and marched his cavalry with the Confederate infantry. Col. Russell's Brigade was in a hot contest but drove the Yankees from their rifle pits. Col. Harrison on the extreme left found no Yankee cavalry.[6]

On November 29, the Confederate brigades engaged in the attacks had to withdraw and go back across the Holston River. General Longstreet ordered the cavalry to move north toward Tazewell. They were to check the advance of the Federals attacking from that direction. Gen. Martin's Cavalry reached Maynardville on the afternoon of November 30. When they arrived, they found General Sam Jones was already engaged in a skirmish. General Martin thought it too late in the day for an attack by his cavalry and did not help General Jones no matter how desperate his condition.[7]

That night General Martin sent General Armstrong's Division around to the right of the Federals. They were to reach the rear before daylight December 1. The remainder of Martin's Cavalry was to attack the front of the Yankees in Maynardville. As dawn broke and the attack became eminent, the Yankees withdrew rapidly. They left a small picket to cover the withdrawal. They were easily captured by Martin's men.[8]

General Armstrong had gotten into the supposed rear of the enemy driving his command into the backside of Maynardville. He found no resistance and linked up again with General Martin. Martin ordered Gen. Armstrong to go northwest toward the Clinch River. Martin sent Gen. Samuel Jones northeast to a place between the enemy and the river. Gen. Jones' command was attacked and prevented from completing his mission. Armstrong was successful in pushing the Federals for several miles and even across the frozen river.

General Martin received orders to return with his cavalry from the Clinch River area back to Knoxville. They arrived back in Knoxville on December 2. The Union army was beginning a siege of Knoxville. Two days after Martin arrived in Knoxville, the Confederates retreated north to Rogersville. General Morgan's Division covered the rear of General Lafayette McLaws' Infantry. They were on the south side of the Holston River. Gen. Martin was on the south side of the river to cover the railroad line as well as the left flank of the army.[9]

As of December 1863, the First Georgia Cavalry was under the command of Gen. James Longstreet. He had placed the cavalry corps under the command of Gen. Martin. The Cavalry Corps was divided into two divisions. The First Georgia Cavalry was in General John T. Morgan's Division. His division included Col. Alfred Russell's Alabama Brigade and Col. Charles Crews' Georgia Brigade. Russell's Brigade contained the First, Third, Seventh, and Fifty-first Alabama Cavalry regiments. Crews' Georgia Brigade contained the following: First Georgia Cavalry, Col. Samuel Davitte; Second Georgia Cavalry, Col. Francis Ison; Third Georgia Cavalry, Col. Robert Thompson; Fourth Georgia Cavalry, Lt. Col. William L. Cook; and Sixth Georgia Cavalry, Col. John Hart.

General Longstreet knew his cavalry needed to forage. On December 10, he recommended that General Martin send his cavalry out for forage. Longstreet advised Martin if he could hold his position near Mossy Creek, it would be a good place to forage the animals. A plus would be keeping the enemy away from the area. Longstreet suggested if Martin could not hold Mossy Creek to go down to Russellville to forage. Longstreet continued with his instructions for Martin to place strong scouting parties to prevent a surprise attack.

Gen. Morgan's Division was in the Russellville area, but they were spread out foraging. While the men were gathering provisions, a brigade of Federal Cavalry began an attack. The First Georgia, Sixth Georgia, and the Third Alabama Cavalry were the only regiments in place to defend against the attacking enemy. The Federals outnumbered the three regiments three to one. The Georgians, commanded by Col. Charles Crews, repulsed the attackers handsomely. The Yankees fled, leaving their dead, wounded, and prisoners with the Confederates. Gen. Martin's report of the attack gave special praise to the First Georgia Cavalry along with the Sixth Georgia and Third Alabama Cavalry. Col. Crews was mentioned in the report especially for his "bravery and skill"[10] displayed during the attack.

The brief battle brought the division back in from foraging, and they all were in their saddles. General Longstreet decided to attack the Yankees at Bean Station which was about nine miles north of Russellville and across the Holston River. On December 13, Longstreet ordered Gen. Martin to get his cavalry into the enemy's rear to operate. When Martin's Cavalry Corps reached the river at May's Ford, they found a brigade of enemy cavalry guarding the ford. Gen. Martin ordered Gen. Morgan to remove them. General Morgan ordered up Captain Jannedine H. Wiggin's 2nd Arkansas Light Battery and Captain Benjamin F. White's Tennessee Horse Artillery batteries and placed them in position. The batteries proceeded to fire on the Yankees in rapid order and soon drove them in great confusion. They did not know which way to run for safety, and in their haste left sixty of their men either dead or wounded. This action delayed Martin's Division from its mission.[11]

By the morning of December 14, the Cavalry Corps still had not finished crossing the Holston River and had not gotten into the enemy's rear. Martin received orders again from Longstreet telling him he was late and to attack the enemy's flank on the Knoxville Road about four miles from Bean Station. General Martin got his corps in order attacking and killing a great number of Yankees. Martin had placed his artillery on a high hill to do the most damage to the Yankee breastworks. Gen. Morgan's Division had been dismounted and moved to attack the Union flank. Wiggin's and White's artillery fired for an hour and a half. With this barrage, the enemy began to retire. As the Federals left the field, they left enough men to prevent a full attack. Because of a lack of coordination with Gen. Micah Jenkins' Infantry Brigade, the cavalry efforts were not as effective as they could have been. Jenkins refused to advance unless he was reinforced which allowed Gen. James Murrell Shackelford's Cavalry time to escape.

On December 15, General Martin was on the Knoxville and River roads in front of the retreating Federals. After driving in the Federal skirmishers, Martin found the Union army in a heavily fortified position on Richland Creek. General Martin decided they were too strong in number, and the terrain was not suitable for cavalry maneuvers so he retired.

After the attack, the Federal generals were looking for Martin's Cavalry Corps as he had done them a great deal of damage. Col. William Palmer, Fifteenth Pennsylvania Cavalry, told General Grant that he thought Martin's position to be near the mouth of Chunky Creek. Palmer thought General Martin might head toward North Carolina by way of French Broad Gap or that he might go to Greeneville, Tennessee.

On December 13, charges were filed against Captain John L. Kerr, Co. G, for improper conduct before the enemy, and he was arrested. General Grant received a message on December 14 that General Martin was in Morristown with five regiments of cavalry. Martin was with the Georgia Brigade. Grant's report said the Georgians were drawn up in a line of battle. The report was true, and General Martin remained there until he received more orders from General Longstreet. On a more pleasant note, Col. Jim Morrison got married on December 21, 1863, to a Mrs. Hattie Berrie near Madison, Morgan County, Georgia.[12]

On December 22, General Longstreet ordered General Martin to have Col. Russell's Alabama Brigade establish pickets from a point four miles east of Dandridge and extending west to a point almost to New Market. Col. Crews' Georgia Brigade was to establish pickets from Dandridge halfway to Morristown. General Armstrong was to establish his pickets to Talbott's Depot on the road from New Market to Morristown. Longstreet wanted all three divisions of cavalry to counterattack the enemy in the rear and flanks.

On December 24, the expected attack came. That morning both General Armstrong and Col. Russell were hit by the Federal army simultaneously. General Armstrong was compelled to withdraw from his assigned position because he was outnumbered and outflanked. He pulled in his pickets from New Market to the eastern side of Mossy Creek. Col. Russell's Alabama Brigade was attacked by 2,000 First Cavalry Brigade commanded by Col. Campbell. In the worst case, Russell was caught by surprise. The Alabama Brigade was in a state of confusion for a while, but Russell pulled them back together in good order and fought the enemy savagely. Not only did they halt the attackers, but they also were able to push them back two miles toward Dandridge.[13]

At the same time Armstrong and Russell were being attacked, Col. Crews had the Georgia Brigade in their saddles. Crews took four regiments containing 600 men and moved out for the enemy's rear. The fifth regiment, Colonel Avery's Fourth Georgia Cavalry, had been sent to Kingston for detached duty. The First Georgia and Sixth Georgia cavalries were in the lead of the column making a dashing charge toward the Yankee artillery. The enemy blazed their cannon at the charging Georgians, but the attackers would not be denied. They captured the artillery and men. The Federal infantry began to fall back from this bold charge. The Federals did recover, rallied themselves, and prepared for a countercharge. The First and Sixth Georgia cavalries were greatly outnumbered by the countercharging Yankees and were soon driven away from the artillery they had just captured. Major Alfred F. Bale, Sixth Georgia, was left for dead during this battle. Major Bale had been shot through the head and had fallen from his horse. His body was later recovered and escorted home by his brother, Lt. C.R. Bale, who was also wounded in this battle.[14]

Before long the other two Georgia Regiments, the Second and Third cavalries arrived on the field with their two pieces of artillery. Col. Crews dismounted the whole Georgia Brigade and put them in a line of battle just like they were infantry. Like infantry, they began to advance upon the enemy barricade. The Georgia boys pushed the Yankees from one fall-back position to another. They finally routed the Federals entirely from the field. The Yankees abandoned one gun and caisson along with their dead and wounded. The enemy escaped capture only because of darkness.

The rout could have been more complete and captured all the enemy had Col. Russell's Alabama Brigade moved up to help. Unfortunately, the courier who was sent to bring the Alabamians never reached Col. Russell. Russell watched the fight and the retreat by 500 Federals moving away from Col. Crews' Georgia Brigade and making their escape.

General Martin noted in his report to General Longstreet that he had never witnessed greater gallantry than that displayed by Col. Charles C. Crews and the officers and men of the First, Second, Third, and Sixth Georgia cavalries.[15] Gen. Martin described the action that day of the Georgia Brigade: "The enemy mounted, three times charged our dismounted men in the open field and were as often repulsed, but not until mingling in our ranks, some of his men were brought to the ground by clubbed guns."[16]

The men of the First Georgia Cavalry were proud of their victory on Christmas Eve at Dandridge, Tennessee. It was hard to realize that the next day would be Christmas Day in such a blood thirsty war. On Christmas Day their thoughts of home and family pulled at their hearts. They longed for this war to be over, and they themselves home with their families and friends. Some wondered if they would ever see their loved ones again.

General William T. Martin wanted an attack on Mossy Creek in order to drive the enemy from that area. General Martin had the men in their saddles and orders issued on December 27, 1863. Unfortunately, a lost courier, a misreading, or a misunderstanding of scrambled orders caused General John T. Morgan to move his division incorrectly, thus making a coordinated effort impossible. This caused General Martin to cancel the entire operation.[17]

Union general Samuel Sturgis received a report about a brigade of cavalry that had been near Dandridge on December 28. Gen. Sturgis sent most of his Second Division down the two roads to Dandridge. Col. Samuel Mott's First Brigade stayed near Mossy Creek. Sturgis noted that General Martin had been encamped on Panther Creek.

On December 29, General Martin moved his full corps and attacked at 9:00 A.M. using all 2,000 men and guns under his command. Martin's Corps attacked Col. Mott's Frist Brigade, Second Division, XXIII Corps, about a quarter of a mile west of Talbott's Station along both sides of the railroad from Mossy Creek to Morristown. General Morgan's Division was on the left of the railroad and were dismounted. General Frank Armstrong was on the right of the line. The field before them had been under cultivation within the past year and was open and rolling. All around the field was a high forest. General Martin complained that he could not maneuver his artillery except near the railroad.[18] The First and Sixth Georgia cavalries met the enemy about one mile east of Panther Springs and drove them toward Mossy Creek.[19]

General Armstrong's Division was to attack the enemy's front with artillery and keep their attention. General Martin took Gen. Morgan's Division around to the enemy's right flank. Mott's Yankees retreated so fast from General Armstrong's attack that Gen. Martin missed the enemy flank. As a result, both divisions charged into the enemy, and the Yankees ran in confusion from the field back to Mossy Creek. The number of enemy engaged was 4,000 men with two batteries of artillery, which was twice the number of the Rebel force.[20]

General Sturgis had given orders that if his men found no rebels in Dandridge they were to return to him. They found none and returned to join the fight midafternoon. The Yankees rallied themselves as units returned and were ready to make a stand. They waited for the Confederates who were not far behind.

Col. Charles Crews and the Georgia Brigade were now on the right side of the railroad with General Armstrong. General Martin had ordered the Georgians to move up toward the enemy position with their artillery until they got within canister range of the enemy who were in the woods. Once in range, Col. Crews and General Armstrong gave their commands the order to charge into the Yankees with their guns blazing.[21]

Col. Alfred Russell's Alabama Brigade had its right flank on the railroad line and its left was extended to the woods across the field. In Russell's front, the enemy had occupied a farmhouse, a barn, and some outhouses. Gen. Martin ordered Russell to attack their position. Col. Russell's Alabama Brigade moved forward, and as they marched, the Yankees were driven from the farm.[22]

The battle raged heavily on both sides of the tracks. Col. Crews' left was being attacked by a brigade of infantry, and Col. Russell's right was engaged by a heavy cavalry charge. The result of these simultaneous assaults caused Morgan's Division to yield some ground. As the brigade of infantry fought with Crews' left flank, another enemy infantry brigade in the Georgians' front proceeded to fix their bayonets and move out into the open field. The Georgians were compelled to give ground as this new force was attacking them.

Gen. Martin could see from his position what was about to happen to the Georgia Brigade. He ordered up the Seventh Alabama Cavalry Regiment and moved it rapidly to a cut of the railroad line. They secured a good position almost fifty yards on the flank of the advancing infantry brigade. When the Alabamians got into a battle line, they poured a galling fire into the Yankee infantry. Col. Crews saw the Federals waiver from this fire and charged his Georgia Brigade in a counterattack. The Georgia Brigade drove the Federals back through the woods killing and wounding a great number. Captain George T. Watts, Co. C, First Georgia Cavalry, was painfully wounded while leading his men in this charge.

Col. Russell's Alabama Brigade held its position while withstanding three enemy charges. After the enemy were repulsed for the third time, all firing stopped for a short while except for the artillery. During this lull, Gen. Martin scouted the enemy's position. He was looking for a weak place for him to probe. Martin found instead General Sturgis to be strongly posted in his front and beyond his flanks. He saw the Federals had three brigades of cavalry, six regiments of infantry, and three batteries of artillery all in line of battle. The enemy artillery was positioned to sweep the entire field. General Martin spotted a reserve of both cavalry and infantry who had not been in the battle across the creek. As Martin pondered the situation, he saw another brigade of cavalry coming down the road to the field from Dandridge in full view of the Confederates.

General Martin made a check of his command. He found that his artillery had exhausted its supply of ammunition except for some canister. The division commanders reported their men had an average of five rounds per man. He discovered that the Third Arkansas Cavalry had no ammunition left at all and had been ordered to the rear. Gen. Martin weighed these factors in his mind, and even though his command had pushed the enemy around that day, he knew he had to withdraw. His men had been fighting hot and steady, without any relief, for seven hours. Gen. Martin did not mind that he was outnumbered, but fresh troops were about to arrive. For him to attack this new brigade with low ammunition was impossible. Now he was faced with giving the retreat order. Doing this in broad daylight was going to be a difficult maneuver.[23]

General Martin gave the order to withdraw to his commanders and told them to protect one another while leaving the field. This would be the only safe way to disengage the enemy. The order was obeyed perfectly. Each regiment fell back in succession to an advantageous point, then held and checked the enemy while the other regiments fell back. The First and Sixth Georgia cavalries covered the retreat from Mossy Creek back to Talbott Station.[24] In General Martin's report, he was especially pleased with their conduct in leaving the field.

Martin said, "While officers and men deserve great credit for their gallantry in the advance, their conduct during this difficult and hazardous movement to the rear entitles them to the highest praise."[25]

The Yankees charged the retreating Confederates one time, and then retired themselves. At dusk, General Martin's Cavalry had been fighting for nine hours. When their ammunition was checked once more, there was less than one round per man remaining.

The next few days brought few engagements for the cavalry and then only slight skirmishes. During this time, Gen. Martin prepared his report of the actions of his corps. In closing the report, Martin told General James Longstreet a large number of his men and officers were ragged and barefooted; some had no blankets or even an overcoat. He continued to report that a large number of his cavalry horses were unshod, and the men had not been paid in six months. Yet, with all those hardships for his men and animals, plus the extreme cold, his men had successfully engaged a superior enemy. But he did not think they could do it again successfully at this time. Special recognition was given Col. Charles Crews in the report, and General Martin placed Crews' name before the War Department for promotion to Brigadier General. Col. Crews had displayed skill in leading the Georgia Brigade and deserved the rank. Gen. Martin added that General John T. Morgan also highly recommended Crews for the promotion.

Col. James J. Morrison, now in Cartersville, Georgia, was recovering from his injuries. He was not able to ride a horse or command cavalry, but he wanted to help his old brigade. He formed a camp nearby as a staging area for members of the Georgia Brigade when reporting in from furlough. Without this camp the men could be designated absent without leave, or even worse, a deserter. Bad things could happen as authorities were looking for deserters.

Col. Morrison also placed notices in local newspapers that men belonging to the Second Cavalry Brigade, which contained the 1st, 2nd, 3rd, 4th, and 6th Cavalry regiments, should report to the Wagon Camp near Cartersville, Ga. From there, he would issue orders and directions to their units. Deserters were being hung or shot during these times.[26]

The First Georgia Cavalry was always on the move and far from the supply depots even when available. Because of this, they had to supply themselves. General John T. Morgan knew the Yankees had stored corn and other needed commodities at a depot across the French Broad River south of Dandridge, Tennessee.[27]

On January 5, 1864, General Morgan took the Georgia and Alabama brigades across Hay's Ferry with their empty wagons to the Federal supply depot. Without much resistance, they hauled away several thousand bushels of corn for their horses and themselves. With their wagons loaded, Morgan's Brigade went back to camp four miles northeast of Dandridge at Beaver Dam. During this short run for supplies, General Morgan learned there was more corn, some 20,000 bushels, plus meat, flour and cattle to be had. The brigade was intent on taking what they needed and then some extra.[28]

Before long the Georgians were well fed, but some still needed shoes and warm clothing. The First Georgia's horses were getting 24 ears of corn per day by January 11, 1864. With this kind of care, the horses and men were getting in good and serviceable condition.[29] Still, the winter was cold and hard on everyone. The ground was so frozen that it was hard as a rock with sharp edges.

Back home in Georgia, Col. Morrison was rounding up troops who had been on furlough. He placed a notice in the *Rome Tri-Weekly Courier*, on January 14, 1864, as follows:

Attention Cavalry

All officers and men belonging to the Second Cavalry Brigade composed of the First, Second, Third, Fourth, and Sixth Georgia Regiments will report immediately at the Wagon Camp near Cartersville, Ga., and await further orders.

J.J. Morrison[30]

On January 15, General Samuel Sturgis moved his command toward Dandridge because their supplies were being pilfered, and he wanted it stopped. General William T. Martin's Corps was located around Dandridge at this time.[31] Gen. Martin informed Gen. James Longstreet that Sturgis was on his way. General Longstreet told Martin to occupy Sturgis' front and hold him as long as he could. Longstreet was concerned because it would be difficult for his infantry to make a forced march that far from Russellville on such short notice. There was also the problem of some of Longstreet's infantrymen having no shoes in which to march across the frozen earth.

General Longstreet rode ahead of his infantry to see just what General Martin had found the enemy doing. When Longstreet arrived at Bull's Gap, he found Martin's Corps strongly engaged with the enemy. Both sides occupied strong positions, but when Longstreet came on the scene, he told Martin to push across the field. He wanted him to occupy the enemy's position on the plateau. Longstreet could not see the Yankee infantry, and he wanted Martin's Cavalry push to flush them out. Martin's Cavalry charged into a heated battle and were able to push the Federals off the plateau. The enemy fell back to the next plateau. This location was even stronger than the first. Still, Longstreet had not seen the enemy infantry and told Martin to attack them again.

General Martin did not think this attack by his cavalry was such a good idea. General Longstreet collected a brigade of Martin's Cavalry to go with him, and he told Gen. Martin to attack Sturgis' front. Martin took Morgan's Cavalry and Armstrong's Cavalry and attacked the front in good order. Gen. Longstreet went around to the rear of Sturgis with his brigade. When Longstreet arrived in the rear, he dismounted the brigade and put them in a single line of battle and marched them forward.

As Longstreet's Cavalry marched across the open field near a farm, a chicken flew up in front of a trooper. While some were startled, the trooper swung at the chicken with his gun and knocked it to the ground. While the chicken lay there unconscious, the soldier, still in stride and in line with the rest of the command, reached down, grabbed the hen, and stuffed it in his haversack to enjoy later.

General Martin pressed hard against General Sturgis' front. Sturgis thought that since Martin was so intent on attacking his front, this would be a good time for him to get into Martin's rear. Now both were trying to get to the other's backside. Gen. Sturgis took part of his command and started for the Confederate rear by a large flanking route. As he galloped to Martin's rear, he was completely surprised to find General Longstreet's Infantry in the road between him and General Martin with a thousand muskets aimed at him. The Confederate infantry opened fire upon Sturgis, and he was barely able to escape being killed or captured.

The fighting continued until after dark. General Sturgis retired his command back to New Market and Strawberry Plains. General Longstreet could not follow Sturgis, as he was out of ammunition and the men had no shoes. After the battle, General Longstreet wrote to the quartermaster and exclaimed how the five brigades of Martin's Cavalry were all in excessive need of shoes, clothing, and blankets.

On January 26, General Morgan still had Col. Archibald Campbell's First Cavalry Brigade in front of him. General Morgan had moved his command to Sevierville a few miles south of Dandridge and across the French Broad River. In front of Morgan on the Newport Road, about three miles out from Sevierville, stood Col. Campbell's force. At this same time, General Frank Armstrong was busy attacking Col. Frank Wolford's cavalry.[32]

Gen. Sturgis was determined to attack and destroy General Morgan's force of Georgia and Alabama cavalry. Sturgis knew he had to strike before Gen. Armstrong could come to Morgan's aid. Morgan's Division had occupied a ridge along the Little Pigeon River near the Hodsden house, which was the stronghold of this position.[33]

In the early morning of January 27, a dense fog rolled in off the river. It was impossible to see through the thick mist, but the Confederate soldier, who laid cold and shivering in his trench, could hear Yankee orders being shouted and the tramping of hooves and feet across the way. Morgan's men made ready to receive the charge they knew would soon be coming. They braced themselves as the enemy cannon belched fire and sent shell whizzing through the fog. Shouts of new orders were heard as Col. Campbell's officers prepared the Yankees for the charge. Captain Eli Lilly's 18th Indiana Battery had provided the firepower for Campbell with rifled guns. Lilly was firing over the charging Yankees' heads into the Rebel fortification.

General Morgan's whole line of Georgia and Alabama cavalry was quickly attacked, and he was forced to fall his men back to a stronger position a few hundred yards to the rear. Morgan's Division dug in on the opposite bank of a creek that was crossed by McNutt's Bridge. General Sturgis sent Col. Oscar LaGrange's Second Brigade on a route which would keep them from being observed by Morgan. He was to make a flank attack on Morgan's new position.[34]

Gen. Morgan saw he was being flanked by LaGrange and fell back to a stronger embankment. As Morgan was falling back, Gen. Sturgis ordered Col. Frank Wolford and Col. Israel Garrard to picket a line between Morgan and Armstrong. This prevented Armstrong from helping Morgan. General Sturgis had now accomplished a great portion of his goal.

The battle raged all during the day, but the now-divided Morgan was not as strong as before. The Georgia and Alabama Brigades were outnumbered and were being outflanked. By 4:00 P.M., Campbell's men, who had been fighting in Morgan's front, charged the position. As the Yankees came in, Morgan's artillery poured heavy canister into their ranks. As bloodied as the Federals were, they still forced Morgan to fall back again. When Col. LaGrange arrived on Morgan's flank, he made a gash in Morgan's line with a fierce saber attack. General Morgan lost about 150 men that day in the bloody battle. As night fell, he withdrew his command from the field. Gen. Morgan continued to withdraw his men for the next few days back north of Dandridge. Morgan's Division was being pursued by General Sturgis, but no further major engagements resulted. Gen. Morgan had to rally his men and get them organized into the fighting unit they had been before their defeat at Sevierville.

Col. Charles Crews reported to General Morgan on January 31, 1864, that 730 men and 63 officers were present for duty in the Georgia Brigade. If he were counting all five regiments in the Georgia Brigade that means each regiment averaged 146 troopers. If the Fourth Georgia Cavalry was not counted, then each regiment averaged 175 troopers.

After this fight in Tennessee, Col. James Morrison learned that his old friend Senator Benjamin Harvey Hill had again submitted his name for promotion to brigadier general.

However, Col. Morrison did not think he could continue to command a division, a brigade, or even a regiment of cavalry. The injuries received during battle could threaten his life if he was injured again, and his pride was injured by less qualified people being promoted in his stead.

In February, General Longstreet had moved his headquarters to Morristown. He realized the state of his cavalry and wished to express his feelings in general about the conduct of the war. On February 6, Longstreet wrote Gen. Robert E. Lee:

> The cavalry of this command is not well organized and is deficient in general officers, in quality and numbers. There are six brigades with but two general officers, Major General W.T. Martin and Brigadier General Morgan.... I deem it my duty therefore to call your attention, to our unprepared condition, to say that if it should be remedied at as early a moment as practicable. The appointment of a proper cavalry leader and three or four brigadiers will give us a very efficient cavalry force. Our material is as good as that I have met with during the war, and with proper officers will be far superior to any cavalry that the enemy has. I have taken the pains to visit the cavalry in some of its fights, and know from personal observation that with proper officers it will be able to contend successfully against the enemy cavalry.... The supplies in this country will be exhausted in a few weeks more, and we shall be obliged to draw them from some other part of the country. The forage is already so scarce that we cannot concentrate our cavalry for active operations.[35]

General Longstreet asked for 10,000 more troops to make a stronger showing against the enemy. Unfortunately, he did not get his wish. Jefferson Davis, on February 19, sent him a telegram ordering him to send General Martin with his cavalry corps to General Joseph E. Johnston near Dalton, Georgia.

General Morgan regrouped his cavalry division and moved away from Sevierville, leaving his trains behind. The Union commanders were confused and concerned when Morgan moved away. General Morgan took his men to the Clinton area. This move was on his way to Georgia. Pvt. James Bunch deserted during this time and took oath on February 24 in Chattanooga.

A letter from Private William H. Hood was mailed home to his beloved parents on February 27 from Clinton. Pvt. Hood complained that his father had not written him since he had gone off to war. Hood reported that his brother John, who was with him, was "a good sturdy boy."[36] Hood also reported that most of his company had gone home on leave and said "there ain't but 25 men with us."[37] Private Hood thought that the command intended on going to Kentucky a few weeks earlier, but the rains and swollen streams prevented it. A sign of better times for the First Georgia Cavalry was indicated in Hood's letter. He said: "Pa we wrote to you to have us a pare of shues made. You needn't to mind it. We can draw shues from the government when we need them. We will draw money tomorrow."[38]

Two men of the First Georgia Cavalry were reported for horse stealing in Rome. Privates W. Garris and J.W. Wright were both from Company A. They were arrested by part of the 8th Texas Rangers and turned over to Col. Cameron, provost marshal of Rome, Georgia. Their punishment was pending as of February 25.[39]

It was not long before General Longstreet's request for general officers paid dividends. On February 29, Special Order No. 49, Item 32, ordered General Alfred Iverson to proceed without delay to Dalton, Georgia. When Iverson arrived, he was to report to General Joseph E. Johnston for assignment to command the Georgia Brigade of Cavalry.[40] General Iverson was still recovering from his mental breakdown after watching his command being slaughtered at Gettysburg on July 1, 1863. He became unfit to command and was sent back to Georgia.

About this same time, General John T. Morgan brought the rest of his division out of Tennessee to Dalton, Georgia, by way of Asheville, North Carolina. He was taking the Georgia Brigade there to meet their new commander. General Martin also made the trip to General Johnston's headquarters to receive his orders.[41] As Pvt. Hood had said, most of the First Georgia Cavalry were home on furlough. They deserved the break from the rigors of war and being in the saddle. Now they were coming back to rejoin the First Georgia Cavalry in Dalton along with newly recruited men and newly acquired horses gathered at the encampment near Cartersville. The First Georgia Cavalry was sent to Blue Mountain, Alabama, to forage and rest the horses.[42]

Col. James Morrison was still active for the First Georgia Cavalry while recuperating from his injuries. He was moving men through camp up to Dalton. The doctors who had examined him advised him to apply for a medical discharge. Col. Morrison protested against this advice as he knew the cause still needed him. The doctors finally prevailed and convinced Morrison that if he reinjured himself, he could be an invalid for the rest of his life. With loathing, Col. Morrison took his pen and wrote his letter of resignation March 22, 1864, to General Samuel Cooper in Richmond, Virginia.

After the letter was sent, gossip began to pass among the Georgia Brigade's officers and men that Col. Morrison had really resigned because young Alfred Iverson had been placed in command of the brigade. Truly, if Morrison did not resent Davidson's and Iverson's promotion and appointment, he should have. Both Morrison and Col. Charles C. Crews had gallantly led the Georgia Brigade, and both deserved the promotion.

Captain George T. Watts, in his letter to General Cooper on March 23, denied the rumor and declared that Col. Morrison's health was in danger. He told Cooper the old warhorse had fought hard for his country and had gallantly led his regiment. Now, he was out to pasture and freed from the anguish and suffering his men would find in the war year yet to come.

Lt. Francis Marion Coulter arrived back in Rome, March 23, after spending six months in a Federal prison at Johnson's Island. He was captured at Mill Springs, Kentucky, May 28, 1863, and exchanged March 10, 1864. He was best known in the community for building the steamer *Pennington*.[43] Captain John L. Kerr, 1st Lt. R.S. Zuber, and 2nd Lt. George Webster were seen in Floyd County with their families and friends along with the men of the Highland Rangers. All were in excellent spirits and glad to be home on furlough.[44]

On Tuesday, March 29, the following article appeared in the *Rome Tri-Weekly Courier*: "Col. J.J. Morrison of the First Georgia Cavalry, who has been acting as Brig. Gen. of the Second Brigade Georgia Cavalry for some time past, has tendered his resignation on account of ill health. We are sorry to hear this from the fact he is a brave officer and good commander, and enjoyed the confidence of the brigade. Brig. Gen. Iverson formally of the State Troops stationed here has been ordered to and assumed command of the brigade. They were to have left Cartersville Saturday. We have not heard whether they did or not. It may not be prudent to state where they are going. Orders have been issued and men sent out to arrest all absentees who are not on furlough. So look out boys."[45]

10

Defending Atlanta

During the month of April 1864, the cavalry was reorganized. General Joseph E. Johnston had divided his Army of Tennessee into three corps: General William Joseph Hardee's Corps, General John Bell Hood's Corps and the Cavalry Corps. The Cavalry Corps was commanded by Gen. Joseph Wheeler.

General Wheeler had divided his corps into three divisions: William Thompson Martin's, John Herbert Kelly's, and William Young Conn Humes'. General Martin's Division was divided into two brigades: John T. Morgan's and Alfred Iverson's. General Morgan commanded his old Alabama Brigade's regiments: First, Third, Fourth, Seventh, and Fifty-first Alabama Cavalry. Gen. Iverson commanded the Georgia Brigade: First Georgia Cavalry, Col. Samuel Davitte; Second Georgia Cavalry, Col. Charles Crews; Third Georgia Cavalry, Col. Robert Thompson; Fourth Georgia Cavalry, Col. Isaac Avery; and Sixth Georgia Cavalry, Col. John Hart.[1]

On April 15, 1864, Colonel James Morrison's resignation was accepted by the War Department, which resulted in Lt. Col. Samuel W. Davitte's promotion to colonel of the First Georgia Cavalry Regiment. Major James H. Strickland was appointed as the lieutenant colonel. Captain Napoleon J. Reynolds had been acting as quartermaster for the First Georgia Cavalry and was promoted to major in the Quartermaster Department and ordered to report to General Wheeler.[2] General Martin reported that his division on April 30 had 169 officers and 1,757 men present for duty. An aggregate of 6,477 were reported to be either present or absent from the division. The average regiment contained 175 effective men at this time for Martin's Division. After the First Georgia Cavalry returned from Alabama, they were posted around Dalton, Georgia. The troops who were on leave of absence, furlough, or recently recruited were to report to Dalton. Many young men were recruited during this time.

Lt. James H. Gilbreath, Co. I, First Georgia Cavalry, had been home on furlough and went by to visit the Othnel Polk Hargis family. Young Hargis had wanted to fight for the South and saw his chance to join the cavalry with Lt. Gilbreath. Hargis asked if he could join Gilbreath's company and found that he could. Gilbreath let Hargis know that he could muster him then and there if he wanted to join. Lt. Gilbreath sat down at a little table in the house, pulled out the necessary papers, wrote down Hargis' name, and told him where to report. After signing, Hargis was now in the cavalry.[3]

Private Hargis was to leave home in a few days to report to the regiment. He told his mother he would have to take the young horse he had raised if he was going to fight in the cavalry. Mrs. Hargis was sad to see her son leave. Her husband had died a few years back and her older sons had already gone off to war. But she knew that she could not hold this son back. She told him to take the horse as he was a good one and would serve him well. Mrs. Hargis filled his knapsack with what food she could, kissed her son good-bye, and urged him to take care of himself.[4]

During this time, the First Georgia Cavalry was getting itself reorganized and training new recruits. General Johnston was concerned about whether General Martin had brought any his artillery with him out of Tennessee.[5] He knew that the Union forces were about to attack him in force, and he needed artillery. Johnston also wanted General Leonidas Polk's command directly under him to give his army more strength.

Not all of the First Georgia Cavalry had gone home on furlough. Some of them were still engaged in patrolling the Oostanaula River from Resaca to Rome. On May 5, Gen. Johnston ordered Gen. Martin to move his headquarters from Cartersville to Rome, as the general wanted Martin to be in charge of the defense of that area.[6]

On May 6, General Martin was instructed to watch for Lt. Col. Felix Robertson, who had three batteries of artillery and was headed toward Cartersville. Martin was to stop him and place his artillery in a strategic position in his line of defense. Martin's Division needed the extra firepower.[7]

On May 7, General Martin received orders that would deeply involve his division, the Georgia and Alabama brigades, in the battle for Atlanta. He was told that the Union Army had moved an entire division that day to LaFayette, and an even larger force was marching to join it. This was the beginning of the campaign around the Confederate left. General Johnston feared General Sherman was moving these divisions to Rome and using the railroads to surround Johnston's army and cut him off from Atlanta.

General Martin received a dispatch from General Johnston's headquarters concerning this movement: "[T]he duty devolves upon you to guard the road and the line from Rome to Calhoun and as Calhoun can be much sooner reached by the enemy from LaFayette than Rome can, he wishes you to move up the river and take a position in the vicinity of Calhoun."[8] General Martin mounted his effective cavalry and moved out toward Calhoun. The men wounded or without horses were left in Rome. Gen. Martin kept a special watch on the fords along the Oostanaula River. The First Georgia Cavalry, with her sister regiments, were the eyes and ears of the Confederate Army.

By May 9, General Martin had his division in place around Calhoun. He was told to cooperate with Gen. James Cantey if the enemy began to engage them. The same day, the Union forces moved to Villianow and sent scouts down John's Creek for eight or ten miles. The enemy scouts reported to their commanders that they could not find any Rebels.[9]

Since General Polk had joined General Johnston's Army of Tennessee, Johnston had wanted General Martin's Cavalry to be placed under Polk's command. He also wanted Gen. Martin to keep the commanding officers at Rome and Resaca informed of the enemy's movement.[10] This required the First Georgia Cavalry to be out on the scout.

The Union Army continued their flanking movement around Dalton, and by May 12 they were moving toward Snake Creek Gap. Gen. Johnston continued to request information from Gen. Martin who was still near Calhoun. Gen. Johnston even asked Gen. Polk to find out all he could from Martin. Johnston wanted Polk to motivate Martin to keep his scouts alert to any step taken by the enemy and report it immediately.

One of the scouting parties from the First Georgia Cavalry consisted of Sergeant Bill

Moore, Private Bill Cavender, and eight others from the regiment. They were in the enemy's rear near Summerville, Georgia. The men and their horses were nearly exhausted from a lack of food and rest. They decided to try to find food and forage. They came to a road that led to a farmhouse far away from the main road. Sergeant Moore placed a couple of men as guards to keep the Yankees from advancing upon them undetected while they investigated the possibility of finding something to eat.[11]

As they rode up to the country home, Bill Cavender was elected to knock on the front door. The lady of the house answered, asking if she could help them. Sergeant Moore told her of their plight and asked if she could spare them any food. In a moment other ladies were at the door to see who they had as visitors. Before long, the scouts were sitting down to a very nice meal. Those dear ladies were delighted to share their food with these fine young men.

The lady of the house told them they could locate feed for their horses in the barn. When the men had finished their meal, they unsaddled their horses to feed them. This was something they rarely did, but on this fine spring day what could go wrong? They felt so far from any harm as they smoked their pipes and shared stories with the ladies. Bill Cavender went to sleep in the shade of the piazza he felt so at ease. Sergeant Moore, however, could not relax. Something just did not feel right to him. It was good he did not relax because suddenly a squadron of about fifteen Yankees burst through the trees. Somehow, they had gotten past the guards without an alarm being given.[12] Sergeant Moore jumped to his feet and yelled at Bill Cavender: "Wake up, Bill. Get your guns. Jump in between the Yankees and the ladies."[13] The enemy started firing indiscriminately at the Rebels and the ladies. Though most of the shots did hit the side of the house, they did not hit anyone, but some of the balls passed through the ladies' dresses.

Sergeant Moore had his men responding. They quickly returned the Yankee fire and killed or wounded several of them. Then they jumped on their horses bareback and charged out with pistols and sabers to capture the remainder of the enemy. A couple of Yankees managed to escape in a scamper through the woods. Sergeant Moore said a quick thanks and good-bye, gathered up the dead and wounded, and took them along with the prisoners to headquarters for questioning.[14]

General Martin told Gen. Polk that his men were across the river and as soon as they encountered the enemy, they would come and report all events to him. Gen. Martin assured Gen. Polk that as quickly as he got the desired information, he would be informed.

On May 12, Captain William M. Tumlin, Co. H, resigned wounded. Captain Tumlin's pride was probably more injured than his body. There was a need in the regiment for a major. All the line officers signed a letter requesting his promotion April 28, 1864. Their request was denied, and Captain John W. Tench was promoted to Major. Captain Tumlin's brother, Lt. Virgil M. Tumlin, commanded Company H.

General Iverson's other scouts in the Georgia Brigade reported to Gen. Martin May 13 that the Yankees were about two miles from Resaca. Col. John R. Hart's Sixth Georgia Cavalry was ordered to mount a battery and go out to attack them.

Private Hargis was arriving about this time in Calhoun to join the First Georgia Cavalry. Hargis reported that he could hear the booming of the cannon from Calhoun as he pressed toward Resaca. Hargis found the First Georgia Cavalry camped below Resaca on the east side of the Oostanaula River. The men of Company I were glad to see young Hargis as most of them were from around where he lived. He found Mathew McDonald and they became mess mates and fought side by side for the rest of the war. Although it was unknown to Hargis, he was about to be a participant for the next year in the fight of his life.

Gen. Martin's Division patrolled the Oostanaula River and scouted John's Valley and on south to Rome.[15] On the night of May 13, General Johnston ordered a party of First Georgia Cavalry to scout for the enemy west of Resaca. The Georgia scouts were to locate the enemy's pickets and report back. Private J.A. Wynn, Company A, First Georgia Cavalry, was in this small party of eight men led by a lieutenant. These First Georgia Cavalry scouts were to go along the Sugar Valley Road until they found the enemy, at which point they were to charge into them and see which way they would retreat. General Johnston wanted to know where Sherman's army was located and in what direction they were moving.[16]

The First Georgia Cavalry platoon of men executed their orders without a man being hurt. They came back to General Johnston's headquarters where the lieutenant reported General Sherman was moving south toward Rome on the west side of the Oostanaula River. General Johnston determined he and Sherman would have a fight the next day.[17]

Early in the morning of May 14, General Johnston sent General Wheeler out to engage the enemy. Gen. Wheeler took General Kelly's Division north and around to the enemy's rear which was across the Conasauga River. The Federals were busy that morning laying out pontoons across the Oostanaula River at Tanner's Ferry. The First Georgia Cavalry was at the river with General John T. Morgan trying to stop them from crossing. The Federals had such a large force that General Morgan needed more men to be effective. General John K. Jackson, who had two infantry regiments, was thrown into the battle. By that afternoon General Morgan's Brigade was forced back as the enemy crossed the river. By nightfall a full division of Federals had crossed the river, but had not yet pressed any further. The Federals camped by the river for the night.[18]

On the morning of May 15, Pvt. Hargis was trying to get his bearings. In doing so, he climbed a hill near the river to see if he could discover anything. While he was up there, he saw a Federal division behind strong breastworks on the west side of the river. The Federals at this location had not crossed the river as the others had the day before. Hargis' eye caught sight of the Sixth Georgia Cavalry, being led by Col. John Hart, in a charge across the river flats toward the breastworks on the east side of the river. As the Sixth Georgia came across the field, Yankees rose up from behind their works and poured lead into the Georgia Regiment.[19]

The distance was far enough that the sounds of gunfire and the sight of the Georgia Regiment falling to the ground made the young private think the entire regiment had been killed. He could not believe his eyes! Suddenly, the Sixth Georgia Cavalry jumped to their feet and ran into the breastworks. The Georgians poured a deadly fire back into the Yankees. With this disaster upon them, the Yankees retreated rapidly from their side of the river. Col. Hart jumped to the top of their breastworks waving his hat and taunting the Yankees as they ran to come back and fight.[20]

The First Georgia Cavalry was near Lay's Ferry that day and helped repel the enemy from the river. General Sherman became disgusted with General Israel Garrard because he failed to cut the rebel railroad which Sherman felt was within his reach. The only thing preventing Garrard from being successful was General Martin's Division of Cavalry.[21]

On May 16, General Martin reported to General Johnston that his scouts had found a large number of enemy infantry, artillery and cavalry moving toward Tanner's and Dobbin's ferries. Martin concluded their intent was to cut General Johnston's line of retreat. General Martin's Cavalry lay in their path and would be the men to foil the Union effort. General Wheeler sent Brig. Gen. John William's Cavalry Brigade over to help Martin's Division resist the enemy.[22]

The tactic for the day was for Johnston to retreat from one position to another. The Confederates would hold long enough to make the Federals deploy their lines of battle. This strategy slowed the Federals' progress and in continuing those tactics the First Georgia Cavalry fell back May 16 to Calhoun. In the town of Calhoun, the Georgians threw up a heavy line of battle. On the south side of town a lighter line was formed. At this time, Bud Jenkins, a private in Company G, First Georgia Cavalry, was detailed to go up on the skirmish line. His brother, Jim, jumped up and volunteered to take his place. Private Hargis described him as "a braver soldier never fired a gun than Jim Jenkins."[23] After a while, the line was ordered in and the retreat continued.

The First Georgia Cavalry trotted down the road toward Adairsville and passed an infantry regiment also falling back. Private Hargis in describing the retreat remarked, "The infantry didn't care much for the cavalry."[24] As Hargis passed, a certain infantryman sweating and trudging down the dusty road with his knapsack on his back looked up and said, "You humped back cavalry, you think you are very fine. Show me some of your sort and I will show you some of mine."[25]

By three o'clock in the afternoon of May 17, General Wheeler pulled his entire cavalry back to the infantry line two miles south of Adairsville. At this time General Benjamin Cheatham's Infantry Division was in front of Adairsville. Wheeler put Gen. Martin's Cavalry Division, the Georgia and Alabama brigades, in line with Cheatham's Infantry. Martin sent his skirmishers out in front of that position.[26]

The fighting continued for the rest of the afternoon in the form of a heavy artillery duel. Some of the men thought the sun would never go down, as they were hoping the cannon would cease firing then. Finally, when dark came, the guns stopped and Gen. Wheeler withdrew his cavalry back to Adairsville to feed the men and horses.

Early in the morning of May 18, Gen. Wheeler drew up his cavalry in line about a mile south of Adairsville. They met the enemy advancing toward them with their skirmishers out in front. Wheeler's men fought until the Federals deployed into full lines of battle. With this development, the Confederates retreated to another position. Gen. Iverson's Georgia Brigade and Gen. Humes' Division were put on the Cassville-Adairsville Road.

In the afternoon at about three o'clock, the Federal skirmishers advanced on the position held by General Martin's Division. The Georgia Brigade, who was on line at the time, handsomely drove them back. That evening Wheeler withdrew his cavalry to the rear to feed the horses and men. He did leave a strong skirmish line in a commanding position to protect the rear. During the day Privates Jesse G. Casey, Co. F; James P. Cooper, Co. I; James W. Echols, Co. H; and William H. Johnson, Co. G, had been captured by Wilder's Cavalry about 9 miles east of Rome at Bass Ferry on the Etowah River.

In the morning of May 19 General Wheeler had his cavalry in line about a mile in front of the infantry near Cassville. The Federal skirmishers appeared from the woods on their front. This time the enemy lines had more men than usual. General Wheeler knew something must be done quickly. He ordered his field guns to open up on the Yankees in rapid fire. This soon drove the Federals back into the woods.

The Federals saw Wheeler's Cavalry was in a strong defensive line; therefore they began to flank him. Again, Wheeler had to withdraw. General Wheeler sent a staff officer to Gen. Martin on the Adairsville Road with orders for him to fall back to the other side of Cassville. Each time Wheeler withdrew, he had his men build temporary breastworks at their new position.[27] The men did this so many times that Hargis said he had carried so many fence rails, he never wanted to see another one.[28]

On May 20, 1864, General Joseph Wheeler received orders for his next mission. The Cavalry Corps was to guard all the roads to the right of the railroad coming from Cartersville. Wheeler sent his cavalry to form lines from Kingston down to the Etowah River and on across the river.[29] During the day the Union Army made no significant attack on the cavalry except on its left. General Sherman was continuing his flank of the Confederate Army. Wheeler's Cavalry was able to hold the line and blocked the Union advance in their sector of the battle. At about five o'clock in the afternoon, Wheeler brought in his cavalry from below the Etowah River and burned the bridge.

Wheeler's Cavalry Corps went into camp near Kingston and rested there for the next couple of days. The corps had been engaged in a heavy battle, and the rest was much appreciated. The camp was not like home. Bullets still whizzed around them like angry hornets and they had to build breastworks, but at least they were out of their saddles.

As the men rested, General Wheeler was making plans for his cavalry to do what it did best, get into the enemy's rear and wreak havoc on him. On the night of May 23, Wheeler selected one hundred men to scout with him to discover the enemy position, strength, and direction of movement. The scouting party moved carefully and remained undetected through the night and early morning. When Wheeler had gathered all the desired information, they returned to the cavalry camp. Wheeler formulated their next move as the men continued their rest by the banks of the Etowah River.

During this lull Private O.P. Hargis went down to the McDonald place. They had been acquaintances of his before the war. When Hargis arrived at the farm, he found Mrs. McDonald standing in the doorway of the smokehouse. She was busy taking down some fine hickory-smoke cured hams and cutting them into sizable slices for the soldiers around the place. When Private Hargis got within eyesight, she recognized him and was so happy to see a familiar face again. They talked about the war and her two sons who were also in the same company as Hargis. After their brief visit, Mrs. McDonald cut four pounds of meat and gave it to Hargis. He reported: "I was glad to get it for I was hungry."[30] After his meal of ham, Hargis went back to the First Georgia Cavalry breastworks.

About the time Hargis got back to the camp, his company was ordered by Gen. Wheeler to go to the Cassville area and drive out all the surplus cattle from there to Cartersville. This was to keep them out of reach of the Federals and to feed the Confederate Army.

At midnight May 24, Gen. Wheeler took a quarter of his command, as directed by Gen. Johnston, on a mission to go to the enemy's rear near Cassville and attack him vigorously. General Johnston wanted to know from the attack if the Union would stand and fight, or run away. Gen. Wheeler ordered Col. Samuel Davitte's First Georgia Cavalry to attack the enemy located at Cass Station. Col. Davitte's mission was to attract the enemy's attention away from Wheeler and the movements of the main body of cavalry corps. While on the way to Cassville, Wheeler saw a large wagon train near Cass Station where the First Georgia Cavalry was to make their diversion.[31]

The First Georgia Cavalry attacked the enemy's advance and drove them back for two and a half miles. The First Georgia Cavalry captured one prisoner, Private Samuel Raney, and two horses. During this attack, "the Yankee drummers beat the long roll,"[32] according to Major Otis Messick, Eleventh Texas Cavalry. Major Messick was sent by Wheeler with the First Georgia. He reported to Wheeler that they had been fighting the 14th Kentucky Cavalry, which was commanded by General Stoneman (Col. Henry C. Lilly). In his message to Wheeler, Messick said, "The First Georgia drove the enemy back on their reserves which were very strong."[33] The prisoner they captured (Private Raney) said his command contained 3,000 cavalry and 15,000 infantry, and that they were all around Cass Station.

The First Georgia Cavalry was forced to fall back when they encountered the Yankee reserve. The Georgians were still involved in heavy skirmishing while they withdrew. Col. Davitte's intent was to rejoin Wheeler at Cassville by taking the Tennessee Road.[34]

Meanwhile, Gen. Wheeler made plans to attack the tremendous wagon train he had discovered. He decided it best not to risk his entire command in the engagement. He attacked with Gen. Kelly's Confederate Cavalry Division, and one regiment to guard his right flank on the Kingston Road. Wheeler led Kelly's Cavalry on a charge into the wagons in the grandest of style. Their guns were blazing and their sabers drawn to cut down the fast retreating enemy. The cavalrymen came in yelling and quickly drove away the Yankee guards and drivers from the wagons. General Wheeler deemed the attack a "complete success."[35] The cavalry was able to capture eighty wagons and brought them away to safety. They set fire to as many wagons because they could not drive all of them to safety.

The Federals were now alert to Wheeler's intrusion and began to press against General Allen's Alabama Brigade. Allen's command was understrength because his men were being used for various details. Gen. Wheeler was delighted he had frightened the Yankees with his bold stroke. He was pleased that the Federals were confused and had burned their remaining wagons and commissary stores themselves. They did this in fear the Rebels might capture them later, a reverse scorched earth action.

General Wheeler could see the Yankee cavalry converging on him in the distance and decided to make a show against them. He gathered the Eighth Texas Cavalry, Major Samuel Christian, and the Second Tennessee Cavalry, Captain John Kuhn, and ordered them to go meet the enemy at a fast trot. When they reached a designated place, if the Yankees showed the slightest desire to wavier, they were to charge them at full speed. Wheeler was pleased at how well Christian and Kuhn carried out his instructions. General Wheeler said the following in his report: "The enemy came up in fine style, and charged with great ferocity. They were met, however, as directed and driven back in utter confusion."[36] The remainder of the Rebel Cavalry joined in the chase killing and wounding a large number of the enemy. Over 100 prisoners were taken during this engagement along with the eighty wagons.

Wheeler moved his cavalry quickly back with the infantry, who were now at Acworth. May 26, Wheeler's Cavalry found itself again dismounted and in line with the main army.[37] They were placed on the right of General Johnston's army on the Acworth-Dallas Road near New Hope Church. The fighting continued as the Union Army kept the pressure coming. After each advance, however, the Yankees would fall back with fewer men than they came with.

The Union pressure continued on the next day as the Yankees made several attacks on the Confederate pickets along the Burnt Hickory Road. General Wheeler moved Gen. Martin's Division of Alabama and Georgia Cavalry brigades to the Burnt Hickory Road to defend against the enemy. Wheeler placed Gen. Kelly's Division on Gen. Martin's right with a space of about two miles inbetween. Wheeler was keeping Humes' Division in reserve. Wheeler had filled the space between the two divisions with Humes' skirmishers. Humes had orders to strike any point where the enemy attacked with the balance of his division.

Before long the Union discovered this weakness in the line. At about 3:00 P.M., the Union cavalry was moving up Pumpkin Vine Creek by the widow Pickett's house. The Union cavalry attacked Humes' skirmishers and was driving them back. General Wheeler saw his lines being threatened and galloped off to the point of attack with a squadron of Humes' Cavalry to reinforce the picket line. When Wheeler got to Pumpkin Vine Creek, he discovered the force attacking to be much larger than he had originally thought. He sent word back to General Humes to dismount one brigade of his cavalry and bring it to the place being attacked. Humes was to move the other brigade to a position between them and Gen. Martin's left. All these movements were made under very difficult battlefield conditions.[38]

While General Humes was moving his brigade into line, General Martin's whole front of Georgia and Alabama cavalry was being attacked. Before Kelly's old entrenchment was filled by General Hiram Grandbury's dismounted Texas Cavalry Brigade, the gap was discovered and attacked by the enemy moving in column up a ravine.

Wheeler ordered a regiment from Humes' Division to counterattack the column, and they quickly obeyed. Humes saw his regiment in distress with their attackers and sent another regiment to their aid. All during these movements, General William Hazen's Second Infantry Brigade of Brigadier General Thomas J. Wood's Third Infantry Division charged the cavalry lines, but they were as often driven off by countercharges. The Georgia and Alabama brigades held their lines all during these confused and perilous moments.

General Wheeler, in writing his report of that day, stated his command captured 32 prisoners and one commissioned officer. The exact number of killed and wounded was unknown. Wheeler noted in the report: "I had 822 men engaged, extending over ground to such length as to enable me to form little more than a line of skirmishers. The enemy we fought proved to be Wood's Division of Howard's Corps. General Howard having moved to that position to turn our right flank. We successfully thwarted this movement, holding this large force of the enemy in check until we were relieved by a division of our infantry to whom we gave up our temporary breastworks and then moved to the right to guard their right flank."[39]

On May 31, the Yankees were on the Marietta Road. Wheeler withdrew a portion of his ranks from the line to attack them and captured 70 during the day. The month of May was spent skirmishing with the enemy all up and down the cavalry lines. The report from Martin's Division for the period of May 6 through May 31 showed 14 killed, 68 wounded, 25 captured, and 43 missing.

The press of the Union Army became heavier than ever before in June 1864. The Army of Tennessee slowly fell back, fighting harder each day. General Joseph E. Johnston's Army would build a fortified position and hold until flanked. They would repeat this process hoping to slow the Union Army. The Confederates desperately wanted to keep General Sherman away from Atlanta. The month of June saw General Johnston's Army fall back to Kennesaw Mountain. General William T. Martin's Cavalry Division guarded the right flank of the army all along the Marietta-Canton Road to the McAfee farm, about eight miles north of Marietta.

The First Georgia Cavalry was camped on the Hartwell Jones farm near the Big Shanty and Marietta-Canton roads intersection. Noonday Creek ran north through this area to the Etowah River. The creek was called "the dead line" by the Confederates and "woe to the Reb or Yank who crossed the line,"[40] according to Private J.A. Wynn of the First Georgia Cavalry.

W.C. Dodson described this period:

> Wheeler was confronted all about his works on June 1st by the 14th and 23rd Corps. The Yankees attacked as usual but the heavy rains slowed them down. They were caught in impassable ground and repulsed. Wheeler's men did capture 40 prisoners. The same result on June 2nd with 37 captured.
>
> On June 3rd, Wheeler's Cavalry was still dismounted in breastworks and were attacked by infantry and cavalry under Gen. Schofield. As the day was closing, Wheeler was attacked again from two points by both infantry and cavalry but they were able to repulse the attackers with artillery and small arms and were able to capture 50 prisoners.
>
> June 4th, the Army changed positions again to near Davis Crossroad and Wheeler's Cavalry covered the withdrawal constantly engaged with the enemy and capturing 43 prisoners.
>
> Jun 5th, General Garrard's Division of Federal Cavalry moved toward Big Shanty Road. Wheeler's Cavalry skirmished, charged, and drove the enemy beyond Big Shanty and captured 45 prisoners.
>
> The next few days were spent in constant battle, skirmish and being attacked but each time they would retire leaving their dead and wounded.
>
> On June 9th, Yankees brought two brigades of infantry, three brigades of cavalry and one battery of artillery. They formed up and charged the whole front of Wheeler's command and sent reeling and again they charged the line but after a storm of lead and iron they retired at dark again leaving dead and wounded on the field.
>
> June 10th, more attacks and more repulsion, but Sherman was moving toward the railroad and extended his left beyond Wheeler's right. Wheeler had to move and took a position near Bell's Ferry and Canton Road.[41]

On June 11, Col. Robert Minty's First Cavalry Brigade of Brigadier General Kenner Garrard's Second Cavalry Division had been pressing south to the crossroads that General Martin's Cavalry Division occupied. General Garrard was concerned about his position and asked Major General James Birdseye McPherson if he should "hold both the Alabama and Big Shanty roads or shall I move down the Marietta Road and hold the Big Shanty Road?"[42] Garrard was concerned by the fact that the roads were some two miles apart and if he were attacked by a large enough force he could not hold both positions. Garrard reminded McPherson that the Big Shanty guarded his left flank, and if he lost that position, the Rebels would be between them.[43]

On June 11, the First Georgia Cavalry was ordered out on a scout to locate the enemy. They found them at Dr. McAfee's house about two miles from the brigade's camp. That morning Col. Minty's Cavalry crossed Noonday Creek. Minty met Col. Davitte's First Georgia Cavalry scouts and drove them for half a mile. At that point they met the remainder of the First Georgia Cavalry, and that blunted their high spirits.[44]

Col. Minty dismounted his Seventh Pennsylvania Cavalry to skirmish heavily with the First Georgia Cavalry. The First Georgia Cavalry was forced to fall back to the Noonday post office. They dismounted and sent their horses to the rear. The First Georgia was formed on both sides of the road behind rail breastworks on the crest of a hill. In front of them was a large wheat field which gave a clear field of fire. The Third and Sixth Georgia cavalries came up on the First Georgia's right in an oak thicket.

Col. Minty pushed Captain Shaffer's Seventh Pennsylvania forward through the woods on the right. Major James Andress was on the left, and Captain Talton's Fourth Michigan Cavalry was ordered to watch the road from Roswell Factory. Col. Minty sent Major Frank Mix with a dismounted battalion of the Seventh Pennsylvania out on the left. The order to advance was given and the Yankee cavalry made progress on the left, but all were eventually thrown back. Private J.A. Wynn described the action: "What the First Georgia did for the Yanks was a plenty. They could not stand it and fell back."[45] The Third and Sixth Georgia charged out at the Yankees and drove them back to their breastworks.

The men of the First Georgia Cavalry were pleased with themselves for throwing back the Yankees, but that moment of relief was short. Before long Private Asa West, a mounted vidette for the First Georgia Cavalry, came riding hard up to General Martin. Gen. Martin was sitting astride his horse talking with his staff. Private Asa West saluted the general and said, "General, the Yankees are in the woods on our right, trying to flank us."[46]

General Martin had just seen the Yankees run from the field and acted toward West as if he did not believe him. Private West was "stung to the quick at the remarks of our General."[47] In Wynn's account of the encounter, he indicated that Private West was a very brave and reliable man. West flashed back at General Martin: "General, by God, you go or send a man with me and I'll show you whether I'm frightened or not."[48]

General Martin was startled by the sharp response of Private West and thought it best to send someone to see what this private had found. General Martin summoned Captain John Tench, now acting as adjunct for the First Georgia Cavalry, to go with West. Captain Tench and West were not gone very long into the woods where West had indicated the enemy was now located. The sounds of guns firing let General Martin know Private West had been truthful.[49]

Col. Minty and his cavalry were making another effort to take the breastworks held by the Georgians. Minty attacked the Sixth Georgia Cavalry who let out a loud Rebel yell as they drove the Yankees again. As Minty retreated, he took his men to within range of the First Georgia Cavalry's guns who administered "them a double dose of medicine that the Sixth Georgia gave."[50] The Yankees continued to fall back across Noonday Creek to the McAfee place.

The Georgia boys thought or hoped the Yankees had had enough for one day, but they were wrong. At noon that day, a courier came galloping up to General Martin with a message. Gen. Martin read the message and excitedly looked up to give orders for the Georgia Brigade to double time to Hartwell Jones' farm. Jones' farm was a mile and a quarter away, and the First Georgia Cavalry was on foot. Unknown to the men in the ranks, the enemy was about to break through to their horses which had been in the rear.

The Fourth Alabama had been guarding a bridge over Noonday Creek on the Big Shanty Road. The Georgia regiments had left their horses there to be guarded by the Alabama Regiment. Since Col. Minty and his cavalry had been beaten by the Georgians, he regrouped his cavalry and decided to attack the smaller force guarding the horses.[51]

Minty's Cavalry came charging into the Fourth Alabama who had to hold their position to protect the bridge and horses. The Alabamians were making a stubborn fight, but they were simply outnumbered. The First Georgia Regiment was running and in the lead to help save the Fourth Alabama and the Georgia horses. The Sixth Georgia Regiment, in the rear, halted on the north side of the grove of woods and then charged in on the right. The First Georgia Regiment went through the grove of trees and through an orchard to the left of the

Alabama Regiment. When the columns were in the proper line, Col. Sam Davitte ordered: "Right flank! Charge!!"[52] Private Wynn said, "We went at them like fighting fire."[53] The Yanks and Rebs were firing so close to one another they could see the kind of weapons the enemy was using. Private Wynn said, "Those mounted were using Navy Pistols and those dismounted had Spencer Seven Shooting rifles."[54] Again the Yankees turned and ran as the Georgia boys gave them hot fire, sharp edges, and Rebel yells.

Col. Minty, who was not to be denied, returned again and finally took the bridge before day's end. He soon lost it, however, when General Garrard ordered Minty to fall back on the Third Brigade west of Noonday Creek.

The First Georgia Cavalry spent the next week fighting and skirmishing daily with the enemy. By June 17, Union intelligence had learned that General Wheeler was making plans for a raid on their railroad somewhere between Dalton and Cleveland, Tennessee. Wheeler had cleared his intentions with General Hardee making sure his cavalry horses were ready for the trip. He sent some scouts to Jasper, Georgia, to learn what they could. Some scouts were hired on the railroad to learn schedules and procedures being used. Other scouts were to find out the number of enemy troops and their direction of movement.

The First Georgia Cavalry continued light skirmishing with the enemy through June 19. That changed when on June 20, General Wheeler's Cavalry, with General Allen's Alabama Cavalry, General Iverson's Georgia Cavalry, Colonel Anderson's Confederate Cavalry, Colonel Hannon's Cavalry, General Williams' Kentucky Cavalry and Colonel Dibrell's Tennessee Cavalry, attacked Col. Robert Minty. They sent Minty back across Noonday Creek. Wheeler caught Col. Minty with his cavalry on the east side of Noonday and ordered Williams', Hannon's and Anderson's brigades to attack the Seventh Pennsylvania and the Fourth Michigan Cavalry. A section of the Chicago Board of Trade Battery under First Lieutenant Trumbull D. Griffin was also attacked. The cavalries fought one another with sabers, hand-to-hand, up close and personal, in a see-saw battle.

Col. Minty deployed Col. Abram Miller's Third Cavalry Brigade (mounted infantry) around the hills near Noonday Creek Bridge. General Allen's Alabama Brigade and General Iverson's Georgia Brigade attacked Minty on his right flank and forced him to fall back on Col. Miller at the bridge. As Col. Minty and his command fell back, Wheeler had all his cavalry dismount and charge into Minty's new position.

Col. Minty had his artillery in place, and the Chicago Board of Trade began to shred the line of Confederates on foot and force them back. Minty knew they would soon return or flank him. He decided it would be best to retreat across the bridge back to his own lines. He acknowledged that he took a heavy loss in this battle, but it should have been more considering the Confederate force he faced. Minty had around 65 men killed. Wheeler captured 120 prisoners, 150 horses, two stands of colors, and lost 15 men killed and 50 wounded.

On June 21, the First Georgia Cavalry resumed its place on the right flank of General Johnston's Army. The word began to spread about the previous day's action against Col. Minty. A lot of people felt Wheeler should have crushed the Yankee cavalry into Noonday Creek. Wheeler felt that his cavalry had performed well by pushing Minty back to his previous position away from the bridge at Noonday Creek.

General Hood's ensuing attack upon the Federals made them more cautious in subsequent attacks. Still, Wheeler's Cavalry was busy skirmishing from dawn until dark.

On June 23, Wheeler's Cavalry attacked the Federals on Bell's Ferry Road. The Rebels carried the first lines of Federal defense. However, the enemy was superior in numbers to Wheeler and began to flank the Confederate attack. This forced Wheeler's men to fall back. The purpose of this attack was to cover General Gideon Pillow's activity. General Pillow was trying to gain the enemy's rear. After the attack, the First Georgia Cavalry assumed its position behind its breastworks and continued its daily skirmishing. Each day was much the same dealing in death.

On June 27, the Federals poured a heavy artillery barrage into General Wheeler's headquarters. That morning's attack was so close to Wheeler that some of his men were killed near his tent by the exploding shells. After the artillery barrage, there came a charge of yelling Yankees. They were hard to convince they should go back to their lines. When the Federals finally withdrew, they left dead men scattered all along the Rebel front. As the sun rose on the last day of June 1864, the enemy opened fire unceasingly upon the Confederates. One Rebel closed a letter home saying he had to stop writing because the Yankees might get careless with their shooting and hit his bottle of ink.

On June 30, Captain George T. Watts and Company C acted as escort for General John Hood around Marietta, Georgia. This was an honor for these men, as they had displayed recent excellent valor.

11

Atlanta

General Joseph E. Johnston's Army of Tennessee was again about to be reshuffled. June 1864 ended with his army in three corps: Gen. Hardee's Corps, Gen. Hood's Corps, and the Cavalry Corps. The cavalry was still commanded by General Joseph Wheeler. Wheeler divided his cavalry into three divisions: General William T. Martin's, General John H. Kelly's, and General William Y.C. Humes'. General Martin's Division was divided into two brigades; General William W. Allen's Alabama Brigade and General Alfred Iverson's Georgia Brigade. The Alabama Brigade included the First, Fourth, Seventh, and Fifty-first Alabama Cavalry regiments and the Twelfth Alabama Battalion of Cavalry.[1] The Georgia Brigade contained First Georgia Cavalry, Col. Samuel Davitte; Second Georgia Cavalry, Col. James Mayo; Third Georgia Cavalry, Col. Robert Thompson; Fourth Georgia Cavalry, Major Augustus R. Stewart; and Sixth Georgia Cavalry, Col. John Hart.[2]

At this time Captain George T. Watts, Co. C, First Georgia Cavalry, was detached to Major General Alexander P. Stewart as his escort. This was an honor for Company C to serve in this capacity. Company C was being recognized for its outstanding valor while recently fighting the Yankees.[3]

On July 1, General Iverson was ordered to keep an eye on the movements of the Union forces he opposed. Lt. Bice returned from his scout to report that General Kenner Garrard had moved his headquarters on Tuesday to Robert McAfee's house.[4] The men of the First Georgia Cavalry were still engaged in skirmishing every day just as they had been in previous days from behind their breastworks.

By July 2, General Johnston had already formulated his plans to fall back to Smyrna. At 1:30 P.M. he sent out a circular to his officers about the move. He ordered the corps commanders to leave enough men to act as a rear guard while the other infantrymen withdrew. The rear guard was to be removed by 1 A.M. the following morning. Wheeler's Cavalry Corps was to be the screen for the last movement from General Hood's left to General William W. Loring's right.[5]

By 4 P.M. July 2, the Federals, sensing a retreat, began an unbelievably ferocious artillery bombardment followed by an infantry attack.[6] The First Georgia Cavalry knew they had to hold their ground to keep the infantry safe. The Yanks were surprised by the torrid fire returned by the cavalry as they advanced on the supposed vacated position. The enemies fought at intervals that afternoon, but each advance was thrown back. That night found no peace for the Confederate cavalry as the artillery shells fell freely all around their lines. The entire infantry was now gone, and the men knew they would have to hold the lines alone.

The next morning, Sherman's men would not be denied. They knew Johnston's Infantry was gone, and they pushed harder toward Atlanta. Wheeler's Cavalry was engaged with the enemy near Marietta. They were trying to slow Sherman's advance. The cavalry fought for two hours dismounted but still the load of the Federals was too heavy. By that night, Wheeler was back in line with the infantry at Smyrna.[7]

July 4 was much the same as the days before; the cavalry was in line with the infantry. General Johnston's headquarters was located at Smyrna Church. Johnston sent a message that he wanted to know who opposed Wheeler. Upon learning that information, he was forced to withdraw, falling back to the Chattahoochee River. Again, Wheeler's Cavalry was the screen for the infantry as they withdrew.[8]

July 5 became one of the most difficult days for the First Georgia Cavalry in a line of difficult days. The Federals had Johnston in retreat. The First Georgia Cavalry, along with Wheeler's Cavalry Corps, was acting as a screen. The Federals had the smell of blood in their nostrils and felt their quarry was treed on the banks of the Chattahoochee River. The Union poured more artillery and men into their effort to end the war. The Fourth Army Corps under General Oliver O. Howard pressed Wheeler and his men hard, but the cavalry held on by fierce fighting. The Rebels fought like cornered animals.[9] They would not yield and fought harder than ever. Pvt. W. Phipps, Co. B, was reported deserted.

On July 9, Wheeler was informed by General Johnston that the army would be moved to the south side of the Chattahoochee River that night and would re-form about three miles south of the river. At 7:15 P.M., Johnston was still crossing the Chattahoochee and held ground from Green's Ferry to Howell's Ferry. He wanted Wheeler to attach to his left line and keep watch up the river as far as practical. Wheeler was to keep the artillery if he needed it, but if not, send it back to the main line.[10]

Finally, seeing the infantry across the river, Wheeler had to get his own men across. They would cross near Pace's Ferry. The order was passed down to prepare to fight on foot. Every fourth man was given the horses and sent across the Chattahoochee. Wheeler sent the others to build barricades and hold General Howard while the wagons crossed the river. Howard attacked with great furry again and again, but he was checked each time.

When the wagon trains and horses were safely across the river, Wheeler ordered the dismounted cavalry to charge into the enemy's advance. The Yankees were caught so completely off guard by this brash attack from their quarry that they retreated. Before the Federals could recover from the attack, Wheeler sent his men scurrying across the pontoon bridge.

General Wheeler was the last to cross the river. He rode the pontoons across as the end was cut from the north bank and allowed to swing south. As Wheeler ran onto the south bank, the Yankees arrived on the north bank, and a heavy exchange of fire by both armies began. This exchange continued for the next few days as Sherman's army moved up to the river.[11] During certain moments or lulls in the battle, both sides would fish in the Chattahoochee River and some even swam together. The Yanks during the evenings had their band play favorite songs which both sides enjoyed. Despite these pleasant moments, the war continued.[12]

Pvt. William Tinney in a letter to his mother tried to explain what was happening. "[W]e fell back on this side of the river and the Yanks on the other bank a facing us. They say our infantry has not crop yet and don't intend to crop without they whip the fight. If we eber fight. The most the soldiers ... the men if anything, I want the fight to come off, it tis coming. I want things decided. I think this fight will decide the war. I don't think it is the plan to file us. I think tho they intend to flank us to death before we can get a fight out of them. This country behind us they cannot [find a] thing to live on. We have destroyed the wheat crops and the corn and I don't know what they will do." Tinney warned his mother: "You must look out for yourself. You must hide out and save all you can."[13]

Sherman sent the Army of the Cumberland to begin crossing at Isham's Ford on July 8, and by the next day they had advanced 800 yards. Wheeler's Cavalry was covering the northeast front of Johnston's Army. Their line stretched twenty miles and was engaged in battle the entire length of their line on July 10. The First Georgia Cavalry was being commanded by Lt. Col. James H. Strickland during this time.

Wheeler thought this 20-mile attack was a ploy by Sherman to hide the true point at which the main attack would come. Each day that followed, the Army of the Cumberland inched forward and crossed more troops over the river. The Sixteenth Corps crossed at Roswell July 14 and began their advance the next day.

The First Georgia Cavalry had spread east toward Decatur. General Iverson had assumed command of General Martin's Division, and he established his headquarters a quarter mile outside the breastworks on the Old Decatur Road. Unknown to the First Georgia Cavalry, intrigue within its own army was at work. President Jefferson Davis, General Braxton Bragg, and General John Bell Hood were conspiring to remove General Joseph E. Johnston.

On July 17, Sherman advanced his army, forcing Johnston back behind Peachtree Creek. Wheeler's headquarters was now at Buckhead. Even Sherman himself could not deliver the blow to the Confederacy that Jefferson Davis was about to strike. Sherman later said: "This is just what we wanted, viz., to fight in open ground, on anything like equal terms, instead of being forced to run up against prepared entrenchments."[14]

The First Georgia Cavalry had been opposing General Grenville Mellen Dodge's XVI Army Corps that day east of Atlanta near Peachtree Creek. During the battle amid the roar of cannon and bursting of shells, Sergeant Bill Moore, Co. G, was killed. Four of his comrades, William Overby, Tom Medley, Joe Wilson and L.M. Lowry, carried his body to Howell's Mill and constructed a crude coffin of roughhewn planks. They buried his body in a small churchyard on Howell Mill Road about a mile and a half from where he received his mortal wound.[15]

On that day, President Davis had General Cooper send General Joseph E. Johnston the following message: "Lt. General J.B. Hood has been commissioned to the temporary rank of General under the late law of congress. I am directed by the Secretary of War to inform you that as you have failed to arrest the advance of the enemy to the vicinity of Atlanta, far in the interior of Georgia and express no confidence that you can defeat or repel him you are hereby relieved from the command of the Army and Department of Tennessee which you will immediately turn over to General Hood."[16]

General Johnston was at his headquarters at the Nelson House when he received the message. That night Gen. Johnston wrote General Order Number 4, which stated: "In obedience to orders of the War Department, I turn over to General Hood the Command of the Army and the Department of Tennessee. I cannot leave this noble army without expressing my admiration of the high military qualities it had displayed…. The enemy has never attacked but to be repulsed and severely punished. You, soldiers have never argued but from your courage, and never counted your foes."[17] Grown men cried as they heard this order being read to them the next day. Johnston's Army loved him, and some generals offered to follow him anyway.

When General Hood replaced General Johnston on July 18, Wheeler's Cavalry Corps consisted of two divisions; Gen. John H. Kelly's Division and Gen. Alfred Iverson's Division. General John William's Cavalry Brigade was also under Wheeler's command. Unfortunately for Wheeler, General Kelly's entire command was detached to guard the Augusta railroad, and General Williams' was detached to General Benjamin Cheatham. That left Wheeler with Iverson's Division consisting of the Georgia and Alabama brigades.[18] General Hood, full of confidence, told Wheeler that Iverson's Division was able to deal with twice their number. He felt they were not cavalry proper but mounted riflemen, trained to dismount and hold an advancing enemy. He bragged that they had learned how to defeat the Federal cavalry without much difficulty.

On July 18, everything seemed to be happening at a faster pace. Wheeler was ordered to burn the bridges or destroy them some way after his command had crossed. On July 19, Gen. Hood sent orders to General Hardee and General Stewart to attack the enemy at 1 P.M. Gen. Cheatham was on the right and told to hold the line. Gen. Wheeler was to give aid anywhere he could to General Cheatham. Wheeler was covering the Confederate right flank and attacked the Federals moving west from Decatur toward Atlanta.

During July 19 and 20, the Georgia and Alabama Cavalry brigades opposed the entire army of General McPherson which consisted of three army corps. McPherson had made his skirmish line so dense that the Confederate cavalry thought them to be lines of battle. General Wheeler asked for reinforcements but got only General Samuel Wragg Fergerson's Brigade. No others could be sent.[19]

On July 20, McPherson advanced heavily upon Wheeler's Command. Wheeler and the Georgia and Alabama Cavalry Brigades engaged Gen. Frank Blair's 17th Corps and desperately blocked their advance. By four o'clock that afternoon, Gen. Fergerson's command, which was on the right, began to fall back. Wheeler dashed to the scene and rallied the men himself. He was able to reestablish the line, and they held it until night.[20]

As the day waned toward dark, Wheeler had his cavalry fall back to a treeless rise known as Bald Hill. They dismounted and dug emplacements from which to defend themselves. Two Brigades of General Walter Gresham's 4th Division attacked the Georgia and Alabama Cavalry brigades and tried to push them off Bald Hill. General Gresham was shot in the left leg while he was inspecting the line.[21]

At daylight, July 21, General Cleburne's Infantry Division had been ordered by General Hood to assume Wheeler's Cavalry position at Bald Hill. Wheeler was ordered to move out to his right and extend the lines. During this changing of positions, General McPherson made his strongest attack.

The situation was compounded because Gen. Cleburne had occupied only a little more than half the ground the Georgia and Alabama brigades had held. The attack came while the cavalry was making its move. Wheeler's men were not even faced toward the enemy. Gen. Fergerson, who was out on the far right, sent word to Wheeler that his right flank was being turned. Wheeler wrote as follows in his report of the attack:

> About daylight the following morning General Cleburne with his Division of infantry came pursuant to General Hood's orders, to relieve me, while I was ordered to extend my line to the right. General Cleburne placed his troops so closely together that only a little more than half my line was occupied by General Cleburne's troops. While changing positions, and before my troops had faced toward the enemy, a general attack was made on my own and

General Cleburne's front. General Ferguson, who was on the right, reported a force turning his right flank, when at the same moment, a general assault of several lines of battle was made by the enemy. Ferguson gave way in some confusion, which exposed the right of Allen's Brigade which with the Georgia Brigade nevertheless fought brilliantly, repulsing a desperate assault and killing the enemy in hand to hand conflicts.[22]

After the enemy was repulsed, they regrouped themselves and made a second assault stronger than the first. The Georgia and Alabama brigades, with the brigades of Cleburne's Division's right flank, were forced back a short distance. The Georgia and Alabama Brigades rallied themselves and charged back into the enemy to retake their previous works. The brigades also captured a Federal Officer and twenty privates. The dead and wounded Yankees lay on the field and even in the brigades' rifle pits. During this action, Lt. Col. James H. Strickland, commanding the First Georgia Cavalry, was mortally wounded while rallying his men to attack the oncoming Yankees. Captain William Thomas York was wounded and carried from the field by his brother, Josiah York, Jr. General Wheeler commented about the battle: "This was a most brilliant feat and the Georgia Brigade deserves great credit for its conduct upon that day."[23]

The Georgia and Alabama boys held their ground for the rest of the day. Late that afternoon, General Cleburne sent his troops to relieve them. The Georgia Brigade was glad to move out of the breastworks and happier yet to learn that Gen. Hood had other plans for this gallant cavalry. While the Georgians were in the rear, they fed themselves, the horses, and prepared for more action.[24]

General Sherman realized that direct assaults on the Confederate lines were getting his men killed, and the Confederate lines were too long to try flanking. With that thought in mind, he decided the best strategy was to destroy the Central of Georgia Railroad east of Atlanta, which was supplying the Confederate Army from Augusta. Sherman sent General James Birdseye McPherson toward Decatur to accomplish that mission.

The night of July 21, the Georgia and Alabama brigades were mounted and moved to the enemy's rear to attack in concert with Gen. Hardee. Hardee had moved his corps up to the flank of the enemy in preparation for his attack. He was slow getting his men into position and could not support Wheeler. He had ordered Wheeler to attack the enemy who were in Decatur at 1:00 P.M. on July 22.[25]

Decatur was to the enemy's extreme left and in the rear of their lines. Hardee told Wheeler that only enemy cavalry was occupying Decatur. General Wheeler thought it best to make his own reconnaissance of the enemy position. Wheeler's scouts found not only cavalry, but also the 20th Corps of Infantry, which was entrenched and occupying the town. Wheeler sent Gen. Hardee a message which described what he had found in Decatur.[26]

Gen. Wheeler dismounted the Georgia and Alabama brigades and Gen. Ferguson's Alabama/Mississippi Cavalry Brigade and moved them into a line for attack. The Federals saw Wheeler's tactics around 1 P.M. and sent out two regiments of infantry to deal with the Rebels. As the fight progressed, Wheeler's Cavalry bested their infantry. The Rebels captured some prisoners and sent the others back running to their previous position. As Wheeler's line pressed forward, the Federals Chicago Board of Trade Artillery welcomed them with a fierce artillery and small-arms fire. After receiving this fire, Wheeler decided it best to flank their barricade. He gave orders to move part of his cavalry to the flank and rear. When all were in position, they made the attack together.[27]

As the lines began to move toward the Yankees, the cannon began their welcome. The Georgia and Alabama brigades gritted their teeth and charged into the galling fire. The advanced line did waver from the fire, but the brave men rallied and pressed forward toward the big guns. As they came charging in, their Rebel yell released their fear and sent it over to the Yanks. Quickly the entire works were carried and 225 prisoners were taken along with all their wagon trains, equipment, cannon, and arms. The Federals were stampeded out of Decatur with the Rebel hounds baying after them. Col. John W. Sprague, Second Brigade, Fourth Division, XVI Corps was awarded the Medal of Honor and promoted to brigadier general for his part in this Union disaster.

As the Georgia and Alabama brigades came into town, three women ran into the street cheering them to go after the fleeing Yankees. General Allen saw them and had some of his men escort the ladies to a cellar out of danger. The shooting was still going on all around them. Private Hargis of the First Georgia related the following: "He found a big pone of egg bread on a stove in a kitchen. He grabbed it and ran back to his company to share with his friends."[28]

As the pursuit continued, three staff officers from Gen. Hardee arrived in succession with directions for Gen. Wheeler to come and reinforce Hardee as soon as possible. Wheeler gathered the available command and galloped off toward Hardee's fight. He left enough of his cavalry in Decatur to hold the town and handle the prisoners.[29]

When Wheeler arrived at Hardee's battle, he threw his cavalry into the lines. They fought warmly with the enemy until the heavy pressure on Hardee was relieved. As night came, Wheeler went into camp for the night. He began to hear rumors that General McPherson had been killed when he was inspecting his lines and came upon Confederate skirmishers. They ordered him to halt and surrender. McPherson had only his orderly with him and decided to make a dash for freedom. He turned his horse to run and a barrage of fire knocked him to the ground mortally wounded. General Hood was sad about the news. McPherson had been his boyhood friend, and they were classmates at West Point 1853.

On July 23, Wheeler's command remained with Hardee until noon. Wheeler received orders for him to attack the Federal cavalry again. With great excitement, the Rebel cavalry were in their saddles in ten minutes ready for the attack. The Georgia and Alabama brigades chased the unseen enemy cavalry for forty miles. At midnight, Wheeler learned the enemy he was to pursue was, and had been, with the main army all along. After chasing a ghost, Wheeler returned his cavalry to the Confederate lines around Atlanta. For the next four days the First Georgia Cavalry skirmished with the enemy from behind earthen works.[30]

12

Sunshine Church

General William T. Sherman was satisfied by the success of his army around Atlanta. By July 26, General John M. Schofield's Army of the Ohio and General George H. Thomas' Army of the Cumberland were holding the Confederates behind the inner entrenchments around Atlanta. Sherman had closed in his armies to prevent them from being separated and attacked piecemeal. Gen. Kenner Garrard's Second Cavalry Division had been active along the Augusta railroad east of Atlanta, tearing up track, burning railcars and bridges. Garrard brought in some Confederate soldiers and horses he had captured to do the work.

General Sherman felt confident the Augusta railroad would be of no use to the Rebel army. He turned his attention on the last supply line to Atlanta, which was the railroad from Macon, Georgia. He moved General George Stoneman from Sandtown to the Army of the Tennessee's left flank. Sherman gave orders to Stoneman to attack the Macon railroad while the infantry made its move against East Point. The combined commands of General Stoneman and Garrard were fully 5,000 men. General Sherman sent General Edward Moody McCook, with the newly arrived General Lovell Rousseau, to the right toward Fayetteville. Both thrusts of the enemy cavalry were to meet on the Macon railroad near Lovejoy and destroy it. General McCook enjoyed his reputation of destroying civilian property.[1]

Sherman was full of confidence and happy as he could be with his cavalry. He felt they could whip all of Wheeler's Cavalry and still execute their missions. As General Stoneman was making ready to leave on the mission, he asked General Sherman if, once the plan was accomplished, he could take his command to Andersonville to free those prisoners of war. Sherman thought for a moment and liked the idea. It sounded good to him, and he felt the idea was within reach of being accomplished. Sherman, underneath whisky breath and whiskers, looked stone cold hard at Stoneman for what seemed forever and warned him to finish his mission first, not to endanger his men, and to send Garrard back to the proper flank of the army when his part of the mission was completed.[2]

General Wheeler and his cavalry were in the trenches with General Hardee's Infantry. On the morning of July 27, the cavalry had just relieved Hardee's entire line. While Wheeler's men moved into the breastwork, Wheeler observed that the Yankees had abandoned their barricades in front of the railroad. They had fallen back to their previous position on the other side. Wheeler knew something was about to happen, but could not think what, where, or when.[3] He nervously watched and waited for his scouts to return. They came in with word of a massive cavalry movement around their right flank. The scouts reported that the Federal Cavalry was being led by General Stoneman. The wheels began to click in the little general's mind. He knew Sherman had to be sending a raiding party south to get at their last supply line. He knew that the only troops who could stop the enemy were now in the trenches. His cavalry had just replaced Hardee's men, and special permission would be needed to get them out.[4]

Wheeler sent word immediately to General Hood of what was taking place. After consideration, Hood sent General Hardee's men back to the lines. Hood told Wheeler to use only the force necessary to accomplish the mission. He also requested Wheeler not go out himself unless he thought most of his command would be needed to stop the enemy. Fightin' Joe was not about to miss the great adventure against the Yankee cavalry.[5]

It did not take long for the cavalry to jump to their saddles and be off after Stoneman and Garrard. By daylight July 28, Wheeler had gotten his men ahead of General Garrard, who was on his way to Jonesboro. Wheeler's Cavalry met the advance of Garrard and drove them across Flat Creek. Garrard realized he was outnumbered and retreated to Flat Rock to await General Stoneman. As he waited, he wondered what had happened to Stoneman. He had been ordered to converge at Lovejoy and destroy the railroad.[6]

Stoneman had instead swung around Covington that same morning with 2,200 of his cavalry and headed toward Macon.[7] Wheeler learned about Stoneman's presence from the captured prisoners of Garrard's Cavalry and knew that Stoneman had to be stopped. While General Wheeler was mulling over what to do, a dispatch arrived from General Francis Asbury Shoup, chief of staff. The message was about General Edward McCook and his threat to the Confederates left near Newnan. With that information and in consideration of his previous orders from General Hood, Wheeler decided to send General Iverson with Col. Charles Crews' Georgia Brigade, General William Allen's Alabama Brigade, and Col. Breckenridge's Kentucky Brigade to go after Stoneman. They were to attack Stoneman wherever they found him.

On July 29, General Garrard could not wait any longer for Stoneman to arrive. Garrard had been skirmishing heavily with Iverson's command and did not know anything of Stoneman so he followed Sherman's orders and returned to Conyers.[8] General Stoneman continued to move his cavalry down the east side of the Ocmulgee River through Jasper and Jones counties to Clinton. From there he sent raiding parties east to the railroad. The Yankees destroyed the bridges over Walnut Creek and the Oconee River. They also destroyed a large number of railcars and locomotives.

General Stoneman took the main body of his force and marched toward Macon. However, Macon was ready for them. The militia had formed across the Ocmulgee River with their old cannon from Fort Hawkins and held Stoneman at bay.[9] Frustration began to overtake Stoneman as he learned that Iverson's Cavalry was in pursuit of him, and he could not get past Macon. He realized he must give up his idea of freeing the Federals at Andersonville Prison. His objective now was to get his command back to Sherman's lines.

General Iverson had selected his battlefield at Sunshine Church near Hillsboro. They began to construct fortifications to receive Stoneman's withdrawing cavalry. Iverson's command built a defensive structure in a V shape with the intent of drawing Stoneman into a trap. The First Georgia Cavalry and the Third Georgia Cavalry occupied positions behind fortifications on the legs of the V. Iverson sent a line of skirmishers out from Allen's Brigade to be bait and draw the Yankees into the trap. General Allen's Alabama Brigade had blocked the Hillsboro Road and was behind a makeshift barricade.[10] The plan began to unfold as Col. Horace Capron's Fourteenth Illinois Cavalry met the Confederate line at dawn on July 31. Allen's Alabama Brigade allowed themselves to be pushed back half a mile into the awaiting arms of the First and Third Georgia Cavalry fortifications on the high ground on the Hillsboro Road. Iverson sent the Fourth Georgia Cavalry to hit the flank and rear of Stoneman's command.[11]

All of Stoneman's command followed Col. Capron into the trap. Once the enemy was in the trap, General Iverson had Captain Benjamin White, Jr.'s Tennessee Battery open up on them with his two six-pounders. This shocked the Union progress. General Stoneman, hearing the cannon's roar, came to the front.[12] He sent Lt. Col. Silas Adams' Eighth Michigan Cavalry to the left. In the movement with Lt. Col. Adams were the First and Eleventh Kentucky Cavalries. These soldiers were particularly anxious because they were to be mustered out of service in two weeks. Many of them had deserted from the Confederate Army and if captured, stood a chance of being shot. Col. James Biddle's Cavalry Brigade was on the right with Capron.

At about 9:30 A.M., Stoneman ordered his cavalry to dismount and march in line to engage the Confederates.[13] It must be noted that most of Stoneman's officers wanted to go around this fortification and back to safety, not to engage General Iverson. Whatever the mood of the officers, General Stoneman was determined to cut his way through this Rebel rabble.

Stoneman's dismounted cavalry scurried up the hill through brush and came charging into Gen. Iverson's position. When the Yankees came into range, the First and Third Georgia Cavalries rose up from behind their barricade and poured a scalding-hot wall of lead into them. The Yankees were thrown back in disbelief that they were still alive, and they did not want to press the issue further. They ran the other way as if their lives depended upon it. Lt. Col. Adams tried to rally them to return, but the Federals had had enough. During this time, General Iverson became ill (we can speculate that it was perhaps from frayed nerves) and put Col. Crews in command. Col. Crews had commanded the Second Georgia Cavalry as well as the Georgia Brigade.

The Georgia Brigade slammed their lines against Stoneman and almost had him surrounded. As the Federal cavalry advanced their push, the men of the Alabama and Georgia Brigades countercharged and crushed their left. A mounted charge by the Fourth Georgia Cavalry on the right made that flank fall back. As the Yankees fell in retreat, the Georgia and Alabama boys gave their Rebel yells and chased after them. The pursuit became so hot that the Yankees threw down their arms to run faster. They were even unable to mount their horses they ran so wildly through the woods. As the Confederates came upon the enemy's horses, they mounted them and continued the chase on horseback.

General Stoneman realized he was surrounded and had summoned his staff by 4:00 P.M. Most of the brigade commanders thought they could cut their way through the Rebel line, but the charge of the Confederates made it almost impossible. Surrender was the only option remaining for most of the command. Stoneman's men were now scattered, making it impossible to communicate with each other. They were also out of ammunition. Even Gen. Stoneman's horse "Beauregard" had been killed.[14]

Stoneman wisely ordered one of his officers to go with a flag of truce to effect the surrender. This would stop the killin, and he hoped, allow some of his men to escape. Although a search was made for a white flag none could be found. General Stoneman, enraged, tore the tail off his own shirt to produce the needed flag. Col. Capron was able to escape with part of his command only to be attacked again at King's Tanyard in Winder. Col. Adams was able to return to Sherman with some of his men.

The captain of the skirmish line saw the flag of truce and ordered a cease fire. The Federal officer came forward and asked for the commanding officer. He was told he was in the rear. The captain sent word back, and soon Col. Crews and his staff rode up. The officers greeted each other with a salute. The Federal officer in a somber voice informed Crews that General Stoneman wished to surrender. Col. Crews restrained his delight and told the officer, "All right, I will go in and receive him."[15] After that, they rode back to Gen. Stoneman's position.[16]

When Col. Crews arrived on the other side of the hill, the men about to be surrendered had stacked their arms and were standing in lines of order. Gen. Stoneman was sitting sullenly upon his reserve horse. He returned Col. Crews' salute as he was approached. Stoneman indicated he was very insulted by having Col. Crews receive his surrender. Stoneman asked if he could surrender to General Iverson. Col. Crews refused his request without a second thought.[17]

After the surrender, everyone was formed up in the road to make their way to Macon. As they were lining up, Stoneman's adjutant, Major Myles Keogh, recognized Col. J. Russell Butler sitting astride his horse watching all the events. Major Keogh spoke up: "Hello, Colonel Butler, how do you do? I'm glad to see you."[18] It was strange to hear a friendly gesture at a time of surrender, but these men had once been classmates at school. That bond overrode their being enemies in the field of battle. The Yankee adjutant went to get a pair of very fine English navy pistols and gave them to Col. Butler. Col. Butler, not thinking of the situation, said, "Thank you, sir! I hope I will do good service with them the next fight I get into."[19]

Major Keogh looked shocked and retorted, "Don't talk to me that way."[20] Col. Butler realized he had offended his old friend and said, "I don't mean if you and I come in contact, I mean among your men."[21] Major Keogh failed to tell Col. Butler that also in his saddlebags was a cache of silver dollars sewn in the lining. This money would sustain the captured officers during their stay at Andersonville Prison. (Myles Keogh was killed at the Battle of Little Big Horn with George A. Custer twelve years later.)[22]

Col. Butler called for three cheers for Col. Crews, which the men heartily gave. Col. Crews had the prisoners marched off to General Iverson's headquarters for him to see. The entire group camped for the night. Col. Crews posted strong guards all around the prisoners to prevent any of them from escaping.[23]

At the end of July 1864, the Army of Tennessee was organized as follows: Hardee's Corp, Gen. Hardee; Lee's Corps, Gen. Stephen D. Lee; Stewarts Corps, Gen. Benjamin F. Cheatham; and Cavalry Corps, Gen. Joseph Wheeler. Wheeler's Cavalry Corps was divided into four Divisions: William T. Martin's, John H. Kelly's, William Y.C. Humes', and William H. Jackson's. Martin's Division was divided into two brigades: William W. Allen's Alabama Brigade and Alfred Iverson's Georgia Brigade. Iverson's Brigade contained First Georgia Cavalry, Col. Samuel Davitte; Second Georgia Cavalry, Col. Charles Crews; Third Georgia Cavalry, Col. Robert Thompson; Fourth Georgia Cavalry, Col. Isaac Avery; and Sixth Georgia Cavalry, Col. John Hart.

On August 1, General Iverson's Cavalry moved the prisoners down the road toward Macon. In their haste to go after Stoneman, the Confederates had not brought enough supplies to sustain both themselves and the prisoners. As they marched down the road, they would pass farms and cornfields. The Confederates and Union alike would go into the field to gather ears of corn to roast. Later in the march, they built fires and roasted the corn and all sat down to eat.[24]

When the column of cavalry with their prisoners finally arrived in Macon, great crowds of people turned out and cheered their gallant cavalry. The ladies of Macon gave a party for them with plenty of food and watermelons, and a grand time was had by all. As the men finished their watermelons, someone impishly washed his buddy's face with a watermelon rind to everyone's delight. Before anyone knew what was happening, the cavalrymen were having a splendid time in a watermelon rind fight. This was the most fun these poor souls had had in three years.[25]

General Iverson turned his prisoners over to the authorities in Macon and sent word to General Hood of the rout and the captured prisoners. Before long the Confederate newspapers were proclaiming Iverson's victory and General Stoneman one of the highest-ranked prisoners of war. Even General Grant clipped the *Richmond Dispatch* on August 3 and sent a copy to both General Sherman and General Halleck.[26]

After the festivities, General Iverson put his cavalry in marching order and set out to rejoin Wheeler near Decatur, Georgia. Wheeler had also enjoyed great success against Gen. McCook near Newnan at Brown's Mill. When Iverson arrived back in Atlanta, his gallant Georgia, Alabama and Kentucky brigades were placed in line between Atlanta and Decatur near the railroad.

The First Georgia Cavalry learned through Col. Sam Davitte that Lt. Col. James H. Strickland, of Coweta County Georgia, had died August 3 from his wounds received during the battle at Bald Hill on July 22. Col. Davitte appointed Captain George T. Watts to act as the lieutenant colonel until the promotion could be authorized. Also on August 3, Captain William T. York, Co. A, died of wounds at Bald Hill, and 1st Lt. Jesse W. Crabb, Co. A, was promoted captain to succeed Captain York. Captain John W. Tench was promoted major.

The First Georgia Cavalry waited for new orders. They were too valuable to hold a line in defense. Wheeler's Cavalry had just delivered a crushing blow to Sherman's army. They wondered what would be next.

13

Raiding Sherman's Rear

General John Bell Hood was delighted with the success of General Wheeler's Cavalry against General Stoneman and General McCook. Those defeats had shattered the effectiveness of the Union cavalry. General Sherman was enraged that his cavalry could not effectively deal with Wheeler's Cavalry. General Hood wanted to follow up the victories and conceived an idea. With Sherman's Cavalry in shambles, now would be a good time for the Confederate cavalry to make its own raid. Hood wanted Wheeler to take his cavalry corps north to destroy the enemy's communications and supply lines from Atlanta to Nashville. Wheeler was to detach units at strategic points where they could continue operations against the enemy lines.[1]

General Wheeler gathered his force, which consisted of Martin's Division and contained the Georgia and Alabama brigades. Wheeler also brought Humes' and Kelly's divisions and William S. Robertson's Brigade. On August 10, Wheeler led his cavalry from their position near Covington, Georgia. His intention was to choke the Federal army to death.

Wheeler's Cavalry Corps traveled to Marietta, and on August 11 they ripped up railroad track for a few miles. They did the same at Cassville and Calhoun. At Calhoun, Col. Moses Hannon's Brigade captured some 1,700 head of cattle and a wagon train. Wheeler ordered Hannon to take the cattle to Ellijay and then around south to the main army. Hannon accomplished this mission even while the Yankee cavalry pursued him. Hannon's Brigade did not rejoin Wheeler.[2]

On August 12, Gen. Martin and Gen. Kelly had confused Gen. Humes as to who would be taking the road to Frogtown, Georgia. Humes had to ask Gen. Wheeler for clarification because his division was to follow one of them to Frogtown. On August 13, Wheeler ordered Gen. Martin to take his division to Tilton and attack the Federal garrison. After taking the garrison, Martin was to begin destroying the railroad from Tilton north toward Dalton.[3] During the night of August 14, General Martin crossed his division, containing the First Georgia Cavalry, at Field's Mill, headed for Tilton. General Wheeler took the remainder of the command to Dalton by way of Old Town. When Martin's Division reached Tilton, they quickly accomplished their first mission. The garrison was captured by the First Georgia Cavalry and to the surprise of the Confederates, it was manned by Negro soldiers. After the prisoners were secured, they started their second mission.

General Martin worked his cavalry hard destroying the rail line as they moved north. General Wheeler approached Dalton and demanded its surrender the afternoon of August 14. Col. Bernard Laibolt, Second Missouri Infantry, refused to surrender and the fight began. Laibolt retreated to a fortified embankment on a hillside outside of town and held off

Wheeler's attacks. The skirmishing continued all night. Wheeler was successful in driving the enemy from Dalton and was able to capture supplies and valuable stores. Unfortunately, not much corn was found to feed the horses. This shortage of food forced Wheeler to move the command.

On August 15, Gen. Wheeler was marching his command when General James B. Steedman attacked with 4,000 infantry. It consisted of two regiments of white and six companies of Negro troops. Steedman drove Wheeler away from Dalton east toward Spring Place. Wheeler was able to withdraw with only a small loss. General Steedman was not so lucky. During the attack, he was wounded.[4]

During this time, General Martin did not stay in contact with General Wheeler. Wheeler became apprehensive as to what had happened to Martin's Division in light of his being attacked. He thought the Federals might have captured Martin's Division. When General Wheeler found Gen. Martin and discovered that he had been very close to him, but made no attempt to communicate or aid him, Wheeler was furious. He had Martin arrested and sent back to Atlanta. After Wheeler disposed of General Martin, he sent the Georgia and Alabama brigades to Spring Place. They were to hold the roads open for Wheeler to be able to retreat eastward if it became necessary.[5]

On August 16, General Edward M. McCook's cavalry attacked Martin's old division near Spring Place, but the Alabama and Georgia brigades were able to throw them off. After the battle, the First Georgia Cavalry ranged from near Spring Place to Dalton and Chattanooga with the division. During their ride, they destroyed everything of any use to the enemy. By the Georgia and Alabama brigades moving constantly, General Steedman was prevented from concentrating his force against General Wheeler. Steedman was afraid to take men from Chattanooga because he thought the Georgia and Alabama brigades might attack. This constant maneuver caused Steedman to march his infantry several times between Dalton and Chattanooga.

Reports were sent to General Sherman about Martin's Division's activities, and on August 16, Sherman sent a message to Col. Green B. Raum to attack Martin. Sherman suggested Martin would quit the fight. It was unknown why Sherman would think such because the gallant fighting tradition of the Georgia and Alabama brigades was established. He possibly wanted to give Raum a false sense of courage, or he did not know Gen. Martin had been removed from command.

General Sherman was wrong about Wheeler's campaign in his rear. Sherman wrote General Halleck: "Wheeler cannot disturb Knoxville or Loudon. He may hurt some minor points, but the whole East Tennessee is a good place for him to break down his horses and a poor place to steal new ones."[6] Little did Sherman dream the trouble Wheeler's men would cause him in the days ahead.

Gen. John E. Smith, following Sherman's orders, moved his Third Infantry Division to Spring Place. He arrived there at 1:30 P.M. and found Wheeler had taken his cavalry corps toward Cleveland, Tennessee. Smith informed Sherman that he had heard cannon fire from the direction of Cleveland but had no idea what it was about.[7]

Once word spread that Wheeler and his cavalry had moved north, the Union command feared the worst and kept the telegraph wires hot. They told all posts to watch for Wheeler and report any sightings. Most feared of all was that Wheeler would take his cavalry to Kentucky. Instead, the general took his force and spread them between Tunnel Hill and Graysville,

Georgia, to destroy the railroad. While in the area, they burned bridges and railroad ties. The burning was hampered by the heavy rains which seemed to never stop.

During this time, promotions were slow, and men where performing duties above their official rank. Acting major John W. Tench was officially a captain on August 16. The gallant officers were being killed, wounded, and worn down by this constant grind of the gristmill of war. Tench was in command of the 3rd Squadron, composed of Companies G and D. He was placed in command by Gen. Wheeler because of his efficiency and gallant conduct. All promotions were subject to the approval of the War Department.

On August 20, Wheeler took his men north. They had kept the railroad closed from Atlanta to Chattanooga for ten days plus another four days to repair it. Wheeler detached 200 men to stay in the area to attack the rail and telegraph lines at night. Wheeler would have stayed there but he was forced out because the place could not support his men and animals. He was afraid that if he did not leave to search for better forage his men would become infantry. Therefore, his cavalry went north to the fertile grounds around the Ocoee and Hiwassee rivers in Tennessee.[8] In this area, forage could be obtained easily.

While around Cleveland, Wheeler learned the Yankees had made considerable preparations for forage to be provided to their army ranging from Cleveland to Loudon. He determined these supplies must be destroyed as part of General Hood's orders. Wheeler's Cavalry Corps attacked Cleveland and destroyed the railroad from there to Charleston.[9] It was hard work for the First Georgia Cavalry to first fight the Yankees and then rip up railroad tracks. They did not mind burning bridges and railcars. After they destroyed all they could, they forded the Hiwassee River to Athens. Their mission was to capture the town and the much needed supplies. They kept items they needed and destroyed the remainder.

Wheeler's Cavalry worked hard fending off enemy attacks and destroying the railroad system from Athens to Loudon. Once Loudon was dealt with, they veered toward Stewart's Landing on the Little Tennessee River. There was a garrison located there which needed to be demolished. After a brief skirmish with about a hundred Yankees, the place was secured. The Confederates cleaned the place out of everything they wanted such as horses, mules, wagons, and stores. While his men worked, Wheeler planned his next move toward Maryville, Tennessee.[10] On the night of August 21, Wheeler had his artillery shell Maryville just to leave a calling card.[11] They moved north toward Dandridge during the night. Wheeler's Cavalry Corps reached Russellville August 22. As the First Georgia Cavalry moved through the area, memories of previous battles crossed their minds.

Wheeler's Cavalry forded the Little Tennessee River easily; the French Broad and Holston Rivers near Knoxville were much too deep to ford. When the cavalry reached the Holston River above Knoxville, the Federals were on the other side to greet them. On August 23, Wheeler's Cavalry charged across the river, driving the enemy before them. Another Federal cavalry unit was hurriedly thrown together in Knoxville to stop Wheeler. The ill-prepared enemy cavalry came out and attacked, but they were easily repulsed. They lost over 100 captured, killed, or wounded.[12]

Gen. John Williams' Kentucky Brigade left Wheeler before the river crossing to go on an expedition of their own. Wheeler was against his leaving, but Williams prevailed with promises of a victory and a speedy return. No matter what Williams accomplished, he never returned; and for the remainder of the expedition, Wheeler's forces were greatly reduced.[13]

After Wheeler passed Knoxville, the Federals feared he would attack the rail and communications around Nashville. The entire area was on alert for Wheeler and his cavalry. General Robert H. Milroy pressed cavalry regiments together to stop him. The Federals were already aware that the telegraph below Loudon had been cut. Some still feared Wheeler was going into Kentucky as he was headed that way.

On August 26, Wheeler brought his cavalry near Jacksboro with what the Federals estimated at 4,000 men.[14] The Rebels attacked the garrison and moved to Bean Station. Wheeler was able to capture a part of General Alvan Cullem Gillem's command in the attack. Wheeler did not hold captives long. He paroled them, and they could not fight until exchanged. Wheeler took his cavalry to the railroad which ran between Chattanooga and Nashville. They went through Sparta on the way to McMinnville and captured two train cars and a number of depots along the way. They drove Yankees from several Post, captured stockades and blockhouses. They destroyed rails, ties, bridges, and telegraph lines.

By August 29, Wheeler was moving near Nashville and still destroying the railroad as they traveled. General Lovell Harrison Rousseau had been trying to catch them to punish Wheeler for all the damage he had caused. Rousseau had a larger force (3,000 men) than Wheeler's command. It was composed of mounted infantry as well as cavalry. Rousseau finally caught up to Wheeler about ten miles from Nashville, and the battle began.[15] After the skirmishers had identified their positions, Rousseau began a general attack on Wheeler. General Wheeler countered by sending Gen. Thomas H. Harrison's Brigade of Humes' Division in a charge into the enemy. This thrust drove the Yankees for two miles. Harrison was able to capture three stands of colors with many prisoners and arms. It took valuable time to parole all the prisoners.

Later that day, Wheeler found a wagon train and captured thirty wagons with mule teams, along with a number of prisoners. The cavalry spent the next day, August 30, working on the railroad and telegraph lines. After they had thoroughly destroyed the lines between Chattanooga and Nashville, they moved over to the rail line between Decatur, Alabama, and Nashville. They set about destroying most of that line between the two strategic cities. Wheeler moved the command, including the Georgia Brigade, to McMinnville on August 31.

The last day of August brought the first request from General Hood for Wheeler to return to his army. Hood felt Wheeler could be more effective closer to him. Wheeler's men were spread all over Tennessee. As a target was destroyed, Wheeler would leave a company of his regiments at that location to continue the destruction. It was not going to be easy to recall his total command.[16]

September 1 Federal reports of an impending attack against Nashville sent the military scurrying around to find enough cavalry to meet Wheeler. That same day, Captain John H. Lester, Co. E, Seventh Alabama Cavalry, Allen's Brigade, was located near Rogersville, Alabama. He sent General Wheeler a message about the movements of General Abel D. Streight and General Rousseau.

One must remember that while Wheeler's Cavalry Corps was in Tennessee, they were attacked by Generals Rousseau, Steedman, John T. Croxton, and Robert Seaman Granger at various places such as Franklin, Lynnville, Campbellsville, and all along the railroad between Nashville and Decatur, Alabama. Even though the Confederate cavalry was sometimes outnumbered four to one, they repelled the Union with each attack. All during this time, the

Federals were never able to completely reconnect their lines of communication or the railroad lines.

The First Georgia Cavalry was destroying the railroad near Mount Pleasant, Tennessee. They were being harassed by the Federals but were able to continue their work. On September 4, several of the First Georgia were wounded or captured there during a skirmish. Pvt. Charles N. Bagwell, Co. E, was wounded in action and captured. Pvt. Wiley Cotton, Co. E, was captured, and 1st Lt. Henry C. Goodwyn, Co. E, was wounded in action and captured.

During these first days of September, General Grant felt that General Nathan B. Forrest had been sufficiently dealt with by General Andrew Jackson Smith's command in Mississippi and requested Smith to turn his attention to Joseph Wheeler.[17] Gen. Smith was informed Wheeler was moving the command into Alabama. Col. Charles Crews, who had been commanding the Georgia Brigade, crossed through Lewisburg, Tennessee,[18] going south into Alabama. As they traveled, the Georgia Brigade continued to destroy railroads and telegraph lines.

General Hood still wanted and needed Wheeler to join him. However, when Wheeler told Hood of his situation of being so spread out and in need of supplies, Hood understood why Wheeler could not return at that time. Gen. Hood sent a message to Wheeler September 13 that the 8,000 horseshoes he needed would be sent to him at Corinth, Mississippi. Gen. Hood still wanted Wheeler's Cavalry to operate against the enemy, and he told Wheeler that General Forrest and General Phillip D. Roddy had the same mission.[19]

During the Tennessee campaign, Wheeler's command increased in number because Tennessee governor Andrew Johnson, later United States president, ordered the state militia into the Federal ranks. This order caused a lot of Tennesseans who had straddled the fence during the war to finally make a decision where to place their allegiance. They joined Wheeler even though his was now a rag-tag outfit. The horses were completely worn out. The men had not stopped long enough to have them shod since leaving Covington, Georgia. Having been on the move since August 10, they had not slept under a tent or a shelter. Prior to that date, they had endured one of the most grueling campaigns of the war. They had fought Sherman's oppressing army from Dalton to Atlanta. A few days prior to this campaign, they had fought and ridden hard at Sunshine Church and Brown's Mill.

General Sherman was having his own problems. The rail lines to Atlanta had been cut almost every day since Wheeler began his campaign. Sherman was in pursuit of Hood and on September 10 wrote General Ulysses S. Grant from Atlanta saying his command needed "rest and pay."[20] Sherman stressed to Grant "our roads are also broken back near Nashville, and Wheeler is not disposed of."[21] Sherman recognized Wheeler's Cavalry's importance by stating, "I do not think we can afford to operate further, dependent on the railroad; it takes so many men to guard it, and even then it is nightly broken by the enemy cavalry that swarm about us."[22] With these problems in mind, Sherman began to formulate his plans to move from Atlanta to possibly Augusta, Savannah, or Mobile, Alabama.

Meanwhile, General Wheeler had his cavalry continue limited operations in north Alabama through September 15. General Hood requested Wheeler move back to him. Hood informed Wheeler that by the following week the left flank of his army would be on the Chattahoochee River. Hood expected Wheeler to join General William Hicks Jackson on the north side of the river.

On September 17, the headquarters for the First Georgia Cavalry was at Russellville,

Alabama. From Russellville, Col. Samuel W. Davitte requested from the War Department that Captain John Tench be promoted as the major for the First Georgia Cavalry. Col. Davitte wanted Tench promoted because George T. Watts' promotion to lieutenant colonel had finally come through. General Wheeler included a note about Captain Tench in the request for promotion. Wheeler said that Captain Tench's promotion to major "would excite others to emulate his valor and skill."[23]

September 20 brought mixed emotions to the great Confederate cavalry leaders Wheeler and Forrest. General Forrest had at one time refused to serve under Wheeler and resigned his commission. General Wheeler was ten years younger than Forrest and an 1859 West Point graduate. At their meeting at Tuscumbia, Alabama, Wheeler might have revealed too much of himself to Forrest. Forrest wrote General Richard Taylor, Department of Alabama and Mississippi, about the meeting later in the day. (General Richard Taylor was the son of President Zachary Taylor.) Forrest stated of Wheeler, "His command is in a demoralized condition."[24] Wheeler must have told everything, as Forrest continued to Gen. Taylor: "He sent General Martin back in arrest and his whole command is demoralized to such an extent that he expresses himself as disheartened and that having lost influence with the troops and being unable to secure aid and co-operation of his officers, he believes it to the interest of the service that he should be relieved of command."[25]

General Forrest estimated Wheeler's command to be a thousand men strong while the enemy, on the same day, reported Wheeler to have between 4,000 and 6,000. Wheeler claimed only 2,000 men in reporting to General Hood the number of cavalry he could bring back with him to Georgia.

Though Forrest was reporting Wheeler as being depressed, the Federals likely had no such thought of his depression or lack of command. They feared his moving to Decatur, Alabama, and attacking them. Their fears came true as Wheeler did attack with the Georgia Brigade and moved on to Huntsville on October 1.

In General Wheeler's report of his Tennessee campaign, he claimed losing only 150 men killed, wounded, or missing for the entire expedition. He claimed 2,000 recruits brought out of Tennessee plus 800 men who had been absent from the army. He continued his report stating while he was behind the enemy lines, he was forced to "engage superior"[26] numbers. He further stated, "In all this work my troops acted well, fought well and worked well."[27] Wheeler paid special tribute to Generals William Y.C. Humes and William W. Allen for their gallantry and good conduct throughout the entire expedition. He then listed the results of his expedition as follows:

1. Causing the enemy to send to their rear to reinforce their garrisons, troops several times as strong as my force.
2. The destruction of the enemy's line of communication for a longer period than any other cavalry expedition however large has done.
3. Capture, destruction or appropriation of stores.
4. Breaking up depots and fortified Post in Tennessee and Georgia.
5. Capture of 1,000 horses and mules, 200 wagons, 600 prisoners, and 1,700 head of beef cattle.
6. Capture and destruction of over 20 trains and cars loaded with supplies.
7. Bringing into service of the Confederate States over 3,000 recruits.[28]

Wheeler ended his report about the Tennessee Campaign that his command also did the following: "averaged 25 miles a day in direct marching, either swam or forded 27 rivers and has captured, killed or wounded three times the greatest effective strength it has ever been able to carry into action."[29]

During the first week of October 1864, General Joseph Wheeler was bringing his cavalry corps back to Georgia as General John Bell Hood had been asking him to do for the past two weeks. Wheeler departed Huntsville, Alabama, and was moving east staying on the north side of the Tennessee River. When the Cavalry Corps reached Lookout Mountain, they crossed the Tennessee River. Once back in Georgia, they began destroying the railroad down to Dalton, Georgia.

On October 2, Wheeler arrived at Dalton and demanded the unconditional surrender of the town to him. Wheeler told Colonel Lewis Johnson, commanding officer, that he had a sufficient force to take the place. General Wheeler neglected to tell Col. Johnson that his artillery had no ammunition. Col. Johnson refused to surrender and braced for the attack. Gen. Wheeler left him with the impression that the terrible attack would be at dawn the next day, and the carnage would be upon him. At dawn, Col. Johnson's command was pleasantly surprised to discover Wheeler had left the vicinity.[30]

Wheeler was pleased his cavalry would not be bothered, because Johnson was bracing for the impending attack. The Federals feared Wheeler might try to capture the 4,000 head of cattle near Adairsville. On the night of October 3, Wheeler had his men camped at Snake Creek Gap near Villanow, Georgia.[31] The next morning, the Coosawatte River was up too high to cross. Wheeler adjusted his plans and moved the command down to the Oostanaula River about four miles west of Cedar Bluff at Edwards Ferry. The command began to cross during the night of October 5 and spent all day October 6 getting completely across. After the crossing, Wheeler took the command through Cave Spring to Lost Mountain. On October 8, General Wheeler was finally reunited with General Hood's army near Cedartown.[32]

On October 9, General Hood wanted Wheeler to move his command back across the Coosa River. Wheeler's Cavalry was to gather all the information they could about the enemy from Kingston to Rome and all along the Etowah River. Wheeler was directed not to allow any citizens to pass through his lines because they might be spies. Hood was most concerned with those citizens who may have come from the direction of Rome. On October 10, Wheeler was to report to Hood at Coosaville to deliver all the information requested.[33]

Wheeler's Cavalry captured Kingston and sent out the scouts. Hood was trying to cut General John M. Corse's communications between Rome and Cartersville. General Corse had blocked Hood at Altoona Pass but had lost one-third of his men, and he had been severely wounded in his face. He lost a cheekbone and an ear in the battle. General Corse feared that since Wheeler had Kingston, he would attack Rome.[34] However, Wheeler did not attack but fell back toward Gen. Hood. He began crossing the river at Coosaville at daylight, October 11, with Generals Stephen D. Lee and William J. Hardee following.

After reporting his findings to Gen. Hood, Wheeler moved his cavalry up to John's Creek below John's Mountain. They were in Villanow by 3:00 P.M.[35] The cavalry was spread all up and down the valley which caused the Federals to be uncertain if Wheeler was going to attack Dalton or Tunnel Hill.[36]

On the morning of October 12, General Hood moved on Resaca where Colonel Clarke

Russell Wever commanded the garrison. At 11:00 A.M. Wheeler attacked Resaca. The attack was savage, and they fought all day. This time Wheeler had ammunition for his artillery, and he used it freely all day.[37] General Hood sent a message to Col. Wever demanding his surrender and advising if he refused, no prisoners would be taken.

Col. Wever knew reinforcements were on the way, and he could hold his position. He replied to General Hood that he was holding and if Hood wanted the place, to come and take it. With that reply, the battle raged again all night. Hood found the reinforcement too strong and moved away.

On October 13, Hood was moving against Dalton. Wheeler sent his advance through Nick-a-jack Gap as Hood's attack started. Hood sent in a demand for surrender to Colonel Lewis Johnson. The garrison surrendered the 751 men of the 44th Colored Infantry. The officers were paroled, but the troops mostly were returned to slavery. After Dalton was secured, Wheeler sent his cavalry against the railroad near Tunnel Hill. When the destruction of the rail line was complete, Wheeler moved his men back to Dirt Town.[38]

Gen. Sherman sent his army to chase Hood after the Dalton attack.[39] On October 16, Gen. Hood's army fell back to Deer Head Cove just across the state line into Alabama. When General Wheeler reached Coosaville, Hood could not make up his mind about sending the cavalry with the pontoons up to the Tennessee River. After four changes in his orders, Gen. Hood finally decided the cavalry should not be going.

Gen. Wheeler had spread his pickets from Coosaville to near Summerville. However, by October 18, they began to fall back toward Gaylesville, Alabama. The Confederate cavalry was being harassed by General Kenner Garrard's Second Cavalry Division. Wheeler's rear guard was attacked early in the morning of October 19. The Confederates fought, scrambled, and skirmished with Garrard as they fell back toward Gaylesville. Wheeler's men cut down large trees to stop Garrard's mounted attack. Garrard dismounted his men to keep up the pressure. They fought all day until dark. The Federals pushed Wheeler to within five miles of Gaylesville.[40]

General Hood ordered Wheeler to slow Garrard down to keep him off his infantry. Wheeler's Cavalry were doing the best they could. Wheeler and Garrard skirmished all day October 20. On October 21, Wheeler's advance occupied a strong position near the Yellow River. The pickets on the Little River had already been forced back by early morning by Brig. Gen. Washington Lafayette Elliott. Wheeler's Cavalry fought hard and defended every position that was defensible. They were forced back because of the overwhelming numbers and the flanking movements of the enemy. The retreat continued to Leesburg.[41]

Wheeler's Cavalry built strong barricades again near Leesburg to protect General Hood's army. General Garrard exacted a heavy toll in blood from the Confederates while Hood moved his infantry to Gadsden. There was no time to care for those dead along the way. Only the living could be helped. The wounded received better care from the Federals than if they had continued to retreat with Hood.

Wheeler's Cavalry spent the next few days screening for Hood's Infantry all the way from Gadsden to the Tennessee River. For the first time since leaving Atlanta, General Alfred Iverson came under Wheeler's wing.[42] Perhaps due to his illness, Iverson had become detached from the Georgia Brigade after the battle at Sunshine Church. Wheeler's Cavalry covered the north side of the Coosa River, all the while shielding Hood's infantry.

General Hood began to think what Sherman would do when he left Atlanta. He thought Sherman might go back to Nashville or Chattanooga, and he felt it was important to keep the line above the Chattahoochee River cut. Hood wanted Wheeler's Cavalry to watch for any sign of advance by the enemy. If they did move, Wheeler was to destroy all mills within ten miles of their line of march. He was also to drive off all cattle and horses from the supposed enemy advance and cut railroad lines.

On October 23, Wheeler's Cavalry was entrenched on the Blount place near Kings Hill, Alabama. The cavalry was confronted by Major General Peter Joseph Osterhaus' Fifteenth Corps. General Osterhaus sent a company to scout Wheeler's position and number. With that information, Osterhaus came back on October 25 with a sufficient force to try Wheeler's strength.[43]

General Wheeler had his skirmishers out in front to engage the enemy as they approached. He wanted his skirmishers to fall back into the earthworks to add strength to his lines. The cavalry was stretched very thin because of the distance that had to be covered. Wheeler's main force was further back beyond Turkeytown. Once Osterhaus began to deploy for a full-scale attack, Wheeler's skirmishers fell into the earthworks as planned.

Wheeler had set his artillery in a position to sweep the entire Turkeytown Valley.[44] The cavalry was dismounted and ready behind the earthworks. As Osterhaus approached, Wheeler's artillery announced their position with a flurry. Osterhaus countered by sending part of his command to flank the Confederates. This flank forced Wheeler to fall back, but for some reason, this time Osterhaus did not pursue.

Wheeler took this time to fall back to Gadsden. Sherman's main army was in chase past Gaylesville. This threat did not allow Wheeler to stop at Gadsden; he had to continue on to Guntersville. This was a bad time for Wheeler's Cavalry as they felt like the fox in the chase. Wheeler had Garrard's Cavalry to contend with as well as the Fifteenth Corps.

Gen. Daniel Weisiger Adams, commander of Central Alabama, located at Talladega, sent Gen. Wheeler a message on October 28, stating that Jacksonville and Blue Mountain were being pressured. Adams was asking for help protecting the railroad as he had no cavalry. Wheeler could not help Adams because he was having his own troubles with Sherman's army trying to trap General Hood. Wheeler's Cavalry stayed near Gaylesville for a few days with only slight skirmishing.

General Wheeler issued from his headquarters in Gadsden Special Order #93. Part two concerned Major John Tench of the First Georgia Cavalry. Major Tench was to go back to the rear where the cavalry had been and locate all the stragglers and men absent from their respective commands. He was then to induce them to return to their units.

On November 2, General Wheeler began to hear from captured Yankees that General Sherman was about to leave Atlanta and take his army to Savannah, Georgia. General Wheeler sent General Hood a message with this information. Gen. Hood still thought Sherman would return to Chattanooga and told Wheeler to work on the railroads and telegraph line between Atlanta and Chattanooga.[45]

Wheeler finally sent his cavalry to Blue Mountain to protect the railroad. He sent Hood a message as to how he had dispatched his cavalry. General Hood approved of the moves and told Wheeler to stop the enemy from progressing south.[46] Wheeler had relocated his headquarters to Jacksonville. From there he sent a message to Gen. John T. Morgan that the cavalry was going back to Georgia to be concentrated near Jonesboro at Lovejoy's.

On November 6, the Georgia Brigade had moved to Carrollton, Georgia, on their way to Jonesboro.[47]

General Hood wired President Davis from Tuscumbia, Alabama, that he was moving to Middle Tennessee and expected to be there by November 9. Hood also stated he thought if General Sherman moved out of Atlanta, it would "be the best thing that could happen for our general good."[48]

14

Sherman Starts for the Sea

On November 7, 1864, the First Georgia Cavalry was still in Alabama with General Joseph Wheeler's Corps. Wheeler's scouts and enemy prisoners were reporting that General William T. Sherman was moving part of his army back toward Atlanta. It had been reported at least three corps were moving south and two corps were moving toward Chattanooga.[1]

When General Wheeler was ordered to Jonesboro, Georgia, General John Bell Hood protested to President Jefferson Davis about this command. On November 13, 1864, General Wheeler arrived in Jonesboro. Upon his arrival, Wheeler began to question General Iverson about the Federal army. Wheeler found that Iverson could tell him nothing of value about Sherman's movements.[2] He reported that from information taken from prisoners and his own personal observations Sherman had been burning something in Atlanta. Wheeler had seen the signs of Captain Orlando Metcalf Poe, Sherman's engineer, at work. Indeed, Captain Poe had thoroughly destroyed Atlanta except for a few dwellings and churches. The people of Atlanta would never forget the destruction Poe did in burning their city.[3]

On November 14, 1864, the march to the sea began. General Sherman sent General Hugh Judson Kilpatrick's Third Cavalry Division toward Jonesboro. He sent General Henry Warner Slocum's Army of Georgia toward Decatur. Sherman's first objective was to move his army to the heart of Georgia, between Macon and Augusta. From there, he could force the Confederates to spread their remaining army thin in protecting the surrounding cities.[4]

On November 15, General Kilpatrick crossed the Flint River and occupied Jonesboro, Georgia.[5] General Wheeler's Cavalry and the Georgia Militia, under General Howell Cobb, had already fallen back to Lovejoy Station. The Georgia Militia had occupied some of the old earthen works that had been constructed by Gen. Hood during his retreat from Atlanta.

The same day the First Georgia Cavalry and the rest of Wheeler's Cavalry Corps received orders concerning the upcoming battle against Sherman and the procedures they were to follow in conducting the war. Instructions included that all mills near the enemy's line of march were to be destroyed. However, no other mill building, corncrib, or any other private property were to be burned or destroyed.[6] Wheeler's command would later be accused of not obeying these orders.

The commanders of the various cavalry units were given instructions while falling back before Sherman. They were to send reliable officers and men one day in advance to assist the citizens in removing themselves and their stock from eminent danger. All cattle, horses, mules, and other stock left by the citizens were to be driven off and a proper receipt given the owner. If no owner could be found, an accurate record of the livestock was to be maintained to aid in reclaiming the animals.[7]

Early in the morning of November 16, Kilpatrick's Third Cavalry Division moved out from Jonesboro heading south toward Lovejoy. Wheeler's Cavalry Corps was in the trenches to receive Kilpatrick. The Yankees charged the Confederate position and were met by a stubborn resistance. After a gallant stand, Col. Eli H. Murray's First Brigade cracked the Confederate line and forced them to fall back to Bear Creek Station. During the battle, Col. Charles Crews' Georgia Brigade lost the two three-inch rifled guns they had captured from General Stoneman at Sunshine Church.[8]

By 4:00 P.M. November 16, Wheeler and his cavalry had checked the fast-advancing enemy cavalry at Bear Creek. As the afternoon progressed, Col. Atkins' Tenth Ohio Cavalry led by Col. Thomas L. Sanderson broke the Confederate lines, forcing Wheeler to fall back to Griffin, about fourteen miles from Bear Creek. General Kilpatrick camped for the night very satisfied with his cavalry and Sherman's plans.

On November 17, Kilpatrick continued his march toward Macon. He attacked Wheeler's cavalry all day. On November 18, Wheeler's headquarters was located in Forsyth. Wheeler was still trying to slow the Federals' progress. Kilpatrick had turned southeast above the Towaliga River and crossed the Ocmulgee River above the mouth of the Towaliga. He moved south again and was in Clinton by November 19, 1864.[9] On this day General Wheeler was still in Forsyth making reports of enemy movements. He sent General Robert Anderson's (Confederate) Cavalry Brigade and Col. Charles Crews' Georgia Cavalry Brigade to Macon. They were to report to General Howell Cobb for his instructions.[10]

General Cobb placed Anderson's Brigade on the Clinton Road on the east side of the Ocmulgee River. They were to observe the enemy movements from that position. Cobb placed Crews' Georgia Brigade on the Milledgeville Road and ordered Col. Crews to engage any raiding party of the enemy which might move toward the railroad.[11]

Later in the day, General Wheeler moved the rest of his command to Macon except for General Samuel Wragg Ferguson's Brigade and Colonel William Campbell Preston Breckenridge's Ninth Kentucky Cavalry Regiment. When Wheeler arrived in Macon at about 11:00 P.M., he found Gen. Hardee had assumed the command of the Department of Georgia, South Carolina, and Florida.[12]

General Wheeler was now commander of the department's Cavalry Corps. His Cavalry Corps had been reduced to only 2,000 men. Much of his former corps were sent with General Nathan B. Forrest who was with General Hood in Tennessee. The corps was divided into three Divisions: General William Allen's, General William Humes', and General Alfred Iverson's. General Allen's Division was divided into three brigades: General Robert Anderson's, Col. James Hagan's, and Col. Charles Crews' Georgia Brigade. Crews' Georgia Brigade was as follows: First Georgia Cavalry, Lt. Col. George T. Watts; Second Georgia Cavalry, Captain George C. Looney; Third Georgia Cavalry, Lt. Col. Robert Thompson; and Sixth Georgia Cavalry, Col. John Hart.

General Hardee ordered Wheeler's Cavalry Corps to attack the enemy on November 20. Wheeler's mission was to discover what the Yankee intentions were with this attack.[13] Early in the morning of November 20, Wheeler moved out with his entire Cavalry Corps except for the Georgia Brigade. He led his men down the Clinton Road from Macon. Almost as soon as they began, their flanks were harassed by small parties of the enemy cavalry. The harassment caused a delay in Wheeler's movement because the effort to drive them away took time. However, this was soon accomplished. Wheeler's Cavalry galloped down the road to Clinton. As they arrived, General Peter Joseph Osterhaus' Fifteenth Corps was moving through the town.[14]

The Yankees did not notice Wheeler's approach until six of Wheeler's cavalrymen dashed upon General Osterhaus' headquarters in an effort to capture Osterhaus himself. The Rebels got to within twenty feet of him before being discovered. They were able to capture only his orderly before being chased away by a squad of enemy cavalry.[15]

Wheeler's advance guard found itself in danger of being cut off by the Federal Cavalry. As fortune would have it, two regiments of Confederate cavalry arrived just in time to drive the Yankees away. This allowed General Wheeler to escape capture himself. Wheeler seized this opportunity, instead of running for safety, to drive the Federal cavalry back upon their infantry. At that point, the Federals rallied and began a countercharge. Each side counter-charged the other until Wheeler satisfied himself by finally pushing the enemy again to their infantry lines at Clinton. After a day of fighting, Wheeler withdrew toward Macon.[16]

Meanwhile, Col. Crews' Georgia Brigade was occupied on the Milledgeville Road. Crews' scouts had located Col. Atkins' Ninety-second Illinois Mounted Infantry led by Lt. Col. Buskirk. They were moving south toward the railroad. Crews had orders from Gen. Hardee to attack the enemy if they moved in that direction. Col. Crews moved the Georgia Brigade to Griswoldville. When they arrived, they set up barricades to engage the enemy. Crews notified Gen. Wheeler of enemy movements and activity. Crews knew Wheeler must be informed his position on the Milledgeville Road had changed, leaving the route to Macon wide open.[17]

From behind the barricades, the Georgia boys waited on Col. Atkins' Mounted Infantry. They observed Lt. Col. Buskirk command the advance, dismount his troops, and form a line of attack. When the Yankees reached a point, the First Georgia Cavalry and her sister regi-ments charged on horseback firing their pistols and slashing their sabers. The Rebels drove the advance from the field in grand style. When the Confederate cavalry met Col. Atkins' entire Second Brigade, Col. Crews had to fall back. Crews rallied his men and charged back into Col. Atkins, driving them from the field. The Yankees found a position they could defend and began to push the Georgia Brigade back through the woods.

Col. Crews found a position for his artillery and began to employ it to keep the Federals at bay. Gen. Wheeler and the cavalry rode upon the field and took charge. Wheeler quickly placed Colonel Harrison's Brigade and Col. Hagan's Alabama Brigade in an unmanned posi-tion between the infantry redoubts. The Yankees charged into the completed lines and were repulsed after a slight skirmish.

That night General Hardee issued Gen. Wheeler orders to take his cavalry corps and drive the enemy from Griswoldville. The following morning, November 21, Wheeler's cavalry attacked and drove the Yankees back to their main column. The Federals counterattacked, forcing Wheeler to withdraw.

General Sherman ordered General Osterhaus to make a demonstration against Gris-woldville. Sherman hoped this would occupy Wheeler and his cavalry. Sherman wanted to move his wagon train toward Gordon unmolested. General Osterhaus ordered General Charles C. Walcutt to move his troops across the railroad to Griswoldville. As Walcutt marched, General Kilpatrick and his cavalry were in front of him. General Kilpatrick had already engaged Wheeler's cavalry that day and was no match for Wheeler and his men. Kil-patrick was driven from the field and had to leave Colonel Jordan's Ninth Pennsylvania Cavalry as a screen to make his withdrawal. General Walcutt had to put his infantry into the fray to stop Wheeler's advance.[18]

While General Walcutt marched toward Griswoldville, General Wheeler placed an advanced brigade of cavalry behind a swampy creek to receive the attack. The Confederates found themselves in a poor position when the attack came. Wheeler had to withdraw the brigade back to his main force. General Walcutt halted his men at the edge of the woods just before entering an open field. Walcutt knew that Wheeler could dash his cavalry better in an open field, and he was not going to give him that advantage.

General Walcutt thought it best to take a position where the creek and swamp could protect his flanks. He had his men build a light breastwork with rails. General Osterhaus, in directing Walcutt, knew once Wheeler realized he was not being pursued, he would come back looking for a fight.

As predicted, Wheeler did return, but with four brigades of infantry, an artillery battalion, and all his cavalry. The attack upon Walcutt was very bloody. The Confederate infantry charged their works, and the Yankee artillery ripped into them as they came. Walcutt's position was too strong to break and that night the Confederates simply moved away.

On November 22, General Alfred Iverson reported to Wheeler the enemy was moving east toward Waynesboro. Iverson reported the position of General Joseph Horace Lewis' Kentucky Brigade and General Hannon's Brigade to Wheeler and confirmed that he would continue to follow Wheeler's instructions to watch the enemy.

Wheeler began to realize the Federals would not make any further demonstrations against Macon. He mounted his cavalry and moved east toward the Oconee River and reached it November 24.[19] Before the First Georgia Cavalry left Macon, Lt. Col. George T. Watts requested supplies and arms from the quartermaster. Watts stated the reason for the request was that he had not had the opportunity until now to supply the First Georgia Cavalry.

Wheeler crossed his cavalry at Blackshear's Ferry on the Oconee River. The crossing took all that day and went into the morning of November 25. The crossing was slow because there were no boats to aid in it. The men had to swim for the other side and in late November the water was very cold.[20]

On November 25, Wheeler received a dispatch from Major General Henry Constantine Wayne stating that an enemy force was marching toward Sandersville. Wheeler was to send help quickly. General Robert Bullock ordered Wheeler to watch the enemy and if they left the railroad and headed toward Augusta, he was to get his cavalry between Augusta and the enemy.

Wheeler sent Lt. Col. John F. Gaines' Brigade immediately to Ball's Ferry to help hold that position, as the enemy was menacing the crossing at that point. Once Wheeler got his command across the Oconee River, he moved to Station #13, Tennille, on the Central of Georgia Railroad. Upon arrival there, General Wheeler sent his scouts and pickets up each road from Tennille by which the enemy could advance.

General Iverson reported from Sandersville that General Allen's Division, containing the Georgia Brigade, was five miles in the rear.[21] Wheeler took his cavalry to the west side of Sandersville. The local troops had already been run off by the Yankees and could not help. Wheeler sent part of his cavalry on the upper road west of Sandersville toward Buffalo Creek.[22] The rest of the cavalry was on the lower road.

The Fourteenth and Twentieth corps under General Slocum were moving on Sandersville from Milledgeville. Wheeler's Cavalry met the enemy about three miles out of town. The Yankees came charging at the Rebels' position, but they stood firm. Once the enemy was stopped, the cavalry charged out at the Yankees and drove them for a mile back to Buffalo Creek upon their infantry. Wheeler's men killed, wounded, or captured about thirty of the enemy plus capturing a number of wagons and horses.

General Wheeler fell back to Sandersville to warn the citizens they lay in Sherman's path. He warned that they should remove all valuables and livestock immediately. Wheeler put his pickets on the west side of town and waited for Sherman.

On the morning of November 26, Sherman's army slowly advanced, pushing the Confederates back through the streets of Sandersville. By late evening, Wheeler was informed by his pickets near the Ogeechee River that Kilpatrick was moving with a large cavalry force toward Augusta. Wheeler had his entire command except for General Iverson's Brigade, and he galloped off to overtake Kilpatrick.

As Sherman passed through Sandersville, he had Captain Orlando M. Poe, of Atlanta fame, burn the courthouse because the Rebels had fired at his troops from the portico. While Sandersville burned, Wheeler chased Kilpatrick. Gen. Kilpatrick did not think he would be overtaken by Wheeler and camped for the night. General Kilpatrick confiscated someone's house and acquired a mistress for a night of pleasure. At about midnight, Wheeler's Cavalry came upon Kilpatrick's pickets posted around the camp.

After the pickets were silenced, the Yankee cavalrymen were unpleasantly awakened as Wheeler's men came crashing through their camp. The Yankees hurriedly ran to their horses, leaving camp equipment, wagons, and some weapons behind. Some of the Federals were not lucky enough to escape to their horses and were chased through the woods. General Kilpatrick, dressed in his drawers, undershirt, and skullcap, jumped out of the house onto a barebacked sorrel horse and barely escaped with his life in a heavy rain of lead. He deserted his mistress, uniform, gilded sword, two ivory-handled revolvers, and his best horse. Later that night, he was able to gather his command together, and they made their way on the lower Augusta Road.

General Wheeler talked with the people who were in the house where Kilpatrick had stopped for the night. In talking with them Wheeler discovered that the Union officers and Kilpatrick had discussed their plans to do great damage to the mills and property in Augusta. The people also told Wheeler Kilpatrick had sent 500 men to Waynesboro to destroy the railroad bridge over Brier Creek.[23] With that information, Wheeler knew Kilpatrick was taking his main force to Augusta. He felt if he could press Kilpatrick hard enough he might turn from Augusta in order to save his command.

General Wheeler walked out of the house into the darkness; he could sense that his men and horses were very tired. He knew that the people of Augusta depended on what his men would do that night. If Wheeler's Cavalry failed to stop Kilpatrick, the strategic city would be destroyed. There was no choice, the order to mount up was given, and the gallant cavalry rapidly galloped out to overtake Kilpatrick.[24]

Kilpatrick posted rear guards in strong positions about 200 to 300 yards apart to deter Wheeler. Kilpatrick hoped the guards would slow Wheeler enough or discourage him entirely from following. He wanted just enough time to allow for the destruction of the vital mills in Augusta.

When Wheeler's men came upon these rear guards, they quickly swept them aside or captured them. The hard riding Confederate cavalry finally caught the Yankee cavalry in the rear and made it warm for Kilpatrick. Wheeler's Cavalry attacked so determinedly Kilpatrick did what Wheeler hoped they would do. They turned away from Augusta.[25]

Kilpatrick turned toward Waynesboro and was so enraged and frustrated by Wheeler's Cavalry he decided to destroy everything he could set a match to and burn it to the ground. However, Wheeler's men continued to chase him hard enough to prevent the planned total destruction. The two enemy cavalries raced from town to town. The Yankees would set the fires, and the Rebs would put them out. Georgia homes, barns, corncribs, mills, and other buildings were the targets. Wheeler's men were able to save some of the buildings about half the time. The chase became so close that Kilpatrick's men did not have enough time to set many fires.[26]

During the night of November 27, Wheeler's men could see the flames of Waynesboro licking up into the night air. General Wheeler and his staff were in the lead of the column. They rushed into Waynesboro and began putting out the flames. Fortunately, they were able to extinguish most of the fires and were able to prevent much damage to the town. Wheeler reported only one home was completely destroyed.

He sent General Hardee a message from Waynesboro that his cavalry was still chasing Kilpatrick, and the enemy were on their way to Millen. Wheeler mounted his cavalry to continue the chase.

Kilpatrick felt Wheeler was not pressing him for the moment and stopped his cavalry and put them to work destroying the railroad between Waynesboro and Millen. While some men worked tearing up track and rails, others were sent out as pickets to keep the command from being surprised as they had been a few nights earlier. When the Confederate cavalry came in to attack, the Federals made a good show and defended their position.

Wheeler was satisfied he had Kilpatrick within reach and had also turned the Federals away from the railroad destruction to his cavalry. Now that Wheeler had their attention, he had to decide how best to attack the Yankee cavalry. He decided to send General Humes' Division around the left flank and to the rear of the enemy. At about three o'clock in the morning of November 28, General Humes was to attack and turn that flank. Wheeler sent two regiments to the right flank and rear with the same orders. The night air was heavy with fog which made it difficult to see. Wheeler's men could not find their way in the darkness and by daylight Kilpatrick had quietly slipped away. Unknown to Wheeler at the time, Kilpatrick had only changed positions to a more favorable place to defend.[27]

Once Wheeler discovered that Kilpatrick had escaped, he sent his scouts out to find him. He sent a line of skirmishers out behind the scouts to be ready for any charges that might be sent against them. Sure enough, as they advanced, Kilpatrick charged part of his cavalry into Wheeler's skirmishers. Wheeler's line held the charge in good fashion and quickly repulsed the Yankee attackers. General Wheeler sent General Humes' Division and General Anderson's Confederate Cavalry Brigade to the enemy flanks. General Wheeler, with General Allen's Division including the Georgia and Alabama brigades by his side, attacked Kilpatrick's front. This gallant charge drove the Yankees from their fortified position.

At last the Confederates had Kilpatrick's Cavalry in their grasp. Many of Kilpatrick's men, however, would not stop and surrender. A rumor had been spread among his command that Wheeler's men did not take prisoners. As a result, many a poor Federal was shot to death trying to make good a futile escape. General Kilpatrick himself came very close to being captured during the attack.[28]

The Rebels continued the pursuit of the routed Federal cavalry. Wheeler halted the chase at the edge of a swamp where Kilpatrick's men had built a crude barricade. From there, Kilpatrick would make his stand. General Wheeler sent his cavalry out as flanking arms to enfold Kilpatrick. With this movement the rout continued, and the stampede was on. Wheeler counted nearly 200 Federals killed, wounded, or captured.

As Sherman's army moved toward Savannah, Georgia, the First Georgia Cavalry was a part of Col. Charles Crews' Georgia Brigade. Crews' Brigade was in Gen. William Allen's Division in Wheeler's Cavalry Corps. General Joseph Wheeler's Corps continued to contain the devastating Federal cavalry. General Judson Kilpatrick was having a most difficult time maintaining order out of the stress Wheeler was creating. As the Federal cavalry fled from their last position, Col. Smith D. Atkins took his Second Brigade across Buckhead Creek near Waynesboro, Georgia. General Kilpatrick was on the other side of the creek with Lt. Col. Lielder A. Jones' Eighth Indiana Cavalry and Col. George S. Acker's Ninth Michigan Cavalry.[29] Wheeler had almost surrounded Kilpatrick on this side of the creek. He would have except Col. William McLemore's Fourth Tennessee Cavalry Regiment of Col. George Dibrell's Brigade failed to gain their rear as ordered. This allowed Kilpatrick time to fall back across the bridge over Buckhead Creek.

General Kilpatrick placed his pickets on the far side of the creek to guard the bridge while his men set fire to it and watched it burn. The Federal cavalrymen had stacked brush underneath the bridge to help in the rapid destruction of this vital link. As Wheeler's Cavalry came in sight, the fire was just beginning to burn hot. Wheeler's advance received a heavy fire from the Yankees on the far bank of the stream. A few brave men jumped from their saddles, ran into the creek to remove the brush from under the bridge, and put the fire out. The others fired at the Yankees to drive them away. Unfortunately, the bridge was badly damaged by the time the fire was out.

As it was, it was impassable for the Cavalry Corps. The men did not just stand there, they began removing the burned-out sections and moving lumber from the good to replace the bad. Some planking was provided from nearby church pews. In about an hour, the first columns of cavalry began to pass over very slowly because Wheeler's men were fighters and not bridge builders, but the bridge held.[30]

Kilpatrick's confidence had increased with his handling of Wheeler. He thought he had finally left Wheeler at the burning bridge, and his pickets would keep the Rebels from crossing. Kilpatrick halted his command about two miles away from the bridge, at Reynolds's Plantation, to feed his horses and men. Before the Federals finished eating, word came to Kilpatrick that Wheeler was now crossing his entire corps across the burned-out bridge. General Kilpatrick could not believe what he was being told. He sent a trusted officer to see if Wheeler was indeed crossing. The officer soon returned with the news Wheeler's Cavalry was truly on its way.[31]

General Kilpatrick was livid. He wanted to teach this tenacious little Rebel general and former roommate at the Point a lesson he would not soon forget. General Kilpatrick put his cavalry in motion to fortify a strong position with barricades. He spread his flanks wide and almost around to his own rear. The Yankees had barely completed these adjustments when Wheeler's cavalry came into sight.

General Wheeler was surprised to find Kilpatrick so near the bridge. He saw the barricades and knew the Yanks wanted a fight. He ordered Colonel George Dibrell to move his division around to the right flank of the enemy. Wheeler directed Dibrell to move behind a line of woods which would act as a screen for his men.

While Dibrell was making his move, Wheeler questioned himself about the large number of missing calvary. Only about 1,200 men had crossed the bridge.[32] On the other hand, night was fast coming which would not leave much time for a good fight. Wheeler decided to strike with the force he had available. He did not want Kilpatrick to escape him again.

As the attack began, Wheeler's men easily drove Kilpatrick's pickets back inside the barricades. As the Confederates advanced, they were met with a very severe fire and fell back. Wheeler re-formed his command for another attack. He placed the Third Arkansas Cavalry led by Major William H. Blackwell in line in front of the Eighth Texas Cavalry led by Lt. Col. Gustave Cook and the Eleventh Texas Cavalry led by Lt. Col. Robert W. Hooks, who were in columns. These regiments were part of Harrison's Brigade led by General Felix Huston Robertson. The cavalry regiments charged, like Hell was after them, into the enemy's blazing guns.[33]

General Kilpatrick called the charge by part of Harrison's Brigade "one of the most desperate cavalry charges I have ever witnessed."[34] General Wheeler said of the charge, "Nothing could have exceeded the gallantry with which these troops responded to the bugle's call and hurled themselves upon the enemy."[35]

The charge drove right into the face of the Union Cavalry. The Federals realized the Rebels were not stopping in their murderous fire so they broke and ran. They ran back across a field into the woods. Kilpatrick rallied his routed men and made another stand. The cover of the forest made it impossible for the cavalry to mount a charge into the heavy thicket.

Wheeler knew he had his quarry treed. All he had to do for victory was to flush him out of the woods. Wheeler sent Colonel Henry M. Ashby's Brigade to their left flank to turn it and take possession of the Louisville Road. That was the road by which Kilpatrick had been retreating. By now it was getting so dark that Col. Ashby occupied the wrong road. He sent word to Wheeler that he held the Louisville Road but in fact he did not. Kilpatrick withdrew during the night back to the safety of Sherman's Infantry.

That night Wheeler was uncertain about what might happen next. He feared an attack by Sherman's Infantry against Augusta, Georgia. Based on that fear, Wheeler posted pickets all along Brier Creek from Waynesboro to Augusta. He posted his main force near Rocky Springs Church. In Gen. Wheeler's report of this action he stated, "Kilpatrick sought the protection of his infantry which he did not venture to forsake again during the campaign, no doubt being too much demoralized to again meet our cavalry."[36]

The following day General Wheeler savored the victory against General Kilpatrick and sent General Braxton Bragg a message about the stampede and almost capturing Kilpatrick. Wheeler told Bragg that he would have captured him "but having a fleet horse he escaped bare headed, leaving his hat in our hands."[37] Wheeler included in the report his loss was about seventy men including General Felix H. Robertson, who was wounded in the elbow.

Wheeler had to content himself by sending his cavalry out to watch for the enemy and harass them at every opportunity. Sherman's Army was spread like locusts across Georgia and were stealing and burning everything in sight at the slightest provocation. Wheeler's Cavalry, in turn, punished the enemy for their deeds at every opportunity.

General Kilpatrick had fallen back with the Fourteenth Army Corps near Louisville. The Federals marched from Louisville to Waynesboro, arriving the morning of December

2.[38] When the Federals arrived near Rocky Creek, Wheeler gave them a good check. His stubborn resistance forced them to move around his left flank. The enemy crossed a bridge over Rocky Creek and marched through the fields to get to Wheeler's rear. Wheeler saw this attempt and realized it would be best to withdraw and fight another day. He had already received General Bragg's message that he was coming with 10,000 men and part of General Wade Hampton's Cavalry. It only made sense to wait for better odds.

General Hardee seemingly was not satisfied with General Wheeler's efforts. On December 3, Hardee made an attempt to impress upon Wheeler the importance of driving the enemy back. Hardee felt that the enemy was getting too close for comfort to Augusta once again. He urged Wheeler to gather in his spread-out cavalry and attack the main body of the Fourteenth Corps commanded by General Jefferson C. Davis.

During these days, General Wheeler's men did not carry enough forage and food with them. Wheeler had allowed his command to spread out at night in order to feed both horses and men. Surviving bullets was much easier than filling bellies in the desolate countryside in which Wheeler's men were fighting.

General Wheeler sent out messengers to find all his brigades and bring them back to him. By late afternoon on December 3, most of them were assembled, and Wheeler moved from his Brier Creek Camp toward Waynesboro. He moved around the town and three miles south, where he found one of Col. Atkins's Second Brigade's regiments camped on the railroad. They were busy taking the railroad apart.

Wheeler called for an attack and drove in their pickets, but he was unable to dislodge them from their position. He was satisfied he had stopped their work on the railroad and withdrew. Later that day after dark, Wheeler thought the Yankees might have resumed their destruction and decided to attack them again. Still he was unable to dislodge the regiment from the tracks. Around midnight, Wheeler brought up his artillery and shelled the Federal camp to good effect.

As dawn began to break on December 4, the Federals started to move toward Wheeler's position, which was about two miles outside Waynesboro. The enemy consisted of both General Davis' Fourteenth Corps and General Kilpatrick's Cavalry Division with Col. Atkins' Brigade in the advance. Wheeler saw the impending danger and quickly called his command together. He dismounted most of his cavalry behind the barricades which had been hastily constructed. He sent out a single regiment as skirmishers to meet the first assault. The regiment had orders to fall back if they met with a heavy force.

Wheeler's Cavalry was barely in position as Col. Atkins began his attack. The lone regiment of skirmishers, upon discovering the full weight behind Atkins, quickly withdrew behind the barricades. Col. Atkins saw the Rebels leaving the field and charged his cavalry into them in an effort to dislodge the Confederates from their crude breastworks. Col. Atkins found the Rebels "to be more strongly posted than was anticipated, and the first attack was a failure,"[39] according to General Kilpatrick.

Three more assaults against the barricades ended with the same results except that Wheeler relied on countercharges, when the timing was correct, to repulse the attacking Yankees. Soon the Federal infantry came into position to attack Wheeler's front. Kilpatrick had dismounted Lt. Col. Buskirk's Ninety-second Illinois Mounted Infantry and put Lt. Col. Sanderson's Tenth Ohio and Colonel Acker's Ninth Michigan Cavalry in columns of fours by battalion and sent them to the right. General Kilpatrick sent Colonel Hamilton's Ninth

Ohio Cavalry to the left to attack General Wheeler's Cavalry Corps flanks. Kilpatrick rolled up the Tenth Wisconsin Battery, under Captain Yates V. Beebe, to within 600 yards of the Confederate barricades.

The scene was staggering to imagine. As usual Wheeler's men did not count the numbers that opposed them and were willing to follow their commander's orders.

The Federals opened fire with their cannon into the flimsy barricades, each cannon belching death and destruction. Wheeler's five pieces of artillery provided only a weak answer to the Federals and were, therefore, withdrawn and sent to the rear. As the Federal cannon roared at the Rebels, Kilpatrick sent his men charging into Wheeler's flanks. At the same time, the infantry moved steadily forward toward the grossly outnumbered Confederates. No matter how valiant Wheeler's men fought, they could not stop their attackers. There were just too many Yankees and not enough bullets.

Wheeler realized the situation was hopeless. He quickly ordered his brigades to withdraw, and each regiment fell back in order. Each took a defensive position to allow the last regiment to fall back. The movement was as successful as possible under the conditions. Each brigade held back the advancing lines until, at last, they were in the town of Waynesboro. Wheeler had his artillery put in front of the town and a crude barricade constructed for his cavalry to fall behind.[40]

As Kilpatrick's Cavalry neared the barricades, Wheeler sent Col. Cook's Eighth Texas Cavalry and Captain Bromley's Ninth Tennessee Battalion to charge the enemy in a final effort to halt their progress. Wheeler reported that the charge "was gallantly done meeting and driving back a charge of the enemy and so staggering him that no further demonstration was made upon us until we were prepared to receive the enemy at our new position north of the town."[41]

Still, no matter how brave or gallant Wheeler's men fought, the results were the same at his new position as at the old. The fighting in town was fast and furious. Kilpatrick was unable to turn Wheeler's flanks, but the strong frontal assault drove the Confederates out of town. Wheeler's Cavalry moved back north to Brier Creek.

During this terrible battle, brigade commander Col. John F. Gaines was severely wounded, along with 200 others, by saber. The Federal loss was reported at 50 killed and 147 wounded. The Federal cavalry was more than double in number to that of Wheeler's Cavalry.[42] Plus, the Federals had a full division or more of infantry which insured Wheeler's defeat that day.

The Federal army stayed in Waynesboro for about three hours after Wheeler's Cavalry withdrew. The Federals were satisfied they had totally destroyed Wheeler and his band of Rebels, as they seemed to scatter in every direction. General Kilpatrick moved south down the road toward Savannah. Once the Federal army moved out of town, Wheeler returned and set up his headquarters. His men, though badly beaten, were not ready to accept defeat.

General Wheeler sent General Joseph Horace Lewis' Brigade of Iverson's Division and Col. William Sugars McLemore's Fourth Tennessee Cavalry to fall back in front of the enemy. They were to warn the people about Sherman and to drive off any unattended stock. Wheeler feared another attack against Augusta and defended her with the remainder of his command. He did send strike forces to hit the flanks and rear of Sherman's army as it crossed Georgia.

Wheeler's Cavalry created enough of a problem for the enemy that they began to block the roads with felled trees and destroyed bridges. Sometimes the Yankees would charge out toward the Rebels, but each time they would be sent back with fewer men and less equipment.[43]

By December 6, General Wheeler had moved his cavalry to Alexander, Georgia. There he met Gen. Braxton Bragg and Bragg told Wheeler to continue his attacks against the Union and to let him know if they crossed the Savannah River. By December 8, Wheeler was near Grahamville where he reported to Gen. Bragg that he did not know if any of the enemy had crossed the river. Wheeler estimated that Kilpatrick's Cavalry Division and General Davis' Fourteenth Corps were on the river road. General Frank Blair's Seventeenth Corps and General Alpheus S. Williams' Twentieth Corps were on the Central of Georgia Railroad, and General Peter J. Osterhaus' Fifteenth Corps were on the middle ground.

On the night of December 6, as General Davis' Fourteenth Corps rested in camp, Wheeler moved his artillery into a good position for an attack. At about midnight, the artillery opened fire on the sleeping Federals. The entire camp was thrown into total confusion. The enemy quickly broke camp and fled into the darkness. In their haste to desert camp, they left most of their clothing, arms, and equipment. The most important discovery in the camp was a dispatch from General Henry Slocum, commander of the Army of Georgia, to General Jefferson C. Davis. The message gave the proposed locations of Sherman's army around Savannah. Wheeler immediately sent the paper to General Hardee who was in the city.[44]

On December 9, a letter of recommendation for the promotion of George T. Watts was forwarded and gave some interesting information about the First Georgia Cavalry. It stated that on October 20, 1863, at Philadelphia, East Tennessee, Lt. Col. Armstead R. Harper was mortally wounded and died October 28. Samuel W. Davitte was promoted to lieutenant colonel and Captain James H. Strickland, the senior captain, was promoted to major. Both came by order of Col. James J. Morrison who was commanding the cavalry force in East Tennessee. On April 15, 1864, Col. James J. Morrison resigned and Samuel W. Davitte was promoted to colonel. Major James H. Strickland was also promoted to lieutenant colonel by Major Gen. William T. Martin commanding the cavalry division. On July 21, 1864, near Atlanta, Lt. Col. Strickland was mortally wounded and died August 3. Captain George T. Watts, Co. C, was recommended for promotion to lieutenant colonel because of his skill and distinguished gallantry at Richmond, Kentucky. On August 30, 1862, he was wounded charging the enemy. At Mossy Creek, East Tennessee, December 29, 1863, he resisted the charge of the enemy. Captain George T. Watts was 35 years of age, born in Jackson County, Georgia, and his home was in Floyd County, Georgia.

The Federal march to Savannah continued, and by December 11, Wheeler was within seventeen miles of the city. General Hardee was in Savannah and about to be surrounded. Hardee told Wheeler to take his cavalry across the river to Hardeeville, South Carolina, and protect his flank from that location.[45] While near Savannah, Col. Sam Davitte of the First Georgia Cavalry requested that all the promotions recommended be approved for the men by the War Department.

General Wheeler continued to harass the enemy but did not move to Hardeeville as ordered. When he got within ten miles of Savannah and surmised he could no longer do harm to the enemy he moved back north and crossed the Savannah River. General Wheeler ordered General Alfred Iverson to remain on the west side of the river and make sure Sherman did not send troops to Augusta without a battle.

On December 13, Wheeler's cavalry crossed at Sister's Ferry on the Savannah River about forty miles north of Savannah.[46] They moved to Izard's Place on the river and from there followed General Hardee's instructions.[47] Wheeler's Cavalry held the line of communication from Huger's Landing to Hardeeville. During this time, the cavalry was being threatened by a division of Sherman's Infantry. Wheeler used his artillery against the enemy and shelled Argyle Island on December 17 and 18. General Wheeler needed and requested more artillery, and General Hardee sent it to him. Gen. Hardee implored Wheeler to hold his position because that was his only line of retreat.

On December 20, General Hardee evacuated the city without Sherman's army ever knowing it. Gen. Sherman was surprised to find the place deserted as he made his final assault. As Hardee was moving, Wheeler began moving all his artillery and ammunition from Tumbridge, Morgan's Landing, and New River Bridge, and also the heavy 9,000-pound guns from Red Bluff.[48]

In closing his report of the Savannah campaign, General Wheeler thanked his division commanders and gave special thanks to Generals William W. Allen, William Conn Humes, Robert H. Anderson, and George G. Dibrell; to Colonels Henry M. Ashby, James Hagan, and Charles C. Crews; and to Lt. Col. Paul F. Anderson. Wheeler mentioned that Gen. William Allen had two horses shot from under him at Waynesboro, Georgia, and had been slightly wounded.[49]

From the above statement, a supposition can be formed that, with Gen. Allen and Col. Crews being singled out, the First Georgia Cavalry was heavily involved in battle with these gallant men as their leaders. In the same report Wheeler gave a brief account of his command activities, which at all times included the First Georgia Cavalry. He stated:

> In closing this report, I will state that during the last five months my command had been without wagons or cooking utensils, with orders to subsist upon the country. Its food had been limited to bread baked upon boards and stones and meat broiled upon sticks. It has not been paid in twelve months and not had the regular issue of clothing which have been made to the infantry. During this time, it has averaged in direct marching sixteen miles a day and being without wagons, has been obliged to pack all forage and rations to camp on horseback, which together with scouting and other duties, would make the average traveling of each soldier at least twenty miles each day. During these five months, my troops have been continuously in the immediate presence of the enemy, fighting nearly every day, and with brilliant success, except in a few instances, when small detachments sent off from my command met vastly superior forces.[50]

Wheeler further described their activities: "During these five months, my command has captured, killed, and wounded more than its own effective strength. It has captured from the enemy in action and carried off the field four pieces of artillery with caissons and battery wagons, 1,200 mules, over 200 wagons, 2,000 head of beef cattle, 3,000 cavalry horses with equipment and over 4,000 stands of arms."[51]

General Wheeler then described how his command lived during those five months: "As we were continually fighting the enemy, our camps could not be designated before nightfall. Details had then to be sent out to procure forage and rations, frequently making it midnight before supper could be prepared for my men, and then they were often compelled to be in the saddle before daylight. No men in the Confederate States have marched more, fought more, suffered more or had so little opportunity for discipline; yet they are today as orderly and as well-disciplined as any cavalry in the Confederate service."[52]

15

Three Runs Swamp

Joe Wheeler was proud of his troops, but particular members of the Confederate command were not so sure about them. During the Savannah Campaign, it was undeniable that groups of men were posing as a part of Wheeler's Cavalry. They robbed and destroyed property that belonged to the citizens of Georgia. The complaints about these ruthless acts filtered back to General Pierre Gustave Toutant Beauregard. Upon hearing these reports, Beauregard became incensed and pronounced Wheeler's command as "worse than useless."[1] General Beauregard did feel General Joseph Wheeler was a tireless and gallant officer, but Wheeler was too young, age 28, to control such a large force of cavalry.

General Beauregard in a letter to General Samuel Cooper, the Confederate inspector general, advised on December 23, 1864, unless Wheeler's "twelve so called brigades can be properly organized into divisions, under good commanders, a large portion of it had better be dismounted forthwith."[2] Beauregard took at face value the accusations against Wheeler without so much as asking him if these crimes were true or not.

Overreacting, Beauregard introduced the idea of 48-year-old General Wade Hampton, or one of his officers, as being the possible commander of Wheeler's Cavalry Corps. General Wheeler knew nothing of the trouble that was brewing for him. He was busy showing compassion for the people already devastated by the ravages of war. He requested of General William J. Hardee, on December 24, that the order "for burning mills and rice, corn and other provisions be reconsidered."[3] Wheeler stated, "The threats of the enemy to burn and destroy all property in South Carolina are of such character if we commence burning the enemy will feel justified in continuing. Will it not be better to give them no provocation to burn? What we would burn in Beaufort District would be of little value to the enemy."[4] On receiving this request, General Hardee thought better of the order and on Christmas Day suspended the burning.

General Wheeler soon learned of the stories about his cavalry corps and began his own investigation to discover who had brought shame to his gallant command. He isolated each brigade in order to watch them and follow their movements. He sent trusted officers to root out the truth behind the allegations made against his cavalry.

On December 25, 2nd Sgt. William Little, Co. F, was officially promoted to 2nd lieutenant. After Christmas, Wheeler's men held onto New River, South Carolina. On December 26, Wheeler sent a detachment to gather in the cattle near Grahamville, SC. On December 28, Wheeler's headquarters was in Hardeeville.

While in Hardeeville, General Wheeler wrote a letter to General Braxton Bragg of his troubles. He felt Bragg would give a sympathetic ear to him and possibly speak up for him to the higher command. In his letter, Wheeler dealt with the charge that his command "*straggled.*"[5] His answer to the charge was this: "This is partially true, but the great cause was the issuing of an illegal order by General Taylor directing General Clinton to organize all absentees from the army into 90 day regiments. This order was of course abused as all illegal orders generally are, and his officers enlisted men directly from my ranks, and this nearly ruined one brigade and had a bad effect upon my entire command."[6] Wheeler was very angry that General Richard Taylor would degrade him and his command for something he himself had caused. The next item Wheeler addressed was the charge of "horse stealing"[7]: "My command captured a great number of horses from the enemy which were the property of citizens. All of these horses are being restored to their owners as rapidly as possible. As the enemy advanced, I sent officers on in advance to advise the citizens to take off their horses and mules. When this duty was neglected, I had details drive them off and thus saved them from the enemy. This stock had been or is being returned to the owners when it is possible to do so."[8]

Wheeler denied burning any mills maliciously as had been charged: "In my anxiety to save property, I placed guards at mills, directing them to remain until the enemy drove them off and only to fire the mill when they saw it was impossible to remain any longer."[9] Finally, he informed Bragg of his command being accused of stealing from the citizens or terrorizing them: "I have positive proof that the country swarmed with organized parties who do not and never did belong to my command. Most of these parties were acting under orders from Governor Brown, but in all their stealing they claimed to belong to Wheeler's Cavalry. I now have the names of sixteen organized parties who steal on my credit. I have now run them off and the difficulty has ceased. Captain Conway, who acted so badly is not and never was in my command. He was acting under orders from Major Norman W. Smith."[10]

Major Norman W. Smith was an appointed officer. He was in the Quartermaster Department serving as chief inspector of field transportation for District 2, CSA and was located in Augusta, Georgia. Supplies were short and means to transport supplies were nonexistent. Major Smith began confiscating foodstuffs and the wagons and mules to haul them away. Confiscation was illegal in Georgia without the signature of Major General Howell Cobb ordering the confiscation of property. On special occasions Major General Joseph Wheeler could sign. Wheeler suspected Major Smith of forging his signature to documents to accomplish his desire to supply the troops. Wheeler hoped these explanations would stop the controversy over him and his cavalry corps.

Meanwhile, Wheeler requested General Hardee to let him advance his line from the New River Bridge to Izard's Place and block all roads below this line. Hardee thought it was a good idea and granted the request on December 29, 1864.[11] Later that day, Hardee received orders from General Beauregard concerning Wheeler. Hardee was to have Wheeler move almost half his command across the Savannah River back into Georgia.

General Wheeler knew about General Beauregard's order back to Georgia and he therefore issued General Order #7. The order contained eight parts including instructions as to the conduct of troops and officers. Wheeler was making double sure his command behaved as the good soldiers he had described in his reports.[12]

General Hardee, now under pressure about General Wheeler, wasted no time in organizing Wheeler's Cavalry Corps. On January 2, 1865, Hardee issued Special Order #1 as the commander of the Department of South Carolina, Georgia, and Florida. The first item dealt with Wheeler and the Cavalry Corps. The corps was divided into three Divisions commanded by General Alfred Iverson, General William Humes, and General William Allen.[13] General Allen's Division consisted of: General Robert Anderson's Confederate Brigade; Colonel Charles C. Crews' Georgia Brigade; and Colonel James Hagan's Alabama Brigade.

The First Georgia was still part of Col. Crews' Georgia Brigade. The brigade contained the following: First Georgia Cavalry, Lt. Col. George T. Watts; Second Georgia Cavalry, Lt. Col. George Looney; Third Georgia Cavalry, Lt. Col. Robert Thompson; and Sixth Georgia Cavalry, Col. John Hart. Lt. Col. George T. Watts's promotion came on December 29, 1864.

On January 8, 1865, General Hardee wrote a letter to President Jefferson Davis. Hardee stated: "Wheeler's Cavalry has been reorganized under my direct supervision and now consists of three divisions and eight brigades. It is a well organized and efficient body. The reports of its disorganization and demoralization are without foundation, and the depredations ascribed to his command can generally be traced to bands of marauders claiming to belong to it. I know nothing at present to add to its effectiveness."[14]

Joe Wheeler was now a lieutenant general and his cavalry corps had been reorganized. His men had new equipment and spirits were running high to free their land of the Yankee invaders. But looming greater every day was the dark side of this new year. Desertions were increasing, Lincoln was reelected, General Robert E. Lee's army had suffered severe defeats, and largest of all was the overwhelming numbers of Union troops.

General Wheeler's Cavalry Corps was located near Hardeeville and New River, South Carolina. Part of the command had moved back to Grahamville, South Carolina. Each day brought skirmishing and probing of Wheeler's lines by Sherman's army.[15] Sherman planned to move to Columbia with much the same design for South Carolina as he had carried out for Georgia. He hoped to link up with General Ulysses S. Grant at Raleigh, North Carolina, and end the war.

On January 3, 1865, General Sherman began sending his troops across the Savannah River. Just before dark that evening, General Robert Anderson, of General William Allen's Division, reported to Wheeler that the Union forces were moving very heavily against him. The crossing consisted of both infantry and cavalry, and they drove Anderson's Confederate Brigade before dark.[16]

On January 4, the Union divisions fell back eight miles below Hardeeville, giving up all the ground they had gained—to the relief of the Confederate Cavalry Brigade. Meanwhile, the Union had moved pontoons across the Savannah River to speed the crossing of the troops.[17]

Wheeler wrote to General Braxton Bragg again defending his command and its commanders. He had great confidence in some of his commanders and some of them he did not like at all, such as General Samuel Wragg Fergerson.[18] The real gut of the letter was about interference with his command. This occasion started with General Hardee. He had recommended to the War Department that Brig. Gen. William C. Young be promoted to major general. Hardee wanted Young to take command of General William Allen's Division, of which the First Georgia Cavalry was a part.[19]

Wheeler stated that General Allen "has served with most distinguished gallantry and ability during the entire campaign winning by his gallantry the confidence of his officers and men."[20] Wheeler remembered being accused of straggling and told General Bragg "General Allen has kept his command better together than General Young."[21]

Four days later, General Hardee placed General William Allen's name in to be promoted to major general. During this same time, General Joseph E. Johnston paid particular attention to the First Georgia Cavalry. On January 7 he remarked on the number of field officers who had been either killed or disabled within the regiment. If he had known their history of always leading in a fight, he would have understood why these gallant men had fallen.

As January went by, Sherman's army prepared to move north. Wheeler's Cavalry became spread out as pickets trying to keep watch on Sherman. By January 20 Wheeler's men ranged from the mouth of the Altamaha River in Georgia to north across the Savannah River to near Walterboro, South Carolina. The First Georgia Cavalry had its headquarters near Matthew's Bluff, South Carolina. Obediah P. Shuford was approved as captain of Company E on January 25, 1865, and Pvt. J.S. Adams, Company E, was captured. Wheeler could not tell if the enemy was going to Charleston or Branchville, South Carolina, but he reported the Yankees were still crossing the Savannah River.

On January 28, General Judson Kilpatrick began his march. He had moved from near the Little Ogeechee River to Robertsville and on to Lawton, on his way to Allendale, South Carolina. He had driven part of Wheeler's Cavalry along the way. Also on this day Col. Sam Davitte's promotion was approved as colonel for the First Georgia Cavalry.

On February 2, 1865, Gen. Allen had established his headquarters at the Maner house. He ordered his pickets to the Orangeburg Road at Owen's Crossroads and at Loper's Crossroads.[22] On February 1, 1865, 1st Lt. Virgil M. Tumlin was dropped from the roll as AWOL since June 1864 by Lt. Col. Watts.

On February 3, General Allen pulled his division back to the Graham house. Col. Crews' Georgia Brigade evidently had not established their position as prescribed by General Wheeler. Gen. Allen was to make sure Crews was in his proper location somewhere in Lower Three Runs Swamp. Gen. Allen had his courier lines established from Blackville and Barnwell Courthouse to Augusta, Georgia.

On February 4, General Wheeler joined Gen. Allen near Springtown, South Carolina, on the road from Buford's Bridge to the railroad. General Wheeler personally put Crews' Georgia Brigade in fortifications at Lower Three Runs Swamp, which was south of Barnwell.[23] Their orders were to resist the enemy's progress toward Augusta. Also at this time the First Georgia Cavalry reported Captain John F. Leak was admitted to Ocmulgee Hospital with chronic nephritis.

General Kilpatrick's Cavalry left Allendale and moved north on the road to Barnwell. Part of the Union command was about to collide with Col. Crews' Georgia Brigade. The enemy units were Major Cramer's First Alabama Cavalry; Major Cheek's Fifth Kentucky Cavalry; Major Rader's Fifth Ohio Cavalry; and Lieutenant Stetson's First Section of the Tenth Wisconsin Battery. These units made up Col. Spencer's Third Brigade. They marched on the left flank of the Yankee division moving north. The other column moving toward Colonel Crews' Georgia Brigade was Colonel Hamilton's Ninth Ohio Volunteer Cavalry and Lt. Col. Buskirk's Ninety-second Illinois Mounted Infantry.

Wheeler put the Georgia Brigade in back of the swamp on the high ground in a well-fortified position. Fortunately, they did not know the full extent of the odds against them. Early in the morning of February 5, there was a low ground fog clinging to the swamp in front of the Georgia Brigade. The greyness gave a ghostly uncertainty to events about to happen. The entrenched Georgia boys could hear the enemy riding to some point in the distance.

Then they heard the orders for the Yankees to dismount and to make ready to cross the swamp and attack.

Meanwhile, back in Augusta, Major Gen. Daniel Harvey Hill, commander of the area forces, was concerned for Augusta. He sent a message to Col. Crews on February 6, outlining his concerns. Augusta's manufacturing provided practically all gunpowder used by the Confederacy, and the Graniteville Mills produced four million yards of cotton cloth a year.[24] Hill was reminding Crews that he was to guard all approaches to the city and not be surprised by the enemy. Hill also informed Crews that the enemy was moving during the night toward Blackville, South Carolina.[25] Col. Crews couldn't have cared less about the Yankees at Blackville because the Blue Bellies marching across the swamp had his full attention.

As the men in blue came out of the shadows of the grey fog, the Georgia boys thought this might be a little like shooting ducks on the water. At this point, the Union troops were up to their waist in cold dark swamp water. Suddenly, the shooting began. At first the Georgia men had the better of position and surprise. As the battle progressed warmly for two hours, the Federal numbers began to play an important role. The Yankees began to envelope Crews' left flank, forcing the Georgia Brigade to fall back. When the Federal artillery shells began to fly into their barricade, there was no doubt it was time to leave.

Col. Crews had his men withdraw in good order and while they fell back, he had them destroy the bridge behind them. Crews hoped this would slow the advancing enemy. Without the bridge the enemy was stopped, and the Georgians fell back toward Augusta. Kilpatrick's Cavalry was not stopped for long. The Yankee cavalry continued their press toward Barnwell. While in Barnwell, Kilpatrick let his arsons do their work and destroy as much property as they could. After Kilpatrick left Barnwell, he sneeringly renamed it "Burn-well"!

Col. Crews had not reported to General Wheeler or General Allen by 8:40 P.M. February 6. General Wheeler had an idea as to why. He knew the main body of the enemy had bypassed him and hit the Georgia Brigade head-on. Wheeler knew there was no way Crews could hold the Federals, and if they swept past the Georgia Brigade, their next move would likely be to hit the railroads.

Later that evening General D.H. Hill, who had learned of Crews' fate, sent a message to encourage Crews to use his good judgment when to withdraw from the enemy. With this encouragement to Crews, Hill again reminded him of how important it was to protect Augusta. He then urged Crews to communicate more often with General Wheeler and himself.[26]

General Wheeler sent General George G. Dibrell's Brigade to reinforce the Georgia Brigade that night. The Georgians were still before the enemy screening Augusta. Wheeler was in the process of putting more of his command between the enemy and Augusta to help the Georgia Brigade. He ordered all the bridges below Holman's Branch destroyed as a further deterrent.[27]

Col. Crews received General Hill's message but misunderstood his intent. Crews sent him a return message telling him he did not understand. Gen. Hill wanted Crews to maintain his position if it was a strong one, but he must maintain the safety of his command and withdraw when it became necessary. In his message, Gen. Hill mentioned that General Alfred Cumming's Infantry Brigade would be at Big Horse Creek on the Beach Island Road. Col. Crews was to report to General Cumming before his cavalry appeared in front of Cumming's Infantry to prevent a disaster of being attacked.[28]

By the morning of February 8, neither Col. Crews nor Gen. Wheeler had communicated with Gen. Hill. Hill hoped General Cumming would have some information for him either from Crews or about the brigade. During this time, General Kilpatrick and his cavalry had been pushing Wheeler and the Georgia Brigade. By 4:00 P.M., Major Lewis M. Dayton and General Kilpatrick had arrived in Williston. Their intent was to destroy the railroad. Dayton reported that General William Allen's Division was in a weak picket between the Edisto and Salkehatchie Rivers.

By February 9, General Allen's Division was located at the Kitchen house about a mile and a half from the Pine Log Bridge. General Allen had asked General Wheeler for further instructions for Col. Crews' Georgia Brigade and Col. James Hagan's Alabama Brigade. However, unknown to General Allen, General Beauregard had orders for Crews. Beauregard had sent instructions through Gen. Hill at 5:00 P.M., February 8. Beauregard wanted Col. Crews to move the Georgia Brigade back to a position in an area around Upper Three Mile Run and connect his left with General Wheeler.

In transmitting the orders, General Hill said, "Hagan's Brigade was stampeded and run off."[29] Hill told Crews this because he should not be looking for Hagan's support. Gen. Hill reminded Col. Crews to not let his left flank be turned and to keep him informed about the Georgia Brigade's movements.[30] Col. Hagan's rout was brought on by his attack on General Kilpatrick at Williston. His effort had little effect on Kilpatrick except to give him the opportunity to deliver a hammer blow to Hagan's Brigade by Col. Spencer's Third Brigade.

By 7:30 that evening no one had heard anything from Col. Crews. General Hill sent a special messenger to Crews that he was to follow Gen. Beauregard's order to move the Georgia Brigade.[31] On February 9, Gen. Beauregard issued another order. This one was to all units explaining their mission. The portion that pertained to Col. Crews' Georgia Brigade was item five. This item outlined that Crews was to withdraw to Upper Three Mile Run. If Crews should be heavily pressed, he was to fall back to Hollow Creek. He could fall back to the infantry if all else failed. Col. Crews was ordered to contact Wheeler's right wing with his left. Lastly, he was by all means to send reports back to command headquarters.[32]

That afternoon General D.H. Hill paid Col. Crews' Georgia Brigade a fine compliment in a message to General Wheeler. General Hill was hoping to rid themselves of Kilpatrick and felt that if Wheeler could again concentrate his cavalry, as at Waynesboro, Georgia, Kilpatrick could be crushed. About Col. Crews, Hill stated, "I have sent an order to Crews to unite with Hagan, and probably something will then be done, as he seems to have a better command."[33]

General Hill had previously mentioned that Col. Hagan's Alabama Brigade had been "badly stampeded"[34] and "ran off causelessly."[35] As a result, General Hill felt that Akin, South Carolina, had been lost to General Kilpatrick. General Hill asked General Allen why he did not bring "Crews' men"[36] to his assistance to defeat General Kilpatrick. Col. Crews' Georgia Brigade was moved to White Pond to buffer the Federal attack. Attack they did, in such fashion that the Georgia Brigade was forced to withdraw to Akin and rejoin General Allen's Division.[37]

On February 10, General Kilpatrick planned to send Col. Smith D. Atkins' Second Brigade to Akin to see if General Allen or General Wheeler occupied the town. General Wheeler, in following Gen. Hill's advice, had concentrated his cavalry near Akin. Wheeler had withdrawn from the town to make it seem empty.

General Wheeler was setting a trap for Kilpatrick. Wheeler had his cavalry form a V formation pointing toward Augusta. Down the center of the V were Park Avenue and the railroad line. Wheeler placed his pickets on the opposite side of town parallel to Williamsburg Street nearest Kilpatrick to draw the enemy into the trap. As the Yankees entered the town, Wheeler would collapse his corps upon the surrounded enemy. The First Georgia Cavalry was in this fight along with General Allen's Division and General Humes' Division.[38]

General Kilpatrick's Division had been camped at Johnson Station, and he was now moving toward Akin. As Col. Atkins approached Akin, he encountered the Rebel pickets and easily drove them as planned by Wheeler. The plan was working fine until an Alabama trooper accidently discharged his weapon which alerted the Federals. Col. Atkins' Cavalry had entered the town and Wheeler had to send his brigades, who were in squadrons, charging down the streets. Wheeler's men were both in front and on the flanks of Col. Atkins.[39]

A main battle area was in front of the present location of the First Baptist Church on Richland Avenue. It was hand-to-hand fighting, with Rebel yells and slashing swords. Captain Yates V. Beebe, Tenth Wisconsin Battery, decided to lob 59 shells into the confusion. The Reverend Henry Cornish of Saint Thaddeus Church reported several shells whizzed by him from a battery on Railroad Avenue. He saw the Confederate cavalry rise in their stirrups with their pistols in hand, yelling and screaming as they drove the Yankees.[40] John Reed, Ninety-second Illinois Mounted Infantry, gave this description of the battle:

> We were within a half-mile of the town of Akin, when we discovered long lines of rebel cavalry. The column halted.... General Kilpatrick came dashing up to the head of the column and desired to know the reason of the halt. Just then a locomotive ran out in plain view near Akin and whistled and whistled. Kilpatrick brought up some artillery and sent a few rifled shells toward the locomotive and into the town. Kilpatrick also called on the 92nd Illinois Silver Cornet Band to play Yankee Doodle. The next thing in order was for the 92nd Illinois to charge into the town.... Now we felt that we were going into a trap, but Kilpatrick took the lead. General Atkins ordered the 9th Ohio into a line of battle on the right of the road, flanking the artillery, and the 9th Michigan Cavalry into line of battle, flanking the artillery on the left of the road, and holding the 10th Ohio Cavalry in reserve. The ladies of the town waved their handkerchiefs in welcome and smilingly invited the officers and men into their houses. But that kind of a welcome was unusual in South Carolina. It was an additional evidence of danger. In the farther edge of the town, the enemy was in line of battle.
>
> After the accidental shot per Reed [the officers] quickly formed the regiment to charge back again to the barricade, the rebels having formed in line in our rear. Every man in the regiment appeared to be conscious that the only way to get out was to assault the rebel line and cut a hole in it. We rode forward to the charge. The rebels awaited our approach until within close range, when they demanded a halt and surrender, and were answered by every man in the regiment pumping into them the eight Spencer bullets in his trusty repeating rifle. It was a desperate charge, and the men fought face to face and hand to hand. Now the brigade bugle sounded and with a yell the 9th Ohio and the 9th Michigan charged into the town of Akin recapturing a great many of the boys that had been taken prisoner.... The rebels at Akin came thundering down upon our four little regiments and the five miles back to camp was a battle field all the way.[41]

Sergeant Charles Waters, of Col. Atkins Second Brigade, described the action: "All this time the Jonnies were getting ready for a scrimmage. As soon as they were ready, a body of them charged furiously upon the Ninety-second Illinois Mounted Infantry. The shock was so great that the Shuckers were obliged to fall back upon our right, in some confusion. The Rebels swarmed around upon their flanks and rear, and they was some close hand-to-hand fighting, the Illinois men clubbing their guns and pounding the heads of their adversaries."[42] Sergeant Pomeroy, a Yankee cavalryman, described the clash: "One cavalry skirmish is much like another. A crash of horses, a flashing of sword blades, five or ten minutes of blind confusion and then those who have not been knocked out of their saddles by their neighbors knees and have not cut off their own horse's head instead of their enemies, find themselves, they know not how, either running away or being run away from."[43]

General Wheeler placed his loss at fifty men killed, wounded, or captured, and the enemy loss at several hundred. Kilpatrick placed Wheeler's loss at 31 killed, 160 wounded, and 60 captured. The loss in Wheeler's men was worth the gains made. They saved Akin from total destruction by Kilpatrick's arsons; and once again, they had saved Augusta, as the enemy made no further demonstration against her. Both cavalries rested for the next few days to recover from the battle. General Kilpatrick offered a flag of truce in order for both sides to recover their dead and wounded. Some of the Yankees had already been buried in churchyards.

On February 14, General Wheeler attacked General Jefferson C. Davis' Fourteenth Corps capturing forty prisoners and breaking their line of battle. On February 15, General Dibrell's Brigade defended the Congree Creek from an advance of the Federal right wing. Wheeler took the Georgia, Alabama, and Texas Brigades against the flank of the attacking enemy. They were able to hold the Federals from making any further advances.

Orders came for Col. Crews to report with his Georgia Brigade to General Cheatham on the Graniteville and Bethlem Road. Upon receiving the orders, Col. Crews sent Gen. Wheeler a message that he was leaving and Colonel Moses W. Hannon's Brigade was now moving into his position.[44] Col. Crews led his brigade off with General Edward Cary Walthall's Division of Stewarts Corps. On February 15, while out on picket, Cpl. William Griffith, Co. A, was WIA near Barnwell, South Carolina.

The Georgia Brigade was in Leesville by February 17. They arrived in Leesville while General Hill was conferring with Major General Pierce Manning Butler Young back in Akin. Hill and Young talked about uniting Young's command with that of Col. Crews. Their mission would be to harass Sherman's rear on the Congree River.[45] The Georgia Brigade, as a result of the decision by General Hill, stayed with General Cheatham. They crossed the Saluda River and moved to Newberry. They had traveled south on the Frog Level Road to within seven miles of Columbia by February 23. Col. Crews halted at that point for several reasons. The first was that the stream was too wide and deep to cross except by swimming. The attempt of crossing would be hazardous at best for fresh horses and men.

Col. Crews heard about a boat that could aid in the crossing and wanted to send for it. He soon found out the boat was fifteen miles above Freshly's Ferry. He still sent his men, but when they got there, they found the boat had been destroyed. Col. Crews advised General Cheatham to build some flatboats to cross his infantry, or he could send them to Freshly's Ferry where they could wade across.[46] Col. Crews' other concern was the enemy's unknown position. He did not want to blunder his command into a battle unprepared. The third problem for the Georgia Brigade was forage. Crews sent scouts out to find the enemy. This was done with little difficulty. Finding food for the brigade was a different matter. The Federals had destroyed almost everything of use, but the Georgians had become accustomed to having their endurance tested.

In numbers, the Georgia Brigade was reduced to less than a full regiment. A regiment usually was a thousand strong. It was estimated Col. Crews had 504 men in his brigade. The "regiments" of the Georgia Brigade were estimated as follows with commander and strength:

- First Georgia Cavalry   Lt. Col. George T. Watts   151
- Second Georgia Cavalry   Lt. Col. F.M. Ison   124
- Third Georgia Cavalry   Lt. Col. J.T. Thornton   122
- Sixth Georgia Cavalry   Col. John R. Hart   47
- Twelfth Georgia Cavalry   Captain James H. Graham   59.[47]

16

The Last Hurrah

On February 25, 1865, Captain Napoleon J. Reynolds, Co. F, had been appointed major and brigade quartermaster of Crews' Georgia Brigade. The First Georgia Cavalry continued with General Benjamin F. Cheatham's Infantry Corps until March 5, 1865. Col. Charles C. Crews received orders from General P.G.T. Beauregard for his Georgia Brigade to join either General Joseph Wheeler or General Wade Hampton, whichever he could find first. Col. Crews knew his men would fight better for Wheeler, therefore, they could not find Hampton. General Hampton, by order of the Confederate government, was to take command of General Wheeler's Cavalry Corps and General Matthew C. Butler's Cavalry Division. This was because of the allegations against Wheeler during the Savannah Campaign.

Col. Charles Crews led the Georgia Brigade across the railroad bridge over the Catawba River en route to Rockingham, North Carolina. Col. Crews was warned to go through Monroe, North Carolina, and avoid Wadesboro because Federal troops had been reported in the area. Travel was difficult along the muddy roads and through the swollen creeks along the way. The weather for the first week of March 1865 had been cold and rainy.

On March 8, General Wheeler was near Rockingham and was moving across the Pee Dee River.[1] The Georgia Brigade found Wheeler and reunited with General William W. Allen's Division. General Wheeler was moving his command by plank road to Fayetteville, North Carolina. He ordered Gen. Allen's Division to send pickets out the road from Rockingham toward Fayetteville, NC. They were to attack General Kilpatrick's Cavalry on the plank road about twenty miles out from Rockingham. General Kilpatrick had been warned by General Sherman to avoid needless battles with the Rebs as Sherman anticipated a war-ending battle near the Virginia border.

On March 9, Gen. Wheeler and Captain Alexander May Shannon's Special Scouts, an elite group of handpicked scouts, spies and secret service men, traveled east on the Morgantown Road and crossed the Lumber River. When they reached a point east of Nicholson Creek along Blue's Road, they discovered Kilpatrick's camp at a place near Monroe's Crossroads.[2] The location is today within the confines of Fort Bragg Military Reservation, North Carolina.[3]

Both Wheeler and Hampton reconnoitered the Yankee camp undetected. They discussed the best way for their cavalry to attack and decided the camp was too near Sherman's main army to attack dismounted. Therefore, they elected to make a mounted attack at daylight.[4]

Orders for the attack were issued. General Wheeler arranged his corps into five attacking columns. He wanted them to cross the large swamp and attack the Yankee camp from the rear. Wheeler ordered General William Y.C. Humes' Division to the extreme right and General Thomas Harrison's Texas Brigade in the center. General William Allen's Division was ordered south of the Morganton Road to attack from that direction. General Hampton placed his command, General Matthew C. Butler's Division, in the center and put General Wheeler in charge of the attack. Wheeler thanked General Hampton for the honor. The order was given to attack at dawn the next morning.[5]

Union Lieutenant Colonel William B. Way's Brigade of about four hundred dismounted cavalry were in charge of the ordnance wagons and the division headquarters wagons. They arrived at Monroe's Crossroads around nine o'clock the stormy night of March 9. They camped in line along the road in front of Charles Monroe's farmhouse. Colonel George E. Spencer's Third Brigade filed past the house and turned off into a large open field about a hundred yards north of Green Springs. Shelter tents were thrown over fence rails and saplings. Pickets were sent out among the pines, and the artillery was parked about fifty yards from the farmhouse. Col. Spencer and his staff made themselves comfortable in the old Monroe home. The Monroes had previously abandoned their home and never came back. Soon, General Kilpatrick and his staff came in and tied their mounts to the porch rail or garden fence. Judson Kilpatrick had as guests the two "lady" friends who had followed him from Savannah, Georgia.[6]

The rains had stopped that morning and a heavy fog covered the Yankee camp. General Humes and General Allen were almost late reaching their appointed position because the heavy rains had made the roads almost impassable. Kilpatrick was up early and came out on the porch in his nightshirt to see if his horse had been fed. The buglers and drummers were standing by to sound reveille. Some Union troopers were just awakening and making coffee when the Rebel cavalry came, fast and unsympathetic, upon the unsuspecting Yankee camp. General Kilpatrick described the attack: "In less than a minute [they] had driven back my people and taken possession of my headquarters, captured artillery and the whole command was flying before the most formidable cavalry charge I have ever witnessed."[7] During the attack General Kilpatrick was almost captured again, but escaped only by running on foot to his cavalry camp in the rear. By the time Kilpatrick arrived, the Yankee camp was also heavily engaged. The Rebels were pushing them into a swamp some 50 yards away.

When the battle seemed won, the Confederates slowed their onslaught to ransack the Yankee camp. That was their mistake! What should have been a complete victory was doomed for failure because no one bothered to find out how deep the bog was that lay between Wheeler's Cavalry Corps and the Yankees. The divisions on the other side could not get into the camp to help. When they tried to cross the bog, some horses and men disappeared never to be seen again. This allowed Kilpatrick enough time to rally his men and retake one of the camps. As a result, the Union cavalry regained their confidence and began to fight.[8]

Lieutenant Ebenezer W. Stetson, Tenth Wisconsin Battery, crawled on hands and knees and managed to reach an artillery fieldpiece parked on a ridge. Entirely alone he loaded, aimed, and fired at the Confederate cavalry. The explosion sent a jolt through the Rebs and enlivened the Yanks. Stetson was soon joined by others to fire a few more rounds, but they were soon silenced by General Butler's troops.[9] The Confederate cavalry's attack, as organized, fell apart because brigades couldn't cross the bog. As a result, Wheeler's Cavalry moved away and Kilpatrick did not follow because he was out of ammunition and in his underwear.

General Humes, General Harrison, Colonel Hagen, Colonel Hannon, Colonel Roberts, and Major John D. Farish were all badly wounded. General Allen and Col. Henry M. Ashby had their horses shot from under them. Hagan's Alabama Brigade lost every field officer and was being commanded by a captain.[10]

During the heat of the battle, General Wheeler repeatedly sent for General Hampton to come with General George Dibrell's Brigade. They were in the rear as the reserve. Hampton was simply too slow coming to aid the outnumbered Confederates. When Dibrell finally arrived, Wheeler took command of them and checked Kilpatrick's men who were advancing on his cavalry. This check allowed the entire command to withdraw unmolested.[11]

General Kilpatrick placed his loss at four officers killed and seven wounded. He had 15 men killed, 61 wounded, and a total of 103 men and officers captured. Kilpatrick counted 80 Confederates killed and 30 captured.[12] He did not give the number of wounded, but a large number can be assumed.

General Wheeler considered the attack a success because after only two hours of very heated battle, they were able to capture 350 Yankee prisoners. They were also able to destroy the supply wagons and run the mules away.[13]

On March 10, General Allen reported to Wheeler the enemy was advancing in his front near Fayetteville, North Carolina.[14] General Wheeler took Allen's Division containing Col. Crews' Georgia Brigade, General Robert H. Anderson's Brigade, and the remains of Colonel Hagan's Alabama Brigade and skirmished heavily with the advancing enemy. Wheeler was forced to withdraw across the Cape Fear River. He burned the bridge to halt the Federals' advance on him. During this fight, General Anderson was wounded.[15]

For the next few days, the Georgia Brigade continued to fall back with General Wheeler. As they fell back, they skirmished heavily with the enemy from the Cape Fear River near Fayetteville to Smith's Mill on the Black River. The Georgians were near Smith's Mill on March 15, 1865.[16]

General Hardee was about four miles south of Averysboro and was being warmly engaged by a force superior to his. Wheeler asked permission of General Hampton to give aid to his old comrade, and Hampton granted the request. Wheeler's Cavalry arrived early in the morning of March 16. The men fought dismounted all day until dark. At that time, Hardee proceeded to withdraw to Smithfield with Wheeler as a screen.[17]

Colonel Ashby's Tennessee Brigade was covering Hardee's rear, and General Allen's Division, with the Georgia Brigade, covered his right flank. General Wheeler was eventually ordered to remain with Hardee until the morning of March 17.

General Hampton feared that the Federals had detachments of cavalry moving up the west side of the Cape Fear River. He thought these Federals would be making an effort to get to the trains in Raleigh. General Hampton informed General Hardee that Col. Crews' Georgia Brigade was in that area and should be able to handle the problem with ease.[18]

Meanwhile, General Wheeler was being pushed out of Averysboro on to Goldsboro. Wheeler had been skirmishing all day in a losing battle. On March 18, he had to double-quick his cavalry to Bentonville. When they arrived, they occupied a position on the right flank of the Confederate army.[19] At the beginning of the battle, they engaged the enemy heavily, but as the day progressed, the fighting became less intense. During the day they were able to capture 40 prisoners.[20]

Wheeler's position was by a stream which was impossible to cross. That night, General

Allen's Division, with Colonel Crews' Georgia Brigade, camped seven miles from Mingo Creek on the Smithfield Road. General Allen had the road picketed against Kilpatrick's cavalry.

On March 19, the Yankees engaged General Allen's Division, but the Yankees were forced to fall back with each charge. By 11:30 A.M. of March 19, General Wheeler took General Allen's and Colonel Ashby's Cavalry Divisions to Mill Creek to secure a bridge before the Federals could destroy it.[21]

On March 20, Wheeler's Cavalry, with Allen and Ashby, checked the advance of a large force of infantry moving on the Goldsboro and Bentonville Road. This force included the Fifteenth and Seventeenth Corps of Sherman's army. The engagement took place to the left of the Confederate army. Wheeler's Cavalry hit the Federals with a gallant charge and fell behind a fence that made a good barricade. During this battle, Wheeler's horse was shot, and he was almost killed. His cavalry was able to hold the Yankee advance all day. That evening General Bragg relieved them with General Robert Hoke's Infantry Division.

Wheeler withdrew his men to a strong position behind Hoke's Infantry. The cavalry built strong breastworks some 1,200 yards long. It took them until daylight of March 21 to complete their work. He put some of the cavalry in the rear mounted and ready to defend any position which became endangered.[22]

By four o'clock that afternoon the entire line was heavily engaged by General Mower's Infantry. Mower was able to force Wheeler's left to give way, and this allowed the Federals to get into the Confederate rear. This was the only line of retreat remaining for the Rebel army remaining. General Wheeler realized that if Mower remained in that zone the entire Confederate army would be lost.[23]

Fighting Joe Wheeler, with Hagan's Alabama Brigade, charged into Mower's left. The brigade was now under the command of General Allen. Wheeler knew this attack had to be bold and would take repeated charges. He could see the Federals in a slow run advancing toward him. All of a sudden, Wheeler's Texas Rangers came galloping across the open field to help. The Rangers reached Mower's skirmishers about 200 yards in front of the Yankee main body. With the greatest of ease, they broke through this line and hit the front of the Federal infantry. At that same instant General Allen led the gallant Alabama Brigade in a hammer blow to Mower's left flank. These blows sent the entire Yankee command in a rapid retreat. General Mower almost became a captured prize during these bold strokes.[24]

During the cavalry attack the Georgia Brigade of Cavalry was in the trenches taking on Sherman's main infantry force. The pressures against them were terrible. Finally, after too long a battle for cavalry in trenches, General Hardee sent General Walthall's Infantry to secure the empty spaces in the line. The Georgians had held all attacks against them and continued for the rest of the day.[25]

At about midnight a cold rain began to fall on the field of battle and the now muddy trenches. Orders came for General Walthall to withdraw his infantry from the breastworks, and soon they began to trudge off in the rain for Smithfield. This left Wheeler's Cavalry alone to defend the breastworks and to check Sherman's entire army. As before in retreat, the cavalry screened for the infantry to allow them to escape to fight another day. That day never came. After this retreat, the Confederate infantry would never fight in another battle.[26]

Before dawn broke on March 22, 1865, the Yankees discovered that the Confederate infantry had disappeared. Lusting for a final victory, Sherman pushed his skirmishers forward against Wheeler's already battered cavalry. In this renewed battle, Wheeler's Cavalry was pushed by superior numbers out of their breastworks toward Mill Creek. Unfortunately, for a number of reasons, the infantry had not retreated very far. Their rear was still in Bentonville at sunup and open to attack. The excuse given for being so slow was that the heavy rains and deep wood hampered their travel.[27]

When General Wheeler discovered the infantry's plight, he calmed his emotions and went to work. He had his cavalry dismount into an unfortified position to again check the rapidly advancing enemy infantry. The rush of Federal infantry was on them and the fighting quickly commenced. Somehow, by 9:00 A.M. the enemy was finally stopped. Wheeler's Cavalry had to yield a mile of real estate, but they stopped them. By 10 A.M., the cavalry had established a new defensive line at Black Creek on the Smithfield Road.

The gallant cavalrymen defended this new front unyieldingly. A strong Federal force beat against them in a heavy storm of battle, but with no gain. The final Yankee charges left many of the dead at Wheeler's front. The dead included three color bearers who were within fifty feet of his barricade. The Federals had had enough and withdrew from the battle and made no further attacks for the rest of the day. The victorious cavalry gave a mighty HURRAH! As they saw their enemy leaving the field, they were thankful to be alive.

The war for Wheeler's Cavalry did not stop at Black Creek. On March 23, General Wheeler had the cavalry as pickets in front of the Confederate army on the other side of Smithfield. The cavalry continued to skirmish but only with foraging or scouting parties for the next few days. On March 28, Col. Crews' Georgia Brigade engaged Col. Spencer's First Alabama Cavalry near Faison's Depot.

On the last day of March 1865, General Allen's Division was detached for a special assignment from Wheeler's Cavalry Corps. Their assignment lasted a week. A minor shuffle in command took place during this time. The First Georgia Cavalry was still part of Col. Crews' Brigade but was commanded by Col. John R. Hart because Col. Crews had been severely wounded. Crews' Brigade was part of Brig. Gen. Allen's Division which also contained Gen. Anderson's Brigade and Hagan's Brigade commanded by Col. David T. Blakely.

Good news came to the First Georgia Cavalry at the end of March. Pvt. Francis M. Clark, Co. A, had been wounded in battle and was now safely home after being discharged disabled. Bad news came to them April 3, 1865. Captain John N. Perkins, who had been severely wounded at Murfreesboro, was now captured. After his recovery, Captain Perkins had been assigned to the Quartermaster Department by the War Department. He had been stationed at Tuscaloosa, Alabama, as part of the First Georgia Cavalry Regiment's Quartermaster Department to send supplies from that depot. Now this source was gone.

On April 9, 1865, the First Georgia Cavalry Regiment was to report to General Hampton. Sherman's army continued its chase of the Confederates toward Raleigh. The First Georgia Cavalry fell back with them still covering their infantry. Once they reached Raleigh, Lt. Col. George T. Watts was ordered to take the First Georgia Cavalry out to the depot a few miles from town to get corn to feed their horses. Once the men arrived at the depot, they proceeded to feed and curry their trusted companions.[28]

Lt. Col. George T. Watts posted pickets to secure the area. Those who were not on picket duty cared for their horses. After the men had pulled the saddles and bridles off the horses, they had a few moments to relax. Suddenly, a bugle call was heard. The men knew that the Yankees were about to pour through the woods any second. Everyone sprang to their horses with saddles and bridles flying. Just as they were able to mount, the Federals broke into sight.[29]

There was no organization as everyone stampeded off in the same direction. Lt. Col. Watts was hoping they could put enough ground between them and the charging Federal cavalry. After a good run for a few miles, Lt. Col. Watts managed to put together a part of the First Georgia Cavalry and turned them around on the Yankees. The Georgia boys came charging back yelling and waving sabers at the Federals.[30]

The crash and clash of sabers broke the air as the First Georgia Cavalry smashed into the Federals. Though the battle was small, to those who fought and died, it was no different than Murfreesboro or Chickamauga. The Georgia Rebels got the better of the Yankees, who had to wrestle themselves away from the Georgians because the remainder of the regiment was about to join the fight.

After the battle, the First Georgia Cavalry went back to Raleigh and rejoined the brigade, which was now commanded by General Wheeler. Early the next morning, the Confederates moved out of town. General Wheeler still had his old enemy General Kilpatrick on his trail. Wheeler put the Alabama Brigade in position to meet Kilpatrick while the rest of the cavalry moved away. The Alabama Cavalry checked and drove Kilpatrick two miles, killing and capturing a good number.

General Wheeler regrouped his cavalry at Morrisville Station, North Carolina, and was attacked there that evening. After a severe skirmish, the enemy retired. The next morning Wheeler moved his men to Chapel Hill. On April 15, the enemy approached, fired a few shots, and then moved away. Wheeler thought this strange until he received orders not to engage the enemy unless attacked. He felt rather empty when he heard the news that General Robert E. Lee had surrendered in Virginia.

On April 17, 1865, General Joseph E. Johnston met with William T. Sherman at the Bennitt farmhouse to discuss the matter of an armistice. They met again April 18 and signed an agreement to stop hostilities. The agreement was more political than military, but it was promptly rejected by Washington because of Abraham Lincoln's murder. On April 26, a military surrender was signed.

Meanwhile, President Jefferson Davis was making his escape from Richmond, Virginia, heading south. Quickly, an escort was arranged consisting of part of Company G, First Georgia Cavalry. Pvt. Lysander Huckaby, Co. G, was a member of that group. After this, they were discharged in Madison, Georgia, in May 1865.

General Wheeler said the following in his report of March 1 through April 15: "Thus ended the Campaign, the War, and the Military Power of the Confederacy. For an entire year my troops had been constantly together enduring, encountering, triumphing. During that year the enemy cavalry had been frequently met and always checked…. The spirit of my brave men was as buoyant, unbroken and determined as in the first days of our country's existence. Unity, concord, good-will, devotion to duty and country, and I might add nearly all elements which grow out of continued success, and which I felt would inspire success to me in the future pervaded my command from the highest officer to the youngest trooper."[31] These thoughts would bode well, as all Confederate troops returned home to an uncertain future.

On April 26, Col. George T. Watts gave the order for the men to come down from the barricades as this was the day of surrender. Some men upon hearing the order simply went home. They could not stand the thought of surrender. Some were glad they survived and could go home. Col. Watts saved the flag of Company C, First Georgia Cavalry, by wrapping the flag around his body and wearing his coat to conceal it from the Yankees.

In the days that followed, Col. John R. Hart took the Georgia Cavalry Brigade down to Salisbury, North Carolina. On April 28, 1865, General Johnston ordered Col. Hart via Crews to move from Salisbury to High Point. On April 29, Crews got a message from General Johnston which stated, "There was to be no surrender, but a cessation of Hostilities."[32] Col. Hart was then ordered to bring the Georgia Cavalry Brigade to Greensboro, North Carolina, in order to receive forage for their horses and mules. General Joseph E. Johnston also wanted to know where the rest of the cavalry could be located, and he requested a reply.

In these last days under the armistice, the First Georgia Cavalry departed for home from many points. The war for them was now over, and some wanted to avoid the term surrender and to take the oath. They took their chances reaching their homes before the Yankees caught them. Private Nathaniel Greenberry Parris had fought the entire war and was given a horse to ride home.

General Joseph E. Johnston explained to Governor Joseph E. Brown of Georgia, in a letter dated April 30, 1865, why he took the road to surrender. Johnston detailed: the disaster in Virginia, the capture of all the workshops for making munitions and repairing arms, the inability to recruit new men, the weight of being opposed by ten times his number, and the inability to supply his own men. To Johnston, there was no hope for victory. He explained that he had made the convention with Sherman "to spare the blood of the gallant little army committed to me, to prevent furthering suffering of our people by destruction and inevitable ruin from the marches of invading armies and to avoid the crimes of waging hopeless war."[33]

General Wheeler closed his report for the end of the war with the following statement: "I cannot express too earnest thanks to my Gallant Officers who had been of most valuable service to me during a long series of campaigns. Major General Allen; General Humes, Dibrell, Anderson and Hagan; I had seen twice wounded while carrying out my orders upon the field. General Robertson, Harrison, and Ashby and Colonels Crews, Cook and Pointer are still disabled from wounds received in the same manner."[34]

That same day, Captain Henry A. North, Company K, First Georgia Cavalry Regiment, sent the men of his company the following letter:

> Gallant Comrades,
>   You have fought for liberty; you have exhibited courage, fortitude and devotion. You were victorious on more than 200 strongly contested fields. You have participated in more than a thousand conflicts-at-arms. You are heroes, veterans, and patriots: The bones of your comrades mark battlefields upon the soils of Kentucky, Tennessee, Virginia, North Carolina, South Carolina, Georgia, Alabama, and Mississippi. You have done all that human exertion could accomplish.[35]

On May 3, 1865, Captain Henry A. North and his orderly First Sergeant James B. Walker were paroled in Charlotte, North Carolina. They rode on horseback to their homes in Coweta County, Georgia. Along the way they discussed the past and the future and seemed more than cheerful. A total of 119 men and officers were paroled that day. The others—the disabled, those who had deserted, and the imprisoned—just drifted away like the morning fog.

The Roster

Men mentioned or depicted in the chapters are referred to in the Index.

Abbott, M.K., 2nd Lt., **A**, Enlisted: 3-62, Cedartown, Ga., by Captain John C. Crabb. Requested tools to shoe horses William Young Conn Humes. 62. Present through 12-31-62. Home on sick furlough and resigned 12-23-62. Successor A.M. Borders.

Abney, John C., Pvt., **D**, Enlisted: 3-62, Dallas, Ga., age 18, by Captain Seawright. Present until 8-62 sick in Loudon, Tenn. Present through 12-63: Detained in Georgia by Gen. Wheeler. Deserted 7-22-64. Paroled: Kingston, Ga. Died: 11-13-1922. Buried: Carnes Chapel, Etowah Co., Ala.

Abrams, John Washington, Pvt., **C**, Enlisted: 3-62, Cave Spring, Ga., by Captain Haynie. Company, Regiment, Government blacksmith. Filed pension: Fulton Co., Ga., 1907. Died: 3-23-1910. Buried: Wax Community, Floyd Co., Ga.

Abrams, Lewis David Henry, Pvt., **C**, Enlisted: 6-63, Cave Spring, Ga., by Lt. Reynolds. Substitute for John Prior. Transferred: Fla. Cavalry, 11-10-62. Lost his weapon in Richmond, Ky., fined $50. Died: 8-30-1885. Buried: Cowan Cemetery, Wayne Co., Mo.

Acre, William J., Pvt., **A**, Paroled: Augusta, Ga., 5-25-1865.

Adams, J.S., Pvt., **E**, Enlisted: 9-64, Jonesboro, Ga., by Captain Wiggins. AWOL 11-4-64. Captured: Sandersville, Ga., 1-25-65. Carried: Hilton Head 2-1-65, Point Lookout, Md. Died: 4-22-1865. Buried: Point Lookout Confederate Cemetery, St. Mary's Co., Md.

Adams, S.A., Pvt., **G**, Captured: Hartwell, Ga., 5-17-1865, paroled.

Adcock, W., Pvt., **D**, Enlisted: 3-62, Dallas, Ga., age 32, by Captain Seawright.

Aderhold, James M., Pvt., **E**, Enlisted 6-6-1861, Campbell Guards, later 21st Ga. Inf. Discharged: Description: age 24, born Campbellton Co., Ga., 5'-0", dark complexion, blue eyes, and brown hair. Enlisted: 1st Ga. Cavalry 3-21-62, Carrollton, Ga., by Captain Blalock. Discharged 9-4-62.

Died: 8-1-1885. Buried: Aderhold Kolk Cemetery, Fulton Co., Ga.

Aderhold, William M., 1st Sgt., **E**, Enlisted: 5-62, Cartersville, Ga., by Captain Blalock. Appointed 1st Sgt. 2-14-63, Col. Morrison. Resigned 10-10-63. Detailed: Brigade QM. Paroled: Charlotte, NC 5-3-1865. Died: 2-9-1895. Buried: Aderhold Kolb Cemetery, Fulton Co., Ga.

Allen, James R., Pvt., **I**, Enlisted: 5-64, Cartersville, Ga., by Captain Leak. Captured: Atlanta 7-21-64. Carried: Nashville; Louisville, 7-31-64; Camp Chase 8-2-64. Released 6-11-1865. Description: home Cass Co., Ga., age 18, dark hair, hazel eyes, 5'-10", dark complexion.

Allen, Nicholas Eugene, Pvt., **K**, Enlisted: 5-62, Cartersville, Ga., by Major Harper. 12-63 with wagon train at Cartersville, Ga. Surrendered: Greensboro, N.C. 4-26-1865. Died: 10-30-1907. Buried: College Park Cemetery, Fulton Co., Ga.

Allen, S.L., Pvt., **E**, Enlisted: 3-62, Carrollton, Ga., by Captain Blalock. Discharged 9-4-62.

Allen, Virgil S., Pvt., **G**, Enlisted: 3-62, Floyd Co., Ga., by Captain Kerr. Never mustered.

Allen, W.A., Pvt., **B**, Enlisted: 3-62 Newnan, Ga. Present through 2-63. 12-63 on Gen. Buckner's staff . WIA: Atlanta 7- 21-64.

Allen, Z.T., Pvt., **G**, Enlisted: 3-62, Floyd Co. by Captain Kerr. Rejected.

Allgood, Elijah William Young, 2nd Lt., **D**, Enlisted: 3-62, Dallas, Ga., age 22, by Captain Seawright. Present through 12-64. Pension: Wounded twice; scout and guide, Gen. Joseph E. Johnston, New Hope Church. Promoted for bravery. At surrender Col. Davitte gave permission to save horses and left early. Paroled: Atlanta. Died: 10-7-1923. Buried: Allgood Methodist Church, Dallas, Ga.

Allgood, James N.S., Pvt., **D**, Enlisted: 2-63, Dallas, Ga., by Lt. Samuel McGregor. Present through 12-64. Surrendered: Greensboro, NC 4-26-1865. Pension: Fulton Co., Ga., 1902.

Allgood, John Edward, Pvt., **E**, Known by marker.

Died: 6-17-1919. Buried: Marietta Campground, Cobb Co., Ga.

Allgood, John Wesley H., Pvt., **D**, Enlisted: 3-62. Died: 7-3-1911. Buried: Allgood Methodist Church, Paulding Co., Ga.

Allgood, John Willis, Pvt., **D**, Enlisted: 2-63, Dallas, Ga., age 25, by Captain Seawright. 12-62 Sick furlough: Paulding Co., Ga., 12-63 detained in Ga. with wagon train by Gen. Wheeler. 12-64 AWOL. Clothing issued 6-7-1864. Pension: Sick furlough 8-1-64 to 5-65. Died: 7-28-1911. Buried: Asbury Cemetery, Carroll Co., Ga.

Allman, Seaborn W. Sr., Captain, **C**, Enlisted: 9-62, Floyd Co., Ga., by Captain Haynie. Mustered: Frankfort, Ky. Elected 2nd Lt. 9-10-62. Promoted 1st Lt. 3-13-63, Col. Morrison. Sick: Thomasville, Ga., 8-3-64. Promoted: Captain of Co. I, 12-21-64 by Col. Davitte. Died: 3-30-1892. Buried: Greenleaf Cemetery, Brownwood, Texas.

Almon, James Hezekiah, Pvt., **B**, Enlisted: 3-62, Newnan, Ga., age 24, by Captain Strickland. Widow pension: KIA: Tennessee late 1864. While on skirmish line, charging the enemy became MIA. His horse came back, but not the rider. His horse, saddle and bridle were sent home. He was never seen again. Monument: Concord Methodist, Carrollton, Ga.

Almon, William Rowe, Pvt., **B**, 4-64, WIA: Atlanta 7-21-1864. Gunshot: right shoulder and arm removing 4 inches of bone. Discharged. Pension: Meriwether Co., Ga., 1912. Buried: Bethel Baptist Church, Rocky Mount, Meriwether Co., Ga.

Amis, John Thomas, Pvt., **B**, Enlisted: 1864, Admitted: General Hospital 11-20-64. Died: 8-22-1888. Buried: Oak Cemetery, Fort Smith, Ark.

Anderson, A.M., Pvt., **F**, Enlisted: 3-62, Gordon Co., Ga., by Col. Morrison.

Anderson, Clark, Pvt., **G**, Enlisted: 3-62, Floyd Co., Ga., by Captain Kerr. Present through 12-62. AWOL 2-63. Received: Louisville 4-10-65, as deserter. Took oath. Description: home Chattooga Co., Ga., 5'-9", blue eyes, dark hair, dark complexion.

Anderson, David, Pvt., **F**, Enlisted: 3-62, Fairmount, Ga., by Col Morrison. Captured: Big Hill, Ky. 8-31-62. Carried: Louisville; Camp Chase 9-12-62; Cairo, Ill. 9-29-62. Exchanged 11-1-62: steamer *Emerald*, Vicksburg. Description: age 18, 5'-11½", hazel eyes, dark hair, light complexion. Took oath 2-24-64. Description: home Pickens Co., Ga., black hair, 6'-1", black eyes, fair complexion. Witness: Pickens Co., Ga., 1899.

Anderson, Robert, Pvt., **F**, Enlisted: 3-62, Fair-

mount, Ga., by Col. Morrison. Present through 10-62. WIA: Left wounded in Ky., and captured fall 1862.

Anderson, Solomon, Pvt., **F**, Enlisted: 3-62, Fairmount, Ga., by Col. Morrison. Captured: Dandridge, Tenn. 2-14-63. Deserter, took oath 2-29-1864.

Ansley, Thomas M., Pvt., **D**, Enlisted: 2-64, Dallas, Ga., by Captain Robert Trammell. 12-64 Detailed: Col. Hill's scouts. Paroled: Charlotte, N.C. 5-3-1865

Arnett, A.W., Pvt., **A**, Paroled: Albany, Ga., 5-10-1865.

Arnett, Edmond Green, Pvt., **A**, Enlisted: 12-63, in field by Captain York. AWOL 12-64. Died: 9-20-1883. Buried: Old Salem Primitive Baptist Church, Chambers Co., Ala.

Arnold, James Davis, Pvt., **K**, Enlisted: 5-62, Camp Morrison by Captain North. WIA: Murfreesboro 7-13-62. 12-63 Sick: Newnan Hospital. 12-64 present. Brother-in law of Captain North. Died: 6-16-1910. Buried: Sharpsburg Baptist Church, Coweta Co., Ga.

Arnold, J.E., Pvt., **K**, Enlisted: 5-62, Camp Morrison, Captain North. Died in service.

Arnold, Thomas Hardeman, Pvt., **K**, Enlisted 5-31-1861: 7th Ga. Inf. WIA: Manassas, Va. 7-21-61. Enlisted: 5-62, 1st Ga. Cavalry, Cartersville by Major Harper. WIA: Decatur, Ga., 7-22-64. Wounded: left leg below groin. Ball passed through pelvis and lodged against spine causing a fistula. 12-64 Provost Duty in Newnan, Ga. Brother-in-law of Captain North. Died: 10-31-1911. Buried: Sharpsburg Baptist Church, Coweta Co., Ga.

Asbury, Thomas Wesley, 2nd Lt., **C**, Enlisted 5-14-61: 8th Ga. Inf., age 20, Floyd Co., Ga. Transferred: 1st Ga. Cavalry 4-64. Appointed 2nd Lt., replace James Marion Reynolds. Acting Adjt.; promoted 2nd Lt. 12-24-64 by Col. Davitte. Surrendered: Salisbury, N.C. 4-26-1865. Died: 9-4-1919. Buried: Cave Spring Cemetery, Floyd Co., Ga.

Ashworth, J.F., Pvt., **G**, Enlisted: 3-62, Floyd Co. by Captain Kerr. Present until 12-63 absent in Ga.

Atkinson, William T., Pvt., **B**, Paroled: Augusta, Ga., 5-20-1865. Buried: Magnolia Cemetery, Collierville, Tenn.

Atwood, Berry Anderson, 2nd Lt., **A**, Enlisted 6-27-1861: 21st Ga. Inf., age 33, Cedartown. Resigned Disabled 8-17-61. Enlisted: 5-62, 1st Ga. Cavalry, Cedartown, by Captain John C. Crabb. 6-62 Sick: Hospital, Loudon, Tenn. Elected 2nd Lt. 7-16-62; appointed Surgeon

8-1-62. Captured: Somerset, Ky. 3-30-63. Carried to City Point, Va., and exchanged 4-14-63. Detailed: with Captain Jesse W. Crabb at hospital 7-31-64. Paroled: Charlotte, N.C. 5-3-1865. Died: 3-2-1889. Buried: Reynolds Cemetery, New York, Texas.

Atwood, Gilbert A., Pvt., **G**, Enlisted: 3-62, Floyd Co. by Captain Kerr. Present until 12-63, in Ga. wounded. AWOL 9-64. Died: 7-20-1882. Buried: Bristol Cemetery, Ellis Co., Texas.

Atwood, Luther Oliver, Pvt., **A**, Enlisted: 4-63, Cedartown, Ga., by Captain York. Hospital sick 8-10-64. Discharged: May 1865. Died: 1-28-1926. Buried: Confederate Field, Sec. 1, Row R, grave #11, Texas State Cemetery, Austin, Texas.

Austin, Gideon Brown., Cpl., **D**, Enlisted: 3-62, Dallas, Ga., age 29, by Captain Seawright. Present until 12-63 absent sick in Ga., 12-64 AWOL. Died after 1900, Paulding Co., Ga.

Austin, Jeremiah "Jerry" Marion, Pvt., **A**, Enlisted: 3-62, Cedartown, Ga., by Captain John C. Crabb. Company, Regimental Blacksmith. 2-63 Transferred from Kingston, Tenn. Hospital to Rome, Ga. Detailed: Government Shop, Rome as Artificer. 12-64 AWOL. Pension: From Nashville, furloughed home disabled sick. Died 1-25-1900. Buried: Cave Spring Cemetery, Floyd Co., Ga.

Austin, John M., Pvt., **D**, Enlisted: 3-62, Dallas, Ga., age 22, by Captain Seawright. Absent 6-62, 8-62 and 2-63: Sick furlough: Paulding Co., Ga., 12-64 AWOL.

Austin, John N., Pvt., **D**, 3-62, Pension: June 1864: Detailed on scout by Captain Bob Tumlin, near Dallas, Ga. Cut off; could not return. Died: after 1904. Buried: Paulding Co., Ga.

Austin, Leanda "Lee" Alfus, Cpl., **D**, Enlisted: 3-62, Dallas, Ga., age 27, by Captain Seawright. Present through 2-63. WIA: Chickamauga 9-19-63. 12-64 AWOL. Surrendered: Charlotte, N.C. 4-26-1865. Died: 3-3-1897. Buried: Harmony Grove Cemetery, Cleburne Co., Ala.

Austin, William Lumpkin, Pvt., **D**, Enlisted: 3-62, Dallas, Ga., age 25, by Captain Seawright. Absent 12-62: Sick in private home. Absent 2-63: Sick furlough: Paulding Co., Ga. Absent 12-63: Detached service in Ga., 12-64 AWOL. Pension: Summer 1864 detailed: Grey's Mill, Paulding Co., Ga., and became cut off. Paroled: Atlanta, Ga., 6-10-65. Died: 4-19-1917. Buried: Yorkville Methodist Church, Paulding Co., Ga.

Austin, Zach, Pvt., **D**, Enlisted: 3-62, Dallas, Ga., by Captain Seawright. Absent 12-62: Furlough in Ga. AWOL 7-63. Widow Pension: Cleburne Co., Ala. 1913.

Aycock, James H., Pvt., **G**, Enlisted: 3-62, Floyd Co., Ga., by Captain Kerr. Present through 12-64. Paroled: Charlotte, N.C. 5-3-1865. Died: 11-6-1900, Polk Co., Ga.

Aycock, William L., Pvt., **G**, Enlisted: 5-64, Rome, Ga., by Col. Cameron. Lost musket 12-64. Paroled: Charlotte, N.C. 5-3-1865. Pension: Floyd Co., Ga., 1911.

Badger, Frank Armon, 1st Lt., **F**, Enlisted: 3-62, Fairmount, Ga., by Col. Morrison. Promoted Sgt. Major 6-6-62. Promoted 3rd Lt. 9-17-62. Promoted 2nd Lt. by Col. Morrison 9-5-63. Promoted 1st Lt. 1-25-64 by Gen. Martin. Paroled: Greensboro, N.C. 5-4-1865.

Baggett, Charles B., 3rd Lt., **D**, Enlisted: 3-62, Dallas, Ga., age 30, by Captain Seawright. Resigned 11-17-62 disabled. Died: 10-30-1920. Buried: Chapel Hill Cemetery, Douglasville, Ga.

Bagwell, Charles N., Pvt., **E**, Enlisted: 3-64, Van Wert, Ga., by Col. Davitte. WIA and captured: Mt. Peasant, Tenn. 9-4-64. Admitted: Way Hospital, Meridian, Miss. Wounded 1-13-65. Surrendered: Raleigh, N.C. 4-26-1865. Died: 5-23-1899. Buried: Pleasant Grove Baptist Church, Villa Rica, Ga.

Bagwell, Samuel, Pvt., **E**.

Bailey, James, Pvt., **K**, Enlisted: 8-62, Newnan, Ga., by Captain North. Present 12-63 and 12-64.

Bailey, James Asbury, Pvt., **G**, Enlisted: 6-62, Camp Morrison by Captain Leak. Present through 10-63. AWOL 12-18-64. Died: 6-10-1930. Buried: Peachtree Road Baptist Church, Lawrenceville, Ga.

Bailey, Jason Thompson, Sgt., **H**, Enlisted: 5-62, Tallapoosa, Ga., by Captain Tumlin. Present until 12-64 WIA. Provost duty: Columbus, Ga., during recovery. Pension: March 1, 1865, regiment captured herd of 200 horses. Detached to care for horses. Cutoff from regiment at surrender. Attached: General Wofford, Kingston, Ga., 5-12-1865; surrendered. Died: 8-3-1909. Buried: Kingston City Cemetery, Bartow Co., Ga.

Bailey, J.T., Pvt., **G**, Enlisted: 5-62, Camp Morrison by Captain Leak. Present through 12-62. Absent 3-63: Detachment Camp.

Bailey, Robert A., Pvt., 1863. Witness on Thomas N. Dobbs pension while living in Cedartown, Ga., 1910.

Bailey, William Pinkney III, Pvt., **H**, Enlisted: 4-62, Tallapoosa, Ga., by Captain Tumlin. Present until 12-62: Absent: sick furlough home. 2-63 AWOL. 12-64 Detached service. Died: 4-6-1891. Buried: Black Oak Cemetery, Grove Oak, Ala.

Baker, Benjamin Wells, Pvt., **C**, Enlisted: 3-62, Cave Spring, Ga., by Captain Haynie. Regimental wagoner. Surrendered: Greensboro, N.C. 4-26-1865. Died: May 1891. Buried: Round Hill Cemetery, Rome, Ga.

Balkman, Joseph Jasper, Pvt., **E**, Enlisted: 11-64, Greenville, Ga., by Captain Watts. Captured: Athens, Ga., 5-8-65. Died: 5-30-1896. Buried: Ellsworth Cemetery, Logan Co., Ark.

Ballew, Washington Lafayette, 1st Lt., **F**, Enlisted: 3-62, Fairmount, Ga., by Col. Morrison. Captured: Powell Valley, Tenn. 6-27-62. Carried: Camp Morton; Vicksburg. Exchanged 11-22-62. Description: age 23, 5'-10", 170 lbs., blue eyes. Promoted 2nd Lt. 9-17-62. Resigned 3-13-1863. Died: 4-12-1915. Buried: Oleander UMC, Marshall Co., Ala.

Ballin (Bollin), Thomas C., Pvt., **F**, Enlisted: 3-62, Fairmount, Ga., by Col. Morrison. Present until 10-62 and 2-63: Absent on sick furlough. Captured: Monticello, Ky. 6-9-63. Carried: Lexington, Camp Chase; Point Lookout, Md. 11-30-63. Exchanged 5-3-64. Admitted: Chimborazo Hospital, Richmond, Va., Chronic diarrhea 5-8-64, furloughed home. Captured at home: Pickens Co., Ga., 5-23-64. Carried: Nashville, Louisville 6-4-64, Rock Island, Ill. Died 9-16-1864: Typhoid pneumonia. Buried: Rock Island Confederate Cemetery, grave #1511.

Banton (Benton), John, Pvt., **I**, Captured: Kingston, Ga., 10-23-64. Carried: Nashville; Louisville; Camp Douglas 11-26-64. Died: typhoid fever, Camp Douglas Prison 12-20-64. Buried: Grave block 2, #291, Chicago City Cemetery, Chicago, Ill.

Barber, John Thomas, Sgt. Major, **B**, Enlisted: 3-62, Newnan, Ga. Promoted 2nd Sgt. 11-1-63. Promoted Sgt. Major 10-31-64. Died: 1878. Buried: Cedar Lane Cemetery, Central State Hospital Cemetery, Baldwin Co., Ga.

Barger, F.A., Sgt. Major, **F&S**, Enlisted: 6-62, Kingston, Tenn., by Col. Morrison. Promoted 8-19-62, Sgt. Major. Last paid 3-1863.

Barker, Rutherford, Pvt., **C**, Enlisted: 3-62, Cave Spring, Ga., by Captain Haynie. KIA: Murfreesboro 7-13-62.

Barksdale, C. David, Pvt., **E**, Enlisted: 3-62, Carrollton, Ga., by Captain Blalock. Present through 12-64. Paroled: Charlotte, N.C. 5-3-1865.

Barnes, Jehu (John), Pvt., **G**, Enlisted: 3-62, Rome, Ga., by Captain Kerr. Present until 2-63 Sick furlough: DeKalb, Ala. Widow pension: Jackson Co., Ala.

Barnes, Ransom, Pvt., **G**, Enlisted: 3-62, Floyd Co., Ga., by Captain Kerr. Blacksmith. Absent 2-63: sick furlough, Floyd Co., Ga. AWOL 7-25-64. Pension: Sever back injury shoeing horses. Served as nurse. Furloughed home 7-1864 and worked in Government shop. Unable to rejoin command as cutoff from Savannah, Ga. Died: 5-12-1899. Buried: Sisk Cemetery, Gordon Co., Ga.

Barnett, B.F., Pvt., **G**, Enlisted: 5-62, Rome, Ga., by Captain Kerr. Absent 6-62: Sick: Loudon Hospital. Absent 2-63: Sick furlough, Rome, Ga. Transferred: Captain Corput's Battery, Cherokee Artillery, 3-4-64.

Barnett, William H.H., Pvt., **G**, Enlisted: 3-62, Floyd Co., Ga., by Captain Kerr. Absent 6-62 Sick: Loudon Hospital. Absent 2-63 Sick furlough, Rome, Ga. Discharged: 3-26-63. Certificate: age 23, 5'-8", fair complexion, blue eyes, brown hair. Buried: Myrtle Hill, Rome, Ga.

Barnett, William P., Pvt., **A**, Enlisted: 3-62, Cedartown, Ga., by Captain John C. Crabb. Absent 8-62 Sick: Kingston, Tenn. Absent 10-62 and 12-62 sick furlough home. AWOL 6-26-64. Pension: Typhoid fever 5-63, Kingston, Tenn. Private home and nursed by John Cambron until he became ill. Discharged: Greensboro, N.C. 4-26-1865. Died: 10-14-1918. Buried: Lime Branch Cemetery, Polk Co., Ga.

Barnette, J.W.W., Pvt., **H**, Enlisted: 4-62, Haralson Co., Ga., by Captain Tumlin. Substitute for Samuel Erwin. Present until 12-63 absent detained in Ga., by Gen. Wheeler.

Barnwell, John T., Jr., Pvt., **H**, Enlisted: 8-62, Dandridge, Tenn., by Captain Tumlin. Captured in Ky.; Carried: Cincinnati. Exchanged: Cumberland Gap 9-13-62. Captured: Knoxville 12-18-63. Carried: Louisville; Rock Island, Ill. Died: 2-14-64, Viola. Buried: Rock Island Confederate Cemetery, grave #495.

Barnwell, John T., Sr., Pvt., **H**, Enlisted: 4-62, Haralson Co., Ga., by Captain Tumlin. Absent 6-62 sick furlough. Present 8-62 through 2-63. AWOL 12-1-63.

Barton, John R., Pvt., **F**, Captured: Boone Co., Ky. 5-7-63. Carried: Point Lookout, Md. for exchange 2-13-1865.

Baskin, Clark W., Sgt., **E**, Enlisted: 3-62, Carrollton, Ga., by Captain Blalock. Present until 2-63 absent with detachment: Kingston, Tenn. Present 12-63 and 12-64. Surrendered: Greensboro, N.C. 4-26-1865. Died: 9-28-1921. Buried: Concord Methodist Church, Carrollton, Ga.

Bateman, David Nathaniel, Pvt., **E**, Enlisted: 3-62, Carrollton, Ga., by Captain Blalock. Present until 12-63, detached service: Teamster. Present 12-64. Surrendered: Greensboro, N.C. 4-26-1865. Died: 10-8-1923. Buried: Duck River Baptist Church, Cullman Co., Ala.

Bates, John Witt, Pvt., **B**, Enlisted: 3-62, Newnan, Ga., age 25, by Captain Strickland. Present until 12-62, detached service: Teamster. WIA: Macon 7-30-64. Died: 4-23-1918. Buried: Forrest Cemetery, Gadsden, Ala.

Beasley, Thomas W., Pvt., **A**, Enlisted: 3-62, Cedartown, Ga., by Captain John C. Crabb. Present through 12-63. AWOL 12-15-64. Pension: Left before surrender to save stock. Died: 11-21-1921. Buried: Greenwood Cemetery, Cedartown, Ga.

Beavers, John Fluker, 1st Lt., **E**, Enlisted: 3-62, Carrollton, Ga., by Captain Blalock. Present until WIA and captured: Somerset, Ky. 3-30-63. Carried: Louisville; City Point, Va. Exchanged 4-18-63. 12-64: Home wounded at war's end, but doing detached service. Died: 1-28-1913. Buried: Mount Vernon Baptist Church, Fairburn, Ga.

Beavers, Robert O., Sr., Pvt., **E**, Enlisted: 4-62, Cartersville, Ga., by Captain Blalock. Captured: Sugar Valley, Ga., 5-14-64.

Beavers, Robert Owen, Jr., Pvt., **E**, Enlisted: 3-62, Carrollton, Ga., by Captain Blalock. Present until discharged: McMinnville, Tenn. 12-2-62. Certificate: age 19, 6'-0", blue eyes, light hair, fair complexion.

Beck, William R., Pvt., **A**, Enlisted: 3-62, Cedartown, Ga., age 30, by Captain John C. Crabb. Transferred: 4-21-62, Captain Elzaphon R. King's Company Artillery. Died: 1-7-1907. Buried: Northview Cemetery, Cedartown, Ga.

Bell, Charles, Pvt., **C**, Deserted near Savannah 10-1-64. Took oath 11-4-64: Chattanooga and admitted: Chattanooga Military Hospital. Released 1-4-1865.

Bell, John D., Pvt., **I**, Enlisted: 5-62, Camp Morrison, by Captain Leak. Present until 3-63 absent: Detachment Camp. Present 12-63 and 12-64. Surrendered: Greensboro, N.C. 4-26-1865. Died: 4-4-1884. Buried: Oak Hill Cemetery, Bartow Co., Ga.

Benson, Thomas, Pvt., **A**, Captured and carried: Vicksburg aboard steamer *Metropolitan*; exchanged 12-2-1862.

Bentley, Elijah, Pvt., **H**, Enlisted: 1-63, Tallapoosa, Ga., by Captain Tumlin. Present until WIA 9-20-64. Died: 4-1-1914. Buried: Bolton Cemetery, Pleasant Grove, Ala.

Bentley, Isaac, 1st Lt., **H**, Enlisted: 4-62, Haralson

Co., Ga., by Captain Tumlin. Absent 6-62 Detached service: Loudon, Tenn. Promoted: 8-5-63, replace George M. Robinson by Col. Morrison. Resigned: 1-25-64. Pension: At surrender, Col. Watts detailed guard a bridge. Died: 8-15-1900. Buried: Kilgore Family Cemetery, Tallapoosa, Ga.

Bentley, Robert Greer, Cpl., **H**, Enlisted: 5-62, Haralson Co., Ga., by Captain Tumlin. Present until 2-63 Detailed: Recruiter for Gen. Pegram. Present 12-63 and 12-64. Died: 8-10-1896. Buried: Jones Chapel, Cullman Co., Ala.

Bentley, William M., Pvt., **H**, Enlisted: 8-63, Dalton, Ga., by Captain Tumlin. AWOL 11-30-63.

Benton, Andrew Hugh, Cpl., **B**, Enlisted: 3-62, Newnan, Ga., age 24, by Captain Strickland. 12-62 and 2-63 Sick furlough: Newnan, Ga. Present 12-63 and 12-64. Died: 12-3-1903. Buried: Benton Family Cemetery, Newnan, Ga.

Benton, Archibald Paul, Sgt., **B**, Enlisted: 3-62, Newnan, Ga., age 37, by Captain Strickland. Present until 2-63 sick furlough: Grantville, Ga. Captured; paroled: Philadelphia, Tn. 10-20-63. 12-64 Teamster for regiment. Paroled: Greensboro, N.C. 5-2-1865. Died: 1-17-1890. Buried: Bingham Family Cemetery, Coweta Co., Ga.

Benton, John W. "Jack," Pvt., **B**, Enlisted: 3-62, Newnan, Ga. Present until 12-63 Detained with wagon train by Gen Wheeler. Present 12-64. Died: 7-19-1901. Buried: Providence Cemetery, Lone Oak, Ga.

Beugh, A.T., Pvt., **A**, Captured; paroled 11-9-62 Warrenton, Va. General Hospital, Petersburg, Va. 11-18-62, Vulnus Incisum head. Returned 12-2-62.

Bird (Byrd), J.O., Pvt., **K**, Enlisted: 3-62, Camp Morrison, by Captain North. Absent 8-62 and 2-63 Sick furlough: Fayette Co. WIA: Mossy Creek, Tn. 12-29-62, Montgomery Hospital.

Bird, Thomas (Solomon), Pvt., **F**, Enlisted: 3-62, Fairmount, Ga., by Col. Morrison. Acting wagon master. Hacket substituted. Captured: Fairmount, Ga., 5-17-64. Carried: Nashville; Louisville; Rock Island, Ill.; City Point, Va. Exchanged 3-6-1865. Witness: Gordon Co., Ga., 1908.

Bishop, Edmond L., Pvt., **D**, Enlisted: 3-62, Dallas, Ga., by Captain Seawright. Present until 12-63 AWOL. 12-64 Detached service. Died: 10-17-1894. Buried: Tillison Cemetery, Gadsden, Ala.

Bishop, George Washington, Pvt., **D**, Enlisted: 3-62, Dallas, Ga., age 23, by Captain Seawright. Present until 8-62 on Scout. Present until 12-64 AWOL. Pension: WIA: shrapnel to his head,

Resaca 1864. A steel plate placed over the wound and never able to rejoin command. Died: 3-5-1913. Buried: Bishop Family Cemetery, Emory, Texas.

Black, David M., Pvt., **E**, Enlisted: 3-62, Carrollton, Ga., by Captain Blalock. Died: 8-6-62, age 19.

Black, W., Pvt., **B**, Enlisted: 5-64, Newnan, Ga., by Lt. Taylor.

Black, William M., Pvt., **E**, Enlisted: 3-62, Carrollton, Ga., Captain Blalock. Present until 2-63 with detachment: Kingston, Tenn. Absent 12-63 sick. Died: 5-14-1896. Buried: Holly Springs Cemetery, Martin Mills, Texas.

Blackmon, Samuel B., Pvt., **H**, Admitted: Ocmulgee-Floyd Hospital, chronic diarrhea 7-21-1864.

Blackstock, John Jasper, Pvt., **E**, Enlisted: 3-62, Carrollton, Ga., Captain Blalock. Present until 9-63 detached service. Captured: Philadelphia, Tn. 9-20-63. Carried: Knoxville; Camp Chase 12-15-1863.

Blalock, James Marion, Captain, **E**, Enlisted: 3-62, Carrollton, Ga., age 37, Lt. Col. Morrison. Present until resigned disabled 12-26-62. Certificate: chronic rheumatism. Died: 6-18-1872. Buried: Carrollton City Cemetery, Carroll Co., Ga.

Blalock, William H., Pvt., **B**, Enlisted: 3-62, Newnan, Ga. Absent 6-62 Detailed: Forage Master, Kingston, Tenn. Discharged 10-25-62: Kingston, Tenn.

Bly, J.M., Pvt., Paroled: Albany, Ga., 5-16-1865.

Bobo, D.M., Pvt., **G**, Enlisted: 5-62, Camp Morrison, Captain Leak. Present until 3-63 Detached service: Brigade wagons. Present 12-63 and 12-64.

Bobo, E.J., Cpl., **G**, Enlisted: 5-62, Camp Morrison, Captain Leak. Present through 12-64. Paroled: Charlotte, N.C. 5-3-1865.

Bobo, John Vann, Cpl., **C**, Enlisted: 3-62, Cave Spring, Ga., Captain Haynie. Promoted: Cpl. 3-31-62. Absent 6-62 sick furlough. Captured: Rome, Ga., 9-15-64. Carried: Nashville; Louisville; Camp Douglas, Ill. Enlisted: U.S. Army, 5th U.S. Vol. Inf. 4-1-1865. Description: born: Elbert Co., Ga., age 35, blue eyes, grey hair, light complexion, 6'-1". Died: 10-1-1902. Buried: Shady Grove Cemetery, Shelby Co., Tx.

Bobo, Martin, Sgt., **C**, Enlisted: 3-62, Cave Spring, Ga., Captain Haynie. Promoted 4th Sgt. 3-31-62. Present until 12-63, sick. WIA: Kentucky.

Bohannon, Alexander Hamilton, Sgt., **B**, Enlisted: 3-62, Newnan, Ga., age 17, Captain Strickland. Orderly for Major Harper. Present until 2-63 Sick furlough: Newnan, Ga. Absent 12-63 Detained with wagons by Gen. Wheeler. Pro-

moted 1st Cpl. 9-1-63. Present 12-64. Surrendered: Greensboro, N.C. 4-26-1865. Died: 5-29-1920. Buried: Oak Hill Cemetery, Newnan, Ga.

Bohannon, Andrew C., Pvt., **B**, KIA: Resaca 5-13-64. Buried: Bohannon Family Cemetery, Newnan, Ga.

Bohannon, Joseph Alavia, Pvt., **B**, Enlisted: 3-62, Newnan, Ga., age 20, Captain Strickland. Absent 6-62 Sick furlough, Grantville, Ga. Present until 2-63, Sick furlough: Newnan, Ga. Absent 12-63 Detained with wagon train by Gen. Wheeler. General Hospital 12-27-64. Paroled: Charlotte, N.C. 5-3-1865. Pension: Suffered a lung hemorrhage during the war. Died: 10-19-1921. Buried: Beula Baptist Church, Carrollton, Ga.

Bohannon, Leander "Lee" Wellington, Pvt., **B**, Enlisted: 3-62, Newnan, Ga., age 17, Captain Strickland. Present until 12-63 Furloughed: Newnan, Ga., by Gen. Longstreet. Absent 12-64 Detached: Provost Guard. Surrendered: Greensboro, N.C. 4-26-1865. Died: 11-12-1912. Buried: Grantville City Cemetery, Coweta Co., Ga.

Boland, Taylor, Pvt., **H**, Enlisted: 4-64, Tallapoosa, Ga., Captain Tumlin. 12-64 AWOL.

Bomar (Bowmer), Edward Armstead, Pvt., **F**, Enlisted 7-3-1861: 11th Ga. Inf. Discharged: measles 10-8-61. Enlisted 3-22-1862: Fairmount, Ga., Col. Morrison. Promoted 2nd Sgt. 9-24-63. Clothing issued 3rd Qtr. 1864. Pension: Surrendered under Gen. Wofford, Cartersville, Ga., 5-1865. Died: 6-10-1895. Buried: McWilliams Cemetery, Villanow, Ga.

Bomar, Edward Owen, Pvt., **E**, Enlisted: 4-64, Oxford, Ala., Col. Davitte. Issued clothing 6-64. WIA: Atlanta 7-64. 12-64 AWOL. Discharged 4-11-1865. Died 6-13-1912. Buried: Hebron UMC, Howells Crossroads, Al.

Bomar, Irvine, Pvt., **E**, Enlisted: 4-62, Cartersville, Ga., Captain Blalock. Present through 2-28-1863.

Bonner, George A., Cpl., **H**, Enlisted: 4-62, Haralson Co., Ga., Captain Tumlin. Present until discharged. Pension: Discharged: Murfreesboro 12-1862 by substitute. Worked gathering salt peter and lead for the Confederate Government. Died: 11-19-1919. Buried: Bonner Cemetery, Roopville, Ga.

Bonner, John Milton, Pvt., **E**, Enlisted: 5-62, Chattanooga, Captain Blalock. Present until WIA and captured; Somerset, Ky. 3-30-63. Carried: Louisville; City Point, Va. Exchanged 4-13-63. Captured: Philadelphia, Tenn. 10-20-63. Carried: Knoxville; Rock Island, Ill. 6-4-64. Took oath and enlisted 2nd U.S. Vol. Inf. for frontier service at Rock Island, Ill. 10-6-1864. Description: born Franklin Co., Ga., age 22, hazel eyes, dark hair, dark complexion, 5'-9". Died: 12-25-1929. Buried: Old Camp UMC, Carroll Co., Ga.

Bonner, Thomas S., Jr., Pvt., **E**, Enlisted: 5-62, Cartersville, Ga., Captain Blalock. Provided substitute 7-26-62. Enlisted 2nd Ga. Cavalry State Guards 7-27-1863. Died: 10-24-1914. Buried: Ashland City Cemetery, Clay Co., Ala.

Bonner, William Smith, Pvt., **E**, Enlisted: 5-62, Cartersville, Ga., Captain Blalock. Died: 6-14-62, Carrollton, Ga.

Boone, Joseph Marion, 2nd Lt., **E**, Enlisted: 7th Ga. Inf. 5-10-1861, Carrollton, Ga. Discharged: 7-16-1862. Certificate: born Carroll Co., Ga., age 23, 5'-8", light complexion, grey eyes, dark hair. Disabled: chronic diarrhea and bronchitis from wading across the Shenandoah River near Manassas, Va. Enlisted: 11-62, 1st Ga. Cavalry: Carrollton, Ga., Captain Blalock. Promoted 2nd Lt. 1-25-64 by Gen. Martin. Present 12-63 and 12-64. Pension: 3-1-1865 Detached to care for 200 horses captured. Cut off and returned to Georgia. Surrendered with Gen. Wofford, Kingston, Ga., 5-12-1865. Died: 3-11-1910. Buried: Macedonia Baptist Church, Newnan, Ga.

Borders, Augustine McDowell, 2nd Lt., **A**, Enlisted: 3-62, Cedartown, Ga., Captain John C. Crabb. Present through 2-63 absent: sick furlough home. Replaced M.K. Abbott. Promoted 8-1-63, Col. Morrison. Succeeded F.M. Clark. Paroled: Charlotte, N.C. 5-3-1865. Died: 3-7-1899. Buried: West End Cemetery, Stephenville, Texas.

Boswell, Stephen "Ster," Pvt., **B**, Enlisted: 3-62, Newnan, Ga., age 33, Captain Strickland. Present until 12-62 and 2-63Detailed: Teamster. Absent 12-63 Detained with wagon train by Gen. Wheeler. Teamster for Gen. Allen 12-64. Surrendered: Greensboro, N.C. 4-26-1865. Pension: Coweta Co., Ga., 1907. Buried: Holly Springs Cemetery, Luthersville, Ga.

Bothwell, David John, Pvt., **C**, Enlisted: 8-63, Knoxville, Captain Watts. 12-63 absent sick. 12-64 present. Died: 1888, Cherokee Co., Ala.

Bothwell, James Ebenezer, Pvt., **C**, Enlisted: 5-62, Cave Spring, Ga., Lt. Reynolds. Absent 6-62 Sick: Loudon, Tenn. Sick furlough 8-62 through 10-62. Present 12-62. Discharged: 2-1-63. Certificate: Age 35, 5'-8", fair complexion, blue eyes, auburn hair. Died: 5-1-1893. Buried: Cedar Hill Cemetery, Leesburg, Ala.

Bowers, Lawson Wilson, Pvt., **B**, Enlisted: 9-62 in Newnan, Ga. Present until 2-63 Sick furlough:

Newnan, Ga. Present 12-63 and 12-64. Surrendered: Greensboro, N.C. 4-26-1865. Died: 2-1-1927. Buried: White Oak Presbyterian Church, Newnan, Ga.

Bowman, C.C., Pvt., **D**, Enlisted: 3-62, Dallas, Ga., age 45, Captain Seawright. Present until 2-63 Sick furlough: Paulding Co., Ga., 12-63 absent, detained in Ga., by Gen. Wheeler. 12-64 absent, detailed service.

Bowman, E.A., Sgt., **F**, Enlisted: 3-62, Fairmount, Ga., Col. Morrison. Present through 2-63. Promoted 2nd Sgt. 9-24-63. 12-64 AWOL.

Bowman, Newton Randolph, Pvt., **H**, Enlisted: 4-62, Haralson Co., Ga., Captain Tumlin. Died 7-4-62, Van Wert, Ga., fever. Buried: Bowman Family Cemetery, Fruithurst, Ala.

Bowman, Wade Hampton, Pvt., **H**, Enlisted: 4-62, Tallapoosa, Ga., Captain Tumlin. Absent 6-62 Sick: Hospital, Knoxville, Tenn. Present until 2-63 Sick furlough: Sweetwater, Tenn. 12-63 absent, detained with wagons by Gen. Wheeler. Present 12-64. Paroled: Talladega, Ala. 6-1-1865. Buried: Bowman Family Cemetery, Fruithurst, Ala.

Boyce, Joseph J., Pvt., **A**, Enlisted: 3-64, in the field, Captain Jesse W. Crabb. Paroled: Charlotte, N.C. 5-3-1865. Died: 11-1-1929. Buried: Oakland Cemetery, Ola, Yell Co., Ark.

Boyd, McDuffie C., Pvt., **K**, Enlisted: 3-62, Newnan, Ga., Captain North. Present until discharged 1-27-63, Kingston, Tenn. Pension: surrendered Macon, Ga., 1865. Died: 4-4-1922. Buried: Ami Cemetery, Menlo, Ga.

Boyd, William H., **F&S**, Enlisted: 4-62, Haralson Co., Ga., Captain Tumlin. Absent 6-62 detached service. Appointed Asst. Surgeon 11-1-62. Stationed: Marietta, Ga., 8-22-64. Paroled: Charlotte, N.C. 5-3-1865. Died: 5-8-1913. Buried: Myrtle Hill, Rome, Ga.

Boyer, Benjamin, Pvt., **I**, Captured: Scottsville, Ala. 10-27-64. Carried: Louisville; Camp Douglas. He escaped in route 10-31-1864. No further record.

Bozeman, James J., Pvt., **B**, Enlisted: 4-62, Cartersville, Ga., Col. Morrison. Present through 12-64. Paroled: Salisbury, N.C. 5-11-1865. Died: 12-11-1913. Buried: Hill View Cemetery, LaGrange, Ga.

Bozeman, Thomas Wright, Pvt., **B**, Enlisted: 3-62, Newnan, Ga., age 18, Captain Strickland. Present through 12-63. Admitted: Ocmulgee Hospital, Macon, Ga., 1-8-65. Released 3-28-65. Home: Meriwether Co., Ga. Discharged 5-4-1865. Died: 11-4-1913. Buried: Andrews Chapel Cemetery, Lauderdale Co., Miss.

Bradfield, R.P., Pvt., **K**, Enlisted: 5-62, Camp Morrison, Col. Morrison. Present through 2-63.

Bradford, Henry M., Pvt., **C**, Enlisted: 5-62, Cave Spring, Ga., Lt. Reynolds. KIA: Murfreesboro 7-13-62.

Bradley, James Joseph, Cpl., **F**, Enlisted: 3-62, Fairmount, Ga., Col. Morrison. Absent 6-62 sick furlough. Present through 12-64. Paroled: Charlotte, N.C. 5-3-1865. Pension: WIA: 9-20-1862, Ky. Gunshot through shoulder settling near spine. Returned to service, but unable to perform well. Died: 6-6-1911, Walker Co, Ga.

Bradley, O.R., Sgt., **F**, Enlisted 5-19-1861: Guntersville, Ala.: 9th Ala. Inf. WIA: Battle of Salem Church, Va. 5-3-1863. Enlisted 1-1-1864: 1st Ga. Cavalry: Sevierville, Tenn., Lt. McWilliams. Promoted 5th Sgt. 7-1-64. Surrendered: Greensboro, N.C. 4-26-1865. Died: 1923 Confederate Soldiers Home. Buried: Marietta Confederate Cemetery, Marietta, Ga.

Bradley, Robert F., Sgt., **F**, Admitted: Ocmulgee Hospital, Macon, Ga., 2-19-65, congenital atrophy and deformity in legs. Returned: 3-10-1865. Home: Upson Co., Ga. Buried: Catholic Cemetery, Savannah, Ga.

Bradshaw, William, Pvt., **A**, Widow pension: Conecuh Co., Ala.

Branch, Edwin R., Pvt., **A**, Enlisted 7-27-1861: Cedartown, Ga., age 24, 21st Ga. Inf. Discharged 10-29-1861. Stated: born Greene Co., Ga., age 24, 5'-11", light complexion, grey eyes, dark hair. Enlisted: 3-62, Cedartown, Ga., Captain John C. Crabb. Present through 10-62. Absent: sick furlough 12-62 and 2-63. WIA: captured; Somerset, Ky. 3-30-63. Carried: Louisville; City Point, Va. Exchanged 4-13-63. Died: smallpox, Athens, Tenn.

Branch, John Lawrence, Surgeon, **F&S**, Enlisted 7-27-61: Cedartown, Ga., age 26, 21st Ga. Inf. as 2nd Lt. Resigned disabled 2-4-62. Enlisted 6-21-62: 1st Ga. Cavalry, Cedartown, Captain John C. Crabb. 6-62 Furlough: Polk Co. Elected 2nd Lt. 7-16-62 successor to Lt. Nathaniel Tracy. Promoted: Regimental Surgeon 8-1-62. Present 12-64. Paroled: Charlotte, N.C. 5-3-65. Died: 8-1-1920. Buried: Branch Family Cemetery, Cedartown, Ga.

Braswell, Hugh H., Pvt., **B**, Enlisted 7-9-1863: 2nd Ga. Cavalry State Troops (Meriwether Volunteers). Enlisted 5-18-64: 1st Ga. Cavalry: Resaca, Ga. Surrendered: Greensboro, N.C. 4-26-1865. Died: 2-28-1925. Buried: Luthersville City Cemetery, Meriwether Co., Ga.

Braswell, William Z., Pvt., **B**, Enlisted: 4-62,

Cartersville, Ga., Col. Morrison. Present 6-62. Absent 8-62 sick furlough home. Absent 10-62 Sick furlough: Luthersville, Ga. Died: Grantville, Ga., 11-12-62.

Brewer, Benjamin A., Pvt., **D**, Enlisted: 3-62, Dallas, Ga., Captain Seawright. Present until 12-63 Sick: hospital Rome, Ga. 12-64 present.

Brewer, William B., Pvt., **G**, Captured: Missionary Ridge 11-24-63. Carried: Louisville 12-2-63; Rock Island, Ill. 12-9-63.

Bridges, Charles, Pvt., **K**, Enlisted: 5-62, Camp Morrison, Captain North. Absent 6-62 Sick furlough: Coweta Co., Ga. Present until 12-63 Sick: Newnan, Ga. Hospital. Died in service.

Bridges, David Watson, Pvt., **G**, Enlisted: 5-62, Camp Morrison, Captain Leak. Present until 3-63 absent: Detachment Camp. Present 10-63 and 12-31-1864. Pension: McMinn Co., Tenn.

Bridges, James M., 1st Sgt., **K**, Enlisted: 5-62, Camp Morrison, Captain North. Died: home 6-30-62 typhoid fever. Buried: Cokes Chapel UMC, Coweta Co., Ga.

Bridges, T.J., Cpl., **G**, Enlisted: 5-62, Camp Morrison, Captain Leak. Present until 3-63 absent: Detachment Camp. 10-63 present. AWOL 12-15-64.

Briscoe, Thomas I.T., Pvt., **G**, Enlisted: 3-62, Rome, Ga., Captain Kerr. Hospital Steward. Absent 6-62 waiting on sick. Present until 2-63 and 12-63 Sick: Floyd Co., Ga. Paroled: Albany, Ga., 5-16-1865. Died: 4-16-1908. Buried: Morgan Methodist Church, Calhoun Co., Ga.

Brittain, Christopher Columbus, Pvt., **B**, Enlisted: 3-62, Newnan, Ga., age 31, Captain Strickland. Present until 2-63 sick furlough: Rocky Mount, Ga. WIA: Mossy Creek, Tn. 12-29-63; Bull's Gap, Tenn. Hospital. WIA: East Tenn. 1-18-1864 left side and right foot; horse KIA and fell on him crushing his chest and body. Light duty. Gen. Hospital 6-2-64. Surrendered: Greensboro, N.C. 4-26-1865. Died: 12-1-1888. Buried: Brittain Family Cemetery, Greenville, Ga.

Brittain, John Marshall, Pvt., **B**, Enlisted: 5-64, Newnan, Ga., Lt. Taylor. Mustered: Resaca, Ga. Surrendered: Charlotte, N.C. 4-26-1865. Died: 2-23-1907. Buried: Bethel Baptist Church, Rocky Mount, Ga.

Brittain, Tyrie L., Pvt., **B**, Enlisted: 3-62 Newnan, Ga. Present 12-62 and 2-63. KIA: Decatur, Ga., 7-21-1864. Buried: Bethel Baptist Church, Rocky Mount, Ga.

Brittain, W.L., Pvt., **B**, Enlisted: 3-62 Newnan, Ga. Absent 12-63 Furloughed: Rocky Mount, Ga., by Gen. Longstreet.

Brittain, William Thomas, Pvt., **B**, Enlisted: 3-62, Newnan, Ga., age 26, Captain Strickland. Present until 2-63 absent: sick furlough, Rocky Mount. Ga. WIA: Kingston, Tn. 11-24-63, sent to Newnan, Ga. Hospital. Absent 12-64 Courier for Gen. Iverson. Surrendered: Greensboro, N.C. 4-26-1865. Died: 2-19-1916. Buried: Beech Creek Cemetery, Cass Co., Tx.

Brooks, Alexander R., Pvt., **A**, Enlisted 4-64, in field, Captain Jesse W. Crabb. AWOL 11-10-64. Pension: Surrendered: Greensboro, N.C. 4-26-1865. Died: 5-30-1885. Buried: Greenwood Cemetery, Cedartown, Ga.

Brooks, James O., Pvt., **F**, Enlisted: 3-62, Fairmount, Ga., Col. Morrison. Absent 6-62 sick furlough. Present 8-62 to 12-62. Deserted 11-24-63: Loudon, Tenn. Took oath 4-2-64. Description: home Gordon Co., Ga., complexion sandy, light hair, blue eyes, 5'-7". Died: 11-17-1905. Buried: Oklahoma. Memorial Headstone: Rocky Face Cemetery, Whitfield Co., Ga.

Brooks, Junius Hillyer, Pvt., **G**, 9-64, Paroled: Savannah 4-1865. Died: 4-2-1937. Buried: Silver Shoals Baptist, Homer, Ga.

Brooks, Lewis "Lew," Pvt., **B**, Enlisted: 3-62, Newnan, Ga., age 26, Captain Strickland. Absent 6-62 Sick furlough: Turin, Ga. Absent 10-62 Sick furlough: Atlanta. Captured: Somerset, Ky. 3-30-63. Carried: Louisville; City Point, Va. Exchanged 4-13-63. KIA: Dandridge, Tn. 12-24-63.

Brooks, William R., Sgt., **E**, Enlisted: 5-62, Cartersville, Ga., Captain Blalock. Present until WIA: Russellville, Tenn. 12-12-63. Died: wounded 1-21-64. Buried: Bethesda Cemetery, Morristown, Tenn.

Broom, Joseph H., Pvt., **E**, Enlisted: 3-62, Carrollton, Ga., Captain Blalock. Acting quartermaster Sergeant 4-1-62 through 7-31-62. Detached service 10-62. Widow pension: On detachment 6-63: Kingston, Tenn. Went home on furlough until reported to Andersonville Prison. Furlough through 11-64. Never returned.

Brown, C.M., Pvt., **C**, Captured: Hartwell, Ga., 5-17-1865, paroled.

Brown, Edward Alexander, Pvt., **A**, Enlisted: Floyd Legion State Guards 8-4-1863, Cedartown, Ga. Next day, enlisted: 1st Ga. Cavalry, Cedartown, Captain York. Absent 10-63 Hospital Camp for Convalescents, Rome, Ga. Detailed: Hospital, Rome. AWOL 10-64. Pension: Discharged, Jackson Port 1865. Buried: Antioch Cemetery, Zion, Ark.

Brown, George L., Pvt., **H**, Enlisted: 4-62, Tal-lapoosa, Ga., Captain Tumlin. Present until 2-63 absent sick furlough. 12-63 Detained in Ga., by Gen. Wheeler. Deserted; took oath 11-24-64, Chattanooga. Description: home Polk Co., Ga., dark complexion, brown hair, blue eyes, 6'-2", age 35. Admitted: Chattanooga Military Prison Hospital 12-14-64. Dismissed 1-4-1865.

Brown, J.E., Sgt., **H**, Enlisted: 4-62, Haralson Co., Ga. Captain Tumlin. Absent 6-62 in Knoxville as Farrier. Promoted: 4th Sgt. 1-28-63. Present 8-62 through 2-63.

Brown, J.F., Pvt., **F**, Admitted: Floyd House, Ocmulgee Hospital, Macon, Ga., 6-6-64. Gunshot: right of right eye.

Brown, James Bartley, Pvt. **A**, Paroled: Talladega, Ala. 5-1865. Pension: Clay Co., Ala. 1907.

Brown, Joseph Miles, Pvt., **H**, Enlisted: 4-62, Haralson Co., Ga. Captain Tumlin. Absent 6-62 Hospital, Knoxville. Discharged 9-1-62. Issued clothing 6-64. Paroled: Talladega, Ala. 6-1-1865. Died: 5-19-1908. Buried: Lower Cane Creek, Cleburne Co., Ala.

Brown, Littleton L., Pvt., **D**, Enlisted: 3-62, Dallas, Ga., age 36, Captain Seawright. Present 6-62 through 12-62 company blacksmith. Present until 12-63 absent furlough: Paulding Co., Ga. 12-64 absent with leave. Died: 4-16-1908. Buried: New Hope Cemetery, Dallas, Ga.

Brown, Nick, Pvt., **B**, Enlisted: 4-62, Cartersville, Ga., Col. Morrison. Present through 12-31-1864.

Brown, Simeon, Pvt., **A**, Enlisted: 3-62, Cedartown, Ga., Captain John C. Crabb. Present 6-62 Blacksmith. Broke courthouse door down, Murfreesboro; WIA 7-13-62. Present 8-62 Asst. Forage Master. Detailed: Quartermaster Dept. Present 12-64. Paroled: Charlotte, N.C. 5-3-1865. Pension: Calhoun Co., Ala.

Brown, T.R., Pvt., **G**, Enlisted: 3-62, Floyd Co., Ga., Captain Kerr. Absent 6-62 Special service, Loudon Hospital. Present 8-62 Detailed: Armory, Rome, Ga., by Gen. Kirby Smith. Died: typhoid fever 11-15-62, Adairsville, Ga.

Brown, William B., Pvt., **B**, Enlisted: 3-62, Newnan, Ga., age 22, by Captain Strickland. Present until KIA: Big Hill, Ky. 8-24-62. Buried: Three Civil War Soldiers Cemetery, Rockcastle, Co., Ky.

Brown, William Henry, Pvt., **F**, Captured: Pine Mountain, Tn. 12-22-62. Carried: Camp Douglas; Vicksburg. Exchanged 1-4-63.

Brown, William Madison, Pvt., **A**, Enlisted: 3-62, Cedartown, Ga., Captain John C. Crabb. Absent sick at home 12-63. AWOL 10-1864. Discharged 1865. Died: 10-15-1923. Buried: Nesmith Cemetery, Cullman Co., Ala.

Bruce, D.A., Pvt., **I**, Enlisted: 4-63, Mosse Creek, Tenn., Captain Leak. Died: Hospital, Kingston, Ga., 10-25-63.

Bruce, J.W., Pvt., **A**, Enlisted: 3-62, Cedartown, Ga. Captain John C. Crabb. Absent 6-62 Sick furlough: Polk Co., Ga. Present through 2-63.

Bruce, Samuel G., Pvt., **I**, Enlisted: 5-62, Camp Morrison, Captain Leak. Present until 3-63 absent: Detachment Camp. Present through 12-64. Surrendered: Greensboro, N.C. 4-26-1865. Rode home with Lt. Glasgow. Pension: DeKalb Co., Ga., 1906.

Bryant, Alfred H., Pvt., **G**, Enlisted: 5-62, Camp Morrison, Captain Leak. Present until 3-63 absent: Detachment Camp. Captured: Fall's Creek, Mill Springs. Ky. 6-3-63. Carried: Lexington; Camp Chase 6-13-63; Johnson's Island; Point Lookout, Md. Exchanged 11-30-63. Admitted: Jackson Hospital, Richmond, Va., rheumatism. Furloughed 30 days. Died: 3-27-1891. Buried: Cedar Grove Cemetery, Kaufman Co., Tx.

Bryant, Andrew J., Cpl., **B**, Enlisted: 4-62, Newnan, Ga., age 25, Captain Strickland. Present until discharged 9-22-62 Kingston, Tenn. Pension: Detailed 10-15-62, Young's Tan Yard, Coweta Co. to make shoes. Discharge: born 1836, 5'-8", fair complexion, blue eyes, light hair. Died: 12-21-1874, Chattooga Co., Ga.

Bryent, Ceberne, Pvt., **D**, Captured in Haralson Co., Ga., 10-17-64. Carried: Camp Douglas, Ill. Applied to take oath 2-1865.

Buchannan, James Jackson, Pvt., **G**, Enlisted: 3-62, Floyd Co., Ga., Captain Kerr. Present until detailed: Robertson's Artillery 11-1-63. Died: 8-10-1918. Buried: Union Dempsey Baptist Church, Clay Co., Ala.

Buford, A.J., Pvt., **I**, Enlisted: 4-63, Mosse Creek, Tenn., Captain Leak. Present through 12-31-1864.

Bulgar, C.L., Pvt., On steamer *Maria Denning*, Vicksburg for exchange 11-15-1862.

Bunch, James, Pvt., Took oath 2-24-64 at Chattanooga. Description: home Pickens Co., Ga., dark complexion, black hair, black eyes, 6'-1".

Bunch, John W., Pvt., **F**, Enlisted: 3-62, Fairmount, Ga., Col. Morrison. Present until 10-62 absent: sick furlough. Present 12-62 through 2-63. Court Martial as bushwhacker 10-2-63. Found guilty but death sentence remitted as evidence not strong enough.

Bunch, William Jefferson, Pvt., **F**, Enlisted: 3-62, Fairmount, Ga., Col. Morrison. Absent 6-62 sick furlough. Present 8-62 through 12-62. Died: 1-27-63, Kingston, Tenn. Buried: Pleasant Grove Baptist Church, Ryo, Ga.

Burdette, John Green, Pvt., **B**, Enlisted: 5-62, Cartersville, Ga., Col. Morrison. Present until 2-63 absent: sick furlough: Grantville, Ga. WIA: Pigeon River, Tenn. 1-27-64, Bulls Gap, Tenn. hospital. Ball entered right hip, fracturing femur, tearing muscle and exiting near knee. Leg became 1 inch shorter. Present 12-64. Surrendered: Greensboro, N.C. 4-26-1865. Died: 1-2-1923. Buried: Allen Lee Memorial UMC, Lone Oak, Ga.

Burdette, Simpson David, Pvt., **B**, Enlisted: 3-62, Newnan, Ga., age 21, Captain Strickland. Present through 12-31-1864. Died: 4-2-1917. Buried: Cedarwood Cemetery, Roanoke, Ala.

Burgess, W.G., Pvt., **F**, Enlisted: 5-64, Marietta, Ga., Lt. Gilbreath. Present 12-64. Paroled: Charlotte, N.C. 5-3-1865.

Burk, John J., Pvt., **A**, Enlisted: 6-62, Cedartown, Ga., Captain John C. Crabb. Present until 2-63 absent: sick furlough at home. 12-63 Teamster. Issued clothing 3rd Qtr. 1864.

Burke, C.H., Pvt., **H**, Paroled: Augusta, Ga., 5-18-1865.

Burke, John H., Pvt., **B**, Enlisted: 3-62, Newnan, Ga., age 30, Captain Strickland. Present until 2-63 absent: sick furlough: Newnan, Ga. 12-63 Detained with wagon train by Gen. Wheeler. 12-64 Teamster for Gen. Hood's supply train. Paroled: Charlotte, NC 5-3-1865. Buried: Oak Hill Confederate Cemetery, Newnan, Ga.

Burnett, Jeremiah M., Pvt., **G**, Enlisted: 5-62, Camp Morrison, Captain Leak. Bugler. Present until 10-63 absent in Ga. Deserted and took oath, 6-2-64 at Chattanooga. Description: home Cass Co., Ga., dark complexion, grey eyes, 5'-5".

Burney, T.S., Pvt., **G**, Enlisted: 3-62, Floyd Co., Ga., Captain Kerr. Present until discharged 8-13-63 substitution of W. H Watson. Re-enlisted: Decatur, Ga., 2-3-1864. Absent 12-64 Courier for Gen. Iverson. Paroled: Charlotte, N.C. 5-3-1865.

Burns, James W., Sgt., **E**, Enlisted: 5-62, Carrollton, Ga., Captain Blalock. Present until 2-63 absent with detachment near Mossy Creek, Tenn. Orderly Sergeant. Present 12-63 and 12-64. Surrendered: Greensboro, N.C. 4-26-1865. Died: 12-17-1918. Buried: New Lebanon Baptist Church, Carroll Co., Ga.

Burns, John E., Pvt., **E**, Enlisted: 8-63, Dalton, Ga., Major Harper. Present through 12-31-1864.

Cain, Ferdinand C., Pvt., **F**, Enlisted: 3-62, Carrollton, Ga., Captain Blalock. Present through 12-63.

Caldwell, Joseph B., Pvt., **A**, Enlisted: 3-62, Cedartown, Ga., Captain John C. Crabb. Absent 6-62 Sick: hospital, Loudon, Tenn. Present 10-62 and 12-62. Promoted 3rd Cpl. 12-31-63. Present through 12-31-1864.

Callaway, J.J., Pvt., **D**, Enlisted: 3-62, Dallas, Ga., age 23, Captain Seawright. Absent 6-62 and 12-62 sick furlough to Paulding Co., Ga. Absent 8-62 sick furlough to Cobb Co., Ga. Discharged 1862.

Cambron, Hugh L., Pvt., **A**, Enlisted: 3-62, Cedartown, Ga., Captain John C. Crabb. Present 6-62 through 12-62 Blacksmith. Present 2-63 Company Artificer. Present 12-63 and 12-64 Blacksmith. Pension: Shoeing and caring for horses; never went on furlough. Surrendered: 4-26-1865 Charlotte, N.C. Died: 12-1-1909. Buried: Singleterry Cemetery, Walker Co., Ga.

Cambron, James, Pvt., **A**, Enlisted: 2-65, Cedartown, Ga., Captain Jesse W. Crabb. Paroled: Charlotte, N.C. 5-3-1865.

Cambron, John A., Pvt., **A**, Enlisted: 3-62, Cedartown, Ga., Captain John C. Crabb. Present 6-62 Blacksmith. Absent 8-62 Sick at Kingston, Tenn. Pension: Assigned to nurse William Barnett, Kingston, Tenn. 5-1863, private home. Discharged: 7-18-63 rheumatism, Sweetwater, Tenn. Died 1-20-1910. Buried: Harmony Baptist, Cedartown, Ga.

Cambron, John Thomas, Pvt., **A**, Enlisted: 6-63, Cedartown, Ga., Captain Hutchins. Present until AWOL 11-10-64. Paroled: Charlotte, N.C. 5-3-1865. Died: 2-21-1924. Buried: Gurley Cemetery, Madison Co., Ala.

Camp, Aaron T., Pvt., **E**, Enlisted: 3-62, Carrollton, Ga., Captain Blalock. Accidentally killed at Wheeler's Gap, Tenn. 5-25-62.

Camp, Edward T., Pvt., **B**, Enlisted: 3-62, Newnan, Ga., age 17, Captain Strickland. Present until 12-63 absent. Captured: Sevierville, Pigeon River, Tenn. 1-27-1864. Carried: Nashville; Louisville; Camp Chase; Rock Island, Ill.; City Point, Va. 3-2-1865; exchanged. At home at war's end. Died 1910. Buried: St. Paul Methodist Church, Whitesburg, Ga.

Camp, H.P., Pvt., **K**, Enlisted: 5-62, Camp Morrison, Captain North.

Camp, Hiram Warner, Sgt., **B**, Enlisted 5-31-1861: 7th Ga. Inf. Discharged 4-15-1862. Certificate: born Coweta Co., Ga., age 20, 6'-4", fair complexion, blue eyes, dark hair. Enlisted: 1st Ga. Cavalry 8-3-62, Newnan, Ga. Present through 12-31-64. Died: 1-1-1908. Buried: Oak Hill Cemetery, Newnan, Ga.

Camp, John Langley, Pvt., **E**, Enlisted: 3-62, Car-

rollton, Ga., Captain Blalock. 8-1-1862 Lewis Phillips substitute. Died: 12-30-1921. Buried: Mount Vernon Baptist Church, Fairburn, Ga.

Camp, Nathan W., Cpl., **B**, Enlisted: 5-62, Cartersville, Ga., Captain Blalock. Present until 2-63 absent sick. Promoted: Cpl. 7-1-64. AWOL 7-12-64. Died 8-10-1888, Douglas Co., Ga.

Camp, Russell Benson Sanford, Pvt., **K**, Enlisted: 5-62, Cartersville, Ga., Major Harper. Present until KIA: Sunshine Church 7-31-64. Buried: Founders Cemetery, Moreland, Ga.

Camp, W.C., Pvt., **B**, Enlisted: 3-62 Newnan, Ga. Present 10-62 through 12-63. Transferred: Co. K. 7-1-63.

Camp, Walker Glenn, Sgt., **K**, Enlisted 5-31-1861 Atlanta: 7th Ga. Inf. Discharged: 6-7-62. Certificate: born Coweta Co., Ga., age 25, 6'-3", dark complexion, grey eyes, black hair. Enlisted: 5-62, Cartersville, Ga., Captain North. WIA: Monticello, Ky. WIA: Sunshine Church 7-31-64. Present 12-63 and 12-64. Paroled: Charlotte, N.C. 5-3-65. Died: 5-31-1911. Buried: Founders Cemetery, Moreland, Ga.

Camp, William H., Pvt., **E**, Enlisted: 5-62, Cartersville, Ga., Captain Blalock. Present until Deserted 2-1-63.

Camp, Wilson L., Pvt., **K**, Enlisted: 5-62, Camp Morrison, Captain North. Absent 6-62 and 2-63 Sick furlough: Campbell Co., Ga. Absent 12-63 Sick: Newnan Hospital. Assigned hospital nurse, Newnan, Ga. Died: 6-5-1914. Buried: Holly Springs Cemetery, Douglasville, Ga.

Campbell, A. Jerry, Pvt., **E**, Enlisted: 3-62, Carrollton, Ga., Captain Blalock. Present: 6-62 and 8-62. Discharged 9-14-62.

Campbell, B.F., Pvt., **A**, Enlisted: 5-64, in field by Captain York. AWOL 11-10-64.

Campbell, James, Pvt., **F**, Enlisted: 3-62, Fairmount, Ga., Col. Morrison. Paid 5-10-1862.

Campbell, Joseph Josiah, Pvt., **F**, Enlisted: 3-62, Fairmount, Ga., Col. Morrison. Sick with Typhoid fever, Knoxville. Sent home to Gordon Co., Ga., 6-25-62. Died: 7-1-1862. Buried: Harmony Cemetery, Calhoun, Ga.

Campbell, J.W., Pvt., **I**, Enlisted: 5-64, Cass Station, Ga., Captain Leak. Died: 8-23-64.

Capps, A.L., Pvt., **G**, Enlisted: 3-62, Floyd Co., Ga., Captain Kerr. Present through 12-31-1864.

Capps, William M., Pvt., **C**, Enlisted: 3-62, Cave Spring, Ga. Captain Haynie. Present until 12-63 absent sick. Clothing issued 1-16-1864.

Carey, O.E., Pvt., **D**, Captured Brookville, Md. 6-30-63. Old Capitol Prison, Washington, D.C. 7-1-63. Took oath; released 12-17-63.

Carlton, Frank Jefferson, Pvt., K, Enlisted 5-31-1861: 7th Ga. Inf. Discharged disabled 6-24-62. Enlisted: 6-62, 1st Ga. Cavalry, Cartersville, Ga., Major Harper. Present until 12-64 absent: Courier for Gen. Iverson.

Carlton, J.V., Pvt., K, Enlisted: 5-62, Camp Morrison, Captain North. Present through 12-31-1862.

Carmical (Carmichael), Abraham Julius, Pvt., K, Enlisted: 5-62, Camp Morrison, Captain North. Absent 6-62 and 2-63 Sick furlough in Coweta Co., Ga. Dropped from the roll 9-25-1863 by Lt. Col. Harper. Died: 4-16-1907. Buried: Mount Olive First Baptist Church, Coosa Co., Ala.

Carmical (Carmichael), James B., Pvt., K, Enlisted: 5-64, Newnan, Ga., Captain York. Surrendered: Greensboro, N.C. 4-26-1865. Died: 9-4-1879. Buried: White Oak ARP, Coweta Co., Ga.

Carmical, Patrick Asberry, Pvt., K, Enlisted: 5-62, Cartersville, Ga., Major Harper. Absent 6-62 Detached service. Present 8-62 through 2-63 Teamster for Brigade. Present 12-63 and 12-64. Pension: Scout upper part South Carolina 3-25-1865, cut off. Captain John D. Ray, 5th Tenn. stated: Joined his command to attack Gen. Wilson's Cavalry, northern Ala. Captured: Oxford, Ala., paroled: April 1865. Died: 10-16-1924. Buried: White Oak ARP, Coweta Co., Ga.

Carmical, Robert, Pvt., K, Enlisted: 5-62, Camp Morrison, Captain North. Present 12-64. Pension: Captain North stated: sick, went home to get well. Enlisted 8-4-1863, Newnan, Ga., 2nd Ga. Cavalry State Guards for 6 months. Rejoined: 1st Ga. Cavalry. Died: 11-13-1905. Buried: White Oak ARP, Coweta Co., Ga.

Carmical, Wesley William, 1st Lt., K, Enlisted: 5-62, Camp Morrison, Captain North. Present until 12-63 absent sick in Newnan, Ga. Hospital. Pension: WIA: New Hope Church, Cassville 5-19-64. Gunshot entered behind left ear and passed through back of neck and out behind right shoulder blade cutting muscles, nerves and injured vertebra. Returned home never to rejoin command. Died: 3-12-1913. Buried: Macedonia Baptist Church, Coweta Co., Ga.

Carmical, William Wesley, Cpl., K, Enlisted: 5-62, Camp Morrison, Captain North. Present except 6-62 and 2-63 absent: Sick furlough in Coweta Co., Ga. Pension: WIA: Campbellsville, Tenn. 9-5-64. Ball entered right cheek and exited left cheek, Florence, Ala. Hospital. Recruiter for the remainder of the war. Died: 9-17-1905. Buried: Union Cemetery, Rye, Ark.

Carrin, T., Pvt., I, Paroled: Augusta, Ga., 5-11-1865.

Carroll, George Wesley , Pvt., D, Enlisted: 3-62, Dallas, Ga., age 23, Captain Seawright. Paid 4-17-1862. Died: 9-3-1920. Buried: Mountain View Baptist Church, Buchanan, Ga.

Carroll, James M., Sgt., H, Enlisted: 4-62, Haralson Co., Ga., Captain Tumlin. Promoted 3rd Sgt. 1-28-63. Present until AWOL 2-5-64. On Knoxville list of deserters taking oath 2-17-64.

Carruth, James E., Pvt., D, Enlisted: 3-62, Dallas, Ga., Captain Seawright. Present until WIA: Richmond, Ky. Died wounded 8-30-1862. Widow pension: Carrying dispatch from Col. Morrison to General Scott on Frankfort to Louisville, Ky. Suspect bushwhackers. Buried: Richmond Cemetery, Section H, mass grave, Madison Co., Ky.

Carruth, William H., Pvt., D, Enlisted: 3-62, Dallas, Ga., Captain Seawright. Present until 12-63 AWOL. KIA: Resaca 6-14-64.

Carter, Joseph, Pvt., D, Enlisted: 3-62, Dallas, Ga., Captain Seawright. Present until 12-62 and 3-63 absent: Sick furlough in Paulding Co., Ga. Captured: Philadelphia, Tenn. 10-20-63. Carried: Camp Nelson; Camp Chase 11-14-63; Rock Island, Ill. 1-17-64. Transferred: New Orleans 5-3-1865, exchanged.

Carter, R.H., Pvt., E, Enlisted 6-14-1861 Phillip's Legion, age 34, Cobb Co., Ga. Accidently shot in his foot and Transferred to 1st Ga. Cavalry. Enlisted: 9-62, Van Wert, Ga., Col. Davitte. Received clothing issue 6-64. 12-64 AWOL.

Cartwright, William J., Pvt., E, Enlisted: 5-62, Carrollton, Ga., Captain Blalock. Present until KIA 8-30-62 Richmond, Ky. Buried: Section H, mass grave, Richmond Cemetery, Madison Co., Ky.

Casey (Cason), Jesse G., Pvt., F, Enlisted: 3-62, Fairmount, Ga., Col. Morrison. Captured: Fairmount, Ga., 5-18-64. Carried: Nashville; Louisville 5-25-64; Rock Island, Ill. 5-27-64. Took oath; joined U.S. Army. Released 11-28-64. Description: home Gordon Co., Ga., dark complexion, grey hair, hazel eyes, 6'-0", age 48.

Cason, Elihu, Pvt., A, Enlisted: 12-62 by Captain Hutchings. Absent 12-62 and 12-63 sick furlough home. AWOL 11-12-1864. Died: 4-12-1897. Buried: Oakland Cemetery, Dallas, Texas.

Cason, Robert J., Pvt., A, Enlisted: 12-62 by Captain Hutchings. Present until 2-63 absent: sick furlough home. 12-31-1864 present.

Cathcart, James F., Pvt., G, Died: 7-29-1895. Buried: Floral Hills Cemetery, Palmetto, Ga.

Cathcart, James Monro, Sr., Pvt., G, Enlisted: 5-62, Camp Morrison, Captain Leak. Present until 3-63 absent with Detachment Camp. 10-63 present. AWOL 11-30-64. Died, buried: Texas, between 1900 and 1910.

Cathcart, Larkin Decatur, Pvt., **D**, Enlisted 3-63: 64th Ga. Inf., Marietta, Ga. Enlisted: 2-64, 1st Ga. Cavalry, Dallas, Ga., Captain Robert Trammell. Clothing issue 7-13-64. 12-31-1864 AWOL. Died: 7-20-1907. Buried: Flint Hill Cemetery, Hiram, Ga.

Cavender, Obediah Morgan, Pvt., **K**, Enlisted: 6-64, Surrendered: Salisbury, N.C. 4-26-65. Died: 5-22-1927. Buried: Elim Baptist Church, Coweta Co., Ga.

Cavender, Seaborn J., Pvt., **K**, Enlisted: 5-62, Cartersville, Ga., Major Harper. Present until 2-63 absent: Sick furlough in Coweta Co., Ga., 12-64 Newnan Hospital. Sharpshooter-killed most Yankees for regiment. Surrendered: Greensboro, N.C. 4-26-1865. Died: 3-6-1929. Buried: Oak Hill Cemetery, Newnan, Ga.

Cavender, William Washington, Pvt., **K**, Enlisted 5-31-61: 7th Ga. Inf. WIA: Manassas, Va. 7-21-1861, canon shell fragment in the head requiring silver plate. Discharged: 3-1-1862. Description: born Coweta Co., Ga., age 20, 6'-0", fair complexion, grey eyes, black hair. Enlisted: 5-62, Cartersville, Ga., Major Harper. Present through 12-62, Col. Morrison's orderly and scout. Absent 2-63 Sick furlough: Coweta Co., Ga., 12-63 Col.'s orderly and scout. 12-64 present. Served in Wheeler's Secret Service. Died: 11-6-1911. Buried: Mount Carmel Methodist, Coweta Co., Ga.

Chambers, James Polk, Pvt., **I**, Enlisted: Floyd Co., Ga., 9-10-1863, Floyd Legion State Guards. Enlisted: 5-64, 1st Ga. Cavalry, Cass Station, Ga., Captain Leak. Absent 1-25-64 Detached service. Paroled: Bainbridge, Ga., 5-20-1865. Description: 5'-9", dark hair, black eyes, dark complexion.

Chandler, Isaac H., Cpl., **H**, Enlisted: 4-62, Haralson Co., Ga., Captain Tumlin. Absent 6-62 sick in hospital. Died: Hospital, Knoxville, Tenn. 6-30-62, fever.

Chandler, Newton J., Pvt., **E**, Enlisted: 5-62, Carrollton, Ga., Captain Blalock. Present until Discharged 1-21-63, Kingston, Tenn. Died: 2-25-1905. Buried: Bowden City Cemetery, Carroll Co., Ga.

Chandler, Thomas J., Pvt., **H**, Enlisted: 4-62, Haralson Co., Ga., Captain Tumlin. Absent 6-62 Sick in hospital, Knoxville, Tenn. KIA: Mt. Vernon, Ky. 8-21-62. Buried: Breastworks Hill Cemetery, London, Ky.

Chapman, Abel, Pvt., **D**, Enlisted: 3-62, Dallas, Ga., age 46, Captain Seawright. Absent 8-62 Sick in Loudon, Tenn. Discharged: 9-22-62, Kingston, Tenn. Had fallen from a horse before enlistment and injury lingered. Born: Lexington Dist., S.C. Age 50, 6'-2", fair complexion, grey hair, grey eyes. Died: 10-1875. Buried: Chapman Family Cemetery (near Basket Creek Baptist Church), Douglas Co., Ga.

Chapman, Robert C., Sgt., **G**, Enlisted: 5-62, Camp Morrison, Captain Leak. Present until 3-63 absent: Detachment Camp. Present 10-63 and 12-64. Admitted: Ocmulgee Hospital, Macon, Ga., 7-14-64, released 7-22-64. Stated: home Bartow Co., Ga. Paroled: Charlotte, N.C. 5-3-1865.

Chavous (Chavons), E., Pvt., **A**, Paroled: Augusta, Ga., 5-19-1865.

Cheatwood, William M., Pvt., **H**, 3-63, Pension: Cleburne Co., Ala.

Cheny, W.D., Pvt., **G**, Enlisted: 3-62, Floyd Co., Ga., Captain Kerr. Absent 6-62 Special service. Present until Discharged: 9-9-62.

Childers, Robert T., Pvt., **A**, Enlisted: 3-62, Cedartown, Ga., Captain John C. Crabb. Asst. commissary. Present until 8-62 absent: sick furlough home. Present 10-62 and 12-62. Absent 2-63 sick furlough home. AWOL 7-3-64.

Chrimer, Jerome, Pvt., **F**, Captured: Hartwell, Ga., 5-20-1865, paroled.

Christian, W.H., Pvt., **B**, Captured: Hartwell, Ga., 5-19-1865, paroled.

Chutwood (Chitwood), Marion, Pvt., **H**, Enlisted: 2-63, Rogersville, Tenn., Captain Tumlin. Substituted by W.E. Smith 2-15-1863.

Clark, D.T., Sgt., **G**, Enlisted: 7-63, Rome, Ga., Captain Kerr. Present 12-63. Issued clothing 6-64. Paroled: Charlotte, N.C. 5-3-1865.

Clark, Francis Marion, 1st Lt., **A**, Enlisted: 3-62, Cedartown, Ga., Captain John C. Crabb. Absent 6-62 and 8-62 Sick furlough in Polk Co., Ga. Promoted 2nd Lt. 12-2-62. Promoted 1st Lt. 8-3-64 by Col. Morrison. 12-64 Wounded in hospital. Pension: WIA 3-65: N.C. Furloughed home disabled. Died: 1-25-1891, Anniston, Ala.

Clark, William J., 1st Sgt., **A**, Enlisted: 3-62, Cedartown, Ga., Captain John C. Crabb. Promoted 3rd Sgt. when T.L. Ward transferred 4-1-62. Present until Discharged: 8-8-62 with a hernia. Description: born Polk Co., Ga., age 24, 5'-8", dark complexion, dark eyes, dark hair. Died: 6-11-1897. Buried: Van Wert Cemetery, Polk Co., Ga.

Clarke, James G., Sgt., **K**, Enlisted: 5-62, Camp Morrison, Captain North. Absent 6-62 Sick in Kingston, Tenn. Present until Discharged: 9-14-62, Kingston, Tenn.

Clayton, William J., Pvt., **H**, Enlisted: 11-63, Tallapoosa, Ga., Captain Tumlin. Present until 12-64

Detached service. Paroled: Talladega, Ala. 6-1-1865. Pension: Cleburne Co., Ala. 1907.

Cleghorn, John Thomas, Pvt., **G**, Enlisted: 5-62, Camp Morrison, Captain Leak. Present until 2-63 absent: Detachment Camp. Absent 10-63 Sick in Ga. AWOL 9-25-64. Died: 7-19-1885. Buried: Oak Hill Cemetery, Cartersville, Ga.

Cleghorn, William Douthit, Pvt., **G**, Enlisted: 5-62, Camp Morrison, Captain Leak. Present through 12-62. Absent 2-1-63 Detached to Brigade battery by Gen. Pegram. Absent 10-63 Sick in Ga. Absent 12-64 on furlough. Pension: 1-1865, Lt. Glasgow detailed carry some captured mules to Gen. Reynolds in Athens, Ga., and became cut off. Attached to Gen. Wofford, surrendered, Kingston, Ga., 5-12-1865. Died: 4-29-1917. Buried: Oak Hill Cemetery, Cartersville, Ga.

Clements, J.S., Pvt., **G**, Enlisted: 3-62, Floyd Co., Ga., Captain Kerr. Present through 12-31-1864. Paroled: Charlotte, N.C. 5-3-1865.

Cline, L.A., Pvt., **D**, Enlisted: 3-62, Dallas, Ga., age 32, Captain Seawright. Present until 12-62 absent: Sick in hospital. Absent 12-63 Detained in Ga., by Gen. Wheeler.

Clontz (Cloutz), Martin L., Pvt., **G**, Enlisted: 3-62, Floyd Co., Ga., Captain Kerr. Present through 12-63 Blacksmith. AWOL 9-1864. Pension: McMinn Co., Tenn. Buried: Varnell Cemetery, Whitfield Co., Ga.

Coats, W.B., Pvt., **H**, Enlisted: 4-62, Haralson Co., Ga., Captain Tumlin. Present until Discharged 9-23-62.

Cobb, James H., Pvt., **E**, Enlisted: 3-62, Carrollton, Ga., Captain Blalock. Present until 2-63 absent with detachment in Kingston, Tenn. Present 12-63 and 12-64. Captured: Athens, Ga., 5-8-65, paroled. Widow's pension claimed surrendered at Greensboro, NC. 4-26-65. Died: 9-28-1907. Buried: Asbury Cemetery, Temple, Ga.

Cobb, John S., Attended Gen. Joseph Wheeler's funeral January 1906.

Cobb, Joseph L., Pvt., **E**, Enlisted: 4-64, Blue Mountain, Ala., Col. Davitte. Present 12-64. Surrendered: Greensboro, N.C. 4-26-1865. Pension: Rode home with Joseph R. McCain. Died: 5-31-1913. Buried: Carrollton City Cemetery, Carroll Co., Ga.

Cobb, William Washington, Pvt., **E**, Enlisted: 5-62, Carrollton, Ga., Captain Blalock. Present until 2-63 absent with detachment at Kingston, Tenn. 12-63 present. July 1864 at Chattahoochee River became ill with chronic diarrhea. Sent to LaGrange, Ga. Hospital. Died: 8-3-1864, LaGrange

and buried. Brother, Joseph, had his body removed to Carroll Co., Ga., 7-65. Buried: Pleasant Grove Baptist Church, Villa Rica, Ga.

Cochran, William Lafayette, Pvt., **A**, 5-64, Surrendered: Kingston, Ga., 5-12-1865. Died: 6-9-1925. Buried: Old Harmony Grove Cemetery, Dallas, Ga.

Coker, James, Pvt., **H**, Enlisted: 1-63, Tallapoosa, Ga., Captain Tumlin. Present until 12-63 absent Detained in Ga., by Gen. Wheeler. 12-64 AWOL.

Coker, William, Pvt., **H**, Enlisted: 4-62, Haralson Co., Ga., Captain Tumlin. Present until 12-62 absent: sick furlough home. Captured: Mossy Creek, Tenn. 1-19-63. Exchanged. Present 2-63. Captured: Pigeon River, Sevierville, Tenn., 1-27-64. Carried: Knoxville; Nashville; Louisville; Rock Island, Ill. 2-15-64. Released: 6-20-1865. Description: home Fair Play, Calhoun Co., Ala., dark complexion, dark hair, blue eyes, 5'-7", age 31.

Colbert, John G., Pvt., **A**, Enlisted 8-4-1863, Bartow Co., Ga. in 10th Battalion Ga. Cavalry State Guards. Enlisted: Cedartown, Ga., age 38, Captain York 12-1-1863. Detailed with Lt. Clark 12-16-64. Paroled: Charlotte, N.C. 5-3-1865.

Cole, Noah, Sgt., **D**, Enlisted: 3-62, Dallas, Ga., age 38, Captain Seawright. Elected 5th Sgt. 8-1-62. Present until home sick with pneumonia, Cobb Co. 2-26-63. Died: 2-27-1863, Cobb Co., Ga.

Cole, William T., Pvt., **B**, Enlisted: 7-63, Grantville, Ga., Lt. Taylor. 12-63 Detained with wagon train by Gen Wheeler. 12-64 AWOL. Died: 5-4-1911. Buried: Oak Hill Cemetery, Newnan, Ga.

Coleman, John Henry, Pvt., **F**, Enlisted: 5-62, Carrollton, Ga., Captain Blalock. 12-63 Captured; paroled. 12-31-1864 AWOL. Died: 1-21-1932. Buried: Hokes Bluff First Baptist Church, Etowah Co., Ala.

Coleman, William Allen, Pvt., **E**, Enlisted: 3-62, Carrollton, Ga., Captain Blalock. Present through 12-64 as Company blacksmith. Pension: In skirmish line when General Stoneman surrendered. Died: 10-30-1917. Buried: Carrollton City Cemetery, Carroll Co., Ga.

Collins, Samuel W., Sgt., **D**, Enlisted: 3-62, Dallas, Ga., age 28, Captain Seawright. Present until 2-63 absent: Sick furlough in Cobb Co., Ga., 12-63 absent sick in Atlanta Hospital. Present 12-64. Surrendered: Greensboro, N.C. 4-26-1865. Pension: Lost Mountain, Cobb Co., Ga., 1895.

Colly (Colley), Aaron D., Pvt., Enlisted 5-10-1862, Cotton Planters Guards, 59th Ga. Inf., Fort Gaines, Ga. 4-64 Transferred: 1st Ga. Cavalry.

Colt, W.B., Pvt., **G**, Paroled: Talladega, Ala. 6-1-1865.

Comer, Robert T., Pvt., **D**, Enlisted: 3-62, Dallas, Ga., Captain Seawright. Present as Teamster until death. Died: Tullahoma, Tenn. 12-18-62. Buried: Confederate Plot, Maplewood Cemetery, Tullahoma, Tenn.

Compton (Crompton), Robert J., Pvt., **D**, Enlisted: 3-62, Dallas, Ga., age 19, Captain Seawright. 6-62 and 12-62 absent: Sick furlough in Paulding Co., Ga. Present 2-63. Captured: Monticello, Ky. 5-1-63. Carried: Louisville 5-7-63; City Point, Va., 6-16-63, for exchange. 12-63 absent Detained in Ga., by Gen. Wheeler. Captured near Dallas, Ga., 5-27-64. Carried: Louisville. Took oath 6-15-64. Description: home Paulding Co., Ga., florid complexion, light hair, grey eyes, 5'-10".

Compton (Crompton), Richard Jehu, Sr., Pvt., **D**, Enlisted: 3-62 Dallas, Ga., age 50, Captain Seawright. 6-62 and 8-62 absent: Sick furlough in Paulding Co., Ga., Ga. Discharged: Kingston, Tenn. 9-22-62. Certificate: age 52, 5'-9", yellow hair, blue eyes. Pension: Lawrence Co., Ala.

Cone, James F., Pvt., **D**, Enlisted: 3-62, Dallas, Ga. Captain Seawright. Present until 12-62 and 2-63 absent: Sick furlough in Paulding Co., Ga.

Cook, Benjamin Franklin, Pvt., **E**, Enlisted: 3-62, Carrollton, Ga., Captain Blalock. Present 6-62 as Blacksmith. Present until Captured near Somerset, Ky. 3-30-63. Carried: Louisville; Fort McHenry, Maryland. Exchanged, 4-13-63. Absent 12-63 on detached service. Absent 12-64 as Corps Headquarters blacksmith. Died: 12-4-1911. Buried: Ranburne First Baptist Church, Cleburne Co., Ala.

Cook, F.L., Pvt., **F**, Enlisted: 3-62, Fairmount, Ga., Col. Morrison. Present until 12-63 AWOL.

Cook, George W., 2nd Lt., **E**, Enlisted: 3-62, Carrollton, Ga., Captain Blalock. Present until 2-63 absent: sick furlough. Admitted to Hospital, Polk Co., Ga., 11-6-63. Promoted 3rd Lt. 9-10-63, Col. Morrison. 12-64 present.

Cook, Henry L., Pvt., **E**, Enlisted: 3-62, Fairmount, Ga., Col. Morrison. Absent 8-62 through 12-62 Sick furlough. 2-63 AWOL.

Cook, J., Pvt., **E**, Enlisted: 7-63, Ebenezer, Tenn., Lt. Col. Harper. 12-63 absent sick. Clothing issued 6-64.

Cook, James A., Pvt., **E**, Enlisted: 1-63, Rogersville, Tenn., Lt. Col. Harper. Present until Captured near Knoxville 12-3-63. Carried: Louisville; Rock Island, Ill. 1-6-64. Enlisted: U.S. Navy. Died in prison 2-10-64. Buried: Rock Island Confederate Cemetery, Rock Island, Ill. Grave #410

Cook, John W., Pvt., **B**, Enlisted: 3-62, Newnan,

Ga., age 28, Captain Strickland. Present until 12-63 admitted to Rome, Ga. Hospital. Present 12-64.

Cook, Reuben J., Cpl., **E**, Enlisted 6-6-1861: 21st Ga. Inf., Campbell Co., Ga., age 22. Discharged 9-30-1861 with Rheumatism. Enlisted: 1st Ga. Cavalry 3-21-1862: Carrollton, Ga., Captain Blalock. Present until Captured in North Carolina 4-25-1865. Carried: Anderson, S.C., and discharged. Died: 3-3-1915. Buried: Bethlehem Baptist Church, Fairburn, Ga.

Cook, Robert Jefferson, Pvt., **F**, Enlisted: 3-62, Fairmount, Ga., Col. Morrison. Present 6-62. Absent 8-62 and 10-62 Sick furlough. Present through 12-63. 12-31-63 AWOL. Living: Grayson Co., Tx.

Cook, Thomas Franklin, Pvt., **F**, Enlisted: 3-62, Fairmount, Ga., Col. Morrison. Deserted: Chattanooga 10-5-63.

Cooper, H.N., Pvt., **K**, Captured: Athens Ga., 5-8-1865, paroled.

Cooper, James, Pvt., **D**, Enlisted: 3-62, Dallas, Ga., age 36, Captain Seawright. Present until 8-62 absent: Sick furlough in Paulding Co., Ga. Died: Big Creek Gap, Tenn. 9-5-1862.

Cooper, James Powers, Sgt., **I**, Enlisted: 5-62, Camp Morrison, Col. Morrison. Present until Detailed to Brigade Battery by Gen. Pegram, 2-1-63. Absent on detached service 10-63. Captured: New Hope Church, 5-18-64. Carried: Nashville; Louisville 5-25-64; Rock Island. Took oath 1-11-65. Description: home Rome, Ga., age 27, 5'-7", brown hair, grey eyes, fresh complexion. Released 6-3-65. Died: 1916. Buried: Dallas Memorial Gardens, Dallas, Ga.

Cooper, John H., Pvt., **I**, Enlisted: 8th Ga. Inf. 5-14-61, Rome, Ga., age 23. Transferred: 1st Ga. Cavalry 9-9-62. Present until 3-63 absent with detachment Camp. Captured: Murfreesboro 1-5-63. Carried: Camp Douglas 3-31-63. On list of deserters. Took oath 12-63 stated home in Floyd Co., Ga.

Cooper, Levi, Sgt., **I**, Enlisted: 3-62, Dallas, Ga., age 26, Captain Seawright. Elected 2nd Sgt. 8-1-62. Present until 12-63 absent: Sick in Ga. hospital. Surrendered: Greensboro, N.C. 4-26-1865. Died: 10-12-1908. Buried: New Hope Baptist Church, Dallas, Ga.

Copeland, Dickson Huie, Cpl., **C**, Enlisted: 5-62, Cave Spring, Ga., Lt. Reynolds. Present through 12-31-64 except for brief AWOL. Elected 1st Cpl. 6-30-63. Died: 12-26-1905. Buried: Cave Spring Cemetery, Floyd Co., Ga.

Corley, John W., Cpl., **G**, Enlisted: 5-62, Rome,

Ga., Captain Kerr. Present until 12-63 absent in Ga. Captured in Floyd Co., Ga. Carried: Louisville on list of deserters 6-4-64. Took oath 6-8-64, released. Description: home Floyd Co., Ga., complexion light, hair light, blue eyes, 5'-9". Died: 1-27-1913. Buried: Pisgah Cemetery, Rome, Ga.

Corley, S.P., Pvt., **G**, Enlisted: 3-62, Floyd Co., Ga., Captain Kerr. Present until admitted to Loudon, Tenn. hospital 7-9-62. During Battle at Danville, Ky. 3-25-63, his horse KIA. Paid $225. 12-63 AWOL.

Corley, W.A., Sgt., **B**, Enlisted: 3-62, Newnan, Ga., 12-63 present. 12-64 blank.

Corley, W.W., Pvt., **G**, Enlisted: 5-62, Floyd Co., Ga., Captain Kerr. Present until 10-62 through 2-63 absent Detailed as Bodyguard for Gen. Kirby Smith. Present 12-63 and 12-64. Paroled: Charlotte, N.C. 5-3-1865.

Cornelius, William T., Pvt., **G**, Died: 11-3-1880. Buried: Myrtle Hill, Rome, Ga.

Cornutt, Edwin (Edward) W., Pvt., **G**, Enlisted: 8-63, Rome, Ga., O.M. Pennington. Present until Captured: Atlanta 7-21-64. Carried: Chattanooga; Nashville; Louisville; Camp Chase 7-31-64. Died: 10-22-64, pneumonia. Buried: Camp Chase Confederate Cemetery, Columbus, Ohio, Row 11, #30, grave #349.

Coston, James J., Pvt., **C**, Enlisted: 5-62, Cave Spring, Ga., Lt. Reynolds. 6-62 present. 8-62 through 2-63 absent sick. 6-63 to 12-63 AWOL. 12-64 present: Blacksmith.

Cotton, Wiley, Pvt., **E**, Captured: Mount Pleasant, Tenn. 9-4-64. Carried: Nashville; Louisville; Camp Chase 9-10-64. Released 6-11-1865. Description: home Jackson Co., Ala., age 18, 5'-9", fair complexion, light hair, blue eyes.

Couch, E. Frank, Cpl., **E**, Enlisted: 9-63 by Captain Kelly. Surrendered: Greensboro, N.C. 4-26-1865. Died: 8-11-1894: Atlanta, Ga.

Coulter, Francis Marion, 2nd Lt., **G**, Enlisted: 5-62, Floyd Co., Ga., Captain Kerr. Promoted 2nd Lt. 12-5-62, Col. Morrison. Present until Captured at Mill Spring, Ky. 5-28-63. Carried: Lexington; Camp Chase; Point Lookout, Md.; exchanged 3-10-64. Statement: age 35, 5'-9", blue eyes, light hair, light complexion. Detailed: Cared for and pilot barges and boats between Rome, Ga., and Greensport, Ala. on Coosa River. Died: 3-1894. Buried: Myrtle Hill, Rome, Ga.

Coursey, B.G., Pvt., **A**, Enlisted: 3-62, Cedartown, Ga., Captain John C. Crabb. Absent 6-62 Sick furlough in Polk Co., Ga. 8-62 to 12-62 present.

Coursey, Edward Graves, Pvt., **A**, Enlisted: 3-62, Cedartown, Ga., Captain John C. Crabb. 2-62 present. 12-63 absent: Cutoff with the wagons. 12-64 present. Substitute. Died: 1-28-1923. Buried: Salem Presbyterian Church, Talladega Co., Ala.

Cox, Calvin S., Pvt., **G**, Enlisted: 5-62, Floyd Co., Ga., Captain Kerr. Present until 12-63 absent: Sick in Floyd Co., Ga. Deserted and took oath: Chattanooga 3-30-1864. Description: home Floyd Co., Ga., 5'-11", blue eyes, brown hair, dark complexion.

Cox, Edward, Pvt., **F**, Enlisted: 8-62, Sparta, Tenn., Captain Reynolds. 10-62 absent: Blacksmith for Regiment. 12-62 through 2-63 absent: Blacksmith for Brigade. 12-63 absent: Detailed to Blacksmith shop in Ga. 12-64 Detailed: make horse shoes for the Regiment. Col. Morrison, witness widow pension: Detailed to get horse shoes for the Regiment at surrender. Died: 3-1-1901. Buried: Decatur City Cemetery, DeKalb Co., Ga.

Cox, James T., Pvt., **I**, Died: 4-12-1925. Buried: Henager Cemetery, DeKalb Co., Ala.

Cox, John M., Pvt., **G**, Enlisted: 3-62, Floyd Co., Ga., Captain Kerr. 6-62 absent: Sick in Loudon, Tenn. hospital. Captured near Clay Village, Ky. 10-4-62, paroled. KIA: Dandridge, Tenn. 12-28-63. Widow pension: Killed outright 12-24-1863, Dandridge, Tenn.

Cox, Jonathan O., Pvt., **G**, Enlisted: 8-62, Kingston, Tenn., Captain Kerr. Present until 2-63 absent: Sick furlough in Floyd Co., Ga. Deserted and took oath 3-30-64: Chattanooga. Description: home Floyd Co., Ga., 5'-7", dark complexion, black hair, black eyes.

Cox, Richard J., Pvt., **G**, Enlisted: 3-62, Floyd Co., Ga., Captain Kerr. Present until 2-63 absent: Sick furlough in Floyd Co., Ga., 12-63 absent: Sick in Ga. Deserted and took oath 3-30-64: Chattanooga. Description: home Floyd Co., Ga., dark complexion, dark hair, grey eyes, 5'-6".

Crabb, Jesse W., Captain, **A**, Enlisted: Cedartown, Ga., age 28, 21st Ga. Inf., 6-27-1861. Discharged disabled 11-18-61. Certificate: born Henry Co., Ga., age 28, 5'-8", light complexion, dark eyes, black hair. Enlisted: 5-62, 1st Ga. Cavalry, Cedartown, Ga., Captain John C. Crabb. Present 6-62 and 8-62. Promoted 1st Lt. 8-3-62 by Col. Morrison. Present 10-62 and 12-62. Absent 2-63 sick furlough in Rome, Ga. 12-63 present. WIA: Sunshine Church 7-31-64. Promoted Captain 8-3-64 by Col. Davitte at death of William T. York. Service to 4-9-65. Died: around 1879. Buried: Barber Cemetery, Van Wert, Ga.

Crabb, John Calaway, Captain, **A**, Enlisted: 3-62, Cedartown, Ga., Lt. Col. Morrison. WIA: Murfreesboro 7-13-62 charging the Court House. Died wounded 7-15-62. Buried: William Anderson's, White Co., Tenn. 8 miles west of Sparta, Tenn. Reinterred: Barber Cemetery, Van Wert, Ga.

Crabb, John W., Pvt., **A**, Enlisted: 3-62, Camp Morrison, Captain John C. Crabb. Substitute for Samuel J. Crabb his father. 6-62 absent: Sick furlough in Polk Co., Ga. Present 8-62 through 12-63. Captured near Cedartown, Ga., 11-20-64. In route to a northern prison, cut a hole in the boxcar to make escape near Marietta, Ga. Paroled: Charlotte, N.C. 5-3-1865. Died: 6-3-1918. Buried: Oak Grove Baptist Church, Cedartown, Ga.

Crabb, Samuel Jackson, Pvt., **A**, Enlisted: Cedartown, Ga., age 45,: 21st Ga. Inf. Enlisted: 3-62, Camp Morrison, Captain John C. Crabb. Substituted for by John W. Crabb, son. Died: 1887. Buried: Oak Grove Cemetery, Cedartown, Ga.

Craig, Samuel R., Pvt., **B**, Enlisted: 3-62, Newnan, Ga. Present through 12-64. Paroled: Charlotte, N.C. 5-3-1865.

Crane, Bartley A., Pvt., **A**, Enlisted: 5-64, Discharged 5-12-1865: Kingston, Ga. Died: 9-8-1915. Buried: Nimblewill Baptist Church, Lumpkin Co., Ga.

Crider, Reuben P., Pvt., **H**, Enlisted: 8-62, Kingston, Tenn., Captain Tumlin. Present 8-62 through 2-63 as Blacksmith. AWOL 9-1-63. 12-64 present.

Crocker, James A., Pvt., **A**, Enlisted: 3-62, Cedartown, Ga., Captain John C. Crabb. Present until 8-62 absent: Sick furlough in Polk Co., Ga. 10-62 to 2-62 present. Captured: Somerset, Ky. 3-30-63. Carried: Louisville; City Point, Va., exchange 4-13-63. 12-63 present. Captured: Atlanta 8-2-64. Carried: Nashville; Louisville 8-13-64; Camp Chase; Point Lookout, Md. 3-18-1865. Died: 10-26-1885. Buried: Friendship Cemetery, Cedartown, Ga.

Crotly (Crotty), **J.**, Pvt., Paroled: Thomasville, Ga., 5-16-65.

Crow, John F., Pvt., **I**, Enlisted: 10th Battalion Cavalry State Guards, Manassas, Ga., 8-4-1863. Enlisted: 5-64, Cass Station, Ga., Captain Leak. AWOL 12-7-64. Died: 5-28-1890. Buried: Bosqueville Cemetery, McLennan Co., Tx.

Crow, William Pickens, Pvt., **I**, Enlisted: 10th Battalion Cavalry State Guards, Manassas, Ga. Enlisted: 6-64, Cass Station, Ga., Captain Leak. AWOL 12-16-1864. Returned and Paroled: Charlotte, N.C. 5-3-1865. Died: 5-23-1923. Buried: Abilene Municipal Cemetery, Abilene, Texas.

Crow, W.W., Pvt., **I**, Enlisted: 12-64, Cass Station, Ga., Captain Leak. Paroled: Charlotte, N.C. 5-3-1865.

Crowell, Josiah F., Pvt., **E**, Enlisted: 3-62, Carrollton, Ga., Captain Blalock. Sent to Hospital in Knoxville with rheumatism. Discharged: 6-19-62, M.A. Shackleford, surgeon. Stated: born Mecklenburg Co., N.C., age 36, 5'-8", red complexion, blue eyes, sandy hair. Pension: 1901 Carroll Co., Ga.

Culpepper, Elijah Milton, Pvt., **B**, Enlisted: 3-62, Newnan, Ga., age 27, Captain Strickland. Absent 6-62 Sick furlough. 8-62 through 2-63 present. Absent 12-63 detailed as Wheelwright in Davidson's Brigade. KIA: Macon, Ga. Pension: Order was given for every fourth man to dismount and step forward. Man next to him hesitated and Culpepper took his place and was killed.

Culpepper, James Daniel, 1st Sgt., **B**, Enlisted: 3-62, Newnan, Ga., age 28, Captain Strickland. Present until 12-63 absent: Detained with wagon train by General Wheeler. Present 12-64. Paroled: Charlotte, N.C. 5-3-1865. Died: 11-1-1903. Buried: Allen-Lee Cemetery, Lone Oak, Meriwether Co., Ga.

Culver, Zack C., Sgt., **H**, Paroled: Augusta, Ga., 5-18-65. Died: 3-18-1901. Buried: Rose Hill Cemetery, Macon, Ga.

Curtis, Daniel Boone, Pvt., **F**, Enlisted: 3-62, Fairmount, Ga., Col. Morrison. Present 5-14-1862. Died 6-30-1906. Buried: Curtis Cemetery, Rising Star, Texas.

Curtis, John Merrill, Pvt., **F**, Enlisted: 3-62, Fairmount, Ga., Col. Morrison. Discharged: Chattanooga 5-4-62. Died: 5-16-1902. Buried: Curtis Cemetery, Gordon Co., Ga.

Curtis, Thomas Newton, Pvt., **F**, Enlisted: 3-62, Fairmount, Ga., Col. Morrison. Discharged at Chattanooga 5-4-1862. Pension: During cavalry drill in Chattanooga, he was ruptured on both sides riding a wild horse, and typhoid fever. Died: 3-8-1907. Buried: Curtis Family Cemetery, Gordon Co., Ga.

Curtis, V.B., Pvt., **F**, Enlisted: 3-62, Fairmount, Ga., Col. Morrison. Discharged: Chattanooga 5-4-62.

Curtis, William Naaman Nathan, Pvt., **F**, Enlisted: 3-62, Fairmount, Ga., Col. Morrison. Sick: typhoid fever 5-29-62, Chattanooga. Developed chorea or St. Vitus Dance. Discharged: 11-7-62. Statement: born Pickens District, S.C., age 30, 5'-10", light complexion, blue eyes, black hair. Died: 1-21-1901. Buried: Curtis Family Cemetery, Gordon Co., Ga.

Cuzzort, Calvin, Pvt., **G**, Enlisted: 3-62, Floyd Co., Ga., Captain Kerr. Rejected 5-62.

Dabbs, Charles T., 2nd Lt., **D**, Enlisted: 3-62, Dallas, Ga., Captain Seawright. Present until 8-62 absent: on scout. Elected 4th Sgt. 8-1-62. Present 10-62 through 2-63. Promoted 2nd Lt. 10-63. WIA: Russellville, Tenn. 12-10-63 in hip. 12-64 absent wounded. Died: 8-25-1890. Buried: Dabbs Family Cemetery, Dallas, Ga.

Dampier, W.M., Pvt., Paroled: Thomasville, Ga., 5-25-65.

Darnell (Darnold), Thomas A., Pvt., **F**, Enlisted: 3-62, Carrollton, Ga., Major Harper. Listed deserted 8-12-63. Transferred: Co. C, 40th Ga. Regt. Inf. Pension: DeKalb Co., Ga. 1910.

Davidson, John P., Pvt., **G**, Enlisted: 3-62, Floyd Co., Ga., Captain Kerr. Present until 2-63 absent: Sick in Floyd Co., Ga. Courier, Gen. Iverson 5-25-1864.

Davidson, S.L., Pvt., **G**, Enlisted: 3-62, Floyd Co., Ga., Captain Kerr. Absent 6-62 Sick in Floyd Co., Ga. Detailed as Courier 10-20-1864 on line service.

Davis, A.H., Jr., Pvt., **G**, Enlisted: 3-62, Floyd Co., Ga., Captain Kerr. Rejected.

Davis, Andrew J., Pvt., **B**, Enlisted: 4-62, Newnan, Ga. Present until 2-63 absent: Sick furlough in Grantville, Ga. Present 12-63 and 12-64. Surrendered: Raleigh, N.C. 4-26-1865. Died: 1-31-1894 Meriwether Co., Ga.

Davis, Chessly W., Pvt., **B**, Enlisted: 3-62, Newnan, Ga. Present until 12-63 Transferred to 34th Ga. Vol. Inf.

Davis, D., Pvt., **K**, Captured: Philadelphia, Tenn.

Davis, D. Hopkins, Pvt., **E**, Enlisted: 5-62, Carrollton, Ga. Present 12-63 through 12-64. Received clothing 6-1864.

Davis, George R., Pvt., **E**, 2-63 present—Substitute for B.S. Smoot. Died 2-10-1863.

Davis, J. Polk, Pvt., **C**, Enlisted: 1-63, Cave Spring, Ga., Captain Haynie. Present until AWOL 10-28-1864.

Davis, James, Pvt., **G**, Enlisted: 11-63, Tenn., by Captain Kerr. 12-63 present. Received clothing 6-1864.

Davis, James W., Pvt., **C**, Enlisted: 3-62, Cave Spring, Ga., Captain Haynie. 6-62 never mustered.

Davis, Jepthie R., Pvt., **B**, Enlisted: 7-63, Newnan, Ga., 12-63 present, but 12-64 blank. Pension: Discharged: Atlanta 1865. Died: 12-29-1915. Buried: Perote Cemetery, Bullock Co., Ala.

Davis, John W., Pvt., **C**, Enlisted: 3-63, WIA twice. Discharged 1865. Living: St. Clair Co., Ala. 1907.

Davis, J.P., Pvt., **B**, Discharged 1865. Lived: Cherokee Co., Ala.

Davis, Samuel, Pvt., **B**, Enlisted: 3-62, Newnan, Ga. Present through 12-64. Discharged: Atlanta 5-1865 by Gen. Wheeler. Died: 6-4-1908. Buried: Goshen Cemetery, Heard Co., Ga.

Davis, Samuel Warren, Pvt., **K**, Enlisted: 5-62, Camp Morrison, Captain North. Present until Captured near Philadelphia, Tenn. 10-20-63. Carried: Camp Chase 11-14-63; Fort Delaware Prison 2-29-64. Exchanged 3-7-1865. Admitted: Jackson Hospital, Richmond, Va. 3-13-1865, Pneumonia. Died: 8-8-1912. Buried: Greer Family Cemetery, DeKalb Co., Ga.

Davis, William T., Pvt., **B**, Enlisted: 7-63, Newnan, Ga. Present 12-63 and 12-31-1864. Died: 7-7-1902. Buried: Luthersville City Cemetery, Meriwether Co., Ga.

Davitte, Jacob Scott, Sgt., **D**, Enlisted: 3-62, Dallas, Ga., age 18, Captain Seawright. Clerk: Post Commissary, Kingston, Tenn. 5-15-62. Present until 2-63 absent: Sick furlough in Polk Co., Ga. Received clothing 7-13-64. 12-64 AWOL. Pension: Asthma. Orderly Sergeant. Surrendered: Greensboro, N.C. 4-26-1865. Died: 2-23-1914. Buried: Davitte Family Cemetery, Polk Co., Ga.

Davitte, Samuel William, Colonel, **F&S**, Enlisted: 3-62, Dallas, Ga., age 30, Captain Seawright. Promoted: Captain 4-1-62 Paymaster and Quartermaster for regiment. Promoted: Major, Col. Morrison 5-2-63 for gallantry in action. Appointed Lt. Col 4-15-64. Appointed Col. 1-28-65. Died: December 1898, Buried: Davitte Family Cemetery, Polk Co., Ga.

Dawson, John N., Sgt., **F**, Enlisted: 3-62, Fairmount, Ga., Col. Morrison. Present through 12-62. Absent 2-63 assigned as Recruiter for Gen. Pegram. Captured: Rome, Ga., 6-10-64, Carried: Nashville; Louisville; Camp Morton, Ind. Released taking oath 2-20-65. Description: dark complexion, black hair, hazel eyes, 5'-7". Died: 12-15-1918. Buried: Glover Hill Cemetery, Jasper, Tenn.

Dawson, Jonas M., Pvt., **F**, Enlisted: 3-62, Fairmount, Ga., Col. Morrison. Died: Knoxville 6-30-62.

Dean, E.P., Surgeon, **C**, 1862 left in Kentucky with sick.

Dean, John H., Pvt., **C**, Enlisted: 3-62, Cave Spring, Ga., Captain Haynie. Present until KIA: Murfreesboro 7-13-62.

Dean, John Thomas, Pvt., **B**, Died: 12-28-1886. Widow filed a pension in Talladega Co., Ala.

Dean, R., Pvt., **B**, Enlisted: 4-62, Newnan, Ga.

Present through 12-63. Absent 12-64 Courier for Gen. Iverson.

Dean, Rayford T., Pvt., **A**, Enlisted: 3-62, Cedartown, Ga., Captain John C. Crabb. Present through 12-62. Absent 2-63 and 12-63 Detailed to Brigade artillery.

Dean, Samuel C., Pvt., **A**, Enlisted: 3-62, Cedartown, Ga., Captain John C. Crabb. Present through 12-62. Absent 2-63 Detailed to Brigade artillery.

Dean, Thomas P., Pvt., **C**, Enlisted: 3-62, Cave Spring, Ga., Captain Haynie. Absent 6-62 Sick furlough in Floyd Co., Ga. Present 8-62 to 2-63. Absent 6-63 sick furlough. Absent 12-63 Special duty for Col. Morrison.

Dean, Virgil H., Pvt., **C**, Enlisted: 3-62, Cave Spring, Ga., Captain Haynie. Present 6-62 to 8-62. Detailed: guard horses for 43 days. Discharged 1-22-1863. Statement: born Spartanburg, S.C., age 32, 6'-0", fair complexion, brown eyes, brown hair.

Dean, Wiley H., Pvt., **G**, Died: 10-7-1864. Buried: Camp Chase Confederate Cemetery, Columbus, Ohio. Grave 258-cc.

Deaton, Andrew, Pvt., **A**, Enlisted 1st Ark. Inf. 4-26-1861, age 24, Benton, Ark. WIA: Murfreesboro 12-31-62. Transferred: 1st Ga. Cavalry. Enlisted: 1-63, Chattanooga by Captain Hutchings. Absent 2-63 with Brigade wagons. Present 12-63. AWOL 5-10-1864. Died: 6-14-1896. Buried: Kentucky Cemetery, Saline Co., Ark.

Deaton, Thomas, Pvt., **A**, Enlisted: 3-62, Cedartown, Ga., Captain John C. Crabb. Present until 10-62 absent: Sick in Kingston, Tenn. Absent 2-63 Brigade wagons-Teamster. Present 12-63. AWOL 5-10-1864.

Deckort, G.W., Pvt., **K**, Pension: Calhoun Co., Ala.

DeLang, Joseph, Pvt., **K**, Enlisted 11-61: 1st La. Cavalry. Transferred: 1st Ga. Cavalry 4-25-63.

Delk, H., Pvt., **K**, Enlisted: 5-62, Camp Morrison, Captain North.

Dempsey, Balaam, Pvt., **F**, Enlisted: 3-62, Fairmount, Ga., Col. Morrison. Deserted 6-15-62, Chattanooga. Took oath. Description: home Gordon Co., Ga., dark complexion, dark hair, black eyes, 6'-1".

Dempsey, Daniel Morgan, Sgt., **C**, Enlisted: 3-62, Cave Spring, Ga., Captain Haynie. Promoted 3rd Cpl. 3-31-62. Present 6-62 and 8-62. Promoted 2nd Sgt. 9-30-62. Present 12-62 and 12-63. Pension: Joined to choose his company. WIA: Mossy Creek, Tenn. 12-29-1863. Died: 1-28-1910. Buried: Highland Cemetery, Piedmont, Ala.

Dempsey, Francis Marion, Pvt., **H**, Enlisted: 4-62,

Haralson Co., Ga., Captain Tumlin. Absent 6-62 Sick furlough. Present 8-62. Discharged 9-23-62.

Dempsey, W.P., Pvt., **H**, Enlisted: 4-62, Haralson Co., Ga., Captain Tumlin. Present until 10-62 absent: Sick in hospital. Absent 2-63 Sick furlough at home.

Dempsey, William B., Pvt., **C**, Enlisted: 3-62, Cave Spring, Ga., Captain Haynie. Present through 6-63. KIA: Chickamauga 9-19-1863.

Dennington, Elias, Pvt., **G**, Enlisted: 3-62, Floyd Co., Ga., Captain Kerr. Rejected. Died: 6-24-1927. Buried: Gassville Cemetery, Baxter Co., Ark.

Dennington, Samuel, Pvt., **G**, Enlisted: 3-62, Floyd Co., Ga., Captain Kerr. Present through 12-62. Absent 2-63 through 12-64 Detached by Gen. Pegram to Marshall's Company of Artillery. Died: 8-27-1928. Buried: Yellville, Ark.

Denson, John, Sgt., **D**, Enlisted: 3-62, Dallas, Ga., age 63, Captain Seawright. Discharged: Kingston, Tenn. 7-4-62. Certificate: born Newberry District, S.C., age 63, 5'-5", fair complexion, dark eyes, grey hair.

Denton, George Washington, Cpl., **D**, Enlisted: 3-62, Dallas, Ga., Captain Seawright. Absent 2-63 Sick furlough in Paulding Co., Ga. Absent 12-63 Sick in Atlanta Hospital. Died: 7-26-1925. Buried: Friendship Baptist Church Cemetery, Upshaw, Ala.

Devine, J.J., Acting Quarter Master, **F&S**, declined.

Dickert, George, W., Cpl., **K**, Enlisted: 5-62, Camp Morrison, Captain North. Present until 2-63 absent: Sick furlough in Coweta Co., Ga. WIA near Russellville, Tenn., and sent to Bristol Hospital 12-12-63. 12-1864 present.

Dickson, William C., Pvt., **D**, Enlisted: 3-62, Dallas, Ga., age 22, Captain Seawright. Asst. Wagon Master 6-15-62. 10-62 and 12-62 absent: Sick furlough in Cobb Co., Ga.

Dillard, Lemuel Smith, Pvt., **G**, Enlisted: 5-62, Camp Morrison, Captain Leak. Present until 3-63 absent at Detachment Camp. Present 12-63 and 12-64. Paroled: Charlotte, N.C. 5-3-1865. Died: 9-24-1911. Buried: Oxford Memorial Cemetery, Lafayette Co., Miss.

Dobbs (Dodd), Burrell Wilhite, 1st Sgt., **H**, Enlisted: 4-62, Haralson Co., Ga., Captain Tumlin. Absent 6-62 Sick furlough. Present 8-62 through 2-63. Absent 12-63 in hospital. Present 12-64. Captured: Greenville, S.C. 5-23-65. Died: 8-9-1896. Buried: Sewell Methodist Church Cemetery, Mansfield, Ga.

Dobbs, James D., Sgt., **E**, Enlisted: 3-62, Carrollton, Ga., Captain Blalock. Present until Captured near Knoxville 12-10-63. Widow pension:

Captured on Retreat from Knoxville to Morristown, Tenn. 3-22-63. Carried: Louisville; Camp Chase; Rock Island Prison, Ill. 1-26-64. 4-1-63 sick with dysentery in prison and never recovered. Died: 6-3-1878 Carroll Co., Ga.

Dobbs, John M., Pvt., **H**, Enlisted: 4-62, Haralson Co., Ga., Captain Tumlin. Present through 8-62. Absent 10-62 Sick furlough home. 12-62 present. Absent 2-63 Sick furlough. Deserted, took oath: Chattanooga 11-18-64. Description: home Polk Co., Ga., dark hair, dark complexion, black eyes, 5'-10". Admitted: Gen. Hospital Chattanooga 12-2-64, variola (smallpox), age 22. Recorded: Died 2-25-1865 but was a witness on widow pension in Gordon Co., Ga., 1891.

Dobbs, Jonathan R., Cpl., **H**, Enlisted: 4-62, Haralson Co., Ga., Captain Tumlin. Present until WIA 1863. Died 8-3-1910. Buried: Acton Cemetery, Hood Co., Tx.

Dobbs, Thomas J., Sgt., **E**, Enlisted: 3-62, Carrollton, Ga., Captain Blalock. Present until Deserted and took oath 11-18-64 at Chattanooga. Description: home Polk Co., Ga., dark complexion, black hair, black eyes, 5'-10". Louisville hospital 6-21-65, typhoid fever. Discharged 6-27-1865.

Dobbs, Thomas N., Pvt., **H**, Enlisted: 9-62. Pension: Served in Georgia Organized Militia. Served under Captain Tumlin. Given 12 days to procure a horse. Fall 1864: blood poison, right hand. Sick with typhoid fever at Tallapoosa, Ga. Captured: at home. Carried: Chattanooga; Nashville. Going further north but the railroad line was broken and war ended then released. Died: 4-18-1937. Buried: Bethlehem Baptist Church, Felton, Ga.

Dobbs, William Martin, Pvt., **H**, Enlisted: 1-63, Bartow Co., Ga., Captain Tumlin. Present until Captured near Dandridge, Tenn. 12-24-63. Carried: Knoxville; Louisville 1-21-64; Rock Island, Ill. 1-26-64. Present at Rock Island 3-13-1865.

Dobbs, William S., Pvt., **I**, Enlisted: 3-62, Camp Morrison, Captain Leak. Pension: Between May and June 1862 became ill with Gastritis at Chattanooga. Sent Home to Cartersville, Ga. Died 6-23-1862.

Dodson, Daniel W., Pvt., **C**, Enlisted: 4-62, Haralson Co., Ga., Captain Tumlin. Present until 2-63 absent: Sick furlough. AWOL 10-1-63. POW at Chattanooga. 8-28-64. On list of deserters 9-1-64. Took oath 9-4-64, Louisville. Description: Captured: Clayton Co., Ala., home Clayton Co., Ala., dark complexion, dark hair, hazel eyes, 5'-7". Died: 11-10-1898. Buried: Mars Hill Cemetery, Cleburne Co., Ala.

Dollar, Ambrose, Pvt., **C**, Enlisted: 3-62, Cave

Spring, Ga., Captain Haynie. Present until 10-62 absent wounded. 12-62 to 2-63 Detailed as Wagoner. Present 6-63 to 12-63. Pension: WIA: Nashville 12-15-64. Shell fragment hit the top of his head fracturing skull. Died: 4-14-1905. Buried: Blackland Cemetery, Foreman, Ark.

Dollar, James Henry, Pvt., **C**, Enlisted: 3-62, Cave Spring, Ga., Captain Haynie. Present until 8-62 absent on wounded furlough. Carried dispatches from Loudon, Tenn. to Kingston. Wounded in left hand losing two middle fingers. Died: 1892, Floyd Co., Ga.

Dollar, Jesse, Pvt., **C**, Enlisted: 3-62, Cave Spring, Ga., Captain Haynie. Died of typhoid fever at Camp Morrison, Cartersville, Ga., 5-10-62.

Dollar, William J., Pvt., **C**, Enlisted: 3-62, Cave Spring, Ga., age 43, Captain Haynie. Present until KIA: Murfreesboro 7-13-62.

Dollar, William J., Pvt., **C**. Son of Ambrose Dollar. Died: 1-7-1911. Buried: Blackland Cemetery, Foreman, Ark.

Dominick, John Robert, Pvt., **K**, Enlisted: 5-62, Camp Morrison, Captain North. Present through 12-64. WIA: Stoneman's raid, left shoulder, Monticello. Surrendered: Greensboro, N.C. 4-26-1865. Died: 9-10-1914, Hall Co., Ga.

Dooley, William, Pvt., **C**, Enlisted: 1-63, Cave Spring, Ga., Captain Haynie. Present until Captured at Atlanta 6-1-64. Carried: Nashville 8-2-64; Lexington 8-12-64; Camp Chase 8-13-64; Point Lookout, Md. 3-18-1865.

Dorough, Jacob W., Pvt., **E**, Enlisted 5-2-1864: Fannin's 1st Ga. Reserve. Description: age 17, 5'-4", fair complexion, blue eyes, light hair. Enlisted: 11-64, 1st Ga. Cavalry, Arbacoochee, Cleburne Co., Ala., by Captain Watts. Present until Captured near Athens, Ga., 5-8-65. Died: 2-25-1894. Buried: Mount Carmel Cemetery, Subiaco, Ark.

Doster, J.G., Pvt., **F**, Enlisted 7-20-1863, Etowah, Ga., Iron Works Artillery, 17th Battalion Georgia State Guards. Enlisted: 5-64, 1st Ga. Cavalry, Decatur, Ga., by Major Andrews. Clothing issued 6-64. 12-31-1864 present.

Driver, Doctor F., Pvt., **H**, Enlisted: 4-62, Haralson Co., Ga., Captain Tumlin. Present through 10-62. Absent 12-62 Sick furlough. Captured: Somerset, Ky. 3-30-63. Carried: Lexington; Camp Chase 6-29-63. Description: 5'-7", age 32, blue eyes, dark hair, sandy complexion. Fort Delaware, 7-14-63. Admitted: Chester Hospital, Penn. 8-10-63, Chronic Dysentery. Died 9-8-63. Buried: Chester Cemetery, Penn., grave 185. Relocated: Philadelphia National Cemetery, Penn.

Ducker, R.C., **E**, Arrested 6-21.

Duckett, **John A.**, Pvt., **F**, Enlisted: 3-62, Fairmount, Ga., Col. Morrison. Absent 6-62 through 12-62 Sick furlough. 2-63 AWOL.

Duckett, **Robert C.**, Pvt., **F**, Enlisted: 3-62, Fairmount, Ga., Col. Morrison. Present until Captured near Powell Valley, Tenn. 6-27-62. Paroled. Present until Deserted 10-5-63, Chattanooga. Enlisted: U.S. 10th Tenn. Cavalry 12-25-1863, Charleston, Tenn., age 23. Died: 12-3-1923. Buried: Mount Isabella Cemetery, Monroe Co., Tenn.

Duckett, **William A.**, Pvt., **F**, Enlisted: 3-62, Fairmount, Ga., Col. Morrison. Present 6-62 and 8-62. 10-62 through 2-63 AWOL as left sick in Ky.

Dudley, **John E.**, Pvt., **F**, Enlisted: 3-62, Fairmount, Ga., Col. Morrison. Present through 12-62. Absent 2-63 through 12-64 Detailed to Captain Marshall's Artillery by Gen. Pegram.

Dudley, **Nicholas**, Pvt., **C**, Enlisted: 21st Ga. Inf. 6-27-1861, age 31, Cedartown, Ga. Discharged: hernia 11-22-61. Certificate: born Oglethorpe Co., Ga., age 33, 6'-0", light complexion, blue eyes, dark hair. Enlisted: 10-62, Cave Spring, Ga., Captain Haynie. Present through 2-63 Company Blacksmith. Captured: Somerset, Ky. 3-30-63. Carried: Louisville; City Point, Va. 4-15-63. Paroled 4-22-63. Present 12-64. Absent 12-31-1864 on detail.

Duke, **Alfred Gaberiel**, Pvt., **G**, Enlisted: 4-64, Oxford, Ala., Lt. Zuber. Present until Paroled: 5-3-1865 Charlotte, N.C. Died: 11-20-1930 at Confederate Soldiers Home, Atlanta. Buried: Duke Family Cemetery, Cobb Co., Ga.

Duke, **Allen Gregory**, Pvt., **G**, Enlisted: 4-64, Paroled: 5-3-1865 Charlotte, N.C. Died: 11-19-1905. Buried: Edgemont Cemetery, Anniston, Ala.

Duke, **Edmund T.**, Pvt., **G**, Enlisted: 8-63, Rome, Ga., by C.M. Pennington. Present until hospitalized 7-14-64. Died at Cannon Hospital, LaGrange, Ga., 8-20-1864 of fibris congestion. Buried: Stonewall Confederate Cemetery, LaGrange, Ga. Row 2, Grave 32. Listed: Edward Duke.

Duke, **James Waldrop**, Pvt., **D**, Died: 5-4-1909. Buried: Mount Moriah Church, Laneburg, Ark.

Duke, **John C.**, Pvt., **D**, Enlisted: 3-62, Dallas, Ga., age 22, Captain Seawright. Present 10-62 and 12-62. Detailed 2-63 Captain Marshall's Brown Horse Artillery. Captured: Ky. 8-15-63. Carried to Fort Delaware; released: 5-5-1865. Statement: light complexion, light hair, blue eyes, 5'-8".

Duke, **Welcome Parks**, Sgt., **H**, Enlisted: 1-63, Cedartown, Ga., Captain Tumlin. Present through

12-31-1864. Died: 12-26-1911. Buried: Duke Family Cemetery, Polk Co., Ga.

Duke, **Wiley**, Pvt., **D**, Enlisted: 3-62, Dallas, Ga., age 27, Captain Seawright. Absent 6-62 and 8-62 Sick furlough. Absent 12-62 and 2-63 Sick furlough in Paulding Co., Ga. Summer 1863 in hospital for 60-90 days. Lost his horse and Col. Davitte sent to infantry. Died: 3-11-1916. Buried: Paulding Co., Ga.

Duncan, **B.P.**, Hung as a spy 7-6-1864 near Chattahoochee River.

Duncan, **James S.**, Pvt., **H**, Enlisted: 4-62, Haralson Co., Ga., Captain Tumlin. Present through 12-62. Absent 2-63 Sick furlough. AWOL 10-15-63. Captured near Moore's Bridge, Ga., 7-31-64. Carried: Camp Chase; Point Lookout, Md.

Duncan, **George W.**, Pvt., **B**, Enlisted: 41st Ga. Inf. 3-4-62, Greenville, Ga. Transferred: 1st Ga. Cavalry 3-62 in Newnan, Ga. Present 12-64. Paroled: 5-31-65 Charlotte, N.C.

Duncan, **Matthew H.**, Sgt., **B**, Enlisted: 41st Ga. Inf. 3-4-62, Meriwether Co., Ga. Enlisted: 1st Ga. Cavalry 3-4-1862 in Newnan, Ga. Captured near Greenville, S.C. 5-23-65, paroled. Died: before January 1875 Meriwether Co., Ga.

Dunn, **James Hardy**, Pvt., **C**, Enlisted: 3-62, Cave Spring, Ga., Captain Haynie. Absent 6-62 Sick in Loudon, Tenn. Present 8-62 through 12-64. Surrendered: Raleigh, N.C. 4-26-1865. Died: 6-2-1926. Buried: Rockmart, Ga.

Dunn, **William P.**, Pvt., **F**, Enlisted: 3-62, Fairmount, Ga., Col. Morrison. Died: Calhoun, Ga., 6-8-62.

Dupree, **Leander Johnson**, Pvt., **A**, Enlisted: 3-64, in field by Captain York. 12-31-1864 present. Died: 1-11-1901. Buried: Ellisville Cemetery, Jones Co., Miss.

Dupriest, **P.R.**, Pvt., **G**, Enlisted: 8-63, Decatur, Ga., by Major Anderson. 12-63 AWOL. 12-31-1864 present. Lost musket 12-21-64.

Dyer, **Alexander**, Pvt., **A**, Enlisted: 3-62, Cedartown, Ga., Captain John C. Crabb. Present 6-62 Blacksmith. Absent 8-62 Sick furlough home. Present 10-62 through 12-63. Captured near Dallas, Ga., 6-2-64. Carried Nashville 6-13-63; Louisville 6-16-64; Rock Island, Ill. 6-24-64; and New Orleans. Exchanged 5-23-1865.

Dyer, **J.L.**, Lt., **E**, Died: 1-4-1865. Buried: Rose Hill Confederate Cemetery, Macon, Ga.

Dykes, **William V.**, Pvt., **C**, Enlisted: 1-63, Cave Spring, Ga., Captain Haynie. Present until Deserted 12-29-63 at Blain's Crossroads, Tenn. On list of deserters in Knoxville, Tenn.

Earp, Richardson, Pvt., **G**, Enlisted: 9-62, Kingston, Tenn., by Captain Kerr. Present until Discharged disabled 2-27-1863. Certificate: born Haywood Co., N.C., age 57, 5'-8", dark complexion, hazel eyes, grey hair. Pension: Cherokee Co., Ala. 1892.

Eason, Augustus C., Pvt., **C**, Enlisted: 2-63, Cave Spring, Ga., by Captain Haynie. Present until Paroled at Talladega, Ala. 6-10-65. Died: 6-4-1932. Buried: Oaklawn Cemetery, Wynnewood, Oklahoma.

Easterwood, William, Pvt., **E**, Enlisted: 3-62, Carrollton, Ga., by Captain Blalock. Present through 12-62. Present as Teamster for Regiment 2-5-63. Listed deserted 3-1-63. Widow pension: Disabled: Abscess or tumor erupting on his side. Captain Blalock discharged him from Spring Hill, Tenn. 4-13-63. Sent home with Nathan Horton and S.L. Allen, September 1863. Died: 11-4-1877 Palmetto, Ga.

Echols, James W., Pvt., **H**, Enlisted: 4-64, Tallapoosa, Ga., by Captain Tumlin. Captured near Calhoun, Ga., 5-18-64. Carried: Nashville; Louisville 5-27-64; Rock Island, Ill. Released 6-21-1865. Description: home Rome, Ga., dark complexion, black hair, grey eyes, 5'-9", age 27. Died: 12-9-1917. Buried: Lutie Cemetery, Wilburton, Oklahoma.

Echols, Robert H., Pvt., **H**, Enlisted: Cobb Co., Ga., age 19, Phillips Legion 6-14-1861. WIA. Enlisted: 1st Ga. Cavalry 4-15-1864, Tallapoosa, Ga., by Captain Tumlin. 12-64 AWOL. Died: 5-22-1873, Franklin Co., Ark.

Eddleman, Emery L., Sgt., **F**, Enlisted: 3-62, Fairmount, Ga., by Col. Morrison. Absent 6-62 on sick furlough. Present 8-62 through 12-62. absent 2-63 with detachment and wagons. Captured near Philadelphia, Tenn. 10-20-63. Exchanged. Captured: Benton, Tenn. 11-30-63. Carried: Nashville; Louisville 12-11-63; Rock Island, Ill. 12-13-63. Released: 6-21-1865. Description: home Manassas, Bartow Co., Ga., ruddy complexion, auburn hair, grey eyes, 5'-8", age 27. Died: 1-13-1901. Buried: Bryan City Cemetery, Brazos Co., Tx.

Edge, William R., Pvt., **B**, Enlisted: 8-63, Haralson Co., Ga., by Lt. Taylor. Absent in Newnan Hospital 12-1-63. Absent 12-64 in hospital. Died: 6-4-1898. Buried: Mount Carmel Methodist Church, Gay, Ga.

Edmunson, J., Pvt., Surrendered: Thomasville, Ga., 5-18-1865, paroled.

Edwards, James F., Pvt., **G**, Enlisted: 6-11-61 Phillips Legion. Fall 1861: Shot through wrist breaking bone, tearing leaders and muscle. Discharged 10-29-61. Enlisted: 5-62, 1st Ga. Cavalry: Camp Morrison by Captain Leak. Discharged 6-5-62, Chattanooga. Died: 11-8-1908. Buried: First Baptist Church, Resaca, Ga.

Edwards, John Fletcher, Pvt., **F**, Enlisted: 5-62. Present until Discharged 3-63 with Disability of spine at Augusta, Ga. Died: 9-1-1890, Bartow Co., Ga.

Edwards, Marcus H., Pvt., **I**, Died: 7-1-1899. Buried: La Fayette City Cemetery, Walker Co., Ga.

Edwards, R.L., Pvt., **G**, Enlisted: 5-62, Camp Morrison by Captain Leak. Lost horse in service. Died: Knoxville 6-25-62. Buried: Bethel Confederate Cemetery, Knoxville, Tenn.

Edwards, William Clarke, 2nd Lt., **I**, Enlisted: 5-62, Camp Morrison by Captain Leak. Present until 2-63 absent with detachment Camp. Present 10-63. Resigned: 1-25-64. Enlisted: 2-2-1864: 8th Ga. Inf. Died: February 1904. Buried: Oak Hill Cemetery, Cartersville, Ga.

Elkins, J.H., Pvt., Paroled: Thomasville, Ga., 5-20-1865. Description: 5'-6", dark hair, dark eyes, fair complexion.

Elledge, John H., Pvt., **A**, Enlisted: 3-62, Cedartown, Ga., by Captain John C. Crabb. Present through 12-63. On list of deserters at Louisville 6-6-64. Captured: Polk Co., Ga. Took oath. Description: home Polk Co., Ga., 5'-8", light complexion, dark hair, grey eyes.

Elledge, Young J., Pvt., **A**, Enlisted: 3-62, Cedartown, Ga., by Captain John C. Crabb. Present until KIA at Somerset, Ky. 3-30-63.

Ellis, Cicero Columbus, Pvt., **C**, Enlisted: 3-62, Cave Spring, Ga., by Captain Haynie. Present 6-62. Absent 8-62 Sick in Loudon, Tenn. Absent sick 10-62 and 12-62. Present 2-63 and 6-63. Absent 12-63 on Special duty for Col. Morrison. Died: 8-4-1924. Buried: Evergreen Cemetery, Paris, Texas.

Ellis, James B., Sgt., **C**, Enlisted: 5-62, Cave Spring, Ga., by Lt. Reynolds. Present 6-62 to Promotion to 3rd Sgt. 5-1-63. Present 12-63. Absent 12-64 on Detachment within Regiment. Died: 8-5-1923. Buried: Evergreen Cemetery, Paris, Texas.

Ellis, S.B., Pvt., **G**, Enlisted: 3-62, Floyd Co., Ga., by Captain Kerr. Absent 6-62 Sick in Loudon, Tenn. Hospital. Present 8-62 through 12-63. Absent: Detailed to make saddles by Gen. Martin 4-26-1864.

Ellis, Samuel D., Pvt., Enlisted: 3-62, Newnan, Ga., age 31, by Captain Strickland. Absent 6-62 on sick furlough in Hogansville, Ga. WIA: Laurel Creek, London, Ky. 8-17-62. Absent 10-62 and 12-62 in Hogansville, wounded. Present 2-63 until Captured near Dandridge, Tenn.

12-24-63. Carried: Knoxville; Louisville 1-21-64; Rock Island, Ill. Exchanged 3-20-1865. Died: 3-8-1893. Buried: Allen Lee Memorial UMC Cemetery, Lone Oak, Ga.

Ellis, Thomas Jefferson, Pvt., **C**, Enlisted: 1-63, Cave Spring, Ga., by Captain Haynie. Present 2-63 and 6-63. Absent 12-63 on Special duty for Col. Morrison. 12-64 present. Died: 1906. Buried: Oakwood Cemetery, Comanche, Texas.

Ellis, William J., Pvt., **B**, Enlisted: 3-62, Newnan, Ga., age 38, by Captain Strickland. Died: Kingston, Tenn. 5-25-62.

Ellis, William Varner, Pvt., **C**, Enlisted: 10-62, Cave Spring, Ga., by Lt. Reynolds. Present through 6-63. MIA from Dandridge, Tenn. 12-18-63. Captured and confined in Knoxville 12-27-63; Louisville, 1-21-64; Camp Chase; Rock Island, Ill. 1-26-64. Died: Rock Island Prison 2-15-64, variola. Buried: Rock Island Confederate Cemetery, Grave # 457.

Ellison, Francis Marion, Pvt., **G**, Enlisted: 9-25-61, 30th Ga. Inf., Fairburn, Ga. Discharged: lumbago 5-11-62. Description: born Fayette Co., Ga., age 28, 6'-1", fair complexion, dark hair, black eyes. Enlisted: 7-63, Rome, Ga., by Captain Kerr. Absent sick 12-63. Absent sick and left near Rome 10-64. Clothing issued 6-64. Died: 6-10-1902. Buried: Garden Valley, Smith Co., Tx.

Elmore, David Eli, Pvt., **C**, Enlisted: 3-62, Cave Spring, Ga., by Captain Haynie. Present until 2-63 absent sick. Present 6-63. WIA: Rockford, Tenn. Present 12-64. Paroled: Charlotte, N.C. 5-3-1865. Died: 8-30-1911. Buried: Hooser Cemetery, Italy, Texas.

Elmore, John, Pvt., **C**, Enlisted: 3-62, Cave Spring, Ga., by Captain Haynie. Present through 2-63. Detailed as Wagoner 2-6-63. 12-63 AWOL. Absent 12-64 Sick since 10-14-64. On Register at Camp Douglas as Died: 2-22-63.

England, H.M., Pvt., **I**, Enlisted: 10-64, Cass Station, Ga., by Captain Leak. Surrendered: Greensboro, N.C. 4-26-1865. Died: 3-21-1936, Bartow Co., Ga.

England, James E., Pvt., **I**, Enlisted: 8-63, Ebenezer, Tenn., by Captain Leak. Present through 12-31-1864.

Erwin, Marcus Blackwell, Sgt., **I**, Enlisted: 7-62, Cartersville, Ga., by Captain Leak. Mustered: Kingston, Tenn. Present through 12-64. Paroled: Charlotte, N.C. 5-3-1865. Died: 1-13-1924. Buried: Crossville Methodist Church, DeKalb Co., Ala.

Erwin, Samuel, Pvt., **H**, J.W.W. Barnette substitute.

Evans, Bennett, Pvt., **B**, 3-62, Pension: At Battle of Gadsden, Ala. September and October 1864, became ill with Typhoid Fever. Was confined to a convalescent camp for 6 weeks. Returned to duty and surrendered: Greensboro, N.C. 4-26-1865. Died: 4-16-1914. Buried: Whitesburg Cemetery, Ga.

Evans, Reuben Vardeman, Pvt., **B**, Enlisted: 3-62, Newnan, Ga., age 20, by Captain Strickland. Present through 2-63. WIA and captured near Kingston, Tenn. 11-24-63. Pension: Shot, during night engagement, through body at Chickamauga and captured. Doctors drew silk handkerchief through wound to clean. Carried: Knoxville; Nashville 4-12-64; Louisville; Camp Chase 4-14-64; City Point, Va., exchanged 2-25-65. Admitted: Gen. Hospital Camp Winder, Richmond, Va. 3-10-65. Died: 5-10-1910. Buried: Founders Cemetery, Moreland, Ga.

Everett, Solomon, Pvt., **G**, Enlisted: 5-64, Resaca, Ga., by Lt. Zuber. Absent sick in hospital, 6-20-1864. Widow: Present at surrender. Died: 4-18-1918. Buried: Everett Springs Baptist Church, Floyd Co., Ga.

Ezzell, Robert Flurnoy, Pvt., **H**, Enlisted: 11-63, Tallapoosa, Ga., by Captain Tumlin. 12-1864 AWOL. Paroled: Talladega, Ala. 3-1865. Died: 11-7-1928. Buried: Old Belgreen Cemetery, Franklin Co., Ala.

Ezzell, T.J., Pvt., **H**, Enlisted: 11-64, Arbacoochee, Ala., by Col. Davitte. 12-64 present.

Fain, Ancil W., Pvt., **F**, Enlisted: 3-62, Fairmount, Ga., by Col. Morrison.

Fannin, John W., Pvt., **D**, Enlisted: 3-62, Dallas, Ga., age 27, by Captain Seawright. Died: 5-23-62 in Paulding Co., Ga. of measles.

Farmer, M., Pvt., **H**, Enlisted: 11-64, Arbacoochee, Ala., by Col. Davitte. 12-31-1864 present.

Farmer, Shadrick "Shade," Pvt., **G**, Enlisted: 3-62, Floyd Co., Ga., by Captain Kerr. Present through 2-63. Extra duty as Forage Master. Became sick with smallpox in Athens, Tenn. June 1863. Confined to an old house in Athens and lingered a few weeks. Died 8-5-63, Athens, Tenn.

Farrow, Asa, Pvt., **C**, Died: 1915. Widow pension: Chambers Co., Ala.

Fason, Benjamin William, Pvt., **B**, Enlisted: 3-62, Newnan, Ga., age 45, by Captain Strickland. Absent sick 6-62 in Hospital, Knoxville. WIA: hip or side at Murfreesboro 7-13-62. Present 8-62. Discharged by age 12-7-62. Certificate: born Wake Co., N.C., age 50, 5'-8", black eyes, grey hair. Died: 9-22-1901. Buried: Eulaton UMC, Anniston, Ala.

Fason, James A., Pvt., **B**, Enlisted: 3-62, Newnan, Ga., age 18, by Captain Strickland. Absent 6-62 at home in Coweta Co., Ga. Horse KIA, paid $150. Present 8-62. Captured and paroled near Loudon, Ky. 9-8-62. Exchanged: Cumberland Gap. 9-16-62. 2-63 AWOL in Coweta Co. 12-63 listed Deserted, but maybe killed in battle.

Felmet, Nathaniel Green, Pvt., **G**, Enlisted: 3-62, Floyd Co., Ga., by Captain Kerr. Present until Captured 6-5-64. On Louisville list of deserters 6-12-64. Took Oath 6-10-64. Description: captured: Gordon Co., Ga., home Gordon Co., Ga., dark complexion, dark hair, hazel eyes, 5'-10". Died: 5-8-1904. Buried: Leonard Cemetery, Fannin Co., Tx.

Ferguson (Furguason), James L., Pvt., **C**, Enlisted: 3-62, Cave Spring, Ga., by Captain Haynie. Extra duty 29 days for striker in shop. Company Blacksmith 4-1-63 to 6-30-63. 12-21-64 present. Buried: Greenwood Cemetery, Cuthbert, Ga.

Fisher, Abner, Pvt., Chattanooga roll of deserters. Took Oath 4-2-1864. Description: home Gordon Co., Ga., sandy complexion, grey hair, hazel eyes, and 5'-8". Died: 1900-1910 Floyd Co., Ga.

Fisherman, Edward H., Pvt., **G**, Captured: Macon, Ga., 4-20-65.

Fitch, Fayette Shepherd, Sgt., **E**, Enlisted: 1st Ga. Inf. Ramsey's 6-1-1861, age 28. Enlisted: 4-62, 1st Ga. Cavalry, Cartersville, Ga., by Captain Blalock. Present through 2-63. Detached to Quartermaster Dept. 3-2-63. Absent 12-63 on Detached service. Present 12-64 at QM Dept. Paroled: Charlotte, N.C. 5-3-1865. Died: 9-26-1885, Harpersville, Ala.

Fitch, G.S., Pvt., **E**, Enlisted: 5-62, Cartersville, Ga., by Major Harper. Paroled: Charlotte, N.C. 5-3-1865.

Flanegan, Joel Sansing, Pvt., **A**, Enlisted: 2-63, Camp Beulah, Tenn., by Captain Hutchings. Absent 12-63 Cut off with the wagons. Present 12-64. Pension: Courier and scout. Discharged 5-26-1865. Died: 3-14-1933. Buried: Edgemont Cemetery, Anniston, Ala.

Flemister, John Wilson, Pvt., **H**, Enlisted: 4-62, Haralson Co., Ga., by Captain Tumlin. Present through 12-62. Absent 2-63 on sick furlough. 12-64 AWOL. Deserted and joined the Union Army. Died: 6-22-1903. Buried: Starrsville Cemetery, Newton Co., Ga.

Flemister, Joseph W., Pvt., **H**, Enlisted: 5-62, WIA: Gunshot, left arm below elbow breaking the radius bone. Paroled: Kingston, Ga. Home: Crystal Springs, Ga., 1907. Died: 12-24-1908 in Floyd Co., Ga.

Floyd, T.R., Pvt., **G**, Enlisted: 5-62, Camp Morrison by Captain Leak. Discharged 6-5-62, Chattanooga.

Floyd, W.M., Pvt., **I**, Enlisted: 5-62, Camp Morrison by Captain Leak.

Fombie, J.H., Sgt., **H**, Enlisted: 5-62, Haralson Co., Ga., by Captain Tumlin. Present through 2-63. Absent 12-63 Detained in Ga., by General Wheeler. AWOL 7-1-1864.

Ford, Richard, Pvt., Enlisted: 4-62, Haralson Co., Ga., by Captain Tumlin. Absent 6-62 and 8-62 in Hospital at Knoxville. Teamster. AWOL 7-1-62. Absent 2-63 Sick at Sweetwater, Tenn.

Forester, F.M., Pvt., **B**, Died: 4-19-1865. Buried in Tenn.

Foster, D.B., Pvt., **H**, Enlisted: 4-62, Haralson Co., Ga., by Captain Tumlin. Present through 12-62. Teamster 2-15-63. Absent 12-63 Detained in Ga., by General Wheeler. 12-64 AWOL.

Foster, E.C., Pvt., **B**, Enlisted: 3-62, Newnan, Ga., age 37, by Captain Strickland. Present through 12-63. Absent 12-64 Detached to Brigade Commissary.

Foster, James Young, Pvt., **F**, Enlisted: 8-63, Sweetwater, Tenn., by Captain Reynolds. Captured: Philadelphia, Tenn. 10-20-63. Carried: Camp Nelson; Camp Chase 11-14-63; Fort Delaware 3-4-64. Died: Fort Delaware Prison 7-3-64, chronic diarrhea. Buried: Finn's Point National Cemetery, Selma, N.J.

Fountain, W.S., Pvt., **G**, Enlisted: 5-62, Camp Morrison by Captain Leak. Present 6-62 and 8-62. Present 10-62 and 12-62 as wagoner. Present 3-63. Detached to Regiment wagons. Absent 12-64 Teamster for Army of Tennessee. Paroled: Charlotte N.C. 5-3-1865.

Franks, Joshua A., Cpl., **G**, Enlisted: 4-62, Floyd Co., Ga., by Captain Kerr. Present through 12-63. Captured near Cassville, Ga., 5-20-64. Carried to Resaca, Nashville 5-27-64; Louisville, 5-31-64; Rock Island, Ill. 6-1-64. Enlisted: U.S. 2nd Vol. Inf. 10-13-1864. Description: age 32, blue eyes, light hair, light complexion, 5'-10", born: Lawrence, SC. Died: 12-6-1873. Buried: Kingston City Cemetery, Bartow Co., Ga.

Free, S.L., Cpl., **B**, Captured, paroled: Hartwell, Ga., 5-18-65.

Freeman, Samuel, Pvt., **D**, Enlisted: 3-62, Dallas, Ga., age 25, by Captain Seawright.

Fuller, Abram J., 2nd Lt., **I**, Enlisted: 5-62, Camp Morrison by Captain Leak. Present through 12-62. Absent 3-63 at Detachment Camp. 10-63 In Arrest. Resigned 7-19-64. Gen. Wheeler ordered him to report to the Brigade at Carrollton, Ga., from Newnan Fuller refused. Fuller said he was under Gen. Hunt's Command and going to Tuscumbia, Ala. Major Tench was ordered to arrest him, but Gen. Hunt tore up order. Lt. Col. Watts, at Matthew's Bluff, S.C., requested dropping A.J. Fuller as absent since 7-10-64. Dropped: 2-14-1865. Died: 1878. Buried: Neches Cemetery, Anderson Co., Tx.

Fuller, George C., Pvt., **F**, Enlisted: 3-62, Fairmount, Ga., by Col. Morrison. Absent 6-62 through 10-62 on sick furlough. Present 12-62 and 2-63. 12-63 AWOL. 12-31-1864 present.

Fuller, Jesse F., Pvt., **F**, Enlisted: 3-62, Fairmount, Ga., by Col. Morrison. Present 6-62 as Teamster for Regiment. Absent 12-63 in Ga. with wagons. Absent 12-64 Detached to Brigade Quartermaster. Paroled: Charlotte, N.C. 5-3-1865.

Fuller, John A., Pvt., **I**, Enlisted: 5-62, Camp Morrison by Captain Leak. Present through 12-62. Absent 3-62 at Detachment Camp. Absent 10-63 in Ga. AWOL 12-7-1864.

Fuller, John R., Pvt., **G**, Filed pension: Cherokee Co., Ala.

Fuller, Steven A., Pvt., **D**, Enlisted: 3-62, Dallas, Ga., age 18, by Captain Seawright. Present 6-62. Absent 8-62 on sick furlough in Paulding Co., Ga. Present 10-62 through 2-63. AWOL 9-1863.

Fuller, Vinson Winston, Pvt., **I**, Enlisted: 23rd Ga. Vol. Inf. 8-31-1861. Captured: Fredericksburg, Va. 5-3-1863. WIA: Sharpsburg, Md. 9-14-63. Gunshot to left thigh. WIA: Ocean Pond, Fla. 2-20-64. Gunshot to right thigh. Enlisted: 8-64, 1st Ga. Cavalry, Decatur, Ga. Surrendered 5-26-1865, Greensboro, N.C. Died: 9-26-1923. Buried: Russell Hill Baptist Church, Sugar Valley, Ga.

Fullwood, John Thomas, Pvt., Enlisted: 3-62, Cedartown, Ga., by Captain John C. Crabb. Present 6-62. Absent 8-62 furlough home. Present 10-62. Absent 12-62 sick furlough home. Present 2-63. Absent 12-63 Cut off with wagons. Captured: Somerset, Ky. 3-30-63. Carried: Louisville, City Point, Va. Exchanged 4-13-63. Captured: Atlanta 7-21-64. Carried: Chattanooga; Nashville 7-29-64; Louisville 7-31-64; Camp Chase; City Point, Va. Exchange 3-4-65. Admitted: Jackson Hospital, Richmond, Va. 3-6-65, chronic diarrhea. Died: 3-23-65. Buried: Hollywood Cemetery, Richmond, Va.

Gaddis, James, Pvt., **F**, Enlisted: 3-62, Fairmount, Ga., by Col. Morrison. Present through 12-63. 12-64 AWOL. Pension: Cherokee Co., Ga., 1897. Discharged: Charlotte, N.C., May 1865. Died: 1903 in Ala.

Gaddis, Nathaniel J., Pvt., **F**, Enlisted: 3-62, Fairmount, Ga., by Col. Morrison. Present 6-62. Absent 8-62 and 10-62 on sick furlough. Present 12-62. Absent 2-63 with detachment and wagons. Absent 12-63 sick. (Possible: Enlisted 12-25-1863 10th Regt. Tenn. Cavalry. Died: 7-14-1864. Buried: New Albany National Cemetery, Floyd Co., Ind.)

Gaines, W.D.P., Pvt., **I**, Enlisted: 3-64, Cass Station, Ga., by Captain Leak. 12-64 present. Paroled: Charlotte, N.C. 5-3-1865.

Gaines, Wylie Anderson, Pvt., **G**, Enlisted: 5-62, Camp Morrison by Col. Morrison. Present 6-62. Died at home of typhoid fever, 7-17-62. Buried: Mount Zion Baptist Church, White Co., Ga.

Gainus, William Jackson, Pvt., **F**, Enlisted: 3-62, Fairmount Ga., by Col. Morrison. Present 6-62. Absent 8-62 and 10-62 on sick furlough. Present 12-62 and 2-63. Deserted and took oath at Chattanooga 4-2-64. Description: home Gordon Co., Ga., dark complexion, dark hair, black eyes, 5'-10". Died: 9-7-1870, Fulton Co., Ga.

Gaither, Nathan, Pvt., **A**, Enlisted: 6th Ky. Cavalry, Captured in Ohio 7-20-1863 on raid with Gen. John Hunt Morgan. Carried: Camp Chase, Camp Douglas. Escaped to Richmond, Va.. Assigned to 1st Ga. Cavalry. Paroled: Charlotte, N.C. 5-3-1865. Married: Mary Dorothy Zollicoffer, daughter General Felix Kirk Zollicoffer. Died: 1-16-1918. Buried: Riverside Cemetery, Hopkinsville, Ky.

Garner, David, Pvt., **A**, Pension: Marshall Co., Ala.

Garrett, James, Pvt., **C**, On list of deserters bound to New York City, on steamer *Arago*, from Hilton Head, S.C. Statement: Came on line 12-17-64, Savannah, Ga.: Captain Marshall's Battery, 1st Ga. Cavalry. Description: Born: Ala., age 17, 5'-10", blue eyes, light hair, light complexion. Sick: bronchitis pneumonia. Admitted: Pace Hospital, Savannah, Ga., 2-1-65. Discharged 2-20-1865

Garrett, William Dewberry, Pvt., **B**, Enlisted: 3-62, Newnan, Ga., age 30, by Captain Strickland. Present 6-62. Present 8-62 as a blacksmith. Present 10-62. Absent 12-62 on extra duty. Absent 2-63 on sick furlough to Grantville, Ga., 12-63 Transferred: 55th Ga. Vol. Inf. Died: 11-19-1905. Buried: Flat Rock Primitive Baptist Church, Rocky Mount, Ga.

Garris, David, Pvt., **A**, Enlisted: 3-62, Cedartown, Ga., by Captain John C. Crabb. Present 6-62. Absent 8-62 and 10-62 Sick in Kingston, Tenn. Present 12-62 and 2-63. Horse KIA at Somerset, Ky. 3-30-63. Absent 12-63 Cutoff with wagons.

On list of deserters carried: Louisville 6-6-64. Captured: Polk Co., Ga. Took oath. Discharge description: home Polk Co., Ga., sandy complexion, auburn hair, blue eyes, 5'-5".

Garris, Elias, Pvt., **A**, Enlisted: 3-62, Cedartown, Ga., by Captain John C. Crabb. Present 6-62 but sick. Present 8-62 and 10-62. Present 12-62 and 2-62 detailed as Brigade Teamster. Absent 12-63 Cutoff with wagons. On list of deserters carried to Louisville 6-6-64. Took oath and discharged 6-8-64. Description: home Polk Co., Ga., dark complexion, dark hair, blue eyes, 5'-7". Pension: Floyd Co., Ga., 1898. Captured, carried: Jeffersonville, Ind. Prison until discharged 5-1865.

Garris, Henry, Pvt., **A**, Enlisted: 3-62, Cedartown, Ga., by Captain John C. Crabb. 6-62 present. Absent 8-62 Sick in Kingston, Tenn. Present 10-62. Present 12-62 and 2-63 detailed as Brigade Teamster. Absent 12-63 Cutoff with wagons. On list of deserters carried to Louisville 6-6-64. Took oath and discharged 6-8-64. Description: home Polk Co., Ga., sandy complexion, brown hair, grey eyes, 5'-7".

Garris, W., Pvt., **A**, Enlisted: 10-63, Chattanooga by Captain York. Absent 12-63 Cutoff with wagons.

Garrison, James Freeborn, Jr., Sgt. Major, **E**, Enlisted: 3-62, Carrollton, Ga., by Captain Blalock. Appointed Sgt. Major 6-5-62. Present 6-62 through 12-63. WIA 7-30-64. Gunshot right forearm fracturing ulna. Wound Suppurating (producing pus) 10-27-64. Died: 2-19-1903. Buried: Caledonia Cemetery, Rusk Co., Tx.

Gay, Henry M., Pvt., **K**, Enlisted 7th Ga. Inf. 5-31-61, Atlanta. Discharged 10-19-61 with broken leg. Certificate: born Ga., age 38, 6'-0", fair complexion, grey eyes, sandy hair. Re-enlisted 8-12-1863. Transferred: 1st Ga. Cavalry, General Longstreet 3-22-1863. Enlisted 8-24-63: 1st Ga. Cavalry, Newnan, Captain North. Transferred back to 7th Ga. Inf. 12-63. Died: 3-28-1893.

Gay, Wiley Jones, Pvt., **K**, Conscripted 8-1-1863, Newnan, 2nd Ga. Cavalry State Guards. Pension: Transferred 3-64: 1st Ga. Cavalry. Surrendered 7-65: Macon, Ga., and discharged. Died: 2-23-1905. Buried: Woolsey Baptist Church, Fayette Co., Ga.

Gay, William Judson, Pvt., **K**, Enlisted: 5-62, Camp Morrison by Captain North. Present through 12-62. WIA: Kingston, Tenn. Absent 2-63 on sick leave in Coweta Co., Ga. Present 12-63. Absent 12-64 Courier for Gen. Iverson. Surrendered: Greensboro, N.C. 4-26-1865. Died: 3-3-1933. Buried: Sharpsburg Baptist Church, Coweta Co., Ga.

Gay, Winston W., 2nd Lt., **K**, Enlisted: 5-62, Camp Morrison by Captain North. Elected 2nd Lt. 5-1-62. Absent 6-62 on sick furlough at home. Present 8-62. Captured near Loudon, Ky. 9-8-62. Exchanged: Cumberland Gap 9-17-62. Present 12-62 and 2-63. WIA and captured near Pigeon River, Sevierville, Tenn. 1-27-64. Hospital "slight flesh wound," hand 1-27-64. Carried: Knoxville; Nashville; Louisville 2-11-64; Camp Chase 2-15-64; Fort Delaware Prison 3-25-64. Released 6-16-1865. Description: home Coweta Co., Ga., ruddy complexion, grey hair, blue eyes, 6'-0". Died: 9-23-1910. Buried: Fredonia Methodist Church, Chambers Co., Ala.

Gentry, Joseph R., Pvt., **E**, Enlisted: 3-62, Carrollton, Ga., by Captain Blalock. Present through 2-63. Captured near Jacksboro, Tenn. 8-27-63. Carried: Camp Nelson; Louisville 9-9-63; Camp Chase; 1-22-64; Rock Island, Ill. 3-2-65 exchanged. Died 10-7-1887. Buried: Gentry-Bloodworth Cemetery, Roopville, Ga.

Gentry, Thomas Jefferson, Pvt., **A**, Enlisted: 2-65, Cedartown, Ga., by Captain Jesse W. Crabb. Paroled: Charlotte, N.C. 5-3-1865. Died: 2-6-1890. Buried: Fellowship Baptist Church, Haralson Co., Ga.

Gibbons, Alfred Ringold, Pvt., **G**, Enlisted: 3-64, Rome, Ga., by Col. Cameron. Attended VMI before enlisting. Captured: Atlanta 7-21-64. Carried: Chattanooga; Nashville; Louisville 7-31-64; Camp Chase. Escaped by jumping from a moving train. Reported killed in Indiana. Recaptured 10 days later and sent to Michigan City. Refused release by not taking oath. Died: 9-26-1932. Buried: Odd Fellows Cemetery, Shelbina, Missouri.

Gibbs, Thomas Preston, Pvt., **B**, Enlisted: 7-63, Newnan, Ga., by Lt. Taylor. 12-31-1864 present. Died: 12-15-1892. Buried: Madison Historical Cemetery, Morgan Co., Ga.

Gibson, Andrew J., Pvt., **A**, Enlisted: 9-63, Cedartown, Ga., by Captain York. Present 12-63. Admitted: Ocmulgee Hospital, Macon, Ga., 7-20-64. Stated: home Polk Co., Ga. Absent 12-64 driving ambulance. Paroled: Charlotte, N.C. 5-3-1865. Died: 1-14-1896. Buried: Rose Hill Cemetery, Rockmart, Ga.

Gibson, James G., Pvt., **A**, Enlisted: 3-62, Cedartown, Ga., by Captain John C. Crabb. Detached: Captain King's Company Light Artillery and promoted 1st Lt..

Gibson, Nicholas M., Pvt., Enlisted: 6-62, Newnan, Ga., by Captain North. Died at home in Coweta Co., Ga., 7-18-62.

Gibson, T., **K**, WIA and captured in East Tenn.

Gibson, William T., Pvt., **A**, Enlisted: Phillip's Legion 6-14-1861, Cobb Co., Ga., age 17. WIA at Sharpsburg 9-17-62. Enlisted 2-1-64, in the field by Captain York. AWOL 7-30-64. Died: 5-5-1912 . Buried: Greenwood Cemetery, Cedartown, Ga.

Gill, George G., 1st Sgt., **C**, Enlisted: 3-62, Cave Spring, Ga., by Captain Haynie. Present through 2-63. Absent 6-63 on furlough in Floyd Co., Ga. Promoted 1st Sgt. 12-26-63. Present 12-31-1864. Died: 10-9-1924. Buried: Old Homer Cemetery, Homer, La.

Gillespie, Green Berry, Pvt., **F**, Enlisted: 8-63, Sweetwater, Tenn., by Captain Reynolds. 12-64 AWOL. Deserted and took oath in Chattanooga 2-14-64. Description: home Gordon Co., Ga., fair complexion, black hair, black eyes, 5'-7". Died: 4-15-1937. Buried: Munford Cemetery, Covington, Tenn.

Gilreath, George Holden, Jr., Pvt., **I**, Enlisted: 12-63, 63rd Ga. Inf. Enlisted 12-64: Cass Station, Ga., by Captain Leak. Paroled: Charlotte, N.C. 5-3-1865. Died: 12-24-1908. Buried: Salem Cemetery, Farmington, Ga.

Gilreath, Hillary Patrick (Paten), Pvt., **G**, Enlisted: 5-62, Camp Morrison by Captain Leak. Discharged 5-20-62 at Chattanooga. Enlisted 8-2-1863: 10th Battalion Ga. Cavalry State Guards. Died: 10-1903. Buried: Oakwood Cemetery, Fort Worth, Texas.

Gilreath, Jabaz, Pvt., **G**, Enlisted: 5-62, Camp Morrison by Captain Leak.

Gilreath, James Henry "Hugh," 1st Lt., **I**, Enlisted: 5-62, Camp Morrison by Captain Leak. Elected 1st Lt. 5-1-62. Present through 3-63. Absent 10-63 sick. Present 12-64. Commanded company at surrender: Greensboro, N.C. 4-26-1865. Elected: Georgia House of Representatives. Died: 12-17-1931. Buried: Oak Hill Cemetery, Cartersville, Ga.

Glasgow, Oliver Union, 2nd Lt., **I**, Enlisted: 5-62, Camp Morrison by Captain Leak. Present through 12-62. Absent 2-63 with detachment Camp. Present 10-63 and 12-64 as Ordnance Sergeant. Promoted: 1-25-64 to succeed William C. Edwards by Col. Davitte. Surrendered: Greensboro, N.C. 4-26-1865. Died: 10-30-1913. Buried: Mount Zion Cemetery, White, Ga.

Glass, Edward Wynn, Pvt., **K**, Enlisted: 11-64, Atlanta by Captain North. 12-31-64 present. Died: 12-24-1904. Buried: Morrow Chapel, Ola, Texas.

Glass, Erastus, Pvt., **K**, Enlisted: 7th Ga. Inf. 5-31-61.

WIA Garnett's Farm, Va. 6-28-62 (Seven Days Battle). Enlisted: 1st Ga. Cavalry 8-10-1864: Newnan, Ga., by Captain North. 12-64 present. Died: 1875, Coweta Co., Ga.

Glass, James Madison, Pvt., **K**, Enlisted: 3-62, Camp Morrison by Captain North. Present through 12-31-1864. Courier for Col. Crews. Surrendered: Greensboro, N.C. 4-26-1865. Died: 8-3-1913. Buried: Oak Hill Cemetery, Newnan, Ga.

Glass, J.P., Pvt., **B**, Enlisted: Meriwether Co., Ga., age 21, 8th Ga. Inf.; 5-18-1861. Resigned 3-28-1862. Enlisted: 1st Ga. Cavalry 8-10-1863, Newnan, Ga., by Lt. Taylor. Captured: Philadelphia, Tenn. 10-20-63. Died: Fort Delaware Prison 4-19-64, smallpox. Buried: Finn's Point Nat. Cemetery, Salem, N.J.

Glass, Robert Edward, Pvt., **K**, Enlisted: 7-64, Atlanta by Captain North. 12-31-1864 present. Married the daughter of Captain North. Died: 5-6-1903. Buried: Sharpsburg Baptist Church, Coweta Co., Ga.

Glass, Thomas Coke, Pvt., **K**, Enlisted: 2-63, Cartersville, Ga., by Major Harper. WIA: Philadelphia, Tenn. 10-20-63 in the foot and sent home. Died: 1914. Buried: Oakland Cemetery, Kaufman Co., Tx.

Glazener, William Lee, Pvt., **I**, Enlisted: 4-64, Oxford, Ala., by Captain Leak. Captured: Atlanta 7-21-64. Carried: Chattanooga; Nashville 7-29-64; Louisville 7-31-64; Camp Chase Ohio. Released 6-11-1865. Description: home Walker Co., Ga., dark complexion, dark hair, hazel eyes, 5'-5", age 18. Died: 8-13-1904. Buried: Post Oak Cemetery, Fairfield, Texas.

Golston, Thomas, Pvt., **C**, Enlisted: 5-62, Cave Spring, Ga., by Lt. Reynolds. Present through 12-31-1864.

Goodwyn, Henry Clay, 1st Lt., **E**, Enlisted: 4-62, Cartersville, Ga., by Col. Morrison. Present 6-62. Appointed 8-62 Sergeant Major for Regiment. Present 10-62 through 2-63. Promoted 2nd Lt. 5-29-63 by Col. Morrison. Absent 12-63 WIA. Promoted 1st Lt. 6-25-64, Gen. Martin. WIA and captured near Mount Pleasant, Tenn. 9-4-64. Carried: Nashville; Louisville 9-1-64; Johnson's Island 9-4-64; City Point, Va. 2-24-65, exchanged. Widow pension stated he was captured at Somerset, Ky., and held at Johnson Island. Died: 10-20-1893, Atlanta, Ga.

Goodwyn, James F., Pvt., **B**, Enlisted: 3-62, Newnan, Ga., age 29, by Captain Strickland. Present 6-62. KIA near Big Hill, Ky. 8-24-1862. Buried: Three Civil War Soldiers Cemetery, Rockcastle Co., Ky.

Goolsby, Peter, Pvt., **H**, Enlisted: 4-62, Tallapoosa, Ga., by Captain Tumlin. Absent 2-63 Detached service at Kingston, Tenn. Absent 12-63 Attached to Captain Marshall's Company Brown Horse Artillery.

Gordon, John W., Pvt., **B**, Enlisted: 3-62 in Grantville, Ga. Absent 12-63 Dalton, Ga. attending Camp of Direction by Gen. Wheeler. Admitted: Empire Hotel Hospital, Atlanta 4-30-64. WIA: Marietta, Ga., 7-4-64. Buried: Catholic Cemetery, Savannah, Ga.

Gordon, William Davis, Pvt., **B**, Enlisted: 3-62 in Newnan, Ga. Present 12-63. WIA during retreat 6 miles below Marietta, Ga., 7-4-64 while on skirmish line. Shot entered below knee and out calf breaking bone, ripping muscle, tendons. Discharged: 8-64. Died: 3-12-1905. Buried: Temperance Congregational Methodist Church, Brown Cemetery, Sand Hill, Ga.

Gordon, Z. Pope, Sgt., **H**, Enlisted: Jones Co., Ga., 8-4-1863, 6th Ga. State Guards. Enlisted: 1st Ga. Cavalry 5-1864. Paroled: Montgomery, Ala. 6-13-1865. Description: 5'-10" auburn hair, hazel eyes, fair complexion. Died: 1911. Buried: Prattville, Ala.

Gorham, Alvin Marion, Pvt., **D**, Enlisted: 3-62, Dallas, Ga., age 25, by Captain Seawright. Present 6-62 and 8-62. WIA near London, Ky. 10-17-62. Sent home to Paulding Co., Ga. Present 2-63. Transferred to Fort Gaines, Ala. 8-1-63. Died: 10-15-1913. Buried: Holly Pond Cemetery, Cullman Co., Ala.

Graham, George P., Pvt., **C**, Enlisted: 10-64, Present: 12-31-1864. Buried: Grange Cemetery, Clarksdale, Miss.

Graham, James Alexander, Chief Bugler, **F&S**, Enlisted: 3-62, Cave Spring, Ga., by Captain Haynie. 6-62 present. Discharged 7-30-62.

Graham, W.H., **K**, On list of deserters sent to Fort Monroe, Va. to Washington, D.C. Captured: Penn's Bridge, S.C. 2-11-65.

Graves, A.S., 2nd Lt., **F**, Appointed 2nd Lt., Gen. Martin. Received clothing issue 6-64. Present 12-64. Requested leave 1-17-64. On roll 2-1865.

Graves, J.H., Pvt., **G**, Enlisted: 3-62, Floyd Co., Ga., by Captain Kerr. 6-62 Never mustered.

Gravely, John L., Pvt., **C**, Enlisted: 1-63, Cave Spring, Ga., by Captain Haynie. Present through 12-63. Absent sick: 9-15-1864. Witness: Polk Co Ga., 1891. Died: 11-11-1903.

Gravley, Anderson, Pvt., **F**, Enlisted: 3-62, Fairmount, Ga., by Col. Morrison. Absent 6-62 through 10-62 on sick furlough. Present 12-62. Absent 2-63 with detachment and wagons.

Absent 12-63 sick. Surrendered: Greensboro, N.C. 4-26-1865. Pension: Chattooga Co., Ga., 1906. Home: Flatwoods, Ga., 1910.

Gravly, Payton Leftwich, Pvt., **F**, Enlisted: 3-62, Fairmount, Ga., by Col. Morrison. Present through 12-62. Absent 2-63 on sick furlough. Present 12-63. 12-64 AWOL. Pension: Floyd Co., Ga., 1907. Home: Flatwoods, Ga., 1910, age 80.

Gray, Charles M., Cpl., **D**, Enlisted: 3-62, Dallas, Ga., by Captain Seawright. Discharged disabled with hernia at Kingston, Tenn. 8-10-62. Certificate: born Gwinnett Co., Ga., age 25, 5'-6", dark complexion, blue eyes, black hair. Died: 5-18-1909. Buried: New Canaan Cemetery, Dallas, Ga.

Gray, Daniel S., Pvt., **D**, Enlisted: 2-63, Dallas, Ga., by Captain Robert Trammell. 12-31-1864 present. Died: 3-20-1873. Buried: Mars Hill Cemetery, Acworth, Ga.

Gray, Garrett, Pvt., **D**, Enlisted: 3-62, Dallas, Ga., age 58, by Captain Seawright. Discharged at Kingston, Tenn. 7-4-62. Certificate: born Laurens District, S.C., age 60, 5'-9", dark complexion, dark eyes, gray hair. Living: Paulding Co. 1870.

Gray, Isaac Newton, Pvt., **D**, Enlisted: 3-62, Dallas, Ga., age 27, by Captain Seawright. Present 6-62. WIA at Murfreesboro 7-13-62. Sent home on wounded furlough. Discharged 12-64 wounded. Died: 8-23-1904. Buried: New Harmony Baptist Church, Hiram, Ga.

Gray, Thomas Franklin, Pvt., **D**, Enlisted: 3-62, Dallas, Ga., by Captain Seawright. Present through 10-62. Absent 12-62 on sick furlough in Paulding Co., Ga. Present 2-63. Absent 12-63 on detail in Ga. Died: 8-28-1903. Buried: Poplar Springs Baptist Church, Hiram, Ga.

Gray, William J., Pvt., **D**, Enlisted: 5-62, Dallas, Ga., by Captain Seawright. Absent 6-62 with leave. Discharged 1862. Died: 4-30-1901. Buried: Flint Hill Methodist Church, Hiram, Ga.

Green, Daniel F., Pvt., **F**, Enlisted: 3-62, Fairmount, Ga., by Col. Morrison. Present 6-62 but Forfeited one month pay due to court martial. Present 8-62. Absent 10-62 as Teamster for Regiment. Present 12-62. Absent 2-63 on sick furlough. Captured near Loudon, Tenn. 12-28-63. Carried: Nashville; Louisville 1-14-64; Rock Island, Ill. 1-20-64. Enlisted: U.S. Navy 5-23-1864. Died: 6-26-1897. Buried: Old Charity Cemetery, Wayne Co., Ky.

Green, Jefferson E., Pvt., **F**, Enlisted: 3-62, Fairmount, Ga., by Col. Morrison. Present through

2-63. Captured during retreat from Kingston, Tenn. 12-5-63. On list of deserters at Knoxville 12-16-63. Took oath. Stated: home Gordon Co., Ga.

Green, John Reynolds, Cpl., **F**, Enlisted: 4-62, Fairmount, Ga., by Col. Morrison. Present 6-62. Absent 8-62 and 10-62 on sick furlough. Present 12-62 and 2-63. Deserted 11-24-63 and Took oath in Chattanooga, 4-2-64. Description: home: Gordon Co., Ga., 5'-9½", blue eyes, sandy hair. Died: 12-28-1899. Buried: Pleasant Grove Baptist Church, Ryo, Ga.

Green, Josiah D., Pvt., **K**, Enlisted: Newnan, Ga., 2nd Ga. Cavalry State Guards. Enlisted: 1st Ga. Cavalry 12-5-1863 by Major Andrews. Absent 12-64 Sick in Forsyth Hospital. Clothing issued 7-13-1864. Surrendered: Greensboro, N.C. 4-26-1865. Died: 12-31-1892. Buried: Roopville City Cemetery, Carroll Co., Ga.

Green, Leroy Hammond, Sgt., **F**, Enlisted: 3-62, Fairmount, Ga., by Col. Morrison. Present through 2-63. Deserted 9-25-63 from Chickamauga. On list of deserters at Knoxville. Took oath 12-16-63. Stated: home Sevier Co., Tenn. Pension: discharged from a camp in Fulton Co., Ga. with free transportation to Calhoun, Ga. Died: 10-28-1907. Buried: Pleasant Grove Baptist Church, Ryo, Ga.

Green, Lewallen, Sgt., **F**, Enlisted: 3-62, Fairmount, Ga., by Col. Morrison. Present through 2-63. Deserted 11-24-63 near Loudon, Tenn. On list of deserters at Chattanooga. Took oath 4-2-64. Description: home Gordon Co., Ga., 5'-4", sandy complexion, brown hair, blue eyes. Widow pension: surrendered near Atlanta 4-65. Died: 4-13-1886. Buried: Green Family Cemetery, Ryo, Ga.

Green, Martin LaFayette, Pvt., **E**, Enlisted: 3-62, Carrollton, Ga., by Captain Blalock. Present through 12-62. Absent 2-63 on furlough. Absent 12-63 Captured and paroled. Present 12-64. Died: 1-3-1914. Buried: Mount Zion Baptist Church, Dallas, Ga.

Green, Thomas Cranford, Pvt., **F**, Enlisted: 4-62 Fairmount, Ga., by Col. Morrison. Present 6-62. Absent 8-62 and 10-62 on sick furlough home. Present 12-62. Absent 2-63 through 12-64 Detached to Marshall's Company of Artillery by Gen Pegram. Captured: July 1863. Carried: Camp Chase; Fort Delaware Prison, Released 6-17-1865. Description: home Gordon Co., Ga., 5'-7", dark complexion, dark hair, blue eyes. Home: Fairmount, Gordon Co., Ga., 1905.

Greenwood, Francis Marion, Pvt., **C**, Enlisted: 1-63, Cave Spring, Ga., by Captain Haynie. Present through 12-64. Paroled: Charlotte, N.C. 5-3-1865. Died: 12-10-1902. Buried: Old Piedmont Cemetery, Piedmont, Ala.

Greenwood, James T., Pvt., **C**, Enlisted: 3-62, Cave Spring, Ga., by Captain Haynie. Present 6-62. Present 8-62 detached as Wagoner. Present 10-62 through 6-63. Absent 12-63 on QM Duty with Captain May. WIA: 9-1-64.

Greenwood, Monroe (T.) G., Pvt., **C**, Enlisted: 3-62, Cave Spring, Ga., by Captain Haynie. Present 6-62. Present 8-62 detailed as Wagoner. Present 10-62 and 12-62 also must Forfeit one month's pay for horse. Captured near Somerset, Ky. 3-30-63. Carried: Louisville, City Point, Va.: exchanged 4-13-63. Present 12-63. Absent 12-64 on Detail with Regiment. Paroled: Charlotte, N.C. 5-3-1865. Died: 1902. Buried: Old Piedmont Cemetery, Piedmont, Ala.

Greenwood, Morris G., Pvt., **C**, Pension: Calhoun Co., Ala.

Gregory, D.N., Pvt., **B**, Captured: Pine Mountain, Tenn. 12-28-62. Carried: Camp Douglas, City Point, Va. Exchange 4-4-1863.

Gresham, David Young, Pvt., **E**, Enlisted: 9-62, Carrollton, Ga., by Captain Blalock. Present through 2-63. Absent 12-63 left sick in Ga. Present 12-64. Surrendered: Greensboro, N.C. 4-26-1865. Died: 5-16-1917. Buried: Concord Methodist Church, Carrollton, Ga.

Gresham (Grisham), Thomas, Pvt., **K**, Enlisted: 5-62, Camp Morrison by Captain North. Present through 12-62 as Wagoner. Absent 2-63 with detachment Camp at Kingston, Tenn.

Griffin, Early A., Pvt., **D**, Enlisted: 3-62, Dallas, Ga., age 21, by Captain Seawright. Present through 12-62. Captured near Stone's River, Murfreesboro 12-31-62. Carried: Camp Douglas, City Point, Va. Exchanged. Absent 8-63 Hospital, Loudon, Tenn. for 7 weeks with measles. Present 12-63. WIA near Adairsville, Ga., 5-15-1864. Left third finger shot off. Captured near Marietta, Ga., 6-17-64. Carried: Nashville; Louisville 6-30-64; Camp Morton 7-1-64; Point Lookout, Md. 2-19-1865, exchanged. Admitted: General Hospital #9, Richmond, Va. 3-2-1865. Surrendered: Greensboro, N.C. 4-26-1865. Died: 11-11-1902. Buried: Oakland Cemetery, Atlanta, Ga.

Griffin, James Prince, 1st Sgt., **E**, Enlisted: 5-62, Cartersville, Ga., by Captain Blalock. Present through 12-64. Paroled: Charlotte, N.C. 5-3-1865. Died: 1907. Buried: Asbury Cemetery, Temple, Carroll Co., Ga.

Griffin, Jesse F., Pvt., **D**, Enlisted: 3-62, Dallas, Ga., age 20, by Captain Seawright. Present 6-62. Absent 8-62 Sick furlough in Paulding Co., Ga. Killed near Marietta, Ga., 10-21-62. Buried: Griffin Family Cemetery, Dallas, Ga.

Griffin, Ransom Lafayette, Sgt., **I**, Enlisted 5-62. Present 10-62 and 12-62. Surrendered: Greensboro, N.C. 4-26-1865. Served under Lt. Gilbreath. Elected Sheriff of Bartow Co., Ga. Died: 10-18-1927. Buried: Oakhill Cemetery, Cartersville, Ga.

Griffin, Reuben Light, Sgt., **G**, Enlisted: 5-62, Camp Morrison by Captain Leak. Present through 12-62. Absent 3-63 on sick furlough. Present 12-63 and 12-64. Surrendered: Greensboro, N.C. 4-26-1865. Died: 4-12-1920. Buried: Carrollton City Cemetery, Carroll Co., Ga.

Griffin, William M., Pvt., **D**, Enlisted: 3-62, Dallas, Ga., age 26, by Captain Seawright. Present 6-62. Absent 8-62 on scout. Absent 2-63 Sick furlough in Floyd Co., Ga. Admitted: Bell Hospital, Rome, Ga., 11-1-63. Clothing issued 7-13-64. Surrendered: Greensboro, N.C. 4-26-1865. Died: 12-21-1900. Buried: Kingston City Cemetery, Bartow Co., Ga.

Griffith, George Washington, Pvt., **A**, Enlisted: Rome, Ga., age 18, 8th Ga. Inf. 5-13-1861. Discharged: tuberculosis 8-15-1862. Enlisted 3-1-1863: 1st Ga. Cavalry, Cedartown, Ga., by Captain Hutchings. Absent 12-63 Cutoff with wagons. Present 12-64. Paroled: Charlotte, N.C. 5-3-1865. Died: 1-29-1919. Buried: Carrollton City Cemetery, Carroll Co., Ga.

Griffith, William, Cpl., **A**, Enlisted: 3-62, Cedartown, Ga., by Captain John C. Crabb. Present through 12-62. Captured near Somerset, Ky. 3-30-63. Carried: Louisville; Fort McHenry, Md.; City Point, Va. Exchanged 4-13-63. WIA near Barnwell, SC 2-15-1865. Ball hit left arm between wrist and elbow breaking both bones. Discharged 4-10-1865. Died: 9-27-1927. Buried: Adger Cemetery, Jefferson Co., Ala..

Grimmett, Edwin S., 2nd Lt., **C**, Enlisted: 3-62, Cave Spring, Ga., by Captain Haynie. Absent 6-62 on sick furlough. Died 7-27-62, age 24. Family: Died 6-28-62. Buried: Ebenezer Cemetery, Cumming, Ga.

Griswald (Greswell), J.S., Pvt., **G**, Enlisted: 3-62, Floyd Co., Ga., by Captain Kerr. Present 6-62 and 8-62. Captured near Clay Village, Ky. 10-4-62. Paroled. Absent 12-62 and 2-63. Witness in Floyd Co., Ga., 1891.

Grogan, David Dejaret, Pvt., **D**, Enlisted: 3-62, Dallas, Ga., age 24, by Captain Seawright. Pres-

ent 6-62. Absent 8-62 through 12-62 Sick furlough in Paulding Co., Ga. Present 2-63. Captured near Sweetwater, Tenn. 10-28-63. Carried: Camp Nelson; Camp Chase 11-14-63; Fort Delaware 3-4-64. Exchanged 3-7-65. Admitted: Wayside Hospital, Richmond, Va. 3-11-1865. Dismissed 3-12-65 with 30 day furlough. Died: 2-23-1914. Buried: Liberty Hill Cemetery, Acworth, Ga.

Gurley, Jonathan, Cpl., **A**, Enlisted: 3-62, Cedartown, Ga., by Captain John C. Crabb. Absent 6-62 Sick furlough in Polk Co., Ga. Present 8-62 through 12-63. Captured near Van Wert, Ga., 11-2-64. Carried: Nashville; Louisville 11-22-64; Camp Douglas Prison 11-26-64. Released 6-17-1865. Description: home Polk Co., Ga., dark complexion, light hair, grey eyes, 6'-0". Died: 2-15-1910. Buried: Mount Olivet Baptist Church, Dallas, Ga.

Gurley, William F., Pvt., **A**, Enlisted: 3-62, Cedartown, Ga., by Captain John C. Crabb. Present 6-62. Absent 8-62 at Kingston, Tenn. Detached with Unserviceable horse. Present 10-62 through 2-63. Absent 12-63 Cutoff with wagons. 12-31-1864 present. Died: 2-6-1892. Buried: Bethel Cemetery, Forney, Ala.

Gurley, William T., Pvt., **A**, Enlisted: 3-62, Cedartown, Ga., by Captain John C. Crabb. Present 6-62. WIA at Murfreesboro 7-13-62. Present through 12-62. Absent 2-63 wounded furlough. Absent 12-63 sick furlough at home. Absent Wounded: 1-3-64. Captured near Rome, Ga., 11-14-64. Carried: Nashville 11-21-64; Louisville 11-24-64; Camp Douglas, Ill. 11-26-64. Released 6-17-1865. Description: home Polk Co., Ga., light complexion, light hair, hazel eyes, 5'-11".

Hacket, James. Pvt., **F**, Enlisted: 3-62, Fairmount, Ga., by Col. Morrison. AWOL 6-30-63.

Hackney, James Augustus, Cpl., **A**, Enlisted: 3-62, Cedartown, Ga., by Captain John C. Crabb. Present 6-62 through 10-62. Absent 12-62 sick furlough at home. Promoted 2nd Cpl. 12-11-62. Captured: Somerset, Ky. 3-30-63. Carried: Louisville, City Point, Va. Exchanged 4-13-63. Present 12-64. Surrendered: Greensboro, N.C. 5-9-1865. Died: 7-16-1892. Buried: Shiloh Baptist Church, Esom Hill, Ga.

Hackney, John F., Pvt., **A**, Enlisted: 3-62, Cedartown, Ga., by Captain John C. Crabb. Exchanged with 21st Ga. Inf. for Cpl. S.J. Crabb. Died: 5-7-1862, chronic dysentery, Lynchburg, Va.

Hackney, J.R., Cpl., **A**, Captured: Somerset, Ky. 3-30-1863. Carried: Louisville 4-13-1863; City Point, Va.; exchanged.

Hailey, F.M., 1Lt., **G**, Captured: Greenville, S.C. 5-18-65, paroled.

Hale, William M. Posey, Pvt., **A**, Enlisted: 3-62, Cedartown, Ga., by Captain John C. Crabb. Present 6-62. KIA attacking Courthouse at Murfreesboro 7-13-62. Buried: Unmarked grave, Courthouse lawn, Murfreesboro, Tenn.

Hall, Jesse B., Pvt., **F**, Enlisted: 3-62, Fairmount, Ga., by Col. Morrison. Present through 2-63. Captured near Dandridge, Tenn. 12-24-63. Carried: Knoxville; Camp Chase 1-1-64. Widow pension: During retreat from Kentucky, guarding rear of army. Attacked by an advance column of enemy cavalry. His horse was killed and he was seen making his way up river, but never seen again. Widow reading *Atlanta Constitution*, saw article from Kentucky newspaper listing Confederate soldiers buried, Nicholasville, Ky. Listed J.B. Hall, 1st Ga. Cav. taken from the headboard. Only notice widow received. Died: 1-28-1864. Buried: Maple Grove Cemetery, Nicholasville, Ky.

Hall, J.P., Pvt., **A**, Enlisted: 12-63, Discharged at Kingston, Ga., 1865. Pension: Lumpkin Co., Ga., 1910.

Hamilton, A., Pvt., **I**, Enlisted: 5-62, Camp Morrison by Captain Leak. Present through 3-63. Absent 10-63 on detached service. Present 12-64. Paroled: Charlotte, N.C. 5-3-1865.

Hamilton, Harry, Pvt., **C**, Captured near Somerset, Ky. 3-30-63. Carried: Louisville; City Point, Va. Exchange 4-13-1863.

Hamilton, John J., Pvt., **C**, Enlisted: 3-62, Cave Spring, Ga., by Captain Haynie. Present through 12-62. Discharged by substitute, Robert Virgil Hamilton, his son. Died: 4-9-1877.

Hamilton, Robert Virgil, Pvt., **C**, Enlisted: 12-62, substitute for John J. Hamilton. Present 2-63 and forfeited one month pay for horse. Captured near Somerset, Ky. 3-30-63. Carried: Louisville; Camp Chase. Released: 5-9-63. Description: age 16, 5'-6", blue eyes, light hair, fair complexion. List: Deserters: Louisville 6-1-63. Took oath 5-3-63. Description: home Floyd Co., Ga., age 16, 5'-8", light hair, light complexion, blue eyes. Absent 6-63 on special duty for Col. Morrison.

Hamilton, W.T., Pvt., **E**, Enlisted: 8-64, Jonesboro, Ga., by Captain Wiggins. 12-31-1864 present.

Hammonds, David, Pvt., **A**, Drowned: Tennessee River 10-64.

Hammonds, H., Pvt., **G**, Enlisted: 4-63 by Captain Kerr. 12-63 present.

Hamon, Joseph S., Cpl., **G**, Enlisted: 10-62, Clinton, Tenn., by Captain Kerr. Present through 12-62. Absent 2-63 Sick in Clinton, Tenn. Hos-pital. Absent 12-63 on furlough. Captured near Atlanta 7-21-64. Carried: Chattanooga; Nashville, 7-29-64; Louisville 7-31-64; Camp Chase 8-2-64; City Point, Va. 3-4-1865, exchanged. Died: 12-5-1928. Buried: Elizabethtown City Cemetery, Hardin Co., Ky.

Hampton, B., Pvt., **K**, Died: 9-6-1864. Buried: Rose Hill Cemetery, Macon, Ga.

Hamrick (Hambrick), Charles Jackson, Pvt., **H**, Enlisted: 4-62, Haralson Co., Ga., by Captain Tumlin. Substitute for Newton J. Tumlin. Died: Knoxville Hospital 7-6-1862, fever. Buried: Mars Hill Cemetery, Cleburne Co., Ala.

Hamrick (Hambrick), James Newton, Pvt., **H**, Enlisted: 2-63, Tallapoosa, Ga., by Captain Tumlin. Absent 12-63. Detained in Ga., by General Wheeler. 12-31-1864 present. Died: 8-29-1883. Buried: Mars Hill Cemetery, Cleburne Co., Ala.

Hamrick (Hambrick), Robert Signor, Sgt., **H**, Enlisted: 4-62, Haralson Co., Ga., by Captain Tumlin. Present through 12-31-1864. WIA and captured. Died 12-22-1908. Buried Valley Grove Cemetery, Cedartown, Ga.

Hamrick (Hambrick), Warren DeKalb, Cpl., **H**, Enlisted: 4-62, Haralson Co., Ga., by Captain Tumlin. Present 6-62. WIA and died near Loudon, Ky. 8-23-62. Buried: Mars Hill Cemetery, Cleburne Co., Ala.

Hamrick (Hambrick), William Harrison, Pvt., **H**, Enlisted: 4-62, Haralson Co., Ga., by Captain Tumlin. Present 6-62 WIA and Horse KIA. Paid $190. Present 8-62 through 2-63. Absent 12-63 Detained in Ga., by General Wheeler. 12-64 present. Pension: At surrender: guarding stock 4-26-1865. Died: 2-25-1913. Buried: Blooming Grove Cemetery, Polk Co., Ga.

Handley, James M., Pvt., **E**, Enlisted: 2-63, Camp Beulah, Tenn., by Lt. Col. Harper. Deserted: 8-19-63. Living: Bowden, Ga., 1870.

Handley, John Randolph, Sgt., **E**, Enlisted: 3-62, Carrollton, Ga., by Captain Blalock. Present through 12-64. Died: 8-23-1887. Buried: Carrollton City Cemetery, Carroll Co., Ga.

Handley, Owen Hilliard Kenion, Pvt., **E**, Enlisted: 3-62, Carrollton, Ga., by Captain Blalock. Present through 12-63. AWOL since 6-4-1864. Died: 7-6-1895. Buried: Livingston Chapel UMC, Crane Hill, Ala.

Hannah, M.M., Pvt., **G**, General Wheeler's escort. Died: 1-1-1864. Buried: Oak Hill Confederate Cemetery, Newnan, Ga.

Hanson, G.D., Pvt., Buried: Confederate Cemetery, Covington, Ga.

Hanson, George Washington, Pvt., **G**, Enlisted:

Floyd Co., Ga., in Floyd Legion State Guards 7-28-1863. Enlisted: 1st Ga. Cavalry 1-7-1864, Rome, Ga., by Lt. Zuber. Absent in Hospital 6-29-64. Received clothing issue 6-64.

Hardaway, Robert Henry, Pvt., **B**, 3-62, Surrendered: Greensboro, N.C. 4-26-1865. Died: 2-11-1905. Buried: Oak Hill Cemetery, Newnan, Ga.

Hardin, Mark A., Captain, **H**, Captured: Gulf of Mexico 4-25-63. Taken: Fort Lafayette, New York Harbor; Fort Warren, Mass. Released 6-10-65.

Hardy, Henry Campbell, Pvt., **G**, Enlisted: 3-62, Floyd Co., Ga., by Captain Kerr. Present through 10-62. Absent 12-62 Wounded furlough in Floyd Co., Ga. 2-63 AWOL. Present 12-63 and 12-64. Died: 4-19-1917. Buried: Caledonia Cemetery, Rusk Co., Tx.

Hardy, W.J., Pvt., **K**, Enlisted: Newnan, Ga., 8-1-1863 in 2nd Ga. Cavalry State Guards. Enlisted: 12-5-1863, 1st Ga. Cavalry by Captain Anderson. 12-31-1864 present.

Hargis, James "Frank" Francis, Pvt., **I**, Enlisted: 6-64, Calhoun, Ga., by Captain Leak. 12-64 present. Pension: Mission with O.P. Hargis at end of war to get horse. Died: 1-14-1925. Buried: Kingston City Cemetery, Bartow Co., Ga.

Hargis, Othnel Polk "Poss," Pvt., **I**, Enlisted: 5-64, Calhoun, Ga., by Captain Leak. 12-64 present. Pension: Went home to get fresh horse on a ten day leave 4-16-1865. Army surrendered before could return. Died: 3-10-1925. Buried: New Smyrna Cemetery, Cobb Co., Ga.

Harkins, Leander J., Pvt., **F**, Enlisted: 3-62, Fairmount, Ga., by Col. Morrison. Present through 12-63. Deserted and took oath 4-2-64 at Chattanooga. Description: home Gordon Co., Ga., 5'-10½". Light complexion, light hair, grey eyes. Living: Comanche Co., Tx. 1910.

Harman, Andrew J., Cpl., **F**, Enlisted: 3-62, Fairmount, Ga., by Col. Morrison. Present through 2-63. Captured near Philadelphia, Tenn. 10-20-63. Carried: Camp Nelson; Camp Chase; Fort Delaware 3-4-64. Exchanged 3-7-1865. Admitted: Wayside Hospital, Richmond, Va. 3-10-65.

Harman, William R., Pvt., **F**, Enlisted: 3-62, Fairmount, Ga., by Col. Morrison. Present through 12-62. Absent 2-63 with detachment and wagons. 12-63 AWOL. On list of deserters and took oath 3-26-64. Description: home Gordon Co., Ga., 5'-11½". Light complexion, brown hair, hazel eyes.

Harper, Alexander Thornton, 2nd Lt., **C**, Enlisted: 3-62, Cave Spring, Ga., by Captain Haynie. Elected 2nd Lt. 3-4-62. Resigned: lung disease

6-13-62. Weighed less than 100 lbs. 1864 Yankees captured him at home, but released when discovered extent of illness. Died: 1-21-1905. Buried: Cave Spring Cemetery, Lavender, Ga.

Harper, Armistead Richardson, Lt. Col. **F&S**, Enlisted: Rome, Ga., age 26, 8th Ga. Inf. 5-14-61. Joined 1st Ga. Cavalry; elected Major 3-30-62. Promoted Lt. Col. 5-28-62. WIA at Philadelphia, Tenn. 10-20-63. Died: 10-28-63. Buried: Myrtle Hill Cemetery, Rome, Ga.

Harper, Jasper, Pvt., **H**, Enlisted: 4-62, Tallapoosa, Ga., by Captain Tumlin. Present 12-62 and 2-63. Horse KIA near Danville, Ky. 7-24-63. Paid $225. Jasper died: 11-20-63.

Harriage, John C., Cpl., **C**, Enlisted: 3-62, Cave Spring, Ga., by Captain Haynie. Promoted 2nd Cpl. 3-31-62. Present through 2-63. Absent 6-63 Quarantined. Absent 12-63 with detachment. Widow pension: Fall 1863: ill with Pneumonia at Bridgeport, Tenn. After 3 or 4 weeks furloughed home. Relapsed at Blue Mountain, Ala. 4-10-64. Sent home and died: 4-24-1864. Buried: Polk Co., Ga.

Harriage, William Henry, Sr., Pvt., **C**, Enlisted: 3-62, Cave Spring, Ga., by Captain Haynie. Absent 6-62 Sick furlough in Floyd Co., Ga. Present 8-62. Discharged 12-22-62 old age and rheumatism. Certificate: born Union District, S.C., age 51, 6'-1½", fair complexion, blue eyes, grey hair. Died; buried, Floyd Co., Ga.

Harris, George, Pvt., **A**, Enlisted: 3-64, in the field by Captain Jesse W. Crabb. 12-31-1864 present.

Harris, J.B.C., Pvt., **I**, Enlisted: 5-62, Camp Morrison by Captain Leak. Present through 12-64. Paroled: Charlotte, N.C. 5-3-1865.

Harris, Samuel, Pvt., **E**, Enlisted: 3-62, Carrollton, Ga., by Captain Blalock. Present through 12-31-1863.

Harrison, T.L., Pvt., **E**, Captured: Athens, Ga., 5-8-65, paroled.

Hart, J.M., Pvt., **E**, Enlisted: 4-64, Oxford, Ala., by Col. Davitte. AWOL 11-4-1864. Pension: Capt. Shuford gave permission, at Choccolocoo, Ala., to get a horse from his sister in Villa Rica, Ga. as his was disabled. When arrived home, the horse was gone and could not return to command.

Harvey, Charles Alexander, Pvt., **E**, Enlisted: 3-62, Carrollton, Ga., by Captain Blalock. Present through 12-31-1864. Died: 12-5-1874, age 32. Buried: Fairburn City Cemetery, Fulton Co., Ga.

Harvey, William Spencer, Pvt., **K**, Enlisted 6-6-1861: Campbellton, Ga., age 16, in 21st Ga. Inf. Enlisted: 1st Ga. Cavalry 5-10-64, Newnan,

Ga., by Captain North. WIA near Knoxville. Present 12-64. Surrendered: Salisbury, N.C. 4-26-65. Died: 2-26-1926. Buried: Fairburn City Cemetery, Ga.

Hathcock, A.M., Pvt., **K**, Enlisted: 5-62, Camp Morrison by Captain North. Absent sick with measles 6-15-62 sent to Knoxville. Sent to Atlanta hospital then home, Fayette Co., Ga. on furlough 6-27-62. Died: Campbell Co., Ga., 7-4-1862.

Hawks, J.P., Pvt., **H**, Enlisted: 2-63, Rogersville, Tenn., by Captain Tumlin. 12-63 AWOL. Pension: WIA. 3-1-1865: Part of Captain Tumlin's company detached to care for 200 captured horses. Cutoff from regiment and departed home, Bartow Co., Ga. Attached: Gen. Wofford's command and surrendered: Kingston, Ga. Witness: Bartow Co., Ga., 1900.

Hayes, J., Pvt., **C**, Enlisted: 3-62, On roll 4-6-1862.

Haynes, James M., Pvt., **B**, Enlisted: 3-62, Discharged: Greensboro, N.C. 4-26-1865. Died: 12-3-1893. Buried: Bethel UMC, Senoia, Ga.

Haynes, Thomas J., Pvt., **E**, Enlisted: 5-62, Carrollton, Ga., by Captain Blalock. Present through 12-62. WIA near Murfreesboro on retreat 1-6-63. Present 12-63 and 12-64. Captured: Athens, Ga., 5-8-65, paroled.

Haynes, William Harrison, Pvt., **E**, Enlisted: 3-62, Carrollton, Ga., by Captain Blalock.

Hayney (Haynie), William Columbus, Pvt., **B**, Enlisted: 9-63, Surrendered: Salisbury, N.C. 4-26-1865. Living: 735 Gordon St. Atlanta 1919. Died: 1-1-1923. Buried: Westview Cemetery, Atlanta, Ga.

Haynie, Milton Henderson, Captain, **C**, Enlisted: 3-62, Cave Spring, Ga., by Lt. Col. Morrison. Elected Captain 3-4-62. Present through 12-62. WIA in Ky. Died: home 3-14-1863, typhoid fever in connection with accidental gunshot wound, age 56. Buried: Family plot: Floyd Co., Ga.

Haynie, Milton Henderson, Jr., Pvt., **C**, Enlisted: 8-62, Cave Spring, Ga., by Captain Haynie. Mustered: London, Tenn. Present 6-63. Absent 12-63 on special duty. 12-31-1864 present. Died: 10-7-1900. Buried: Oak Hill Cemetery, Newnan, Ga.

Hazlett, John M., Pvt., **A**, Enlisted: 3-62, Cedartown, Ga., by Captain John C. Crabb. Absent 6-62 Sick in Loudon, Tenn. in hospital. Present 8-62. Absent 10-62 through 12-63 on sick furlough at home. Died 1864, exposure.

Hedgepeth, Charles Frank, Pvt., **D**, Died: October 1900.

Hedgepeth, William N., Pvt., **D**, Enlisted: 3-62, Dallas, Ga., age 44, by Captain Seawright. Present 6-62.

Absent 8-62 Sick furlough in Paulding Co., Ga. Captured near Clay Village, Ky. 10-4-62. Paroled. Absent 2-63. Detailed with Artillery in Knoxville. WIA near Kingston, Tenn. 11-28-63. Captured near Kingston, Tenn. 12-3-63. Sent to U.S. General Hospital, Chattanooga: gunshot wound, right foot, fractured bone. Arrived: Louisville, 2-20-64; Fort Delaware 3-7-64. Reported dead: Fort Delaware: measles 3-13-64. (Here it gets interesting!) 6-4-1896 Pension: 18 months service before capture, chronic rheumatism. Escaped exchanging identification with a dead prisoner! Died: 6-15-1910. Buried: Muscadine, Ala.

Henap, H., Pvt., **G**, Enlisted: 3-62, Cave Spring, Ga., by Captain Haynie. Paroled: Charlotte, N.C. 5-3-1865.

Henderson, Augustus C., Pvt., **C**, Enlisted: 5-62, Cave Spring, Ga., by Lt. Reynolds. Present through 6-63. Absent 12-63 with detachment. 12-31-1864 present.

Henderson, G.W., Pvt., **C**, Enlisted: 9-64, Present 12-31-1864.

Hendrix, George Washington, Pvt., **K**, Enlisted: 5-62, Camp Morrison by Captain North. Present 6-62. Discharged.

Hendrix, Henry H., Pvt., **K**, Enlisted: 5-62, Camp Morrison by Captain North. Absent 6-62 Sick in Coweta Co., Ga. Present 8-62 through 12-62. 2-63 AWOL in Coweta Co. Present 12-63 and 12-64. Living: Coweta Co., Ga., 1880.

Hendrix, Henry W., Pvt., **C**, Enlisted: 2-63, Cave Spring, Ga., by Captain Haynie. Present 6-63. Admitted: Ocmulgee Hospital, Macon Ga., 7-8-1864. Transferred: home Polk Co., Ga., 7-22-64. Present 12-64.

Hendrix (Hendricks), Thomas Jefferson, Pvt., **I**, Enlisted: 5-63, Calhoun, Ga., by Captain Leak. Mustered: Oxford, Ala. Present 12-64. Surrendered: Greensboro, N.C. 4-26-1865. Died: 3-28-1911. Buried: Dewey Baptist Church, Bartow Co., Ga.

Hendrix, Thomas W., Pvt., **A**, Enlisted: 3-62, Cedartown, Ga., by Captain John C. Crabb. Present through 2-63. Captured near Somerset, Ky. 3-30-63. Carried: Louisville 4-13-63; City Point, Va. Exchange 4-14-63. Captured near Rome, Ga., 7-14-64. Carried: Nashville 10-23-64; Louisville 10-26-64; Camp Douglas 10-29-64. Released: 6-17-1865. Description: home Floyd Co., Ga., 6'-0", dark complexion, dark hair, blue eyes.

Hendrix, William J., Pvt., **C**, Enlisted: 5-62, Cave Spring, Ga., by Lt. Reynolds. Present 6-62 and 8-62 Detailed as Wagoner. Present 10-62 through 6-63. Absent 12-63 sick. Present 12-64.

Hennon, J.L., Pvt., **I**, Enlisted: 5-62, Camp Morrison by Captain Leak. Present through 12-62. Absent 3-63 at Detachment Camp. Present 10-63. WIA at Sunshine Church 7-31-64.

Henson, Andrew B., Pvt., **G**, Enlisted: 3-62, Floyd Co., Ga., by Captain Kerr. Absent 6-62 Sick in Loudon, Tenn. Hospital. Present 8-62 through 12-62. Absent 2-63 Sick furlough in Floyd Co., Ga. Absent 2-63 in Ga. Received clothing issue 6-64. Pension: In raid into North Ga. and Tenn. to burn bridges and supplies. Surrendered: Raleigh, N.C. 4-26-1865. Died: Grayson Co., Tx. 6-1871.

Herrill, N.P., Pvt., **E**, Captured: Athens, Ga., 5-8-1865, paroled.

Herring, Haston Y., Pvt., **B**, Enlisted: 3-62 in Newnan, Ga. WIA near Philadelphia, Tenn. 10-20-63, and sent to Newnan, Ga. Hospital. Paroled: Augusta, Ga., 5-19-1865. Died: 4-11-1890. Buried: Oak Hill Cemetery, Newnan, Ga.

Herring, Jesse Marion, Pvt., **B**, Enlisted: 3-62, Newnan, Ga., age 19, by Captain Strickland. Present through 12-62. Absent 2-63 Sick furlough in Newnan, Ga. WIA near Philadelphia, Tenn. 10-20-63, and sent to Hospital in Newnan, Ga. Present 12-64. Surrendered: Hillsboro, NC 4-26-1865. Died: 12-29-1894. Buried: Oak Hill Cemetery, Newnan, Ga.

Herring, Samuel, Pvt., **K**, Enlisted: 5-62, Camp Morrison by Captain North. Present through 12-63. WIA at Decatur, Ga., 7-21-1864. Gunshot: right leg, posterior of thigh, breaking bone 2 inches above knee and exit at joint. Died: 4-10-1909 Coweta Co., Ga.

Hertin, C., Pvt., **K**, Enlisted: 5-62, Camp Morrison by Captain North.

Hicks, Jefferson N., Pvt., **H**, Enlisted: 8-62, Kingston, Tenn., by Captain Tumlin. Present 10-62. Died: 1909. Buried: Mars Hill Primitive Baptist Church, Cleburne Co., Ala.

Hicks, James W., Pvt., **I**, Enlisted: 9-64, Surrendered: Greensboro, N.C. 4-26-1865. Died: 8-7-1898. Buried: Pine Log Cemetery, Rydal, Ga.

Hicks, Thomas Erwin, Pvt., **H**, Enlisted: 4-62, Tallapoosa, Ga., by Captain Tumlin. Present 12-62 and 2-63. Absent 12-63 Detained in Ga., by General Wheeler. 12-64 present. Died: 2-16-1908. Buried: Mars Hill Primitive Baptist Church, Cleburne Co., Ala.

Hicks, T.J., Pvt., **H**, Enlisted: 8-62, Kingston, Tenn., by Captain Tumlin. Present 2-63. Absent 12-63 Detained in Ga., by General Wheeler. 12-31-1864 present.

Hickson, James, Pvt., **K**, Captured: Knoxville 8-7-63. Carried: Nashville; Louisville. Took oath. Enlisted: Federal Army 8-12-1863. (Possible: James Hixson, enlisted: 10th U.S. Tenn. Cavalry 2-29-1864. Description: born in Walker Co., Ga., age 20, blue eyes, dark hair, fair complexion, 5'-9".)

Hickson, Samuel, Pvt., **I**, Captured: Knoxville 8-7-63. Carried: Nashville; Louisville 8-11-63. Took oath. Enlisted: Federal Army 8-12-1863. (Possible: Samuel Hixson, enlisted: U.S. 10th Tenn. Cavalry 8-12-1863, age 26. Died: 3-15-1865. Captured: Broomtown Valley, Chattooga Co., Ga., and murdered. Possibly for desertion from Confederate Army.)

Higginbotham, Andrew Jackson, Pvt., **C**, Enlisted: 3-62, Cave Spring, Ga., by Captain Haynie. Present 6-62. Promoted: Regimental bugler 7-1-62. Absent 2-63 sick. Present 6-63 through 12-64 and Detailed with Regiment. Died: 3-24-1899. Buried: Whitefield Cemetery, Haskell Co., Ok.

Higginbotham, Henry Oliver, Pvt., **I**, Enlisted: 1-64, Calhoun, Ga., by Captain Leak. Present 12-64. Surrendered: Greensboro, N.C. 4-26-1865. Died: 12-18-1908. Buried: Jersey UMC, Jersey, Ga.

Higginbotham, Joseph H., Pvt., **I**, Enlisted: 8-64 in Decatur, Ga. Surrender: Greensboro, N.C. 5-26-1865. Died: 1-20-1939. Buried: Sugar Valley Baptist Church, Gordon Co., Ga.

Higgins, Mills (Miles) Alberto, Pvt., **E**, Enlisted: 5-62, Cartersville, Ga., by Captain Blalock. Present through 12-62. Absent 2-63 on furlough. Absent 12-63 Captured and paroled. AWOL 11-4-64. Pension: Paroled: Atlanta, Ga., 5-1865. Died: 4-30-1913. Buried: Friendship Cemetery, Lawrence Co., Ala.

Higgins, Thomas J., Pvt., **E**, Captured: Carroll Co., Ga., 8-10-64. Carried: Nashville 8-30-64; Louisville 9-2-64; Camp Chase. Paroled: New Orleans 5-2-1865.

Hill, James L., Pvt., **E**, Enlisted: 4-62, Carrollton, Ga., by Captain Blalock. KIA near Richmond, Ky. 8-31-62. Buried: Richmond, Ky. Cemetery, Mass grave section H.

Hill, M.P., Pvt., **G**, Enlisted: 3-62, Floyd Co., Ga., by Captain Kerr. Present 6-62 and 8-62. Discharged: 9-62, age 40 as unable to perform army duty. Pension: Floyd Co., Ga., 1896.

Hill, Payton C., Pvt., **H**, Enlisted: 6-64, Tallapoosa, Ga., by Captain Tumlin. Captured: Atlanta 7-21-64. Carried: Chattanooga; Nashville, 7-29-64; Louisville 7-30-64; Camp Chase 8-2-64. Died: Camp Chase Prison 2-4-65, pneumonia. Buried: Camp Chase Confederate Cemetery, Columbus, Ohio. Row 26 #65 grave 1048.

Hindsman, Benjamin Homer, Pvt., **B**, Enlisted: 3-62, Newnan, Ga., age 25, by Captain Strickland. Absent 6-62 Sick furlough in Grantville, Ga. WIA near Big Hill, Ky. 8-24-62. Absent 10-62 and 12-62 Wounded furlough in Grantville, Ga. Discharged 2-14-63. Died: 4-1-1916. Buried: New Hope Cemetery, Eden, Ala.

Hindsman, Felix E., Cpl., **B**, Enlisted: 3-62, Newnan, Ga., age 21, by Captain Strickland. Present through 2-63. Transferred: 55th Ga. Vol. Inf. 8-15-63, Col. Davitte. Died: 12-11-1909. Buried: Southview Cemetery, Moreland, Ga.

Hindsman, James Knox Polk, Pvt., **B**, Enlisted: 5-64, Newnan, Ga., by Lt. Taylor. 12-31-1864 present. Living: Coweta Co., Ga., 1870.

Hindsman, Michael C., 1st Sgt., **B**, Enlisted: 3-62, Newnan, Ga., age 25, by Captain Strickland. Absent 6-62 Sick furlough in Newnan, Ga. Present 8-62 through 12-62. Discharged: 7-18-63: Knoxville. Pension: Surrendered: Greensboro, N.C. 4-26-1865. Died: 3-7-1901. Buried: Luthersville City Cemetery, Meriwether Co., Ga.

Hindsman, Peter S., Pvt., **B**, Enlisted: 3-62, Newnan, Ga., age 18, by Captain Strickland. Present through 12-63. WIA in both thighs and captured in Atlanta 7-21-64. Admitted: 17th U.S. Army Hospital, Marietta, Ga., 9-2-64. Carried: Nashville 10-27-64; Louisville 10-31-64; Camp Douglas 11-1-64. Discharged 6-17-1865. Description: home Coweta Co., Ga., 5'-9", light complexion, light hair, blue eyes. Died 10-2-1866. Age 23. Buried: Founders Cemetery, Moreland, Ga.

Hines, James M., Pvt., **B**, Enlisted: 41st Ga. Inf. 3-4-1862, Meriwether Co., Ga. Listed Absent in Captain Strickland's Cavalry Company. Transferred: 1st Ga. Cavalry 3-62. Enlisted: Newnan, Ga., age 19, by Captain Strickland. Present 6-62. Died: Meriwether Co., Ga. 8-3-62.

Hines, John T., Pvt., **B**, Enlisted: 3-62, Newnan, Ga., age 26, by Captain Strickland. Present through 12-62. Absent 2-63 Sick furlough in Grantville, Ga. Present 12-63 and 12-64. Pension: Left before surrender. Paroled: Atlanta 1865. Died: 3-12-1916: Luthersville, Ga.

Hinesley, John Jefferson, Pvt., **E**, Enlisted: 8-63, Ebenezer, Tenn., by Lt. Col. Harper. Present 12-63 and 12-64. Died: 5-7-1910. Buried: Fox Cemetery, Stone Co., Ark.

Hinesley, Thomas H., 2nd Lt., **E**, Enlisted: 3-62, Carrollton, Ga., by Captain Blalock. Present through Promotion 2nd Lt. 10-24-62. Present 12-62. Absent 2-63 sick. Resigned: 8-3-63 with chronic hepatitis. Died 7-23-1898. Buried: Hinesley Cemetery, Cross Plaines, Ga.

Hipp (Hipps), Andrew Jackson, Sgt., **D**, Enlisted: 3-62, Dallas, Ga., age 39, by Captain Seawright. Present through 12-63. Horse KIA near Monticello, Ky. 5-1-63 paid, $300. Captured at Atlanta 7-21-64. Marched to Chattanooga. Carried by train: Nashville 7-29-64; Louisville 7-31-64; Camp Chase 8-2-64; City Point, Va. 3-4-1865 Released 5-65. Died: 5-30-1895. Buried: Flint Hill Cemetery, Hiram, Ga.

Hobbs, A.H., Pvt., **A**, Enlisted: 2-63, Cedartown, Ga., by Captain Hutchings. Absent 12-63 Sick. Captured 8-64.

Hobbs, William Andrew, Pvt., **A**, Enlisted: Cobb Co., Ga., age 16, Phillips' Legion 8-4-1861. Enlisted: 2-63, 1st Ga. Cavalry, Cedartown, Ga., by Captain Hutchings. Absent 12-63 sick. Captured: Rome, Ga., 9-27-64. Carried: Nashville; Louisville; Camp Douglas 10-29-64. Discharged 5-11-65. Description: home Paulding Co., Ga., 5'-7", fair complexion, black hair, blue eyes. Died: 1-14-1926. Buried: Salt Lake City Cemetery, Salt Lake City, Utah.

Hodges, J.A., Pvt., **K**, Enlisted: 5-62, Camp Morrison by Captain North. WIA near Richmond, Ky., by bushwhackers also his horse KIA, paid $170. Absent 8-62 wounded furlough. Present 10-62 Acting Orderly Sgt. Present through 12-31-1864. Transferred: 32nd Ga. Inf. Transfer revoked 2-3-1865.

Hodges, John Robert, Pvt., **K**, Enlisted: 5-62, Cartersville, Ga., by Lt. Col. Harper. Absent 12-63 Detained with wagon train by General Wheeler. KIA at Sunshine Church 7-31-1864.

Hodges, Martin Greene, Pvt., **B**, Enlisted: 3-62, Newnan, Ga., age 20, by Captain Strickland. Present through 12-64. Surrendered: Yadkin River, Salisbury, N.C. 4-26-1865. Died: 5-14-1904. Buried: Myrtle Hill Cemetery, Hogansville, Ga.

Hogan, C.C., Pvt., **B**, Enlisted: 4-62, Cartersville, Ga., by Col. Morrison. Present 6-62 and 8-62. Absent 10-62 WIA, MIA left sick at Frankfort, Ky.

Hogg, William, Pvt., **A**, Enlisted: 12-62, Cedartown, Ga., by Captain Hutchings. Absent 2-63 Sick. Present 12-63. KIA at Atlanta 7-21-64.

Hogue, Stephen Kelly, 2nd Lt., **C**, Enlisted: 3-62, Cave Spring, Ga., by Captain Haynie. Promoted 4th Cpl. 3-31-62. Present 6-62. Promoted 1st Sgt. 8-10-62. Present 10-62 and 12-62. Absent 2-63 Sick. Captured near Somerset, Ky. 3-30-63. Carried: Louisville; City Point, Va. Exchanged 4-13-63. Promoted 2nd Lt. 12-26-63, Col. Davitte. Surrendered: Greensboro, N.C. 4-26-1865. Witness: Polk Co., Ga., 1901.

Holcomb, Asa, Pvt., **G**, Enlisted: 3-62, Floyd Co., Ga., by Captain Kerr. Present through 2-63. Captured near Mill Springs, Ky. 5-28-63. Carried: Lexington; Camp Chase 6-10-63; Point Lookout, Md. 11-30-63. Description: age 36, 5'-11", dark eyes, dark complexion, dark hair. Exchanged: 2-13-1865. Arrived at Camp Lee, near Richmond, Va., 2-65

Holcombe, James Madison, Pvt., **H**, Enlisted: 4-62, Haralson Co., Ga., by Captain Tumlin. Present through 10-62. Absent 12-62 sick furlough home. Present 2-63. Absent 12-63 Detained in Ga., by General Wheeler. Died: 10-17-1890. Buried: Little Vine Cemetery, Bremen, Ga.

Holcombe, Jonathan C., Pvt., **E**, Enlisted: 5-62, Carrollton, Ga., by Captain Blalock. Present 2-63. WIA near Mossy Creek, Tenn. 12-29-1863; taken to a private home where he died 1-13-64, Morristown, Tenn.

Holland, William A., Pvt., **B**, Enlisted: 3-62, Newnan, Ga., age 31, by Captain Strickland. Present 6-62. WIA: Big Hill, Ky. 8-24-62. Absent 10-62 Wounded furlough in Newnan, Ga. Absent 12-62. Wounded furlough in Grantville, Ga. Present 2-63. Absent 12-63 Detained with wagon train by General Wheeler. 12-64 present. Died: 1867. Buried: Founders Cemetery, Moreland, Ga.

Holleman, Charles B.C., Pvt., **E**, Enlisted: 3-62, Carrollton, Ga., by Captain Blalock. Present through 8-62. Discharged 10-11-62 physically disabled. Died: 2-10-1896 Coweta Co., Ga.

Hollis, John B., Pvt., **E**, Enlisted: 3-62, Fairmount, Ga., by Col. Morrison. Present through 12-62. Absent 3-63 at Detachment Camp. Present 10-63. Deserted 8-20-64.

Hollis, William J., Pvt., **I**, Enlisted: 5-62, Camp Morrison by Captain Leak. Present 6-62. Died: 7-5-62: Loudon, Ky. Buried: Turkeytown Memorial Gardens, Gadsden, Ala.

Holman (Hallman), Joel E., Cpl., **K**, Enlisted: 5-62, Camp Morrison by Captain North. Absent 6-62 Sick furlough in Coweta Co., Ga. Present 8-62 through 12-63. Absent 12-64 in Newnan, Ga. Hospital. Pension: During fall back to Atlanta, became sick and sent to hospital in Atlanta by Captain North. After release returning to command, reached Branchville, S.C., and war ended. Pension: Pike Co., Ga., 1907.

Holmes, Gamaliel Wyatt, Pvt., **G**, Died: 11-3-1890. Buried: Myrtle Hill Cemetery, Rome, Ga.

Holmes, William J., Pvt., **G**, Enlisted: 3-62, Floyd Co., Ga., by Captain Kerr. Present 2-63. Captured near Mill Springs, Ky. 5-28-63. Carried:

Lexington; Camp Chase 6-10-63; Johnson's Island 6-14-63; Point Lookout, Md. 11-24-63. Description: age 38, 5'-8", blue eyes, dark hair, fair complexion. Admitted: War Camp Hospital, Point Lookout, Md. 9-19-64, chronic diarrhea. Died: 10-24-64. Buried: Point Lookout Confederate Cemetery, Scotland, Md. (Listed: 1 La. Cav.)

Holt, Cicero, Surgeon, **F&S**, Appointed Surgeon 4-27-61: 21st Ga. Inf. Resigned 2-20-62. Joined 1st Ga. Cavalry. Absent 6-62 in LaGrange, Ga. sick. Living in Clarke Co., Ga., 1870.

Hood, John, Pvt., **I**, Enlisted: 12-62, Cartersville, Ga., by Captain Leak. Present through 10-63. Absent on Detached service 6-1-1864.

Hood, William H., Sgt., **I**, Enlisted: 5-62, Camp Morrison by Captain Leak. 6-62 discharged. Mustered back 12-4-62: Cartersville, Ga. Admitted: Ocmulgee Hospital, Macon Ga., 10-5-63, WIA. Present 10-63. Present 12-64. Paroled: Charlotte, NC 5-3-1865.

Hooper, C.W., Sgt., **G**, 3-62, Ordnance sergeant.

Hooper, James P., Pvt., **G**, Pension: Cullman Co., Ala.

Hopkins, J.D., Pvt., **B**, Enlisted: 5-64, Newnan, Ga., by Lt. Taylor. 12-31-1864 present. Died: 7-14-1906. Buried: Bethel Baptist, Rocky Mount, Ga.

Hopkins, William, Pvt., **H**, Enlisted: 4-64, Tallapoosa, Ga., by Captain Tumlin. 12-31-1864 AWOL.

Hopson, Thomas G., Pvt., **B**, Enlisted: 4-62, Cartersville, Ga., by Col. Morrison. Present 12-62. Absent 2-63 Sick furlough in Grantville, Ga. WIA near Russellville, Tenn. 12-12-63. Sent to Newnan, Ga. Hospital. Received clothing issue 1864.

Horsley, Robert Russell, Pvt., **E**, Enlisted: 3-62, Carrollton, Ga., by Captain Blalock. Present through 12-62. Absent 2-63 Detachment at Kingston, Tenn. Present 12-63 and 12-1864. Died: 3-28-1907. Buried: Hinesly Cemetery, Cross Plains, Ga.

Horton, David W., Pvt., **A**, Enlisted: 3-62, Cedartown, Ga., by Captain John C. Crabb. Present 6-62. Absent 8-62 sick furlough home. Absent 10-62 Sick in Kingston, Tenn. Present 2-63. Captured near Somerset, Ky. 3-30-63. Carried: Louisville; City Point, Va. Exchanged 4-13-1863.

Horton, Nathan, Pvt., **E**, Enlisted: 3-62, Carrollton, Ga., by Captain Blalock. Present through 8-62. Absent 10-62 sick furlough home. Present 12-62. Discharged sick 2-18-63. Died: 7-23-1926. Buried: Crossroads Cemetery, West Point, Ala.

House, Benjamin F., Sgt., **F**, Enlisted: 3-62, Fairmount, Ga., by Col. Morrison. Absent 6-62 sick furlough. Present 8-62 through 2-63. Absent 12-63 in Ga. with wagons. Paroled: Charlotte, N.C. 5-3-1865.

House, Seaborn, Pvt., **D**, Enlisted 4th Ga. State Troops 10-25-61. Discharged. Enlisted: 3-62, Dallas, Ga., age 40, by Captain Seawright. Present 6-62. Absent 8-62 on scout. Present 10-62 and 12-62. WIA in left hand 1862. Absent 2-63 in Hospital at Kingston, Tenn. Absent 12-63 Detained in Ga., by General Wheeler. 12-31-64 AWOL. Died: 1902. Buried: Greenwood Cemetery, Hopkins Co., Tx.

Howard, James, Pvt., **E**, Enlisted: 3-62, Carrollton, Ga., by Captain Blalock. Present 6-62 and 8-62. Discharged 10-3-62.

Howell, Elisha Wright, Cpl., **E**, Enlisted: 3-62, Carrollton, Ga., by Captain Blalock. Present through 12-64. WIA at New Hope Church 5-19-64. Paroled: Charlotte, N.C. 5-3-1865. Died: 8-22-1907. Buried: Hebron Cemetery, Howell's Crossroads, Ala.

Hubbard, Burton William, Pvt., A, Enlisted: 4-64, in field by Captain York. AWOL 9-64. Died: 1897. Buried: Lambert Cemetery, Carrollton, Ga.

Hubbard, John W., Pvt., A, Enlisted: 7-63 by Captain Hutchings. Absent 12-63 Sick. Clothing issued: Gen, Hospital, Montgomery Springs, Va. 2-10-1864.

Hubbard, William Ray, Pvt., A, Enlisted: 8-63 by Captain Hutchings. Absent 12-63 at Capitol in Milledgeville, Ga. a Senator from: Polk, Paulding and Haralson, Ga. Resigned: when elected. Died: 4-14-1902. Buried: Van Wert Baptist, Rockmart, Ga.

Huckaby, E., Pvt., **G**, Enlisted: 3-62, Floyd Co., Ga., by Captain Kerr. Present through 12-62. Present 2-63 Detailed as Teamster. Absent 12-63 in Ga. Absent 12-64 Detailed to Robertson's Artillery.

Huckaby, Lysander Samuel, Pvt., **G**, 3-62, Pension: WIA (right knee): Murfreesboro 7-13-62. Detailed: Wiggin's Battery, 1st Ga. Cavalry 8-64. Detached with part of his company to escort, President Jefferson Davis 5-65. Discharged at end of service at Madison, Ga. May 1865. Died: 9-28-1929. Buried: Cedar Creek Baptist Church, Cave Spring, Ga.

Huddleston, J.B., Pvt., **F**, Enlisted: 5-64, Decatur, Ga., by Major Andrews. Absent 12-64 in Hospital wounded.

Huggins, James W., Pvt., **F**, Enlisted: 9-64, Greenbush, Walker Co., Ga., by Col. Davitte. Present 12-64. Surrendered: Salisbury, N.C. 4-26-1865. Died: 2-17-1909. Buried: Pleasant Hill Cemetery, LaFayette, Ga.

Huggins, William, Pvt., **A**, Enlisted: 4-62, Haralson Co., Ga., by Captain John C. Crabb.

Hughen, William C., Pvt., **K**, Enlisted: 5-62, Cartersville, Ga., by Major Harper. Absent 6-62 Sick furlough in Coweta Co., Ga. Present through 12-31-1864. Died: 5-7-1911. Buried: Westview Cemetery, Atlanta, Ga.

Huley, J., Pvt., **A**, Enlisted: 3-63, in field by Captain York. AWOL 6-64.

Hulsey, Jennings T., Pvt., **A**, Enlisted: 3-62, Cedartown, Ga., by Captain John C. Crabb. Present 6-62. Absent 8-62 sick furlough home. Absent 10-62 Sick in Loudon, Tenn. Absent 12-62 sick furlough home. Present 2-63. Absent 12-63 Cut off with wagons. AWOL 7-20-64. Paroled: Charlotte, N.C. 5-3-1865. Died: 3-26-1923. Buried: Mountain View Baptist Church, Dallas, Ga.

Hunt, Ashbury P., Sgt., **C**, Enlisted: 3-62, Cave Spring, Ga., by Captain Haynie. Present through 8-62 and Promoted 4th Cpl. 8-10-62. Present through 6-63 and Promoted 4th Sgt. 5-1-63. Present 12-63 and 12-64. Witness: Polk Co., Ga., 1891.

Hunt, Benjamin Franklin, Pvt.(Major), **F**, Enlisted 1861: 8th Batt. Ga. Inf. Elected: Major 5-6-1861. Resigned 3-30-1863 to join 1st Ga. Cavalry to be with son. Enlisted: 8-63, Sweetwater, Tenn., by Captain Reynolds. Pension: Saturday morning 9-19-63 at Chickamauga Creek, Jay's Mill, shot through the body and died. Body brought home about 15 miles from battlefield 9-21-63. Buried home burial ground, 9-24-1863, Walker Co., Ga. South of Villanow, Ga.

Hunt, William H., Pvt., **F**, Died: 1925. Buried: Peavine Cemetery, Rock Spring, Ga.

Hunt, William R., Pvt., **F**, Enlisted: 3-62, Fairmount Ga., by Col. Morrison. Present through 12-62. Present 2-63 Detached as Col. Harper's orderly. Present through 12-1864.

Hunt, William W., Cpl., **C**, Enlisted: 3-62, Cave Spring, Ga., by Captain Haynie. Present through 6-63 and promoted 3rd Cpl. 6-30-63. Absent 12-63 with detachment. Left regiment 7-64.

Hunter, George C., Pvt., **K**, Enlisted 7th Ga. Inf. 5-31-1861, Atlanta. Discharged 7-16-62. Enlisted 1st Ga. Cavalry 5-1-62, Cartersville, Ga., by Major Harper. Absent 6-13-63 furloughed home. KIA at Sunshine Church 7-31-64.

Hunter, Robert F., Pvt., **K**, Enlisted 8-1-1864, Newnan, Ga., 2nd Regt Cavalry Ga. State Guards.

Enlisted: 1st Ga. Cavalry 5-1-64, Newnan, Ga., by Captain North. WIA at Decatur, Ga., 7-22-64. Sent to Newnan, Ga. Hospital two months, gunshot wound, right hip. Furloughed home, Newnan, Ga. Witness: Coweta Co., Ga., 1887.

Hutcherson, George W., Pvt., Enlisted: 3-62, Cave Spring, Ga., by Captain Haynie. Present 6-62. Discharged 8-10-62.

Hutcherson, H.D., Pvt., **D**, Enlisted: 3-62, Dallas, Ga., age 23, by Captain Seawright. Present through 2-63. Absent 12-63 Detained in Ga., by General Wheeler. 12-64 present.

Hutchings, William M., Captain, **A**, Enlisted: 3-62, Cedartown, Ga., by Captain John C. Crabb. Elected 1st Lt. 3-4-62. Present 6-62. WIA: Murfreesboro 7-13-62. Absent 8-62 Wounded furlough: Polk Co., Ga. Promoted: Captain, death of John C. Crabb. Absent 10-62 and 12-62 wounded furlough. Present 2-63. Resigned 5-1-63: Disabled, wounded forearm. Living: Polk Co., Ga., 1870.

Hyde, George W., Pvt., **K**, Enlisted: 5-62, Cartersville, Ga., by Captain North. Present through 12-62. Absent 2-63 Sick furlough: Meriwether Co., Ga. Present 12-63 as Company blacksmith. Absent 12-64 sick: Erysipelas (skin disease). Paroled: Charlotte, N.C. 5-3-1865. Pension: Heard Co., Ga., 1895; witness 1897.

Ingram, George C., Pvt., **K**, Enlisted: 55th Ga. Inf. 5-8-62, Meriwether Co., Ga. Enlisted: 8-63, Cartersville, Ga., by Major Harper. Absent 12-63 Detained in Ga. with Wagon Train by General Wheeler. KIA: Resaca, Ga., 5-13-1864.

Ingram, Martin Little, Pvt., **H**, Enlisted: 4-62, Haralson Co., Ga., by Captain Tumlin. Present through 2-63. Absent 12-63 Detained in Ga., by General Wheeler. 12-64 AWOL. Family claim: Surrendered 5-65. Died 5-12-1918. Buried: Old Province Cemetery, Forney, Ala.

Ingram, William A., Pvt., **E**, Enlisted: 3-62, Carrollton, Ga., by Captain Tumlin. Present 6-62 as wagoner. Present through 12-62 as Teamster. Present 2-63 and 12-63. Absent 12-64 Sick. WIA in Georgia. Discharged: 4-26-1865. Pension: Cullman Co., Ala.

Isbell, George Munroe, Pvt., **H**, Enlisted: 4-64, Tallapoosa, Ga., by Captain Tumlin. Absent 12-64 Sick. Surrendered: Greensboro, N.C. 4-26-1865. Died: 10-3-1922. Buried: Euharlee Presbyterian Church, Bartow Co., Ga.

Isbell, Jeremiah H. (Marion), Pvt., **H**, Enlisted: 5-62, Haralson Co., Ga., by Captain Tumlin. Present through 12-62. Absent 2-63 sick furlough. AWOL 10-20-63. Present 12-64. Pension:

2-1865 Co. H was detailed to recruit captured stock and on detail at surrender. Died: 4-22-1913. Buried: Shiloh Baptist Church, Eson Hill, Ga.

Isbell William, Pvt., **A**, Enlisted: 8-63, Cedartown, Ga., by Captain York. Present through 12-64. Paroled: Charlotte, N.C. 5-3-1865.

Ivy (Ivie), Elisha Floyd, Pvt., **F**, Enlisted: 3-62, Fairmount, Ga., by Col. Morrison. Absent though 10-62 sick furlough. WIA near Stones River, Murfreesboro 1-1-63. Left wounded and Died: 2-63.

Izzell, F.N., Pvt., **H**, Enlisted: 11-63, Kingston, Tenn., by Captain Tumlin. 12-31-1863 present.

Jackson, Alonzo C., Pvt., **B**, Enlisted: 3-62 in Newnan, Ga. Present through 12-64. Surrendered: Greensboro, N.C. 4-26-1865. Died: 1-28-1919. Buried: Forsyth City Cemetery, Monroe Co., Ga.

Jackson, James Madison, 2nd Lt., **H**, Enlisted: 4-62, Haralson Co., Ga., by Captain Tumlin. Present through 12-62. Promoted Orderly Sergeant 1-28-63. Promoted 8-5-63 2nd Lt., Col. Morrison. WIA: legs (left hip joint) 12-12-63, Russellville, Tenn. Certificate: Gunshot: fractured; upper third, left thigh, shorting leg by 3". Died: 7-22-1886. Buried: Elim Baptist Church, Handy, Ga.

Jackson, J.L., Surgeon.

Jackson, John M., Pvt., **E**, Enlisted: 3-62, Carrollton, Ga., by Captain Blalock. Present through 2-63. Captured near Somerset, Ky. 3-30-63. Carried: Louisville; City Point, Va. 4-13-1863; exchanged.

Jackson, William Perry, Pvt., **F**, Enlisted: 10-63, Chattanooga by Lt. McWilliams. Present through 12-64. Surrendered: Greensboro, N.C. 4-26-1865. Died: 3-20-1926. Buried: New Hope Church, Gray, Ga.

Jacobs, Anderson, Pvt., **E**, Enlisted: 3-62, Carrollton, Ga., by Captain Blalock. Present through 8-62. Discharged 10-3-62. Died: 1934: Russell Co., Ala.

Jacobs, James F., Cpl., **K**, Enlisted: 5-62, Camp Morrison by Captain North. Present through 12-62. Absent 2-63 Sick furlough in Coweta Co., Ga. Captured near Somerset, Ky. 3-30-63. Carried: Louisville; City Point, Va. 4-13-1863; exchanged.

Jacobs, William B., Sgt., **E**, Enlisted: 3-62, Carrollton, Ga., by Captain Blalock. Present through 2-63. WIA near Mossy Creek, Tenn. 12-29-63. Died: Bull's Gap, Tenn. Hospital 1-17-64.

James, William, Pvt., **I**, Enlisted: 12-62, Camp Morrison by Captain Leak. Present through

12-64. Pension: Col. Davitte led him and several others to leave before surrender to cross Mississippi River and join other fighting units to continue war. Paroled: Kingston, Ga. May 1865. Died: 8-26-1925, Fulton Co., Ga.

Jarrell, Jacob Redding, Pvt., **A**, Enlisted: 3-62, Cedartown, Ga., by Captain John C. Crabb. 6-62 Sick furlough in Polk Co., Ga. Present through 12-62. Absent 2-63 sick furlough home. Absent 12-63 Cut off with wagons. Deserted 11-20-64. Pension: Polk Co., Ga., 1897 stated he was at surrender. Died: 1900-1910 Polk Co., Ga.

Jenkins, James Madison, Cpl., **I**, Enlisted: 5-62, Camp Morrison by Captain Leak. Present through 12-31-1864. Died: 2-25-1891. Buried: Myrtle Hill, Rome, Ga.

Jenkins, John Thomas, Pvt., **I**, Enlisted: 9-64, Surrendered: Salisbury, N.C. May 1865. Died: 7-30-1896. Buried: Myrtle Hill, Rome, Ga.

Jenkins, William Francis (Bud), Pvt., **I**, Enlisted: 5-62, Camp Morrison by Captain Leak. Present through 12-31-1864. Pension: Sick with measles and typhoid fever. Died: 5-23-1900 Floyd Co., Ga.

Jennings, F.A.B., 1st Lt., **K**, Surrendered: Augusta, Ga., 5-23-1865, paroled.

Jett, Stephen L., Pvt., **E**, Enlisted: 3-62, Carrolton, Ga., by Captain Blalock. Present through 2-63. Absent 12-64 Detached to Government Shop.

Johns, Benjah Marshall, Pvt., **A**, Enlisted: Cedartown, Ga., 21st Ga. Inf. 6-27-61. Discharged: 11-22-61 with tuberculosis. Certificate: born Pittsylvania Co., Va., age 22, 5'-8", sallow complexion, grey eyes, dark hair. Enlisted: 1st Ga. Cavalry 12-1-62, Cedartown, Ga., by Captain Hutchings. Absent 12-62 sick furlough home. Discharged 2-18-63. Received clothing issue 3rd Qtr. 1864. KIA: Atlanta 7-20-1864. Buried: Greenwood Cemetery, Barnesville, Ga.

Johns, Grandberry, Pvt., **C**, Enlisted: 3-62, Cave Spring, Ga., by Captain Haynie. Died: 4-20-62 typhoid fever, Cave Spring, Ga.

Johnson, A., Pvt., **H**, Enlisted: 5-64, Tallapoosa, Ga., by Captain Tumlin. Clothing issued 6-64. 12-64 AWOL.

Johnson, Asa R., Pvt., **K**, Enlisted: 5-62, Newnan, Ga., by Captain North. Present through 8-62. Discharged 9-22-62 age 50. Certificate: born 1812, S.C., 5'-5", fair complexion, blue eyes, light hair. Signed: Lt. W.W. Carmical, commander of detachment at Kingston, Tenn.

Johnson, James L.B., Pvt., **A**, Enlisted: 3-62, Cedartown, Ga., by Captain John C. Crabb. Absent 6-62 Sick furlough: Calhoun Co., Ala. Discharged 8-8-62.

Johnson, J.P., Pvt., **G**, Enlisted: 5-62, Camp Morrison by Captain Leak. Present through 12-62. Absent 3-63 Detachment Camp. Present through 12-64. Paroled: Augusta, Ga., 5-23-1865.

Johnson, J.W., Sgt., **G**, Enlisted: 5-62, Camp Morrison by Captain Leak. Present through 12-62. Absent 3-63: Detachment Camp. Absent 12-63: Detached to guard horses in Ga. Present 12-64. Surrendered: Greensboro, N.C. 4-26-1865. Died: 6-23-1904, Gordon Co., Ga.

Johnson, L.C., Pvt., **G**, Enlisted: 12-63, Decatur, Ga., by Major Andrews. Absent 12-64 Detailed to attend disabled horses and sent to Eufaula, Ala. 9-15-64. Paroled: Albany, Ga., 5-7-1865. Description: 5'-11½", grey hair, blue eyes, dark complexion.

Johnson, Nathaniel "Nat" J., Pvt., **H**, Enlisted: 8-62, Kingston, Tenn., by Captain Tumlin. Substitute for Jonathan Dobbs. Present 12-63. Clothing issued Gen. Hospital, Liberty Va. 3-7-64. AWOL 12-31-1864. Died: 8-29-1915. Buried: New Harmony Cemetery, Heflin, Ala.

Johnson, Snelling A., Pvt., **K**, Enlisted: 1-64, Cartersville, Ga., by Captain North. Present 12-64. Paroled: Charlotte, N.C. 5-3-1865.

Johnson, Thomas Lafayette, Sgt., **F**, Enlisted: 3-62, Fairmount, Ga., by Col. Morrison. Absent through 10-62 sick furlough. Present 12-62 through 12-64. Appointed 1st Cpl. 7-1-63. Pension: WIA 7-21-64 Atlanta; Surrendered: Greensboro, N.C. 4-26-1865. Rode home with O.R. Bradley. Died: 7-7-1928. Buried: Johnson Cemetery, Gordon Co., Ga.

Johnson, William, Pvt., **I**, Enlisted: 5-62, Mustered 12-62 at Cartersville, Ga. Present through 12-64. Paroled: Charlotte, N.C. 5-3-1865. Pension: WIA: Blaine's Crossroads, Tenn. 12-1862. In line of battle, horse was shot, reared up and fell backwards on him injuring right shoulder. Discharged. Pension: 1902, Bartow Co., Ga.

Johnson, William H., Pvt., **G**, Enlisted: 3-62, Floyd Co., Ga., by Captain Kerr. Present through 2-63. Absent 12-63 in Ga. Captured 5-18-64 by Wilder's Cavalry 9 miles east, Rome, Ga. at Bass Ferry on Etowah River. 5-18-64. Carried: Nashville; Louisville; Rock Island, Ill. Released 5-22-1865. Description: age 27, 5'-9", dark complexion, black hair, grey eyes. Died: 8-1907, Walker Co., Ga.

Johnson, William R., Pvt., **F**, Enlisted: 12-62, Spring Creek, Tenn., by Captain Reynolds. Died: 2-8-63, Kingston, Tenn.

Jones, Frank C., Pvt., **K**, Enlisted: 4-63, Mouse (Mossy) Creek, Tenn., by Captain Leak. Present

12-63. Absent 12-64 Sick: Macon, Ga. Hospital. Paroled: Charlotte, N.C. 5-3-1865.

Jones, Henry, Pvt., **E**. (Possible: Brother, William Moses Jones and John Thomas Jones. Enlisted in 7th Ga. Inf. for 12 months. Discharged 6-62. Died: 6-26-1910. Buried: Pine Grove Primitive Baptist Church, Cherokee Co., Ala.)

Jones, Isaac Newton, Jr., Pvt., **A**, Enlisted: 5-62, Camp Morrison by Captain John C. Crabb. Present through 2-63. Absent 12-63 Cut off with wagons. Captured: Atlanta 7-20-64. Carried: Chattanooga; Nashville; Louisville; Camp Chase 8-2-64. Transferred 3-4-1865 City Point, Va., exchanged. Oklahoma Pension Board inquired.

Jones, Isaac Y., Pvt., **E**, Filed pension: Cleburne Co., Ala. Died: 8-22-1897.

Jones, James Jethro Peter, Cpl., **E**, Enlisted: 5-62, Cartersville, Ga., by Captain Blalock. Present through 12-62. Absent 2-63 Detachment: Kingston, Tenn. Captured: Atlanta 7-21-64. Carried: Chattanooga; Nashville; Louisville; Camp Chase 8-2-64. Transferred 3-4-1865: City Point, Va., exchanged. Received: Wayside Hospital, Richmond, Va. 3-11-1865. Died: 11-29-1907. Buried: Jones/Watson Family Cemetery, Whitesburg, Ga.

Jones, John A., Pvt., **K**, Enlisted 7th Ga. Inf. 5-31-61, Atlanta. Enlisted: 5-62, Cartersville, Ga., by Major Harper. Present through 8-62. Present 10-62 and 12-62: Wagoner. Absent 12-63 and 12-64: Teamster for Brigade. Paroled: Charlotte, N.C. 5-3-1865.

Jones, John Thomas, Pvt., **E**, Enlisted: 5-62, Cartersville, Ga., by Captain Blalock. Surrendered: Raleigh, N.C. 4-26-1865. Died: 3-20-1921. Buried: St. Paul Methodist, Whitesburg, Ga.

Jones, Nathaniel Cornelius, Pvt., **E**, Enlisted: 5-62, Cartersville, Ga., by Captain Blalock. Present through 12-63. WIA 12-31-63: East Tenn. WIA: New Hope Church, Ga., 5-19-1864. Gunshot: arm, broken and useless. 2-3 inches bone removed. Discharged. Died: 9-1-1910. Buried: Jones Family Cemetery, Stonewood, Carroll Co., Ga.

Jones, Robert Haywood, Pvt., **G**, Enlisted: 3-64, Cartersville, Ga., by Captain Lamar. Present 12-64 and Lost 1 short Enfield rifle 12-21-64. Died: 7-15-1914, Hunt, Texas.

Jones, T. Frank, Pvt., **A**, Enlisted: 3-62, Cedartown, Ga., by Captain John C. Crabb. Present 6-62. Absent 8-62 Sick: Kingston, Tenn. Present 10-62 through 2-63. Absent 12-63. Cut off with wagons. Present 12-64. Surrendered: Greensboro, N.C. 4-26-1865. Died: 4-12-1914. Buried: Rose Hill Cemetery, Rockmart, Ga.

Jones, Thomas Wells, Pvt., **D**, Enlisted: 3-62, Dallas, Ga., by Captain Seawright. Present 10-62 and 12-62. Absent 2-63 Sick furlough: Paulding Co., Ga. 12-63 Sick: Atlanta Hospital. Pension: Nearly lost sight, left eye, in battle. Sick: 5-64, Dallas, Ga., and sent home. Discharged: Kingston, Ga., 5-1865.

Jones, Wiley, Pvt., **D**, Enlisted: 3-62, Dallas, Ga., age 23, by Captain Seawright. Present 6-62 as Teamster. Absent 8-62 on scout. Present 10-62 through 2-63. AWOL 2-63. Died: 4-21-1904. Buried: Jones Cemetery, Dallas, Ga.

Jones, William Daniel, Pvt., **G**, Enlisted: 8-64, Covington, Ga., by Lt. Webster. Present 12-64. Surrendered: Raleigh, N.C. 4-26-1865. Died: 6-1-1925. Buried: Myrtle Hill, Rome, Ga.

Jones, William H., Sgt., List: deserted 9-3-1864, Chattanooga, took oath. Description: light complexion, light hair, blue eyes, 5'-11". Released: 6-17-1865.

Jones, William M., Pvt., **K**, Enlisted: 8-63, Newnan, Ga., by Captain North. Present 12-63 and 12-1864.

Jones, William Moses, Sgt., **E**, Enlisted: 3-62, Carrollton, Ga., by Captain Blalock. Present 8-62 and 10-62. Transferred: 4-64, 1st Regt. Ga. State Troops. Died: 12-18-1917. Buried: Carrollton City Cemetery, Carroll Co., Ga.

Jordan, H.R., Pvt., **F**, Surrendered: Augusta, Ga., 5-19-1865, paroled.

Jordan, Isaac, Pvt., **H**, Enlisted: 1-63, Kingston, Tenn., by Captain Tumlin. Absent 2-63: Detached service, Kingston Tenn. Absent 12-63: Detached with Battery. Substitute for James S. Tumlin 1-14-1863.

Junior, A., Pvt., **C**, Paroled: Talladega, Ala. 6-1-1865.

Junior, Austin, Pvt., **H**, Enlisted: 4-62, Haralson Co., Ga., by Captain Tumlin. Present through 8-62. Discharged: 10-62. Died: 1884. Buried: Shoal Creek Cemetery, Cleburne Co., Ala.

Junior, Henry, Pvt., Enlisted: 4-62, Haralson Co., Ga., by Captain Tumlin. Died: 6-30-62, Knoxville hospital: fever.

Keith, Abselom Blye, Sgt., **E**, Enlisted: Tallapoosa, Ga. Served until Spring 1864 when furloughed home and stayed until end of war. Died: 8-12-1923. Buried: Central Baptist Church, Trussville, Ala.

Keith, Joel Mackey, Pvt., **H**, Enlisted: 1863, Discharged 1865. Paroled: Talladega, Ala. Died: 6-22-1923, Jefferson Co., Ala.

Kelley, B.M., Pvt. POW: Camp Morton; Johnson's Island; Vicksburg. Exchanged 11-22-1862 aboard steamer *Charm*.

Kelley, Henry B., Pvt., **H**, Surrendered: Augusta, Ga., 5-27-1865, paroled.

Kelley, Thomas M., Captain, **F**, Enlisted: 3-62, Carrollton, Ga., by Captain Blalock. Elected 2nd Lt. 3-21-62. Promoted 1st Lt. 8-6-62, death of Andrew C. Velvin by Gen. Maxey. Present through 12-62. Absent 2-63 sick. Promoted: Captain, resignation James M. Blalock 12-12-63 by Gen. Pegram. Resigned: 1-25-64. Died: 1-31-1911. Buried: Jordan Memorial Cemetery, Carroll Co., Ga.

Kelly, William E., Pvt., **C**, Enlisted: 5-62, Cave Spring, Ga., by Lt. Reynolds. Present through 8-62 without a horse. Present 10-62 and 12-62. Absent 2-63: Detailed: Captain Marshall's Company Brown Horse Artillery. Captured: Big Hill, Ky. 7-30-63. Carried: Louisville 8-3-63; Camp Chase 8-7-63; Fort Delaware 3-4-64. Released 5-5-1865. Description: home Cherokee Co., Ala., 5'-8", fair complexion, blue eyes, auburn hair.

Kemp, James G., Pvt., **D**, Enlisted: 3-62, Dallas, Ga., by Captain Seawright. Present 8-62 and 10-62. Absent 12-62 Sick furlough: Paulding Co., Ga. Absent 12-63 Sick: Atlanta Hospital. Living: Acorn Tree District, Paulding Co., Ga., 1880.

Kennedy, James, Pvt., **I**, Enlisted: 5-62, Camp Morrison by Captain Leak. Present through 12-62. Absent 3-63: Detachment Camp. Detailed Company blacksmith 8-10-63. Present 10-63 and 12-64. Surrendered: Greensboro, N.C. 4-26-1865. Died: 2-21-1880. Buried: Oak Hill Cemetery, Cartersville, Ga.

Kerr, Andrew A., Pvt., **H**, Enlisted: 4-62, Haralson Co., Ga., by Captain Tumlin. Present 6-62. WIA: Loudon, Ky., left leg, 8-17-62. Furlough: Ala. Absent 10-62 through 12-63 wounded furlough. Clothing issued 6-64. 12-64 present. Died: 8-27-1906. Buried: Mars Hill Cemetery, Cleburne Co., Ala.

Kerr, John L., Captain, **G**, Enlisted: Rome, Ga., 3-13-1862 by Lt. Col Morrison. Company called Highland Rangers. Elected Captain 3-13-62. WIA: Murfreesboro 7-13-62. Present through 2-63. Present 12-63 and 12-64. Arrested: 12-13-63 misbehavior before enemy. Paroled: Charlotte, N.C. 5-3-1865.

Kilgore, Francis Marion, Pvt., **H**, Enlisted: 8-62, Kingston, Tenn., by Captain Tumlin. Present through 2-63. AWOL 8-25-63. Died: 2-14-1913. Buried: Kilgore Family Cemetery, Haralson Co., Ga.

King, James L., Pvt., **G**, Enlisted: 5-64, Rome, Ga., by Col. Cameron. Clothing issued 6-64. Sick: hospital 7-7-1864.

King, Nathan, Pvt., **B**, Enlisted: 3-62, Newnan, Ga., age 36, by Captain Strickland. Absent 6-62: Hos-

pital Loudon, Tenn. Discharged 7-5-62 Loudon, Tenn. Certificate: born Taliaferro Co., Ga., age 37, 5'-9", fair complexion, brown eyes, light hair, boot maker. Pension: Coweta Co., Ga., 1906.

King, W.H., Pvt., **G**, Enlisted: 3-62, Floyd Co., Ga., by Captain Kerr. Present 6-62. Discharged: 8-6-62 disabled. Certificate: born Gwinnett Co., Ga., age 28, 5'-10", fair complexion, blue eyes, auburn hair.

Kingsbery, Charles Samuel, Pvt., **E**, Enlisted: 3-62, Carrollton, Ga., by Captain Blalock. Present through 12-62. Absent 2-63: Detached: Commissary Dept. Present 12-63. Present 12-64 Detailed to Commissary Dept. Paroled: Charlotte, N.C. 5-3-1865. Died: 8-25-1908. Buried: Oakland Cemetery, Atlanta, Ga.

Kingsbery, Joseph, Sgt., **E**, Enlisted: 5-62, Carrollton, Ga., by Captain Blalock. Present 12-62 as Regimental Commissary. Appointed Sgt. 11-1-62. Absent 2-63 sick furlough home. Present 12-63 and 12-64: Detailed to Commissary Dept. Paroled: Charlotte, N.C. 5-3-1865. Died: 1-4-1929. Buried: Oakland Cemetery, Atlanta, Ga.

Kingston, T.H., Pvt., Surrendered: Thomasville, Ga., 5-24-1865.

Kinman, James Polk, Pvt., **I**, Enlisted: 5-62, Camp Morrison by Captain Leak. Present through 12-62. Absent 3-63: Detachment Camp. Captured: Somerset, Ky. 3-30-63. Carried: Louisville; City Point, Va. Exchanged 4-13-63. WIA: Chickamauga 9-19-63. Gunshot: left foot, inside below ankle; lodged at second bone from little toe. Present 12-64. Paroled: Charlotte, N.C. 5-3-1865. Died: 7-4-1917. Buried: Kinman Cemetery, Lily Pond, Ga.

Kirby, John Terrell, Pvt., **B**, Died: 12-25-1902. Buried: Oak Hill Cemetery, Newnan, Ga.

Kirby, Moses Russell, Pvt., **B**, Died: 4-28-1921. Buried: Hill View Cemetery, LaGrange, Ga.

Kirk, George W., Pvt., **D**, Enlisted: 2-64, Dallas, Ga., by Captain Robert F. Trammell. 12-64 AWOL. Surrendered: Greensboro, N.C. 4-26-1865. Died: 10-18-1905. Buried: Allgood Methodist Church, Dallas, Ga.

Kline, Leander A., Pvt., **D**, Sick in Knoxville, never recovered. Died: 11-11-1898. Widow pension: Etowah Co., Ala.

Knight, Matthew, Pvt., **C**, Enlisted: 3-62, Cave Spring, Ga., by Captain Haynie. Present 6-62. Present 8-62 as Wagoner. Present 10-62 and 12-62. Discharged 1-22-63. Died: 10-28-1883, Meriwether Co., Ga.

Lackey, W.J., Pvt., **G**, Enlisted: 4-62, Camp Morrison by Captain Leak. Absent 6-62 Discharged.

Reenlisted: Served until 5-1865 with Cowan's Scouts. Paroled: Kingston, Ga., 5-1865. Pension: Calhoun Co., Ala. 1900.

Lackey, W.L., Pvt., **G**, WIA: Cartersville, Ga., 1864. Pension: Calhoun Co., Ala.

Laird, James, Pvt., **C**, Captured: Greenville, S.C. 5-23-1865, paroled.

Lake, J.C., Pvt., **C**, Enlisted: 9-64, in field by Captain Watts. 12-31-1864 present.

Lamar, L.L., Sgt., **A**, Enlisted: 2-63, Hancock Co., Ga., by Captain Hutchings. Appointed Acting Orderly Sgt. Present 12-64 and Appointed Acting Commissary by Col. Davitte. Paroled: Charlotte, N.C. 5-3-1865.

Lambert, Noah Augustus, Pvt., **B**, Enlisted: 4-62, Cartersville, Ga., by Col. Morrison. Present through 2-63. Absent in Rome, Ga. Hospital 11-12-63. Present 12-64. Pension: WIA: Macon, Ga., 1864. Gunshot through right chest. 5-65 detailed by Col. Watts: collect tithes for army in Meriwether Co., Ga.

Land, Zedekiah, Pvt., Pension: Captured: Cobb Co., Ga., 1-19-64. Captured: Paulding Co., Ga. Took oath: Chattanooga 7-11-1864. Description: home Paulding Co., Ga., light complexion, dark hair, blue eyes, 5'-7". Died: 1909. Buried: New Canaan Cemetery, Dallas, Ga.

Lanier, James Crawford, Sgt., **D**, Enlisted: 10-63, Served for eighteen months. Died: 10-23-1912. Buried: Lanier Cemetery, Grasmere, Ala.

Lankford, Edwin P., Pvt., **D**, Enlisted: 3-62, Dallas, Ga., age 26, by Captain Seawright. Present 6-62. Absent 8-62 Sick furlough: Paulding Co., Ga. AWOL 9-63. Clothing issued 6-7-64. 12-64 present.

Lard, James M., Pvt., **E**, Enlisted: 3-62, Carrollton, Ga., by Captain Blalock. 4-17-1862 paid $50. bounty.

Lassetter (Lassiter), William Cheadle, Pvt., **E**, Enlisted: 8-63, Ebenezer, Tenn., by Lt. Col. Harper. Present 12-63. Absent 12-64 Sick. Died: 2-16-1888. Buried: St. Paul Methodist Church Cemetery, Whitesburg, Ga.

Lawrence, Cicero Homer, Pvt., Attended 1911 Veterans meeting Ark. Died: 7-21-1926. Buried: Oak Cemetery, Fort Smith, Ark.

Leak, Barnett, Pvt., **G**, Enlisted: 4-62, Floyd Co., Ga., by Captain Kerr. Absent 6-62 Rejected. Died: 4-26-1895. Buried: Salmon Cemetery, Floyd Co., Ga.

Leak, John Fletcher, Captain, **I**, Enlisted: Camp Morrison 5-1-1862 by Lt. Col. Morrison. Elected Captain 5-1-62. Present through 12-62. Absent 2-63 sick furlough. Absent 10-63 Detached serv-

ice: Bartow Co., Ga. Absent 12-64 sick. Granted permission to go before Medical board for retirement 2-1865. Admitted: Ocmulgee Hospital, Macon, Ga., 2-4-65. Diagnosed: chronic nephritis. Discharged: 4-18-1865. Died: 6-27-1904. Buried: Carmel Cemetery, Spring Garden, Ala.

Leake, James H., 2nd Lt., **D**, 3-62, WIA, sent home by Captain Robert Trammell. Never returned. Died: 1917. Buried: Norman Park, Colquitt Co., Ga.

Ledbetter, Charles D., Pvt., **F**, Enlisted: 3-62, Fairmount, Ga., by Col. Morrison. Present 6-62. Absent 8-62 and 10-62. Horse KIA: Somerset, Ky. 3-30-63. Paid 8-20-63 $250. Present through 12-63. Captured: Resaca, Ga., 8-14-64. On list of deserters at Louisville 9-1-64. Took oath; discharged 9-4-1864. Description: home Gordon Co., Ga., 5'-10", blue eyes, light hair, light complexion.

Ledbetter, Humphrey Posey, Pvt., **F**, Enlisted: 3-62, Fairmount, Ga., by Col. Morrison. Absent 6-62. Present through 12-62. Absent 12-63 in Ga. with wagons. Living: Gordon Co., Ga., 1870.

Lester, James Q. (O.), Pvt., **E**, Enlisted: 3-62, Carrollton, Ga., by Captain Blalock. Present 6-62. Absent 10-62: Left in Ky. 2-63 AWOL. Captured: Pennington Gap, Lee Co., Va. 3-21-64. Carried: Louisville 3-29-64, Camp Chase 4-3-64. Died: Camp Chase Prison 12-3-64, smallpox. Buried: Camp Chase Confederate Cemetery, Columbus, Ohio. Grave # 549.

Lester, Joseph Henry, Pvt., **D**, Enlisted: 3-62, Dallas, Ga., age 22, by Captain Seawright. Present 6-62: Teamster. Present through 12-62. AWOL 2-63.

Lewis, Baylis Washington Harrison, Cpl., **F**, Enlisted: 3-62, Fairmount, Ga., by Col. Morrison. Absent through 10-62 sick furlough. Present 12-62 and 2-63. Captured: Somerset, Ky. 3-30-63. Carried: Louisville 4-13-63; City Point, Va. Exchanged 4-13-63. Returned to regiment and captured. Took oath 2-14-64. Description: home Gordon Co., Ga., dark complexion, brown hair, light eyes, 5'-9". Enlisted: U.S. 10th Tenn. Cavalry 4-10-1864. Age 22, born: Cass Co., Ga. Died: 11-15-1915. Buried: Big Hurricane Cemetery, Brookwood, Ala.

Lewis, Henry F.T., Pvt., **D**, Enlisted: 3-62, Dallas, Ga., age 19, by Captain Seawright. Teamster 5-1-62. Present through 12-62. Absent 2-63 Sick furlough: Paulding Co., Ga. Absent 12-63 Detained in Ga., by General Wheeler. Absent 12-64 Detached with Battery.

Lewis, James, Pvt., **I**, Enlisted: 3-64, Cass Station, Ga., by Captain Leak. Deserted 3-1-64.

Lewis, J.S., Pvt., **D**, Enlisted: 3-62, Dallas, Ga., by Captain Seawright. Present through 10-62. Captured: Clay Village, Ky. 10-4-62, paroled 1-11-63. AWOL 1-64.

Lewis, M.R., Sgt., **A**, Enlisted: 3-62, Cedartown, Ga., by Captain John C. Crabb. Absent 6-62 Sick furlough: Polk Co., Ga. Discharged 6-3-62. Buried: Ammons Family Cemetery, Polk Co., Ga.

Lewis, Tarlton, 1st Lt., **F**, Enlisted: 3-62, Fair Mount, Ga., by Col. Morrison. Elected 2nd Lt. 3-22-62. Absent 6-62 sick furlough. Present 8-62 and 10-62. Promoted 1st Lt. 9-17-62, by Col. Morrison. WIA in Ky. Left wounded and Died: 12-25-62.

Lewis, W.T., Pvt., **I**, Enlisted: 5-62, Camp Morrison by Captain Leak. Present through 10-63. Absent 12-64 sick. Surrendered: Greensboro, N.C. 4-26-1865. Died: 12-24-1894, Floyd Co., Ga.

Liles, F.D.(aka. **Virgil D.**), Pvt., **F**, Enlisted: 1-64, Sevierville, Tenn., by Lt. McWilliams. Captured: Gordon Co., Ga. Carried: Chattanooga 7-29-64. On list of deserters at Louisville 8-3-64. Took oath, released 8-4-1864. Description: home Gordon Co., Ga., light complexion, light hair, grey eyes, 5'-8½".

Liles, William W., Pvt., Deserted, took oath: Chattanooga 5-29-1864. Description: home Gorgon Co., Ga., fair complexion, light hair, blue eyes, 5'-6".

Linn, Frank, Pvt., **A**, Captured: Macon, Ga., 4-20-1865.

Linn, James H., Sgt., **F**, Enlisted: 3-62, Fairmount, Ga., by Col. Morrison. Present through 12-62. Detailed: Acting Commissary Dept. 9-10-62. Absent 2-63 on furlough. Appointed Sgt. 9-6-63. Captured: Philadelphia, Tenn. 10-20-63. Carried: Camp Nelson; Camp Chase 11-14-63; Rock Island, Ill. Prison 1-24-1864.

Lipscomb, Nathan, Pvt., **B**, Enlisted: 3-62, Newnan, Ga., age 28, by Captain Strickland. Absent 6-62: Detailed as Asst. Forage master. Kingston, Tenn. Present 8-62. Absent 10-62 Sick furlough: LaGrange, Ga.

Lisle, E., 1st Sgt., **C**, Enlisted: 3-62, Present 4-6-1862.

Lisle (Lyle), W.A., Pvt., **G**, Enlisted: 3-62, Floyd Co., Ga., by Captain Kerr. Present 6-62. Died: 8-26-62, Sparta, Tenn., bilious fever. Father John P. Lyle, Eldridge, Ala.

Little, Elijah Marion, Pvt., **H**, Enlisted: 4-62, Haralson Co., Ga., by Captain Tumlin. Substitute. Present through 2-63. Absent 12-63 sick furlough. 12-64 AWOL. Pension: Sick: chronic diarrhea, Fall 1864. Furloughed home and never

returned. Died: 8-28-1886. Buried: Mount Zion West, Tallapoosa, Ga.

Little, John, Pvt., **D**, Enlisted: 3-62, Dallas, Ga., age 18, by Captain Seawright. Paid 4-17-1862.

Little, John Calvin, Pvt., **D**, Enlisted, 3-62, Dallas, Ga., age 21, by Captain Seawright. Present 6-62. Absent 8-62 on scout. Present 10-62 and 12-62. Absent 2-63 Sick furlough: Paulding Co., Ga. KIA: Mossy Creek, Tenn. 12-29-63.

Little, John William, Pvt., **H**, Enlisted: Buchanan, Ga., 35th Ga. Inf. 9-19-61. WIA: Manassas, Va. 8-29-62. Enlisted 6-1-63: Tallapoosa, Ga., by Captain Tumlin. AWOL 10-15-1863. Died: 3-10-1907. Buried: East Mount Cemetery, Greenville, Texas.

Little, Thomas Jefferson, 2nd Lt., **H**, Enlisted: 4-62, Tallapoosa, Ga., by Captain Tumlin. Elected 2nd Lt. 4-19-62. Absent 6-62 Sick: Chattanooga. Certificate: typhoid pneumonia, Dr. Boyd. Resigned: 8-15-63. Died: 7-9-1874. Buried: Mount Zion West Cemetery, Haralson Co., Ga.

Little, William, 2nd Lt., **F**, Enlisted: 3-62, Fairmount, Ga., by Col. Morrison. Present through 10-62. Captured: Frankfort, Ky. 10-16-62. Carried: Vicksburg 11-29-62, steamboat, Mary Crane, exchanged. Description: age 21, 5'-9½", grey eyes, dark hair, light complexion. Present 2-62 and 12-63. Appointed 2nd Lt., by Col. Morrison. Promoted by Gen. Martin 1-25-64.

Lloyd, John W., Pvt., **B**, Enlisted: 3-62, Newnan, Ga., age 30, by Captain Strickland. Present through 12-62. Absent 2-63 Sick furlough: Rocky Mount, Ga. Present 12-63. Absent 12-64 Courier for Gen. Iverson.

Lockridge, George W., Pvt., **I**, Enlisted: 8-62, Kingston, Tenn., by Captain Leak. Present through 12-62. Absent 3-63 Sick furlough.

Logan, A., Pvt., **A**, 6-62, Courier.

Logan, Riley Thomas, Pvt., **A**, Enlisted: 6-62, Rome, Ga., by Lt. Hutchings. Present 2-63. Present 12-63 Col. Morrison's orderly. AWOL 11-20-64. Surrendered: Greensboro, N.C. 4-26-1865. Died: 1-27-1919. Buried: Myrtle Hill, Rome, Ga.

Long, B.A., Pvt., **G**, Captured 4-30-1865 Macon, Ga.

Long, D.A., Sgt., **G**, Enlisted: 3-62, Floyd Co., Ga., by Captain Kerr. Absent 6-62 through 10-62 Sick furlough: Coosa Co., Ga. Discharged disabled: 12-4-62. Certificate: born Pike Co., Ga., age 30, 5'-11", fair complexion, grey eyes, light hair. Admitted: Ocmulgee Hospital 10-29-63, fever. Discharged 10-31-63.

Looney, James B., Pvt., **D**, Captured: Greenville, S.C. 5-23-1865, paroled.

Lorren, George A., Pvt., **H**, Enlisted: 4-62, Tallapoosa, Ga., by Captain Tumlin. Present through 8-62. Absent 10-62 Discharged.

Lorren, Warren Jefferson, Pvt. **H**, Enlisted: 11-63, Died: 11-22-1914. Buried: Oak Level UMC, Cleburne Co., Ala.

Loveless, Harrison Abner, Sgt., **G**, Enlisted: 5-62, Camp Morrison by Captain Leak. Present through 12-64. Paroled: Charlotte, N.C. 5-3-1865. Died: 2-4-1910 Bartow Co., Ga.

Lovinggood, Benjamin Marion, Sgt., **D**, Enlisted: 3-62, Dallas, Ga., age 25, by Captain Seawright. Died: 11-1-1920. Buried: Whitmire Methodist Church, Salem, S.C.

Lowery (Lancy), Lewis Monroe, Pvt., **G**, Enlisted: 8-63, Rome, Ga., by Captain Kerr. Absent 12-63 in Ga. Captured: Rome, Ga., 10-6-64. Carried: Lexington; Louisville 10-25-64; Camp Douglas 10-28-64. Released: 6-17-1865. Description: home Floyd Co., Ga., dark complexion, dark hair, grey eyes, 5'-4". Died: Clarksville, Texas 1895.

Lumpkin, T., Pvt., **A**, Enlisted: 8-63, Cedartown, Ga., by Captain York. 12-31-1863 present.

Lumpkin, William J., Pvt., **C**, Enlisted: Cave Spring, Ga., Floyd Legion State Guards 7-11-1863. Enlisted: 9-64, 1st Ga. Cavalry by Captain Watts. 12-31-1864 present.

Lumpkin, William Saulsberry, Pvt., **G**, Enlisted: 3-62, Floyd Co., Ga., by Captain Kerr. Absent 6-62 Sick: Rome, Ga. Discharged: Kingston, Tenn. 8-6-62. Certificate: born Oglethorpe Co., Ga., age 36, 5'-10", florid complexion, grey eyes, red hair. Diagnosed: consumption with hemorrhage. Died: 1-2-1895. Buried: Oakland Cemetery, Atlanta, Ga.

Lyle, Evans Hugh, 1st Lt., **C**, Enlisted: 3-62, Cave Spring, Ga., by Lt. Reynolds. Promoted 1st Sgt. 3-31-62. Present 6-62 through 6-63. Promoted 2nd Lt. 5-15-63. Assigned duty as 1st Lt. 8-3-64. Present 12-64. Promoted by Col. Davitte 12-21-64. Died: 12-29-1883. Buried: Cave Spring Cemetery, Floyd Co., Ga.

Lynch, N.A., Pvt., **B**, Enlisted: 3-64, Newnan, Ga., by Lt. Taylor. 12-31-1864 AWOL.

Lynch, Rufus Wade, Pvt., **B**, Enlisted: 1-63, Surrendered: Greensboro, N.C. 4-26-1865. Attended 1911 Veterans meeting Ark. Died: 3-28-1929. Buried: Oak Hill Cemetery, Griffin, Ga.

Lyon, Starling M., Pvt., **A**, Enlisted: 3-62, Cedartown, Ga., by Captain John C. Crabb. Absent 6-62 sick furlough home. Present 10-62 through 12-64. Company teamster. Paroled: Charlotte, N.C. 5-3-1865. Died: 8-24-1911. Buried: Pleasant Hope Cemetery, Rome, Ga.

Lyon, Thomas P., Pvt., **A**, Enlisted: 3-62, Cedartown, Ga., by Captain John C. Crabb. Present 6-62. Absent 8-62 Sick: Loudon, Tenn. Absent 10-62 and 12-62 sick furlough home. Present 2-63 through 12-31-1864. WIA, captured: Ky. Died: Polk Co., Ga. after 1880.

Lyons, Richard M., 1st Sgt., **A**, Enlisted: 5-62, Cedartown, Ga., by Captain John C. Crabb. Present 6-62. In three man charge. Absent 8-62 Sick: Kingston, Tenn. Promoted 1st Sgt. 8-1-62. Absent 12-62 and 2-63 sick furlough home. Present 12-63. AWOL 11-10-1864.

Maas, Richard, Pvt., Deserted, took oath 11-9-62. Paroled.

Macier, T., Pvt., **B**, Enlisted: 7-63, Grantville, Ga., by Lt. Taylor. KIA: Chickamauga 9-19-1863.

Madden, Franklin G., Pvt., **A**, Enlisted: 2-63, Cedartown, Ga., by Captain York. 12-31-1864 present. Living: Polk Co., Ga., 1870.

Maddox, William, Pvt., **A**, During Retreat from Ky. to Tenn. he was knocked off his horse and trampled by running horse. Chest injured. Pension: Cullman Co., Ala. 1893.

Maffitt, James C., Pvt., **B**, Enlisted: 5-64, Newnan, Ga., by Lt. Taylor. Pension: on scout with 12 men at surrender. Surrendered: North Carolina 4-1865. Elected Sheriff: Meriwether County. Died: Meriwether Co., Ga. after 1919.

Magouirk, H., Pvt., **A**, Enlisted: 3-64, Cedartown, Ga., by Captain Jesse W. Crabb. Present 12-64. Paroled: Charlotte, N.C. 5-3-1865.

Mann, Henry A. "Ike," Pvt., **K**, Enlisted: 5-62, Camp Morrison, age 42, by Captain North. WIA: Loudon, Tenn. Died 6-12-62 at home in Coweta Co., Ga.

Mann, John W., Cpl., **A**, Enlisted: 3-62, Cedartown, Ga., by Captain John C. Crabb. Present 6-62. Absent 8-62 Detailed with sick horses, Kingston, Tenn. Absent 10-62 on leave. Absent 12-13-62: Detailed to Government Shop, Rome, Ga. Iron Works.

Manning, Allen B., Pvt., **D**, Enlisted: 3-62, Dallas, Ga., by Captain Seawright. Present through 10-62. Absent 12-62 Sick furlough: Paulding Co. AWOL since 10-62. Died: 11-29-1908. Buried: Bluff Springs Cemetery, Rosston, Ark. Marker: Manning Cemetery, Hiram, Ga.

Manning, James M., Pvt., **D**, Enlisted: 3-62, Dallas, Ga., age 24, by Captain Seawright. Present 6-62. Absent 10-62 and 12-62 Sick furlough: Paulding Co., Ga. AWOL since 10-62. Died: 1873. Buried: Manning Cemetery, Hiram, Ga.

Manning, John M., Pvt., **D**, Enlisted: 3-62, Dallas, Ga., age 22, by Captain Seawright. Present 6-62.

Died at home 10-21-62 Paulding Co., Ga. Buried: Manning Cemetery, Hiram, Ga.

Marony, **B.D.**, Pvt., **A**, Enlisted: 11-62, Cedartown, Ga., by Captain Hutchings. Present 12-62. Absent 2-63 with Brigade wagons. Absent 12-63 Cut off with wagons. Detached by Gen. Davidson 5-10-64. Discharged: 1865. Pension: Calhoun Co., Ala. 1896.

Martin, **Albert**, Pvt., **K**, Enlisted: 5-62, Camp Morrison by Captain North. Present through 8-62. Captured: London, Ky. 9-8-62; exchanged, Cumberland Gap 9-17-62. Present through 12-64. Pension: Contracted Catarrh (Asthma). Died: 3-17-1895. Buried: Tranquil Cemetery, Coweta Co., Ga.

Martin, **David Reuben**, Pvt., **K**, Enlisted: 11-63, Surrendered: N.C. Died: 9-9-1894. Buried: Martin Cemetery, Carroll Co., Ga.

Martin, **R.F.**, Pvt., **K**, Enlisted: 6-64, Marietta, Ga., by Captain North. 12-31-1864 AWOL.

Martin, **William A.**, Pvt., **G**, Enlisted: 5-62, Chattanooga by Captain Kerr. Absent 6-62 Sick: Floyd Co., Ga. Present through 12-63. Arrested 12-22-64. Paroled: Charlotte, N.C. 5-3-1865. Died: 5-20-1914. Buried: Highland Cemetery, Ozark, Arkansas.

Martin, **William C.**, Pvt., **E**, Enlisted: 3-62, Carrollton, Ga., by Captain Blalock. Present 6-62 as wagoner. Present through 12-62. Absent 2-63: Teamster for Brigade. Deserted 9-10-63.

Martin, **William W.**, Pvt., **E**, Enlisted: 4-64, Oxford, Ala., by Col. Davitte. 12-31-1864 present.

Martin, **Z.**, Pvt., **I**, Paroled: Talladega, Ala. 5-27-1865

Mashburn, **Francis Marion**, Pvt., **B**, Enlisted: 4-62, Cartersville, Ga., by Col. Morrison. Present through 2-63. WIA: Kingston, Tenn. 11-24-63. Sent to Newnan, Ga. Hospital. Surrendered: 4-26-1865. Died: 2-24-1909. Buried: New Lebanon Baptist, Carroll Co., Ga.

Mason, **J.G.**, Pvt., **K**, Enlisted: 5-62, Camp Morrison by Captain North.

Mathews, **George W.**, Pvt., **A**, Enlisted: 3-62, Cedartown, Ga., by Captain John C. Crabb. Present 6-62. Absent 8-62 sick furlough home. Absent 10-62 Sick: Loudon, Tenn. KIA: Dandridge, Tenn. 12-24-1863.

Mathis, **George**, Pvt., WIA: Mossy Creek, Tenn. 12-29-1863.

Matthews, **Ezekiel**, Pvt., **C**, Captured: Missionary Ridge 11-25-63. Carried: Nashville; Louisville 12-7-63; Rock Island, Ill. 12-20-63. Exchanged 3-2-1865. Admitted: Jackson Hospital, Richmond, Va. 3-11-65 with ascites (liver disease).

Died: 1-19-1883. Buried: First Baptist Church, Lilburn, Ga.

Matthews, **Robert**, Pvt., **D**, Enlisted: 5-64, Dallas, Ga., by Captain Robert F. Trammell. 12-31-64 present.

Matthews, **W.C.**, Pvt., **D**, Enlisted: 3-62, Dallas, Ga., age 28, by Captain Seawright. Present 6-62. Absent 2-63 Sick furlough: Paulding Co., Ga. Absent 12-63 Detained in Ga., by General Wheeler. 12-64 AWOL.

Matthews, **William C.**, Pvt., **D**, Enlisted: 3-62, Dallas, Ga., by Captain Seawright. Discharged 9-27-62, Kingston, Tenn. Certificate: born Newton Co., Ga., age 32, 5'-10", dark complexion, hazel eyes, black hair. Pension: Summer 1862 sick with measles; settling in eyes rendering virtually blind. Died: 7-15-1902. Buried: New Hope Baptist Church, Dallas, Ga.

Mattux, **William**, Pvt., **A**, Enlisted: 3-62, Cedartown, Ga., by Captain John C. Crabb. Absent 6-62 Sick furlough: Polk Co., Ga. Present through 2-63. Absent 12-63 Cut off with wagons. Deserted: 11-20-64.

Maulding, **B.M.**, Pvt., **F**, Enlisted: 3-62, Fairmount, Ga., by Col. Morrison. Absent 6-62 sick furlough. Present through 2-63. Absent 12-63 and 12-64. Detailed with Engineers, Dalton, Ga..

May, **Samuel Meredith**, Captain, **F&S**, Enlisted: 3-62, Rome, Ga., by Captain Kerr. Elected 3rd Lt. 3-13-62. Promoted 2nd Lt. 6-20-62. Absent 6-62 sick furlough. Present through 2-63. Appointed: Acting Quartermaster for Regiment succeeding Sam Davitte. Promoted Captain 5-2-63. Present 12-64. Paroled: Charlotte, N.C. 5-3-1865. Died: 8-13-1877. Buried: Myrtle Hill, Rome, Ga.

McAdams, **William**, Pvt., **A**, Enlisted: 2-63, Cedartown, Ga., by Captain Hutchings. Present 12-63 and 12-31-1864.

McAllister, **W.A.**, Pvt., **B**, 1862, Surrendered: Salisbury, N.C. 4-26-1865. Pension: Carroll Co., Ga., 1902. (Possible: Died: 3-22-1904. Buried: St. Paul Methodist Church Cemetery, Whitesburg, Ga.)

McAlister, **William T.**, Pvt., **B**, Enlisted: 3-62, Newnan, Ga., age 24, by Captain Strickland. Absent 6-62 Detailed: Wagoner, Kingston, Tenn. Present 8-62. Absent 10-62 detailed: Teamster. Absent 12-62. Present 12-63 and 12-64. Paroled: Charlotte, N.C. 5-3-1865.

McCain (**McLain**), **John Milton**, Pvt., **D**, Enlisted: Acworth, Ga., 18th Ga. Inf. 9-1-1861. WIA: 7-3-63, Gettysburg. Captured, carried: David's Island Prison, N.Y. Exchanged. Enlisted: Dallas,

Ga., 1st Ga. Cavalry, 8-1-1864. Pension: At Yadkin River, N.C. at surrender. Went home, paroled, Kingston, Ga. Died: 12-1918. Buried: Mars Hill Cemetery, Acworth, Ga.

McCain, Joseph Reid, Cpl., **E**, Enlisted: 3-62, Carrollton, Ga., by Captain Blalock. Present through 12-64. Surrendered: Salisbury, N.C. 4-26-1865. Died: 9-13-1920. Buried: Asbury Cemetery, Temple, Ga.

McCarty (McCarthy), William, Pvt., **G**, Enlisted: 2-64. Captured: Scottsville, Ala. 10-27-64. Carried: Louisville 11-9-64; Camp Douglas 11-12-64. Stated: Deserted for Amnesty Proclamation. Took oath 3-1-1865. Description: home DeKalb Co., Ga., 5'-10", fair complexion, black hair, brown eyes.

McCarver, A.L., Pvt., **C**, Enlisted: 10-64, Present 12-31-1864.

McClain (McCain), Andrew Hamilton, Pvt., **E**, Enlisted: 3-62, Carrollton, Ga., by Captain Blalock. Present through 8-62. Absent 10-62 Left sick in Ky. Captured: Lexington, Ky. 10-27-62. Carried: Louisville 11-5-62; Vicksburg 11-12-62, aboard steamer *Metropolitan*. Description: age 20, 5'-11½", dark complexion, dark eyes, light hair. Died: Cairo, Ill. 11-22-1862. Buried: Oak Woods Cemetery, Chicago, Ill.

McClain, James Allen, Pvt., **G**, 1911 Veterans meeting Ark. Died: 10-9-1920. Buried: Pisgah Cemetery, Pottsville, Ark.

McClure (McLure), Martin Van Buren, 1st Sgt., **E**, Enlisted: 3-62, Carrollton, Ga., by Captain Blalock. Resigned as 1st Sgt. 6-5-62. Present through 12-62. Absent 2-63 with detachment: Kingston, Tenn. Died: 11-11-1920. Buried: Stripling Chapel UMC, Carrollton, Ga.

McCollum, John W., Pvt., **H**, Enlisted: 4-62, Haralson Co., Ga., by Captain Tumlin. Present through 2-63. Captured: Dandridge, Tenn. 12-24-63. Carried: Knoxville 12-27-63; Camp Chase; Louisville; Rock Island, Ill. 1-26-1864.

McCollum, John W., Pvt., **K**, Enlisted: 5-62, Camp Morrison by Captain North. Died at home in Coweta Co., Ga., 7-13-62, typhoid fever.

McCormick, J.A., Pvt., **A**, Enlisted: 8-63, Cedartown, Ga., by Captain York. Absent 12-63 sick. In Hospital sick 7-20-1864. Captured: Macon, Ga., 4-30-1865.

McCormick, Joseph P., Sgt., **A**, Enlisted: Cedartown, Ga., age 21, 21st Ga. Inf. 6-27-1861. Discharged: 11-22-61, fistula-in-ano. Certificate: born Troup Co., Ga., age 21, 5'-10", light complexion, blue eyes, dark hair. Enlisted: 1st Ga. Cavalry 5-14-62, Cedartown, Ga., by Captain

John C. Crabb. Present through 12-62. Absent 2-63 Detached as recruiter. Present 12-63. KIA: Decatur, Ga. 7-22-1864.

McCurry, James M., Pvt., **A**, Enlisted: 1-63, Cedartown, Ga., by Captain Hutchings. Present through 12-64. Pension: 2-65 Hospital with measles and broken arm. Absent 3-65, Sick furlough home. Pension: 1907, Polk Co., Ga.

McCurry, Pleasant W., Pvt., **A**, Enlisted: 3-62, Cedartown, Ga., by Captain John C. Crabb. Absent 6-62 Sick in hospital: Loudon, Tenn. Present 2-63 as Teamster. Absent 12-63 Detailed: hospital nurse. Present 12-64. Surrendered: Smithfield, N.C. 4-26-1865. Died: 3-19-1904. Buried: Blooming Grove Cemetery, Polk Co., Ga.

McDaniel, Jeff W., Pvt., **I**, Enlisted: 4-62, Camp Morrison by Captain Leak. Present 6-62 as Farrier. Present through 12-62. Absent 2-63 sick furlough. Present 10-63 and 12-64. Surrendered: Greensboro, N.C. 4-26-1865. Died: 1884. Buried: Paulding Co., Ga.

McDaniel, John M., Pvt., **B**, Enlisted: 5-63, Newnan, Ga., by Lt. Taylor. Absent in Newnan, Ga. Hospital 11-28-63. Absent 12-64 in General Hospital. Surrendered: Greensboro, N.C. 4-26-1865. Died: 12-1907, Kingston, Ga.

McDonald, Matthew J., Pvt., **I**, Enlisted: 1-64, Cass Station, Ga., age 14, by Captain Leak. Captured: Savannah, Ga., 12-21-64. Carried: Hilton Head, S.C.; Fort Delaware 3-12-1865. Released 6-16-1865. Description: home Upson Co., Ga., light complexion, dark hair, grey eyes, 5'-4".

McDougal, Robert, Pvt., **F**, Captured: Greenville, S.C. 5-23-1865, paroled.

McEntire, Phillip N., Pvt., **A**, Tombstone: 1st Ga. Cavalry. Pension: 1st Ga. State Troops. Died: 1-8-1914. Buried: Oostanaula UMC, Shannon, Ga.

McEver, Brice Collins, Pvt., **I**, 10-64, Pension: Col. Davitte lead him and several others to leave 4-16-1865 and head west to join other fighting units to continue war. Paroled: Kingston, Ga. May 1865. Died: 7-10-1918. Buried: White Methodist, Bartow Co., Ga.

McFadden, S.B., Attended Gen. Joseph Wheeler's funeral January 1906.

McGahee, W.T., Pvt., **B**, Enlisted: 3-62, Newnan, Ga., age 18, by Captain Strickland. Present through 12-62. Absent 2-63 Detached: Brigade Artillery. Pension: 5-63 Detached: Huwald's Battery, Joe Wheeler's Flying Artillery. 12-63 Detached: Captain Marshall's Battery, Brown Horse Artillery, Lt. Col. Harper. 12-64 Detached: Benjamin

White's Light Artillery. Surrendered 4-15-1865 Hamburg, S.C. Pension: Fulton Co., Ga., 1905.

McGarrity, J.S., Pvt., **A**, Enlisted: 2-64, in field by Captain York. 12-31-1864 present.

McGhee, Robert R., Pvt., **G**, Enlisted: 3-62, Floyd Co., Ga., by Captain Kerr. Present through 12-31-1864 Company Blacksmith. Surrendered: Greensboro, N.C. 4-26-1865. Died: 2-23-1899. Buried: Livingston UMC, Floyd Co., Ga.

McGregor, Augustus Silas, Sgt., **A**, Enlisted: 5-62, Cedartown, Ga., by Captain John C. Crabb. Present through 12-31-1864. Promoted 5th Sgt. 12-31-62. WIA: Somerset, Ky. 3-30-63. WIA, right hip and left thigh, 7-22-64 Atlanta, Ga. Disabled. Elected Sheriff of Polk Co., Ga., 1868. Died: 10-29-1914. Buried: Woodlawn Cemetery, Tampa, Fla.

McGregor, Samuel D., 1st Lt., **D**, 3-62. Died: 1874. Buried: Old High Shoals Baptist Church, Dallas, Ga.

McGregor, Samuel R., 1st Lt., **D**, Enlisted: 3-62, Dallas, Ga., age 21, by Captain Seawright. Elected 2nd Lt. 3-8-62. 8-62 Sick furlough: Paulding Co., Ga. Promoted 1st Lt. 7-13-62, replace Robert Trammell. Present 10-62 and 12-62. Dropped from roll 7-20-1864. Pension: Surrendered: Goldsboro, N.C. 4-26-1865. Died: 7-18-1921. Buried: Bullard Cemetery, Powder Springs, Ga.

McGuffee, Z.F., Pvt., **G**, Enlisted: 3-62, Floyd Co., Ga., by Captain Kerr. Present through 12-62. Captured: Richmond, Ky. 8-24-62. Carried: Lexington; Camp Morton 8-28-62; Camp Butler, Ill. Description: home Floyd Co., Ga., age 25, 5'-8", fair complexion, blue eyes, black hair. Exchanged: Vicksburg 9-23-62. Absent 2-63 Detailed: Marshall's Battery by Gen. Pegram. AWOL 11-1-1864.

McGuire, Thomas, Pvt., **G**, Captured: Scottsville, Ala. 10-27-64. Carried: Louisville 11-9-64; Camp Douglas 11-12-64. Statement: Deserted: Amnesty Proclamation. Description: dark complexion, grey hair, blue eyes, 5'-10½". Released: 5-12-1865.

McJunkin, Erasmus H., Pvt., **A**, Enlisted: 3-62, Cedartown, Ga., by Captain John C. Crabb. Present 6-62. Absent 8-62 Sick: Kingston, Tenn. Absent 10-62 and 12-62 sick furlough home. 2-63 AWOL. Pension: September to November 1862, in camp at Kingston, Tenn. with consumption. Discharged. Died: 8-11-1880. Buried: Morgan McJunkin Family Cemetery, Polk Co., Ga.

McKee, A.G., Cpl., **H**, Captured: Hartwell, Ga., 5-17-1865, paroled.

McKee, James A., Pvt., **H**, Enlisted: 4-62, Haralson Co., Ga., by Captain Tumlin. Present through 2-63. WIA: Big Hill, Ky. 8-12-62. Absent 12-63

Detailed: Hospital nurse. Died: 1-16-1891. Buried: Turkeytown UMC, Hokes Bluff, Ala.

McKelvey (McIlvey), Josiah, Pvt., **C**, Enlisted: 3-62, Cave Spring, Ga., by Captain Haynie. Present 6-62. Absent 8-62 Sick: Loudon, Tenn. Present 10-62 and 12-62. KIA: Monticello, Ky. 5-1-1863.

McKelvey, George P., Pvt., **I**, Enlisted: 8th Battalion Ga. Inf. 5-13-1862. Enlisted: 12-64, 1st Ga. Cavalry, Cass Station, Ga., Captain Leak. Paroled: Charlotte, N.C. 5-3-1865.

McKibbins, James M., Pvt., **C**, Enlisted: 3-62, Cave Spring, Ga., by Captain Haynie. Present through 12-31-1864. Danville, Ky. 3-24-63, horse KIA. Paid $175.

McLain, J.M., Pvt., **D**, Enlisted: 8-64, Dallas, Ga., by Captain Robert F. Trammell. 12-31-1864 present.

McLane, J., Pvt., **G**, Enlisted: 5-64, Resaca, Ga., by Lt. Zuber. Absent 12-31-1864 Detailed to drive cattle at Macon, Ga., 11-28-1864.

McMillan, Wilson Lumpkin, Pvt., **F**, Enlisted: 3-62, Fairmount, Ga., by Col. Morrison. Present through 12-64, Blacksmith. Paroled: Charlotte, N.C. 5-3-1865. Died: 8-28-1880. Contracted Lung disease in service. Buried: Jerusalem Baptist Church, Jasper, Ga.

McMillen (McMillan), George W., Sgt. Major, **F&S**, Enlisted: 8-62, Dallas, Ga., by Captain Robert F. Trammell. Present through 2-63. Somerset, Ky. 3-29-63, horse KIA. Paid $350. Absent 12-63 Detained in Ga., by General Wheeler. Appointed Sgt. Major 7-1-63. Captured: Atlanta 7-21-64. Carried: Chattanooga; Nashville 7-29-64; Louisville 7-31-64; Camp Chase 8-2-1864; City Point, Va. 3-4-1865, exchanged. Died: 11-5-1911. Buried: Mars Hill Cemetery, Acworth, Ga.

McMillen, Robert Huie, 1st Sgt., **D**, Enlisted: 3-62, Dallas, Ga., by Captain Seawright. Present through 2-63. Absent 12-63 Detached: Hospital, Russellville, Tenn. 12-64 present. Died: 7-13-1907. Buried: Mars Hill Cemetery, Cobb Co., Ga.

McMillin, P.H., Pvt., **F**, Enlisted: 9-64, Newnan, Ga., by Captain McWilliams. Present 12-64. Paroled: Charlotte, N.C. 5-3-1865.

McWhorter (McWhorten), R.E., Pvt., **F**, Enlisted: 5-64, Decatur, Ga., by Major Anderson. 12-31-1864 present.

McWilliams, Edwin D., Pvt., **F**, Enlisted: 3-62, Fairmount, Ga., by Col. Morrison. Present through 2-63. Absent 12-63 Sick. 12-31-1864 present.

McWilliams, H.C., Pvt., **F**, 2-64, Widow's pension: Watter's Scouts. (1st Ga. Cavalry) for 14 months.

Surrendered: Kingston, Ga. Died: 11-13-1913. Buried: McWilliams Cemetery, Villanow, Ga.

McWilliams, John Harvey, Pvt., **B**, Enlisted: 3-62 in Newnan, Ga. Present through 12-31-1864. Died: 5-4-1927. Buried: Pine Crest Cemetery, Atlanta, Texas.

McWilliams, William, F., Died: 1-25-1878. Buried: McWilliams Cemetery, Villanow, Ga.

McWilliams, William M., Captain, **F**, Enlisted: 3-62, Fairmount, Ga., by Col. Morrison. Present through 8-62. Elected 2nd Lt. 9-19-62. Promoted 1st Lt.; death of Tarlton Lewis 12-25-62. Present 12-62 and 2-63. Promoted Captain by Gen. Martin 1-24-64, replace Nap. J. Reynolds. Present 12-64. Paroled: Charlotte, N.C. 5-3-1865. Pension: Broke camp 4-26-65 and went home. Paroled: Kingston, Ga. May 1865. Died: 1919. Buried: Young Cemetery, Walker Co., Ga.

Meadows, E.S., Pvt., **B**, Enlisted: 5-64, Newnan, Ga., by Lt. Taylor. 12-31-1864 present.

Medlin, Pleadious M. Thomas, Pvt., **G**, Enlisted: 3-62, Floyd Co., Ga., by Captain Kerr. Present through 12-31-1864. Lost one Austrian rifle. Surrendered: Greensboro, N.C. 4-26-1865. Died: 6-7-1909. Buried: Smyrna Memorial Cemetery, Cobb Co., Ga.

Meecham, David L., Pvt., **B**, KIA 10-20-1863; Philadelphia, Tenn.

Meeks, Benjamin Franklin, Pvt., **C**, Enlisted: 5-62, Cave Spring, Ga., by Lt. Reynolds. Absent 6-62 and 8-62 Sick furlough: Floyd Co., Ga. Present 10-62 and 12-62. Discharged 12-31-62.

Merrell, George Washington, Pvt., **E**, Enlisted: 5-62, Carrollton, Ga., by Captain Blalock. Present through 12-62. Absent 2-63 sick furlough home. Present 12-63. Absent 12-64 Sick. Pension: Sick furlough at home at surrender. Left at Cane Creek, Ala., covered with camp boils. Unable to ride horse. Died: 12-15-1918. Buried: Pleasant Grove Baptist, Villa Rica, Ga.

Merrell, William Perry, Pvt., **E**, Enlisted: 4-64, Oxford, Ala., by Col. Davitte. 12-64 present. Pension: Detached: Drive cattle from Savannah to Greensboro, NC, and surrendered. Died: 4-23-1932. Buried: Tallapoosa Primitive Baptist, Carroll Co., Ga.

Metcalf, A.W., Pvt., Enlisted: 3-62, Floyd Co., Ga., by Captain Kerr. Present through 12-62. Present 12-63 and 12-64. Pension: During service sick with measles. Surrender: Greensboro, NC 4-26-1865. Died: 2-16-1875. Buried: Cave Spring Cemetery, Floyd Co., Ga.

Mewborn, W.A., Pvt., **D**, Enlisted: 3-62, Dallas, Ga., age 23, by Captain Seawright. Present 6-62.

Absent 8-62 Sick furlough: Paulding Co., Ga. Present 10-62 and 12-62. AWOL 2-63.

Michum, David L., Pvt., **B**, Enlisted: 3-62, Newnan, Ga., age 30, by Captain Strickland. Present through 12-62. Present 2-63 Detailed Teamster. Captured: Philadelphia, Tenn. 10-20-63. Carried: Camp Nelson; (Admitted: Hospital 11-11-63, Pleurisy); Louisville; Rock Island, Ill. 12-5-63. Died 1-17-64, chronic diarrhea, Rock Island Prison. Buried: Rock Island Confederate Cemetery, Grave #213.

Milam, Thomas J., Pvt., **I**, Mustered: 7-63, Sweetwater, Tenn. Surrendered: Greensboro, N.C. 4-26-1865. Pension: Bartow Co., Ga., 1908. Buried: Euharlee Presbyterian Church, Bartow Co., Ga.

Milam, W.S., Pvt., **I**, Enlisted: 4-63, Mouse (Mossy) Creek, Tenn., by Captain Leak. Absent 10-63 Sick in Ga. AWOL 12-18-1864.

Miller, George W., Pvt., **E**, Enlisted: 3-62, Carrollton, Ga., by Captain Blalock. Present through 12-62. Absent 2-63 Sick furlough: Paulding Co., Ga. Present 12-62. Absent 12-64 Detached service. Surrendered: Greensboro, N.C. 4-26-1865.

Miller, James J., Pvt., **H**, Enlisted: 4-62, Haralson Co., Ga., by Captain Tumlin. Present through 2-63. AWOL 10-15-63. Received clothing issue 6-64. 12-64 AWOL. Buried: Oak Level UMC, Cleburne Co., Ala.

Millican, Andrew Jackson, Pvt., **E**, Enlisted: 1-63, Decatur, Ga., by Major Hardee. Present through 12-64. Pension: Columbia Co., Arkansas. Died: 1-3-1932.

Millican, Charles Findley, Sgt., **C**, Enlisted: 3-62, Cave Spring, Ga., by Captain Haynie. Promoted 5th Sgt. 3-31-62. Present through 2-63. Discharged: 7-15-63, Sweetwater, Tenn. Certificate: born Elbert Co., Ga., age 45, 6'-0", dark complexion, black eyes, grey hair; chronic Nephritis and hernia. Died: 5-2-1887. Buried: Jackson Chapel, Cedartown, Ga.

Millican, James Franklin, Pvt., **C**, Enlisted: Floyd Legion 7-11-1863, Floyd Co., Ga. Enlisted: 5-64 1st Georgia Cavalry. Present 12-31-1864. Surrendered: Greensboro, N.C. 4-26-1865. Died: 2-21-1928. Buried: Old Antioch Cemetery, Floyd Co., Ga.

Milner, William A., Pvt., **I**, Enlisted: 5-62, Camp Morrison by Captain Leak. Present through 2-63. Absent 3-63 Detachment Camp. Absent 10-63 Detached with sick, Loudon, Tenn. to accompany to Ga. Enlisted: 4th Ga. Reserves 5-10-64.

Milner, William R.A., Pvt., **I**, Enlisted: 8-63,

Ebenezer, Tenn., by Captain Leak. WIA: Kingston, Tenn. 11-24-63. Absent 12-64 WIA. Died: 10-10-1916. Buried: Columbiana Cemetery, Shelby Co., Ala.

Minshew, James Allen, Pvt., **E**, Died: 2-22-1928. Buried: Reeves Chapel UMC, Pittsburg, Texas.

Minshew, James Allen, Pvt., **E**, Enlisted: 3-62, Carrollton, Ga., by Captain Blalock. Present through 2-63. Captured: Knoxville 12-18-63. Carried: Knoxville 12-20-63; Louisville 1-25-64; Rock Island, Ill. 1-26-1864. Died: 5-4-1864, chronic diarrhea. Buried: Rock Island Confederate Cemetery. Grave #1118.

Mohon, John C., Pvt., **D**, Enlisted: 3-62, Dallas, Ga., age 28, by Captain Seawright. Present through 10-62. Absent 12-62 Special duty in Cobb Co., Ga. Present 2-63. Absent 12-63 Detained in Ga., by General Wheeler. WIA: Somerset, Ky. 3-30-63. Gunshot: right hip. Captured: Marietta, Ga., 6-23-64. Carried: Nashville 7-12-64; Louisville 7-14-64; Camp Douglas 7-16-64. Discharged: 5-16-1865. Died: 10-16-1909. Buried: Midway Cemetery, Lost Mountain, Ga.

Moncrief, William R., Pvt., **B**, Enlisted: 3-62, Newnan, Ga., age 19, by Captain Strickland. Absent 6-62 Hospital: Loudon, Tenn. Present 8-62. Captured: Clay Village, Ky. 10-4-62, paroled. Absent 12-62. Present 2-63. Dropped from roll 12-63, Major Strickland. Pension: WIA: London, Ky. 8-27-63. Gunshot: right hand severing index finger, thumb. Hospital: LaGrange, Ga. to end of war. Died: 7-15-1921. Buried: Hill View Cemetery, LaGrange, Ga.

Monfort, Alexander, Pvt., **A**, Enlisted: 5-62, Camp Morrison by Captain John C. Crabb. Milton Mullins, substitute 6-25-62. Died: 7-1-1894. Buried: Liberty UMC, White Plains, Ga.

Monfort, Oscar L., Pvt., **A**, Enlisted: 3-62, Cedartown, Ga., by Captain John C. Crabb. Present 6-62. KIA: Murfreesboro, 7-13-62.

Montgomery, Bailey Christopher, 1st Lt., **C**, Enlisted: 3-62, Cave Spring, Ga., by Captain Haynie. Resigned disabled: 6-14-62. Died: 6-20-1904. Buried: Sandy Mountain Cemetery, Llano Co., Tx.

Montgomery, C.S., Pvt., **G**, Enlisted: 3-62, Floyd Co., Ga., by Captain Kerr. Absent 6-62 Sick furlough: Floyd Co., Ga. Present 8-62 and 10-62. Discharged disabled 11-6-62.

Montgomery, R.S., Pvt., **I**, Enlisted: 5-62, Camp Morrison by Captain Leak.

Montgomery, William H., Pvt., **C**, Enlisted: 3-62, Cave Spring, Ga., by Captain Haynie. Absent 6-62 Sick furlough: Floyd Co., Ga. Present

through 12-62. Absent 2-63 sick. Present 6-63. Absent 12-63 sick. Surrendered: Salisbury, N.C. 5-3-1865. Died soon after.

Moore, Bennett C., 1st Sgt., **G**, Enlisted: 3-62, Floyd Co., Ga., by Captain Kerr. Present through 12-62. Promoted 1st Sgt. 12-1-62. Present 2-63. Captured: Somerset, Ky. 3-30-63. Carried: Louisville; City Point, Va. Exchanged 4-13-63. Captured: Gwinnett Co., Ga. On list of deserters: took oath 6-12-64. Description: home Gwinnett Co., Ga., dark complexion, auburn hair, hazel eyes, 6'-1".

Moore, H.B., Pvt., **D**, Enlisted: 3-62, Dallas, Ga., by Captain Seawright. Present 10-62. Absent 12-62 Sick furlough: Paulding Co., Ga. Absent 2-63 Detailed to accompany J.W. Allgood home. Absent 12-63 Sick: Atlanta Hospital. Clothing issued 7-13-64. 12-64 AWOL.

Moore, Henry T., Pvt., **G**, Enlisted: 5-62, Rome, Ga., by Captain Kerr. Absent 6-62 Sick: Loudon, Tenn. Hospital. Present 8-62 and 10-62. Absent 12-62 sick furlough. Present 2-63. 12-63 AWOL. AWOL 11-5-64. Pension: Surrendered 4-26-1865, Raleigh, N.C. Died: 11-8-1909, Rome, Ga.

Moore, Jerry A., Pvt., **D**, Enlisted: 3-62, Dallas, Ga., by Captain Seawright. Present through 8-62. Absent 10-62 Sick furlough: Paulding Co., Ga. Absent 12-62 Sick furlough: Cobb Co., Ga. Present 2-63. Captured: Somerset, Ky. 3-30-63. Carried: Louisville; City Point, Va. Exchanged 4-13-63. KIA: Resaca, Ga., 6-64.

Moore, J.J., Cpl., **I**, Enlisted: 5-62, Camp Morrison by Captain Leak. Present through 10-63. Absent 12-64 Detached service since 6-10-64. Surrendered: Greensboro, NC 4-26-1865. Died: 6-23-1892, Bartow Co., Ga.

Moore, John, Pvt., **I**, Enlisted: 8-63, Ebenezer, Tenn., by Captain Leak. Absent 10-63 Detached service in Ga. Present 12-64 Teamster.

Moore, John C., Pvt., **G**, Enlisted: 6-62, Calhoun, Ga., by Major Dunwoody. Present through 12-62. Discharged 8-13-63, substitution. Certificate: born Buncombe Co., N.C., age 50, 5'-9", fair complexion, grey eyes, grey hair.

Moore, Marion Jackson, Pvt., **G**, Enlisted: 2-63, Rome, Ga., by C.M. Pennington. Absent 12-63 in Ga. Died in service 1864.

Moore, Mitchael Lee, Pvt., **C**, Enlisted: 10-64. Present 12-64. Discharged 5-4-1865. Died: 2-7-1933. Buried: Glenwood Cemetery, Tupelo, Miss.

Moore, T.A., Pvt., **I**, Enlisted: 1-64, Newport, Tenn., by Captain Leak. Absent 12-64 Detached service since 6-10-64.

Moore, William, Pvt., **G**, Enlisted: 5-62, Camp

Morrison by Captain Leak. Present through 10-62. Died: McMinnville, Tenn. 12-15-62.

Moore, William "Bill" R., Sgt., **G**, Enlisted: 5-62, Rome, Ga., by Captain Kerr. Present through 12-62. Promoted 3rd Sgt. 12-1-62. Present 2-63. Captured: Knoxville on scout. Took oath 11-17-63, released. Rejoined: regiment. Absent 12-63 Sick furlough: Floyd Co., Ga. KIA: Battle Peachtree Creek 7-17-1864. Buried: Northside Park Baptist Church, 1877 Howell Mill Rd. , Atlanta, Ga.

Morgan, George W., Pvt., **A**, Enlisted: 3-62, Cedartown, Ga., by Captain John C. Crabb. Discharged. Polk Co., Ga., 1910

Morgan, Isaac, Pvt., **D**, Enlisted: 3-62, Dallas, Ga., age 24, by Captain Seawright. Present through 2-63. AWOL 11-63. Clothing issued 7-13-64. 12-64 AWOL.

Morgan, Joseph Marion, Pvt., **A**, Enlisted: 3-62, Cedartown, Ga., by Captain John C. Crabb. Present through 2-63. Captured: Somerset, Ky. 3-30-63. Carried: Louisville 4-30-63; City Point, Va. Exchanged 5-6-63. Absent 12-63 Home wounded. AWOL 11-10-64. 1880 Fish Creek, Polk Co., Ga.

Morgan, Tillman, Pvt., **D**, 3-62, Enlisted: Dallas, Ga., by Captain Seawright. Present through 12-62. Absent 2-63 Sick furlough: Paulding Co., Ga. AWOL 6-20-63. Widow's pension: Surrendered: Greensboro, N.C. 4-26-1865. Died: 1878 Polk Co., Ga.

Morgan, William Harrison, Pvt., **A**, Enlisted: 5-62, Cedartown, Ga., by Captain John C. Crabb. Present 6-62. WIA: left hip, Murfreesboro 7-13-62 and captured. Absent 10-62 prisoner on parole and wounded. Absent 12-62 wounded at home. Present 2-63. Absent 12-63 Hospital wounded. Captured: Somerset, Ky. 3-30-63. Paroled. WIA: Mossy Creek, Tenn. 12-29-63. WIA 6-1-64. Both ankles wounded and in back, ball passing through lung. Never returned. Died: 6-9-1907. Buried: Iron City, Seminole Co., Ga.

Morris, Edward A., Cpl., **K**, Enlisted: 5-62, Camp Morrison by Captain North. Present through 2-63. WIA: Murfreesboro 7-13-62. Absent 12-63 with wagon train, Cartersville, Ga., by General Wheeler. Captured: Resaca, Ga., 8-1-64. Captured while piloting boat Gen. Rosser. Carried: Nashville; Louisville 10-25-64; Camp Douglas, Ill. 10-29-64. Discharged 5-17-1865. Description: home Campbell Co., Ga., fair complexion, brown hair, hazel eyes, 6'-0". Died: 8-10-1914. Buried: Old Camp UMC, Carroll Co., Ga.

Morris, Henry J., Pvt., **A**, Enlisted: 3-62, Cedar-

town, Ga., by Captain John C. Crabb. Present 6-62. Company Bugler. KIA: Murfreesboro 7-13-62.

Morris, Loverick, Pvt., **G**, Enlisted: 3-62, Floyd Co., Ga., by Captain Kerr. Absent 6-62 Sick: Loudon, Tenn. Hospital. Present 8-62 and 10-62. Absent 12-62 Sick furlough: Floyd Co., Ga. AWOL 2-63. Captured: Mill Springs, Ky. 5-28-63. Carried: Lexington; Camp Chase 6-10-63; Johnson's Island. Took oath 4-12-64, Point Lookout, Md. Description: age 37, 5'-8", dark complexion, light hair, black eyes. Pension: Etowah Co., Ala. 1909.

Morris, Willis, Pvt., **G**, Enlisted: 3-62, Floyd Co., Ga., by Captain Kerr. On list of deserters at Louisville 6-12-64. Took oath 6-13-64. Description: home Floyd Co., Ga., dark complexion, dark hair, hazel eyes, 5'-11".

Morris, William Taylor, **D**, Enlisted 2-65, Died: 1928. Buried: Brooksville Baptist Church, Blount Co., Ala.

Morrison, James J., Colonel, **F&S**, 3-62, Major in 4th Battalion Ga. Inf. 7-19-61, evolved into 21st Ga. Inf., Lt. Colonel. Resigned 3-30-62. Organized First Georgia Cavalry Regiment, Lt. Colonel. Resigned: injured (hernia) shell exploded near him throwing him from horse at full gallop 4-15-64. Died: 9-3-1910. Buried: Woodlawn Cemetery, Eastman, Ga.

Morrison, Jesse, Pvt., **F**, 8-1-1863, 4th Battalion Ga. State Guards. Captured: Anderson, S.C. 5-19-1865, paroled.

Morrison, W.H., Pvt., **G**, Enlisted: 3-62, Floyd Co., Ga., by Captain Kerr. Present through 8-62. Absent through 2-63 Detailed: Clerk, Provost Marshall Office, Kingston, Tenn.

Morrow, Leonard, Pvt., **G**, Enlisted: 3-62, Floyd Co., Ga., by Captain Kerr. Present through 8-62. Discharged disabled 9-9-1862.

Morton, G.W., Pvt., **A**, Enlisted: 3-63, in field by Captain York. 12-31-1864 present.

Moseley, John P., Pvt., **H**, Reference folder and in 1st Ga. Inf.

Moss, J.C., Cpl., **H**, Enlisted: 4-62, Haralson Co., Ga., by Captain Tumlin. Absent through 8-62 sick furlough. Absent 10-62 Sick: Hospital, Loudon, Tenn. Absent 2-63 Hospital, Atlanta. 12-64 AWOL. Issued clothing 6-24-64. Captured: Macon, Ga., 4-30-1865.

Mountain, John F., Pvt., **C**, Enlisted: 2-63, Floyd Co., Ga., by Captain Haynie. Present 6-63. Absent 12-63 with detachment Cut off from Command.

Mullenix, James T., Pvt., **E**, Enlisted: 3-62, Carrollton, Ga., by Captain Blalock. Present through 10-62. Joined 26th Bat. Ga. Inf. 8-15-1863, Carrollton, Ga., age 45. Died: 2-17-1906. Buried: Whitesburg Cemetery, Carroll Co., Ga.

Mullenix, John O., Pvt., **E**, Enlisted 1861: 26th Bat. Ga. Inf., discharged, measles. Enlisted: 7-62, 1st Ga. Cavalry, Clinton, Tenn. Discharged 12-20-62, sick. Pension: In Hospital at West Point, Ga. with measles. Provost Duty at surrender. Witness: Carroll Co., Ga., 10-9-1924. Buried: Stripling Chapel UMC, Carrollton, Ga.

Mullinax, A., Pvt., **G**, Enlisted: 4-64, Oxford, Ala., by Lt. Zuber. Absent: Sick in hospital 7-2-1864.

Mullinax, D.O., Pvt., **F**, Enlisted: 4-64, Haralson Co., Ga., by Captain Tumlin.

Mullinix, Benton O., Pvt., **F**, Enlisted: 3-62, Fairmount, Ga., by Col. Morrison. Captured: Powell's Valley, Tenn. 6-27-62. Carried: Camp Morton. Listed as Deserter 6-21-1862. Absent 12-63 Sick.

Mullins, Milton, Cpl., **A**, Enlisted: 3-62, Cedartown, Ga., by Captain John C. Crabb. Present 6-62. Substitute for Alexander Munford 6-5-62. Present through 12-62. Promoted 4th Cpl. 12-31-62. Present 2-63. Captured: Champion Hill, Ky. 5-17-63. Carried: Fort Delaware. Took oath, discharged 7-3-1863.

Munford, John T., Pvt., **G**, Enlisted: 5-62, Camp Morrison by Captain Leak. 3-63 Detachment Camp. Detached service 9-20-1864. Pension: At surrender detailed: Hospital Surgeon. Died: 10-21-1904. Buried: Cassville Cemetery, Bartow Co., Ga.

Murchison, John D., Pvt., **H**, Enlisted 6-13-61: 18th Ga. Inf., Camp McDonald. Discharged 12-11-1861, inefficiency. Enlisted: 4-62, 1st Ga. Cavalry, Haralson Co., Ga., by Captain Tumlin. Present through 12-62. WIA: Stones River, Murfreesboro 1-1-63. Absent 12-63 Detained in Ga., by General Wheeler. 12-64 AWOL. Died: October 1900. Buried: Raccoon Creek Church, Taylorsville, Ga.

Murphey, C.M., Pvt., **I**, Enlisted: 5-62, Camp Morrison by Captain Leak. Present through 12-62. Absent 3-63 Detachment Camp. Present 10-63. AWOL 12-18-64.

Nall, Hiram Madison, Sgt., **B**, Enlisted: 55th Ga. Inf. 5-3-1861, Grantville, Ga. Transferred: 1st Ga. Cavalry, Newnan, Ga., 7-13-63. Present 12-63 and 12-64. Horse kicked him in leg 3-1865, furloughed home. Died: 12-4-1912. Buried: Allen Lee Memorial UMC, Lone Oak, Ga.

Nalley, Bailus (Bailey) M., Pvt., **F**, Enlisted: 3-62, Fairmount, Ga., by Col. Morrison. Captured: Powell's Valley, Tenn. 6-27-62. Paroled. Present

2-63 and 12-63. Deserted and took oath 2-64. Enlisted: U.S. 10th Regt. Tenn. Cavalry, 2-15-1864, age 20, Chattanooga. Involved in "Skeered Corn Murders," August 1865, Pickens and Gordon Co., Ga. Died: Pulaski Co., Ill. 1-1-1927

Nalley, Benson M., Pvt., **F**, Horse KIA: Somerset, Ky. 3-30-63. Paid $200. at Camp Ebenezer, Tenn. 8-20-63. Horse KIA: Stubenville, Ky. 5-30-63. Paid $200. 8-24-63. Took oath: Chattanooga 2-4-64. Description: home Pickens Co., Ga., fair complexion, black hair, blue eyes, 5'-4". Severely wounded in "Skeered Corn Murders."

Nalley, Elijah, Pvt., **F**, Enlisted: 7-63, Sweetwater, Tenn., by Captain Reynolds. Present 12-63. Deserted and took oath: Chattanooga 4-2-1864. Description: home Pickens Co., Ga., age 19, light complexion, sandy hair, blue eyes, 5'-7". Enlisted: U.S. 10th Regt Tenn. Cavalry, 3-1-1864. Killed 8-1865, "Skeered Corn Murders."

Nance, J.T., Pvt., **G**, Enlisted: 5-62, Camp Morrison by Captain Leak. Discharged 5-1-1862.

Nance, Thomas Jefferson, Pvt., **I**, Enlisted: 5-62, Discharged 10-12-1862. Died: 5-4-1909. Buried: Pleasant Valley Cemetery, Cherokee Co., Ala.

Nations, James Madison, Pvt., **A**, Captured: Rome, Ga., 9-13-64. Carried: Nashville 11-21-64; Louisville 11-22-64; Camp Douglas 11-26-64. Discharged 8-18-1865. Died: 3-19-1917. Buried: West Hill Cemetery, Dalton, Ga.

Neal, Abraham Harrison, Pvt., **G**, Enlisted: 5-62, Camp Morrison by Captain Leak. Present through 10-63 as Regimental Butcher. AWOL 11-18-1864. Died: 7-31-1914. Buried: Pleasant Hill Cemetery, Lafayette, Ga. Monument: 8th Ga. Inf. but no record of service.

Neal, Andrew Jackson, Pvt., **G**, Enlisted: 5-62, Camp Morrison by Captain Leak. Discharged 9-62. Died: 10-19-1898. Buried: Greenwood Community Cemetery, Weatherford, Texas.

Neal, Charles Asbury "Berry," Sgt., **G**, Enlisted: 5-62, Camp Morrison by Captain Leak. Present through 12-64. Surrendered: Kingston, Ga., 4-1865. Died: 3-11-1910. Buried: Russell Hill Baptist, Gordon Co., Ga.

Neely, Crayton Alonzo, Pvt., **K**, Enlisted: 3-63, Cartersville, Ga., by Lt. Col. Harper. Absent 12-63 Detained with wagon by General Wheeler. Absent 12-64 sick furlough home. Discharged 4-26-1865. Pension: Henry Co., Ala.

Neely, John H., Pvt., **K**, Enlisted: 11-64, Newnan, Ga., by Captain North. Present 12-64. WIA. Surrendered: Salisbury, N.C. 4-26-1865. Died: 7-12-1934. Buried: Sharpsburg Baptist Church, Coweta Co., Ga.

Nelson, Ashley S., Cpl., **E**, Enlisted: 3-62, Carrollton, Ga., by Captain Blalock. Present through 12-62. Absent 2-63 Detachment at Kingston, Tenn. WIA 12-12-63, Russellville, Tenn. Present 12-63 and 12-64. Pension: Marshall Co., Ala. 1896. Died: 4-19-1899. Buried: Ware Cemetery, Tolosa, Texas.

Nelson, N. Halley, Cpl., **E**, Enlisted: 5-62, Carrollton, Ga., by Captain Blalock. Present through 12-62. Absent 2-63 sick furlough. WIA: Mossy Creek, Tenn. 12-29-63. Gunshot: left hip near joint fracturing bone rendering leg 4 inches shorter. 90 days in hospital then furloughed home. Captured: Anderson, S.C. 5-3-1865, paroled. Pension: 1905, Haralson Co., Ga.

Nelson, Noel, Pvt., **H**, Enlisted: 4-62, Haralson Co., Ga., by Captain Tumlin. Present through 12-62. Absent 2-63 and 12-63 sick furlough. 12-64 AWOL. Died: 11-23-1890. Buried: Mars Hill Cemetery, Cleburne Co., Al.

Nevels, John, Pvt., **H**, Enlisted: 5-62, Haralson Co., Ga., by Captain Tumlin.

New, Jesse N., Pvt., **D**, Enlisted: 3-62, Dallas, Ga., by Captain Seawright. Present 2-63. Absent 12-63 WIA and sent to Atlanta Hospital.

Newborn, William A., Pvt., **D**, Captured 11-62.

Neyman, William G., 1st Sgt., **G**, Enlisted: 3-62, Floyd Co., Ga., by Captain Kerr. Present through 12-62. Promoted 2nd Sgt. 12-1-62. Present 2-63 and 12-63. WIA 9-64. Discharged 5-1-1865. Pension: Jackson Co., Ala. 1899.

Nicholas, Charles E., Pvt., **B**, Captured: Nashville 12-15-64. Carried: Louisville 12-19-64; Camp Douglas 12-23-64. 1-2-1865 stated: always loyal, conscripted, and deserted to Gen. Thomas Army, Nashville 12-16-64.

Nobles, L., Pvt., **G**, Enlisted: 7-63, Rome, Ga., by Captain Kerr. 12-63 present. Absent 12-64 Sick: Gadsden, Ala.

Norman, William Zacheriah, Pvt., **E**, Enlisted: 3-62, Carrollton, Ga., by Captain Blalock. Present through 2-63. 12-63 WIA. Absent 12-64 Detached with disabled horses. Paroled: Albany, Ga., 5-7-1865. Pension: Sick with measles summer 1864. At Atlanta, relapsed, with chronic diarrhea. Died: 8-18-1887. Buried: Mount Carmel Church, Cross Plains, Ga.

Norris, Cornelius Abner, Cpl., **B**, Enlisted: 4-62, Cartersville, Ga., by Col. Morrison. Present through 12-31-1864. Died: 7-30-1898. Buried: Glenwood Cemetery, Thomaston, Ga.

Norris, Julius Cicero, Pvt., **B**, Enlisted 5-15-1862, Savannah, Ga., 13th Ga. Inf. WIA: Sharpsburg 9-17-1862. WIA: 7-27-63, age 20. Enlisted: 5-64

in Newnan, Ga. Surrendered: Bentonville, N.C. 4-1865. Died: 12-1-1932. Buried: Luthersville City Cemetery, Meriwether Co., Ga.

North, B.A., Pvt., **K**, WIA: Akin, S.C.

North, Edward Owen, Sgt., **K**, Enlisted: 5-62, Camp Morrison by Captain North. Present through 12-62. Absent 12-63 Furlough: Fayetteville, Ga. Present 12-64. Surrendered: Salisbury, N.C. 4-26-1865. Died: 2-26-1895. Buried: Fayetteville City Cemetery, Fayette Co., Ga..

North, George Pennington, Pvt., **K**, Enlisted: 10-64, Newnan, Ga., by Captain North. Present 12-1864. Discharged 1865. Living: Montgomery Co., Ala. 1907.

North, Henry Anthony, Captain, **K**, Enlisted: 3-62, Camp Morrison by Lt. Col. Morrison. Elected Captain 5-1-62. Present through 2-62. Absent 12-63 Sick: Newnan, Ga. Hospital. Present 12-64. Paroled: Charlotte, N.C. 5-3-1865. Died: 2-17-1909. Buried: Sharpsburg Baptist Church, Coweta Co., Ga.

North, Marcus Bolden, Pvt., **K**, Enlisted: 5-62, Camp Morrison by Captain North. Absent 6-62 Captured: Loudon, Tenn., paroled. Present through 12-62. Absent 2-63 with leave in Coweta Co., Ga. Present 12-63 and 12-64. Died: 2-10-1900. Buried: Old Camp UMC, Carroll Co., Ga.

North, Needham Angier, Pvt., **K**, Enlisted: 5-62, Camp Morrison by Captain North. WIA 5-62. Horse KIA, paid $200. Present 8-62 through 12-62. Absent 2-63 with leave in Coweta Co., Ga. WIA: Chickamauga 9-19-63. Gunshot to thigh. WIA 12-29-63, Mossy Creek, Tenn. Sent to Bull's Gap Hospital. Gunshot: through right foot and into left foot. Sent home to Provost Duty, Newnan, Ga. Died: 3-6-1922. Buried: Sharpsburg Baptist Church, Coweta Co., Ga.

North, Robert Abraham J., Pvt., **K**, Enlisted: 5-62, Camp Morrison by Captain North. Official Record: Died: Travisville, Tenn., measles 8-28-1862. Death not reported, resulted him being reported KIA: Richmond, Kentucky 8-30-1862, buried mass grave. However, R.A.J. North, Died 8-28-1862, Buried: Chanute—Campbell Cemetery, Pickett Co., Tenn.

North, Robert Allen, Pvt., **K**, Enlisted: 5-62, Camp Morrison by Captain North. Absent 6-62 Captured and Paroled: Loudon, Tenn. Present 8-62. Captured: London, Ky. 9-8-62. Exchanged. Present 12-62. Discharged 8-14-63. Re-Enlisted 8-1-63, Knoxville: Captain North. Present 12-64. WIA: Savannah, Ga., 1-19-65. Gunshot: left heel destroying bone, causing amputation and gunshot: right big toe. Sent to Augusta, Ga. hospital. Died: 12-5-1908. Buried: Sharpsburg Baptist Church, Coweta Co., Ga.

North, Thomas Glenn, Pvt., **K**, Enlisted: 2-64, Newnan Ga., by Captain North. Surrendered: Greensboro, NC 4-26-1865. Died: 2-5-1904. Buried: Sharpsburg Baptist, Coweta Co., Ga.

Northcutt, Jesse J., Pvt., **D**, Enlisted: 3-62, Dallas, Ga., age 22, by Captain Seawright. Present through 8-62. Captured: Clay Village, Ky. 10-4-62, paroled. Absent 12-62. Present 2-63. Captured: Knoxville 12-1-63. Carried: Rock Island Prison, Ill. 1-6-64. Died: 2-20-64, Variola. Buried: Rock Island Confederate Cemetery, Grave #540.

Norwood, James A., Pvt., **B**, Enlisted: 7-63 in Grantville, Ga. Present 12-63 and 12-64.

Norwood, P.K., Pvt., **B**, Enlisted: 7-63 in Grantville, Ga. Present 12-63 Ordnance Sgt. 12-64 present.

Norwood, Thomas A., Pvt., **B**, Enlisted: Atlanta 5-22-1861, age 16, Atlanta Greys, 8th Ga. Inf. WIA: Manassas, Va. 7-21-1861. Discharged. Enlisted: 7-63 in Grantville, Ga. KIA: Philadelphia, Tenn. 10-20-63. Buried: Norwood Family Cemetery, Grantville, Ga.

O'Bryne, L.C., Pvt., **H**, Paroled: Talladega, Ala. 5-29-1865.

O'Donnell, John, Pvt., **K**, Captured: Decherd, Tenn. 7-3-63. Carried: Nashville 7-10-63; Louisville 7-15-63; Camp Chase 8-10-63. Took oath: 6-10-64. Description: home Hamilton Co., Tenn., light complexion, light hair, grey eyes, 5'-9". Released 12-31-1864.

Oliver, James H., Pvt., **C**, Enlisted: 3-62, Cave Spring, Ga., by Captain Haynie. Present 6-62 Blacksmith. Present 8-62 and 10-62. Present 12-62 Detailed: wagoner. Present 2-63. Present 6-63 Teamster for Regiment. Absent 12-63. AWOL 10-25-1864.

Omberg, Adolph A., Pvt., **G**, Enlisted: 8-63, Rome, Ga., by C.M. Pennington. Absent 12-63 sick. Present 12-64. Paroled: Charlotte, N.C. 5-3-1865. Died: 1-9-1885. Buried: Myrtle Hill, Rome, Ga.

O'Rillion, Fred, 2nd Lt., **A**, Captured: Mill Springs, Ky. 5-29-63. Carried: Johnson's Island; City Point, Va. 2-24-1865, exchanged.

Orr, Alexander Lynn, Pvt., **D**, Enlisted: 3-62, Dallas, Ga., age 25, by Captain Seawright. Present through 8-62. Absent 10-62 and 12-62 Sick furlough: Cobb Co., Ga. Present 2-63 through 12-64. Surrendered: Yadkin River, N.C. 4-26-1865. Died: 6-8-1910. Buried: Mars Hill Cemetery, Acworth, Ga.

Orr, David Woodburn, Pvt., **D**, Enlisted: 3-62, Dallas, Ga., age 27, by Captain Seawright. Pres-

ent through 8-62. Absent 10-62 and 12-62 Sick furlough: Cobb Co., Ga. Present 2-63 and 12-63. Absent 12-64 Captured; exchanged. Died: 1-29-1907. Buried: Mars Hill Cemetery, Acworth, Ga.

Orr, Joseph L., Pvt., **D**, Enlisted: 8-63, Dallas, Ga., by Lt. McGregor. Absent 12-63 Sick, Atlanta Hospital. 12-64 present. Died: 2-20-1900. Buried: Old Stone Cemetery, Ringgold. Ga.

Overby, Marquis de LaFayette, Pvt., **G**, Enlisted: 3-62, Floyd Co., Ga., by Captain Kerr. Present through 2-63 Present 12-63 Wagon driver. Absent on 30 day furlough. Died: 2-28-1887. Buried: Jones Valley Cemetery, Goldthwaite, Texas.

Overby, William Alexander, Pvt., **G**, Enlisted: 5-62, Chattanooga by Captain Kerr. Absent 6-62 Sick, Floyd Co., Ga. Present through 2-63. Absent 12-63 in Ga. Present 12-64. Paroled: Charlotte, N.C. 5-3-1865. Died: 5-25-1910; Rome, Ga.

Owen, Brice Marshall, Pvt., **B**, Enlisted: 3-62, Newnan, Ga., age 18, by Captain Strickland. Absent 6-62 through 2-63 Sick furlough: Luthersville, Ga. WIA: Chickamauga 9-19-63, Newnan, Ga. Hospital. 12-64 present. Died: 1-30-1909. Buried: Hollonville Cemetery, Pike Co., Ga.

Owen, James Oliver, Pvt., **H**, Enlisted: 4-62, Haralson Co., Ga., by Captain Tumlin. Present through 12-63. 12-31-1864 AWOL. Pension: Discharged 5-1-1865. Died: 7-13-1923. Buried: Harmony Grove Cemetery, Cleburne Co., Ala.

Owens, John, Pvt., **H**, Enlisted: 4-62, Haralson Co., Ga., by Captain Tumlin. Absent 6-62 Detached service, Loudon, Tenn. Present through 12-63. Captured: Dicks River, Ky. 3-28-63. Carried: Louisville; City Point, Va.; exchanged 4-13-63. 12-64 AWOL. Pension: Cherokee Co., Ala. 1899. Stated: discharged 5-1864.

Padgett, John Wesley, Pvt., **G**, Enlisted: Rome, Ga., age 23, 8th Ga. Inf. 5-13-61. WIA. Discharged. Enlisted: 1st Ga. Cavalry 3-13-62, Floyd Co., Ga., by Captain Kerr. Present through 12-62. Absent 2-63 on furlough. Absent 12-63 in Ga. On list of deserters at Chattanooga. Took oath 3-30-64. Description: home Floyd Co., Ga., sandy complexion, sandy hair, blue eyes, 5'-8". Died: 8-19-1900. Buried: Sand Springs Cemetery, Floyd Co., Ga.

Pain, J.K., Pvt., **G**, Enlisted: 10-64, Dirt Town, Ga., by Lt. Webster. 12-31-1864 present.

Pankey, J.C., Pvt., **A**, Enlisted: 2-64, Cedartown, Ga., by Captain York. 12-31-1864 present. Died: 2-17-1865. Buried: Magnolia Cemetery, Confederate Sq., row 5 , grave 11, Augusta, Ga.

Pannell, Wiley, Pvt., **G**, Enlisted: 3-62, Floyd Co., Ga., by Captain Kerr. Present 6-62 Wagon driver. Present through 2-1863.

Paris, Nathaniel Calvin, Pvt., **D**, Enlisted 5-62. Kicked by horse injuring leg. Discharged 11-64 at Savannah, Ga. Worked in Potash mines for Confederate Government until end of war. Died: 3-27-1911. Buried: New Canaan Baptist Church, Hiram, Ga.

Parker, John, Pvt., **A**, Enlisted: 5-64, in field by Captain York. 12-31-1864 present.

Parker, Sam, Pvt., **A**, Enlisted: 11-64, in field by Captain Jesse W. Crabb.

Parker, Thomas D., Pvt., **F**, Enlisted: 3-62, Fairmount, Ga., by Col. Morrison. Absent through 12-62 sick furlough. On Roll as Deserted 7-62 but also on Register of Discharged Soldiers 9-9-62. Captured: Fairmount, Ga., 5-17-64. Carried: Nashville 5-24-64; Louisville 5-28-64; Rock Island Prison, Ill.; exchanged 2-15-1865.

Parker, William C., Sgt., **E**, Enlisted: 3-62, Carrollton, Ga., by Captain Blalock. Present 6-62 through 2-1863.

Parker, William M., Pvt., **F**, Enlisted: 4-63, Sweetwater Valley, Tenn., by Captain Reynolds. Captured: Fairmount, Ga., 5-17-64. Carried: Nashville; Louisville 5-24-64; Rock Island Prison, Ill. 5-27-64. Erroneously reported exchanged with name of man who substituted himself 2-25-65. Released 5-26-1865. Description: home Fairmount, Gordon Co., Ga., light complexion, dark hair, hazel eyes, 5'-7", age 21. Died: 5-1-1914. Buried: Bethesda Baptist, Red Bud, Ga.

Parlier, J.W.T., Pvt., **G**, Enlisted: 5-62, Camp Morrison by Captain Leak. Present through 12-62. Absent 2-63 Detachment Camp. 10-63 AWOL.

Parmer, F.O., Pvt., **H**, Paroled: Montgomery, Ala. 6-14-1865. Description: 5'-7", dark hair, grey eyes, dark complexion.

Parris, Francis Marion, Pvt., **D**, Enlisted: 3-62, Dallas, Ga., by Captain Seawright. Present through 12-62. Absent 2-63 Sick furlough: Paulding Co., Ga. Absent 12-63 Sick: Atlanta Hospital. On list of deserters at Louisville 7-16-64. Released 7-18-64. Description: home Cobb Co., Ga., sallow complexion, black hair, grey eyes, 5'-7". Pension: December 1863, Parris almost froze to death while on picket duty. Could not get off his horse or speak. Died: 2-9-1875. Buried Mount Vernon Baptist, Paulding Co., Ga.

Parris, Nathaniel Greenberry, Pvt., **D**, Enlisted: 3-62, Dallas, Ga., age 25, by Captain Seawright. Present through 12-63. Absent 12-64 with leave. Surrendered: Durham Station, N.C. 4-26-1865.

Died: 7-8-1915. Buried: Chosea Springs Community Cemetery, Calhoun Co., Ala.

Pate, Hollis M., Pvt., **K**, Enlisted: 5-62, Camp Morrison by Captain North. Died: 4-5-1895. Buried: Historic Heritage Garden Cemetery, Douglasville, Ga.

Pate, Thomas Mitchell, Pvt., **F**, Died: 1-8-1905 . Buried: Mount Pleasant Cemetery, Coosa Co., Ala.

Patterson, Charles Davis, Pvt., **C**, 4-62, Died: 1886. Buried: Pine Grove Cemetery, Cullman Co., Ala.

Patterson, D.M., Pvt., **A**, Paroled: Columbus, Miss. 5-26-1865.

Patterson, Francis M., Pvt., **G**, Enlisted: 5-62, Camp Morrison by Captain Leak. Present through 12-62. Absent 2-63 sick furlough. Present 10-62 and 12-64. Admitted: Ocmulgee Hospital, Macon, Ga., 7-14-1864, pleurisy. Released 7-22-64. Home: Walker Co., Ga.

Patterson, George Washington, Pvt., **I**, Enlisted: 1-63, Kingston, Tenn., by Lt. Edwards. Present through 12-64. Pension: WIA: Atlanta 7-21-1864. Ball broke 9th rib; passed through lower lobe of lung, exited body. Died: 8-30-1936. Buried: LaFayette City Cemetery, Walker Co., Ga.

Paxton, John H., 1st Lt., **F**, Enlisted: 3-62, Fairmount, Ga., age 42, by Col. Morrison. Elected 1st Lt. 3-22-62. Present 6-62. Absent 8-62 sick. Resigned disabled 9-1-62: Gravel and urinary colloid (kidney stones). Captured: Carried to Chattanooga. Signed oath 2-26-1864. Description: home Pickens Co., Ga., dark complexion, dark hair, grey eyes, 5'-6".

Payne, F.N., Sgt., **F**, Captured: Athens, Ga., 5-8-65, paroled.

Pearson, W., Pvt., **B**, Enlisted: 7-64, Newnan, Ga., by Lt. Taylor. 12-31-1864 present.

Peavy, Thomas Hightower, Pvt., **B**, Enlisted: 3-4-1862, Newnan, Ga., 41st Ga. Inf. Discharged by substitute 12-7-62. Certificate: born Jasper Co., Ga., age 34, blacksmith, 5'-10", fair complexion, blue eyes, dark hair. Enlisted 3-4-62: 1st Ga. Cavalry, Newnan, Ga., by Captain Strickland. Present 12-62 and 2-63. Absent 12-63 and 12-64 Blacksmith, Detailed: Government Shop, Rutledge, Ga., Major Davitte. Died: 1871. Buried: Presbyterian Church, Senoia, Ga.

Peek, Robert H., Pvt., **A**, Enlisted: 3-64, Cedartown, Ga., by Captain Jesse W. Crabb. Present 12-64. Surrendered: Salisbury, N.C. 4-26-1865. Died: 11-23-1880 Polk Co., Ga.

Peek, Thomas Mayburn, Pvt., **A**, Enlisted: 3-62, Cedartown, Ga., by Captain John C. Crabb. Absent

6-62 and 8-62 Sick furlough: Newton Co., Ga. Present 10-62 and 12-62. Absent 12-63 Detailed: Government shop, Cunyard, wheelwright. A man came into the shop with smallpox. Peek caught it and died: 12-9-1863, Atlanta, Ga.

Penny, J.R., Cpl., **G**, Enlisted: 3-62, Floyd Co., Ga., by Captain Kerr. Elected Cpl. 3-31-62. Rejected.

Pepper, James M., 1st Lt., G, Enlisted: 3-62 in Rome, Ga. Present through 8-62. Absent 10-62 Acting Adjt. Gen., Col. Allston. 12-62 promoted: Asst. Adjt. Gen. Buried: Myrtle Hill Cemetery, Rome, Ga.

Perdue, James Polk, Pvt., **B**, Enlisted: 4-64 in Newnan, Ga. Present 12-64. Surrendered: Greensboro, N.C. 4-26-1865. Died: 6-30-1931. Buried: Pleasant Grove Baptist, Joel, Ga.

Perkins, John N., Captain, **F&S**, 4-62, WIA: Murfreesboro 7-13-62. Ball entered front left shoulder passing through body between heart and spine to under right arm. Disabled from field service. Absent 12-64 Detached service: Quartermaster Dept., Tuscaloosa, Ala. Captured: Tuscaloosa 4-3-1865. Carried: Macon, Ga., 5-2-1865, paroled. Died: 2-15-1896. Buried: Myrtle Hill Cemetery, Rome, Ga.

Perkins, J.T., Pvt., **A**, Deserted: 11-22-64; Hilton Head, S.C. On list of deserters for steamer *Fulton* going to New York. Received 2-3-1865. Description: born Macon, Ga., age 18, grey eyes, brown hair, fair complexion, 5'-9".

Perry, James L., Pvt., **A**, Surrendered: Kingston, Ga., 5-1865. Witness: Dawson Co., Ga., 1919.

Phelps, Reuben, Pvt., **B**, Enlisted: 3-62, Newnan, Ga., age 38, by Captain Strickland. Present through 12-63. WIA: Resaca, Ga., 5-13-64. Gunshot, left thigh. Admitted: General Hospital, Charlottesville, Va. 10-21-64. Left leg amputated.

Phillips, Daniel Pinkney, Pvt., **G**, Enlisted: 3-64, Cartersville, Ga., by Lt. Zuber. Blacksmith. Issued clothing: Cannon Hospital, Union Spring, Ala., patient. Present 12-64. Surrendered: Raleigh, N.C. 4-26-1865. Died: 7-29-1911. Buried: Pleasant Valley North Cemetery, Rome, Ga.

Philips, J.L., Pvt., **G**, Enlisted: 5-64, Rome, Ga., by Col. Cameron. AWOL 8-64.

Philips, S.P., Pvt., **F**, Enlisted: 10-64, Jonesboro, Ga., by Captain McWilliams. 12-31-1864 present.

Phillips, Jeremiah S., Pvt., **A**, Enlisted: 3-62, Camp Morrison by Captain John C. Crabb. Present through 12-62. Absent 2-63 Detailed: Recruiter. Absent 12-63 Cut off with wagons. Absent 12-64 Teamster for Gen. Martin 8-10-1864. Paroled:

Meridian, Miss. 5-11-1865. Home: Cedartown, Ga. Widow pension: Jefferson Co., Ala. 1904.

Phillips, Lewis, Pvt., **F**, Enlisted: 8-62, Carrollton, Ga., by Captain Blalock. Substitute for John L. Camp 8-1-62. Present through 2-63. Deserted: 3-13-63.

Phillips, Robert A., Pvt., **G**, Enlisted: 3-62, Floyd Co., Ga., by Captain Kerr. Present through 8-62. Captured: Clay Village, Ky. 10-4-62, paroled. Present through 12-64. Paroled: Charlotte, N.C. 5-3-1865. Died: 2-12-1904. Buried: Whooping Creek Primitive Baptist, Carrollton, Ga.

Phillips, Robert Crayton, Pvt., **G**, 4-62, Surrendered: Raleigh, N.C. 4-26-1865. Died: 3-3-1891, Floyd Co., Ga.

Phipps, W., Pvt., **B**, Captured: Marietta, Ga., 7-5-64. Carried: Camp Douglas 10-27-64. Claimed Deserted for Amnesty Proclamation.

Picket, J., Pvt., **F**, Enlisted: 5-64 in Decatur, Ga. 12-31-64 AWOL.

Pickett, Benjamin W., 2nd Lt., **D**, Enlisted: 3-62, Dallas, Ga., age 35, by Captain Seawright. In Three Man Charge. Present through 12-62. Elected 2nd Lt. 8-5-62, succeeding S.R. McGregor. Absent 2-63 Sick furlough: Paulding Co., Ga. KIA: Chickamauga 9-19-63. Buried: New Hope Cemetery, Dallas, Ga.

Pinkard, Peter J., Pvt., **D**, Enlisted: 3-62, Dallas, Ga., age 19, by Captain Seawright. Present through 2-63. WIA: Philadelphia, Tenn. 10-20-63. Ball entered right thigh causing amputation near body. Died: 9-22-1910. Buried: Yorkville Methodist Church, Paulding Co., Ga.

Pitner, Albert Gilbert, Jr., Pvt., **G**, Enlisted 7-14-63, Rome, Ga., Floyd Legion. Died: 11-29-1878. Buried: Myrtle Hill Cemetery, Rome, Ga., 1st Ga. Cavalry service by tombstone.

Pittman, O.J., Pvt., **D**, Enlisted: 3-62, Dallas, Ga., age 37, by Captain Seawright. Absent through 8-62 Detailed: Clerk, QM Dept. Present 10-62 through 2-63. Absent 12-63 Detained in Ga., by General Wheeler. Issued clothing 6-7-1864.

Pitts, Meedy, Pvt., **E**, Enlisted: 7-62, Carrollton, Ga., by Captain Blalock. Substitute for Thomas Bonner 7-26-62. Present through 12-62. 2-62 AWOL. Absent 12-63 WIA. Clothing issued 8-23-63.

Plant, John Anthony, Cpl., **B**, Enlisted: 3-62, Newnan, Ga., age 40, by Captain Strickland. Present through 12-62. Absent 2-63 Sick furlough: Grantville, Ga. 12-64 present. Diagnosed: chronic nephritis. Placed on Lite duty. Died. 8-17-1893. Buried: Meriwether Co., Ga.

Poarch, S.D., Pvt., **G**, Enlisted: 5-62, Camp Morrison by Captain Leak. Present through 12-62. Absent 3-63 Detachment Camp.

Polk, Franklin Marion, Pvt., **B**, Enlisted: 3-62 in Newnan, Ga. Present through 2-63. Captured: Pigeon River, Tenn. 1-27-64. Carried: Knoxville; Nashville; Louisville 2-15-64; Rock Island, Ill. 2-18-64. Admitted: Jackson Hospital, Richmond, Va., pneumonia 3-11-1865. Died: 2-1-1922. Buried: Cook Springs Baptist, St. Clair Co., Ala.

Pollard, Pickens, Pvt., **C**, Enlisted: 2-63, Cave Spring, Ga., by Captain Haynie. Present through 6-63. Absent 12-63 Supposed to be with detachment, but became cut off from command.

Potts, James H., Pvt., **F**, Enlisted: 7-63, Sweetwater, Tenn., by Captain Reynolds. 12-63 and 12-64 AWOL.

Potts, William C., Pvt., **E**, Enlisted: 3-62, Carrollton, Ga., by Captain Blalock. Present through 12-62. Present 2-63 Teamster for Regiment. Died 5-7-1863.

Powell, Mark, Cpl., **D**, Enlisted: 3-62, Dallas, Ga., age 45, by Captain Seawright. Present 6-62. Absent 8-62 Sick furlough: Paulding Co., Ga. Present 10-62. AWOL 12-62. Present 2-63. AWOL 12-1-63. Pension: Col. Davitte, witness 2-1897, Powell served to end of war. Surrendered: Raleigh, N.C. 4-26-1865. Died: May 1904, Polk Co., Ga.

Powell, William, D, KIA: 1864.

Power, David P., Pvt., **B**, Enlisted: 3-62, Newnan, Ga., age 22, by Captain Strickland. Absent 6-62 Sick furlough: Newnan, Ga. Present through 2-63. Absent 12-63 Detained with wagon train by General Wheeler. Absent in Hospital 12-5-1864. Surrendered: Greensboro, N.C. 4-26-1865. Died: 12-25-1901. Buried: Carrollton City Cemetery, Carroll Co., Ga.

Presley, William Johnson, Pvt., **F**, Enlisted: 3-62, Fairmount, Ga., by Col. Morrison. Absent 6-62 sick furlough. Present through 12-62. Absent 2-63 Recruiting for Gen. Pegram. Present 12-63 and 12-64. Died: 1909. Buried: West Hill Cemetery, Sherman, Texas.

Price, James S., Pvt., **K**, Enlisted: 5-62, Camp Morrison by Captain North. Present through 12-62. Absent 2-63 on leave in Coweta Co., Ga. Captured: Philadelphia, Tenn. 10-20-63. Carried: Camp Nelson; Camp Chase 11-14-63; Rock Island, Ill. 1-17-64. Exchanged. Admitted: Jackson Hospital, Richmond, Va. 3-6-1865, debilitas.

Prichard, J.R., Pvt., **D**, Enlisted: 9-62, Dallas, Ga., by Captain Robert F. Trammell. Present 10-62. Absent 12-62 on leave in Paulding Co., Ga. Present 2-63 Detailed to Brigade Wagons. Absent

12-63 Detained in Ga., by General Wheeler. 12-64 AWOL.

Prichett, William N., Pvt., **C**, Enlisted: 3-62, Cave Spring, Ga., by Captain Haynie. Present 6-62. Absent 8-62 on furlough home. Present 10-62. Absent 12-62 Transferred: 1st Ala. Cavalry. Present 2-63 Detailed wagoner. Absent 12-63 Sick. Pension: Transferred 10-1864, 3rd Maryland Artillery (no record). Surrendered: Meridian, Miss.

Prickett, William Wiley P., Pvt., **C**, Enlisted: 8-62, Cave Spring, Ga., by Captain Nap. Reynolds. Mustered: Kingston, Tenn. Present through 12-62. Pension: Scout for Gen. Wheeler, North Ga., 6-64. Captured; carried: Camp Morton, Ind., and held. Died: 1-7-1929. Buried: New Hope Baptist Cemetery, Acworth (North), Bartow Co., Ga.

Prikett (Prichard), W.L., Cpl., **D**, Enlisted: 3-63 in Knoxville.

Prior, John Taylor, Pvt., **C**, Enlisted: 3-62, Cave Spring, Ga., by Captain Haynie. Discharged 6-62 Lewis D.H. Abrams substituted. Died: 11-5-1910. Buried: Masonic Cemetery, Deer Creek, Oregon.

Proctor, G.W., Pvt., **H**, Enlisted: 4-62, Haralson Co., Ga., by Captain Tumlin. Present through 12-62. Absent 2-63 Sick furlough. Absent 12-63 sick. 12-64 AWOL.

Proctor, Henry, Pvt., **E**, Enlisted: 3-62, Carrollton, Ga., by Captain Blalock. Present through 12-63. Clothing issued 6-1864.

Proctor, Hiram G., Pvt., **H**, Enlisted: 1-63, Kingston, Ga., by Captain Tumlin. Present 2-63. AWOL 12-1-63. Died: hospital 8-30-1864.

Pruett, S.E., Pvt., **G**, Enlisted: 5-62, Camp Morrison by Captain Leak. Present: 6-62 through 12-62. 3-63 AWOL.

Pruett (Pruitt), Wilson Lumpkin, Cpl., **D**, Enlisted: 3-62, Dallas, Ga., by Captain Seawright. Present through 12-62. Absent 2-63 Sick furlough: Paulding Co., Ga., bronchitis. 12-63 present. Died 12-23-1905. Buried: Skirum UMC, Dawson, Ala.

Pruitt, W.H., Pvt., **G**, Enlisted: 3-62, Floyd Co., Ga., by Captain Kerr. Present through 12-62. AWOL 2-63. Absent 12-63 in Ga. Clothing issued 6-64.

Pryor, William A., Pvt., **K**, Captured: Knoxville 8-7-63. Carried: Nashville; Louisville 8-10-63. Took oath. Enlisted: Federal Army 8-12-1863, age 26, 10th Regt. Tenn. Cavalry.

Puckett, William Ellis, Pvt., **I**, Enlisted: 5-62, Camp Morrison by Captain Leak. Present through

10-63. AWOL 6-1-64. Pension: Joined, Big Shanty. Horse KIA: Murfreesboro 7-13-1862. Rawlins's Mill, Cumberland River, Ky.; Went fishing with three others, 25 Yankees attacked, shooting and capturing all. Puckett played dead. Walked 100 miles to rejoin regiment. WIA: New Hope Church 5-19-64, hospitals: Atlanta and Macon, Ga. Surrendered: Kingston, Ga., 1865. Died: 1-28-1928. Buried: Sunset Hills Cemetery, Valdosta, Ga.

Pullin, John T., Pvt., **B**, Enlisted: 3-62, Newnan, Ga., by Captain Strickland. Present through 8-62. Absent 10-62 Sick furlough: Luthersville, Ga. Discharged 12-8-62. Died: 4-24-1873. Buried: Hogan-Word Family Cemetery, Hogansville, Ga.

Pullin, W. Tillman, Pvt., **B**, Enlisted: 3-62, Newnan, Ga., by Captain Strickland. Present through 10-62. Absent 12-62 and 2-63 Sick furlough: Grantville, Ga., 12-63 Dropped from roll by Major Strickland. Last paid 6-30-1863. Died before 1870.

Pullin, William M., Pvt., **B**, Enlisted: 3-62, Newnan, Ga., by Captain Strickland. Present through 12-62. Absent 2-63 Sick furlough: Hogansville, Ga. 12-63 Dropped from roll by Major Strickland. Recommended for hospital duty. Disabled: indolent ulcer, right leg 1-2-1864. Living: Volusia, Fla. 1900.

Puryear, Hamilton Young, Pvt., **F**, Enlisted 7-3-1861, Atlanta: 11th Ga. Inf. Bounty: born Walker Co., Ga., age 18, 5'-10", grey eyes, light hair, light complexion. Typhoid fever, discharged. Enlisted: 1st Ga. Cavalry, 5-1-64: Big Shanty, Ga., by Lt. McWilliams. Present 12-64. Surrender: Greensboro, N.C. 4-26-1865. Pension: Captain McWilliams broke camp, headed home. Paroled: Kingston, Ga. May 1865. Died: 12-29-1909. Buried: Puryear Cemetery, Walker Co., Ga.

Puryear, Henry Clay, Sgt., **F**, Enlisted: 3-62, Fairmount, Ga., by Col. Morrison. Present through 12-62. Absent 2-63 Detachment and wagons. Captured: Philadelphia, Tenn. 10-20-63. Carried: Camp Nelson; Camp Chase 11-14-63; Fort Delaware Prison 3-4-64. Released 6-15-1865. Description: home Walker Co., Ga., sallow complexion, light hair, blue eyes, 6'-0". Witness: Walker Co., Ga., 1891. Died: 4-5-1903, Ga.

Puryear, John Jasper, Pvt., **F**, Enlisted: 3-62, Fairmount, Ga., by Col. Morrison. Present through 2-63. Absent 12-63 In Ga. with wagons. 12-64 present. Buried: Mount Carmel Cemetery, Wolfe City, Texas.

Puryear, William Harrison, Pvt., **F**, Enlisted: 3-62, Fairmount, Ga., by Col. Morrison. Present

through 8-62. WIA: 10-25-62. Died: 11-1-62. Buried in Virginia.

Putnam, Thomas Whitney, Cpl., **C**, Enlisted: 3-62, Cave Spring, Ga., by Captain Haynie. Present through 2-63. Promoted 1st Cpl. 3-16-63. 12-63 present. KIA during 1863.

Pyles, Thomas J., Pvt., **G**, Enlisted: 5-62, Cartersville, Ga., by Captain Leak. Discharged: 9-27-62. Certificate: Delicate constitution, kidney disease. Description: age 42, 5'-8", fair complexion, blue eyes, dark hair.

Pyron, W.B., Pvt., **B**, Enlisted: 3-62, Newnan, Ga., age 25, by Captain Strickland. Absent 6-62 Sick furlough: Turin, Ga. Furloughed 30 days: 7-13-62, Loudon, Tenn.

Rabun, R.L., Pvt., **G**, Enlisted: 3-62, Floyd Co., Ga., by Captain Kerr. Died: Big Creek Gap, Tenn. 6-2-62, Pneumonia.

Ragsdale, Charles David, Pvt., **K**, Enlisted: 1st Ga. Inf. Regt. Ramsey's (Newnan Guards) 3-18-61, Newnan, Ga. Enlisted 1st Ga. Cavalry 5-3-62: Camp Morrison by Captain North. Present through 12-31-64. Best Vidette. Pension: Coweta Co., Ga. 1899.

Ragsdale, George Washington, 2nd Lt., **D**, Enlisted 5-31-1861: 7th Ga. Inf. Enlisted: 3-62, Dallas, Ga., by Captain Seawright. Present through 2-63. Captured: Philadelphia, Tenn. 10-20-63. Died: 4-24-1907. Buried: Glenwood Cemetery, Green Forest, Ark.

Ragsdale, Johnathan Harrison, Pvt., **D**, Enlisted: 8-63, Dallas, Ga., by Lt. McGregor. Absent 12-63 Sick: Atlanta Hospital. 12-64 present. Pension: Camped at Yadkin River, N.C. at surrender. Went home, paroled: Kingston, Ga. Died: 12-10-1928. Buried: Mars Hill Cemetery, Acworth, Ga.

Rainwater, William Joseph, Pvt., **D**, Enlisted: 3-62, Dallas, Ga., age 17, by Captain Seawright. Present 6-62. Absent 8-62 and 2-63 Sick furlough: Paulding Co., Ga. Present 10-62 and 12-62. AWOL 9-1-63. Widow Pension: Home sick with measles 9-1-64. Returned to duty 10-64, relapsed and turned into typhoid fever. Sent to hospital, Bainbridge, Ga.; died 10-26-1864.

Rakestraw, Calvin B., 2nd Lt., **D**, Enlisted: 3-62, Dallas, Ga., age 36, by Captain Seawright. Present through 2-63. Promoted 2nd Lt. 9-19-62 by Col. Morrison. WIA: Dandridge, Tenn. 1-12-64. WIA: Atlanta 7-22-64. Paroled: Charlotte, N.C. 5-3-1865. Died: 12-16-1901. Buried: Poplar Springs Cemetery, Hiram, Ga.

Rakestraw, Ivey Richard, Pvt., **D**, Deserted: Atlanta 1864. Took oath and released, Chattanooga 11-18-64. Description: 5'-10", black hair, and hazel eyes. Died: 5-12-1899. Buried: Mount Tabor Cemetery, Dallas, Ga.

Rakestraw, James R., Pvt., **D**, Enlisted: 5-62, Dallas, Ga., by Captain Seawright. Absent 6-62 Sick furlough: Paulding Co., Ga. Absent 8-62 Sick: Loudon, Tenn. Present 10-62 through 2-63. Absent 12-63 Detained in Ga., by General Wheeler. Deserted and took oath 11-18-64 at Chattanooga. Description: home Paulding Co., Ga., light complexion, black hair, hazel eyes, and 5'-10". Died: 7-29-1923. Buried: Ball Ground Community Cemetery, Cherokee Co., Ga.

Rakestraw, John, Pvt., **D**, Enlisted: 5-62, Dallas, Ga., by Captain Seawright. Present 6-62. Absent 8-62 Sick furlough: Cobb Co., Ga. Present 10-62 and 12-62. Absent 2-63 Detailed: Recruiter. Present 12-63 and 12-64. POW: Chattanooga, General Hospital 12-14-1864, age 30. Met future wife walking home from the war. She directed him to his destroyed home. Died: 2-8-1932. Buried: Poplar Springs Baptist, Hiram, Ga.

Rakestraw, John W., Sgt., **D**, Enlisted: 3-62, Dallas, Ga., by Captain Seawright. Present through 2-63. WIA: Philadelphia, Tenn. 10-20-63. 12-64 AWOL. Clothing issued 7-13-1864. Pension: Fighting day and night, Crew's Brigade, S.C. and N.C., eyes inflamed from exposure and gunpowder could not see to call roll as orderly sergeant. Captain Robert Trammell excused him from duty 3-65. Died: 7-5-1904. Buried: New Canaan Baptist Church, Hiram, Ga.

Rakestraw, Leroy, Pvt., **D**, Enlisted: 5-62, Dallas, Ga., by Captain Seawright. Absent 6-62 Sick furlough: Paulding Co., Ga. Present through 12-63. AWOL 12-64. Pension: Left regiment before surrender. Called away from the works and told of surrender and went home. Confederate Soldier Home 11-2-1910. Died: 11-22-1912. Buried: Paulding Co., Ga.

Rakestraw, William Jr., Cpl., **D**, Enlisted: 5-62, Dallas, Ga., by Captain Seawright. Absent 6-62 Sick furlough: Paulding Co., Ga. Absent 8-62 Sick: Loudon, Tenn. Present through 12-63. Issued clothing 7-13-64. Deserted and took oath 11-18-64, Chattanooga. Description: home Cobb Co., Ga., dark complexion, black hair, black eyes, 6'-0". Prison General Hospital, Chattanooga 12-18-64, dismissed 1-4-65, age 26. On list of deserters at Louisville 2-20-65. Released 2-21-1865. Died: 2-20-1901. Buried: Bullard Cemetery. Powder Springs, Ga.

Rakestraw, William Sr., Pvt., **E**, Enlisted: 3-62, Carrollton, Ga., by Captain Blalock. Present through 12-62. Absent 2-63 sick furlough. Pres-

ent 12-63. Captured: Atlanta 7-22-64. Took oath 2-14-65.

Ramsey, John, Pvt., **H**, Enlisted: 7-64, Tallapoosa, Ga., by Captain Tumlin. 12-31-1864 AWOL.

Randall, John James, Pvt., **A**, Enlisted: 2-63, Cedartown, Ga., by Captain Jesse W. Crabb. Surrendered: Greensboro, NC 4-26-1865. Died: 8-11-1925, Halls Station, Bartow Co., Ga.

Rankin, Robert C., Pvt., Widow pension: Cleburne Co., Ala. 1891.

Ray, Lavender Roy, Captain, **H**, Enlisted 1st Ga. Inf. 7-6-61. Enlisted 1st Ga. Cavalry 4-19-62, Tallapoosa, Ga., by Captain Tumlin. Present 6-62. Absent 8-62 and 10-62 Sick: Newnan, Ga. Absent 2-63 sick furlough. Absent 12-63 Detailed: Ordnance Depot, Atlanta 7-18-63. Employed at Atlanta Arsenal by Gen. Buckner. Appointed Adjutant: 1st Ga. Cavalry 7-3-64. Assigned action ordnance officer, Iverson's Brigade 10-16-64. Paroled: Augusta, Ga., 5-2-65. Died: 5-27-1916. Buried: Oak Hill Cemetery, Newnan, Ga.

Reaves (Reeves), James H., Pvt., **D**, Enlisted: 3-62, Dallas, Ga., age 23, by Captain Seawright. Present through 8-62. Absent 10-62 and 12-62 Sick furlough: Paulding Co., Ga. Present 2-63 and 12-63. Issued clothing 7-13-64. AWOL 12-31-1864.

Reed, W.P., Cpl., **K**, Enlisted: 3-62, Camp Morrison by Captain North. Present through 12-31-1864.

Reese, Henry, Pvt., **K**, 5-62, WIA: Resaca 6-14-1864. Surrendered: Greensboro, N.C. 4-26-1865. Died: 10-2-1928, Coweta Co., Ga.

Reese, W.H., Pvt., **K**, Enlisted: 5-62, Cartersville, Ga., by Major Harper. Present through 8-62. Absent 10-62 and 2-63. Sick furlough: Coweta Co., Ga. Present 12-62. Absent 2-63 sick furlough: Coweta Co., Ga. Present 12-63. Admitted: Oglethorpe Barracks, Savannah for discharge exam 1-22-63. Denied. Present 12-64. Dismounted with wagon train. Paroled: Charlotte, N.C. 5-3-1865.

Reeves, Augustus A., Pvt., **K**, Enlisted: Griffin, Ga., age 22, 13th Ga. Inf. 7-8-1861. Discharged 10-19-61 Tuberculosis. Description: 6' tall, light complexion, dark hair and eyes. Enlisted 5-1-62: Camp Morrison by Captain North. Discharged 5-30-62, Chattanooga. Died: 2-11-1917. Buried: Westview Cemetery, Atlanta, Ga.

Reeves, John, Pvt., **G**, Enlisted: 3-62, Floyd Co., Ga., by Captain Kerr. Present through 8-62. Absent 10-62 Left sick, Bloomfield, Ky. 9-20-62. Captured sick: Bloomfield 10-11-62. Carried: Louisville; Vicksburg on steamboat, Mary Crane, exchanged 11-29-62. Description: age 18, 5'-10½", and sick.

Reeves, M.W., Pvt., K, Enlisted: 5-62, Cartersville, Ga., by Major Harper. WIA, captured in skirmish at Leaches' Ford, Powell River, Tenn. 6-19-62. Carried: Camp Morton; Johnsons Island Prison. Died: 10-30-62. Buried: Johnson Island Confederate Cemetery, Marblehead, Ohio.

Reeves, Mal, K, KIA: Russellville, Tenn. 12-12-1863.

Reid, Henry T., Cpl., E, Enlisted: 3-62, Carrollton, Ga., by Captain Blalock. Present through 2-63. Absent 12-63 Sick. Present 12-31-1864.

Reid (Reed), Henry Wyatt, Pvt., E, Enlisted: 4-64, Oxford, Ala., by Col. Davitte. Present 12-31-1864. Pension: 56th Ga. Inf., substitute, John T. Dale as father was ill. Joined Captain Shuford's Company. Surrendered: Greensboro, N.C. 4-26-1865. Died: 6-1-1908. Buried: Holly Springs Primitive Baptist Church, Carroll Co., Ga.

Reid, Leonodes, Pvt., E, Enlisted: 3-62, Carrollton, Ga., by Captain Blalock. Present through 12-62. Absent 2-63 sick furlough. 12-63 present. Clothing issued 6-1864.

Reid, Robert A., Cpl., I, Died: 7-25-1924. Buried: Hebron Cemetery, Howell's Crossroads, Cherokee Co., Ala.

Reynolds, Benajah Houston, Pvt., C, Enlisted: 3-62, Cave Spring, Ga., by Captain Haynie. Present 6-62. WIA: 7-13-62 Murfreesboro. Gunshot: seven inches from spine, left side, passed through across spine to six inches, right side, exit. Admitted: Bell Hospital, Rome, Ga., 3-24-63. Furloughed 30 days: P.O. Booker's Store, Ga. Discharged disabled 8-15-63. Died: 11-15-1898. Buried: Tin Top Cemetery, Tarrant Co., Texas.

Reynolds, B.G., Attended Gen. Joseph Wheeler's funeral January 1906.

Reynolds, D., Pvt., C, Enlisted 3-63, Present 4-6-1863.

Reynolds, James C., Pvt., A, Captured: Rome, Ga., 9-13-64. Carried: Nashville 11-21-64; Louisville 11-22-64; Camp Douglas 11-26-64. Took oath. Enlisted: 6th U.S. Vols. Inf. 3-29-1865. Description: born Floyd Co., Ga., age 22, blue eyes, fair complexion, light hair, 5'-9".

Reynolds, James M., Pvt., G, Enlisted: 3-62, Floyd Co., Ga., by Captain Kerr. 6-62 Rejected.

Reynolds, James Marion, 2nd Lt., C, Enlisted: 3-62, Cave Spring, Ga., by Captain Haynie. Present 6-62. Appointed 2nd Lt., death of Edwin S. Grimmett 6-27-62. Present 8-62. Absent 10-62 Sick furlough: Floyd Co., Ga. Present 12-62 and 2-63. WIA: Dandridge, Tenn. 12-24-63. Died: 12-27-63. Buried: Battlefield, Dandridge, Tenn.

Reynolds, John S., Pvt., I, Enlisted: 4-62, Camp Morrison by Captain Leak. Present through

12-62. Absent 3-63 Detachment Camp: Blacksmith. 12-63 AWOL. Pension: Surrendered: Goldsboro, N.C. 4-26-1865. Pension: Fulton Co., Ga., 1910.

Reynolds, Lewis R., Pvt., C, Enlisted: 3-62, Cave Spring, Ga., by Captain Haynie. Present through 8-62. WIA: 8-18-62: Richmond, Kentucky. Gunshot: left wrist cutting off hand. Amputated arm below elbow. Present 12-62 Regimental wagoner. Present 2-63. Absent 12-63. Absent 12-64 unfit for duty. Pension: Floyd Co., Ga., 1902. Buried: New Prospect Cemetery, Floyd Co., Ga.

Reynolds, Napoleon J., Major, F, Enlisted: Rome, Ga., Floyd Sharp Shooters, became 21st Ga. Inf. Elected 2nd Lt. 6-24-61. Resigned 4-30-62. Enlisted: 5-62, 1st Ga. Cavalry, Fairmount, Ga., by Col. Morrison. Elected Captain 3-22-62. Present through 12-63. Absent 12-63. Appointed Major; Brigade Quartermaster, Crews' Brigade. Paroled: Brigade Hq. 5-3-1865.

Reynolds, P.H., Pvt., H, Enlisted: 4-62, Haralson Co., Ga., by Captain Tumlin. Present through 12-31-1863.

Reynolds, S.J., Cpl., D, Enlisted: 3-62, Dallas, Ga., age 38, by Captain Seawright. Present 6-62. Absent 8-62 Sick furlough: Paulding Co., Ga. Discharged disabled 9-22-62, Kingston, Tenn. Certificate: born in Ga., age 38, 5'-6", dark complexion, black hair, black eyes.

Reynolds, Simon, Sgt., C, Enlisted: 3-62, Cave Spring, Ga., by Captain Haynie. Promoted 3rd Sgt. 3-31-62. Ordnance Sgt. 7-1-62. Present 8-62 through 2-63. Absent 12-63 with detachment. Admitted: Floyd House Hospital, Macon, Ga., 9-21-1864, chronic diarrhea, general debilitated and emaciated, from Talladega, Ala.

Reynolds, Thomas Charles, Pvt., H, Enlisted: 4-62, Tallapoosa, Ga., by Captain Tumlin. Present through 2-63 as Farrier. Present 12-63. Issued clothing 6-64. 12-64 AWOL. Died: 10-9-1909. Buried: Glenfield Cemetery, New Albany, Miss.

Richardson, Hugh W., Pvt., C, Enlisted: 3-62, Cave Spring, Ga., by Captain Haynie. Absent 6-62 Furlough: Floyd Co., Ga. Present 8-62. Died: 10-10-1896. Buried: Lyerly Cemetery, Chattooga Co., Ga.

Richardson, Jesse L., Pvt., D, Enlisted: 3-62, Dallas, Ga., by Captain Seawright. Present 10-62. Present 12-62. Detailed nurse at hospital. Absent 2-63 Sick furlough: Paulding Co., Ga. Absent 12-63. Detailed as Teamster. Present 12-64. Paroled: Charlotte, N.C. 5-3-1865. Living: Walton Co., Ga., 1870.

Richardson, Morgan J., Pvt., C, Enlisted: 3-62,

Cave Spring, Ga., by Captain Haynie. Discharged 6-62.

Richardson, William Hugh, Pvt., **C**, Enlisted: 3-63, Cave Spring, Ga., by Captain Haynie. Present through 12-31-64. Pension: WIA: Kingston, Ga., shell fragment 6-18-1864. Leg above knee; traveled down tearing joint; exiting leg. Crippled thereafter. Died: 2-8-1900. Buried: Lyerly Cemetery, Chattooga Co., Ga.

Richardson, W.W., Pvt., **K**, Enlisted: 5-62, Camp Morrison by Captain North. First in company to kill a Yankee with a sword. Present through 2-63. Absent 12-63 Detained with wagon train by General Wheeler. Issued clothing 6-7-64. 12-31-1864 AWOL.

Riddle, James W., Pvt. On list of deserters that took oath 4-2-64. Description: home Gordon Co., Ga., sandy complexion, brown hair, grey eyes, 6'-0".

Riddle, Vaden H., 1st Sgt., **F**, Enlisted: 3-62, Fairmount, Ga., by Col. Morrison. Present through 12-63. Resigned: 1st Sgt. 9-6-63. Absent 12-64 Detailed to Brigade Quartermaster. Paroled: Charlotte, N.C. 5-3-1865.

Riggs, Alexander Hamilton Stephens, Pvt., **E**, Enlisted: 5-64, Marietta, Ga., by Captain Shuford. Absent 12-64 sick. Died: 7-27-1903. Buried: Bethel Baptist Church, Temple, Ga.

Riley, William, Pvt., **C**, Enlisted: 9-62, Cave Spring, Ga., by Lt. Reynolds. Mustered: Kingston, Tenn. Present through 12-63. Absent 12-64 Detailed within Regiment. Surrendered: Salisbury, N.C. 4-1865. Died: 3-27-1915, Walker Co., Ga.

Rivers, Kolb, Pvt., **C**, Enlisted: 10-64. Present 12-64, not paid.

Robberts, John, Pvt., **G**, Enlisted: 5-62, Camp Morrison by Captain Leak. Present through 3-63. Captured: Fall Creek, Mill Springs, Ky. 6-3-63. Carried: Lexington; Camp Chase 6-13-63; Johnsons Island 6-20-63; City Point, Va. 2-24-65, exchanged.

Roberson, William, Pvt., **B**, Enlisted: 3-62, Newnan, Ga., age 21, by Captain Strickland. Present through 12-62. Absent 2-63 Sick furlough: Grantville, Ga. Present 12-63. WIA: Atlanta 7-21-64. Admitted to General Hospital.

Roberts, Charles, Pvt., **D**, Enlisted: 5-62, Dallas, Ga., by Captain Seawright. Died of measles, Clinton, Tenn. 5-26-62. Physician T. Briscoe approved charge of $5. for coffin by J.J. Kennedy.

Roberts, James, Pvt., **H**, Enlisted: 3-63, Tallapoosa, Ga., by Captain Tumlin. AWOL 9-14-63. Last paid 6-30-63.

Roberts, J.J., Pvt., **G**, Enlisted: 5-62, Camp Mor-

rison by Captain Leak. Present through 12-62. WIA: Murfreesboro (Stones River) 1-1-63. Captured: Jacksboro, Tenn. 8-27-63. Carried: Camp Nelson 9-5-63; Louisville 9-5-63; Rock Island, Ill. 1-24-64. Exchange 3-13-1865.

Roberts, Joseph H., Pvt., **G**, Paid Clerk, extra duty, Savannah 1-31-64 through 7-31-1864, by Gen. Beauregard.

Roberts, N., Pvt., **C**, 3-62, Present 4-6-1862.

Roberts, Roland, Pvt., **H**, Living: Roanoke, Ala. 1921. Pension: Randolph Co., Ala.

Roberts (Robberts), William E., Pvt., **I**, Enlisted: 9-62, Kingston, Tenn., by Captain Leak. Present through 10-63.

Robertson, Archibald, Pvt., **H**, Captured: Jacksboro, Tenn. 8-3-63. Carried: Camp Nelson; Louisville 8-25-63; Camp Chase 9-2-63; Rock Island, Ill. 1-24-64. Exchanged 3-2-1865.

Robertson, James P., Pvt., **B**, Enlisted: 4-62, Cartersville, Ga., by Col. Morrison. Present 6-62 became ill and sent home. Died 7-22-62, Meriwether Co., Ga.

Robertson, John, Pvt., **B**, Enlisted: 3-62, Newnan, Ga., by Lt. Taylor. Present 6-62. Absent 8-62 and 10-62 Sick furlough: Grantville, Ga. Discharged: Epilepsy 2-19-63, Rogersville, Tenn. Re-enlisted 8-22-63. Discharged: 10-10-63. Certificate: born Meriwether Co., Ga., age 25, fair complexion, 5'-8" tall, blue eyes, light hair. Died: 4-24-1912. Buried: Luthersville City Cemetery, Meriwether Co., Ga.

Robertson, M., Pvt., **B**. Present 12-62. Absent 2-63 Sick furlough: Grantville, Ga. Present 12-63. WIA: 7-21-1864: Atlanta. Admitted General hospital.

Robertson, Washington, Pvt., **B**, Enlisted: 3-62. Absent 2-63 Sick furlough: Grantville, Ga. Severely WIA: Atlanta 7-21-1864. Carried off battlefield, General Hospital, never returned. Died: 3-9-1885, Meriwether Co., Ga.

Robertson, William H., Pvt., **B**, Enlisted: 3-62, Newnan, Ga., age 21, by Captain Strickland. Present through 8-62. Died: 3-2-1885, Meriwether Co., Ga.

Robinson, George Michael, 1st Lt., **H**, Enlisted: 4-62, Tallapoosa, Ga., by Captain Tumlin. Absent 6-62 Detached duty, Knoxville. Present through 2-63. 12-62 Signed as commanding company. Resigned 8-5-63. Died: 11-16-1917. Buried: Oakwood Cemetery, Austin, Texas.

Robinson, William, Pvt., **G**, Enlisted: 3-62, Floyd Co., Ga., by Captain Kerr. Present through 2-63. Absent 12-63 in Ga. Absent 12-64 Scout service since 10-64.

Robinson, William B., Pvt., **K**, Enlisted: 5-62, Camp Morrison by Captain North. Absent 6-62 Furlough: Fulton Co., Ga. Present through 10-62. Present 12-62 Wagoner. Present 2-63 and 12-63 Teamster. Present 12-64 Ordnance Teamster. Paroled: Charlotte, N.C. 5-3-1865. Died: 4-5-1909. Buried: Johns Creek Baptist, Chamblee, Ga.

Rollins, W.L., Pvt., **D**, Enlisted: 3-62, Dallas, Ga., by Captain Seawright. Present 10-62. Absent 12-62 Sick furlough: Paulding Co., Ga. Present 2-63. Captured during retreat from Kingston, Tenn. 12-8-63. On list of deserters in Knoxville, took oath 12-16-63. Died: 11-1-1905. Buried: Mount Zion Baptist Church, Dallas, Ga.

Rope (Rape), Thomas A., Pvt., On list of deserters at Chattanooga that took oath 3-30-64. Description: home Catoosa Co., Ga., dark complexion, brown hair, dark eyes, 5'-7".

Rose, William, Pvt., **H**, Enlisted: 9-62, Kingston, Tenn., by Captain Tumlin. Absent 12-62 sick furlough home. Present 2-63 and 12-63. Present 12-64 Detailed to gather forage for horses.

Rowe, Allen Jackson, Pvt., **B**, Enlisted: 3-62, Newnan, Ga., age 24, by Captain Strickland. Present through 8-62. WIA: Big Hill, Ky. 8-24-62. Absent through 12-63 wounded Furlough, Rocky Mount, Ga. Present 12-64 Forage Master for regiment. Surrendered: Salisbury, N.C. Died: 2-7-1909. Buried: New Hope Methodist Church, Meriwether Co., Ga.

Rowper (Roper), James H., Pvt., **K**, Captured: Fairmount, Ga., 5-17-64. Carried: Nashville; Louisville 5-25-64; Rock Island, Ill. 5-27-64; City Point, Va. Exchanged 3-2-1865.

Sanders, Arnold C., Sgt., **D**, Enlisted: 3-62, Dallas, Ga., by Captain Seawright. Detailed: accompany Noah Cole home 2-26-63. Absent 12-63 Detached service. 12-64 AWOL. Captured; exchanged. Promoted Sergeant 1-6-65. Died: 6-13-1897. Buried: Jones Chapel, Cullman Co., Ala.

Sanders, Elijah William, Pvt., **C**, Enlisted: 3-62, Cave Spring, Ga., by Captain Haynie. AWOL 12-1-64. Pension: Resigned, became Baptist minister. Died: 2-26-1931. Buried: Riverside Cemetery, Iredell, Texas.

Sanders, Stephen Marion "Bud," Pvt., **A**, Enlisted: 2-63, Cedartown, Ga., by Captain Hutchings. Present through 12-63. 12-64 AWOL. Pension: Surrendered near Salisbury, N.C. 4-26-1865. Died: 8-23-1919. Buried: Antioch Baptist Church, Polk Co., Ga.

Sanders, William B., Pvt., **C**, Enlisted: 3-62, Cave Spring, Ga., by Captain Haynie. Present 6-62.

Present 8-62 Wagoner. Present 10-62. Absent 12-62 detached: Quartermaster department. Present through 12-64.

Satterfield, Isaac, Pvt., **H**, Enlisted: 4-62, Tallapoosa, Ga., by Captain Tumlin. Present through 12-62. Absent 2-62 sick furlough. Absent 12-63 detached: Shoe shop.

Saunders, Johnson, Confederate Soldiers Home, Atlanta, Ga., 1901.

Scoggins (Scogin), James J., Pvt., **B**, Enlisted: 3-62, Newnan, Ga., age 28, by Captain Strickland. Present 6-62. Present 8-62, but had been on sick furlough. Present through 2-63. Absent in Newnan, Ga. Hospital 10-21-63. Present 12-64. Surrendered: Greensboro, NC 4-26-1865. Died: 8-6-1918. Buried: Luthersville City Cemetery, Meriwether Co., Ga.

Scott, J.J., Pvt., **F**, Enlisted: 3-62, Fairmount, Ga., by Col. Morrison. Present 12-62. Absent 2-63 sick furlough. Deserted: Loudon, Tenn. 11-24-63. Issued clothing 6-64. 12-64 AWOL. Died: 1882. Buried: Old High Shoals Baptist Church, Dallas, Ga.

Scott, Lewis, Pvt., **A**, Enlisted: 3-62, Cedartown, Ga., by Captain John C. Crabb. Present 6-62. Absent 8-62 Home wounded accidently through 12-62. Absent 2-63 Brigade Teamster. Absent 12-63 Cut off with wagons. AWOL 8-64. Died: 2-4-1914. Buried: Hixson Cemetery, Franklin Co., Ark.

Scott, Mark Waits, Pvt., **A**, Enlisted: 3-64, Oxford, Ala., by Captain York. 12-64 present. Pension: Going with Gen. Wheeler; Mississippi to continue fight. Surrendered: Greensboro, N.C. 4-26-1865. Living: Atlanta, Ga., 1910.

Scott, Mathew, Pvt., **A**, Enlisted: 7-63, Cedartown, Ga., by Captain York. Present 12-63 and 12-64. Paroled: Charlotte, N.C. 5-3-1865 Died: 3-16-1901. Buried: Hagin Cemetery, Polk Co., Ga.

Scott, R., Pvt., **A**, Enlisted: 3-64, in field by Captain York. Hospital sick 6-18-1864.

Scott, Samuel Hunter, 3 lt., **A**, Enlisted: Phillips Legion 5-6-1862. Enlisted: Cedartown, Ga. 10-16-63, 1st Ga. Cavalry by Captain York. Present 12-63 and 12-64. Paroled: Charlotte, N.C. 5-3-1865. Died 4-12-1910. Buried: Phillips Cemetery, Falls County, Texas.

Scott, Thomas J., Pvt., **F**, Enlisted: 3-62, Fairmount, Ga., by Col. Morrison. Present through 12-62. Deserted 2-63. Reported back 3-4-63. Deserted: Loudon, Tenn. 11-24-63. 12-64 AWOL.

Seals, Thomas, Sgt., **H**, Admitted: Ocmulgee—Floyd Hospital 7-21-1864, diarrhea.

Seavey, William, Pvt., **A**, Enlisted: 2-63, Rome, Ga., by Captain Hutchings. Present 2-63. Absent

12-63 Hospital wounded. Absent 12-64 detached to Gen. Davidson 5-64. Died: 6-25-1878. Buried: Myrtle Hill, Rome, Ga.

Seawright, William Robert, Captain, **D**, Enlisted: 3-62, Dallas, Ga., age 30, by Lt. Col. Morrison. Present 6-62. KIA: Murfreesboro 7-13-62. Born: Abbeville, S.C. Robert Trammell succeeded him.

Segars (Seagers), Miles Jackson, Pvt., **E**, Enlisted: 3-62, Carrollton by Captain Blalock. Present through 12-31-1864. Died: 1-12-1917. Buried: Herring Cemetery, Hartselle, Ala.

Self, Henry L., Pvt., **H**, Enlisted: 4-64, Tallapoosa, Ga., by Captain Tumlin. Captured: Dallas, Ga., 5-21-64. Carried: Nashville; Rock Island, Ill. 6-9-64. Died: Rock Island Prison, 8-6-64, typhoid fever. Buried: Rock Island Prison Confederate Cemetery, Grave #1378.

Selman, J.W., Pvt., **G**, Enlisted: 12-63, Decatur, Ga., by Major Anderson. AWOL 11-64.

Sewell, E., Pvt., **B**, Enlisted: 4-64, Newnan, Ga., by Lt. Taylor. General Hospital 11-20-1864.

Sewell, James Davis, Pvt., **B**, Enlisted: 4-64 in Newnan, Ga. Present 12-64. Surrendered: Greensboro, N.C. 4-26-1865. Died: 1-2-1918. Buried: Carrollton City Cemetery, Carroll Co., Ga.

Sewell, James Henry, Pvt., **B**, Enlisted: 3-62, Newnan, Ga., age 24, by Captain Strickland. Died: Hospital: Grantville, Ga., 6-22-62, fever. Buried: Lone Oak Cemetery, Meriwether Co., Ga.

Sewell, John Asbury, Sgt.. **B**. Enlisted 7-61 2nd Ga. Inf. Discharged disabled 12-61. Enlisted: 3-62, Newnan, Ga. WIA: left shoulder, neck and jaw, Mossy Creek, Tenn. 12-29-63. Hospital, Bull's Gap, Tenn. 12-31-64 present. Died: 7-11-1923. Buried: Fredonia Cemetery, Union Co., Ark.

Sewell, J.W., Pvt., **K**, Enlisted: 5-62, Cartersville, Ga., by Major Harper. Absent 6-62 Sick: Coweta Co., Ga. Present 8-62. Absent 10-62 Sick furlough: Fulton Co., Ga. Present 12-62. Captured 7-3-1864; carried: Chattanooga 7-9-1864.

Sewell, Milton Newton, Pvt., **B**, Enlisted: 4-64, Newnan, Ga., by Lt. Taylor. General Hospital 11-20-64. Paroled: Atlanta 1865. Died: 11-8-1925. Buried: Shady Grove Cemetery, Leesburg, Ala.

Sewell, Thomas Marion, Pvt., **K**, Enlisted: 5-62, Camp Morrison by Captain North. Absent 6-62 sick furlough home. Horse KIA; paid $175. Present 8-62 and 10-62. Absent 2-63 Sick furlough: Fulton Co., Ga. Present 12-63. Captured: Russellville, Tenn. 4-2-64. Carried: Nashville; Louisville; Camp Douglas 7-15-64. Died: Camp Douglas Prison, Ill. 9-11-64, chronic diarrhea. Buried: Chicago, Ill. City Cemetery, Grave #1343.

Shackleford, M.A., Surgeon, **F&S**, Enlisted 5-62,

Appointed by Col. Morrison. Resigned 11-21-62. Succeeded, Dr. W.H. Boyd.

Shaw, Edward H., Pvt., **B**, Enlisted: 3-62, Newnan, Ga., age 27, by Captain Strickland. Present through 12-31-64. Died: 4-19-1896. Buried: Holly Springs Cemetery, Coweta Co., Ga.

Shaw, Gilbert W., Pvt., Paroled 9-26-1862.

Shaw, John, Pvt., **E**, Enlisted: 3-62, Carrollton, Ga., by Captain Blalock. Present 6-62 as Blacksmith. Present through 2-63. Deserted 9-30-63.

Shaw, John H., Pvt., **A**, Enlisted 5-13-1862, Rome, Ga., 1st Conf. Vol. Inf. Widow's Pension: Transferred: 12-64, 1st Ga. Cavalry. Left Regiment 4-23-65 to save his horse, with J.A. Wynn. Died: 6-26-1914. Buried: Jackson Chapel Cemetery, Cedartown, Ga.

Shaw, William Wesley, Pvt., **E**, Enlisted: 3-62, Carrollton, Ga., by Captain Blalock. Present through 12-62: Company blacksmith. Captured: Ky. 8-15-62. Held in Cincinnati. Exchanged at Tazewell, Tenn., by Gen. Morgan. Present 2-63. Present 12-63 and 12-31-64.

Sheldon, P.B., Pvt., **C**, Enlisted: Cave Spring, Ga., Floyd's Legion 8-1-1863. Enlisted: 1st Ga. Cavalry, March 27, 1864. 12-31-64 present.

Shell, Thomas Edward, Pvt., **K**, Enlisted: 12-64, Newnan, Ga., by Captain North. 12-31-1864 present. Died: 6-14-1901. Buried: Tranquill Cemetery, Coweta Co., Ga.

Shield, C., Pvt., Captured: Athens, Ga., 5-8-1865, paroled.

Shipp, Jesse, Pvt., **D**, Enlisted: 3-62, Dallas, Ga., age 22, by Captain Seawright. Discharged 4-17-1862. Living: Paulding Co., Ga. 1870.

Shipp, Joseph Richard, Pvt., **D**, Enlisted: 3-62, Dallas, Ga., age 29, by, Captain Seawright. Absent 6-62 through 12-62 Sick furlough: Paulding Co., Ga. Present 2-63. Absent 12-63 Sick: Atlanta Hospital. 12-64 AWOL. Died: 3-18-1901. Buried: Poplar Springs Cemetery, Hiram, Ga.

Shipp, William M., Pvt., **D**, Enlisted: 3-62, Dallas, Ga., age 24, by Captain Seawright. Present through 2-63. Captured: Philadelphia, Tenn. 10-20-63. Carried: Camp Nelson; Camp Chase 11-14-63; Rock Island, Ill. 1-17-64. Released: 6-16-1865. Description: home Powder Springs, Cobb Co., Ga., fair complexion, light hair, grey eyes, 5'-8". Died: 1-10-1903. Buried: Mount Zion Baptist Church, Warrior, Ala.

Shiver, J.J., **F&S**, Enlisted: 5-62, Centerville, Ga., by Captain Kerr. Present through 2-63. Commissary of Subsistence.

Shoebert, William, Pvt., **E**, Widow Pension: Marshall Co., Ala. 1924.

Shoemaker (Shoemake), Martin H., Pvt., **C**, Enlisted: 3-62, Cave Spring, Ga., by Captain Haynie. Absent 6-62 sick furlough. Discharged disabled 8-10-62.

Shoemaker (Shoemake), Talton Gilmore, Pvt., **H**, Enlisted: 4-62, Haralson Co., Ga., by Captain Tumlin. Present through 1-62. Absent 12-62 sick furlough home. Present 2-63. 12-63 Detained in Ga., by General Wheeler. Deserted and took oath 10-26-64. Description: home Calhoun Co., Ala., complexion light, hair light, eyes blue, 5'-7". Living: Cleburne Co., Ala. 1880.

Shropshire, Charles J., Pvt., **K**, Enlisted 5-31-1861: Atlanta, 7th Ga. Inf. WIA Manassas, Va., 7-21-61. Certificate: born Coweta Co., Ga., age 20, 5'-4", fair complexion, grey eyes, light hair. Enlisted: 1st Ga. Cavalry 5-62, Cartersville, Ga., by Major Harper. KIA: Mossy Creek, Tenn. 12-29-63. Buried: Bethesda Presbyterian Church, Morristown, Tenn.

Shropshire, Walton F., Pvt., **K**, Enlisted: 5-62, Cartersville, Ga., by Major Harper. Present through 12-31-1864. Surrendered: Bentonville, N.C. 5-4-1865. Died: 1-1-1907. Buried: Cokes Chapel UMC, Sharpsburg, Ga.

Shropshire, William Robert, Pvt., **K**, Enlisted: 11-64, Newnan, Ga., by Captain North. Present 12-64. Surrendered; paroled: Bentonville, N.C. 5-4-1865. Died: 4-2-1913. Buried: Oakland Cemetery, Atlanta, Ga.

Shuford, Obediah P., Captain, **E**, Enlisted: 3-62, Carrollton, Ga., by Captain Blalock. Present through 12-64. Elected 3rd Lt. 3-62. Promoted 2nd Lt. 10-24-62 by Gen. Maxey. Promoted 1st Lt. by Col. Morrison 5-29-63. Promoted Captain 1-25-64, by Gen. Martin. Paroled: Charlotte, N.C. 5-3-1865. Died: 3-17-1886. Buried: Ramsaur Cemetery, Lincolnton, N.C.

Sides, James K. Polk, Pvt., **H**, Enlisted: 3-63, Tallapoosa, Ga., by Captain Tumlin. Absent 12-64 Detailed service as Cattle Driver.

Simmons, Benjamin R., Pvt., **C**, Enlisted: 3-62, Cave Spring, Ga., by Captain Haynie. Present 6-62: Teamster. Present through 2-63. Absent 12-63 special duty. Absent 12-64: Detailed within Department. Detached to drive cattle at surrender, Macon, Ga. Discharged: Savannah, Ga., 4-1865. Died: 10-31-1909. Buried: Jackson Chapel Cemetery, Cedartown, Ga.

Simmons, John W., Sgt., **C**, Enlisted: 3-62, Cave Spring, Ga., by Captain Haynie. Promoted 2nd Sgt. 3-31-62. Present through 6-63. Absent 12-63 sick. Captured: Knoxville 12-18-63. Carried: Louisville 12-18-63; Rock Island, Ill. 1-26-64.

Exchanged 3-20-65. Surrendered: Greensboro, N.C. 4-26-1865. Died: Polk Co., Ga., 9-19-1884.

Simmons, William Joshua, Pvt., **C**, Enlisted: 3-62, Cave Spring, Ga., by Captain Haynie. Present through 8-62. Absent 10-62 sick. Present 12-62 through 6-63. Captured: Dandridge, Tenn. 11-12-63. Carried: Knoxville; Camp Chase 1-1-64; Rock Island, Ill. Paroled: Talladega, Ala. 5-17-1865. Died: 1894 (wagon accident), Donley Co., Tx.

Simms, Newton W., Pvt., **A**, Enlisted: 3-62, Cedartown, Ga., by Captain John C. Crabb. Present 6-62. Absent 8-62 Sick: Kingston, Tenn. Absent 10-62 and 12-62: Sick furlough. Absent 2-63: with Brigade wagons. Absent 12-63: Cut off with wagons. Captured: Stilesboro, Ga., 6-7-64 by Col Wilder's Cavalry. Carried: Nashville; Louisville; Rock Island, Ill. 6-24-64. Enlisted: U.S. Navy 7-6-64.

Simpler, Valentine Van, Pvt., **E**, Enlisted: 3-62, Carrollton, Ga., by Captain Blalock. Discharged disabled 6-19-62. Mental issues. Certificate: age 38, 6'-1", sallow complexion, blue eyes, brown hair. Signed, M.A. Shackelford.

Sims, A. Beulus, Pvt., **A**, Enlisted: 6-64, Cedartown, Ga., by Captain York. Captured: Stilesboro, Ga., 10-2-64. Carried: Nashville; Louisville; Camp Chase 10-22-1864.

Sims, J.M., Sgt., Enlisted: 3-62, Newnan, Ga., age 26, by Captain Strickland. Present through 12-31-1864. Promoted 1st Sgt. 11-1-63.

Sizemore, W.G., Pvt., **H**, Enlisted: 4-62, Tallapoosa, Ga., by Captain Tumlin. Present 6-62: Teamster. Present through 2-63. Absent 12-63: Detached to drive beef cattle. Parole: Talladega, Ala. 5-24-1865.

Skinner, J.J., Pvt., **G**, Enlisted: 5-62, Cartersville, Ga., by Captain Kerr. Present through 12-62. Discharged 2-16-63, Rogersville, Tenn.

Skinner, R., Pvt., Paroled: Thomasville, Ga., 6-16-1865.

Sligh, J.E., Pvt., **D**, Enlisted: 3-62, Dallas, Ga., age 23, by Captain Seawright. Received bounty 4-17-1862.

Sloan, J.H., Pvt., **C**, Enlisted: 3-64, Cave Spring, Ga., by Captain Watts. Absent 12-64: Detailed within regiment.

Smith, Alexander Hamilton. Pvt., **H**, Enlisted: 4-62, Tallapoosa, Ga., by Captain Tumlin. Present through 12-62. Present 2-63: Teamster since 2-15-63. Absent 12-63: Detached with wagons. Absent 12-64: Detached service. Captured: Wattsburg, Tenn. 6-18-63. Died: 2-17-1894. Buried: Ellijay City Cemetery, Gilmer Co., Ga.

Smith, Basil, Pvt., **B**, Enlisted: 7-63, Grantville,

Ga., by Lt. Taylor. Present 12-63. Absent at General Hospital 3-18-64. Died: 1-24-1915. Buried: Founders Cemetery, Moreland, Ga.

Smith, Byron, Pvt., **G**, Enlisted: 5-62, Camp Morrison by Captain Leak. Present through 6-63. Captured: Fall Creek, Mill Springs, Ky. 6-3-63. Carried: Lexington 6-13-63; Johnson's Island 6-20-63; Camp Chase; Point Lookout, Md. 10-30-63; Sandusky, Ohio 11-4-63. Exchanged 2-3-1865. Present 2-65 with regiment. Discharged: Greensboro, N.C. 4-26-1865. Died: 2-3-1926. Buried: Lea Cemetery, Gillsburg, Miss.

Smith, Charles, Pvt., **I**, 11-62, Deserted 8-14-64, Knoxville. Description: home Marietta, Ga., age 17, 5'-6", eyes blue, hair light. Held as a pretend Rebel Deserter. Paroled Newton, N.C. 4-19-1865.

Smith, F.W., Cpl., **K**, Enlisted: 5-62, Newnan, Ga., by Captain North. Present through 2-63. Absent 12-63 WIA sent to Bull Gap, Tenn. Hospital. , then furloughed home. Present 12-64.

Smith, Henry R., Pvt., **G**, Enlisted: 3-62, Floyd Co., Ga., by Captain Kerr. Present through 12-62. Absent 2-63: Detached at Kingston, Tenn. 12-63 present.

Smith, Henry T., Pvt., **E**, Enlisted: 3-62 by Captain Blalock. Present 6-62. Transferred: 8-5-1862.

Smith, Isaac H., Pvt., **K**, Enlisted: 8-63, Newnan, Ga., by Captain North. Discharged 11-23-63. Certificate: born Ga., 35 yr. old, 5'-10", light complexion, blue eyes, dark hair.

Smith, J.A., Pvt., **I**, Enlisted: 5-64 by Captain Leak. AWOL 12-7-1864.

Smith, James, Pvt., **H**, Enlisted: 4-62, Haralson Co., Ga., by Captain Tumlin. Present through 10-62. Absent 12-62 Sick furlough home. Absent 2-63: Sick at Rome, Ga. AWOL 3-1-63. POW: Released at Talladega, Ala. 5-24-1865.

Smith, James B., Pvt., **K**, Died: 1909. Buried: Cokes Chapel UMC, Sharpsburg, Ga.

Smith, J.E., Pvt. POW: Captured in Fayetteville, N.C. 3-11-1865. On list of deserters from Fort Monroe, Va. sent to Washington, D.C. 4-2-65. Took oath 4-5-1865.

Smith, Jesse W., Pvt., **C**, Enlisted: 6-63, Cave Spring, Ga., by Captain Haynie. Absent: Sick in hospital 7-6-63. Absent 4-64: Polk Hospital, Rome, Ga.

Smith, J.J., Pvt., **K**, Enlisted: 5-62, Camp Morrison.

Smith, J.K., Pvt., **K**, Enlisted: 8-63, Newnan, Ga., by Captain North. Absent 12-63 Detailed: Nurse, Atlanta Hospital. Discharged 12-2-1863.

Description: age 33, 5'-10", blue eyes, dark hair, farmer.

Smith, John, Pvt., **H**, Enlisted: 4-62, Haralson Co., Ga., by Captain Tumlin. Absent 6-62 Hospital, Knoxville. Present through 12-62. Absent 2-63 sick furlough. Absent 12-64 sick. Captured: Penn's Bridge, S.C. 2-11-65. On list of deserters: Fort Monroe, Va. Took oath 4-5-1865.

Smith, John Erwin Patton, Pvt., **K**, Enlisted: 5-62, Cartersville, Ga., by Major Harper. Present through 12-62. WIA: Murfreesboro (Stones River) 1-1-63 and furloughed home. Absent 12-63: Transferred to 55th Ga. Inf. Died: 12-12-1921. Buried: Ellijay City Cemetery, Gilmer Co., Ga.

Smith, J.T.M., Pvt., **A**, Enlisted: 3-62, Cedartown, Ga., by Captain John C. Crabb. Present 6-62. Captured: Murfreesboro 7-13-62. Absent 10-62: Prisoner on parole. Absent 12-62: Sick furlough home. Absent 2-63: Hospital: Kingston, Tenn. Absent 12-63: Cut off with wagons. Died: 11-27-1919. Buried: Bethel Baptist Church, Bainbridge, Ga.

Smith, J.W., Pvt., **G**, Enlisted: 5-62, Camp Morrison by Captain Leak. Present through 12-62. Captured: Somerset, Ky. 3-30-63. Carried: City Point, Va. Paroled 4-14-63. Description: home Houston Co., Ga., age 44, fair complexion, dark hair, blue eyes, 5'-5". Captured: Salisbury, N.C. 4-12-65. Carried: Camp Chase; released 6-13-1865. Pension: Madison Co., Ala.

Smith, Langdon Quinn, Pvt., **G**, Enlisted: 5-62, Camp Morrison by Captain Leak. Present through 12-1864. Died: 7-26-1902. Buried: Lea Cemetery, Gillsburg, Miss.

Smith, Martin M., Pvt., **E**, Enlisted: 3-62, Carrollton, Ga., by Captain Blalock. Present through 12-62. Absent 2-63 Detachment: Kingston, Tenn. Present 12-63 and 12-64.

Smith, Peter M., Pvt., **K**, Enlisted: 5-62, Camp Morrison by Captain North. Absent 6-62 Home sick: Coweta Co., Ga. Discharged disabled 9-22-62. Reenlisted 2-63. Present 12-63. Absent 12-64: Carroll Co., Ga. with white swelling and discharge.

Smith, R. Lang, Pvt., **I**, Enlisted: 3-64, Cass Station, Ga., by Captain Leak. KIA: Calhoun, Ga., 5-27-64.

Smith, R.F., Pvt., **I**, Enlisted: 1-64, Cass Station, Ga., by Captain Leak. AWOL 12-18-1864.

Smith, R.I., Pvt., **G**, Captured: East Point, Ga., 9-8-64.

Smith, Robert, Sgt., **G**, Enlisted: 5-62, Camp Morrison by Captain Leak. Elected 3rd Sgt. 3-31-62.

Present through 12-62. Absent 3-63 Detachment Camp. Present 10-63. AWOL 12-18-64.

Smith, Robert H., Pvt., **K**, Enlisted: 5-62, Camp Morrison by Captain North. Present through 12-1864. Buried: Spring Hill Cemetery, Naples, Texas.

Smith, Robert W., Pvt., **A**, Enlisted: 3-62, Cedartown, Ga., by Captain John C. Crabb. Absent 6-62 Polk Co., Ga.: sick furlough. Present through 12-62. Absent 2-63 sick furlough home. Absent 12-63 Cut off with wagons. AWOL 11-10-1864. Pension: Surrendered: Bennitt Place, N.C. 1865. Buried: Bethel Church, Bainbridge, Ga.

Smith, Samuel E., Sgt., **G**, Enlisted: 5-62, Camp Morrison by Captain Leak. Present through 12-62. Absent 3-63 Detachment Camp. Present 10-63. AWOL 6-25-1864. Died: 1-31-1912. Buried: Rose Hill Cemetery, Rockmart, Ga.

Smith, S.W., Pvt., **C**, Enlisted: Chattanooga. Absent 12-63 Sick. Paroled: Albany, Ga., 5-22-1865.

Smith, Thomas Zachariah, Pvt., **G**, Enlisted: 3-62, Floyd Co., Ga., by Captain Kerr. Present 6-62: Blacksmith. WIA: Murfreesboro 7-13-62. Gunshot: left leg. Absent 10-62 and 12-62: Wounded furlough: Floyd Co., Ga. Present 2-63 and 12-63. Captured: Floyd Co., Ga., 5-25-64. Carried: Louisville 6-6-64. Deserter, took oath 6-8-64. Description: home Floyd Co., Ga., complexion dark, hair dark, eyes grey, 5'-11". Died: 3-29-1891. Buried: Pleasant Hill Cemetery, Nevada, Texas.

Smith, T.J., Attended Gen. Joseph Wheeler's funeral January 1906.

Smith, W.E., Pvt., **H**, Enlisted: 4-62, Haralson Co., Ga., by Captain Tumlin. Absent 6-62 Detailed services. 12-62 present.

Smith, W.G., Pvt., **G**, Enlisted: 3-62, Floyd Co., Ga., by Captain Kerr. Present through 2-62. Absent 12-63 Sick: Floyd Co., Ga. Absent 12-64: Detailed: Provost Duty in Columbus, Ga.

Smith, W.H., Pvt., **K**, Enlisted: 5-62, Camp Morrison by Captain North.

Smoot, Benjamin Sylvester, Pvt., **E**, Enlisted: 3-62, Carrollton, Ga., by Captain Blalock. Present through 8-62. Substituted by George R. Davis 9-1-62. Substitute: died 2-10-63. Joined 2nd Ga. Cavalry State Guards. Died: 2-12-1908. Buried: Hillside Cemetery, Anniston, Ala.

Spalding, Hiram Tilman, Pvt., **A**, Enlisted: 3-62, Cedartown, Ga., by Captain John C. Crabb. Present 6-62. Absent: Sick with measles and discharged 7-4-62. Certificate: born Elbert Co., Ga., age 28, 5'-3", sallow complexion, dark eyes, black hair, school teacher. Died: 1-28-1872. Buried: Forrest Cemetery, Gadsden, Al.

Spalding, William "Willie" Eugene, Pvt., **F&S**, Enlisted 6-27-1861, age 17, 21st Ga. Inf., Polk Co. 10-30-63, L.G. Capers, Surgeon, recommended to Col. Morrison he be appointed to him. John Branch, Surgeon approved. Appointed Hospital Seward 12-22-1863. Present 12-31-1864. Died: 2-5-1893. Buried: Kimball Cemetery, Bosque Co., Tx.

Spann, J.M., Cpl., Captured: Flint River Bridge 4-19-1865.

Sparks, Doctor Banks, Pvt., **C**, Enlisted 8-12-1861: 19th Ala. Inf., Kirk's Grove, Ala. Enlisted: 8-62, Cave Spring, Ga., by Captain Haynie. Present through 12-63. AWOL 10-64, joined Gen. Clanton's command. Died: 12-15-1905. Buried: Bethel Cemetery, Maypearl, Texas.

Sparks, Thomas C., Pvt., **C**, Enlisted 5-14-1861: 8th Ga. Inf., age 18, Rome, Ga. 1st Ga. Cavalry, Enlisted: 10-62, by Lt. Reynolds. Present through 12-63. Present 12-6: Detail within Regiment. Buried: Cave Spring Cemetery, Floyd Co., Ga.

Spier, Jackson P., Pvt., **E**, Enlisted: 3-62, Carrollton, Ga., by Captain Blalock. Present through 8-62: Clerk for Col. Benjamin Allston. WIA: Tazewell, Tenn. 10-21-62. Present 12-62 and 2-63. Absent 12-63: Detached: Office, 3rd Cavalry Brigade. Absent 12-64: Detached: Quartermaster Dept. Paroled: Charlotte, N.C. 5-3-1865. Died: 4-3-1908. Buried: Fairburn, Ga.

Spier, Martin Vann Buren, Pvt., **K**, Enlisted: Fayette Co., Ga., 10th Ga. Inf. Discharged 7-2-1861. Enlisted: 5-62, Cartersville, Ga., by Major Harper. Absent 6-62 sick. Present 8-62. Captured: Richmond, Ky. 10-1-62. Exchanged. 2-63 AWOL in Fayette Co., Ga. Absent 12-63: Detained with wagon train by General Wheeler. KIA near Fairburn, Ga.

Spencer, Abner, Pvt., **K**, Enlisted: 5-62, Cartersville, Ga., by Maj. Harper. Deserted: McMinnville, Tenn. 7-15-62.

Spencer, H., Pvt., **H**, Enlisted: 4-64, Tallapoosa, Ga., by Captain Tumlin. 12-64 AWOL.

Sprewell (Spruill), Gabriel Newton, Pvt., **E**, Enlisted: 3-62, Carrollton, Ga., by Captain Blalock. Present 6-62: Wagoner. Present 8-62. Present 10-62 and 12-62: Teamster. Died: Dickard, Tenn. 1-20-1863.

Stallings, John, Pvt., **K**, Enlisted: 5-62, Camp Morrison by Captain North.

Stallings, John M., 2nd Lt., **B**, Enlisted: 3-62, Newnan, Ga., age 24, by Captain Strickland. Absent 2-63: Detached: Acting surgeon, Kingston, Tenn. WIA: Knoxville 11-24-63. Present 12-64. Promoted 3rd Lt. 11-6-64. Promoted 2nd Lt.

12-21-64 by Col. Davitte. Surrendered: Greensboro, N.C. 4-26-1865. Pension: Coweta Co., Ga., 1910.

Stallings, J.W., Surgeon, **F&S**.

Stanford, William P., Pvt., **F**, Enlisted: 8-64, Decatur, Ga., by Maj. Andrews. 12-31-1864 present. Pension: Detailed: Courier for Gen. D.B. Frye, Augusta, Ga. Discharged: Augusta, Ga. May 1865. Pension: Columbia Co., Ga., 1907.

Steadham (Stidham), Thomas Cleveland, Pvt., **E**, Enlisted: 5-62, Cartersville, Ga., by Captain Blalock. Present through 12-62. Absent 2-63: Detached: Captain Marshall's Battery. Present 12-63. Captured: Cassville, Ga. 5-20-64. Carried: Nashville; Louisville; Rock Island, Ill. 6-1-64. Took oath: 10-25-1864. Description: home Carroll Co., Ga., age 30, 6'-0", fair complexion, dark hair, blue eyes. Died: 5-7-1904. Buried: Pleasant Grove Baptist Church, Villa Rica, Ga.

Steed, Alexander McCoen, Pvt., **E**, Enlisted: 5-62, Cartersville, Ga., by Captain Blalock. Present through 12-62. Present 2-63: Substitute J.C. Holcomb. Discharged 11-1863. Died: 11-22-1902. Buried: Sardis Methodist Church, Clay Co., Ala.

Steed, Calvin Lane, Pvt., **A**, Served: 1st Ga. Cavalry 1862 to 1864. Transferred: 1st Ala. Battalion. Died: 10-17-1892. Buried: Steed Cemetery, Oak Level, Ala.

Steedly, James P., Pvt., **F**, Enlisted: 3-62, Fairmount, Ga., by Col. Morrison. Present through 12-62. Captured: Monticello, Ky. 5-5-63. Carried: Lexington; Johnson's Island 6-20-63; Point Lookout, Md. 10-30-63. Took oath; released 4-11-64.

Steedly, William, Pvt., **F**, Enlisted: 3-62, Fairmount, Ga., by Col. Morrison. Absent 6-62 through 12-62 Sick furlough. Deserted 7-1862.

Step, T., Pvt., **A**, Enlisted: 11-64, in field by Captain Jesse W. Crabb. Absent 12-64: Detailed: cattle driver.

Stephens, H.W., Pvt., **B**, Enlisted: 7-64, Newnan, Ga., by Lt. Taylor. 12-64 present.

Stephens, John E., Pvt., **K**, Enlisted: 5-62, Camp Morrison by Captain North. Died at home: Coweta Co., Ga., 6-22-62.

Stephenson, W.J., Pvt., **K**, Enlisted: 8-63, Newnan, Ga., by Captain North. Present 12-63 and 12-64.

Stevens, Elisha Lambert, Pvt., **B**, Enlisted: 3-62, Newnan, Ga., age 20, by Captain Strickland. Present 6-62 and 8-62. WIA: Big Hill, Ky. 8-24-62. Absent 10-62: wounded furlough, Grantville, Ga. Absent 2-63 Grantville, Ga., sick furlough. Present 12-63 and 12-64. Died: 1883. Buried: New Hope Cemetery, Pell City, Ala.

Stevens, John, Pvt., **B**, Enlisted: 3-62, Newnan, Ga., age 29, by Captain Strickland. Present through 12-31-64.

Stevens, Joseph Benjamin, Pvt., **B**, Enlisted: 7-64, Newnan, Ga., by Lt. Taylor. Present 12-64. Surrendered: Greensboro, N.C. 4-26-1865. Died: Baldwin County Asylum for the Blind 12-27-1913. Buried: Southview Cemetery, Moreland, Ga.

Stevens, William Henry, Pvt., **B**, Enlisted: 7-64 in Newnan, Ga. 12-31-1864 present. Died: 12-7-1912. Buried: Pell City, Ala.

Stewart, George W., Pvt., **G**, Enlisted: 5-62, Camp Morrison by Captain Leak. Present through 12-62. Absent 3-63: Detachment Camp. Captured: Gordon Co., Ga. Carried: Louisville. Took oath 9-26-64. Description: home Gordon Co., Ga., blue eyes, dark hair, fair complexion, 5'-9".

Stewart, J.J., Sgt., **K**, Enlisted: 5-62, Camp Morrison by Captain North. Absent 6-62: sick furlough home. Absent 8-62: Hospital, Atlanta. Discharged disabled: McMinnville, Tenn. 11-14-1862.

Stewart, John, Pvt., **F**, Enlisted: 3-62, Fairmount, Ga., by Col. Morrison.

Stokes, Francis Marion, Pvt., **F**, Enlisted: 5-62, Fairmount, Ga., by Col. Morrison. Absent May 1862, Cartersville, Ga: Sick with measles. Relapsed and furloughed home 12-62. Died 5-4-1863, Gilmer Co., Ga.

Stokes, Nathan L., Pvt., **F**, Enlisted: 3-62, Fairmount, Ga., by Col. Morrison. Captured: Powell Valley, Tenn. 6-27-62. Widow statement: On picket, Cumberland Gap, taken 6-22-62. Federal: arrested 6-22-62 Cumberland Gap, age 26, 140 lbs. 5'-7", blue eyes. Camp Marion 6-26-62, deserted. Exchanged 11-1-62 aboard steamer *Emerald*, Vicksburg. Died: 5-4-1863.

Stone, Ephraim, Pvt.. **F**, Enlisted: 3-62, Fairmount, Ga., by Col. Morrison. Deserted 6-15-62, Chattanooga.

Stone, George W., Pvt., **F**, Enlisted: 3-62, Fairmount, Ga., by Col. Morrison. Absent 6-62: sick furlough. Present 8-62. Absent 10-62: sick furlough. Absent 12-62 and 2-63: Left sick in Ky. AWOL.

Stone, Nathan L., Pvt., **F**, Enlisted: 3-62, Fairmount, Ga., by Col. Morrison. Present through 2-63. Captured on retreat from Kingston, Tenn. 12-5-63. Knoxville: deserters 12-16-1863. Stated: Home, Gordon, Co., Ga.

Stone, William Henry, Pvt., **F**, Enlisted: 3-62, Fairmount, Ga., by Col. Morrison. Discharged 6-62 by Substitute, Samuel Stuart. Died: 1-20-1927. Buried: Bethel Baptist Church, Rocky Mount, Ga.

Storey, H.H., Pvt., **E**, Captured between Chickasaw Landing and Macon, Ga. at Flint River Bridge 4-19-1865.

Strickland, Enoch Solomon, Pvt., **E**, Enlisted: 3-62, Carrollton, Ga., by Captain Blalock. Present through 2-63. Absent 12-64: Detached: blacksmith to government shop. Died: 4-21-1900. Buried: Fairburn City Cemetery, Fulton Co., Ga.

Strickland, Ezekiel Henry, Pvt., **B**, Enlisted: 3-62. Absent 2-63: Sick furlough: Luthersville, Ga. Absent: Assigned as Asst. Surgeon 9-20-63 in Hospital, Milledgeville, Ga. Could no longer ride horse. Paroled: Milledgeville, Ga., 5-1865. Pension: Troup Co., Ga., 1912.

Strickland, Ezekiel Livingston, Pvt., **B**, Enlisted: 10-62 in Newnan, Ga. Captured: Philadelphia, Tenn. 10-20-63. Carried: Camp Nelson; Camp Chase 11-14-63; 3-4-64 Fort Delaware. Released 6-7-1865. Description: home Meriwether Co., Ga., 5'-6", brown eyes, auburn hair, light complexion. Died: 7-7-1909, Ga.

Strickland, James F., Pvt., **A**, Enlisted: 3-62, Cedartown, Ga., by Captain John C. Crabb. Absent 6-62 Polk Co., Ga.: Sick furlough. Discharged disabled: 8-7-62, kidney disease. Certificate: blue eyes, black hair, light complexion, 6'-0". Widow: Bright's disease; discharged 12-1862. Died: 7-5-1883. Buried: Pleasant Grove Methodist Church, Yorkville, Ga.

Strickland, James H., Lt. Col., **B**, Enlisted: 3-62 in Newnan, Ga., age 31, by Lt. Col. Morrison. Elected Captain 3-62. Present through 10-62. Appointed Major 9-13-62. Absent 2-63: Detached service. Promoted Lt. Col. 4-15-64 by Gen. Martin. WIA: Battle, Bald Hill, Atlanta 7-22-64. Gunshot through the groin, G.W. McWade, surgeon. Died: 8-3-64, Bowersville, Ga. Buried: Bohannan Family Cemetery, Newnan, Ga.

Strickland, John Mercer, 2nd Lt., **B**, Enlisted: 3-62, Newnan, Ga., age 24, by Captain Strickland. Present through 2-63. Present 12-63: Promoted 2nd Lt. 10-28-63 by Col. Morrison. Died: 10-24-1912. Buried: Bethel Baptist Church, Rocky Mount, Ga.

Strickland, Julius Floyd, Pvt., **B**, Enlisted: 3-62, Newnan, Ga., age 25, by Captain Strickland. Present through 12-31-1864. Died: 10-25-1910. Buried: Strickland Town Cemetery, Meriwether Co., Ga.

Strickland, J.W., 2nd Lt., **B**, Enlisted: 3-62, Newnan, Ga., age 24, by Captain Strickland. Promoted 2nd Lt. 10-28-63. Present through 12-31-64.

Strickland, Thomas Jefferson, Pvt., **B**, Enlisted 4th Regt. Ga. State Troops 10-25-61. Enlisted 34th Ga. Inf. 5-13-62, Grantville, Ga. Captured: Vicksburg 7-4-63. Enlisted: 1st Ga. Cavalry 10-16-63, Newnan, Ga. Present 12-63. WIA: Atlanta 7-21-64. Admitted: hospital. Died: 12-29-1898. Buried: Strickland Cemetery, Whitesburg, Ga.

Stricklin (Strickland), James, Pvt., **D**, Captured: Ringgold, Ga., 1-28-64. Admitted: U.S. General Hospital, Nashville 2-2-64, chronic diarrhea. Died: Nashville Prison 2-9-64, Pleura Pneumonia. Buried: Nashville City Cemetery, grave #6250.

Stricklin, James F., Pvt., **A**, Hospital, Eufaula, Ala. 8-23-1864.

Stuart (Stewart), Samuel, Pvt., **F**, Enlisted: 3-62, Fairmount, Ga., by Col. Morrison. Present through 8-62. Absent 10-62: Detached service. Present 12-62. Absent 2-63: with detachment and wagons. 12-63 Acting Hospital Steward.

Sullivan, Hamilton G., Pvt., **B**, Enlisted: 8-63, Haralson Co., Ga., by Lt. Taylor. Present 12-63 and 12-64. Pension: WIA: last day of war. Carried: from field to hospital. Hit near spine. Paroled: Greensboro, N.C. 5-2-1865. Died: 2-27-1902. Buried: Senoia City Cemetery, Coweta Co., Ga.

Summerhill, G., Pvt., **D**, Captured; exchanged aboard steamer *Metropolitan*, Vicksburg, 12-4-1862.

Summerhill, James L., Pvt., **D**, Enlisted: 3-62, Dallas, Ga., age 21, by Captain Seawright. Present through 8-62. Captured: Clay Village, Ky. 10-4-62. Paroled 10-7-62: Hardinsville, Ky. Absent 12-62 on parole. Present 2-63. Absent 12-63 Sick: Atlanta Hospital. Transferred: 41st Ga. Inf. 4-1864. Died: 4-14-1913. Buried: Mount Tabor Methodist Church, Dallas, Ga.

Summerville, John F., Sgt., **A**, Enlisted: 3-62, Cedartown, Ga., by Captain John C. Crabb. Promoted: 3rd Cpl. 4-5-62. Present through 12-62. Promoted: 1st Cpl. 12-31-62. Present 2-63 and 12-63. Promoted: 4th Sgt. Roll 12-31-1864. Paroled: Charlotte, N.C. 5-3-1865. Died: 1-28-1910, Haralson Co., Ga.

Suttles, J.T., Pvt., **F**, Enlisted: 7-64, Atlanta by Captain McWilliams. Present 12-64. Surrendered: Salisbury, N.C. 5-26-1865. Witness: Walker Co., Ga., 1911.

Taff, William L., Pvt., **A**, Enlisted: 8-63, Cedartown by Captain York. Present 12-63 and 12-64. Blacksmith since 11-10-64. Paroled: Charlotte, N.C. 5-3-1865.

Talbert (Tolbert), Josiah Thomas, Pvt., **E**, Enlisted: 9th Ga. Artillery. Enlisted: 3-62, 1st Ga. Cavalry, Carrollton, Ga., by Major Harper. Once on scout, Guerrillas chased him for 5 miles. Captured:

Knoxville 12-3-63. Carried: Knoxville 12-6-63; Louisville 12-29-63; Rock Island, Ill. 1-6-64. Released 5-21-1865. Description: home Carroll Co., Ga., age 29, blue eyes, black hair, dark complexion, 5'-6½". Died: 6-15-1915 Atlanta, Fulton Co., Ga.

Talbot (Tolbot), E.H., Pvt., **K**, Captured: Richmond, Ky. Shipped: Vicksburg. Exchanged 12-4-62 aboard steamer *Metropolitan*. Age 28, 5'-8¾", grey eyes, dark hair, light complexion.

Talley, D.H., Sgt., **H**, Enlisted: 4-62, Haralson Co., Ga., by Captain Tumlin. Present through 8-62. Discharged 10-6-62.

Tanner, McDaniel, Pvt., **H**, Enlisted: 2-63, Tallapoosa, Ga., by Captain Tumlin. Present 2-63. WIA: Mossy Creek, Tenn. 12-24-63. Ball entered left shoulder, cut through collar bone, turned down inside ribs and lodged just below heart. Kicked by a horse causing hernia. Discharged disabled 12-64. Died: 3-13-1894. Buried: Mars Hill Primitive Baptist Church, Cleburne Co., Ala.

Taylor, James, Pvt., **F**, Enlisted: 5-64, Marietta, Ga., by Captain McWilliams. 12-64 present.

Taylor, James W., 1st Lt., **B**, Enlisted: 3-62, Newnan, Ga., age 28, by, Captain Strickland. Present through 12-62. Present 2-63: sent to General Hospital. Absent 12-63: Promoted 10-28-63 by Col. Morrison replacing John W. Trammell. Dr. Taylor was studying to become a medical doctor. At Stegall's Ferry, Ky., amputated a man's arm while in battle with aid of two ladies and a saw. The man survived. Refused many promotions to stay with his men. Left near Waynesboro, Ga. near end of war by Gen. Martin to Post Duty, Palmetto, Ga. Surrendered: Kingston, Ga. Died: 12-15-1925. Buried: Luthersville City Cemetery, Meriwether Co., Ga.

Taylor, John, Pvt., **C**, Enlisted: 11-62, Cave Spring, Ga., by Captain Haynie. Absent 2-63 sick. Present 6-63. Absent 12-63 Sick. Absent sick: 9-14-1864.

Teagle, Nathaniel, Pvt., **B**, Enlisted: 5-64, Newnan, Ga., by Lt. Taylor. Absent 12-64 sent to Hospital 11-15-1864. Died: 1-13-1889. Buried: Luthersville City Cemetery, Meriwether Co., Ga.

Tench, John Walter, Major, **K**, Enlisted 1st Ga. Inf.(Ramsey's) 6-1-61. Enlisted: 5-62, 1st Ga. Cavalry, Camp Morrison by Captain North. Elected 3rd Lt. 6-62. Present through 12-62. WIA: Mill Springs, Ky. 5-28-63, right thigh. WIA: Stubenville, Ky. 6-15-63. Absent 12-63 Furloughed, Newnan, Ga. Judge Advocate Martin's Division. Promoted Captain by Gen. Mar-

tin, 8-15-64, for gallantry and efficient conduct. Promoted Major 12-21-64 by General Wheeler. Recommended by Col. Davitte. WIA in hand: Union, S.C. 1865. Surrendered: Greensboro, N.C. 4-26-1865. Died: 4-8-1926. Buried: Evergreen Cemetery, Gainesville, Fla.

Tench, Rubin Montmornci, Sgt., **K**, Enlisted 1st Ga. Inf. (Ramsey's) 6-1-61. Enlisted: 1st Ga. Cavalry 5-1-62, Camp Morrison by Captain North. Present through 8-62. Elected 2nd Sgt. 6-62. WIA: Murfreesboro 7-13-62. Gunshot: left arm above wrist and exit at elbow, fracturing bone. Absent 10-62 and 12-62 sick furlough. Absent 2-63 with detachment: Kingston, Tenn. Absent 12-63 Furloughed: Newnan, Ga., 12-31-64 present. Died: 5-18-1910. Buried: Tench Cemetery, Coweta Co., Ga.

Terry, Alfred, Pvt., **D**, Enlisted: 8-62, Dallas, Ga., by Captain Robert F. Trammell. Mustered: Big Creek Gap, Tenn. Present through 10-62. Discharged 11-15-62: Sparta, Tenn. Absent 12-63 Sick: Atlanta hospital. Captured: Cobb Co., Ga. Carried: Nashville, took oath 6-24-64. Description: home Cobb Co., Ga., 6'-3", blue eyes, light hair, light complexion. Paroled: 6-1865. Died: 1-27-1899. Marker: Crossroads Baptist Church, Dallas, Ga. Buried: County Line UMC, Cobb Co., Ga.

Terry, Napoleon Bonaparte, Pvt., **G**, Enlisted: 3-62, Floyd Co., Ga., by Captain Kerr. Present through 12-31-1864. Died: 9-12-1904. Buried: Bluff Cemetery, Bagwell, Texas.

Thacker, J., Pvt., **D**, 8-63, Enlisted: Dallas, Ga., Captain Robert F. Trammell. AWOL 9-1-1863.

Thomas, Aug. O., Pvt., **K**, Enlisted: 8-63, Knoxville by Captain North. Admitted: Ocmulgee Hospital, Macon, Ga., 5-21-64. Present 12-63 and 12-64. Paroled: Montgomery, Ala. 5-16-1865. Description: 5'-10", blue eyes, dark hair, fair complexion.

Thomas, James H., Pvt., **I**, Captured: Athens, Ga., 5-8-65, paroled.

Thompson, John, Pvt., **H**, Captured. Exchanged on steamer *Metropolitan*, Vicksburg. 12-2-62. Paroled: Charlotte, N.C. 5-3-1865.

Thompson, John E., Pvt., **H**, Enlisted: 4-62, Haralson Co., Ga., by Captain Tumlin. Present through 8-62. Absent 10-62 WIA. Present 12-62 and 2-63: Teamster. Absent 12-63: Detached service with wagons. 12-64 present.

Thompson, P.B., Pvt., **H**, Enlisted: 4-62, Haralson Co., Ga., by Captain Tumlin. Present through 12-30-1863.

Thompson, Thomas T., Cpl., **H**, Enlisted: 4-62, Haralson Co., Ga., by Captain Tumlin. Present through 2-63. Promoted: 3rd Cpl. 1-28-63. Absent 12-63 and 12-64 WIA. Buried: Upper Cane Creek Cemetery, Fruithurst, Ala.

Thompson, William, Pvt., **H**, Enlisted: 8-63, Dalton, Ga., by Captain Tumlin. Elected Clerk of Inferior Court, Haralson Co. 2-3-64. Discharged 5-7-64. 12-64 AWOL. Moved to Texas.

Thornton, Augustus Sterling Clayton, Pvt., **E**, WIA: Atlanta. Admitted: Ocmulgee—Floyd Hospital, Macon, Ga., 7-21-1864. Died: wounded and typhoid fever. Buried: Magnolia Cemetery, Augusta, Ga.

Thornton, Y., Pvt., **B**, Enlisted: 3-62 in Newnan, Ga. 12-64 present.

Thurman, Ansalem A., Pvt., **A**, Enlisted: 3-62, Cedartown, Ga., by Captain John C. Crabb. Present 6-62. KIA: Murfreesboro 7-13-62.

Thurman, Marcus D., Pvt., **K**, Enlisted: 8-64, Newnan, Ga., by Captain North. Present 12-64. Surrendered: Greensboro, N.C. 4-26-1865. Pension: Campbell Co., Ga., 1919.

Tidwell, Mansell D., Sgt., **D**, Enlisted: 3-62, Dallas, Ga., age 23, by Captain Seawright. Present through 12-62. WIA: Murfreesboro. 7-13-62. Elected Cpl. 8-1-62. Absent 2-63 Sick furlough: Paulding Co., Ga. 12-63 present. Died: 1-12-1917. Buried: Noble Hill Cemetery, Maryville, Ala.

Timmons (Timons), James, Pvt., **C**, 6-64, Present 12-64. Last paid 6-30-1864.

Timmons, Robert T., Pvt., **H**, Enlisted: 4-62, Haralson Co., Ga., by Captain Tumlin. Present through 12-31-1864.

Tinney, Joseph Thomas, Pvt., **B**, Enlisted: 7-63 in Newnan, Ga., age 41. Present 12-63. Absent at General Hospital 10-28-64. Died: 1-15-1898. Buried: Hubbard Cemetery, Shelby Co., Ala.

Tinney, Wiley Clark, Pvt., **B**, Enlisted: 3-62, Newnan, Ga., age 21, by Captain Strickland. Absent 6-62 Grantville, Ga., sick furlough. Present through 12-62. Absent 2-63: Detached: Brigade artillery. 12-63 present. Living 1880 Harris Co., Ga.

Tinney, William T., Pvt., **B**, Enlisted: 3-62 in Newnan, Ga. Present 6-62. Absent: WIA, London, Ky. 8-17-62; Shot: lower back near spine. Absent 10-62 and 12-62 Grantville, Ga., wounded furlough. Present 12-63 and 12-64. Died: 11-30-1916. Buried: Wilsonville Cemetery, Shelby Co., Ala.

Tolbert, Phillip H., Sgt., **D**, Enlisted: 3-62, Dallas, Ga., age 23, by Captain Seawright. Absent 6-62 Sick at Barboursville, Ky. Present 8-62. Absent 10-62 and 12-62: Left sick in Ky. and Captured at Richmond, Ky. 10-28-62. Exchanged. Absent 2-63: Paulding Co., Ga. on sick furlough. 12-63 present.

Tomlin, Arkin Aquilla, Sgt., **K**, Enlisted: 1st Ga. Inf. 3-18-61, Newnan, Ga. Enlisted: 1st Ga. Cavalry 5-3-62, Camp Morrison by Captain North. Present through 12-31-1864. WIA: Murfreesboro. 7-13-1862. Died: 3-21-1914. Buried: Friendship Cemetery, Cale, Ark.

Tomlin, Garley W., Pvt., **D**, Enlisted: 3-62, Dallas, Ga., by Captain Seawright. Present 6-62. Absent 8-62 Sick furlough: Paulding Co., Ga. Present 10-62 through 2-63. Absent 12-63 Detained in Ga., by General Wheeler. 12-64 AWOL. Pension: Col. Davitte allowed to leave without surrender to save horse. Died: 12-19-1919. Buried: Yorkville Methodist Church, Paulding Co., Ga.

Tomlin, Pierce S., Pvt., **B**, Enlisted: 3-62, Newnan, Ga., age 24, by Captain Strickland. Present 6-62 as Company wagoner. Present 8-62 through 12-62: Detailed as Teamster. Absent 2-63: Sick furlough in Newnan, Ga. Present 12-63 and 12-64. Surrendered: Greensboro, NC 4-26-1865. Died: 2-6-1913. Buried: Founders Cemetery, Moreland, Ga.

Tomlingson, John, Pvt., **H**, Enlisted: 8-63, Dalton, Ga., by Captain Tumlin. AWOL 12-1-1863.

Tomlinson, James Johnson, Pvt., **G**, Enlisted: 3-62, Floyd Co., Ga., by Captain Kerr. Absent 6-62 and 12-62: Sick in Floyd Co., Ga. Present 8-62 and 10-62. Present 2-63. Captured: Mill Springs, Ky. 5-28-63. Carried: Lexington 6-10-63; Camp Chase 6-14-63; Point Lookout, Md.; exchanged 2-18-1865. Description: age 27, 5'-10½", dark eyes, hair, and complexion. Died: 12-8-1910. Buried: Lindale Cemetery, Bowie, Texas.

Tomlinson, Simpson Grove, Sgt., **G**, Enlisted: 3-62, Floyd Co., Ga., by Captain Kerr. Present through 12-62. Promoted: 4th Sgt. 12-1-62. Captured: Mill Springs, Ky. 5-28-63. Carried: Lexington 6-10-63; Camp Chase; Point Lookout, Md. 10-30-63. Exchanged 2-13-1865. Description: age 25, 5'-10", blue eyes, light hair, fair complexion. Died: 1870, Red River Co., Tx.

Torrence, Andrew Jackson, Pvt., **E**, Enlisted: 4-62, Cartersville, Ga., by Captain Blalock. Present through 12-30-1863.

Torrence, J.T., Pvt., **E**, Enlisted: 3-62, Carrollton by Captain Blalock.

Tracy, Nathaniel H., 2nd Lt., **A**, Enlisted: 3-62, Cedartown, Ga., by Captain John C. Crabb. Absent 6-62 Sick furlough: Cedartown, Ga. Resigned 7-16-62. Certificate: disease of eyes. Died: 2-1873. Buried: Macedonia Baptist Church, Webster Co., Ga.

Trammell, E.S., Pvt., **B**, Enlisted: 3-62 in Newnan,

Ga. Present 12-63. WIA: Atlanta 7-21-64. Died: 8-12-1897. Buried: Center Point Baptist Church, Walker Co., Ga.

Trammell, John William, Major, **B**, Enlisted: 3-62, Newnan, Ga., age 31, by Captain Strickland. Present through 12-63. Elected 1st Lt. 3-31-62. Promoted Captain 10-27-63 succeeded Captain Strickland. Promoted Major by Col. Morrison to command Detachment. Paroled: Charlotte, NC, 5-3-1865. Died: 10-1-1896. Buried: Luthersville City Cemetery, Meriwether Co., Ga.

Trammell, Robert F., Captain, **D**, Enlisted: 3-62, Dallas, Ga., age 32, by Captain Seawright. Present through 12-62. WIA: Murfreesboro. 7-13-62. Promoted Captain 7-13-62 by Col. Morrison to replace Captain Seawright. Absent 12-63 sick furlough in Ga. Absent 12-64 Detached service. Captured 5-8-65: Athens, Ga. Died: 10-28-1885. Buried: Harmony Baptist Church, Empire, Ala.

Trimble, William Wiley, Pvt., **G**, Enlisted: 5-62, Camp Morrison by Captain Leak. Present through 12-62. Present 3-63: Detailed with Brigade wagons. Absent 10-63 in Ga. Present 12-64. Paroled: Charlotte, N.C. 5-3-1865. Died: 10-31-1907. Buried: Poplar Springs Cemetery, Adairsville, Ga.

Trout, Sanford C., Pvt., **C**, Enlisted: 3-63, Cave Spring, Ga., by Captain Haynie. Captured: Somerset, Ky. 3-30-63. Carried: Lexington; Camp Chase; Fort Delaware 7-14-63; Point Lookout, Md. Exchange 4-27-64. Taken: Richmond, Va. Chimborazo Hospital #3. V.S., right elbow. Absent 12-64 On detail. Applied to be a hospital steward. Buried: Witherspoon Cemetery, Vandervoort, Ark.

Tumlin, Henry Imri, Pvt., **H**, Enlisted: 4-62, Haralson Co., Ga., by Captain Tumlin. Substitute for John E. Kerr. Absent 6-62 and 10-62 Detached service. Present 8-62. Enlisted: 7-27-63, 2nd Ga. Cavalry State Guards. Died: 6-4-1881. Buried: Davistown Cemetery, Old Davisville, Ala.

Tumlin, James Spencer, 1st Sgt., **H**, Enlisted: 4-62, Haralson Co., Ga., by Captain Tumlin. Present through 12-62. Discharged by substitute: Isaac Jordan 1-14-1863. Enlisted: 7-27-1863, 2nd Ga. Cavalry State Guards. Died: 7-5-1909. Buried: Carrollton City Cemetery, Carroll Co., Ga.

Tumlin, Newton Jasper, Pvt., **H**, Enlisted: 4-62. Discharged: May 10, 1862, by substitute Charles J. Hambrick who died 7-6-1862. Drafted into Floyd Legion State Guards, 7-28-1863. Died: 3-26-1905. Buried: Carrollton City Cemetery, Carroll Co., Ga.

Tumlin, Virgil Meggs, 1st Lt., **H**, Enlisted: 19th Ga. Inf. 6-11-61. Transferred: 1st Ga. Cavalry 9-15-62: Clinton, Tenn. Elected 2nd Lt. 8-5-63, 1st Lt. AWOL 6-64. Dropped 2-1-65. Pension: Fall 1864, crossing Chattahoochee River, outpost duty, nearly captured but narrowly escaped to Mississippi. Joined Captain Norwood, Ross's Brigade. Surrendered 1865: Jackson, Miss. Died: 5-19-1921. Buried: Westview Cemetery, Atlanta, Ga.

Tumlin, William Marion, Captain, **H**, Enlisted 6-10-1861: 19th Ga. Inf. (Kingston Vols.), 2nd Lt. Enlisted 4-19-62: 1st Ga. Cavalry, age 26, by Lt. Col. Morrison. Present through 2-63. WIA: Resaca 6-14-64 sent to Cuthbert Hospital, Macon, Ga. Requested 2 month leave for rheumatism. The probable real injury was to his pride for being Passover for promotion to Major. From Oxford, Ala., the line officers of the regiment signed a letter requesting his promotion, but it went to Captain John W. Tench. Resigned: 2-16-65 wounded. Pension: Chatham Co., Ga., 1906.

Turner, Joseph, Pvt., **A**, Captured: Franklin, Tenn. 12-18-64. Admitted: U.S. General Hospital, Nashville, age 25, pneumonia 12-24-64 with scrofula (tuberculosis in neck lymph nodes). Transferred: Prison, Nashville 4-11-1865.

Underwood, Harvey N. "Newt," Pvt., **H**, 4-62, Died: 12-17-1916, Cleburne Co., Ala.

Underwood, Henry N., Pvt., **H**, Enlisted: 4-62, Haralson Co., Ga., by Captain Tumlin. Present through 8-62. Captured: Cumberland Gap 9-13-62. Carried: Cincinnati; paroled 10-16-62. Absent 10-62 on parole. Present 2-63: Teamster since 2-15-63. Absent 12-63 and 12-64: Detached service with wagons. Paroled: Talladega, Ala. 6-1-1865.

Underwood, Henry P., Pvt., **H**. Died, chronic diarrhea. Home: Monroe Co., Miss.

Underwood, I., Pvt., **A**, Paroled 5-24-1865, Talladega, Ala.

Underwood, James R., Pvt., **G**, Enlisted: 5-62, Camp Morrison by Captain Leak. Present through 12-62. Absent: Sick with fever in Hospital: Kingston, Tenn. Absent 3-63: Detachment camp. Present 10-63. Deserted 7-20-64. Died: Bartow Co., Ga., 6-13-1868.

Underwood, John P., Pvt., **H**, Enlisted: 4-62, Haralson Co., Ga., by Captain Tumlin. Present through 8-62. Captured; paroled 9-4-62. Captured: Shelbyville, Ky. 9-11-62. Carried: Louisville; Camp Chase 9-26-62. Exchanged aboard steamer *Emerald*, Vicksburg 11-1-62 . Description: age 23, 5'-8", blue eyes, dark hair, light complexion. Absent 12-62 on parole. Present 2-63.

Absent 12-63 Detained in Ga., by General Wheeler. Died: 12-16-1871, Cleburne Co., Ala.

Upshaw, A.L., Pvt., **B**, Enlisted: 3-62 in Newnan, Ga. Absent 12-63: Detained with wagons by General Wheeler. 12-64 present.

Upshaw, Allen C., Pvt., **B**, 3-62. Received clothing issue June 1864. Died: 2-19-1899. Buried: Upshaw Family Cemetery, Luthersville, Ga.

Upshaw, John A., Pvt., **B**, Enlisted: 3-62, Newnan, Ga., age 26, by Captain Strickland. Present through 12-63. Died: 2-14-1903. Buried: Tallapoosa Co., Ala.

Upshaw, John R., Pvt., **B**, Enlisted: 4-62, Cartersville, Ga., by Col. Morrison. Present through 12-62. Absent 2-63 Newnan, Ga.: sick furlough. Present 12-63. Present 12-64: Courier for Col. Crews. Paroled: Charlotte, NC 5-3-1865. Died: 6-6-1898. Buried: Columbiana Cemetery, Shelby Co., Ala.

Upshaw, Robinson Valentine, Pvt., B, Enlisted: 3-62, Newnan, Ga., age 16, by Captain Strickland. Present through 12-63 when Dropped from roll by Major Strickland. Re-enlisted 11-20-64: Luthersville, Col. Davitte. (Father seems to have requested him home as youngest son.) Present 12-64. Paroled 5-3-65, Charlotte, N.C. Died: 10-16-1901. Buried: Fairview Cemetery, Shawnee, Ok.

Upshaw, Turner L., Pvt., **K**, Enlisted: Atlanta, 7th Ga. Inf. 5-31-1861. WIA 7-21-61, Manassas, Va. Enlisted: 5-63, 1st Ga. Cavalry, Cartersville, Ga., by Major Harper. Present 12-64. Murdered by brother Nathan 12-28-1869. Buried: Upshaw Family Cemetery, Luthersville, Ga.

Valentine, Armstead R., Pvt., **G**, Enlisted: 8-63 in Rome, Ga. Present 12-63. Captured: Rome 10-8-64. Carried: Nashville 11-21-64; Louisville; Camp Douglas 11-24-64. Discharged: 6-17-65. Description: home Floyd Co., Ga., 5'-10", blue eyes, light hair, fair complexion. Died: 8-4-1898.

Varner, J.T., Pvt., **I**, Captured 12-24-63: Dandridge, Tenn. Carried: Camp Chase 1-1-64.

Vaughan, John W., Pvt., **E**, Surrendered: Kingston, Ga., 5-12-1865. Died: 9-27-1887. Buried: Vaughan Cemetery, Bartow Co., Ga.

Velvin, Andrew C., 1st Lt., **E**, Enlisted: 3-62, Carrollton, Ga., by Captain Blalock. Elected 1st Lt. 3-21-1862. Died: 8-6-62, Carrollton, Ga., disease. Succeeded by Thomas M. Kelly.

Venable, Charles Wesley, Pvt., **I**, Enlisted: 5-64, Cass Station, Ga., by Captain Leak. Deserted 5-22-64. Living: Bartow Co., Ga. 1870.

Venable, James Knox Polk, Pvt., **G**, Enlisted: 5-62 in Bartow Co., Ga. Present through 12-62.

Absent 3-63: Detachment Camp. Absent 10-62 in Ga. Deserted 5-24-64. Pension: 1914, Texas.

Venable, Thomas Wiley, Sgt., **G**, Enlisted: 5-62, Camp Morrison by Captain Leak. Present through 8-62 as QM Sgt. Present 10-62 and 12-62. Absent 3-63 sick furlough. Present 12-63. Deserted 5-25-64. Pension: Hamilton Co., Tenn. Died: 1910. Buried: Forest Hills Cemetery, Chattanooga, Tenn.

Waddell, Alford (Alfred) L., Pvt., **E**, Enlisted: 5-62, Cartersville, Ga., by Captain Blalock. Present 6-62. Absent 8-62 and 10-62 wounded furlough home. 12-62 WIA, Knoxville. Died: 1904. Buried: Old Albertville Cemetery, Marshall Co., Ala.

Waddle, L.C., Pvt., **E**, Enlisted: 5-62, Cartersville, Ga., by Captain Blalock. Present through 12-63. Died: WIA 1-24-64.

Wade, Andrew Jackson, Pvt., **A**, Enlisted: 3-62, Cedartown, Ga., by Captain John C. Crabb. Present 6-62: Teamster for headquarters. Absent 8-62 Kingston, Tenn. sick. Absent 10-62 and 12-62: Home wounded accidentally. Captured: Somerset, Ky. 3-30-63. Carried: Louisville; City Point, Va. Exchanged 4-13-63. Absent 12-63: Detailed to Commissary Dept. AWOL 11-10-1864. Died: 9-15-1886. Buried: Balch Cemetery, Alvarado, Texas.

Wade, Joseph A., Pvt., **A**, Enlisted: 11-64 by Captain Jesse Crabb. Discharged: Kingston, Ga., 4-1865. Died: 8-8-1926. Buried: Erin Springs Cemetery, Garvin Co., Ok.

Waldrop, Stephen Holmes, Pvt., **B**, Enlisted: 3-62, Newnan, Ga., by Captain Strickland. Present through 12-62. Absent 2-63 Newnan, Ga.: sick furlough. Present 12-63. Present 12-64: Teamster for Gen. Hood. Surrendered: Greensboro, N.C. 4-26-1865. Died: 12-17-1906. Buried: Carrollton City Cemetery, Carroll Co., Ga.

Walea, Thomas Lamar, Pvt., **F**, Enlisted: 2nd Regt. State Line. Discharged: Certificate 6-16-63: age 20, 5'-6", fair complexion, blue eyes, light hair. Enlisted: 5-64, 1st Ga. Cavalry, Decatur, Ga., by Major Anderson. 12-64 AWOL. Paroled: Augusta, Ga., 5-20-65. Died: 12-7-1921. Buried: Walea Family Cemetery, Emanuel Co., Ga.

Walker, C.C., Pvt., **G**, Enlisted: 5-62, Camp Morrison by Captain Leak. Present 6-62: Wagoner. Died: Bartow Co., Ga., 7-5-62.

Walker, J.A., 1st Sgt., **K**, Enlisted: 5-62, Camp Morrison by Captain North. Present through 2-63. WIA, 7-64 near Fishing Creek, Sunshine Church, Ga.

Walker, James, Pvt., **G**, Enlisted: 3-62, Floyd Co., Ga., by Captain Kerr. Absent 6-62 Sick: Loudon,

Tenn. Hospital. Present through 12-62. Absent 2-63 Sick: Floyd Co., Ga. Admitted: St. Mary's Hospital, LaGrange, Ga., 6-17-64. Present 12-64. Paroled: Charlotte, N.C. 5-3-1865.

Walker, James Burton, 1st Sgt., **K**, Enlisted: Newnan, 7th Ga. Inf. 7-30-61. Enlisted: 12-62, 1st Ga. Cavalry: Cartersville, Ga., by Major Harper. Present through 12-64. WIA Sunshine Church 7-31-64, Hospital, three months. Surrendered: Greensboro, N.C. 4-26-1865. Died: 12-8-1915. Buried: Tranquil Cemetery, Coweta Co., Ga.

Walker, Robert A., Pvt., **K**, Admitted: Saint Mary's Hospital, LaGrange, Ga., 6-17-64. Dismissed 7-18-1864 and returned to duty.

Walker, Robert Noah, Pvt., **K**, Enlisted: 5-62, Cartersville, Ga., by Major Harper. Present 8-62. Captured; paroled: London, Ky. 9-8-62. Present 12-62 and 2-63. Died with fever, 8-26-1863. Buried: White Oak Presbyterian Church, Newnan, Ga.

Walker, Thomas W., Pvt., **A**, Enlisted: 4-63, Cedartown, Ga., by Captain Hutchings. 12-63 present. Pension: While drilling to form line of battle; Dirt Town, Ga.; horse stumbled and fell on right ankle crushing the bone. Pension: Meriwether Co., Ga., 1906.

Wallace, W.H., Pvt., **G**, Captured 11-16-63. Carried: Knoxville, deserted. Released: taking oath 11-17-63.

Walthall, Leonard H., Cpl., **B**, Enlisted: 3-62, Newnan, Ga., age 23, by Captain Strickland. Present through 12-31-1864. Died: 12-3-1890. Buried: White Oak Presbyterian Church, Newnan, Ga.

Walthall, William Morgan, Pvt., **K**, Enlisted: 5-62, Cartersville, Ga., by Major Harper. Present through 12-32-1864. Secretary for Captain North. Died: 7-3-1889. Buried: Floral Hills Cemetery, Palmetto, Ga.

Ward, D.Y., Pvt., **H**, Enlisted: 9-63, Tallapoosa, Ga., by Captain Tumlin. Absent 12-63: Detailed as Nurse, hospital.

Ward, M. Hamp, Pvt.. **K**, Enlisted: 5-62, Camp Morrison by Captain North. Present through 2-63: Blacksmith. Absent 12-63: Detailed: Government Shop, Rutledge, Ga. Absent 12-31-1864: Detailed: Government Shop, Wilmington, N.C. Paroled: Talladega, Ala. 5-20-1865. Widow pension: Cleburne Co., Ala. 1920.

Ward, T.L., Sgt., **D**, Enlisted: 3-62, Cedartown, Ga., by Captain John C. Crabb.

Warnock, Jasper M., Pvt., **I**, Enlisted: 3-63, Moore Creek, Tenn., by Lt. Fuller. Present through 12-64. Surrendered: Salisbury, N.C. 4-1865.

Died: 2-1-1903. Buried: Mount Tabor Cemetery, Floyd Co., Ga.

Warren, George W., Pvt., **G**, Enlisted: 3-62 in Floyd Co., Ga. Present through 2-63. Absent 12-63 Sick: Floyd Co., Ga. Present 12-64. Paroled: Charlotte, N.C. 5-3-1865. Witness: Floyd Co., Ga., 1918.

Warren, John K.A., Pvt., **G**, Enlisted: 3-62, Floyd Co., Ga., by Captain Kerr. Present through 8-62. Absent 10-62 and 12-62 Sick: Floyd Co., Ga. 2-63 AWOL. Absent 12-63 Sick.

Warren, W.P., Pvt., **G**, Enlisted: 4-64 in Rome, Ga. Absent 12-64: Sick in hospital since 7-17-1864.

Watkins, Andrew G., Pvt., **H**, Enlisted: 2-63, Clinton, Tenn., by Captain Tumlin. Captured: Chattooga Co., Ga., 1-22-64. Carried: Nashville; Louisville; Rock Island, Ill. 3-18-64. Said he was on the wrong side. Joined U.S. Navy 5-26-1864.

Watkins, William A., Pvt., **C**, Captured: Cherokee Co., Ala. 10-22-64. Received: Camp Douglas, Ill. 11-26-64. Enlisted: 5th USA Vol. Inf. 4-6-1865.

Watson, Thomas, Pvt., **G**, Enlisted: 3-62, Floyd Co., Ga., by Captain Kerr. Absent 6-62 Sick: Rome. Present through 12-62. Absent 2-63: Sick: Kingston, Tenn.

Watson, William H., Pvt., **G**, Enlisted: 8-62 in Kingston, Tenn. Substitute for T.S. Burney. Absent 12-62: Sick in Versailles, Ky. since 10-10-62. Died: 1-3-1863. Buried: Versailles Cemetery, Woodford Co., Ky.

Watters, Henry Pinkney, Pvt., **G**, Enlisted: 5-62, Rome, Ga., by Captain Kerr. Absent 6-62: Sick: Floyd Co., Ga. Present through 12-63. Captured and paroled in Ky. while on scout 10-64. Witness: Widow pension: Sent to tear up railroads south of Nashville. Atlanta on scout, cut off with Joseph S. Wilson and never returned to regiment. Died: 7-28-1922. Buried: Pleasant Valley North Cemetery, Rome, Ga.

Watters, N.S., Pvt., **I**, Enlisted: 3-64, Cass Station, Ga., by Captain Leak. Present 12-64. Surrendered: Greensboro, N.C. 4-26-1865. Pension: Floyd Co., Ga., 1905.

Watters (Waters), Sebaston, Pvt., **G**, Enlisted: 5-62, Camp Morrison by Captain Leak. Present through 12-62. Absent 3-63: Detachment Camp. Present 10-63. AWOL 12-7-64.

Watters, W.H., Pvt., **G**, Enlisted: 3-62, Floyd Co., Ga., by Captain Kerr. Absent 6-62 Sick: London, Ky. Hospital. Captured: Lebanon, Ky. 9-21-62. Carried: Louisville; Vicksburg. Exchanged 9-29-62 aboard steamer *Emerald*. Description: Age 20, blue eyes, light hair, light complexion, 5'-10¾". Present through 12-63. Absent 10-64 on scout mission.

Watters, William, Pvt., **G**, Enlisted: 4-64 in Rome, Ga. Present 12-64. Paroled: Charlotte, N.C. 5-3-1865.

Watts, George Troup, Lt. Col., **C**, Enlisted: 3-62, Cave Spring, Ga., by Captain Haynie as a private. Present through 8-62. Promoted 2nd Lt. 9-10-62, resignation Alexander Harper. Present through 3-63. Present 6-63: Promoted Captain at death of Milton H. Haynie. Absent 12-63 on leave. Escort: Lt. Gen. Hood 6-30-64, Marietta, Ga. Recommended Lt. Col. by Col. Davitte for skill and valor and promoted 12-21-64 by Gen. Wheeler. Commander 1st Ga. Cavalry Regiment at end of war. Paroled: Charlotte, N.C. 5-3-1865. Died: 4-22-1880. Buried: Cave Spring Cemetery, Floyd Co., Ga.

Watts, James Cowart, Pvt., **C**, Enlisted: 2-64, Cave Spring, Ga., by Captain Watts. Present 12-64. Paroled: Charlotte, N.C. 5-3-1865. Died: 9-16-1890. Buried: Unionville Cemetery, Lincoln Parish, La.

Watts, J.W.S., Pvt., **C**, Enlisted: 7-63, Floyd Co., Ga., by Captain Haynie. Absent 12-63 Sick. Present 12-64. Paroled: Charlotte, N.C. 5-3-1865.

Weach, Robert C, Surgeon, **F&S**.

Weatherly, Benjamin Franklin, Ordnance Sergeant, **A**, Enlisted: 3-62, Cedartown, Ga., by Captain John C. Crabb. Absent 6-62 Sick: Loudon, Tenn. Hospital. Present through 2-63. Absent 12-64 Detailed with Major Reynolds. Paroled: Charlotte, N.C. 5-3-1865. Died: 3-10-1926. Buried: Lone Oak Cemetery, Hunt Co., Tx.

Weatherly, Orvin Joseph Burton, Pvt., **A**, Enlisted 1st Ala. Cavalry. Transferred, 1st Ga. Cavalry, with brother and uncle, Captain John C. Crabb. Enlisted: 1-63, Cedartown, Ga. Present 2-63. Absent 12-63 Cut off with wagons. AWOL 12-1-64. Died: 9-5-1918. Buried: Lone Oak Cemetery, Hunt Co., Tx.

Weathers, L., Sgt., **G**, 3-62, Present 4-12-1862.

Weathington, Leroy Campbell, Pvt., **D**, Enlisted: Camp McDonald, age 26, 19th Ga. Inf., 6-25-1861. Discharged 10-2-1861. Description: age 26, 5'-10", dark complexion, dark hair, black eyes. Enlisted: 3-62, Dallas, Ga., age 27, by Captain Seawright. Present 6-62. Absent 8-62 Sick furlough: Paulding Co., Ga. Present 10-62 through 2-63. Absent 12-63 Detained in Ga., by General Wheeler. AWOL 6-28-64. Captured: Paulding Co., Ga., as Deserter. Took oath 9-4-64, Louisville. Description: home Paulding Co., Ga., 5'-10", blue eyes, dark hair, light complexion. Died: 9-19-1906, Crossville, DeKalb Co., Ala.

Weaver, William Henry, Pvt., **B**, Captured: Mur-freesboro 12-31-62; exchanged or escaped. Captured: Danville, Ky. 1-2-63. Carried: Lexington; Vicksburg. Exchanged 1-5-63. Captured: Jacksboro, Tenn. 12-28-63.

Webb, J.M., Sgt., G, Enlisted: 3-62, Floyd Co., Ga., by Captain Kerr. Present 6-62. Died of congestion of the brain 7-9-62.

Webb, Levi W., Cpl., **G**, Enlisted: 3-62, Floyd Co., Ga., by Captain Kerr. Present through 2-63. Captured: Somerset, Ky. 3-30-63. Carried: Louisville; City Point, Va. Exchanged 4-14-63. Captured: Dandridge, Tenn. 12-24-63. Carried: Knoxville; Camp Chase; Rock Island, Ill. New Orleans from Camp Douglas, Ill.; exchange 5-23-1865. Died: 6-14-1892. Buried: Centre Cemetery, Cherokee Co., Ala.

Webster, George Addison, 2nd Lt., **G**, Enlisted: 5-62, Rome, Ga., by Captain Kerr. Absent 6-62 Sick in Rome, Ga. Present through 2-63. Promoted 9-5-63 for gallantry at Chickamauga by Col. Morrison. During 1864 his Captain was under arrest and 1st Lt. was sick, therefore; he commanded the company. Present 12-64. Surrendered: Greensboro, N.C. 4-26-1865. Died: 5-12-1925. Buried: Decatur Cemetery, DeKalb Co., Ga.

Weems, W.F., Chaplin, **F&S**, Resigned: Certificate 5-15-62. Afflicted: Hypertrophy, left ventricle, heart.

Welch, Matthew, Pvt., **K**, Captured: Cowan, Tenn. 7-4-63. POW: Carried: Nashville; Louisville; Camp Chase. On list of deserters that Took oath 11-23-64. Description: home Muscago (Muscogee) Co., Ga., 5'-7", grey eyes, lite hair, lite complexion, age 32.

Wells, Edwin W., Pvt., **E**, Enlisted: 3-62, Carrollton, Ga., by Captain Blalock. Present through 12-64. Paroled: Charlotte, N.C. 5-3-1865. Died: 5-8-1906. Buried: Carrollton City Cemetery, Carroll Co., Ga. Elected Mayor, Carrollton, Ga.

Wells, J.F., Pvt., **K**, Enlisted: 5-62, Camp Morrison by Captain North.

Wells, Samuel S., Pvt., **K**, Enlisted: 5-62, Cartersville, Ga., by Major Harper. Present through 2-63: Teamster for Regiment. Absent 12-63. Present 12-64 with Gen. Hood's supply train. Discharged: Salisbury, N.C. 5-4-1865. Witness: Coweta Co., Ga., 1891.

Wells, Thomas J., Pvt., **B**, Enlisted: 3-62, Newnan, Ga., by Captain Strickland. Present 6-62: Company blacksmith. Absent 8-62 Sick furlough: Meriwether Co., Ga. Absent 10-62 Sick furlough: Savannah, Ga. Absent 2-63 Sick furlough Newnan, Ga. Absent 12-63: Detailed blacksmith for Davidsons Brigade. Absent 12-64: Detailed: Govt. Shop, Rutledge, Ga.

West, A.J., Colonel, **F&S**, Captured: Athens, Ga., 5-8-65, paroled.

West, Alex, Pvt., **G**, Enlisted: 3-62, Floyd Co., Ga., by Captain Kerr. 4-62 Camp McDonald, Rejected.

West, Asa, Pvt., **A**, Vidette. Served: end of war. Living: Cedartown, Ga., 1880.

West, Benjamin T., Pvt., **A**, Enlisted: 3-62, Cedartown, Ga., by Captain John C. Crabb. Present 6-62 acting Wagon Master. Absent 8-62: Wagon master: Kingston, Tenn. Present 10-62. Absent 12-62 Regiment: wagon master. Present 2-63: Acting Wagon Master. Absent 12-63. Present 12-64. Paroled: Charlotte, N.C. 5-3-1865. Died: 3-30-1903. Buried: West Family Cemetery, Cedartown, Ga.

West, Jonathan Francis Marion, Pvt., **F**, Died: 11-6-1911. Buried: Ebenezer Baptist Church, Gilmer Co., Ga.

West, Middleton E., Pvt., **C**, Enlisted: 3-62, Cave Spring, Ga., by Captain Haynie. Present 6-62. Absent 8-62 Sick: Loudon, Tenn. Present 10-62 and 12-62: Teamster. Present through 12-64. Died: 3-31-1898. Buried: West Family Cemetery, Cedartown, Ga.

West, W.C., Pvt., **C**, Enlisted: 3-62. Present 4-6-1862.

Wethers (Weathers), Lawson H., Sgt., **G**, Enlisted: 3-62, Floyd Co., Ga., by Captain Kerr. Present 6-62. Died: Kingston, Tenn. 7-15-62, bilious fever. Body given to Logan Weathers, father.

Wheat, Henry C., Pvt., **K**, Enlisted: 11-64, Newnan, Ga., by Captain North. 12-64 present.

Wheeler, J.J., Pvt., **H**, Enlisted: 4-62, Haralson Co., Ga., by Captain Tumlin. Present through 2-63. AWOL 9-16-63. Paroled: Talladega, Ala. 5-25-1865. Buried: Friendship Primitive Baptist Church, Hiram, Ga.

Wheeler, James M., Pvt., **H**, 4-62, Enlisted: 4-62, Haralson Co., Ga., by Captain Tumlin. Substitute for Lewis Ramsey. Present 6-62. Discharged: (ruptured) 8-6-62; Kingston, Tenn. Paroled: Talladega, Ala. 5-25-1865.

Whisenhunt, Phillip Marion, Pvt., **E**, Enlisted: 5-62, Cartersville, Ga., by Captain Blalock. Present through 12-63. Captured: East Tenn. 2-1-64. Carried: Morristown, Tenn. (deserter); Knoxville 3-15-1864. Died: Before 6-3-1900, Haralson Co., Ga.

White, J.K.H., Pvt., **F**, Enlisted: 9-64, Villanow, Ga., by Col. Davitte. 12-64 present.

White, John Belle, Pvt., **C**, Enlisted: 3-62, Cave Spring, Ga., by Captain Haynie. Absent 8-62

and 10-62: Sick in Floyd Co., Ga. Present 12-62: Detailed with wagons since 12-15-62. Present 2-63. Absent 6-63 in Floyd Co., Ga. to purchase horse. Present 12-63 and 12-64. Paroled: Kingston, Ga. May 1865. Died: 11-17-1920. Buried: Livingston Cemetery, Floyd Co., Ga.

White, Milton, Pvt., **F**. POW: Captured: Philadelphia, Tenn. 10-20-63. Carried: Fort Delaware Prison. Died: 1-19-1908. Buried: White Cemetery, Chattooga Co., Ga.

White, Newton, Pvt., **I**, Died: 6-29-1889. Buried: White Cemetery, Walker Co., Ga.

White, William, Pvt., **A**, Enlisted: 3-63, Cedartown, Ga., by Captain Hutchins. POW: Captured: Philadelphia, Tenn. 10-20-63. Carried: Camp Nelson; Camp Chase 11-14-63; Rock Island, Ill. 1-22-64.

Whitehead, John R.J., Pvt., **A**, Enlisted: 3-63, Cedartown by Captain York. Present 12-63 and 12-64. WIA. Paroled: Charlotte, N.C. 5-3-1865.

Whitehead, Raleigh W., Sgt., Enlisted: 3-62, Cedartown, Ga., by Captain John C. Crabb. Present 6-62. Absent 8-62 Kingston, Tenn. sick. Present 10-62: Acting Forage Master. Present 12-62: Detailed on special duty. Present 12-63 WIA. AWOL 11-10-64. Paroled: Charlotte, N.C. 5-3-1865. Died: 4-15-1878. Buried: Family Cemetery, Hwy. 27 and Adams Rd., Cedartown, Ga.

Whitehead, Robert Seybourn, Pvt., **A**, Enlisted: 3-62, Cedartown, Ga., by Captain John C. Crabb. Substitute for R.W. Whitehead. Absent 12-63 Cut off with wagons. Present 12-64. Surrendered: Greensboro, N.C. 4-26-65. Died: 1931. Buried: Granbury Cemetery, Hood Co., Tx.

Whorton, Francis M., Sgt., **C**, Enlisted: 5-62 in Cave Spring, Ga. Present through 6-63. Promoted 2nd Cpl. 3-15-63. Absent 12-63. Present 12-64: Detailed within Regiment. Died: 7-9-1905. Buried: Roscoe Cemetery, Nolan Co., Tx.

Whorton, Jackson Beverly, Pvt., **C**, Enlisted: 1-63, Cave Spring, Ga., by Captain Haynie. Present through 12-63. AWOL 12-31-1864. POW: Fort Delaware Prison 8-4-64. Pension: Transferred: Escort, Gen. Stewart for the war. Buried: Carmel Cemetery, Spring Garden, Ala.

Whorton, John H., Pvt., **C**, Enlisted: 3-62, Cave Spring, Ga., by Captain Haynie. Present 6-62: Company Teamster. Present until Discharged: 12-31-62, sick. Died: 10-25-1896, Floyd Co., Ga.

Whorton, Lafayette W., Pvt., **C**, Enlisted: 3-62, Cave Spring, Ga., by Captain Haynie. Present through 12-63. Died: 1915. Buried: Deep Creek Cemetery, Boyd, Texas.

Wigley, William Eccles, Pvt., **D**, Enlisted: 3-62, Dallas, Ga., age 26, by Captain Seawright. Present through 10-62. Absent 12-62: sick in hospital. Absent 2-63 Sick furlough: Paulding Co., Ga. Captured: Loudon, Tenn. 12-1-63. Escaped and rejoined unit. Absent 12-64: Captured. Died: 11-23-1918. Buried: Ridge Park Cemetery, Hillsboro, Texas.

Wiley, James, Pvt., **A**, Enlisted: 10-63, Vansant, Ga., by Captain York. 12-63 present.

Wiley, T.T., Pvt., **K**, Enlisted: 11-64, Newnan, Ga., by Captain North. 12-64 present.

Wilkins, James W., Pvt., **C**, Enlisted: 3-62, Cave Spring, Ga., by Captain Haynie. Present through 2-63. KIA: Somerset, Ky. 3-30-63.

Wilkins, William A., Pvt., **C**, Enlisted: 3-62, Cave Spring, Ga., by Captain Haynie. Present through 2-63. Captured: Somerset, Ky. 3-30-63. Carried: Louisville; City Point, Va.; exchanged 4-13-62. Present 12-63. Captured: Cherokee Co., Ala. 10-20-64. Carried: Nashville; Camp Douglas 11-23-64. Died, consumption 7-1881, Polk Co., Ga.

Willard, Milton P., Sgt., **H**, Enlisted: 4-62, Haralson Co., Ga., by Captain Tumlin. Present 6-62. MIA: 6-30-62. POW: Camp Morton. Stated he deserted at Cumberland Gap 7-1-62 sent Vicksburg 11-22-62.

Williams, Butler LaFayette, Pvt., **F**, Enlisted: 5-10-62, Villa Rica, Ga.: 56th Ga. Inf. Transferred 8-63: 1st Ga. Cavalry. Enlisted: Dallas, Ga., by Captain Robert F. Trammell. AWOL 9-63. 12-64 AWOL. Discharged: 4-65. Died: 9-14-1919. Buried: Friendship Baptist Church, Odenville, Ala.

Williams, Elihue M., Sgt., E, Enlisted: 3-62, Carrollton, Ga., by Captain Blalock. Present through 8-62. Discharged with rheumatism 10-24-62. Certificate: born Laurens District, S.C., age 35, 5'-11", dark complexion, blue eyes, dark hair. Died: 5-22-1865 shot in back at home. Buried: Williams Family Cemetery, Mount Carmel. Carroll Co., Ga.

Williams, George, Pvt., **H**, Captured: Penn's Bridge, S.C. 2-11-65. Carried: New Bern, N.C.; Point Lookout, Md. Released 6-21-1865. Description: home Butler Co., Ala., 5'-9½", dark complexion, black hair, hazel eyes.

Williams, George W., Pvt., **D**, Enlisted: 3-62, Dallas, Ga., age 22, by Captain Seawright. Absent 6-62 through 10-62 Sick furlough: Paulding Co., Ga. Absent 12-62 sick in hospital. Died: 10-30-1901. Buried: Allgood Methodist Church, Dallas, Ga.

Williams, Henry Roland, Pvt., **E**, Enlisted: 4-64, Carrollton, Ga., by Captain Shuford. Present 12-64. Paroled: Charlotte, N.C. 5-3-1865. Description: tall, red hair. Died: 5-19-1901. Buried: Jordan Memorial Family Cemetery, Carroll Co., Ga.

Williams, Horatio H., Sgt., **K**, Enlisted: 5-62, Camp Morrison by Captain North. Absent 6-62: Sick furlough home. Present 8-62. Captured: London, Ky. 9-8-62. Exchanged 9-16-62, Cumberland Gap. Present 12-63 and 12-64. Surrendered: Greensboro, NC 4-26-1865. Died: 4-15-1896. Buried: County Line Cemetery, Temple, Ga.

Williams, J.A., Pvt., **B**, Received clothing 2-27-1864.

Williams, James A., Pvt., **H**, Enlisted: 4-62, Haralson Co., Ga., by Captain Tumlin. Died: Cartersville, Ga., 5-31-62, fever.

Williams, James Carter, Pvt., **B**, Enlisted: 5-4-62, Meriwether Co., Ga.: 55th Ga. Inf. Enlisted: 8-63, Knoxville by Lt. Taylor. Paroled: Talladega Ala. 6-20-65. Died: 5-12-1924. Buried: First Baptist Church, Haralson, Ga.

Williams, J.C., Pvt., **A**, Enlisted: 3-62, Cedartown, Ga., by Captain John C. Crabb. A substitute for James Young 7-1-62. Charged the Court House at Murfreesboro and severely WIA. Discharged because of wounds 8-8-62.

Williams, J.C., Pvt., **B**, Enlisted: 3-62, Newnan, Ga. Enlisted 7-16-63: Knoxville. Present 12-63 and 12-64. Paroled: Talladega, Ala. 6-20-65.

Williams, J.H., Pvt., **E**, 1864, At surrender in hospital "The Rock," Macon, Ga. Died: 12-19-1915, Meriwether Co., Ga.

Williams, J.J., Pvt., **H**, Enlisted: 9-63, Tallapoosa, Ga., by Captain Tumlin. AWOL 10-14-1863.

Williams, John Coffee, Pvt., **A**, Enlisted: 3-62, Cedartown, Ga., by Captain John C. Crabb. Substitute for James Young 7-1-62. WIA: Murfreesboro 7-13-62, six places. Gunshot: right arm breaking bone result amputation below elbow. Discharged: 8-8-62. Pension: 1902, Polk Co., Ga.

Williams, John E., Pvt., **H**, Enlisted: 4-62, Haralson Co., Ga., by Captain Tumlin. Present through 12-62. Absent 2-63: Sick furlough.

Williams, J.T., Pvt., **A**, Prison at war's end.

Williams, Newton J., Pvt., **H**, Enlisted: 4-62, Haralson Co., Ga., by Captain Tumlin. Present through 12-62. Absent 2-63 Detached service: Hospital. Absent 12-63: Detained in Ga., by General Wheeler. Absent 12-64: Detached service. Died: 1-12-1913. Buried: Mars Hill Cemetery, Cleburne Co., Ala.

Williams, Newton W., Pvt., **C**, Enlisted: 3-62,

Cave Spring, Ga., by Captain Haynie. Present through 12-62. Absent 2-63: Detached as Brigade Wagoner. Present 12-63.

Williams, R., Pvt., **K,** Enlisted: 5-62, Camp Morrison by Captain North.

Williams, W.H., Pvt., **F,** Enlisted: 10-62, Carrollton, Ga., by Captain Blalock. Present through 12-62. Absent 2-63: Detached to Captain Marshall's Battery through 12-64.

Williams, William W., Pvt., **C,** Enlisted: 5-62 in Cave Spring, Ga. Present through 12-62. Absent 2-63: Detached to artillery service. Present 6-63. Absent 12-63: Detached service. Present 12-64. Furloughed home 2-26-1865. Pension: Floyd Co., Ga., 1909.

Williams, William Wesley, Pvt., **E,** Enlisted: 3-62, Carrollton, Ga., by Captain Blalock. Present through 2-63. Wounded, legs. Discharged 4-9-1865. Died 12-13-1918. Buried: Welti Presbyterian Church, Cullman Co., Ala.

Williams, W.J., Pvt., **H,** Enlisted: 4-62, Haralson Co., Ga., by Captain Tumlin. Absent 6-62: Detached service. Present through 12-62. Substituted for 2-28-63.

Williams, Zachary T., Pvt., **A,** Enlisted: 3-62, Cedartown, Ga., by Captain John C. Crabb. Present through 2-63. Absent 12-63: Cut off with wagons. Captured: Haralson Co., Ga. Carried: Chattanooga; Louisville 6-6-64, as Deserter. Took oath 6-8-64. Description: home Haralson Co., Ga., 5'-7", complexion dark, hair dark, eyes black. Died: 7-17-1927. Buried: Bremen City Cemetery, Haralson Co., Ga.

Willingham, James (S.) C., Pvt., **B,** 4-64, Present 12-64. Discharged: ulcers and unable to ride, Dr. Branch. Died: 12-15-1932. Buried: Allen Lee Memorial UMC Cemetery, Lone Oak, Ga.

Willingham, William Samuel, Sgt., **B,** Enlisted: 3-62, Newnan, Ga., age 28, by Captain Strickland. Present through 12-62. Absent 2-63: Rocky Mount, Ga. on sick furlough. Absent 12-64: Courier for Gen. Iverson. During surrender between Gen. Iverson and Gen. Crews Headquarters. Died: 3-27-1896, Meriwether Co., Ga.

Willis, John F., Pvt., **A,** Enlisted: 3-62, Cedartown, Ga., by Captain John C. Crabb. Present through 2-63. Absent 12-63: Cut off with wagons. AWOL 11-1-64. Pension: Attached to Gen. Wofford's command, surrendered 5-12-1865, Kingston, Ga. Pension: Bartow Co., Ga., 1907.

Willis, Walter T., Pvt., **K,** Enlisted 10-8-61 4th Regt. Ga. State Troops. Enlisted: 5-62, Cartersville, Ga., by Major Harper. 9-19-63, Chickamauga during charge, thrown from horse. Run

over by following horses. Captured: Pigeon River, Tenn. 1-27-64. Carried: Nashville; Camp Chase; Rock Island, Ill. 2-18-64. Released: 6-20-1865. Statement: home Coweta Co., Ga., age 20, 5'-8", dark hair, blue eyes, fresh complexion. Died: 8-17-1918. Buried: Cokes Chapel UMC., Sharpsburg, Ga.

Willis, W.W., Pvt., **H,** 2-64, Transferred: 12th Ala. Inf.

Wills, John W., Pvt., **D,** Enlisted: 9-62, Dallas, Ga., by Captain Robert F. Trammell. Present through 10-62. Absent 12-62: Paulding Co., Ga. on leave. AWOL 10-1-62. Last paid 6-30-1863.

Wilson, Allen, Pvt., **D,** Admitted: Ocmulgee— Floyd Hospital, Macon Ga. 7-21-1864.

Wilson, George W., Sgt., **D,** Enlisted: 8-62, Dallas, Ga., by Captain Robert F. Trammell. Present through 2-63. Present 12-63: Appointed 5th Sgt. 12-13-63. Captured: Sevierville, Tenn. 1-27-64. Carried: Nashville; Louisville; Camp Chase; Rock Island, Ill. 2-15-64. Admitted: Camp Winder General Hospital, Richmond, Va. 3-16-1865.

Wilson, John J., Pvt., **G,** Enlisted: 3-62, Floyd Co., Ga., by Captain Kerr. Present 6-62. Wounded accidentally 7-20-62, Kingston, Tenn. Absent 10-62 and 12-62: Wounded furlough: Floyd Co., Ga. Present 12-63. Absent 12-64: WIA near Rome, Ga., 10-64. Died: 4-2-1877. Buried: Clark Co., Ark.

Wilson, Joseph Sanford, Sgt., **G,** Enlisted: 12-62, McMinnville, Tenn., by Captain Kerr. Present through 12-63. Captured: Collierville, Tenn. 11-3-63. Admitted: Alton, Ill. Prison Hospital 11-16-63, Typhus Pneumonia. Dismissed 11-24-63. Paroled. Absent 10-64: on Scout. Pension: With Regiment until Atlanta 1864 became Cut off with Henry Pink Watters. Never returned. Died: 1-11-1934. Buried: DeGray Cemetery, Clark Co., Ark.

Wilson, William A., Pvt., **G,** Enlisted: 5-62, Camp Morrison by Captain Leak. Present through 12-62. 3-63 AWOL. Died: 1890. Buried: Bethesda Cemetery, Amity, Ark.

Wimpee, David Henry, Pvt., **G,** Enlisted: 3-62, Floyd Co., Ga., by Captain Kerr. Present 6-62: Extra duty doing wood work. Present 8-62. Absent 10-62 through 2-63: Sick furlough: Rome, Ga. Pension: Wheeler, Ark. 1901.

Wimpee, George Washington, Pvt., **G,** Enlisted: 3-62, Floyd Co., Ga., by Captain Kerr. Present 6-62: Extra duty doing wood work. Present through 2-63. Absent 12-63 and 12-64: Sick in Cedartown, Ga. since 11-1-64. Surrendered;

paroled: Kingston, Ga. Died: Walker Co., Ga., 1900.

Wimpee, Matthew (Mahew)Allen, Jr., Pvt., **G**, Enlisted: 3-62, Floyd Co., Ga., by Captain Kerr. Absent 6-62: Sick: Rome, Ga. Present 8-62. Absent 10-62 through 2-63: Sick furlough: Rome, Ga. Discharged disabled: 2-1863. Enlisted 7-14-1863, Floyd Legion. Died: 11-23-1912. Buried: Myrtle Hill Cemetery, Rome, Ga.

Windham (Windom), George Washington, Pvt., **B**, Enlisted: 4-62, Cartersville, Ga., by Col. Morrison. Present through 10-62. Absent 12-62 and 2-63: Atlanta Hospital. Absent 12-63: Detained with wagon train by General Wheeler. Transferred: artillery within 1st Ga. Cavalry. Died: 10-1-1908. Buried: Bethel Baptist Church, Rocky Mount, Ga.

Windham (Windom), Marion W., Cpl., **H**, Enlisted: 4-62, Haralson Co., Ga., by Captain Tumlin. Present through 12-62. Resigned 1-23-63. Absent 12-63 WIA. 12-64 AWOL.

Windom, Francis Marion, Pvt., **H**, Enlisted: 4-63, Detached to go with Gen. Hood, Franklin, Tenn. 8-64. Advance guard, Col. Jones, 3rd Texas Cavalry. Surrendered: Meridian, Miss. Died: 8-1-1923. Buried: Bethany Cemetery, Haralson Co., Ga.

Wingard, James Sumptner, Pvt., **A**, Enlisted: 11-64, in field by Captain Jesse W. Crabb. Paroled: Charlotte, N.C. 5-3-1865. Died: 10-11-1928. Buried: Cobb Cemetery, Thornton, Texas.

Winnett, Elkanah "Luke" K., Pvt., **H**, Enlisted: 4-62, Haralson Co., Ga., by Captain Tumlin. Present through 12-62. AWOL 2-63. Absent 12-63: Detained in Ga., by General Wheeler. Captured: Cartersville, Ga., 5-25-64. Carried: Nashville; Louisville; Rock Island, Ill. 6-9-64. Died: Rock Island Prison 8-23-64, Erysipelas. Buried: Confederate Cemetery, Rock Island, Ill. Grave # 1443.

Wisner, Jacob Daniel, Pvt., **D**, Enlisted: 3-62, Dallas, Ga., age 17, by Captain Seawright. Present through 2-63. AWOL 9-1-63. Pension: Captured 1863. Paroled. Transferred: 1st Confed. Cavalry. Died: 7-14-1914. Buried: New Hope Baptist Church, Dallas, Ga.

Wisner, J.M., Pvt., **D**, Enlisted: 3-62, Dallas, Ga., age 28, by Captain Seawright. Present until Discharged 11-6-62, Sparta, Tenn.

Wisner, James, Pvt., **D**, 3-62, Sick furlough, Col. Morrison 3-64. Died: 6-2-1866, Greene Co., Ala.

Witcher, Benjamin W., Pvt., **B**, Enlisted: 3-62, Newnan, Ga., by Captain Strickland. Present until Discharged: 9-28-62, Kingston, Tenn. Died: 1897. Buried: Abilene Missionary Baptist Church, Carroll Co., Ga.

Witcher, Hezekiah W., **F&S**, Regiment surgeon appointed 5-28-62, Col. Morrison. Present 6-62. KIA: Murfreesboro. 7-13-62. In charge against Court House, shot off his horse. Died ten minutes later. Buried: Ammons Family Cemetery, Polk Co., Ga.

Witcher, Osborn R., Pvt., **C**, Enlisted: 3-62, Cave Spring, Ga., by Captain Haynie. Present through 2-63. WIA: Monticello, Ky. Died: wounded, Rome, Ga., 6-9-63.

Witcher, Taliaferro, Pvt., **C**, Enlisted: 3-62, Cave Spring, Ga., by Captain Haynie. Present through 2-63. Absent 12-63: Special duty. 12-31-1864 present. Died: 1921. Buried: Lakeside Cemetery, Canon City, Colorado.

Witherington, Lee C., **D**, Deserted 1863.

Witherington, Sizemore, **D**, Deserted 1863.

Witzell (Wetzel), G.W., Cpl., **G**, Enlisted: 3-62, Floyd Co., Ga., by Captain Kerr. Present through 10-62. Absent 2-63: Captured and paroled in Ky. POW: Cincinnati: exchanged at Cumberland Gap 10-16-63.

Witzell, P.W., Pvt., **G**, Enlisted: 3-62, Floyd Co., Ga., by Captain Kerr. Present 6-62. Absent 8-62: Wounded accidentally 7-30-62, Kingston, Tenn. Absent through 12-64 Wounded in Floyd Co., Ga.

Wofford, J.C., Cpl., **G**, Enlisted: 5-62, Camp Morrison by Captain Leak. Present through 10-63.

Wood, Robert C., **F&S**, Surgeon

Wood, W.A., Pvt., **F**, Enlisted: 5-64, Decatur, Ga., by Major Anderson. 12-64 AWOL.

Wood, William, Pvt., **D**, Enlisted: 3-62, Dallas, Ga., age 17, by Captain Seawright. Present through 8-62. Captured: London, Ky. 9-21-62. Paroled 10-7-62. AWOL 11-63.

Wooten, W. Dave, Pvt., **G**, Enlisted: 5-62, Camp Morrison by Captain Leak. Present through 12-62. Absent 3-63: Wounded furlough—Shot accidentally on picket. Absent 10-63: Wounded. Present 12-64. Tennessee pension board made inquiry.

Wortham, Andrew Daria, Pvt., **B**, Enlisted: 3-62, Newnan, Ga., age 33, by Captain Strickland. Discharged: Cartersville, Ga., 4-15-62. Died: 1-10-1897. Buried: Columbiana Cemetery, Shelby Co., Ala.

Wortham, Christopher Columbus, Pvt., **B**, Enlisted: 3-62, Grantville, Ga. Absent 12-63: Newnan Hospital since 12-5-63. Absent 12-64: General Hospital since 7-1-64. Died: 10-2-1893, Meriwether Co., Ga.

Wortham, Francis "Frank" Benjamin, 2nd Lt., **B**, Enlisted: 3-62, Newnan, Ga., age 27, by Captain

Strickland. Present through 12-63. Promoted 2nd Lt. 10-28-63 by Col. Morrison succeeding James W. Taylor. Surrendered: Greensboro, N.C. 4-26-1865. Died: 7-11-1879. Buried: Luthersville City Cemetery, Meriwether Co., Ga.

Wortham, Thomas Nelson, Pvt., **B**, Enlisted: 4-62, Cartersville, Ga., by Col. Morrison. Present through 8-62. Absent 10-62 through 2-63: Sick furlough: Luthersville, Ga. Absent 12-63: Newnan, Ga. Hospital. Surrendered: Raleigh, N.C. 4-26-1865. Died: 4-16-1909. Buried: Luthersville City Cemetery, Meriwether Co., Ga.

Wragg, James Langdon, Pvt., **G**, Enlisted: 10-64, Dirt Town, Ga., by Col. Davitte. Present 12-64. Paroled: Charlotte, N.C. 5-3-1865. Died: 9-15-1908. Buried: Davis Chapel Cemetery, Panola Co., Miss.

Wragg, L.R., 1st Sgt., **G**, Enlisted: 3-62, Floyd Co., Ga., by Captain Kerr. Present 6-62. Absent 8-62 and 10-62: WIA: McMinnville, Tenn. 7-20-62. Absent 12-62: Resigned as 1st Sgt. 12-1-62. Absent 2-63 in Floyd Co., Ga. AWOL 12-18-64. Paroled: Charlotte, N.C. 5-3-1865.

Wright, A.Y., Pvt., **G**, Enlisted: 5-62, Camp Morrison by Captain Leak. Died: Knoxville 6-26-1862.

Wright, George W., Pvt., **B**, Enlisted: 7-63 in Newnan, Ga. Present 12-63. Died: Catoosa Hospital, Griffin, Ga., 7-14-64, chronic "Diarrahoea." Buried: Flat Rock Primitive Baptist Church, Rocky Mount, Ga.

Wright, J.B., Sgt., **H**, Enlisted: 4-62, Camp Morrison by Captain Tumlin. Present through 12-62. Promoted Cpl. 1-28-63. Present 2-63. AWOL 12-63. Deserted and took oath: Knoxville 2-17-1864.

Wright, John A., Pvt., **K**, Enlisted: 8-63, Dallas, Ga., by Captain Kelly. Captured: Pigeon River, Tenn. 1-27-64. Carried: Nashville; Louisville; Camp Chase 2-4-64; Rock Island, Ill. 2-18-64. Died: 3-24-64, Erysipelas. Buried: Rock Island Prison Confederate Cemetery, Grave #915.

Wright, Newton M., Pvt., **A**, Enlisted: 4-64, in field by Captain York. AWOL 8-64. Paroled: Charlotte, NC 5-3-1865. Died: 4-30-1898. Greenwood Cemetery, Cedartown, Ga.

Wright, William C., Pvt., **K**, Enlisted: Newnan, Ga.: Ramsey's 1st Ga. Inf. 3-18-61. Enlisted: 5-62, Camp Morrison by Captain North. Present 6-62. WIA: Murfreesboro 7-13-62. Present through 2-63. Absent 12-63: Teamster for Brigade. Present 12-64. Paroled: Charlotte, N.C. 5-3-65.

Wright, William H., Pvt., **B**, Enlisted: 3-62, Newnan, Ga., age 24, by Captain Strickland. Absent 6-62 and 2-63: Sick furlough: Newnan, Ga. Pres-

ent 8-62 through 12-62. Absent 12-63: Detained with wagon train by General Wheeler. Present 12-64: Teamster for Regiment. Paroled: Charlotte, N.C. 5-3-1865. Pension: Spring, 1862: Chattanooga, sick, measles. Surrendered: Greensboro, N.C. 4-26-1865. Pension: Heard Co., Ga., 1912.

Wright, W.T., Tanner, Paroled: Albany, Ga., 5-15-1865.

Wright, Zacheus T., Pvt., **G**, Enlisted: 5-62, Camp Morrison by Captain Leak. Present through 12-62 as Wagoner. Absent 3-63: Detachment Camp. Present 10-63 and 12-64. Surrendered: Greensboro, N.C. 4-26-1865. Pension: Marshall Co., Ala.

Wynn, H.C., Pvt., **E**, Enlisted: 5-62, Cartersville, Ga., by Captain Blalock. Present through 12-62. Absent 2-63: Detachment: Kingston, Tenn. Absent 12-63: Detached service: Fort Valley, Ga. as Wheelwright. Absent 12-64: Detached: Govt. Shop.

Wynn, Julius "Jule" A., Pvt., **A**, Enlisted: 2-64, in field by Captain York. WIA: Kennesaw Mountain, Ga., 5-1864. AWOL 9-64. Pension: Left early from Greensboro, NC to save horse with J.H. Shaw. Died: 8-3-1918. Buried: Greenwood Cemetery, Cedartown, Ga.

Wynne, T.M., Pvt., **D**, Enlisted: 3-62, Dallas, Ga., age 38, by Captain Seawright. Absent 6-62: Sick furlough: Paulding Co., Ga. Discharged: 10-27-62: Loudon, Tenn..

Yancey, Marshall Orle, Pvt., **B**, Enlisted: 3-62 in Newnan, Ga. Present through 2-63. Absent 12-63: Detained with wagon train by General Wheeler. Present 12-64. Paroled: Charlotte, N.C. 5-3-1865. Died: 6-7-1907. Buried: Forest Park Cemetery, Clayton Co., Ga.

York, Abraham Huddleston, Pvt., **A**, Enlisted 11-61: Nunnally's Battalion. Enlisted: 3-62, 1st Ga. Cavalry, Cedartown, Ga., by Captain John C. Crabb. Present 6-62. First up courthouse stairs at Murfreesboro 7-13-62. Absent through 12-62: Detached: Commissary Dept. Absent 2-63: with Brigade wagons. Present 12-63. AWOL 12-64. Surrendered: Greensboro, N.C. 4-26-1865. Died: 8-18-1925. Buried: Van Wert Cemetery, Rockmart, Ga.

York, David Marshall, Pvt., **B**, Enlisted: 3-62 in Newnan, Ga. Present through 2-63. WIA 12-15-63, Bean Station. Tenn. Gunshot above right eye crushing skull and popping bone fragments; Bull's Gap, Tenn. Hospital. 12-64 present. Died: 2-18-1908. Buried: Flat Rock Primitive Baptist Church. Rocky Mount, Ga.

York, Jasper Newton, Sgt., **A**, Enlisted: 3-62, Cedartown, Ga., by Captain John C. Crabb. Present 6-62. Broke courthouse door down, Murfreesboro 7-13-62. Absent 8-62: Kingston, Tenn. sick. Present 10-62. Absent 12-62: Sick furlough home and Promoted 12-31-62: 2nd Sgt. Present 12-63 and 12-64. Developed tuberculosis during war. Died: 1867, Florida. Tombstone: Van Wert Cemetery, Rockmart, Ga.

York, John N., Pvt., **K**, Enlisted: 5-62, Cartersville, Ga., by Major Harper. Present through 10-62. Absent 12-62: Sick furlough: Luthersville, Ga. Present 12-63 and 12-64. Discharged: Atlanta, May 1865. Died: July 25, 1903. Buried: Bethel Cemetery, Heard Co., Ga.

York, Josiah Cowan, Jr., Pvt., **A**, Enlisted 6-14-1861, Cobb Co., Ga., age 19,: Phillips Legion. Wounded in eye at Gettysburg by bayonet of comrade. Transferred: 2-64 to brother, Captain William York's company. Josiah carried wounded brother Captain William York from battlefield and remained with him. 12-64 AWOL. Died: 8-8-1922. Buried: Centralhatchee Cemetery, Heard Co., Ga.

York, Larkin Blake, Sgt., **A**, Enlisted: 5-62, Cedartown, Ga., by Captain John C. Crabb. Absent 6-62 and 8-62: Sick furlough: Paulding Co., Ga. Present 10-62 and 12-62. Promoted 4th Sgt. 12-31-62. Absent 2-63: Sick furlough home. Enlisted 7-22-1863, Floyd's Legion. Died: 11-22-1903. Buried: Van Wert Cemetery, Rockmart, Ga.

York, Singleton B., Pvt., **B**, Enlisted: 3-62, Newnan, Ga., age 35, by Captain Strickland. Present 6-62 and 8-62: Blacksmith. Present through 12-64: Company blacksmith. WIA. Died: 4-24-1895. Buried: Brittain Family Cemetery, Greenville, Ga.

York, William Thomas, Captain, **A**, Enlisted: 3-62, Cedartown, Ga., by Captain John C. Crabb as Private. Absent 6-62 and 8-62: Acting Commissary. Present 10-62: Acting Commissary. Present 12-63: Promoted Captain by Col. Morrison 5-21-63. WIA 7-20-64, Peachtree Creek, Atlanta. Died 8-3-64 Kingston Hospital, Barnesville, Ga. Buried: Greenwood Cemetery, Barnesville, Ga.

Young, Allen Jacob, Pvt., **E**, Enlisted: 3-62, Carrollton, Ga., by Captain Blalock. Present through 12-62. Absent 2-63: Detailed: Commissary Dept. Present 12-63. Captured: Georgia 8-14-64. Carried: Camp Chase. Discharged 4-10-1865. Died: 10-17-1911. Buried: Shiloh Cemetery, Lawrence Co., Ala.

Young, F.M., Pvt., **F**, Enlisted: 7-63, Decatur, Ga.

Present 12-63. Absent 12-64: Detached: Brigade Ordnance. Witness: Walker Co., Ga., 1891.

Young, George E., Pvt., **B**, Enlisted: 3-62, Newnan, Ga., age 28, by Captain Strickland. Present through 8-62. WIA: Big Hill, Ky. 8-24-62. Gunshot: left side ribs. Carried from field paralyzed arm and leg for period of time. Furloughed: Newnan, Ga. wounded. Present 12-62 through 12-64. Surrendered: Greensboro, N.C. 4-26-1865. Died: 5-25-1913. Buried: White Oak Presbyterian Church, Newnan, Ga.

Young, James, Pvt., **A**, Enlisted: 3-62, Cedartown, Ga., by Captain John C. Crabb. 6-62 present. Transferred: Home Guards.

Young, James Wesley C., Pvt., **E**, Enlisted: 3-62, Carrollton, Ga., by Captain Blalock. Present through 8-62. Injured thrown from horse: Louden, Tenn. Discharged 9-4-62. Enlisted: 10th Ga. Cavalry State Guards 7-27-1863. Died: 12-28-1896. Buried: Corinth Baptist Cemetery, Randolph Co., Ala.

Young, Nathan H., Pvt., **B**, Enlisted 3-62 in Newnan, Ga. Present through 12-64. Surrendered: Raleigh, N.C. 4-26-1865. Died: 2-5-1913. Buried: White Oak Presbyterian Church, Newnan, Ga.

Youngblood, W.M., Pvt., **C**, Enlisted: 4-64, Cave Spring, Ga., by Captain Watts. Absent 12-64 since 11-15-64. Paroled: Charlotte, N.C. 5-3-1865.

Zuber, Daniel H., Pvt., **A**, Enlisted: 3-62, Cedartown, Ga., by Captain John C. Crabb. WIA: Murfreesboro 7-13-62. Thought to be dead and placed in coffin. Had to be turned to fit as too tall and began to bleed. Discharged wounded, 11-20-62. Died: 1-24-1911, Kilgore, Texas.

Zuber, Robert Bigham, Pvt., **G**, Enlisted: 21st Ga. Inf. 10-27-63. Discharged: underage 6-24-64. Enlisted 1st Ga. Cavalry 11-9-64, Cedartown, Ga. by Col. Davitte. Paroled: Charlotte, N.C. 5-3-65. Died: 1907. Buried: Forrest Cemetery, Gadsden, Ala.

Zuber, R.S., 1st Lt., **G**, Enlisted: 4-62 in Rome, Ga. Present through 12-62. Promoted 2nd Lt. 6-20-62 by Col. Morrison. Absent 2-63 and 12-63: Sick furlough: Rome, Ga. Present 12-64: Promoted 1st Lt. WIA 7-30-64. Paroled: Charlotte, N.C. 5-3-1865.

Zuber, Thomas A., Pvt., **G**, Enlisted: Calhoun, Ga., 4-20-63, 8th Ga. Inf. Battalion. Discharged as minor 6-20-1863. Enlisted: 5-64, 1st Georgia Cavalry, Calhoun, Ga., by Lt. Zuber. Absent 12-64: Detailed by Gen. Allen as Provost Guard 9-64. Paroled: Charlotte, N.C. 5-3-1865.

Chapter Notes

Chapter 1

1. Edward McPherson, clerk of the House of Representatives, *The Political History of the United States of America During the Great Rebellion* (New York: Philip and Solomon's, D. Appleton, 1864), 25–26.

2. *Ibid.*

3. *Ibid.*

4. Henry W. Thomas, *History of the Doles: Cook Brigade of Northern Virginia C.S.A.* (Atlanta: Franklin, 1903), 342.

5. *Ibid.*, 343.

6. *Ibid.*

7. *Ibid.*

8. Col. James J. Morrison's file in the records of the Twenty-first Georgia Infantry in the Civil War Room of the Georgia State Archives, Atlanta, Georgia.

9. This advertisement appeared in the February 20, 1862, issue of the *Rome (GA) Courier*. A copy of this newspaper was found in the Carnegie Library, Rome, Georgia.

10. Letter to the editor appears in the *Rome (GA) Courier,* March 6, 1862, Carnegie Library, Rome, Georgia.

11. Advertisement in the March 13, 1862, issue of the *Rome (GA) Courier.*

12. Notice, April 1, 1862, *Rome (GA) Courier.*

13. *Rome (GA) Courier,* April 18, 1862.

14. Advertisement, April 25, 1862, *Rome (GA) Weekly Courier,* Carnegie Library, Rome, Georgia.

15. *Rome (GA) Courier,* May 8, 1862.

16. Notice, May 8, 1862, *Rome (GA) Courier.*

17. *Ibid.*

18. *Official Records, War of the Rebellion*, Volume 10, part 2, p. 438.

19. *Official Records, War of the Rebellion*, Volume 52, part 2, p. 314.

20. *Official Records, War of the Rebellion*, Volume 10, part 2, p. 553.

21. Letter written July 28, 1862, by Pvt. Jesse B. Hall from Knoxville, Tennessee, to his parents (letter courtesy of Steve Hall).

22. *Ibid.*

23. *Official Record, War of the Rebellion*, Volume 16, Part 2, p. 679.

24. *Ibid.*, Part 2.

25. *Ibid.*, 700.

26. *Ibid.*, 699.

27. Letter written June 22, 1862, by Pvt. William T. Tinney from Loudon, Tennessee, to his parents (letter courtesy of Tamera Tinney Caine).

28. *Ibid.*

29. *Ibid.*

30. *Ibid.*

31. Letter written June 27, 1862, by Pvt. William T. Tinney from Loudon, Tennessee, to his brother Richard (letter courtesy of Tamera Tinney Caine).

32. *Ibid.*

33. *Official Record, War of the Rebellion*, Volume 16, Part 2.

34. *Rome (GA) Courier,* November 18, 1862. This clipping was found in Col. James J. Morrison's file in the Civil War Records in the Georgia Archives, Atlanta.

35. Letter written July 28, 1862, by Pvt. Jesse B. Hall from Knoxville, Tennessee, to his parents (letter courtesy of Steve Hall).

36. *Official Record, War of the Rebellion*, Volume 16, Part 2.

37. *Ibid.*

Chapter 2

1. *Official Record, War of the Rebellion*, Volume 28, Part 2, p. 722, correspondence from Gen. Kirby Smith to Col. James Morrison July 6, 1862.

2. *Official Record, War of the Rebellion*, Volume 16, Part 1, report from Brig. Gen. N.B. Forrest to Major Gen. E. Kirby Smith, commanding, July 22, 1862.

3. *Ibid.*

4. *Ibid.*

5. Report of Major Baxter Smith commanding two companies of Spiller's Artillery to Col. Nathan B. Forrest after the Battle of Murfreesboro.

6. *Rome (GA) Weekly Courier,* August 1, 1862, taken from the *Knoxville Register,* written by Captain Milton Haynie.

7. *Rome (GA) Tri-Weekly Courier,* August 14, 1862, written by Lt. John W. Tench, July 20, 1862, from Lebanon, Tennessee.

8. *Ibid.*, 2.

9. *Official Record, War of the Rebellion*, Volume 16, Part 1, report of Brig. Gen. T.T. Crittenden on action July 13, 1862.

10. *Ibid.*

11. *Rome (GA) Tri-Weekly Courier,* August 14, 1862.

12. *Official Record, War of the Rebellion*, Volume 16, Part 1.

13. *Ibid.*, report of Lt. Col. John G. Parkhurst, Ninth Michigan Infantry, on action July 13, 1862.

14. *Ibid.*

15. *Rome (GA) Tri-Weekly Courier,* August 14, 1862.

16. *Rome (GA) Weekly Courier,* November 18, 1862, written by Lt. John W. Tench on November 11, 1862.

17. *Official Record, War of the Rebellion*, Volume 16, Part 1.

18. *Ibid.*

19. *Official Record, War of the Rebellion*, Volume 16, Part 1.

20. *Ibid.*, 805.

21. *Rome (GA) Weekly Courier,* August 1, 1862.

22. *Ibid.*

23. *Ibid.*

24. *Official Record, War of the Rebellion*, Volume 16, Part 1.

25. *History of Livingston County, Michigan* (Philadelphia: Everts and Abbott, 1880) 82.

26. *Official Record, War of the Rebellion*, Volume 16, Part 1, p. 808.

27. *Ibid.*

28. *Ibid.*

29. *Rome (GA) Weekly Courier*, November 18, 1862, written by Lt. John W. Tench on November 11, 1862.

30. *Rome (GA) Tri-Weekly Courier*, July 24, 1862.

31. Nathan B. Forrest, Brig. Gen., Second Cavalry Brigade Report, McMinnville, Tennessee, July 24, 1862.

32. *Rome (GA) Tri-Weekly Courier*, August 14, 1862, letter to editor, July 20, 1862, from Lt. John W. Tench.

33. Nathan B. Forrest, Brig. Gen., Second Cavalry Brigade Report, McMinnville, Tennessee, July 24, 1862.

34. *Ibid.*

35. *Official Record, War of the Rebellion*, Volume 16, Part 1, p. 818.

36. *Ibid.*, 736.

37. *Ibid.*, 829.

38. *Ibid.*, 818, Wheeler's orders to Col. Morrison, July 29, 1862.

Chapter 3

1. *Rome (GA) Courier*, August 1, 1862.

2. *Official Record, War of the Rebellion*, Volume 16, Part 1, p. 938.

3. *Rome (GA) Tri-Weekly Courier*, September 23, 1862.

4. *Ibid.*

5. *Official Record, War of the Rebellion*, Volume 16, Part 1, p. 938.

6. *Rome (GA) Tri-Weekly Courier*, September 23, 1862.

7. *Ibid.*

8. *Ibid.*

9. *Ibid.*

10. *Ibid.*

11. *Ibid.*

12. *Rome (GA) Weekly Courier*, November 18, 1862, Col. James J. Morrison's report to Col. John S. Scott, August 22, 1862.

13. *Rome (GA) Courier*, August 1, 1862.

14. *Ibid.*

15. *Ibid.*

16. *Ibid.*

17. *Rome (GA) Weekly Courier*, November 18, 1862, letter from Lt. John W. Tench written November 11, 1862.

18. *Official Record, War of the Rebellion*, Volume 16, Part 1, p. 938.

19. *Ibid.*, 944.

20. *Ibid.*, 938.

21. *Ibid.*

22. *Ibid.*, 944.

23. *Ibid.*

24. *Rome (GA) Tri-Weekly Courier*, November 18, 1862.

25. *Official Record, War of the Rebellion*, Volume 16, Part 1, p. 909.

26. *Rome (GA) Tri-Weekly Courier*, November 18, 1862.

27. *Ibid.*, November 20, 1862, Col. James J. Morrison, report to Col. John S. Scott, August 31, 1862.

28. *Rome (GA) Tri-Weekly Courier*, November 18, 1862, letter to editor from Lt. John W. Tench written November 18, 1862.

29. *Ibid.*

30. *Official Record, War of the Rebellion*, Volume 16, Part 1, p. 938.

31. *Ibid.*

32. *Ibid.*

33. *Ibid.*

34. *Ibid.*, 944.

35. *Rome (GA) Tri-Weekly Courier*, October 20, 1862.

36. *Ibid.*

37. *Ibid.*

38. *Rome (GA) Tri-Weekly Courier*, November 5, 1862.

39. *Official Record, War of the Rebellion*, Volume 16, Part 1, p. 938, report of Col. John S. Scott, September 11, 1862.

40. *Ibid.*, 933.

41. *Ibid.*, 974.

42. *Ibid.*, 977.

43. *Official Record, War of the Rebellion*, Volume 16, Part 1, p. 961.

44. CWSAC, Battle Summaries, Munfordville, http://www.nps.gov/hps/abpp/battles/ky008.htm (accessed 8/14/2011).

45. *Rome (GA) Tri-Weekly Courier*, October 20, 1862.

Chapter 4

1. *Official Record, War of the Rebellion*, Volume 16, Part 2, p. 850.

2. *Ibid.*, 915.

3. *Rome (GA) Weekly Courier*, October, 2, 1862, report of Col. J.J. Morrison from Boston, Kentucky.

4. *Ibid.*

5. *Ibid.*

6. *Ibid.*

7. *Ibid.*

8. *Ibid.*, Report October 17, 1862, from Camp Frost, Kentucky.

9. *Ibid.*

10. *Rome (GA) Weekly Courier*, November 20, 1862, Col. James J. Morrison's report to Col. John S. Scott, October 17, 1862.

11. *Ibid.*

12. *Official Record, War of the Rebellion*, Volume 16, Part 2, p. 943.

13. *Ibid.*, Volume 28, Part 2, p. 917.

14. *Ibid.*, Volume 16, Part 2, p. 615.

15. *Ibid.*, 943.

16. *Ibid.*, 917.

17. *Rome (GA) WeeklyCourier*, November 6, 1862.

18. *The Rome (GA) Tri-Weekly Courier*, November 2, 1862.

19. *Ibid.*

20. Letter to the editor, *Rome (GA) Courier*, November 18, 1862. Letter was written by Lt. John Tench, November 11, 1862, from Camp Haynie, Tennessee.

21. *Ibid.*

22. *Ibid.*

23. *Ibid.*

24. *Ibid.*

25. *Official Record, War of the Rebellion*, Volume 20, Part 1, p. 94.

26. *Ibid.*, 15.

27. *Official Record, War of the Rebellion*, Volume 20, Part 2, p. 429.

28. *Rome (GA) Tri-Weekly Courier*, December 11, 1862.

29. *Essays: Brigadier General John Pegram, Lee's Paradoxical Cavalier.* http://www.ehistory.osu.edu/uscw/library/paradoxical_cavalier.cfm (accessed 7/28/2011).

30. *Official Record, War of the Rebellion*, Volume 20, Part 1, p. 663.

31. *Ibid.*, 664.

32. *Official Record, War of the Rebellion*, Volume 20, Part 2, p. 663.

33. Longacre, Edward G., *Cavalry of the Heartland: The Mounted Forces of the Army of Tennessee* (Yardley, PA: Westholme), 2009.

34. *Official Record, War of the Rebellion*, Volume 20, Part 2, p. 429.

35. *Official Record, War of the Rebellion*, Volume 20, Part 1, p. 667.

36. *Ibid.*

37. *Ibid.*

38. *Rome (GA) Tri-Weekly Courier*, January 3, 1863.

39. *Official Record, War of the Rebellion*, Volume 20, Part 1, p. 669.

40. William H. Hood file, Georgia State Archives, Atlanta, letter written home January 16, 1863, from Kingston, Tennessee.

41. *Ibid.*

42. *Ibid.*

43. *Ibid.*

44. James J. Morrison file, Civil War Room, Georgia State Archives, Atlanta.

Chapter 5

1. *Official Record, War of the Rebellion*, Volume 23, Part 2, p. 623.
2. *Ibid.*, 647.
3. *Ibid.*
4. *Rome (GA) Tri-Weekly Courier*, February 17, 1863.
5. *Official Record, War of the Rebellion*, Volume 23, Part 2, p. 96, correspondence of James F. Robinson, governor of Kentucky, March 1863.
6. *Ibid.*
7. *Ibid.*, 116, correspondence of Major Gen. H.G. Wright, March 6, 1863.
8. *Ibid.*, 121.
9. *Ibid.*, 126.
10. *Rome (GA) Tri-Weekly Courier*, March 3, 1863.
11. *Ibid.*, 12, correspondence of Major Gen. W.S. Rosecrans, March 10, 1863.
12. *Official Record, War of the Rebellion*, Volume 23, Part 1, p. 171.
13. *Ibid.*, 172.
14. *Ibid.*
15. *Ibid.*
16. *Ibid.*
17. *Official Record, War of the Rebellion*, Volume 23, Part 2, p. 181.
18. *Ibid.*
19. *Official Record, War of the Rebellion*, Volume 23, Part 1, p. 172.
20. *Ibid.*
21. *Ibid.*
22. *Ibid.*
23. *The Rome (GA) Tri-Weekly Courier*, April 18, 1863. Correspondence by Captain William M. Footmen, Near Monticello, Kentucky, April 4, 1863.
24. *Official Record, War of the Rebellion*, Volume XXIII, Part 1, 173.
25. *Ibid.*
26. *Official Record, War of the Rebellion*, Volume XXIII, Part 2, 171.
27. *Rome (GA) Weekly Courier*, April 24, 1863. The correspondent to the editor requested that the *Courier* publish communications between Captain William M. Footman and General John Pegram.
28. *Ibid.*
29. *Ibid.*
30. *Official Record, War of the Rebellion*, Volume 23, Part 1, p. 173.
31. *Ibid.*, 174.
32. *Official Record, War of the Rebellion*, Volume 23, Part 2, p. 215, correspondence of A.E. Burnside to P.H. Watson, assistant of war, April 6, 1863.

Chapter 6

1. *Rome (GA) Courier*, May 19, 1863, letter to editor of the *Atlanta Confederacy*, written May 8, 1863, signed "O."
2. *Official Record, War of the Rebellion*, Volume 23, Part 2, p. 286.
3. *Rome (GA) Courier*, May 19, 1863.
4. *Ibid.*
5. *Ibid.*
6. *Ibid.*
7. *Ibid.*
8. *Ibid.*
9. *Ibid.*
10. *Ibid.*
11. *Ibid.*
12. *Ibid.*
13. *Ibid.*
14. *Ibid.*
15. *Ibid.*
16. *Ibid.*
17. *Ibid.*
18. *Ibid.*
19. *Official Record, War of the Rebellion*, Volume 23, Part 2, p. 810.
20. *Ibid.*, 813.
21. *Ibid.*, Part 1, p. 314.
22. *Ibid.*, Part 2, p. 820, correspondence to Major General John Pegram from General Dabney H. Maury, May 5, 1863.
23. *Ibid.*
24. *Official Record, War of the Rebellion*, Volume 23, Part 2, p. 836.
25. Samuel W. Davitte file, Civil War Room, Georgia State Archives, Atlanta.
26. *Ibid.*
27. *Rome (GA) Tri-Weekly Courier*, May 26, 1863.
28. Letter from Col. Samuel W. Davitte to General S. Cooper from near Russellville, Alabama, September 17, 1864, recommending Captain John W. Tench's promotion to Major.
29. *Official Record, War of the Rebellion*, Volume 23, Part 1, p. 371.
30. *Rome (GA) Tri-Weekly Courier*, June 18, 1863.
31. *Official Record, War of the Rebellion*, Volume 23, Part 2, p. 881.
32. *Ibid.*, 459.
33. *Ibid.*, 887.
34. *Rome (GA) Tri-Weekly Courier*, May 26, 1863.
35. *Ibid.*, June 16, 1863.
36. *Ibid.*, July 3, 1863.

37. *Official Record, War of the Rebellion*, Volume 23, Part 2, p. 520.
38. James J. Morrison file, Civil War Room, Georgia Archives, Atlanta.

Chapter 7

1. *Rome (GA) Tri-Weekly Courier*, August 13, 1863.
2. *Ibid.*, August 18, 1863.
3. *Official Record, War of the Rebellion*, Volume 30, Part 4, p. 537.
4. *Ibid.*, 568.
5. *Ibid.*, 587.
6. *Ibid.*, Part 3, p. 441.
7. *Ibid.*, 461.
8. *Ibid.*, 496.
9. *Ibid.*, Part 2, p. 528.
10. Robert Selph Henry, *First with the Most: Forrest* (Indianapolis: Bobbs Merrill, 1944), 178.
11. *Official Record, War of the Rebellion*, Volume 30, Part 1, p. 727.
12. Henry, *First with the Most*, 178.
13. *Official Record, War of the Rebellion*, Volume 30, Part 1, p. 446.
14. R.T. Logan file, Civil War Room, Georgia State Archives, Atlanta.
15. *Ibid.*
16. *Ibid.*
17. *Ibid.*
18. *Ibid.*
19. *Ibid.*
20. *Ibid.*
21. *Official Record, War of the Rebellion*, Volume 30, part 1, p. 446.
22. *Ibid.*, Part 2, p. 49.
23. *Rome (GA) Courier*, September 15, 1863.
24. *Official Record, War of the Rebellion*, Volume 30, Part 4, p. 647.
25. *Ibid.*, Part 2, p. 31.
26. *Ibid.*, Part 1, p. 922.
27. *Ibid.*, Part 2, p. 528.
28. John W. Minnish, *Pegram's Confederate Brigade at Chickamauga* (1930), OCLC number 32172068.
29. *Ibid.*
30. *Ibid.*
31. *Ibid.*
32. *Ibid.*
33. *Official Record, War of the Rebellion*, Volume 30, Part 2, p. 528.
34. Minnish, *Pegram's Confederate Brigade.*
35. *Official Record, War of the Rebellion*, Volume 30, Part 2, p. 529, report of General John Pegram, September 24, 1863.
36. Henry, *First with the Most*, 183.
37. Minnish, *Pegram's Confederate Brigade.*

38. *Official Record, War of the Rebellion*, Volume 30, Part 1, p. 157.

39. *Ibid.*, Part 2, p. 529, report of General John Pegram, September 24, 1863.

40. *Ibid.*

41. *Official Record, War of the Rebellion*, Volume 30, Part 2, p. 530, report of Col. John S. Scott, September 22, 1863.

42. *Ibid.*, 529.

43. *Official Record, War of the Rebellion*, Volume 30, Part 2, p. 724, report of General Joseph Wheeler, October 30, 1863.

44. *Ibid.*

45. *Official Record, War of the Rebellion*, Volume 30, Part 2, p. 723.

46. *Rome (GA) Tri-Weekly Courier*, October 20, 1863.

47. *Official Record, War of the Rebellion*, Volume 30, Part 2, p. 723.

48. *Ibid.*, 724.

49. *Ibid.*

50. *Ibid.*

51. *Ibid.*, 709.

52. *Ibid.*, 724.

53. *Ibid.*, 686.

54. *Ibid.*

55. *Official Record, War of the Rebellion*, Volume 30, Part 2, p. 727, report of Col. George B. Hodge, October 11, 1863.

Chapter 8

1. *Rome (GA) Tri-Weekly Courier*, October 27, 1863, Lt. John W. Tench report to the *Southern Confederacy*.

2. *Official Record, War of the Rebellion*, Volume 31, Part 1, p. 8.

3. *Ibid.*

4. *Ibid.*, pp. 13–14.

5. *Ibid.*, 13, report of Col. James J. Morrison.

6. *Ibid.*, 14.

7. *Official Record, War of the Rebellion*, Volume 31, Part 1, p. 6.

8. *Ibid.*, 8.

9. A.R. Harper file, Georgia State Archives, Atlanta.

10. *Rome (GA) Tri-Weekly Courier*, October 27, 1863.

11. *Ibid.*

12. *Ibid.*

13. *Official Record, War of the Rebellion*, Volume 31, Part 1, p. 13.

14. *Ibid.*, 14.

15. *Ibid.*

16. *Ibid.*

17. *Official Record, War of the Rebellion*, Volume 31, Part 1, p. 8.

18. *Ibid.*, 9.

19. Letter to the editor of the *Atlanta Confederacy*, dated October 22, 1863. The special correspondent from Morrison's Cavalry signed "JWT" (probably John Tench).

20. Letter to the editor of the *Atlanta Confederacy*, dated October 20, 1863.

21. *Rome (GA) Tri-Weekly Courier*, October 27, 1863.

22. *Official Record, War of the Rebellion*, Volume 31, Part 1, p. 13.

23. *Ibid.*

24. *Ibid.*, Part 3, p. 578.

25. *Ibid.*, 600–601.

26. *Ibid.*, 601.

27. *Ibid.*

28. *Ibid.*, 604–605.

29. *Rome (GA) Tri-Weekly Courier*, November 3, 1863, report from Lt. Col. S. W. Davitte in the *Atlanta Confederacy*.

30. *Official Record, War of the Rebellion*, Volume 31, Part 3, p. 628.

31. Newspaper article about the dedication of a monument to Sgt. Bill Moore, August 22, 1900, Robert L. Rodgers, Scrapbook Collection, Georgia State Archives and History, Atlanta.

32. *Ibid.*

33. *Official Record, War of the Rebellion*, Volume 31, Part 3, p. 634.

34. *Ibid.*, 638.

35. *Ibid.*, 891.

Chapter 9

1. *Official Record, War of the Rebellion*, Volume 31, Part 1, p. 545.

2. *Ibid.*, Part 3, p. 737.

3. *Ibid.*

4. *Ibid.*, Part 1, p. 545.

5. *Ibid.*

6. *Ibid.*

7. *Ibid.*, 546.

8. *Ibid.*

9. *Ibid.*

10. *Ibid.*, Part 1, p. 546, report of Major General William T. Martin.

11. *Ibid.*

12. *Rome (GA) Tri-Weekly Courier*, December 28, 1863.

13. *Official Record, War of the Rebellion*, Volume 31, Part 1, p. 547.

14. *Ibid.*

15. *Ibid.*

16. *Ibid.*

17. *Ibid.*

18. *Ibid.*

19. *Rome (GA) Tri-Weekly Courier*, January 5, 1864.

20. *Official Record, War of the Rebellion*, Volume 1, p. 548.

21. *Ibid.*

22. *Ibid.*

23. *Ibid.*

24. *Rome (GA) Tri-Weekly Courier*, January 5, 1864.

25. *Official Record, War of the Rebellion*, Volume 31, Part 1, p. 549, report of General William T. Martin, January 8, 1864.

26. *Rome (GA) Tri-Weekly Courier*, January 5, 1864.

27. *Official Record, War of the Rebellion*, Volume 32, Part 2, p. 44.

28. *Ibid.*, 44–45.

29. *Ibid.*, Part 1, p. 68.

30. *Rome (GA) Tri-Weekly Courier*, January 14, 1864.

31. *Official Record, War of the Rebellion*, Volume 32, Part 2, p. 127.

32. *Ibid.*, Part 1, p. 135.

33. *Ibid.*, 136.

34. *Ibid.*

35. *Ibid.*, Part 2, pp. 681–682, correspondence of General James Longstreet.

36. William H. Hood Collection, Civil War Room, Georgia State Archives, Atlanta.

37. *Ibid.*

38. *Ibid.*

39. *Official Record, War of the Rebellion*, Volume 32, Part 2, p. 818.

40. *Ibid.*, Part 3, p. 32.

41. *Rome (GA) Tri-Weekly Courier*, March 29, 1864.

42. *Ibid.*, March 24, 1864.

43. *Ibid.*

44. *Rome (GA) Tri-Weekly Courier*, March 26, 1864.

45. *Ibid.*, March 29, 1864.

Chapter 10

1. *Official Record, War of the Rebellion*, Volume 38, Part 3, p. 642.

2. *Rome (GA) Tri-Weekly Courier*, April 23, 1864.

3. O.P. Hargis, "A Georgia Farm Boy in Wheeler's Cavalry," *Civil War Times Illustrated* 7, no. 7 (November 1968).

4. *Ibid.*

5. *Official Record, War of the Rebellion*, Volume 38, Part 4, p. 659.

6. *Ibid.*, 663–664.

7. *Ibid.*, 668.

8. *Ibid.*, p.674, correspondence to Major Gen. Martin, May 7, 1864.

9. *Official Record, War of the Rebellion*, Volume 38, Part 4, p. 96.

10. *Ibid.*, 674.

11. Clipping from unknown newspaper, August 22, 1900. Scrapbook, Robert L. RODGERS Collection,

Civil War Room, Georgia Department of Archives, Atlanta.

12. *Ibid.*

13. *Ibid.*

14. *Ibid.*

15. *Official Record, War of the Rebellion*, Volume 38, Part 4, p. 171.

16. (Pvt.) J.A. Wynn, personal paper file, Georgia State Archives and History, Atlanta.

17. *Ibid.*

18. *Official Record, War of the Rebellion*, Volume 38, Part 3, p. 945.

19. O.P. Hargis, "A Georgia Farm Boy in Wheeler's Cavalry," *Civil War Times Illustrated* 7, no. 7.

20. *Ibid.*

21. *Official Record, War of the Rebellion*, Volume 38, Part 4, p. 197.

22. *Ibid.*, Part 3, p. 945.

23. Hargis, "A Georgia Farm Boy."

24. *Ibid.*

25. *Ibid.*

26. *Official Record, War of the Rebellion*, Volume 38, Part 3, p. 946.

27. *Ibid.*

28. Hargis, "A Georgia Farm Boy."

29. *Official Record, War of the Rebellion*, Volume 38, Part 3, p. 946.

30. Hargis, "A Georgia Farm Boy."

31. *Official Record, War of the Rebellion*, Volume 38, Part 3, p. 947, correspondence to Major General Wheeler from Major O.M. Messick, May 24, 1864.

32. *Ibid.*

33. *Ibid.*

34. *Official Record, War of the Rebellion*, Volume 38, Part 3, p. 947.

35. *Ibid.*

36. *Ibid.*

37. *Ibid.*, 948.

38. *Ibid.*

39. *Ibid.*

40. (Pvt.) J.A Wynn, "Memories," J.A. Wynn file, Civil War Room Georgia State Archives, Atlanta.

41. W.C. Dodson, ed., *Campaigns of Wheeler and His Cavalry, 1862–1865* (Atlanta: Hudgins, 1899), 189–190.

42. *Official Record, War of the Rebellion*, Volume 38, Part 2, p. 821, correspondence to Major General McPherson from Gen. Garrard, June 18, 1864.

43. *Ibid.*

44. Dodson, ed., *Campaigns of Wheeler*, 189–190.

45. *Ibid.*

46. *Ibid.*

47. *Ibid.*

48. *Ibid.*

49. *Ibid.*

50. *Ibid.*

51. *Ibid.*

52. *Ibid.*

53. *Ibid.*

54. *Ibid.*

Chapter 11

1. *Official Record, War of the Rebellion*, Volume 38, Part 3, p. 647.

2. *Ibid.*

3. *Ibid.*, 652.

4. *Ibid.*, Part 5, p. 858.

5. *Ibid.*, 860.

6. Dodson, ed., *The Campaigns of Wheeler.*

7. *Ibid.*

8. *Ibid.*

9. *Ibid.*

10. *Ibid.*

11. Hargis, "A Georgia Farm Boy."

12. *Ibid.*

13. (Pvt.) William T. Tinney, personal letter, June 22, 1862 (letter courtesy of Tamera Tinney Caine).

14. William Tecumseh Sherman, *Memoirs of General W.T. Sherman* (New York: C.L. Webster, 1891), 72.

15. Rodgers, Scrapbook Collection, Georgia State Archives and History, Atlanta.

16. *Official Record, War of the Rebellion*, Volume 38, Part 5, p. 886, correspondence to Gen. Joseph E. Johnston received July 17, 1864.

17. *Official Record, War of the Rebellion*, Volume 38, Part 5, p. 887, General Order #4, issued by Gen. Joseph E. Johnston, July 17, 1864.

18. *Official Record, War of the Rebellion*, Volume 38, Part 3, p. 951.

19. *Ibid.* 952.

20. *Ibid.*

21. Civil War Historic Markers Across Georgia, "Engagement at Bald (or Leggett's) Hill," http://www.lat34north.com/HistoricMarkers/CivilWar/EventDetails.cfm? (accessed October 8, 2013).

22. *Official Record, War of the Rebellion*, Volume 38, Part 3, p. 952, report of Gen. Joseph Wheeler.

23. *Ibid.*

24. *Ibid.*

25. *Ibid.*

26. *Ibid.*

27. *Ibid.*

28. Hargis, "A Georgia Farm Boy."

29. *Official Record, War of the Rebellion*, Volume 38, Part 3, p. 953.

30. *Ibid.*

Chapter 12

1. *Official Record, War of the Rebellion*, Volume 38, Part 1, p. 75.

2. *Ibid.*

3. *Ibid.*, Part 3, p. 953.

4. *Ibid.*

5. *Ibid.*

6. *Ibid.*, Part 1, p. 75.

7. *Ibid.*, Part 2, p. 925.

8. *Ibid.*, Part 1, p. 76.

9. *Ibid.*, Part 3, p. 972.

10. David Evans, *Sherman's Horsemen: Union Cavalry Operations in the Atlanta Campaign* (Bloomington: Indiana University Press, 1996), 324.

11. *Official Record, War of the Rebellion*, Volume 38, Part 2, p. 916.

12. Evans, *Sherman's Horsemen*, 324.

13. *Ibid.*

14. *Official Record, War of the Rebellion*, Volume 38, Part 2, p. 917.

15. Hargis, "A Georgia Farm Boy," *Civil War Times Illustrated* Vol. 7, No. 8 (December 1968).

16. *Ibid.*

17. *Ibid.*

18. *Ibid.*

19. *Ibid.*

20. *Ibid.*

21. *Ibid.*

22. Myles Keogh, *Three Wars, Two Continents, One Irish Soldier*, myleskeogh.org.

23. Hargis, "A Georgia Farm Boy."

24. *Ibid.*

25. *Ibid.*

26. *Official Record, War of the Rebellion*, Volume 38, Part 5, p. 339.

Chapter 13

1. *Official Record, War of the Rebellion*, Volume 38, Part 3, p. 957.

2. *Ibid.*

3. *Ibid.*, 958.

4. *Ibid.*, Part 5, p. 967.

5. *Ibid.*, Part 3, p. 957.

6. *Official Record, War of the Rebellion*, Volume 39, Part 2, p. 262, correspondence to General Halleck from Gen. Sherman, August 17, 1864.

7. *Official Record, War of the Rebellion*, Volume 38, Part 5, p. 561.

8. *Ibid.*, Part 3, p. 958.

9. *Ibid.*, 959.

10. *Ibid.*

11. *Official Record, War of the Rebellion*, Volume 39, Part 2, p. 284.

12. *Official Record, War of the Rebellion*, Volume 38, Part 3, p. 959.

13. *Ibid.*

14. *Official Record, War of the Rebellion*, Volume 39, Part 2, p. 303.

15. *Official Record, War of the Rebellion*, Volume 38, Part 3, p. 959.

16. *Ibid.*, 960.

17. *Official Record, War of the Rebellion*, Volume 39, Part 2, p. 341.

18. *Official Record, War of the Rebellion*, Volume 38, Part 5, p. 816.

19. *Official Record, War of the Rebellion*, Volume 39, Part 2, p. 827.

20. *Ibid.*, 341, correspondence to General Grant from General Sherman September 10, 1864.

21. *Ibid.*

22. *Ibid.*

23. Letter in John M. Tench file, Civil War Room, Georgia State Archives, Atlanta, letter from General Wheeler to Gen. Allen concerning Tench's promotion.

24. *Official Record, War of the Rebellion*, Volume 39, Part 2, p. 859, correspondence to Gen. Taylor from Gen. N.B. Forrest, September 20, 1864.

25. *Ibid.*

26. *Official Record, War of the Rebellion*, Volume 38, Part 3, p. 960, report of Maj. Gen. Joseph Wheeler.

27. *Ibid.*

28. *Ibid.*, 961.

29. *Official Record, War of the Rebellion*, Volume 39, Part 3, p. 784.

30. *Ibid.*, 57.

31. *Ibid.*, 51.

32. *Official Record, War of the Rebellion*, Volume 39, Part 1, p. 806.

33. *Ibid.*, 809.

34. *Ibid.*, Part 3, p. 186.

35. *Ibid.*, 208.

36. *Ibid.*, 214.

37. *Ibid.*, 233.

38. *Ibid.*, 252.

39. *Ibid.*, 292.

40. *Ibid.*, 364.

41. *Ibid.*, 387.

42. *Ibid.*, 842.

43. *Ibid.*, 742.

44. *Official Record, War of the Rebellion*, Volume 39, Part 3, p. 445.

45. *Ibid.*, 882–883.

46. *Ibid.*, 892.

47. *Ibid.*, 890.

48. *Ibid.*, 891, correspondence to Jefferson Davis from Gen. Hood from Tuscumbia, Alabama, November 6, 1864.

Chapter 14

1. *Official Record, War of the Rebellion*, Volume 39, Part 3, pp. 891, 903–904.

2. *Ibid.*, 918.

3. *Ibid.*

4. *Official Record, War of the Rebellion*, Volume 44, Part 1, p. 8.

5. *Ibid.*, 362.

6. *Ibid.*, 859.

7. *Ibid.*

8. *Ibid.*, 362.

9. *Ibid.*, 406.

10. *Ibid.*

11. *Ibid.*

12. *Ibid.*

13. *Ibid.*, 870.

14. *Ibid.*, 406.

15. *Ibid.*, 407.

16. *Ibid.*

17. *Ibid.*

18. *Ibid.*

19. *Ibid.*

20. *Ibid.*

21. *Ibid.*, 898.

22. *Ibid.*

23. *Ibid.*, 408.

24. *Ibid.*

25. *Ibid.*

26. *Ibid.*

27. *Ibid.*

28. *Ibid.*

29. *Official Record, War of the Rebellion*, Volume 44, p. 364.

30. *Ibid.*, 409.

31. *Ibid.*, 364.

32. *Ibid.*, 409.

33. *Ibid.*

34. *Official Record, War of the Rebellion*, Volume 44, p. 364, General Judson Kilpatrick's report, November 15–December 4, 1864.

35. *Official Record, War of the Rebellion*, Volume 44, p. 409, report of Joseph Wheeler December 24, 1864.

36. *Ibid.*

37. *Official Record, War of the Rebellion*, Volume 44, p. 910, correspondence to General Bragg from General Wheeler, November 29, 1864, from west of Buckhead Church.

38. *Official Record, War of the Rebellion*, Volume 44, p. 409.

39. *Ibid.*, p. 365, report of General Judson Kilpatrick.

40. *Ibid.*, 410.

41. *Official Record, War of the Rebellion*, Volume 44, p. 410, report of General Joseph Wheeler. December 24, 1864.

42. *Ibid.*

43. *Ibid.*

44. *Ibid.*

45. *Ibid.*, 949.

46. *Ibid.*, 955.

47. *Ibid.*, 960.

48. *Ibid.*, 411.

49. *Ibid.*

50. *Ibid.*, 412, report of General Joseph Wheeler.

51. *Ibid.*

52. *Ibid.*

Chapter 15

1. *Official Record, War of the Rebellion*, Volume 44, p. 979, correspondence from General Beauregard to General Cooper, December 23, 1864.

2. *Ibid.*

3. *Official Record, War of the Rebellion*, Volume 44, p. 975, correspondence to General Hardee from General Wheeler near Savannah, Georgia, December 24, 1864.

4. *Ibid.*

5. *Official Record, War of the Rebellion*, Volume 44, p. 998, correspondence to Gen. Braxton Bragg from Gen. Wheeler in Hardeeville, South Carolina, December 28, 1864.

6. *Ibid.*

7. *Ibid.*

8. *Ibid.*

9. *Ibid.*

10. *Ibid.*

11. *Official Record, War of the Rebellion*, Volume 44, p. 1002.

12. *Ibid.*

13. *Official Record, War of the Rebellion*, Volume 47, Part 2, p. 987.

14. *Ibid.*, Part 2, p. 1000, correspondence to Jefferson Davis from Gen. Hardee, January 8, 1865.

15. *Official Record, War of the Rebellion*, Volume 47, Part 1, p. 1115.

16. *Ibid.*

17. *Ibid.*

18. *Official Record, War of the Rebellion*, Volume 47, Part 2, p. 1012.

19. *Ibid.*, 987, correspondence to Braxton Bragg from General Wheeler, January 4, 1865.

20. *Ibid.*

21. *Ibid.*

22. *Official Record, War of the Rebellion*, Volume 47, Part 2, p. 1080.

23. *Ibid.*, 1097.

24. Pete Peter, "History of the Battle of Aiken," http://www.drmclient.com/battleof aiken/history-detail.html (accessed 3/12/2012).

25. *Official Record, War of the Rebellion*, Volume 47, Part 2, p. 1105.

26. *Ibid.*, 1106.

27. *Ibid.*, 1109.

28. *Ibid.*, 1113–1114.

29. *Official Record, War of the Rebellion*, Volume 47, Part 2, p. 1123, correspondence to Col. C.C. Crews

from Gen. D.H. Hill, Augusta, Georgia, February 8, 1865, 5:00 P.M.

30. *Ibid.*

31. *Ibid.*

32. *Ibid.*, 1137.

33. *Official Record, War of the Rebellion*, Volume 471, Part 2, p. 1136, correspondence to Gen. Joseph Wheeler from Gen. D.H. Hill, February 9, 1865, 6:00 P.M.

34. *Ibid.*

35. *Ibid.*

36. *Official Record, War of the Rebellion*, Volume 47, Part 2, p. 1147, correspondence to General Allen from Gen. D.H. Hill, February 10, 1865, 2:30 P.M.

37. *Ibid.*, 1147.

38. Peter, "History of the Battle of Akin."

39. *Ibid.*

40. *Ibid.*

41. *Ibid.*

42. Wilbur F. Hinman, *The Story of the Sherman Brigade* (Alliance, OH: Published by the Author, 1897), 911.

43. *Ibid.*

44. *Official Record, War of the Rebellion*, Volume 47, Part 2, p. 1200.

45. *Ibid.*, 1214.

46. *Ibid.*, 1261.

47. History/Organization of the Armies, 34, http://www.bennettpla cehistoricsite.com (accessed 6/13/2013).

Chapter 16

1. *Official Record, War of the Rebellion*, Volume 47, Part 1, p. 1130.

2. W.C. Dodson, ed., *The Campaigns of Wheeler and His Cavalry, 1862–1865* (Atlanta: Hudgins, 1899), 344.

3. William Preston Mangum, "Kill Cavalry's Nasty Surprise," *America's Civil War* (November 1996).

4. *Ibid.*

5. Dodson, ed., *The Campaigns of Wheeler*, 344.

6. Douglas D. Scott, William J. Hunt, Jr., and John H. Jameson, Jr., *The Civil War Battle at Monroe's Crossroads, Fort Bragg, North Carolina: A Historical Archeological Perspective*, chapter 3, "The Battle and Land Use of Monroe's Crossroads," United States Department of the Army, 161 Airborne Corps (Fort Bragg, NC), Southeast Archeological Center (U.S.), place and publisher not identified, 1998, http://www.nps.gov/seac/mc-archweb/ch3/index.htm (accessed 12/13/2011).

7. *Official Record, War of the Rebellion*, Volume 47, Part 1, p. 861, report of Major General Judson Kilpatrick.

8. Mangum, "Kill Calvary's Nasty Surprise."

9. *Ibid.*

10. Dodson, ed., *The Campaigns of Wheeler*, 345.

11. *Ibid.*, 346.

12. *Official Record, War of the Rebellion*, Volume 47, Part 1, p. 862.

13. *Ibid.*, 1131.

14. *Ibid.*, 1126.

15. *Ibid.*, 1130.

16. *Ibid.*, 1131.

17. *Ibid.*

18. *Official Record, War of the Rebellion*, Volume 47, Part 2, p. 1415.

19. Dodson, ed., *The Campaigns of Wheeler*, 350.

20. *Official Record, War of the Rebellion*, Volume 47, Part 1, p. 1130.

21. *Ibid.*, 1128.

22. *Ibid.*, 1131.

23. *Ibid.*

24. *Ibid.*

25. *Ibid.*

26. *Ibid.*

27. *Ibid.*

28. Hargis, "A Georgia Farm Boy in Wheeler's Cavalry.".

29. *Ibid.*

30. *Ibid.*

31. *Official Record, War of the Rebellion*, Volume 47, Part 3, p. 852. Correspondence to Georgia Governor Brown, April 30, 1865.

32. *Official Record, War of the Rebellion*, Volume 47, Part 3, p. 851, correspondence to Col. Crews, Salisbury, North Carolina, April 29, 1865.

33. *Ibid.*

34. *Official Record, War of the Rebellion*, Volume 47, Part 1, p. 1032, report of Gen. Joseph Wheeler, March 1–April 15, 1865.

35. Letter to Company K, First Georgia Cavalry Regiment, from Captain Henry A. North, commanding.

Bibliography

Atlanta (GA) Confederacy, 1863.

Avery, I.W. *History of the State of Georgia from 1850–1881: Embracing the Three Important Epochs*. New York: Brown and Derby, 1881.

The Battle and Land Use of Monroe's Crossroads. http://74.6.238.254/search/srpeache?ei=UFT-8&p=major+cramer+first=alabama=cavalry (accessed 12/13/2011).

Battle of Monroe's Crossroads. http:en.wikipedia.org/wiki/Battle_of_Monroe%27s_Crossroads (accessed 12/12/2011).

Battle of Mossy Creek. http://en.wikipedia.org/wiki/Battle_of_Mossy_Creek (accessed 7/28/2011).

Batty, George Magruder. *A History of Rome and Floyd County, State of Georgia, United States of America*. Floyd Co., GA: Webb and Vary Company, 1921.

Breiner, Thomas L. *The Battle of Perryville: Bragg's Kentucky Invasion*. http://www.battleofperryville.com/invasion.html (accessed 7/29/2011).

Brown, Joseph M. *The Mountain Campaigns in Georgia*. Buffalo, NY: Western and Atlantic Railroad, 1886.

Civil War Historic Markers Across Georgia. "Engagement at Bald (or Leggett's) Hill." http://www.lat34north.com/HistoricMarkers/CivilWar/EventDetails.cfm?EventKey=18640721&EventTitle=Engagement%20at%20(or%20Legett's)%20Hill (accessed October 8, 2013).

Cleburne County Al. Archives Military Records. 1st Georgia Cavalry. http://www.usgwarchives.org/al/alfiles.htm (accessed 7/27/2011).

Collins in North Carolina and Georgia. "The Scared Corn-Ryo Murders." http://nc-ga-collins.weebly.com/the-scared-corn-ryo-murders.html (accessed 8/17/2013).

Cruickshank, Stewart. "Pegram's Kentucky Expedition and the Battle of Dutton's Hill." *The Lost Cause: The Journal of the Kentucky Division, Sons of Confederate Veterans*, March 21, 2009. http://thelostcauseky.blogspot.com/2009/03/pegrams-kentucky-expedition-battle-of.html (accessed 11/12/2011).

CWSAC. Battle Summaries: Munfordville. http://www.nps.gov/hps/abpp/battles/ky008.htm (accessed 8/14/2011).

Davitte, (Col.) Samuel W. Personal papers. Georgia Department of Archives and History, Atlanta.

Dodson, W.C., ed. *The Campaigns of Wheeler and His Cavalry, 1862–1865*. Atlanta: Hudgins, 1899.

Essays: Brigadier General John Pegram, Lee's Paradoxical Cavalier. http://ehistory.osu.edu/uscw/library/paradoxical cavalier.cfm (accessed 7/28/2011).

Evans, Clement A. *Confederate Military History: A Library of Confederate State History*. Atlanta: Confederate, 1899.

Evans, David. *Sherman's Horsemen: Union Cavalry Operations in the Atlanta Campaign*. Bloomington: Indiana University Press, 1996.

Family Data. http://wc.rootsweb.ancestry.com/cgi-bin/igm.cgi (accessed 7/14/2009).

Family Search. https://familysearch.org/search/records (accessed 10/12/12).

Find a Grave. http://www.findagrave.com/cgi-bin/fg.cgi (accessed 8/23/2009).

First Georgia Cavalry, Confederate Service Records. http://www.fold3.com/title_31/georgia (accessed 11/25/2011).

Hall, (Pvt.) Jesse B. Personal letter from Knoxville, Tennessee, July 28, 1862 (courtesy of Steve Hall).

Hargis, O.P. "A Georgia Farm Boy in Wheeler's Cavalry." *Civil War Times Illustrated* 7, nos. 7 (November 1968), 8 (December 1968).

Harper, (Lt. Col.) Armstead R. Personal Papers. Georgia State Archives and History, Atlanta.

Hathaway, Michael J. *Surprise Attack at the Monroe Farm*. http://www.civilwaralbum.com/misc13/monroes_crossroads_surprise.htm (accessed 12/15/2011).

Hawkins, Anthony. *Of Savage Fury: The Battle of Richmond, Kentucky*. Ashcamp, KY: Hawkins Historical Publications, 2004.

Henderson, Lillian. *Roster of the Confederate Soldiers of Georgia, 1861–1865*. Hapeville, GA: Longina and Porter, 1959.

Henry, Robert Selph. *First with the Most: Forrest*. Indianapolis: Bobbs-Merrill, 1944.

Hinman, Wilbur F. *The Story of the Sherman Brigade*. Alliance, OH: Published by the Author, 1897.

History of Livingston County, Michigan. Philadelphia: Everts and Abbott, 1880. Digitized by Google.

History/Organization of the Armies. http://www. bennettplacehistoricsite.com (accessed 6/13/2013).

Hood, John B. (General, CSA). "The Defense of Atlanta." In *Battles and Leaders of the Civil War*. Vol. 4. Edited by Robert Underwood Johnson and Clarence Clough Buel. NY: Century, 1888.

Hood, (Pvt.) William H. Personal Papers. Georgia Department of Archives and History, Atlanta.

Huwald's Tennessee Mountain Howitzer Battery Homepage. "Huwald's Battery, Tennessee Mountain Howitzers." http://dixieweb.com/Camp1513/huwald.htm (accessed 6/12/2013).

Lenoir, William Ballard. *History of Sweetwater Valley*. Sweetwater, TN, 1916. http://www.ebooksread. com/authors-eng/william-ballard-lenoir/history-od-sweetwater-valley (accessed 6/12/2013).

Logan, (Pvt.) R.T. Personal papers. Georgia Department of Archives and History, Atlanta.

Longacre, Edward G. *Cavalry of the Heartland: The Mounted Forces of the Army of Tennessee*. Yardley, PA: Westholme, 2009.

Longstreet, James. *From Manassas to Appomattox: Memoirs of the Civil War in America*. Philadelphia: J.B. Lippincott, 1896.

Mangum, William Preston. "Kill Cavalry's Nasty Surprise." *America's Civil War* (November 1996).

Mathews, Byron H. *The McCook-Stoneman Raid*. Philadelphia: Dorrance, 1976.

McPherson, Edward. *The Political History of the United States of America During the Great Rebellion*. New York: Philip and Solomon's, D. Appleton, 1864.

Minnish, John W. *Pegram's Confederate Brigade at Chickamauga*. 1930. OCLC number 32172068.

Morrison, (Colonel) James J. Personal Papers. Georgia Department of Archives and History, Atlanta.

Myles Keogh: Three Wars, Two Continents, One Irish Soldier. myleskeogh.org (accessed 10/12/12).

9th Michigan Volunteer Infantry Regiment. http:// en.wikipedia.org/wiki/9th_Michigan_Volunteer_Infantry_Regiment (accessed 11/2/2011).

No Better Place to Die: The Battle of Stones River. http://books.google.com/books?id=CvZ4yzYqvesc&ipg=Pa172@ots=sLl_ko_JP8&dq=wheeler's%20raid%20around%20Rosecrans%20December%20%20Starkweather&pg=PA172#v=onepage&q&f=false (accessed 12/29/2011).

North, (Captain) Henry A. Letter to Company K, First Georgia Cavalry Regiment, 1865.

Obituary of William Washington Cavender. *Confederate Veteran* No. 4 (April 1912): 181.

Peter, Pete. "History of the Battle of Aiken." http://www.drmclient.com/battleofaiken/history-detail.html (accessed 3/12/2012).

Poole, John Randolph. *Cracker Cavaliers: The 2nd Georgia Cavalry Under Wheeler and Forrest*. Macon, GA: Mercer University Press, 2000.

Roberts, Lucien E. *A History of Paulding County*. Dallas, GA: Published by Author, 1933.

Rodgers, Robert L. Scrapbook Collection, Georgia State Archives and History, Atlanta.

Rome (GA) Courier, 1862–1864.

Rome (GA) Tri-Weekly Courier, 1862–1864.

Rome (GA) Weekly Courier, 1862–1864.

Sanfilippo, Diane. "Bios: Captain William Thomas York." http://www.usgwarchives.net/ga/gafiles. hmt (accessed 1/20/2012).

Scott, Douglas D., William J. Hunt, Jr., and John H. Jameson, Jr. *The Civil War Battle at Monroe's Crossroads, Fort Bragg, North Carolina: A Historical Archeological Perspective*. United States Department of the Army. XVIII Airborne Corps. Fort Bragg, NC; Southeast Archeological Center (U.S.). Place and Publisher not identified. 1998. http://www.nps.gov/seac/mc-archweb/ch3/index.htm (accessed 12/13/2011).

Scott, P. Shannon's Scouts. Online Archive of Terry's Texas Rangers. http://www.terrystexasrangers. org/histories/mhtsw/shannons_scouts.html (accessed 12/15/2011).

"Secession! The Story of Georgia's Secession from the United States, 1861." http://ngeorgia.com/history/secession.html (accessed 10/31/2011).

Sherman, William Tecumseh. *Memoirs of General W.T. Sherman*. New York: C.L. Webster, 1891.

Smith, (Major) Baxter. Report to Colonel Nathan Bedford Forrest after the Battle of Murfreesboro, Tennessee, July 13, 1862.

Soldiers and Sailors Database. http://nps.gov/civilwar/soldiers-and-sailors-database.htm (accessed 2/24/2011).

Tench, Major John W. Personal Papers. Georgia State Archives and History, Atlanta.

Thomas, Henry W. *History of the Doles: Cook Brigade of Northern Virginia, C.S.A.* Atlanta: Franklin, 1903.

Tinney, (Pvt.) William T. Personal letter from Loudon, Tennessee, June 22, 1862, and June 27, 1862 (courtesy of Tamera Tinney Caine).

USGWARCHIVES. http://www.usgwarchives.net/search.cgi/searchga.htm (accessed 11/12/12).

Ventura, Mike. *Alexander May Shannon and Shannon's Scouts*. http://www.geocities.ws/crittercompany org/shannons_scouts.htm (accessed 12/15/2011).

Walden, Geoffrey R. *Death of General Felix K. Zollicoffer*. History-Mill Springs Battlefield Association, October 19, 2009. http://www.millsprings.net/history/death-of-gen-felix-k-zollicoffer (accessed 7/28/2011).

The War of the Rebellion: A Compilation of the Official Records of the Union and Confederate Armies. 128 volumes. Washington, DC: U.S. Government Printing Office, 1898.

West, Mike, ed. *Forrest Rides to Murfreesborough's Rescue*. http://www.murfreesboropost.com/forrest-rides-to-murfreesborough-s-rescue-cms-5191 (accessed 8/5/2011).

Wheeler's Late Raid: Its Failure; Incidents Connected

With It; Sketch of Gen. Wheeler. http://www.nyti mes.com/1864/10/03/news/wheeler-s-late-raid-its-failure-incidents-connected-with-it (accessed 12/6/2011).

Wilson, J.S. *The Battle of Sunshine Church.* August 13, 2009. http://themonticellonews.com/the-battle-of-sunshine-chirch-p6101-116.htm (accessed 8/7/2011).

Wynn, (Pvt.) J.A. Personal Papers. Georgia State Archives and History, Atlanta.

York Family. Information contributed by Diane Stark Sanfilippo. E-mail, 2-14-2014.

Young, Bennett Henderson. *Confederate Wizards of the Saddle: Being Reminiscences and Observations of One Who Rode with Morgan*Kennesaw, GA: Continental, 1958.

Index

Photographs of 1st Cavalry men are indicated by page numbers in **bold italics**. *See also the Roster*